# INTERNATIONAL BIBLIOGRAPHY
## OF THE SOCIAL SCIENCES

# BIBLIOGRAPHIE INTERNATIONALE
## DES SCIENCES SOCIALES

# Publications of the ICSSD / Publications du CIDSS

International Bibliography of the Social Sciences / Bibliographie Internationale des Sciences Sociales.

[published annually in four parts / paraissant chaque année en quatre parties. Until 1961 / Jusqu'en 1961: UNESCO, Paris].

*International bibliography of sociology / Bibliography internationale de sociologie* [red cover / couverture rouge]. Vol. 1: 1951 (Publ. 1952).
*International bibliography of political science / Bibliographie internationale de science politique* [grey cover / couverture grise]. Vol. 1: 1952 (Publ. 1954).
*International bibliography of economics / Bibliographie internationale de science économique* [yellow cover / couverture jaune]. Vol. 1: 1952 (Publ. 1955).
*International bibliography of social and cultural anthropology / Bibliographie internationale d'anthropologie sociale et culturelle* [green cover / couverture verte]. Vol. 1: 1955 (Publ. 1958).

Other series / Autres collections:

International Political Science Abstracts / Documentation Politique Internationale.

[quarterly / trimestriel. Basil Blackwell, Oxford].

Confluence, Surveys of research in the social sciences / Confluence, états des recherches en sciences sociales.

[semi-annual / semestriel. Mouton, The Hague-Paris.]

Documentation in the Social Sciences / Documentation dans les Sciences Sociales.

[UNESCO, Paris].

*Catalogue des sources de documentation juridique dans le monde / A register of legal documentation in the world* (2nd Ed. / 2e édition 1957).
*Liste mondiale des périodiques spécialisés dans les sciences sociales / World list of social science periodicals* (2nd Ed. / 2e édition 1957).
*International repertory of social science documentation centres / Répertoire internationale des centres de documentation de sciences sociales* (1952).
*International register of current team research in the social sciences / Répertoire international des recherches collectives en cours dans le domaine des sciences sociales* (1955).

# INTERNATIONAL BIBLIOGRAPHY
## OF THE SOCIAL SCIENCES

# BIBLIOGRAPHIE INTERNATIONALE
## DES SCIENCES SOCIALES

# 1973

## International Bibliography of
# ECONOMICS

## Bibliographie internationale de
# SCIENCE ÉCONOMIQUE

### VOL. XXII

Prepared by the
International Committee for Social Science Information and Documentation

Établie par le
Comité international pour l'information et la documentation en sciences sociales

## LONDON : TAVISTOCK PUBLICATIONS
## CHICAGO : ALDINE PUBLISHING COMPANY

*Manuscrit prepared under the auspices of the International Economic Association by the ICSSD with the financial support of Unesco (Subvention 1974, DG/3.2/41/53)*

*Manuscrit préparé sous les auspices de l'Association Internationale de Science Économique par le CIDSS avec l'aide financière de l'Unesco (Subvention 1974, DG/3.2/41/53)*

ISBN 422 74790 4

# TABLE OF CONTENTS
# TABLE DES MATIÈRES

# PREFACE

We take pleasure in thanking, here, the institutions and economists of many countries who have informed us of their publications and have thus facilitated the drafting of this twenty-second volume of the *International Bibliography of Economics*.

Our thanks are also due to those who have either written directly to the Managing Editor's office or sent information through Unesco's Science Cooperation Offices for South Asia and the Middle East.

As it is not possible to give a full list, we wish at least to mention certain institutions whose help has been especially valuable in bringing to our knowledge a given country's, or even a given region's publications on economics: *Belgrade*, the University; *Brussels*, Institut de Sociologie Solvay; *Bucarest*, Biblioteca Centrală de Stat; *Budapest*, Magyar Tudományos Akadémia, Közgazdaságtudományi Intézet; *Buenos Aires*, Universidad, Facultad de Ciencias económicas; *Helsinki*, Kauppakorkeakoulu; *Jerusalem*, Eliezer Kaplan School of Economics and Social Sciences; *London*, London School of Economics and Political Science; *Madrid*, Instituto Balmes; *Moscow*, Akademija Nauk Sojuza Sovetskih Socialističeskih Respublik; *Paris*, Fondation Nationale des Sciences Politiques; *Rio de Janeiro*, Centro Latino-Americano de Pesquisas em Ciências Sociais; *Tokyo*, National Commission for Unesco; and *Warsaw*, Szkola Glowna Planowania i Statystiki.

We appeal to all scientific or university institutions in other countries which might be prepared to render us the same service.

We further wish to express our gratitude to several distinguished persons who have collaborated particularly closely with the Editor: Dr. H. Uniejewska (Warsaw); Dr. Tamás Földi (Budapest); Dr. Manuel Diégues Jr. (Rio de Janeiro); Dr. Miloš Samardžija (Belgrade); Dr. Yoshio Muto (Tokyo); Dr. Oreste Popescu (Bogotà); Mrs. Inessa A. Chodosh (Moscow); and Professor Carmelo Viñas y Mey (Madrid).

It seems only fair to mention here those who have, this year, once again, selected and coded the bibliographical material and prepared the manuscript: Agnès d'Eszláry de Tiszaföldvar, Regina Frank, Germaine George and Geneviève Mordini.

# PRÉFACE

Il nous est agréable de remercier ici les institutions et les économistes de nombreux pays qui nous ont informés de leurs publications, et ont ainsi facilité la rédaction de ce volume de la *Bibliographie internationale de science économique*.

Ces remerciements s'adressent à tous ceux qui ont écrit directement au siège du secrétariat de rédaction ou communiqué des renseignements par l'intermédiaire des postes de coopération scientifique de l'Unesco pour l'Asie méridionale et pour le Moyen-Orient.

Ne pouvant procéder à une énumération complète, nous nous contenterons de mentioner certaines institutions dont le concours à été particulièrement important en ce qu'il nous a permis de connaître les publications économiques d'un pays ou même d'une région: *Belgrade*, Université; *Bruxelles*, Institut de Sociologie Solvay; *Bucarest*, Biblioteca Centrală de Stat; *Budapest*, Magyar Tudományos Akadémia, Közgazdaságtudományi Intézet; *Buenos Aires*, Universidad, Facultad de Ciencias económicas; *Helsinki*, Kauppakorkeakoulu; *Jérusalem*, Eliezer Kaplan School of Economics and Social Sciences; *Londres*, London School of Economics and Political Science; *Madrid*, Instituto Balmes; *Moscou*, Akademija Nauk Sojuza Sovetskih Socialističeskih Respublik; *Paris*, Fondation Nationale des Sciences Politiques; *Rio de Janeiro*, Centro Latino-Americano do Pesquisas em Ciências Sociais; *Tokyo*, Commission nationale pour l'Unesco; *Varsovie*, Szkola Glowna Planowania i Statystyki.

Nous faisons appel à toutes les institutions scientifiques ou universitaires des autres pays qui seraient disposées à nous rendre le même service.

Nous tenons, en outre, à exprimer notre reconnaissance à plusieurs personnalités qui ont collaboré de façon particulièrement étroite avec la rédaction, à savoir: le Dr. H. Uniejewska (Varsovie), Dr. Tamás Földi (Budapest), le Dr. Manuel Diégues Jr. (Rio de Janeiro), le Dr. Miloš Samardžija (Belgrade), le Dr. Yoshio Muto (Tokyo), le Dr. Oreste Popescu (Bogotà), Mme Inessa A. Chodosh (Moscou), le professeur Carmelo Viñas y Mey (Madrid).

Il est juste de mentionner ici les personnes qui ont, cette année encore, recensé et traité les données bibliographiques et préparé le manuscrit : Agnès d'Eszláry de Tiszaföldvár, Regina Frank, Germaine George, Geneviève Mordini.

| | | |
|---|---|---|
| Academy of Management Journal | *Acad. Manag. J.* | Eugene, Ore. |
| Accounting Review | *Accting R.* | Columbus, Ohio |
| Acta geographica. Bulletin officiel de la Société de Géographie | *Acta geogr.* | Paris |
| Acta juridica | *Acta jur. (Budapest)* | Budapest |
| Acta oeconomica | *Acta oecon.* | Budapest |
| Acta politica | *Acta polit.* | Amsterdam |
| Acta sociologica | *Acta sociol.* | København |
| Actualité économique | *Actual. écon.* | Montréal |
| Actualités industrielles lorraines | *Ajtual. industr. lorraines* | Metz |
| Administración y Desarrollo | *Adm. y Desarr.* | Bogotà |
| Administration | *Administration (Dublin)* | Dublin |
| Administration | *Administration (Paris)* | Paris |
| Administration Science Quarterly | *Adm. Sci. Quart.* | Ithaca, N.Y. |
| Affari esteri | *Aff. est.* | Roma |
| Africa | *Africa (London)* | London |
| Africa | *Africa (Madrid)* | Madrid |
| Africa | *Africa (Roma)* | Roma |
| Africa Quarterly | *Afr. Quart.* | New Delhi |
| Africa today | *Afr. today* | Denver, Col. |
| African Affairs | *Afr. Aff.* | London |
| African Review | *Afr. R.* | Dar Es Salaam |
| African Studies Review | *Afr. Stud. R.* | Boston, Mass. |
| Africana Bulletin | *Africana B.* | Warszawa |
| Afrika heute | *Afr. heute* | Bonn |
| Afrika Spectrum | *Afr. Spectrum* | Hamburg |
| Afrique et Asie | *Afr. et Asie* | Paris |
| Aggiornamenti sociali | *Aggiorn. soc.* | Milano |
| Agrarwirtschaft | *Agrarwirtschaft* | Braunschweig |
| Agricultural Economics Research | *Agric. Econ. Res.* | Washington, D.C. |
| Akita Daigaku Kenkyu Kiyô | *Akita Daigaku Kenkyu Kiyô* | Akita |
| Aktual'nye Voprosy Teorii Progressa | *Aktual. Vopr. Teor. Progr.* | Kujbyšev |
| Almanach | *Almanach* | Berlin |
| Aménagement du Territoire et Développement régional | *Aménag. Territ. Dévelop.* | St Martin d'Héres |
| América indígena | *Amér. indíg.* | México |
| América latina | *Amér. lat.* | Rio de Janeiro |
| American Anthropologist | *Amer. Anthropol.* | Washington, D.C. |
| American behavioral Scientist | *Amer. behav. Scientist* | Princeton, N.Y. |
| American economic Review | *Amer. econ. R.* | Menasha, Wis. |
| American Economist | *Amer. Economist* | New York |
| American historical Review | *Amer. hist. R.* | New York |
| American Journal of agricultural Economics | *Amer. J. agric. Econ.* | Menasha, Wis. |
| American Journal of Economics and Sociology | *Amer. J. Econ. Sociol.* | New York |
| American Journal of international Law | *Amer. J. int. Law* | Washington, D.C. |
| American Journal of political Science | *Amer. J. polit. Sci.* | Detroit, Mich. |

| | | |
|---|---|---|
| American Journal of Sociology | *Amer. J. Sociol.* | Chicago, Ill. |
| American political Science Review | *Amer. polit. Sci. R.* | Washington, D.C. |
| American Politics Quarterly | *Amer. Polit. Quart.* | Beverly Hills, Cal. |
| American Psychologist | *Amer. Psychol.* | Washington, D.C. |
| American Scholar | *Amer. Scholar* | Washington, D.C. |
| American sociological Review | *Amer. sociol. R.* | New York |
| American Sociologist | *Amer. Sociologist* | Washington, D.C. |
| Amministrare | *Amministrare* | Milano |
| Amministrazione italiana | *Amm. ital.* | Roma |
| Anales de Economía | *A. Econ. (Madrid)* | Madrid |
| Anales de la Cátedra Francisco Suarez | *A. Cátedra Francisco Suarez* | Granada |
| Analíse social | *Anal. soc.* | Lisbõa |
| Analyse et Prévision | *Anal. et Prévis.* | Paris |
| Analyse financière | *Anal. financ.* | Paris |
| Annales (Économies — Sociétés — Civilisations) | *Annales* | Paris |
| Annales africaines | *A. afr.* | Dakar |
| Annales d'Études internationales | *A. Ét. int.* | Genève |
| Annales de Droit | *A. Dr.* | Bruxelles |
| Annales de Droit internatonal médical | *A. Dr. int. médic.* | Monaco |
| Annales de Géographie | *A. Géogr.* | Paris |
| Annales de Sciences économiques appliquées | *A. Sci. écon. appl.* | Louvain |
| Annales de l'Économie collective | *A. Écon. coll.* | Liège |
| Annales de l'Université de Madagascar. Série de Droit et des Sciences économiques | *A. Univ. Madagascar. Sér. Dr. Sci. écon.* | Tananarive |
| Annales de l'Université des Sciences sociales de Toulouse | *A. Univ. Sci. soc. Toulouse* | Toulouse |
| Annales de la Faculté de Droit de Liège | *A. Fac. Dr. Liège* | Liège |
| Annales de la Faculté de Droit et des Sciences économiques de Lyon | *A. Fac. Dr. Sci. écon. Lyon* | Lyon |
| Annales internationales de Criminologie | *A. int. Criminol.* | Paris |
| Annales Universitatis Mariae Curie-Skłodowska | *A. Univ. M. Curie-Skłodowska* | Lublin |
| Annales Universitatis Scientiarum budapestiensis de Rolando Eötvös nominatae. Sectio geographica | *A. Univ. Sci. budapest. Sect. geogr.* | Budapest |
| Annali della Facoltà di Economia e Commercio dell'Università di Messina | *A. Fac. Econ. Com. Messina* | Messina |
| Annali di Sociologia | *A. Sociol. (Milano)* | Milano |
| Annals of economic and social Measurement | *A. econ. soc. Measurement* | New York |
| Annals of the American Academy of political and social Science | *A. Amer. Acad. polit. soc. Sci.* | Philadelphia, Pa. |
| Annals of the Association of American Geographers | *A. Assoc. Amer. Geogr.* | Lawrence, Kan. |
| Année sociologique | *Année sociol.* | Paris |
| Annuaire de l'Afrique du Nord | *Annu. Afr. Nord* | Aix-en-Provence |
| Annuaire de l'URSS | *Annu. URSS* | Strasbourg |
| Annuaire internationale de la Fonction publique | *Annu. int. Fonction publ.* | Paris |
| Annuaire suisse de Science politique | *Annu. suisse Sci. polit.* | Genève |
| Annuario di Politica internazionale | *Annu. Polit. int.* | Milano |
| Antitrust Bulletin | *Antitrust B.* | New York |
| Anuario del Instituto de Ciencias penales y criminológicas | *Anu. Inst. Cienc. pen. criminol.* | Caracas |
| Aperçus sur l'Économie tchécoslovaque | *Aperçus Écon. tchécosl.* | Prague |
| Aportes | *Aportes* | Paris |

| | | |
|---|---|---|
| Arbeit und Arbeitsrecht | *Arbeit u. Arbeitsrecht* | Berlin |
| Arbeit und Sozialpolitik | *Arbeit u. soz.-Polit.* | Baden-Baden |
| Arbor | *Arbor* | Madrid |
| Archiv des öffentlichen Rechts | *Archiv öff. Rechts* | Tübingen |
| Archiv des Völkerrechts | *Archiv Völkerrechts* | Tübingen |
| Archiv für Kommunalwissenschaften | *Archiv Kommunalwiss.* | Stuttgart |
| Archiv für Rechts- und Sozialphilosophie | *Archiv Rechts- u. soz.-Philos.* | Berlin-Neuwied-am-Rhein |
| Archives de Philosophie du Droit | *Archiv. Philos. Dr.* | Paris |
| Archives de Sciences sociales des Religions | *Archiv. Sci. soc. Relig.* | Paris |
| Archives de Sociologie des Religions | *Archiv. Sociol. Relig.* | Paris |
| Archives européennes de Sociologie / European Journal of Sociology / Europäisches Archiv für Soziologie | *Archiv. europ. Sociol.* | Paris |
| Archives internationales de Sociologie de la Coopération / International Archives of Sociology of Cooperation / Archivio internazionale di Sociologia della Cooperazione | *Archiv. int. Sociol. Coop.* | Paris |
| Archivo de Derecho público y Ciencias de la Administración | *Archiv. Der. publ. Cienc. Adm.* | Caracas |
| Argument | *Argument* | Karlsruhe |
| Artha Vijñana | *Artha Vijñana* | Poona |
| Asia Quarterly | *Asia Quart.* | Bruxelles |
| Asian Affairs. Journal of the Royal Central Asian Society | *Asian Aff.* | London |
| Asian Survey | *Asian Surv.* | Berkeley, Calif. |
| Aspects statistiques de la Région parisienne | *Aspects statist. Région paris.* | Paris |
| Association de Cadres dirigeants de l'Industrie pour le Progrès social et économique. Bulletin | *Assoc. Cadres dir. Industr. B.* | Paris |
| Atlantic Community Quarterly | *Atlantic Community Quart.* | Washington |
| Aussenpolitik | *Aussenpolitik* | Stuttgart |
| Aussenwirtschaft | *Aussenwirtschaft (St Gallen)* | St Gallen |
| Australian and New Zealand Journal of Sociology | *Austral. New Zealand J. Sociol.* | Melbourne |
| Australian economic Papers | *Austral. econ. Pap.* | Adelaide |
| Australian economic Review | *Austral. econ. R.* | Melbourne |
| Australian Journal of agricultural Economics | *Austral. J. agric. Econ.* | Armindale, N.S.W. |
| Australian Journal of Politics and History | *Austral. J. Polit. Hist.* | Sydney |
| Australian Outlook | *Austral. Outlook* | Melbourne |
| Australian Quarterly | *Austral. Quart.* | Sydney |
| AWR Bulletin | *AWR Bull.* | Paris |
| Azija i Afrika segodnja | *Azija i Afr. segod.* | Moskva |
| | | |
| BACIE Journal | *BACIE J.* | London |
| Balkan Studies | *Balkan Stud.* | Thessalonique |
| Banca nazionale del Lavoro. Quarterly Review | *Banca naz. Lav. quart. R.* | Roma |
| Bancaria | *Bancaria* | Roma |
| Bangladesh economic Review | *Bangladesh econ. R.* | Dacca |
| Bank of England quarterly Bulletin | *Bank England quart. B.* | London |
| Bank of Finland monthly Bulletin | *Bank Finland mthly B.* | Helsinki |
| Bank of London and South America Review | *Bank London South Amer. R.* | London |

| | | |
|---|---|---|
| Banker | *Banker* | London |
| Bankers' Magazine | *Bankers' Mag.* | London |
| Banque | *Banque* | Paris |
| Banque des États de l'Afrique centrale. Études et Statistiques | *Banque États Afr. centr. Ét. Statist.* | Paris |
| Banque française et italienne pour l'Amérique du Sud | *Banque franç. ital. Amér. Sud* | Paris |
| Banque française et italienne pour l'Amérique du Sud. Études économiques | *Banque franç. ital. Amér. Sud Ét. écon.* | Paris |
| Bayern in Zahlen | *Bayern in Zahlen* | München |
| Behavioral Science | *Behav. Sci.* | Ann Arbor, Mich. |
| Behavioral Science Notes | *Behav. Sci. Notes* | New Haven, Conn. |
| Beiträge zur Konfliktforschung | *Beitr. Konfliktforsch.* | Köln |
| Bénélux. Bulletin trimestriel économique et statistique | *Bénélux B. trim. écon. statist.* | Bruxelles |
| Berichte des deutschen Industrie Instituts zur Sozialpolitik | *Ber. dtsch. Industr. Inst. soz.-Polit.* | Köln |
| Berkeley Journal of Sociology | *Berkeley J. Sociol.* | Berkeley, Calif. |
| Berufliche Bildung | *Berufl. Bildung* | Düsseldorf |
| Berufsbildung | *Berufsbildung* | Berlin |
| Betriebswirtschaftliche Forschung und Praxis | *Betriebswirtsch. Forsch. u. Praxis* | Göttingen |
| Biuletyn Instytutu Gospodarstwa Społecznego | *Biul. IGS* | Warszawa |
| Bjulleten' inostrannoj kommerčeskoj Informacii Priloženie | *B. inostr. kommerč. Inform. Prilož.* | Moskva |
| Black Politician | *Black Politician* | Los Angeles, Calif. |
| Blätter für deutsche und internationale Politik | *Blätt. dtsche u. int. Polit.* | Köln |
| Boletim do Instituto Joaquim Nabuco de Pesquisas sociais | *Bol. Inst. Joaquim Nabuco Pesq. soc.* | Recife |
| Boletim econômico e financeiro | *Bol. econ. financ.* | São Paulo |
| Boletín de Documentación del Fondo para la Investigación económica y social | *Bol. Docum. Fondo Investig. econ. soc.* | Madrid |
| Boletín de Estudios económicos | *Bol. Estud. econ. (Bilbao)* | Bilbao |
| Boletín de Estudios latinoamericanos | *Bol. Estud. latinoamer.* | Amsterdam |
| Boletín de Londres | *Bol. Londres* | London |
| Boletín de la Facultad de Derecho y Ciencias sociales | *Bol. Fac. Der. Cienc. soc. (Córdoba)* | Córdoba |
| Boletín del Museo social argentino | *Bol. Mus. soc. argent.* | Buenos Aires |
| Boletín informativo de Ciencia política | *Bol. inform. Cienc. polít.* | Madrid |
| Boletín mensual de Estadística | *Bol. mens. Estadíst.* | Bogotá |
| Boletín mexicano de Derecho comparado | *Bol. mexic. Der. comp.* | Mexico |
| Boletín tecnico, Instituto para la Formación y Aprovechamiento de Recursos humanos | *Bol. tecn. Inst. Formación Aprovech. Recursos hum.* | Panama |
| Boletín uruguayo de Sociología | *Bol. urug. Sociol.* | Montevideo |
| British Journal of industrial Relations | *Brit. J. industr. Relat.* | London |
| British Journal of political Science | *Brit. J. polit. Sci.* | London |
| British Journal of social and clinical Psychology | *Brit. J. soc. clinic. Psychol.* | London |
| British Journal of social Psychiatry and Community Health | *Brit. J. soc. Psychiatry* | London |
| British Journal of Sociology | *Brit. J. Sociol.* | London |
| Brookings Papers on economic Activity | *Brookings Pap. econ. Activity* | Washington, D.C. |
| Bulletin d'Information de la Région parisienne | *B. Inform. Région paris.* | Paris |

| | | |
|---|---|---|
| Bulletin d'Information du Comité central du Parti ouvrier polonais unifié | *B. Inform. Comité centr. Parti ouvr. polon. unif.* | Varsovie |
| Bulletin d'Information du Comité et de l'Agence du Bassin Rhône-Méditerrannée-Corse | *B. Inform. Comité Agence Bassin Rhône-Méditer.-Corse* | Pierre-Bénite |
| Bulletin de Conjoncture régionale | *B. Conjonct. région. (Rennes)* | Rennes |
| Bulletin de Documentation. Grand Duché de Luxembourg | *B. Docum. (Luxembourg)* | Luxembourg |
| Bulletin de Liaison et d'Information de l'Administration centrale de l'Économie et des Finances | *B. Liaison Inform. Adm. centr. Écon. Finances* | Paris |
| Bulletin de Statistique | *B. Statist. (Bruxelles)* | Bruxelles |
| Bulletin de l'Association des Géographes français | *B. Assoc. Géogr. franç.* | Paris |
| Bulletin de l'Institut fondamental d'Afrique noire | *B. Inst. fondam. Afr. noire* | Dakar |
| Bulletin de l'Institut international de l'Administration publique | *B. Inst. int. Adm. publ.* | Paris |
| Bulletin du Centre d'Études et de Recherches psychotechniques | *Bull. CÉRP* | Paris |
| Bulletin du Centre européen de la Culture | *B. Centre europ. Cult.* | Genève |
| Bulletin du STATEC | *Bull. STATEC* | Luxembourg |
| Bulletin économique et social du Maroc | *B. écon. soc. Maroc* | Rabat |
| Bulletin for Indonesian economic Studies | *B. Indon. econ. Stud.* | Canberra |
| Bulletin for international fiscal Documentation | *B. int. fisc. Docum.* | Amsterdam |
| Bulletin, international Association for educational and vocational Guidance | *B. int. Assoc. educ. vocat. Guidance* | Luxembourg |
| Bulletin, international Institute for Labour Studies | *B. int. Inst. Lab. Stud.* | Geneva |
| Bulletin interparlementaire | *B. interparl.* | Genève |
| Bulletin mensuel Économie et Statistique agricoles | *B. mens. Écon. Statist. agric.* | Rome |
| Bulletin of economic Research | *B. econ. Res.* | Hull |
| Bulletin of Peace Proposals | *B. Peace Propos.* | Oslo |
| Bulletin of the African Institute of South Africa | *B. Afr. Inst. South Afr.* | Pretoria |
| Bulletin of the Oxford University Institute of Economics and Statistics | *B. Oxford Univ. Inst. Econ. Statist.* | Oxford |
| Bundesarbeistblatt | *Bundesarbeitsblatt (Bonn)* | Bonn |
| Bundesarbeitsblatt | *Bundesarbeitsblatt (Stuttgart)* | Stuttgart |
| Business and Society Review | *Busin. Soc. R.* | Boston, Mass. |
| Business Economist | *Busin. Economist* | Oxford |
| Business Horizons | *Busin. Horizons (Bloomington)* | Bloomington |
| Cahiers africains d'Administration publique. Études | *C. afr. Adm. publ. Ét.* | Tanger |
| Cahiers d'Études africaines | *C. Ét. afr.* | La Haye-Paris |
| Cahiers d'Outre-Mer | *C. O.-Mer* | Bordeaux |
| Cahiers de Bruges | *C. Bruges* | Bruges |
| Cahiers de Droit européen | *C. Dr. europ.* | Louvain |
| Cahiers de Sociologie économique | *C. Sociol. écon.* | Le Havre |
| Cahiers de Sociologie et de Démographie médicales | *C. Sociol. Démogr. médic.* | Paris |

| | | |
|---|---|---|
| Cahiers de Tunisie | *C. Tunisie* | Tunis |
| Cahiers de l'Institut français des Sciences administratives | *C. Inst. franç. Sci. adm.* | Paris |
| Cahiers du Communisme | *C. Communisme* | Paris |
| Cahiers du Monde hispanique et luso-brésilien | *C. Monde hisp. luso-brésil.* | Toulouse |
| Cahiers économiques de Bruxelles | *C. écon. Bruxelles* | Bruxelles |
| Cahiers économiques et sociaux | *C. écon. soc. (Kinshasa)* | Kinshasa |
| Cahiers internationaux de Sociologie | *C. int. Sociol.* | Paris |
| Cahiers Laënnec | *C. Laënnec* | Paris |
| Cahiers Vilfredo Pareto | *C. V. Pareto* | Genève |
| Cahiers zaïrois d'Études politiques et sociales | *C. zaïr. Ét. polit. soc.* | Lumubashi |
| Cahiers zaïrois de la Recherche et du Développement | *C. zaïr. Rech. Dévelop.* | Kinshasa |
| California Management Review | *Calif. Manag. R.* | Los Angeles, Calif. |
| Canadian geographical Journal | *Canad. geogr. J.* | Ottawa |
| Canadian Journal of African Studies / Revue canadienne d'Études africaines | *Canad. J. Afr. Stud.* | Ottawa |
| Canadian Journal of agricultural Economics | *Canad. J. agr. Econ.* | Toronto |
| Canadian Journal of Economics | *Canad. J. Econ.* | Toronto |
| Canadian Journal of political Science | *Canad. J. polit. Sci.* | Toronto |
| Canadian public Administration | *Canad. publ. Adm.* | Toronto |
| Canadian Slavonic Papers | *Canad. Slavonic Pap.* | Ottawa |
| Canadian Yearbook of international Law | *Canad. Yb. int. Law* | Vancoover |
| Capitol Studies | *Capitol Stud.* | Washington, D.C. |
| Carribean Studies | *Carib. Stud.* | Puerto Rico |
| Carnets de l'Enfance | *Carnets Enfance* | Paris |
| Case Western Reserve Journal of international Law | *Case West. J. int. Law* | Cleveland, Ohio |
| Catalyst | *Catalyst* | Buffalo-New York |
| Čelovek i Obšéestvo | *Čelovek i Obšč.* | Leningrad |
| Central Bank of Ireland quarterly Bulletin | *Centr. Bank Ireland quart. B.* | Dublin |
| CÉRÈS Nord-Pas-de-Calais | *CÉRÈS Nord-Pas-de-Calais* | Lille |
| Challenge | *Challenge* | New York |
| Changing Latin America | *Changing Latin Amer.* | New York |
| Child Welfare | *Child Welfare* | New York |
| China Quarterly | *China Quart.* | London |
| China Report | *China Rep.* | New Delhi |
| Chirigaku Hyôron | *Chirigaku Hyôron* | Tokyo |
| Chronique de Politique étrangère | *Chron. Polit. étr.* | Bruxelles |
| Ciencias administrativas | *Cienc. adm. (La Plata)* | La Plata |
| Civilisations | *Civilisations* | Bruxelles |
| Civiltà cattolica | *Civiltà catt.* | Roma |
| Civitas | *Civitas (Romnheim)* | Mannheim |
| Civitas | *Civitas (Mana)* | Roma |
| Co-existence | *Co-existence* | Ontario-Chicago, Ill. |
| Collections de l'INSÉE | *Coll. INSÉE* | Paris |
| Colombo Law Review | *Colombo Law R.* | Colombo |
| Columbia Essays in international Affairs | *Columbia Essays int. Aff.* | New York |
| Columbia Journal of transnational Law | *Columbia J. transnat. Law* | New York |
| Columbia Journal of World Business | *Columbia J. Wld Busin.* | New York |
| Columbia Journalism Review | *Columbia J-ism R.* | New York |
| Columbia Law Review | *Columbia Law R.* | New York |
| Commentary | *Commentary* | New York |
| Common Market Law Review | *Common Market Law R.* | Leyden |
| Communautés | *Communautés* | Paris |

| | | |
|---|---|---|
| Communications | Communications | Paris |
| Community and Development Journal | Community Develop. J. | Manchester |
| Comparative Education Review | Comp. Educ. R. | Kent, Ohio |
| Comparative political Studies | Comp. polit. Stud. | Beverly Hills, Calif. |
| Comparative Politics | Comp. Polit. | Chicago, Ill. |
| Comparative Studies in Society and History | Comp. Stud. Soc. Hist. | The Hague-Ann Arbor, Mich. |
| Comptes-rendus trimestriels des Séances de l'Académie des Sciences d'Outre-Mer | C. R. trim. Acad. Sci. O.-Mer | Paris |
| Comunità | Comunità | Milano |
| Comunità internazionale | Comunità int. | Roma |
| Conflict Studies | Conflict Stud. | London |
| Confronter | Confronter | Paris |
| Conjuntura economica | Conjunt. econ. | Rio de Janeiro |
| Connexions | Connexions | Paris |
| Consommation. Annales du CREDOC | Consommation | Paris |
| Construction, Aménagement | Construct. Aménag. | Paris |
| Contemporary Review | Contemp. R. | London |
| Contemporary Sociology | Contemp. Sociol. | Washington, D.C. |
| Contradictions | Contradictions | Paris |
| Contrepoint | Contrepoint | Paris |
| Contributions to Indian Sociology. New Series | Contrib. Ind. Sociol. New Ser. | Bombay |
| Contropiano | Contropiano | Roma |
| Convivium | Convivium (São Paulo) | São Paulo |
| Coopération | Coopération | Paris |
| Cooperation and Conflict | Coop. and Conflict | Stockholm |
| Coopération et Développement | Coop. et Dévelop. | Paris |
| Cornell Journal of social Relations | Cornell J. soc. Relat. | Ithaca, N. Y. |
| Correspondance municipale | Corresp. municip. | Paris |
| Courrier des Pays de l'Est | Courr. Pays-Est | Paris |
| Creditanstalt Bankverein Wien. Wirtschaftsberichte | Creditanstalt Bankver. Wien Wirtsch.-Ber. | Wien |
| Cristianismo y Sociedad | Crist. y Soc. | Montevideo |
| Criterio | Criterio | Buenos-Aires |
| Critica marxista | Crit. marx. | Roma |
| Critica sociale | Crit. soc. (Milano) | Milano |
| Critica sociologica | Crit. sociol. (Roma) | Roma |
| Critique | Critique | Paris |
| Critique de l'Économie politique | Crit. Écon. polit. | Paris |
| Critique socialiste | Crit. social. (Paris) | Paris |
| Cuadernos américanos | Cuad. amér. | México |
| Cuadernos de Economía | Cuad. Econ. (Barcelona) | Barcelona |
| Cuadernos de Estudios políticos | Cuad. Estud. polít. | Barcelona |
| Cuadernos de Ruedo ibérico | Cuad. Ruedo ibér. | Paris |
| Cuadernos de la Realidad nacional | Cuad. Real. nac. | Santiago de Chile |
| Cuadernos para el Diálogo | Cuad. Diálogo | Madrid |
| Cuadernos para el Diálogo extra-ordinario | Cuad. Diálogo extraord. | Madrid |
| Culture et Développement | Cult. et Dévelop. | Louvain |
| Culture française | Cult. franç. | Paris |
| Current Affairs Bulletin | Curr. Aff. B. | Sydney |
| Current History | Curr. Hist. | Philadelphia, Pa. |
| Dados | Dados | Rio de Janeiro |
| Daedalus. Journal of the American Academy of Arts and Sciences | Daedalus | Cambridge, Mass. |
| De Economia | De Economia | Madrid |

| | | |
|---|---|---|
| Défense nationale | *Déf. nat.* | Paris |
| Defensor Legis | *Defensor Legis* | Helsinki |
| Democrazia e Diritto | *Democr. e Dir.* | Roma |
| Demográfia | *Demográfia* | Budapest |
| Demografía y Economía | *Demogr. y Econ.* | México |
| Demografičeskie Tetrady | *Demogr. Tetrady* | Kiev |
| Demografie | *Demografie* | Praha |
| Demography | *Demography (Ann Arbor)* | Ann Arbor |
| Demosta | *Demosta* | Praha |
| Den'gi i Kredit | *Den'gi i Kred.* | Moskva |
| Derecho de la Integración | *Der. Integr.* | Buenos-Aires |
| Desarollo económico | *Desarr. econ.* | Buenos-Aires |
| Desarrollo indoamericano | *Desarr. indoamer.* | Bogotá |
| Deutsche Aussenpolitik | *Dtsche Aussenpolit.* | Berlin |
| Deutsche Jugend | *Dtsche Jugend* | München |
| Deutsche Studien. Verteljahreshefte für vergleichende Gegenwartskunde | *Dtsche Stud.* | Lüneburg |
| Deutsche Zeitschrift für Philosophie | *Dtsche Z. Philos.* | Berlin |
| Deutschland Archiv | *Deutschland Archiv* | Köln |
| 2000, Revue de l'Aménagement du Territoire | *2000 R. Aménag. Territ.* | Paris |
| Developing Economies | *Develop. Econ.* | Tokyo |
| Development and Change | *Develop. and Change* | The Hague |
| Développement et Civilisations | *Dévelop. et Civilis.* | Paris |
| Dialogue | *Dialogue (Washington)* | Washington |
| Dimensions économiques de la Bourgogne | *Dim. écon. Bourgogne* | Dijon |
| Diogène | *Diogène* | Paris |
| Direction et Gestion des Entreprises | *Dir. Gestion Entr.* | Paris |
| DISP. Dokumentation- und Informationstelle für Planungsfragen | *DISP* | Zürich |
| Dissent | *Dissent* | New York |
| Djeich (El) | *Djeich* | Alger |
| Documentation française illustrée | *Docum. franç. illustr.* | Paris |
| Documentation sur l'Europe centrale | *Docum. Europ. centr.* | Louvain |
| Documentos políticos | *Doc. polít.* | Bogotá |
| Documents. Revue des Questions allemandes | *Documents (Cologne)* | Cologne |
| Documents CEPESS. Centre d'Études politiques, économiques et sociales | *Doc. CÉPESS* | Bruxelles |
| Documents de la CEGOS | *Docum. CEGOS* | Puteaux |
| Documents européens | *Docum. europ.* | Paris |
| Donauraum | *Donauraum* | Salzburg |
| Dossier Mundo | *Doss. Mundo* | Barcelona |
| Dossiers de l'Économie lorraine | *Doss. Écon. lorraine* | Nancy |
| Dossiers de la Politique agricole commune | *Doss. Polit. agric. commune* | Paris |
| Dossiers documentaires | *Doss. docum.* | Alger |
| Dritte Welt | *Dritte Welt* | Meisenheim |
| Droit bulgare | *Dr. bulg.* | Sofia |
| Droit et Liberté | *Dr. et Liberté* | Paris |
| Droit social | *Dr. soc.* | Paris |
| East Africa Journal | *East Africa J.* | Nairobi |
| East African economic Review | *East. Afr. econ. R.* | Nairobi |
| Eastern Anthropologist | *East. Anthropol.* | Lucknow |
| Eastern European Economics | *East. Europ. Econ.* | New York |
| Échanges internationaux et Développement | *Échanges int. Dévelop.* | Toulouse |
| Econometrica | *Econometrica* | Chicago, Ill. |

| | | |
|---|---|---|
| Economía | *Economía (Quito)* | Quito |
| Economia e Lavoro | *Econ. e Lav. (Padova)* | Padova |
| Economia internazionale | *Econ. int. (Genova)* | Genova |
| Economia internazionale delle Fonti di Energia | *Econ. int. Fonti Energia* | Milano |
| Economía y Administración | *Econ. y Adm.* | Concepción |
| Economia y Desarrollo | *Econ. y Desarr.* | La Habana |
| Economic Affairs | *Econ. Aff.* | Calcutta |
| Economic Analysis and Policy | *Econ. Anal. Pol.* | St. Lucia, Australia |
| Economic and political Weekly | *Econ. polit. Wkly* | Bombay |
| Economic and social Review | *Econ. soc. R.* | Dublin |
| Economic Bulletin. National Bank of Egypt | *Econ. B. (Cairo)* | Cairo |
| Economic Bulletin for Asia and the Far East | *Econ. B. Asia Far East* | Lake Success, N. Y. |
| Economic Bulletin for Latin America | *Econ. B. Latin Amer,* | New York |
| Economic Bulletin of Ghana | *Econ. B. Ghana* | Accra |
| Economic Development and cultural Change | *Econ. Develop. cult. Change* | Chicago, Ill. |
| Economic Geography | *Econ. Geogr. (Worcester)* | Worcester, Mass. |
| Economic Journal | *Econ. J.* | London |
| Economic quarterly Review | *Econ. quart. R.* | Amsterdam |
| Economic Record | *Econ. Rec.* | Melbourne |
| Economic Review | *Econ. R. (Helsinki)* | Helsinki |
| Economic Studies Quarterly | *Econ. Stud. Quart.* | |
| Económica | *Económica (La Plata)* | La Plata |
| Economica | *Economica (London)* | London |
| Economie | *Economie (Tilburg)* | Tilburg |
| Économie appliquée | *Écon. appl.* | Paris |
| Économie et Humanisme | *Écon. et Human.* | Caluire |
| Économie et Politique | *Écon. et Polit.* | Paris |
| Économie et Statistique | *Écon. et Statist.* | Paris |
| Économie — Géographie | *Écon. Géogr.* | Paris |
| Économie régionale. Poitou-Charentes | *Écon. région. Poitou-Charentes* | Poitiers |
| Économie rurale | *Écon. rur.* | Paris |
| Economisch en sociaal Tijdschrift | *Econ. soc. Tijds.* | Antwerpen |
| Economist (De) | *Economist (Haarlem)* | Haarlem |
| Economy and Society | *Econ. and Soc.* | London |
| Educación | *Educación* | Caracas |
| Éducation et Culture | *Éduc. et Cult.* | Strasbourg |
| Éducation permanente | *Éduc. perm.* | Nancy |
| Educational Education and Information | *Educ. Educ. Inform.* | Geneva |
| Educational Technology | *Éduc. Technol.* | Englewood-Cliffs |
| Égypte contemporaine | *Égypte contemp.* | Le Caire |
| Einheit | *Einheit* | Berlin |
| Ekistics | *Ekistics* | Athens |
| Ekonomi Journal | *Ekon. J.* | Kuala Lumpur |
| Ėkonomičeskie Nauki | *Ėkon. Nauki* | Moskva |
| Ekonomicko-matematický Obzor | *Ekon.-matem. Obzor* | Praha |
| Ėkonomika i matematičeskie Metody | *Ėkon. matem. Metody* | Moskva |
| Ėkonomika i Organizacija promyšlennogo Proizvodstva | *Ėkon. Org. promyšl. Proizvodstva* | Novosibirsk |
| Ėkonomika sel'skogo Hozjajstva | *Ėkon. sel'sk. Hoz.* | Moskva |
| Ekonomisk Revy | *Ekon. R. (Stockholm)* | Stockholm |
| Ekonomiska Samfundets Tidskrift | *Ekon. Samfund. Ts.* | Helsinki |
| Ekonomist | *Ekonomist (Zagreb)* | Zagreb |
| Ekonomista | *Ekonomista (Warszawa)* | Warszawa |
| Ekonomska Misao | *Ekon. Misao* | Beograd |

| | | |
|---|---|---|
| Ekonomska Revija | Ekon. R. (Ljubljana) | Ljubljana |
| Encounter | Encounter | London |
| Energy Policy | Energy Pol. | Guildford |
| Engineering Economist | Engin. Economist | Hoboken, N. J. |
| Épistémologie sociologique | Épistémol. sociol. | Paris |
| Épithéorissi dimossion Dikaion kaì Diikitikon Dikaion | Épithéor. dimos. Dikaion Diikit. Dikaion | 'Athênaï |
| Era socialistă | Era social. | Bucuresti |
| Ésope | Ésope | Paris |
| Espace géographique | Espace géogr. | Paris |
| Espaces | Espaces | Paris |
| Espaces et Sociétés | Espaces et Soc. | Paris |
| Espoir | Espoir | Paris |
| Esprit | Esprit | Paris |
| Est | Est (Milano) | Milano |
| Est-Ovest | Est-Ovest | Trieste |
| Estadística | Estadística (Washington) | Washington |
| Estrategía | Estrategía | Buenos Aires |
| Estudios | Estudios (Montevideo) | Montevideo |
| Estudios andinos | Estud. andin. | La Paz |
| Estudios cooperativos | Estud. coop. | Madrid |
| Estudios de Derecho | Estud. Der. (Medellín) | Medellín |
| Estudios de la Seguridad social | Estud. Segur. soc. | Ginebra |
| Estudios geográficos | Estud. geogr. | Madrid |
| Estudios internacionales | Estud. int. | Santiago de Chile |
| Estudios sindicales y cooperativos | Estud. sindic. coop. | Madrid |
| Estudos sociais e corporativos | Estud. soc. corpor. | Lisbõa |
| Ethics. An international Journal of social, political and legal Philosophy | Ethics | Chicago, Ill. |
| Ethnies | Ethnies | Nice |
| Ethnology | Ethnology | Pittsburgh, Pa. |
| Études | Études (Paris) | Paris |
| Études de Planning familial | Ét. Planning famil. | New York |
| Études de Radio-Télévision | Ét. Radio-Télévis. | Bruxelles |
| Études de la Région parisienne | Ét. Région paris. | Paris |
| Études économiques | Ét. écon. (Mons) | Mons |
| Études et Documents (Éducation nationale) | Ét. et Doc. (Éduc. nat.) | Paris |
| Études et Statistiques. Bulletin mensuel. Cameroun Afrique équatoriale. Banque centrale | Ét. Statist. Cameroun Afr. équat. Banque centr. | Paris Paris |
| Études internationales | Ét. int. | Québec |
| Études normandes | Ét. normandes | Le Havre |
| Études polémologiques | Ét. polémol. | Paris |
| Études régionales. Supplément au Bulletin. Conjoncture économique dans la Région de Bretagne | Ét. région. Suppl. B. Conjonct. écon. Bretagne | Rennes |
| Études rurales | Ét. rur. | Paris |
| Études slaves et est-européennes | Ét. slaves est-europ. | Montréal |
| EURE. Revista latinoamericana de Estudios urbano-regionales | EURE | Santiago de Chile |
| Europa-Archiv | Europa-Archiv | Frankfurt-am-Main |
| Europaïsche Rundschau | Europ. Rdschau | Wien |
| Europarecht | Europarecht | München |
| Europe-France Outre-Mer | Europe-France O.-Mer | Paris |
| European demographic Information Bulletin | Europ. demogr. Inform. B. | The Hague |
| European economic Review | Europ. econ. R. | Bruxelles |
| European Journal of political Research | Europ. J. polit. Res. | Amsterdam |

| | | |
|---|---|---|
| European Journal of social Psychology | *Europ. J. soc. Psychol.* | The Hague |
| European Training | *Europ. Training* | Bradford |
| Examen de la Situación económica de México | *Exam. Sit. econ. México* | México |
| Expansion régionale | *Expans. région. (Paris)* | Paris |
| Explorations in economic History | *Explor. econ. Hist.* | Richmond, Va. |
| Express Rhône-Alpes | *Express Rhône-Alpes* | Lyon |
| | | |
| Family Coordinator | *Family Coordinator* | Eugene, Ore. |
| Family Process | *Family Process* | Baltimore, Md. |
| Federal Reserve Bank of St Louis | *Fed. Reserve Bank St Louis* | St Louis, Mo. |
| Federal Reserve Bulletin | *Fed. Reserve B.* | Washington, D. C. |
| Filosofskie Nauki | *Filos. Nauki* | Alma-Ata |
| Finance and Development | *Finance and Develop.* | Washington, D. C. |
| Finanse | *Finanse* | Warszawa |
| Finansy SSSR | *Finansy SSSR* | Moskva |
| Finante Finante şi Credit | *Finante şi Cred.* | Bucureşti |
| Finanzarchiv | *Finanzarchiv* | Tübingen |
| Finsk Tidskrift | *Finsk Ts.* | Åbo |
| Fiscalité européenne | *Fisc. europ.* | Nice |
| Földrajzi Értesítő | *Földrajzi Értes.* | Budapest |
| Folia oeconomica cracoviensia | *Fol. oecon. cracov.* | Kraków |
| Food Research Institute Studies | *Food Res. Inst. Stud.* | Stanford, Calif. |
| Foreign Affairs | *For. Aff.* | New York |
| Foreign Policy | *For. Pol.* | New York |
| Formation-France | *Formation-France* | Paris |
| Formazione e Lavoro | *Formazione e Lav.* | Roma |
| Foro internacional | *Foro int.* | México |
| Fortune | *Fortune* | Chicago, Ill. |
| France-Forum | *France-Forum* | Paris |
| Frankfurter Hefte | *Frankfurt. H.* | Frankfurt-am-Main |
| Frères du Monde | *Frères du Monde* | Bordeaux |
| Futures | *Futures (Guildford)* | Guildford |
| Futuribili | *Futuribili* | Roma |
| Futurist | *Futurist* | Washington, D. C. |
| Futuro presente | *Futuro presente* | Madrid |
| | | |
| Gallup Opinion Index | *Gallup Opin. Index* | Princeton, N. J. |
| Gazette | *Gazette (Amsterdam)* | Amsterdam |
| Gegenwartskunde | *Gegenwartskunde* | Opladen |
| Gendai to Shiso | *Gendai to Shiso* | [Nihon] |
| General Systems | *Gen. Systems* | New York |
| Genève-Afrique | *Genève-Afr.* | Genève |
| Geographical Journal | *Geogr. J.* | London |
| Geographical Review | *Geogr. R.* | New York |
| Géographie et Recherche | *Géogr. et Rech.* | Dijon |
| Georgia Augusta | *Georgia Augusta* | Göttingen |
| German economic Review | *German econ. R.* | Tübingen |
| German foreign Policy | *German for. Pol.* | Berlin, FR |
| Gérontologie | *Gérontologie* | Paris |
| Giornale degli Economisti e Annali di Economia | *G. Economisti* | Padova |
| Gledišta | *Gledišta* | Beograd |
| Godišnik na ekonomski ot Fakultet (Skopje) | *Godiš. ekon. Fak. (Skopje)* | Skopje |
| Gospodarka planowa | *Gosp. planowa* | Warszawa |
| Government and Opposition | *Gvt and Opposition* | London |
| Group Psychotherapy and Psychodrama | *Group Psychother.* | Beacon, N. Y. |
| Growth and Change | *Growth and Change* | Lexington, Ky. |

| | | |
|---|---|---|
| Guyana Journal | *Guyana J.* | Georgetown |
| Habitation | *Habitation* | Paris |
| Hamburg in Zahlen | *Hamburg in Zahlen* | Hamburg |
| Hamburger Jahrbuch für Wirtschafts- Geselschaftspolitik | *Hamburg. Jb. Wirtsch.- u. Ges.-Polit.* | Hamburg |
| Handel wewnętrzny | *Handel wewn.* | Warszawa |
| Handel zagraniczy | *Handel zagran.* | Warszawa |
| Harper's Magazine | *Harper's Mag.* | New York |
| Harvard Business Review | *Harvard Busin. R.* | Boston, Mass. |
| Harvard Business School Bulletin | *Harvard Busin. School B.* | Boston, Mass. |
| Harvard educational Review | *Harvard educ. R.* | Cambridge, Mass. |
| Harvard Law Review | *Harvard Law R.* | Cambridge, Mass. |
| Heuristics | *Heuristics* | De Kalb |
| Higher Education | *Higher Educ.* | Amsterdam |
| Hikaku Bunka Kenkyû Kiyô | *Hikaku Bunka Kenkyû Kiyô* | Tokyo |
| History and Theory | *Hist. and Theory* | Middletown, Conn. |
| History of political Economy | *Hist. polit. Econ.* | Durham, N. C. |
| Hitotsubashi Journal of Economics | *Hitotsubashi J. Econ.* | Tokyo |
| Hitotsubashi Journal of social Studies | *Hitotsubashi J. soc. Stud.* | Tokyo |
| Hô to Seiji | *Hô to Seiji* | Nishinomiya |
| Hogaku | *Hogaku* | [Nihon] |
| Hôgaku Kenkyû | *Hôgaku Kenkyû* | Tokyo |
| Hogaku Ronso | *Hogaku Ronso* | Kyoto |
| Hôgaku Shinpô | *Hôgaku Shinpô* | Tokyo |
| Hogaku Zasshi | *Hogaku Zasshi* | [Nihon] |
| Homme et Société | *Homme et Soc.* | Paris |
| Hommes et Migrations | *Hommes et Migr.* | Paris |
| Hommes et Migrations. Documents | *Hommes et Migr. Doc.* | Paris |
| Hommes et Technique | *Hommes et Techn.* | Paris |
| Homo | *Homo* | Toulouse |
| Hôpital à Paris | *Hôpital Paris* | Paris |
| Hosei Ronshu | *Hosei Ronshu* | [Nihon] |
| Hôsôgaku Kenkyû | *Hôsôgaku Kenkyû* | Tokyo |
| Human Context | *Hum. Context* | London |
| Human Organization | *Hum. Org.* | New York |
| Human Relations | *Hum. Relat.* | London |
| Humanisme | *Humanisme* | Paris |
| Humanisme et Entreprise | *Human. et Entrepr.* | Paris |
| Humanizm Pracy | *Human. Pracy* | Warszawa |
| Idéologie | *Idéologie* | Rome |
| Igreja e Missão | *Igreja e Missão* | Cucujães |
| Illinois agricultural Economics | *Ill. agric. Econ.* | Urbana, Ill. |
| IMF Staff Papers | *IMF Staff Pap.* | Washington, D. C. |
| Impact, Science et Société | *Impact* | Paris |
| Impacts | *Impacts* | Angers |
| Impresa | *Impresa* | Roma |
| Improving human Performance, a Research Quarterly | *Improving hum. Perform. Res. Quart.* | Washington, D. C. |
| Impuestos de la Hacienda pública | *Impuestos Hac. públ.* | Madrid |
| India Quarterly | *India Quart.* | New Delhi |
| Indian co-operative Review | *Ind. coop. R.* | New Delhi |
| Indian economic Journal | *Ind. econ. J.* | Bombay |
| Indian Journal of Adult Education | *Ind. J. Adult Educ.* | New Delhi |
| Indian Journal of agricultural Economics | *Ind. J. agric. Econ.* | Bombay |
| Indian Journal of industrial Relations | *Ind. J. industr. Relat.* | New Delhi |

| | | |
|---|---|---|
| Indian Journal of political Science | *Ind. J. polit. Sci.* | Lucknow |
| Indian Journal of Politics | *Ind. J. Polit.* | Aligarh |
| Indian Journal of public Administration | *Ind. J. publ. Adm.* | New Delhi |
| Indian Journal of social Research | *Ind. J. soc. Res.* | Baraut |
| Indian Labour Journal | *Ind. Lab. J.* | Simla |
| Indian Management | *Ind. Manag.* | New Delhi |
| Indian political Science Review | *Ind. polit. Sci. R.* | Delhi |
| Indicateurs de l'Économie du Centre | *Indicateurs Écon. Centre* | Paris |
| Indonesia | *Indonesia* | Ithaca, N. Y. |
| Industria | *Industria* | Milano |
| Industria e Produtividade | *Industr. e Produtiv.* | Rio de Janeiro |
| Industrial and commercial Training | *Industr. com. Training* | Guilsborough |
| Industrial and Labor Relations Review | *Industr. Lab. Relat. R.* | Ithaca, N. Y. |
| Industrial Egypt | *Industr. Egypt* | Cairo |
| Industrial Gerontology | *Industr. Gerontol.* | Washington, D. C. |
| Industrial Law Journal | *Industr. Law J.* | London |
| Industrial Relations | *Industr. Relat. (Berkeley)* | Berkeley, Calif. |
| Industrial Relations Journal | *Industr. Relat. J.* | London |
| Industrie | *Industrie* | Bruxelles |
| Industries et Travaux d'Outre-Mer | *Industr. Trav. O.-Mer* | Paris |
| Industry of free China | *Industry free China* | Taipei |
| Información comercial española | *Inform. com. esp.* | Madrid |
| Información jurídica | *Inform. jur. (Madrid)* | Madrid |
| Information Bulletin (of the Council of Europe) | *Inform. B.* | Strasburg |
| Information géographique | *Inform. géogr.* | Paris |
| Informationen | *Informationen* | Bad-Godesberg |
| Informations constitutionnelles et parlementaires | *Inform. constit. parl.* | Genève |
| Informations SIDA | *Inform. SIDA* | Lille |
| Informations sociales | *Inform. soc. (Paris)* | Paris |
| Informations universitaires et professionnelles internationales | *Inform. univ. profes. int.* | Paris |
| Instant Research on Peace and Violence | *Instant Res. Peace Violence* | Tampere |
| Institut international d'Études sociales. Bulletin | *Inst. int. Ét. soc. B.* | Genève |
| Institute of Development Studies. Bulletin | *Inst. Develop. Stud. B.* | Brighton |
| Insurgent Sociologist | *Insurgent Sociologist* | |
| Integration | *Integration* | Augsburg |
| Inter-American economic Affairs | *Inter-Amer. econ. Aff.* | Washington, D. C. |
| Intermountain economic Review | *Intermountain econ. R.* | [USA] |
| Internasjonal Politikk | *Int. Polit. (Bergen)* | Bergen |
| International Affairs | *Int. Aff. (London)* | London |
| International and comparative Law Quarterly | *Int. comp. Law Quart.* | London |
| International Conciliation | *Int. Conciliation* | New York |
| International economic Review | *Int. econ. R.* | Osaka |
| International Journal | *Int. J.* | Toronto |
| International Journal of comparative Sociology | *Int. J. comp. Sociol.* | Leiden |
| International Journal of contemporary Sociology | *Int. J. contemp. Sociol.* | Ghaziabad |
| International Journal of Group Psychotherapy | *Int. J. Group Psychother.* | New York |
| International Journal of Middle East Studies | *Int. J. Mid. East Stud.* | London |
| International Journal of Politics | *Int. J. Polit.* | New York |
| International Journal of Sociology | *Int. J. Sociol.* | New York |

| | | |
|---|---|---|
| International Journal of Sociology of the Family | *Int. J. Sociol. Family* | Lucknow |
| International Labour Review | *Int. Lab. R.* | Geneva |
| International Migration Review | *Int. Migration R.* | New York |
| International Organization | *Int. Org.* | Boston, Mass. |
| International Problems | *Int. Probl. (Belgrade)* | Belgrade |
| International Problems | *Int. Probl. (Tel-Aviv)* | Tel-Aviv |
| International Relations | *Int. Relat. (London)* | London |
| International Relations | *Int. Relat. (Prague)* | Prague |
| International Review of Education | *Int. R. Educ.* | The Hague |
| International Review of History and political Science | *Int. R. Hist. polit. Sci.* | Meerut |
| International Review of Sociology | *Int. R. Sociol.* | Dekalb, Ill. |
| International social Development Review | *Int. soc. Develop. R.* | New York |
| International social Security Review | *Int. soc. Secur. R.* | Geneva |
| International social Work | *Int. soc. Wk* | Bombay |
| International socialist Review | *Int. social. R.* | New York |
| International Studies | *Int. Stud. (New Delhi)* | New Delhi |
| International Studies | *Int. Stud. (Stockholm)* | Stockholm |
| International Studies Quarterly | *Int. Stud. Quart.* | Detroit, Mich. |
| International Trade Review | *Int. Trade R.* | New York |
| International Spectator | *Int. Spectator* | 's-Gravenhage |
| Internationales Afrika Forum | *Int. Afrika Forum* | München |
| Internationales Asien Forum | *Int. Asien Forum* | München |
| Internationales Recht und Diplomatie | *Int. Recht u. Diplom.* | Hamburg |
| Inter-Nord | *Inter-Nord* | Paris |
| Intertax | *Intertax* | Paris |
| Investigación económica | *Invest. econ.* | México |
| Inwestycje i Budownictwo | *Invest. i Budown.* | Warszawa |
| IPW Berichte | *IPW Ber.* | Berlin |
| Iskusstvo Kino | *Isk. Kino* | Leningrad |
| Israel Law Review | *Israel Law R.* | Jerusalem |
| Issues | *Issues* | New York |
| Issues and Studies | *Issues and Stud.* | Taîpeh |
| Istina | *Istina* | Paris |
| Istorija SSSR | *Ist. SSSR* | Moskva |
| Istruzione tecnica professionale e Realizzazioni | *Istr. tecn. profess. Realiz.* | Torino |
| Izvestija Akademii Nauk SSSR. Serija ekonomičeskaja | *Izv. Akad. Nauk SSSR Ser. ekon.* | Moskva |
| Izvestija Akademii Nauk Turkmenskoj SSR. Serija obščestvennyh Nauk | *Izv. Akad. Nauk Turkmen. SSR Ser. obšč. Nauk* | Ašhabad |
| Izvestija Sibirskogo Otdelenija Akademii Nauk SSSR. Serija obščestvennyh Nauk | *Izv. Sib. Otdel. Akad. Nauk SSSR. Ser. obšč. Nauk* | Novosibirsk |
| Izvestija Tomskogo politehničeskogo Instituta im. S.M. Kirova | *Izv. Tomsk. politehn. Inst.* | Tomsk |
| Jahrbuch des öffentlichen Rechts der Gegenwart | *Jb. öff. Rechts* | Tübingen |
| Jahrbuch für Geschichte der sozialistischen Länder Europas | *Jb. Gesch. sozial. Länd. Europas* | Berlin |
| Jahrbuch für Geschichte und Geographieunterricht | *Jb. Gesch. u. Geogr.-Unterr.* | [Deutschland] |
| Jahrbuch für internationales Recht | *Jb. int. Recht* | Göttingen |
| Jahrbuch für Ostrecht | *Jb. Ostrecht* | München |
| Jahrbuch für Sozialwissenschaft | *Jb. soz.-Wiss.* | Göttingen |
| Jahrbuch für Wirtschaftsgeschichte | *Jb. Wirtsch.-Gesch.* | Berlin |

| | | |
|---|---|---|
| Jahrbücher für Nationalökonomie und Statistik | *Jb-r nat.-Ökon. u. Statist.* | Stuttgart |
| Japan-Interpreter | *Japan-Interpreter* | Tokyo |
| Japan Quarterly | *Japan Quart.* | Tokyo |
| Japon Économie | *Japon Écon.* | Tokyo |
| Jewish Journal of Sociology | *Jew. J. Sociol.* | London |
| Jimbun Gakuho | *Jimbun Gakuho* | Tokyo |
| Jinbun Kenkyû | *Jinbun Kenkyû* | Osaka |
| Jogtudományi Közlöny | *Jogtud. Közl.* | Budapest |
| Journal de la Société de Statistique de Paris | *J. Soc. Statist. Paris* | Paris |
| Journal des Caisses d'Épargne | *J. Caisses Épargne* | Paris |
| Journal du Droit international | *J. Dr. int.* | Paris |
| Journal of the scientific Study of Religion | *J. scient. Study Relig.* | New Haven, Conn. |
| Journal of Administration Overseas | *J. Adm. Overseas* | London |
| Journal of African History | *J. Afr. Hist.* | London |
| Journal of African Law | *J. Afr. Law* | London |
| Journal of agricultural Economics | *J. agric. Econ.* | Manchester |
| Journal of American Studies | *J. Amer. Stud.* | Cambridge, Eng. |
| Journal of applied behavioral Science | *J. appl. behav. Sci.* | New York |
| Journal of Asian and African Studies | *J. Asian Afr. Stud.* | Toronto |
| Journal of Asian Studies | *J. Asian Stud.* | Ann Arbor, Mich. |
| Journal of biosocial Science | *J. biosoc. Sci.* | Oxford |
| Journal of Black Studies | *J. Black Stud.* | Los Angeles, Calif. |
| Journal of Business | *J. Busin.* | Chicago, Ill. |
| Journal of Business Finance | *J. Busin. Finance* | London |
| Journal of Business Policy | *J. Busin. Pol.* | London |
| Journal of Common Market Studies | *J. Common Market Stud.* | Oxford |
| Journal of Commonwealth political Studies | *J. Commonwealth polit. Stud.* | Leicester |
| Journal of Communication | *J. Communication* | Lawrence, Kan. |
| Journal of comparative Administration | *J. comp. Adm* | Beverly Hills, Calif. |
| Journal of comparative Family Studies | *J. comp. Family Stud.* | Calgary, Alta. |
| Journal of Conflict Resolution | *J. Conflict Resol.* | Ann Arbor, Mich. |
| Journal of constitutional and parliamentary Studies | *J. const. parl. Stud.* | New Delhi |
| Journal of Consumer Affairs | *J. Consumer Aff.* | Columbia, Miss. |
| Journal of contemporary Asia | *J. contemp. Asia* | Stockholm |
| Journal of contemporary Business | *J. contemp. Busin.* | Washington, D. C. |
| Journal of contemporary History | *J. contemp. Hist.* | London |
| Journal of criminal Law, Criminology and Police Science | *J. crim. Law Criminol. Police Sci.* | Chicago, Ill. |
| Journal of cross-cultural Psychology | *J. cross-cult. Psychol.* | Bellingham, Wash. |
| Journal of developing Areas | *J. develop. Areas* | Macomb, Ill. |
| Journal of Development Studies | *J. Develop. Stud.* | London |
| Journal of economic Education | *J. econ. Educ.* | New York |
| Journal of economic History | *J. econ. Hist.* | New York |
| Journal of economic Issues | *J. econ. Issues* | Austin, Texas |
| Journal of economic Literature | *J. econ. Liter.* | Menasha, Wis. |
| Journal of economic Theory | *J. econ. Theory* | New York-London |
| Journal of Economics and Business | *J. Econ. Busin.* | Philadelphia |
| Journal of educational Research | *J. educ. Res.* | Madison, Wis. |
| Journal of experimental social Psychology | *J. exper. soc. Psychol.* | London-New York |
| Journal of Finance | *J. Finance* | Chicago, Ill. |
| Journal of financial and quantitative Analysis | *J. financ. quant. Anal.* | Seattle, Wash. |
| Journal of human Relations | *J. hum. Relat.* | Wilberforce, Ohio |

| | | |
|---|---|---|
| Management international Review | *Manag. int. R.* | Wiesbaden |
| Management Science | *Manag. Sci.* | New York |
| Manchester School of economic and social Studies | *Manchester Sch. econ. soc. Stud.* | Manchester |
| Manpower Journal | *Manpower J.* | New Delhi |
| Marga | *Marga* | Colombo |
| Marquette Business Review | *Marquette Busin. R.* | Milwaukee, Wis. |
| Marxism today | *Marxism today* | London |
| Massacommunicatie | *Massacommunicatie* | |
| Matekon | *Matekon* | White Plains, N. Y. |
| Mawazo | *Mawazo* | Kampala |
| Méditerranée | *Méditerranée* | Aix-en-Provence |
| Međunarodni Problemi | *Međun. Probl.* | Beograd |
| Meijigakuin Ronsô | *Meijigakuin Ronsô* | Tokyo |
| Meijô-Daigaku Jingabun Tokusyûgo | *Meijo-Daigaku Jinbun Tokusyûgo* | Nagoya |
| Mémoires et Documents. Centre de Documentation cartographique et géographique | *Mém. et Doc.* | Paris |
| Mens en Maatschappij | *Mens en Mij* | Amsterdam |
| Mens en Onderneming | *Mens en Onderneming* | Leiden-Haarlem |
| Merkur | *Merkur* | Stuttgart |
| Metodologičeskie Voprosy Nauki | *Metod. Vopr. Nauki* | Saratov |
| Metra | *Metra* | Paris |
| Metroeconomica | *Metroeconomica* | Trieste |
| Meždunarodnyj Ežegodnik. Politika i Ėkonomika | *Meždun. Ėžeg. Polit. Ėkon.* | Moskva |
| Mezinárodni Vztahy | *Mezin. Vztahy* | Praha |
| Miasto | *Miasto* | Warszawa |
| Middle East Journal | *Mid. East J.* | Washington, D. C. |
| Middle East technical University Studies in Development | *Mid. East techn. Univ. Stud. Develop.* | |
| Middle Eastern Studies | *Mid. East. Stud.* | London |
| Midwest Journal of political Science | *Midwest J. polit. Sci.* | Detroit, Mich. |
| Midwest Review of public Administration | *Midwest R. publ. Adm.* | Parkville, Mo. |
| Migrations internationales | *Migr. int.* | La Haye |
| Milbank Memorial Fund Quarterly | *Milbank Memor. Fund Quart.* | New York |
| Militärgeschichte | *Militärgeschichte* | Berlin |
| Minerva | *Minerva* | London |
| Mirovaja Ėkonomika i meždunarodnye Otnošenija | *Mir. Ėkon. meždun. Otnoš.* | Moskva |
| Modern Age | *Mod. Age* | Chicago, Ill. |
| Modern Asian Studies | *Mod. Asian Stud.* | London |
| Modern Law Review | *Mod. Law R.* | London |
| Modern Occasions | *Mod. Occasions* | Cambridge, Mass. |
| Modern Review | *Mod. R. (Calcutta)* | Calcutta |
| Monatsberichte der Deutschen Bundesbank | *Monatsber. dtschen Bundesbank* | Frankfurt-am-Main |
| Monatsberichte des Österreichischen Instituts für Wirtschaftsforschung | *Monatsber. österr. Inst. Wirtsch.-Forsch.* | Wien |
| Monde moderne | *Monde mod.* | Paris |
| Mondes en Développement | *Mondes en Dévelop.* | Genève |
| Mondo aperto | *Mondo aperto* | Roma |
| Moneda y Crédito | *Moneda y Créd.* | Madrid |
| Moneta e Credito | *Moneta e Cred.* | Roma |
| Monthly Labor Review | *Mthly Lab. R.* | Washington, D. C. |
| Monthly public Opinion Surveys | *Mthly publ. Opin. Surv.* | New Delhi |

| | | |
|---|---|---|
| Monthly Review | *Mthly R.* | New York |
| Moorgate and Wall Street | *Moorgate and Wall Street* | London |
| Mouvement social | *Mouvement soc.* | Paris |
| Mouvement syndical mondial | *Mouvement synd. mond.* | Paris |
| Mulino | *Mulino* | Bologna |
| Muslim World | *Muslim Wld* | Hartford, Conn. |
| | | |
| Narody Azii i Afriki | *Narody Azii Afr.* | Moskva |
| National civic Review | *Nat. civic R.* | New York |
| National Institute economic Review | *Nat. Inst. econ. R.* | London |
| National Tax Journal | *Nat. Tax J.* | Lancaster, Pa. |
| National Westminster Bank quarterly Review | *Nat. Westminster Bank quart. R.* | London |
| Natural Resources Journal | *Natur. Resources J.* | Albuquerque, N. M. |
| Naučnye Doklady vysšej Školy. Ékonomičeskie Nauki | *Nauč. Dokl. vysš. Školy ėkon. Nauki* | Moskva |
| Naučnye Doklady vysšej Školy. Filosofskie Nauki | *Nauč. Dokl. vysš. Školy filos. Nauki* | Moskva |
| Naučnye Doklady vysšej Školy. Naučnyj Kommunizm | *Nauč. Dokl. vysš. Školy nauč. Kommunizm* | Moskva |
| Naučnye Trudy Novosibirskogo pegagogičeskogo Instituta | *Nauč. Trudy Novosib. pedag. Inst.* | Novosibirsk |
| Naučnye Trudy Sverdlovskogo pedagogičeskogo Instituta | *Nauč. Trudy Sverdlovsk. pedag. Inst.* | Sverdlovsk |
| Naučnye Trudy (Taškentskij Universitet) | *Nauč. Trudy (Taškent. Univ.)* | Taškent |
| Naučnye Zapiski Taškentskogo Instituta narodnogo Hozjajstva | *Nauč. Zap. Taškent. Inst. nar. Hoz.* | Taškent |
| Naučnyj Kommunizm | *Nauč. Kommunizm* | Moskva |
| Nebraska Journal of Economics and Business | *Nebraska J. Zcon. Busin.* | [USA, Neb.] |
| Nef | *Nef* | Paris |
| Neue Gesellschaft | *Neue Gesellsch.* | Bielefeld |
| Neue Praxis | *Neue Praxis* | Neuwied |
| Neues Forum | *Neues Forum* | Wien |
| Neues rotes Forum | *Neues rotes Forum* | Heidelberg |
| New Hungarian Quarterly | *New Hungar. Quart.* | Budapest |
| New Left Review | *New Left R.* | London |
| New Outlook | *New Outlook* | Tel-Aviv |
| New Politics | *New Polit.* | New York |
| New South | *New South* | Atlanta, Ga. |
| New York University Law Review | *New York Univ. Law R.* | New York |
| New Zealand economic Papers | *New Zealand econ. Pap.* | Wellington |
| New Zealand Journal of public Administration | *New Zealand J. publ. Adm.* | Wellington |
| Newstate | *Newstate* | |
| Nigerian Journal of economic and social Studies | *Niger. J. econ. soc. Stud.* | Ibadan |
| Nôkei Ronshû | *Nôkei Ronshû* | Hokkaidô |
| Nord e Sud | *Nord e Sud* | Milano-Napoli |
| Norois | *Norois* | Poitiers |
| Note d'Économie régionale Champagne-Ardenne | *Note Écon. région. Champagne-Ardenne* | Reims |
| Note d'Information, Centre d'Études et de Recherches sur les Qualifications | *Note Inform. Centre Ét. Rech. Qualif.* | Paris |
| Notes and Documents, United Nations Unit on Apartheid | *Notes Docum. UN Unit Apartheid* | New York |
| Notes d'Information et Statistiques. Banque centrale de l'Afrique de l'ouest | *Notes Inform. Statist. Banque centr. Afr. Ouest* | Paris |

| | | |
|---|---|---|
| Notes et Arguments | *Notes et Arguments* | Paris |
| Notiziario della Confederazione generale dell'Industria italiana | *Notiz. Confeder. gen. Industr. ital.* | Roma |
| Nouvelle Critique | *Nouv. Crit.* | Paris |
| Nouvelle Optique | *Nouv. Optique* | Montréal |
| Nouvelle Revue des deux Mondes | *Nouv. R. deux Mondes* | Paris |
| Nouvelle Revue international | *Nouv. R. int.* | Paris |
| Novaja i novejšaja Istorija | *Nov. novejš. Ist.* | Moskva |
| Nowe Drogi | *Nowe Drogi* | Warszawa |
| Nuestro Tiempo | *Nuestro Tiempo* | Madrid |
| Nuisances et Environnement | *Nuisances et Environ.* | Paris |
| Nuovo Mezzogiorno | *Nuovo Mezzogiorno* | Roma |
| | | |
| Ocean Development and international Law Journal | *Ocean Develop. int. Law J.* | Washington, D. C. |
| Öffentliche Verwaltung | *Öff. Verw.* | Stuttgart |
| Økonomi og Politik | *Økon. og Polit.* | København |
| Opština | *Opština* | Beograd |
| Optima | *Optima* | Johannesburg |
| Optimum | *Optimum* | Ottawa |
| Options méditerrannéennes | *Options méditerr.* | Paris |
| Orbis | *Orbis* | Philadelphia, Pa. |
| Ordo. Jahrbuch für die Ordnung von Wirtschaft und Gesellschaft | *Ordo* | Düsseldorf |
| Orientação 2 | *Orientação 2* | Rio de Janeiro |
| Orientamenti sociali | *Orientam. soc.* | Roma |
| Orientation scolaire et professionnelle | *Orientat. scol. profes.* | Paris |
| Oriente moderno | *Oriente mod.* | Roma |
| Osaka Kyoiku Daigaku Kiyô | *Osaka Kyoiku Daigaku Kiyô* | Osaka |
| Österreichische Osthefte | *Österr. Osth.* | Wien |
| Österreichische Zeitschrift für Aussenpolitik | *Österr. Z. Aussenpolit.* | Wien |
| Österreichisches Institut für Wirtschaftsforschung. Monatsberichte | *Österr. Inst. Wirtsch.-Forsch. Mber.* | Wien |
| Osteuropa | *Osteuropa* | Stuttgart |
| Osteuropa Recht | *Osteuropa Recht* | Stuttgart |
| Osteuropa Wirtschaft | *Osteuropa Wirtsch.* | Stuttgart |
| Osteuropäische Rundschau | *Osteurop. Rdsch.* | München |
| Oxford agrarian Studies | *Oxford agr. Stud.* | Oxford |
| Oxford Bulletin of Economics and Statistics | *Oxford B. Econ. Statist.* | Oxford |
| Oxford economic Papers | *Oxford econ. Pap.* | Oxford |
| Oyô Tô Keigaky | *Oyô Tô Keigaky* | Tokyo |
| | | |
| Pacific Affairs | *Pacific Aff.* | New York |
| Pacific Community | *Pacific Community* | Tokyo |
| Pacific sociological Review | *Pacific sociol. R.* | San Diego, Calif. |
| Pacific Viewpoint | *Pacific Viewpoint* | Wellington |
| Pakistan Horizon | *Pakistan Horizon* | Karachi |
| Panorama CDC | *Panorama CDC* | Paris |
| Panorama démocrate chrétien | *Panorama démocr. chr.* | Rome |
| Paperi ja puu | *Paperi ja puu* | Helsinki |
| Parliamentarian | *Parliamentarian* | London |
| Parliamentary Affairs | *Parl. Aff.* | London |
| Parole et Société | *Parole et Soc.* | Paris |
| Patronat | *Patronat* | Paris |
| Patterns of Prejudice | *Patterns of Prejudice* | London |
| Paysans | *Paysans* | Paris |

| | | |
|---|---|---|
| Peace and the Sciences | *Peace and Sci.* | Vienna |
| Penant. Revue de Droit des Pays d'Afrique | *Penant* | Paris |
| Pensamiento político | *Pensamiento polít.* | Mexico |
| Pensamiento y Acción | *Pensamiento y Acción* | Santiago de Chile |
| Pensée (La). Revue du Rationalisme moderne | *Pensée* | Paris |
| Pensiero politico | *Pensiero polit.* | Firenze |
| PEP Broadsheet | *PEP Broadsheet* | London |
| Permanences | *Permanences* | Paris |
| Personnel | *Personnel (Paris)* | Paris |
| Personnel Administration and public Personnel Review | *Personnel Adm. publ. Personnel R.* | Chicago, Ill. |
| Personnel and Guidance Journal | *Personnel Guidance J.* | Washington, D. C. |
| Personnel Journal | *Personnel J.* | Swathmore, Pa. |
| Personnel Management | *Personnel Manag. (Epping)* | Epping |
| Personnel Management | *Personnel Manag. (London)* | London |
| Personnel Practice Bulletin | *Personnel Practice B.* | Melbourne |
| Personnel Review | *Personnel R.* | Epping |
| Perspectives | *Perspectives (New Delhi)* | New Delhi |
| Perspectives | *Perspectives (Unesco)* | Paris |
| Perspectives économiques de l'OCDE | *Perspect. écon. OCDE* | Paris |
| Perspectives internationales | *Perspect. int.* | Ottawa |
| Perspectives polonaises | *Perspect. polon.* | Varsovie |
| Philippine economic Journal | *Philippine econ. J.* | Manila |
| Philippine Economy Bulletin | *Philippine Econ. B.* | Manila |
| Philippine Journal of public Administration | *Philippine J. publ. Adm.* | Manila |
| Philippine social Sciences and Humanities Review | *Philippine soc. Sci. Human. R.* | Quezon City |
| Philosophy and public Affairs | *Philos. publ. Aff.* | New York |
| Philosophy of the social Science | *Philos. soc. Sci.* | Aberdeen |
| Phylon | *Phylon* | Atlanta, Ga. |
| Planeación y Desarrollo | *Plan. y Desar.* | |
| Planification, Habitat, Information | *Planif. Habitat Inform.* | Paris |
| Planning and Development in the Netherlands | *Planning Develop. Netherl.* | Assen |
| Planning Outlook | *Planning Outlook* | Newcastle-upon-Tyne |
| Plánované Hospodarstvi | *Plán. Hospod.* | Praha |
| Planovanie i Povyšenie effektivnosti obščestvennogo Proizvodstva | *Plan. Povys. ěffekt. obšč. Proizvodstva* | Moskva |
| Planovoe Hozjajstvo | *Plan. Hoz.* | Moskva |
| Point économique de l'Auvergne | *Point écon. Auvergne* | Clermont-Ferrand |
| Points d'Appui pour l'Économie Rhône-Alpes | *Points Appui Écon. Rhône-Alpes* | Paris |
| Policy and Politics | *Pol. and Polit.* | London |
| Policy Science | *Pol. Sci.* | Santa Monica, N. Y. |
| Policy Studies Journal | *Pol. Stud. J.* | Urbana, Ill. |
| Polish Perspectives | *Polish Perspect.* | Warsaw |
| Polish Review | *Polish R.* | New York |
| Polish sociological Bulletin | *Polish sociol. B.* | Warsaw |
| Politea | *Politea* | Caracas |
| Politica del Diritto | *Polit. Dir.* | Bologna |
| Politica ed Economia | *Polit. ed Econ.* | Roma |
| Politica internazionale | *Polit. int. (Milano)* | Milano |
| Political Affairs | *Polit. Aff.* | New York |
| Political Quarterly | *Polit. Quart.* | London |
| Political Science | *Polit. Sci. (Wellington)* | Wellington |

| | | |
|---|---|---|
| Political Science annual | *Polit. Sci. ann.* | New York |
| Political Science Quarterly | *Polit. Sci. Quart.* | New York |
| Political Science Review | *Polit. Sci. R.* | Jaipur |
| Political Science Reviewer | *Polit. Sci. R-er* | Hampden-Sydney, Virginia |
| Political Studies | *Polit. Stud. (Oxford)* | Oxford |
| Politicka Misao | *Polit. Misao* | Beograd |
| Politico | *Politico* | Pavia |
| Politics and Society | *Polit. and Soc.* | Washington |
| Politiek Perspectief | *Polit. Perspect.* | Den Hague |
| Politiikka | *Politiikka* | Helsinki |
| Politik und Zeitgeschichte (Aus) | *Polit. u. Zeitgesch.* | Bonn |
| Politique aujourd'hui | *Polit. aujourd.* | Paris |
| Politique étrangère | *Polit. étr.* | Paris |
| Politische Meinung | *Polit. Meinung* | Köln |
| Politische Rundschau | *Polit. Rdsch.* | Bern |
| Politische Studien | *Polit Stud. (München)* | München |
| Politische Vierteljahresschrift | *Polit. Vjschr.* | Heidelberg-Köln-Opladen |
| Politische Vierteljahresschrift. Sonderheft | *Polit. Vjschr. Sonderh.* | Heidelberg-Köln-Opladen |
| Polity | *Polity* | Amherst, Mass. |
| Pologne et les Affaires occidentales (La) | *Pologne Aff. occid.* | Poznan |
| Population | *Population* | Paris |
| Population et Famille / Bevolking en Gezin | *Popul. et Famille / Bevolk. en Gezin* | Bruxelles |
| Population Studies | *Popul. Stud.* | London |
| Praca i Zabezpieczenie społeczne | *Praca Zabezp. społecz.* | Warzawa |
| Prace naukowe wyzszej Szkoły ekonomicznej w Wrocławiu | *Prace nauk. wyzsz. Szkoly ekon. Wrocław.* | Wrocław |
| Pravovedenie | *Pravovedenie* | Leningrad |
| Preuves | *Preuves* | Paris |
| Previdenza sociale | *Previd. soc.* | Roma |
| Previdenza sociale nell'Agricoltura | *Previd. soc. Agric.* | Roma |
| Problemas del Desarrollo | *Probl. Desarr.* | Mexico |
| Probleme economice | *Probl. econ. (Bucureşti)* | Bucureşti |
| Problèmes sociaux congolais | *Probl. soc. congolais* | Lumumbashi-Bruxelles |
| Problèmes sociaux zaïrois | *Probl. soc. zaïr.* | Lumumbashi |
| Problemi del Socialismo | *Probl. Social. (Milano)* | Milano |
| Problems of Communism | *Probl. Communism* | Washington |
| Problemy ekonomiczne | *Probl. ekon. (Warszawa)* | Warszawa |
| Problemy ekonomiki Gruzii | *Probl. ěkon. Gruzii* | Tbilisi |
| Problemy Filosofii i naučnogo Kommunizma | *Probl. Filos. nauč. Kommunizma* | Krasnojarsk |
| Problemy Mira i Socializma | *Probl. Mira Social.* | Moskva |
| Problemy naučnogo Kommunizma | *Probl. nauč. Kommunizma* | Moskva |
| Problemy organizacji | *Probl. organ.* | Warszawa |
| Proceedings of the Academy of political Science | *Proc. Acad. polit. Sci.* | New York |
| Proche-Orient. Études économiques | *Proche-Orient Ét. écon.* | Beyrouth |
| Proche-Orient. Études juridiques | *Proche-Orient Ét. jur.* | Beyrouth |
| Professions et Entreprises | *Professions et Entr.* | Paris |
| Profils de l'Économie Nord-Pas-de-Calais | *Profils Écon. Nord-Pas-de-Calais* | Lille |
| Programmed Learning and educational Technology | *Programmed Learning educ. Technol.* | London |
| Projet | *Projet* | Paris |
| Promotion rurale | *Promotion rur.* | Paris |

| | | |
|---|---|---|
| Przegląd komunikacyjny | *Przegl. komunik.* | Warszawa |
| Przegląd socjologiczny | *Przegl. socjol.* | Lódz |
| Przegląd statystyczny | *Przegl. statyst.* | Warszawa |
| P.S. Newsletter of the American political Science Association | *P.S. Newsl.* | Washington, D. C. |
| PSU Documentation | *PSU Docum.* | Paris |
| Psychometrika | *Psychometrika* | Richmond, Virg. |
| Public Administration | *Publ. Adm. (London)* | London |
| Public Administration | *Publ. Adm. (Sydney)* | Sydney |
| Public Administration in Israel and aborad | *Publ. Adm. Israel abroad* | Jerusalem |
| Public Administration Review | *Publ. Adm. R.* | Chicago, Ill. |
| Public Choice | *Publ. Choice* | Blacksburg, Va. |
| Public Interest | *Publ. Interest* | New York |
| Public Law | *Publ. Law (London)* | London |
| Public Opinion Quarterly | *Publ. Opin. Quart.* | Princeton, N. J. |
| Public Personnel Management | *Publ. Personnel Manag.* | Chicago, Ill. |
| Public Policy | *Publ. Pol.* | Cambridge, Mass. |
| Public Welfare | *Publ. Welfare* | London |
| Publications de la Faculté de Droit et d'Économie d'Amiens | *Publ. Fac. Dr. Écon. Amiens* | Amiens |
| Publius | *Publius* | Bremen |
| Publizistik | *Publizistik* | Münster-in-Westfalen |
| Punto final | *Punto final* | Santiago de Chile |
| Quaderni di Azione sociale | *Quad. Azione soc.* | Roma |
| Quaderni di Sociologia | *Quad. Sociol.* | Torino |
| Quality and Quantity | *Quality and Quantity* | Padova |
| Quarterly Journal of Administration | *Quart. J. Adm.* | Ibadan |
| Quarterly Journal of Economics | *Quart. J. Econ.* | Cambridge, Mass. |
| Quarterly Review of agricultural Economics | *Quart. R. agric. Econ.* | Canberra |
| Quarterly Review of Economics and Business | *Quart. R. Econ. Busin.* | Champaign, Ill. |
| Queen's Quarterly | *Queen's Quart.* | Kingston, Ont. |
| Questions actuelles du Socialisme | *Quest. act. Socialisme* | Paris |
| Quindicinale di Note e Commenti, Centro Studi Investimenti sociale | *Quindic. Note Commenti Centro Studi Invest.* | Roma |
| Rabočij Klass i sovremenny Mir | *Rabočij Klass sovrem. Mir* | Moskva |
| Race | *Race* | London |
| Ramparts | *Ramparts* | San Francisco, Calif. |
| Rassegna di Statistiche del Lavoro | *Rass. Statist. Lav.* | Roma |
| Rassegna economica | *Rass. econ. (Napoli)* | Napoli |
| Rassegna italiana di Sociologia | *Rass. ital. Sociol.* | Firenze |
| Rassegna sindicale Quaderni | *Rass. sind. Quad.* | Roma |
| Rasy i Narodny | *Rasy i Nar.* | |
| Ratio. Rivista di Scienze dell'Amministrazione e Teoria dell'Impresa | *Ratio* | Firenze |
| Raumforschung und Raumordnung | *Raumforsch. u.-Ordnung* | Bad-Godesberg |
| Razón y Fe | *Razón y Fe* | Madrid |
| Réalités franc-comtoises | *Réalités franc-comtoises* | Besançon |
| Realtà economica | *Realtà econ.* | Milano |
| Recent Sociology | *Recent Sociol.* | New York |
| Recherche sociale | *Rech. soc. (Libreville)* | Libreville |
| Recherches économiques de Louvain | *Rech. écon. Louvain* | Louvain |
| Recherches internationales à la Lumière du Marxisme | *Rech. int.* | Paris |

| | | |
|---|---|---|
| Recherches sociographiques | *Rech. sociogr.* | Québec |
| Recherches sociologiques | *Rech. sociol.* | Louvain |
| Recht in Ost und West | *Recht in Ost West* | Berlin |
| Reflets de l'Économie franc-comtoise | *Reflets Écon. franc-comtoise* | Paris |
| Reflets et Perspectives de la Vie économique | *Reflets Perspect. Vie écon.* | Bruxelles |
| Regional and urban Economics. Operational Methods | *Region. urb. Econ.* | Amsterdam |
| Regional Science Association. Papers and Proceedings | *Region. Sci. Assoc. Pap. and Proc.* | Cambridge, Mass. |
| Regional Studies | *Region. Stud.* | Oxford |
| Relations | *Relations* | Montréal |
| Relations industrielles | *Relat. industr.* | Québec |
| Remarques africaines | *Remarques afr.* | Bruxelles |
| Rencontre. Chrétiens et Juifs | *Rencontre* | Paris |
| Rencontres franco-allemandes | *Rencontres franco-allem.* | Paris |
| Repères. Économie du Languedoc-Roussillon | *Repères Écon. Languedoc-Roussillon* | Montpellier |
| Res publica | *Res publ.* | Bruxelles |
| Reserve Bank of India Bulletin | *Reserve Bank India B.* | Bombay |
| Review of economic Studies | *R. econ. Stud.* | Edinburgh |
| Review of Economics and Statistics | *R. Econ. Statist.* | Cambridge, Mass. |
| Review of Income and Wealth | *R. Income Wealth* | New Haven |
| Review of Marketing and agricultural Economics | *R. Mkting agric. Econ.* | Sydney |
| Review of Politics | *R. Polit.* | Notre Dame, Ind. |
| Review of radical political Economics | *R. radic. polit. Econ.* | Ann Arbor, Mich. |
| Review of religious Research | *R. relig. Res.* | New York |
| Review of social Economy | *R. soc. Econ.* | Chicago, Ill. |
| Review of the economic Conditions in Italy | *R. econ. Condit. Italy* | Rome |
| Revija za Sociologiju | *R. Sociol.* | Zagreb |
| Revista brasileira de Economia | *R. brasil. Econ.* | Rio de Janeiro |
| Revista brasileira de Estatística | *R. brasil. Estatíst.* | Rio de Janeiro |
| Revista brasileira de Estudos políticos | *R. brasil. Estud. polít.* | Belo Horizonte |
| Revista, Camara de Comercio de Bogotà | *R. Cam. Com. Bogotà* | Bogotà |
| Revista de Administração de Emprêsas | *R. Adm. Emprêsas* | Rio de Janeiro |
| Revista de Administração municipal | *R. Adm. municip. (Rio de Janeiro)* | Rio de Janeiro |
| Revista de Administração pública | *R. Adm. publ. (Rio de Janeiro)* | Rio de Janeiro |
| Revista de Administración pública | *R. Adm. públ. (Madrid)* | Madrid |
| Revista de Ciência política | *R. Ciênc. polít.* | Rio de Janeiro |
| Revista de Ciencias sociales | *R. Cienc. soc. (Puerto Rico)* | Puerto Rico |
| Revista de Ciencias sociales | *R. Cienc. soc. (Rio Piedras)* | Rio Piedras |
| Revista de Derecho y Ciencias políticas. Universidad de San Marcos | *R. Der. Cienc. polít.* | Lima |
| Revista de Direito administrativo | *R. Dir. adm.* | Rio de Janeiro |
| Revista de Economía latinoamericana | *R. Econ. latinoamer.* | Caracas |
| Revista de Economía política | *R. Econ. polít. (Madrid)* | Madrid |
| Revista de Economía y Estadística | *R. Econ. Estadíst.* | Cordóba (Argentina) |
| Revista de Estudios agro-sociales | *R. Estud. agro-soc.* | Madrid |
| Revista de Estudios de la Vida local | *R. Estud. Vida loc.* | Madrid |
| Revista de Estudios políticos | *R. Estud. polít.* | Madrid |
| Revista de Estudios sociales | *R. Estud. soc.* | Madrid |
| Revista de Filozofie | *R. Filoz.* | Bucureşti |
| Revista de Fomento social | *R. Fomento soc.* | Madrid |
| Revista de Historia de América | *R. Hist. Amér.* | México |

| | | |
|---|---|---|
| Revista de Información económica mundial | *R. Inform. econ. mund.* | London |
| Revista de Occidente | *R. Occidente* | Buenos Aires |
| Revista de Planeación y Desarrollo | *R. Plan. Desarr. (Bogotà)* | Bogotà |
| Revista de Política internacional | *R. Polít. int. (Madrid)* | Madrid |
| Revista de Política social | *R. Polít. soc.* | Madrid |
| Revista de Psicología general i aplicada | *R. Psicol. gen. apl.* | Madrid |
| Revista de Seguridad social | *R. Segur. soc.* | Buenos-Aires |
| Revista de Statistică | *R. Statist. (Bucureşti)* | Bucureşti |
| Revista de Trabajo | *R. Trab. (Madrid)* | Madrid |
| Revista de la Academia diplomática del Perú | *R. Acad. diplom. Perú* | Lima |
| Revista de la Facultad de Derecho | *R. Fac. Der. (Caracas)* | Caracas |
| Revista de la Facultad de Derecho de México | *R. Fac. Der. México* | México |
| Revista de la Facultad de Direito | *R. Fac. Dir. (São Paulo)* | São Paulo |
| Revista de la Integración | *R. Integr.* | Buenos Aires |
| Revista de la Universidad. Externado Colombia | *R. Univ. Externado Colombia* | Bogotà |
| Revista del Banco Central de Venezuela | *R. Banco Centr. Venezuela* | Caracas |
| Revista del Banco de la República | *R. Banco Repúbl.* | Bogotà |
| Revista del Instituto de Ciencias sociales | *R. Inst. Cienc. soc.* | Barcelona |
| Revista do Serviço público | *R. Serv. públ.* | Rio de Janeiro |
| Revista española de Derecho internacional | *R. esp. Der. int.* | Madrid |
| Revista española de la Opinión pública | *R. esp. Opin. públ.* | Madrid |
| Revista geográfica | *R. geogr. (Rio de Janeiro)* | Rio de Janeiro |
| Revista iberoamericana de Seguridad social | *R. iberoamer. Segur. soc.* | Madrid |
| Revista internacional de Sociología | *R. int. Sociol. (Madrid)* | Madrid |
| Revista javeriana | *R. javer.* | Bogotà |
| Revista juridica de Buenos Aires | *R. jur. Buenos Aires* | Buenos Aires |
| Revista latinoamericana de Ciencia política | *R. latinoamer. Cienc. polít.* | Santiago de Chile |
| Revista latinoamericana de Ciencias sociales | *R. latinoamer. Cienc. soc.* | Santiago de Chile |
| Revista latinoamericana de Psicología | *R. latinoamer. Psicol.* | Bogotá |
| Revista latinoamericana de Sociología | *R. latinoamer. Sociol.* | Buenos Aires |
| Revista mexicana de Seguridad social | *R. mexic. Segur. soc.* | México |
| Revista mexicana de Sociología | *R. mexic. Sociol.* | México |
| Revista mexicana del Trabajo | *R. mexic. Trab.* | México |
| Revista paraguaya de Sociología | *R. parag. Sociol.* | Asunción |
| Revista peruana de Derecho internacional | *R. peru. Der. int.* | Lima |
| Revista SENAI | *Rev. SENAI* | Rio de Janeiro |
| Revista sindical de Estadística | *R. sind. Estadíst.* | Madrid |
| Revue administrative | *R. adm.* | Paris |
| Revue algérienne du Travail | *R. algér. Trav.* | Alger |
| Revue belge de Droit international | *R. belge Dr. int.* | Bruxelles |
| Revue belge de Sécurité sociale | *R. belge Sécur. soc.* | Bruxelles |
| Revue d'Allemagne | *R. Allem.* | Paris |
| Revue d'Économie et de Droit immobilier | *R. Écon. Dr. immob.* | Paris |
| Revue d'Économie et de Gestion | *R. Écon. Gestion* | Nice |
| Revue d'Économie politique | *R. Écon. polit. (Paris)* | Paris |
| Revue de Défense nationale | *R. Déf. nat.* | Paris |
| Revue de Droit contemporain | *R. Dr. contemp.* | Bruxelles |
| Revue de Géographie alpine | *R. Géogr. alpine* | Grenoble |
| Revue de Géographie de Lyon | *R. Géogr. Lyon* | Lyon |

| | | |
|---|---|---|
| Revue de Science financière | *R. Sci. financ.* | Paris |
| Revue de l'Économie du Centre-Est | *R. Écon. Centre-Est* | Dijon |
| Revue de l'Économie méridionale | *R. Écon. mérid.* | Montpellier |
| Revue de l'Est | *R. Est* | Paris |
| Revue de l'Institut de Sociologie | *R. Inst. Sociol.* | Bruxelles |
| Revue de l'Occident musulman et de la Méditerranée | *R. Occident musul. Méditerr.* | Aix-en-Provence |
| Revue de l'Université d'Ottawa | *R. Univ. Ottawa* | Ottawa |
| Revue de l'Université de Bruxelles | *R. Univ. Bruxelles* | Bruxelles |
| Revue de la Commission internationale des Juristes | *R. Commiss. int. Juristes* | La Haye |
| Revue de la Coopération internationale Impôts | *R. Coop. int.* | Londres |
| Revue de la Société d'Études et d'Expansion | *R. Soc. Ét. Expans.* | Liège |
| Revue des Droits de l'Homme | *R. Dr. Homme* | Paris |
| Revue des Études coopératives | *R. Ét. coop.* | Paris |
| Revue des Ingénieurs | *R. Ingén.* | Paris |
| Revue des Pays de l'Est | *R. Pays Est* | Bruxelles |
| Revue des Sciences économiques | *R. Sci. écon.* | Liège |
| Revue des Sciences sociales de la France de l'Est | *R. Sci. soc. France Est* | Strasbourg |
| Revue des Travaux de l'Académie des Sciences morales et politiques | *R. Trav. Acad. Sci. mor. polit.* | Paris |
| Revue du Droit public et de la Science politique en France et à l'étranger | *R. Dr. publ. Sci. polit.* | Paris |
| Revue du Marché commun | *R. Marché commun* | Paris |
| Revue du Tourisme | *R. Tourisme* | Berne |
| Revue du Travail | *R. Trav. (Bruxelles)* | Bruxelles |
| Revue économique | *R. écon. (Paris)* | Paris |
| Revue économique de Madagascar | *R. écon. Madagascar* | Tananarive |
| Revue économique de la Banque nationale de Paris | *R. écon. Banque nat. Paris* | Paris |
| Revue économique du Sud-Ouest | *R. écon. Sud-Ouest* | Bordeaux |
| Revue économique et sociale | *R. écon. soc.* | Lausanne |
| Revue économique franco-suisse | *R. écon. fr.-suisse* | Paris |
| Revue financière | *R. financ.* | Alger |
| Revue française d'Études politiques africaines | *R. franç. Ét. polit. afr.* | Paris |
| Revue française de Science politique | *R. franç. Sci. polit.* | Paris |
| Revue française de Sociologie | *R. franç. Sociol.* | Paris |
| Revue française de l'Énergie | *R. franç. Énergie* | Paris |
| Revue française des Affaires sociales | *R. franç. Aff. soc.* | Paris |
| Revue française du Marketing | *R. franç. Mkting* | Paris |
| Revue générale | *R. gén.* | Bruxelles |
| Revue générale de Droit international public | *R. gén. Dr. int. publ.* | Paris |
| Revue générale de l'Air et de l'Espace | *R. gén. Air Espace* | Paris |
| Revue générale des Assurances terrestres | *R. gén. Assur. terr.* | Paris |
| Revue générale des Chemins de Fer | *R. gén. Chem. de Fer* | Paris |
| Revue géographique des Pyrénées et du Sud-Ouest | *R. géogr. Pyrénées* | Toulouse |
| Revue hellénique de Droit international | *R. hell. Dr. int.* | Athènes |
| Revue hospitalière de France | *R. hospital. France* | Lyon |
| Revue internationale de Droit comparé | *R. int. Dr. comp.* | Paris |
| Revue internationale de Politique criminelle | *R. int. Polit. crim.* | New York |
| Revue internationale de Sociologie / International Review of Sociology | *R. int. Sociol. (Rome)* | Rome |

| | | |
|---|---|---|
| Revue internationale des Sciences administratives | *R. int. Sci. adm.* | Bruxelles |
| Revue internationale des Sciences sociales | *R. int. Sci. soc.* | Paris |
| Revue juridique et économique du Sud-Ouest. Série juridique | *R. jur. écon. Sud-Ouest Sér. jur.* | Bordeaux |
| Revue juridique et politique Indépendance et Coopération | *R. jur. polit.* | Paris |
| Revue militaire générale | *R. milit. gén.* | Paris |
| Revue nouvelle | *R. nouv.* | Tournai |
| Revue politique et parlementaire | *R. polit. parl.* | Paris |
| Revue roumaine d'Études internationales | *R. roum. Ét. int.* | Bucarest |
| Revue roumaine des Sciences sociales. Série Science juridique | *R. roum. Sci. soc. Sér. Sci. jur* | Bucarest |
| Revue roumaine des Sciences sociales. Série Sociologie | *R. roum. Sci. soc. Sér. Sociol.* | Bucarest |
| Revue socialiste | *R. social.* | Paris |
| Revue syndicale suisse | *R. synd. suisse* | Berne |
| Revue Tiers-Monde | *R. Tiers-Monde* | Paris |
| Revue trimestrielle de Droit commercial | *R. trim. Dr. com.* | Paris |
| Revue trimestrielle de Droit européen | *R. trim. Dr. europ.* | Paris |
| Revue tunisienne de Sciences sociales | *R. tunis. Sci. soc.* | Tunis |
| Ricerche economiche | *Ric. econ.* | Venezia |
| Risô | *Risô* | Tokyo |
| Risparmio | *Risparmio* | Roma |
| Rivista di Diritto agrarie | *Riv. Dir. agr.* | Firenze |
| Rivista di Diritto finanziaro e Scienza delle Finanze | *Riv. Dir. finanz.* | Milano |
| Rivista di Economia agraria | *Riv. Econ. agr.* | Roma |
| Rivista di Politica agraria | *Riv. Polit. agr,* | Bologna |
| Rivista di Politica economica | *Riv. Polit. econ.* | Roma |
| Rivista di Psicologia sociale e Archivio italiana di Psicologia generale e del Lavoro | *Riv. Psicol. soc.* | Torino |
| Rivista di Sociologia | *Riv. Sociol.* | Roma |
| Rivista di Studi politici internazionali | *Riv. Studi polit. int.* | Firenze |
| Rivista geografica italiana | *Riv. geogr. ital.* | Firenze |
| Rivista giuridica del Lavoro e della Previdenza sociale | *Riv. giur. Lav. Previd. soc.* | Roma |
| Rivista internazionale di Filosofia politica e sociale e di Diritto comparato | *Riv. int. Filos. polit. soc. Dir. comp.* | Bologna |
| Revista internazionale di Scienze economiche e commerciali | *Riv. int. Sci. econ. com.* | Milano-Padova |
| Rivista internazionale di Scienze sociali | *Riv. int. Sci. soc.* | Milano |
| Rivista italiana di Scienza politica | *Riv. ital. Sci. polit.* | Bologna |
| Rivista trimestrale di Diritto pubblico | *Riv. trim. Dir. pubbl.* | Milano |
| Rocky Mountain social Science Journal | *Rocky Mountain soc. Sci. J.* | Fort Collins, Colo. |
| Roczniki Instytutu Handlu wewnetrznego | *Roczn. Inst. Handlu wewn.* | Warszawa |
| Round Table | *Round Table* | London |
| Ruch prawniczy, ekonomiczny i socjologiczny | *Ruch prawn. ekon. socjol.* | Poznan |
| Rue | *Rue* | Paris |
| Rural Africana | *Rur. Afr.* | East Lansing |
| Rural Sociology | *Rur. Sociol.* | Lexington, Ky. |

| | | |
|---|---|---|
| SAIS Review | *SAIS Rev.* | Washington, D. C. |
| Santé de l'Homme | *Santé de l'Homme* | Paris |
| Sbornik aspirantskih Statej Instituta Filosofii Akademija Nauk SSSR | *Sb. aspirant. Statej Inst. Filos. Akad. Nauk SSSR* | Moskva |
| Sbornik naučnyh Trudov Èrevanskogo politehničeskogo Instituta. Serija obščestvennyh Nauki | *Sb. nauč. Trud. Èrevan. politehn. Inst. Ser. obšč. Nauki* | Èrevan |
| Sbornik naučnyh Trudov (Permskij politehničeskij Institut) | *Sb. nauč. Trud. (Perm. politehn. Inst.)* | Perm' |
| Scandinavian political Studies | *Scand. polit. Stud.* | Helsinki |
| Schweizer Monatshefte | *Schweiz. Mh.* | Zürich |
| Schweizer Rundschau | *Schweiz. Rdsch.* | Soleure |
| Schweizerische Zeitschrift für Volkswirtschaft und Statistik | *Schweizer. Z. Volkswirtsch. Statist.* | Basel |
| Schweizerisches Archiv für Verkehrswissenschaft und Verkehrspolitik | *Schweizer. Archiv. Verkehrswiss. u. -Polit.* | Zürich |
| Science and public Affairs | *Sci. publ. Aff.* | |
| Science and Society | *Sci. and Soc.* | New York |
| Sciences sociales. Académie des Sciences de l'URSS | *Sci. soc. (Moscou)* | Moscou |
| Scientific American | *Scient. Amer.* | New York |
| Scienze sociali | *Sci. soc. (Bologna)* | Bologna |
| Scottish Journal of political Economy | *Scott. J. polit. Econ.* | Edinburgh |
| Scuola e Città | *Scuola e Città* | Firenze |
| Seguridad social | *Segur. soc. (México)* | México |
| Seishin-Eisei Kenkyû | *Seishin-Eisei Kenkyû* | Tokyo |
| Seminar | *Seminar* | New Delhi |
| Service social | *Serv. soc. (Québec)* | Québec |
| Service social dans le Monde | *Serv. soc. Monde* | Bruxelles |
| Sextant. Cahiers statistiques de la Bretagne | *Sextant* | Rennes |
| Shakai Fukushi Hyôron | *Shakai Fukushi Hyôron* | Osaka |
| Shakai Kagaku Ronsyu | *Shakai Kagaku Ronsyu* | Osaka |
| Shakai Kagaku Tôkyû | *Shakai Kagaku Tôkyû* | Tokyo |
| Shakaifukushi | *Shakaifukushi* | Tokyo |
| Shakaigaku Hyôron | *Shakaigaku Hyôron* | Tokyo |
| Shakaigaku Kenkyû Nenpô | *Shakaigaku Kenkyû Nenpô* | Fukuoka |
| Shakaigaku Tokyû | *Shakaikagaku Tokyû* | Tokyo |
| Shisô | *Shisô* | Tokyo |
| Shisô no Kagaku | *Shisô no Kagaku* | Tokyo |
| Shogaku Ronsô | *Shogaku Ronsô* | Tokyo |
| Shôkei Gakusô | *Shôkei Gakusô (Osaka)* | Osaka |
| Sicurezza sociale | *Sicur. soc.* | Roma |
| Simulation and Games | *Simul. and Games* | Beverly Hills, Calif. |
| Síntesi economica | *Síntesi econ.* | Roma |
| Sistemnyj Metod i sovremennaja Nauka | *Sistem. Metod sovrem. Nauka* | Novosibirsk |
| Situazione economica provinciale | *Sit. econ. provinc.* | Milano |
| Skandinaviska enskilda Banken quarterly Review | *Skand. ensk. Bank. quart. R.* | Stockholm |
| Slavic Review | *Slavic R.* | New York |
| Small Industry Bulletin for Asia and the Far East | *Small Industr. B. Asia Far East* | Bangkok |
| SMUH Bulletin trimestriel | *SMUH Bull. trim.* | Paris |
| Sociaal Maandblad Arbeid | *Soc. Maandbl. Arb.* | Alphen-aan-den-Rijn-Rotterdam |
| Social Action | *Soc. Action* | Poona |
| Social and economic Studies | *Soc. econ. Stud.* | Kingston |

| | | |
|---|---|---|
| Social Biology | *Soc. Biology* | New York |
| Social Casework | *Soc. Casewk* | New York |
| Social Compass | *Soc. Compass* | The Hague |
| Social Forces | *Soc. Forces* | Chapel Hill, N. C. |
| Social Policy | *Soc. Pol.* | New York |
| Social Problems | *Soc. Probl.* | New York-Rochester, Mich. |
| Social Research | *Soc. Res* | New York |
| Social Science | *Soc. Sci. (Winfield)* | Winfield |
| Social Science and Medicine | *Soc. Sci. Medic.* | Boston, Mass. |
| Social Science Information / Information sur les Sciences sociales | *Soc. Sci. Inform. / Inform. Sci. soc.* | Paris |
| Social Science Quarterly | *Soc. Sci. Quart.* | Austin, Tex. |
| Social Science Research | *Soc. Sci. Res.* | Ann Arbor, Mich. |
| Social Security Bulletin | *Soc. Secur. B.* | Washington |
| Social Service Review | *Soc. Serv. R.* | Chicago, Ill. |
| Social Studies, Irish Journal of Sociology | *Soc. Stud.* | Naas |
| Social Theory and Practice | *Soc. Theory Practice* | Tallahassee, Fla. |
| Social Work | *Soc. Wk (Albany)* | Albany, N. Y. |
| Sociale Wetenschappen | *Soc. Wetensch.* | Tilburg |
| Socialisme | *Socialisme* | Bruxelles |
| Socialist Revolution | *Social. Revol.* | San Francisco, Calif. |
| Socialističeskaja Zakonnost | *Social. Zakonn.* | Moskva |
| Socialističeskij Trud | *Social. Trud* | Moskva |
| Socialt Tidsskrift | *Soc. Tss.* | København |
| Société de Banque suisse. Bulletin | *Soc. Banque suisse B.* | Bâle |
| Société royale d'Économie politique de Belgique | *Soc. roy. Écon. polit. Belgique* | Bruxelles |
| Society | *Society* | St Louis, Mo. |
| Society and Leisure | *Soc. and Leisure* | Prague |
| Socijalizam | *Socijalizam* | Beograd |
| Socio-economic Planning Sciences | *Socio-econ. Plan. Sci.* | New York |
| Sociologia | *Sociologia (Roma)* | Roma |
| Sociologia internationalis | *Sociol. int. (Berlin)* | Berlin |
| Sociologia neerlandica | *Sociol. neerland.* | Assen |
| Sociologia ruralis | *Sociol. rur.* | Assen |
| Sociological Analysis | *Sociol. Anal. (San Antonio)* | San Antonio, Tex. |
| Sociological Analysis | *Sociol. Anal. (Sheffield)* | Sheffield |
| Sociological Bulletin | *Sociol. B. (Bombay)* | Bombay |
| Sociological Focus | *Sociol. Focus* | Akron, Ohio |
| Sociological Inquiry | *Sociol. Inquiry* | Toronto |
| Sociological Quarterly | *Sociol. Quart.* | Carbondale, Ill. |
| Sociological Review | *Sociol. R.* | Keele |
| Sociological Yearbook of Religion in Britain | *Sociol. Yb. Relig. Britain* | London |
| Sociologičeskie Issledovanija | *Sociol. Issled.* | Sverdlovsk |
| Sociologický Časopis | *Sociol. Čas.* | Praha |
| Sociologie du Travail | *Sociol. Trav.* | Paris |
| Sociologie et Sociétés | *Sociol. et Soc.* | Montréal |
| Sociologija | *Sociologija* | Beograd |
| Sociologija sela | *Sociol. sela* | Zagreb |
| Sociologus. Zeitschrift für empirische Soziologie, socialpsychologische und ethnologische Forschung | *Sociologus* | Berlin |
| Sociology | *Sociology (Kyoto)* | Kyoto |
| Sociology | *Sociology (London)* | London |
| Sociology and social Research | *Sociol. soc. Res.* | Los Angeles, Calif. |
| Sociology of Education | *Sociol. Educ.* | Washington, D. C. |

| | | |
|---|---|---|
| Sociometry | *Sociometry* | New York |
| Sondages | *Sondages* | Paris |
| Sophia economic Review | *Sophia econ. R.* | Tokyo |
| Sosiaalinen Aikakauskirja | *Sos. Aikakausk.* | Helsinki |
| Sosiologia | *Sosiologia* | Helsinki |
| South African international Quarterly | *South Afr. int. Quart.* | Johannesburg |
| South African Journal of Economics | *South Afr. J. Econ.* | Johannesburg |
| South African Outlook | *South Afr. Outlook* | Lovedale |
| South Asian Review | *South Asian R.* | London |
| South Asian Studies | *South Asian Stud.* | Jaipur |
| Southeast Asia | *Southeast Asia* | Carbondale, Ill. |
| Southern Quarterly | *South. Quart.* | Hattiesburg, Miss. |
| Sovetskaja Ětnografija | *Sov. Ětnogr.* | Moskva |
| Sovetskoe Gosudarstvo i Pravo | *Sov. Gos. Pravo* | Moskva |
| Soviet and Eastern European foreign Trade | *Sov. East. Europ. for. Trade* | White Plains, N. Y. |
| Soviet Jewish Affairs | *Sov. Jew. Aff.* | London |
| Soviet Sociology | *Sov. Sociol.* | New York |
| Soviet Studies | *Sov. Stud.* | Glasgow |
| Soziale Welt | *Soz. Welt* | Dortmund |
| Sozialistische Politik | *Sozial. Polit.* | Berlin |
| Sozialwissenschaftliches Jahrbuch für Politik | *Soz.-wiss. Jb. Polit.* | München |
| Soziologisches Institut des Universität Zürich. Bulletin | *Soziol. Inst. Univ. Zürich B.* | Zürich |
| Spectrum | *Spectrum* | Bangkok |
| Spettatore internazionale | *Spettatore int.* | Roma |
| Spółdzielczy Kwartalnik Naukowy | *Spóld. Kwartal. Nauk.* | Warszawa |
| Sprawy miedzynarodowe | *Spr. miedzyn.* | Warszawa |
| Sri Lanka Labour Gazette | *Sri Lanka Lab. Gaz.* | Sri Lanka |
| SŠA | *SŠA* | Moskva |
| Staat (Der) | *Staat* | Berlin |
| Staat und Recht | *Staat u. Recht* | Potsdam |
| Städtetag | *Städtetag* | Stuttgart |
| Staff Papers | *Staff Pap.* | Washington, D. C |
| Stanovništvo | *Stanovništvo* | Beograd |
| Statistika | *Statistika (Praha)* | Praha |
| Statistique et Développement. Pays de la Loire | *Statist. et Dévelop.* | Paris |
| Statistiques et Études financières | *Statist. Ét. financ.* | Paris |
| Statistiques et Études financières. Série bleue | *Statist. Ét. financ. Sér. bleue* | Paris |
| Statistiques et Études financières. Série rouge | *Statist. Ét. financ. Sér. rouge* | Paris |
| Statistiques et Études financières. Études économiques. Série orange | *Statist. Ét. financ. Ét. écon. Sér. orange* | Paris |
| Statistiques pour l'Économie normande | *Statist. Écon. normande* | Rouen |
| Statistische Praxis | *Statist. Praxis* | Berlin |
| Statisztikai Szemle | *Statiszt. Szle* | Budapest |
| Stato sociale | *Stato soc.* | Roma |
| Statsvetenskaplig Tidskrift | *Statsvet. Ts.* | Lund |
| Storia e Politica | *Storia e Polit.* | Milano |
| Stratégie | *Stratégie* | Paris |
| Studi di Sociologia | *Studi Sociol.* | Milano |
| Studi Emigrazione | *Studi Emigr.* | Roma |
| Studi parlamentari e di Politica costituzionale | *Studi parl. Polit. costit.* | Roma |
| Studia demograficzne | *Studia demogr.* | Warszawa |
| Studia finansowe | *Stud. finans.* | Warszawa |

| | | |
|---|---|---|
| Studia socjologiczne | *Stud. socjol.* | Warszawa |
| Studies in comparative and local Government | *Stud. comp. loc. Gvt* | The Hague |
| Studies in comparative Communism | *Stud. comp. Communism* | Los Angeles, Calif. |
| Studies in comparative international Development | *Stud. comp. int. Develop.* | New Brunswick |
| Studies in Soviet Thought | *Stud. Soc. Thought* | Friburg |
| Studies of Broadcasting | *Stud. Broadcast.* | Tokyo |
| Studii şi Čercetări economice | *Stud. Cerc. econ.* | Bucureşti |
| SUD. Information économique Provence Côte d'Azur Corse | *SUD. Inform. écon. Provence-Côte d'Azur-Corse* | Paris |
| Survey. A Journal of Soviet and East European Studies | *Survey* | London |
| Survey of current Business | *Surv. curr. Busin.* | Washington, D. C. |
| Survival | *Survival* | London |
| Swedish Economy | *Swedish Econ.* | Stockholm |
| Swedish Journal of Economics | *Swedish J. Econ.* | Stockholm |
| Synopsis | *Synopsis* | Bruxelles |
| Synthèses | *Synthèses* | Bruxelles |
| Syrie et Monde arabe | *Syrie et Monde arabe* | Damas |
| Systematics | *Systematics* | London |
| Szociológia | *Szociológia* | Budapest |
| | | |
| Teachers College Record | *Teachers College Rec.* | New York |
| Techniques et Développement | *Techn. et Dévelop.* | Paris |
| Technological Forecasting | *Technol. Forecasting* | New York |
| Télévision et Éducation | *Télévis. et Éduc.* | Paris |
| Temas políticos y sociales | *Temas polít. soc.* | Madrid |
| Tempi moderni | *Tempi mod.* | Roma |
| Temps modernes | *Temps mod.* | Paris |
| Tendances | *Tendances* | Paris |
| Tendances de la Conjoncture | *Tendances Conjonct.* | Paris |
| Teorija in Praksa | *Teorija in Praksa* | Ljubljana |
| Terra | *Terra* | Helsinki |
| Terre malgache / Tany malagasy | *Terre malgache / Tany malagasy* | Tananarive |
| Terzo Mondo | *Terzo Mondo* | Milano |
| Testimonianze | *Testimonianze* | Firenze |
| Theory and Decision | *Theory and Decision* | Dordrecht |
| Third World | *Third World* | London |
| Three Banks Review | *Three Banks R.* | Edinburgh |
| Tidskrift utgiven av juridiska | *Ts. jur. For. Finland* | Helsinki |
| Tiers-Monde | *Tiers-Monde* | Paris |
| Tijdschrift voor Economie | *Tijds. Econ.* | Leuwen |
| Tijdschrift voor economische en sociale Geografie | *Tijds. econ. soc. Geogr.* | Rotterdam |
| Tijdschrift voor sociale Wetenschappen | *Tijds. soc. Wetensch.* | Ghent |
| Tôhoku Fukushi Daigaku Ronsô | *Tôhoku Fukushi Daigaku Ronsô* | Sendai |
| Tokaidaigaku Kiyô | *Tokaidaigaku Kiyô* | Tokyo |
| Tokyo-Gakugei-Daigaku Kenkyû Kiyô | *Tokyo-Gakugei-Daigaku Kenkyû Kiyô* | Tokyo |
| Toxicomanies | *Toxicomanies* | Québec |
| Tôyô Bunka Kenkyûjo Kijô | *Tôyô Bunka Kenkyûjo Kiyô* | Tokyo |
| Trabalho | *Trabalho* | Luanda |
| Transaction-Society | *Transact. Soc.* | St. Louis, Mo. |
| Transports | *Transports* | Paris |
| Travaux du Colloque international de Droit comparé | *Trav. Colloque int. Dr. comp.* | Ottawa |

| | | |
|---|---|---|
| Travaux et Jours | *Trav. et Jours* | Beyrouth |
| Travaux et Recherches (Documentation française) | *Trav. et Rech.* | Paris |
| Trimestre económico | *Trim. econ.* | México |
| Trudy Altajskogo politehničeskogo Instituta | *Trudy Altajsk. politehn. Inst.* | Barnaul |
| Trudy Burjatskogo Instituta obščestvennyh Nauk | *Trudy Burjat. Inst. obšč. Nauk* | Ulan-Ude |
| Trudy Gor'kogo vysšego partijnoj Skoly | *Trudy Gor'k. vysš. part. Školy* | Gor'kij |
| Trudy Kafedry politekonomii Moskovskogo ekonomiko-statističeskogo Instituta | *Trudy Kaf. politekon. Moskov. ekon. statist. Inst.* | Moskva |
| Trudy Tallinskogo politehničeskogo Instituta | *Trudy Tallinsk. politehn. Inst.* | Tallin |
| Trudy Ufimskogo aviacionnogo Instituta | *Trudy Ufimsk. aviac. Inst.* | Ufa |
| Trybuna spółdzielcza | *Tryb. spółd.* | Warszawa |
| Turkish Yearbook of international Relations | *Turk. Yb. int. Relat.* | Ankara |
| Turvallisuupolitiikka | *Turvallisuuspolitiikka* | Helsinki |
| Tutela del Lavoro | *Tutela Lav.* | Roma |
| Tutzinger Studien | *Tutzing. Stud.* | München |
| | | |
| Učenye Zapiski (Jaroslavskij tehnologičeskij Institut) | *Učen. Zap. (Jarosl. tehnol. Inst.)* | Jaroslav |
| Učenye Zapiski Kafedr marksistko-leninskoj Filosofii Vysšej Partijnoj Školy pri CK KPSS i mestnyh Vysših partijnyh Škol | *Učen. Zap. Kaf. marks.-lenin. Filos. Vysš. Part. Školy CK KPSS mest. vysš. part. Škol* | Moskva |
| Učenye Zapiski Kafedr obščestvennyh Nauk Vuzov Leningrada. Problemy naučnogo Kommunizma | *Učen. Zap. Kaf. obšč. Nauk Vuzov Leningr. Probl. nauč. Kommunizma* | Leningrad |
| Učenye Zapiski (Kazanskij pedagogičeskij Institut) | *Učen. Zap. (Kazan. pedag. Inst.)* | Kazan' |
| Učenye Zapiski (Kurskij pedagogičeskij Institut) | *Učen. Zap. (Kursk pedag. Inst.)* | Kursk |
| Učenye Zapiski Permskogo Institut | *Učen. Zap. Perm. Inst.* | Perm' |
| Učenye Zapiski (Taškentskij pedagogiceskij Institut) | *Učen. Zap. (Taskent. pedag. Inst.)* | Taškent |
| Učenye Zapiski Tomskogo Universiteta. Problemy social'nyh issledovanij | *Učen. Zap. Tomsk. Univ. Probl. soc. Issled.* | Tomsk |
| Ulkopolitiikka | *Ulkopolitiikka* | Helsinki |
| UN. Revista de la Dirección de Divulgación cultural | *UN Rev. Dir. Divulg. cult.* | Bogotá |
| United Asia | *United Asia* | Bombay |
| Universidad | *Universidad* | Santa Fe |
| Universidad de Antioquía | *Univ. Antioquía* | Medellín |
| Universitas. Pontifica Universidad católica javeriana | *Universitas (Bogotá)* | Bogotá |
| Urban Affairs annual Review | *Urb. Aff. ann. R.* | Beverly Hills, Calif. |
| Urban Affairs Quarterly | *Urb. Aff. Quart.* | Beverly Hills, Calif. |
| Urban Studies | *Urb. Stud.* | Edimburgh |
| Urbanisation et Environnement | *Urbanis. et Environ.* | Paris |
| Urbanisme | *Urbanisme* | Paris |
| Urbanistica | *Urbanistica* | Torino |
| Uzbekistonda iztimoii Fanlar | *Uzbek. ižtim. Fanlar* | Taškent |
| | | |
| Verfassung und Recht in Übersee | *Verfassung u. Recht Übersee* | Hamburg |
| Verfassung und Verfassungswirklichkeit | *Verfassung u. -Wirklichkeit* | Köln |

| | | |
|---|---|---|
| Veritas | *Veritas* | Buenos Aires |
| Verwaltung | *Verwaltung* | Heidelberg |
| Vestnik Akademii Nauk SSSR | *Vestn. Akad. Nauk SSSR* | Moskva |
| Vestnik Leningradskogo | *Vestn. Leningr. Univ.* | Leningrad |
| Vestnik Leningradskogo Universiteta. Serija Ékonomiki, Filosofii i Pravo | *Vestn. Leningr. Univ. Ser. Ékon. Filos. Pravo* | Leningrad |
| Vestnik Moskovskogo Universiteta. Serija Ékonomika | *Vestn. Moskov. Univ. Ser. Ékon.* | Moskva |
| Vestnik Moskovskogo Universiteta. Serija Filosofija | *Vestn. Moskov. Univ. Ser. Filos.* | Moskva |
| Vestnik Moskovskogo Universiteta. Serija Istorija | *Vestn. Moskov. Univ. Ser. Ist.* | Moskva |
| Vestnik Moskovskogo Universiteta. Serija Žurnalistika | *Vestn. Moskov. Univ. Ser. Žurnal.* | Moskva |
| Vestnik Moskovskogo Universiteta. Teorija naučnogo Kommunizma | *Vestn. Moskov. Univ. Teorija nauč. Kommunizma* | Moskva |
| Vestnik Statistiki | *Vestn. Statist.* | Moskva |
| Vie économique | *Vie écon. (Berne)* | Berne |
| Vie italienne | *Vie ital.* | |
| Vie sociale | *Vie soc.* | Paris |
| Vierteljahresberichte | *Vierteljahresberichte* | Hannover |
| Vierteljahreshefte für Zeitgeschichte | *Vjh. Zeitgesch.* | Stuttgart |
| Vierteljahreshefte zur Wirtschafts- forschung | *Vjh. Wirtsch.-Forsch.* | Berlin |
| Vita e Pensiero | *Vita e Pensiero* | Milano |
| Vita sociale | *Vita soc.* | Firenze |
| Vitalité française | *Vitalité franc.* | Paris |
| Vivre en France | *Vivre en France* | Paris |
| Vnešnjaja Torgovlja | *Vnešn. Torg.* | Moskva |
| Voprosy Bor'by prestupnost'ju | *Vopr. Bor'by prestupnost'ju* | Moskva |
| Voprosy Cenoobrazovanija | *Vopr. Cenoobraz.* | Moskva |
| Voprosy Ékonomiki | *Vopr. Ékon.* | Moskva |
| Voprosy Ékonomiki Dal'nego Vostoka | *Vopr. Ékon. Dal'n. Vost.* | Vladivostok |
| Voprosy Filosofii | *Vopr. Filos.* | Moskva |
| Voprosy Geografii Belorussii | *Vopr. Geogr. Belorus.* | Minsk |
| Voprosy Istorii | *Vopr. Ist.* | Moskva |
| Voprosy Istorii i Teorii nacional'nyh Otnošenij v SSSR | *Vopr. Ist. Teorii nac. Otnoš. SSR* | Ulan-Udě |
| Voprosy Istorii KPSS | *Vopr. Ist. KPSS* | Moskva |
| Voprosy Literatury | *Vopr. Lit.* | Moskva |
| Voprosy Metodologii Nauki | *Vopr. Metod. Nauki* | Tomsk |
| Voprosy Metodologii obščestvennyh i gumanitarnyh Nauk | *Vopr. Metod. obšč. gumanit. Nauk* | Kalinin |
| Voprosy naučnogo Ateizma. Institut naučnogo Ateizma Akademii obščestvennyh Nauk pri CK KPSS | *Vopr. nauč. Ateizma* | Moskva |
| Voprosy obščestvennyh Nauk | *Vopr. obšč. Nauk* | Kiev |
| Voprosy Psihologii | *Vopr. Psychol.* | Moskva |
| Voprosy Teorii i Metodov ideologičeskoj Raboty | *Vopr. Teorii Metod. ideol. Raboty* | Moskva |
| Vorgänge | *Vorgänge* | Hamburg |
| Vozes. Revista católica de Cultura | *Vozes* | Petropolis |
| Vues sur l'Économie d'Aquitaine | *Vues Écon. Aquitaine* | Paris |
| | | |
| Waseda Hôgaku | *Waseda Hôgaku* | Tokyo |
| Weg und Ziel | *Weg u. Ziel* | Wien |
| Wehrkunde | *Wehrkunde* | München |
| Weltwirtschaft | *Weltwirtschaft* | Kiel |
| Weltwirtschaftliches Archiv | *Weltwirtsch. Archiv* | Kiel |

| | | |
|---|---|---|
| Western economic Journal | *West. econ. J.* | Los Angeles, Calif. |
| Western political Quarterly | *West. polit. Quart.* | Salt Lake City, Utah |
| Wiadomosci statystyczne | *Wiadom. statyst.* | Warszawa |
| Wiener Tagebuch | *Wiener Tagebuch* | Wien |
| Wiez | *Wiez* | Warszawa |
| Wirtschaft und Recht | *Wirtsch. u. Recht* | Zürich |
| Wirtschaft und Statistik | *Wirtsch. u. Statist.* | Stuttgart |
| Wirtschaftsdienst | *Wirtsch.-Dienst* | Hamburg |
| Wirtschaftswissenschaft | *Wirtsch.-Wiss.* | Berlin |
| Wissenschaftliche Zeitschrift der Hochschule für Ökonomie | *Wiss. Z. Hochschule Ökon.* | Berlin, FR |
| Wissenschaftlicher Dienst Südosteuropa | *Wiss. Dienst Südosteuropa* | München |
| WIST. Wirtschaftswissenschaftliches Studium | *WIST* | München |
| World Affairs | *Wld Aff.* | Washington, D. C. |
| World marxist Review | *Wld marx. R.* | Toronto |
| World Politics | *Wld Polit.* | Princeton, N. J. |
| World Survey | *Wld Surv.* | London |
| World today | *Wld today* | London |
| World Yearbook of Education | *Wld Yb. Educ.* | London |
| Worldview | *Worldview* | New York |
| WSI Mitteilungen | *WSI Mitt.* | Köln |
| | | |
| Yale Law Journal | *Yale Law J.* | New Haven, Conn. |
| Yale Review | *Yale R.* | New Haven, Conn. |
| Yamaguchi Kyoiku Gakubu Kenkyu Ronsô | *Yamaguchi Kyoiku Gakubu Kenkyu Ronsô* | Yamaguchi |
| Ydin | *Ydin* | Helsinki |
| Yearbook of World Affairs | *Yb. Wld Aff.* | London |
| Yorkshire Bulletin of economic and social Research | *Yorkshire B. econ. soc. Res.* | Manchester |
| Youth and Society | *Youth and Soc.* | Los Angeles, Calif. |
| Yugoslav Survey | *Yugosl. Surv.* | Belgrad |
| | | |
| Zagadnienie Ekonomiki rolnej | *Zagadn. Ekon. roln.* | Warszawa |
| Zaïre-Afrique | *Zaïre-Afr.* | Kinshasa |
| Zbornik pravnog Fakulteta u Zagrebu | *Zb. prav. Fak. Zagrebu* | Zagreb |
| Zeitschrift für Agrargeschichte und Agrarsoziologie | *Z. Agrargesch. u.-Soziol.* | Frankfurt-am-Main |
| Zeitschrift für ausländisches öffentliches Recht und Völkerrecht | *Z. ausländ. öff. Völkerrecht* | Stuttgart |
| Zeitschrift für Betriebswirtschaft | *Z. Betriebswirtsch.* | Wiesbaden |
| Zeitschrift für Geschichtswissenschaft | *Z. Gesch.-Wiss.* | Berlin |
| Zeitschrift für Parlamentsfragen | *Z. Parlamentsfragen* | Opladen |
| Zeitschrift für Politik | *Z. Polit.* | Köln-Wien-Zürich |
| Zeitschrift für Rechtspolitik | *Z. Rechtspolit.* | München |
| Zeitschrift für Sozialpsychologie | *Z. soz.-Psychol.* | Frankfurt-am-Main |
| Zeitschrift für Soziologie | *Z. Soziol.* | Stuttgart |
| Zeitschrift für Wirtschafts- und Sozialwissenschaften | *Z. Wirtsch.- u. soz.-Wiss.* | Berlin |
| Zeitschrift für den Erdkundeunterricht | *Z. Erdkundeunterricht* | Berlin |
| Zeitschrift für die gesamte Staatswissenschaft | *Z. ges. Staatswiss.* | Tübingen |
| Zeszyty naukowe Szkoły g'ównej Planowania i Statystyki | *Zesz. nauk. Szkoły główn. Plan. Statyst.* | Warszawa |
| Zeszyty naukowe wyższej Szkoły ekonomicznej w Katowicach | *Zesz. nauk. wyższ. Szkoły ekon. Katowic.* | Katowice |
| Zeszyty naukowe wyższej Szkoły ekonomicznej w Krakówie | *Zesz. nauk. wyższ. Szkoły ekon. Kraków.* | Kraków |

| | | |
|---|---|---|
| Zeszyty naukowe wyższej Szkoły ekonomicznej w Poznańiu | *Zesz. nauk. wyższ. Szkoły ekon. Poznań* | Poznań |
| Zukunft | *Zukunft* | Wien |
| Zukunfts- und Friedensforschung | *Zukunfts- u. Friedensforsch.* | Hannover |

# CLASSIFICATION SCHEME[1]
# PLAN DE CLASSIFICATION[1]

---

1. All such headings as are not represented this year by even a single entry will be omitted in the body of the bibliography. / Toute rubrique qui ne sera pas, cette année, représentée par une étude sera omise dans le corps de la bibliographie.

## H Production (goods and services)
## Production (biens et services)

**I**       **Prices and markets**
**Prix et marchés**

| J | **Money and finance** |
|---|---|
| | **Monnaie et finance** |

| J.o | General works / Ouvrages généraux | |
| J.o1 | Theoretical studies / Études théoriques . . . . . . | 3979–3999 |
| J.o2 | Monetary situation: descriptive studies / Situation monétaire : études descriptives . . . . . . . . . . . | 4000–4004 |

| J.1 | Money / Monnaie | |
| J.11 | General monetary theory / Théorie monétaire générale . . . | 4005–4020 |
| J.12 | Monetary systems and standards / Systèmes et standards monétaires | |
| J.13 | Issue of money / Émission de monnaie. . . . . . . | 4022 |
| J.14 | Quantity of money / Volume de la monnaie . . . . . | 4023–4031 |
| J.15 | Monetary dynamics / Dynamique monétaire | |
| J.151 | Theory / Théorie | |
| J.1510 | General studies / Études générales . . . . . . | 4032–4050 |
| J.1511 | Inflation-deflation / Inflation-déflation . . . . . . | 4051–4094 |
| J.152 | Descriptive studies: inflation-deflation, anti-inflationary policies / Études descriptives: inflation-déflation, politiques anti-inflationnistes | |
| J.16 | Money market / Marché monétaire . . . . . . | 4124–4128 |
| J.161 | Discount rate / Taux d'escompte . . . . . . . | 4129–4131 |

| J.2 | Credit / Crédit | |
| J.21 | Bank structure / Structure bancaire | |
| J.210 | General studies / Études générales . . . . . . | 4132–4138 |
| J.211 | Bank systems / Systèmes bancaires . . . . . . | 4139–4165 |
| J.212 | Central banks / Banques . . . . . . . | 4166–4172 |
| J.213 | Other public banking establishments, nationalized banks / Autres institutions bancaires publiques, banques nationalisées . . . | 4173–4177 |
| J.214 | Private banks / Banques privées . . . . . . . | 4178–4179 |
| J.215 | Savings banks / Caisses d'épargne . . . . . . | 4180–4188 |
| J.216 | Bank operations / Technique bancaire . . . . . . | 4189–4201 |
| J.22 | Credit: theory and operations / Le crédit : théorie, opérations de crédit | |
| J.220 | General studies / Études générales . . . . . . . | 4202–4203 |
| J.221 | Evolution of credit: local studies / Évolution de crédit : études localisées . . . . . . . . . . . | 4204–4210 |
| J.222 | Short-term credit, discount / Crédit à court terme, opérations d'escompte | |
| J.223 | Medium-term credit / Crédit à moyen terme . . . . | 4211–4212 |
| J.224 | Long-term / Crédit à long terme | |
| J.23 | Specialized credit agencies and operations / Organismes et opérations de crédit spécialisées | |
| J.231 | Consumer credit. Pawn houses / Crédit à la consommation. Crédit municipal . . . . . . . . . . . . | 4213–4219 |
| J.232 | Agricultural credit / Crédit agricole . . . . . . | 4220–4227 |
| J.233 | Industrial and commercial credit / Crédit industriel et commercial | 4228–4229 |
| J.234 | Co-operative credit / Crédit coopératif | |
| J.235 | Building credit / Crédit à la construction | |
| J.236 | Mortgage and real estate credit / Crédit hypothécaire, crédit foncier | |
| J.24 | Credit control and policy / Contrôle et politique du crédit . . | 4230–4235 |

| J.3 | Insurance / Assurances . . . . . . . . . | 4236–4245 |

| J.4 | Stock market / Marché financier | |
| J.41 | Institutions, legislation and policy / Institutions, législation et politique | |
| J.411 | Investment trust / Sociétés d'investissement . . . . | 4246–4250 |
| J.412 | Securities: legislation / Régime des valeurs mobilières . . . | 4251–4252 |
| J.42 | Economic functions and equilibrium / Fonctions économiques et équilibre | |

# A PRELIMINARIES
# PRÉLIMINAIRES

## A.1 REFERENCE BOOKS (DICTIONARIES, ENCYCLOPEDIAS, DIRECTORIES, etc.)
## OUVRAGES DE RÉFÉRENCE (DICTIONNAIRES, ENCYCLOPÉDIES, ANNUAIRES, etc.)

1    BAUDHUIN, F. *Dictionnaire de l'économie contemporaine.* Verviers, Editions Gérard et Cş, 72, 343 p.

2    COVENEY, J.; MOORE, S. J. *Glossary of French and English management terms / Lexique de termes anglais français de gestion.* London, Longman, 72, xii-146 p.

3    RYNERN, G. VON (ed.). *Wörterbuch zur politischen Ökonomie* (Dictionary of political economy). Opladen, Westdeutscher Verlag, 73, 492 p.

4    GUHA, P. S. *Directory of economic research centres in India.* Calcutta, Information Research Academy, 72, 426 p.

5    HENNI, M. *Dictionnaire des termes économiques et commerciaux, français-anglais-arabe, avec index des mots-clés anglais et arabes.* Beyrouth, Librairie du Liban, 72, 409 p.

6    HERSANT, G. *Les 50 mots-clés de la science économique.* Toulouse, Privat, 72, 152 p.

7    MAYER, G. *Dizionario di economia* (Dictionary of economics). Roma, Bulzoni, 72, 218 p.

8    PARIKH, K. C. *Dictionary of business and management.* Bombay, N. M. Tripathi, 72, xi-403 p.

9    SHALLALAH, Y. *Dictionnaire pratique, français-arabe: droit, commerce, finances, suivi d'un vocabulaire arabe-français.* Alexandrie, Etablissement al-Maaref, 73, 1368-xlviii-269 p.

10    SOPIRA, A. *Rusko-slovenský ekonomický* (Russian-Slovak dictionary of economics). Bratislava, SPN, 748-1 p.

11    TEZENAS DU MONTCEL, H. *Dictionnaire des sciences de la gestion.* Paris, Mame, 72, 332 p.

12    UNITED STATES. Department of Commerce. *Dictionary of economic and statistical terms.* Washington, Government Printing Office, 73, 83 p.

13    ZAHN, H. E. *Euro-Wirtschafts-Wörterbuch; deutsch, english, französisch / Dictionary of economics and business / Dictionnaire de l'économie et des affaires.* Frankfurt-am-Main, F. Knapp, 73, xiii-702 p.

## A.2 BIBLIOGRAPHY, DOCUMENTATION, PERIODICALS
## BIBLIOGRAPHIE, DOCUMENTATION, PÉRIODIQUES

[See also / Voir aussi: 1751, 1758, 2597, 2793, 2802, 3381, 5197, 6417]

14    BILLINGS, B. B.; VIKSNINS, G. G. "The relative quality of economics journals: an alternative rating system", *West. econ. J.* 10(4), dec 72 : 467-469.

15    FRANKENA, M.; BHATIA, K. "Journal articles from Canadian economics departments" *West. econ. J.* 10(3), sep 72 : 352-363.

16    LOTTE, J. "Les problèmes de l'information économique en France", *Impact* 5(3), 1973 : 65-71.

17    LOVELL, M. C. "The production of economic literature: an interpretation", *J. econ. Liter.* 11(1), mar 73 : 27-55.

18    MARESKI, S.; FERRARO, O. H. *Bibliografía sobre datos y estudios económicos en el Paraguay* (Bibliography on economic data on studies in Paraguay). Asunción Centro Paraguayo de Documentación Social, 72, 82 1.

19    MOORE, W. J. "The relative quality of economics journals: a suggested rating system", *West. econ. J.* 10(2), jun 72 : 156-169.

20    PREDETTI, A. *L'informazione economica di base* (Basic economic information). Milano, A. Giuffrè, 72, iii-85 p.

21    PROTOPOPESCU, V. V.; STOICA, D. *Sistemul de informare economică și procesul de luare a deciziilor în întreprindere* (System of economic information and decision-making process in the enterprise). Bucureşti, Editura didactică şi pedagogică, 72, 239 p.

22    RATH, V. *Index of Indian economic journals, 1916-1965.* Poona, Gokhade Institute of Politics and Economics; Orient Longman, 71, liv-302 p.

23    SCHWEIZERISCHE GESELLSCHAFT FÜR STATISTIK UND VOLKSWIRTSCHAFT; EIDGENÖSSISCHES STATISTISCHES AMT. *Schweizerische Bibliographie für Statistik und Volkswirtschaft / Bibliographie suisse de statistique et d'économie politique.* Bern, 73, 219 p.

24    SKEELS, J. W.; TAYLOR, R. A. "The relative quality of economics journals: an alternative rating system", *West. econ. J.* 10(4), dec 72 : 470-473.

25    TEREBUCHA, E. *Wstęp do ogólnej teorii informacji mikro-ekonomicznej* (Introduction to the general theory of microeconomic information). Warszawa, Paûstwowa Wydawnictwo Naukowe, 73, 120 p.

26    VAISTO, E. *Organisaatio-opin ja yrityksen hallinnon kirjallisuus Suomessa vuosil ta 1945-1970 / Bibliography of organization and administration in Finland 1945-1970.* Helsinki, Kauppakorkeakoulu; Jakelu, Kyriiri, 72, 180(1) p.

27    VAISTO, E. *Suomen liiketaloustieteellinen kirjallisuus 1971 / Business literature in Finland 1971.* Helsinki, Kauppakorkeakoulun Kirjasto, 72, iii-10 p.


### A.3    CONFERENCES, MEETINGS, ASSOCIATIONS
###        CONGRÈS, COLLOQUES, ASSOCIATIONS

[See also / Voir aussi: 2391, 3384, 4056]

28    COATS, A. W.; COATS, S. E. "The changing social composition of the Royal Economic Society, 1890-1960, and the professionalization of British economics", *Brit. J. Socio.* 24(2), jun 73 : 165-187.


### A.4    TEACHING AND RESEARCH INSTITUTIONS
###        ORGANISMES D'ENSEIGNEMENT ET DE RECHERCHE

[See also / Voir aussi: 2347, 2516, 3514, 3562]

29    BECKER, H. A. "Observation by informants in institutional research", *Quality and Quantity* 6(1), jun 72 : 157-169.

30    CHOLAJ, H. "A közgazdaságtudomány helyzete, feladatai Lengyelországban" (The situation and the tasks of economic science in Poland), *Közgazd. Szle* 20(9), sep 73 : 1096-1106.

31    FREIER, U.; LEWICKI, B. *Volkswirtschaftslehre im Rundfunk; Analysen und Materialien* (Political economy teaching on the radio: analysis and materials), Frankfurt-am-Main, Dipa-Verlag, 72, 159 p.

32    GALBRAITH, J. K. "Power and the useful economist", *Amer. econ. R.* 63(1), mar 73 : 1-11.

33    HOUGH, R. R. *What economists do.* New York, Harper and Row, 72, viii-167 p.

34    JOHNSON, G. L.; ZERBY, L. K. *What economists do about values; case studies of their answers to questions they don't dare ask.* East Lansing, Department of Agricultural Economics, Michigan State University, 73, vii-255 p.

35    JUZUFOVIČ, G. K. *Ekonomičeskie metody upravlenija naučnymi issledovanijami v stranah-členah SEV* (Economic methods of scientific research management in the Comecon countries). Leningrad, Izdatel'stvo Leningradskogo Universiteta, 73, 120 p.

36    KOLANOWSKA, B.; JAROMIN, J. "Nauczanie dyscyplin finansowych w wyzszych szkołach ekonomicznych" (Teaching of financial sciences in higher economic schools), *Finanse* (2), 1973 : 44-56. [Poland].

37    LEWANDOWSKI, J. "Ocena stanu badaû i dorobkhy oraz dalsze zadania i kierunki rozwoju podstawowych nauk ekonomicznych" (Present state, achievements, further objectives and development trends of theoretical economics: review and appraisal), *Ekonomista* (2), 1973 : 329-350.

38    Lisikiewicz, J. "Stan i rozwój ekonomik branzowych i badaû stosowanych w latach 1951-1971" (State and prospects of the various sectors of economic science and applied economics, 1951-1971), *Ekonomista* (2), 1973 : 351-389.

39    Livingstone, I. *et al.* (eds.). *The teaching of economics in Africa.* London, Chatto and Windus, 73, 192 p.

40    Maxwell, G. W.; Winnett, W. L. (eds.). *Relevance in the education of today's business student.* Washington, National Business Education Association, 73, x-292 p.

41    Norton, H. S. *The world of the economist.* Columbia, University of South Carolina Press, 73, xii-169 p.

42    Oliver, J. M. *The principles of teaching economics.* London, Heinemann Educational, 73, viii-87 p.

3

# B  METHODS
# MÉTHODES

## B.1  GENERAL METHODOLOGY
## MÉTHODOLOGIE GÉNÉRALE

### B.10  Scope, value and method (and relations to other sciences)
### Objet, valeur et méthode (rapports de l'économie avec les autres sciences)

[See also / Voir: 4390]

43  BLACK, R. D. C.; COATS, A. W.; GODDWIN, C. D. W. (eds.). *The marginal revolution in economics; interpretation and evaluation*. Durham, N. C., Duke University Press, 73, viii-367 p.

44  BLANCHFIELD, W. C.; OSER, J. *Economics: reality through theory*. New York, Harcourt Brace Jovanovich, 73, x-387 p.

45  BOWEN, H. R. "Toward a humanist economics", *Nebraska J. Econ. Busin.* 11(4), 1972 : 9-24.

46  CHOŁAJ, H. "O roli, zadaniach i warunkach rozwoju nauk ekonomicznych" (The role, objectives and conditions of the development of economic sciences), *Ekonomista* 2, 1973 : 279-327.

47  DENIS, H. (ed.). *La formation de la science économique*. Paris, Presses universitaires de France, 73, 340 p.

48  FEDORENKO, N. "Aktual'nye problemy razvitija sovetskoj ekonomičeskoj nauki" (Present problems of development of Soviet economic science), *Vopr. Ekon.* 25 (7), jul 73 : 50-63.

49  GOUDZWAARD, B. "Economie en vooruitgangsidee" (Economics and the idea of progress), *Economist (Haarlem)* 120(1), jan-feb 72 : 1-26.

50  GRENDI, E. (ed.). *L'antropologia economica* (Economic anthropology). Torino, G. Einaudi, 72, lxiii-299 p.

51  GUTTMAN, H. *Cercetări de sociologie economică* (Research on economic sociology). București, Editura științifică, 72, 175 p.

52  Bibl. XXI.-131. HADLEY, G.; KEMP, M. C. *Variational methods in economics*. CR: W. A. BROCK, *J. econ. Liter.* 10(4), dec 72 : 1230-1231.

53  HEILBRONER, R. L. "Economics as a value-free science", *Soc. Res.* 40(1), 1973 : 129-143.

54  HUNT, E. K.; SCHWARTZ, J. G. (eds.). *A critique of economic theory; selected readings*. Harmondsworth, Penguin, 72, 476 p.

55  HUNT, E. K.; SHERMAN, H. J. *Economics. An introduction to traditional and syndical views*. London-New York, Harper and Row, 72, xxii-647 p. CR: D. E. KAUN, *J. econ. Liter.* 11(2), jun 73 : 525-526.

56  HUTCHINSON, H. D. *Economics and social goals; an introduction*. Chicago, Science Research Associates, 73, 512 p.

57  KAGEL, J. H. "Token economies and experimental economics", *J. polit. Econ.* 80(4), jul-aug 72 : 779-785.

58  KLANT, J. J. *Spelregels voor economen. De logische structuur van economische theorieen* (Rules for the economist. The logical structure of economic theories). Leiden, Stenfert Kroese, 73, viii-211 p.

59  LANCASTER, K. *Modern economics: principles and policy*. Chicago, Rand McNally, 73, xix-741 p.

60  LATOUCHE, S. "Linguistique et économie politique", *Homme et Soc.* 28, apr-jun 73 : 51-70.

61 Leontief, W. "Ipotesi teoriche ed aspetti trascurati della scienza economica" (Theoretical hypothesis and neglected aspects of economic science), *Econ. int. (Genova)* 25(3), aug 72 : 397-407.

62 Mehta, J. K. *The infra-structure of economics.* Allahabad, Chugh Publications, 72, ii-ii-341 p. [Rev. and enl. ed. of a work originally published under title : *A philosophical interpretation of economics.*]

63 Miller, R. LeR. *Economics today.* San Francisco, Canfield Press, 73, xvii-750 p.

64 Morgenstern, O. "Thirteen critical points in contemporary economic theory: an interpretation", *J. econ. Liter.* 10(4), dec 72 : 1163-1189.

65 Myrdal, G. *Against the stream: critical essays on economics.* New York, Pantheon Books, 73, x-336 p.

66 Naylor, T. H. "Experimental economics revisited", *J. polit. Econ.* 80(2), mar-apr 72 : 347-352.

67 Parkin, M.; Nobay, A. R. (eds.). *Essays in modern economics.* London, Longman, 73, xii-399 p.

68 Perroux, F. *Pouvoir et économie.* Paris, Bordas, 73, ix-139 p.

69 Ruzička, J. "Metodologické otázky ekonomické sociologie a psychology prace v souvislosti s rízením" (Methodological problems of economic sociology and psychology of work in connection with management), *Sociol. Čas.* 9(4), 1973 : 396-403.

70 Schachter, G. "Some developments in economic science since 1965: methods, ideas approaches", *Amer. J. Econ. Sociol.* 32(3), jul 73 : 331-335.

71 Shannon, R. D. (ed.). *Economics today: editorial columns from the Greenville news.* Clemson, S. C. College of Industrial Management and Textile Science Press, Clemson University, 73, xv-148 p.

72 Smith, T. "Politics, economics and political economy", *Gvt and Opposition* 8(3), été 73 : 263-279.

73 Šoškić, B. *Ekonomska analiza* (Economic analysis). Beograd, Fakultet organizacio nih nauka; Privredno-finansijski vodič Oeconomica, 72, 2 vols.

74 *Technique économique et finalité humaine. Vers une démarche opératoire.* Namur, CERUNA, Gembloux, Éditions Duculot, 72, 277 p.

75 Tenzer, O. *Úvod do metody myšlení pro ekonomy* (Introduction to research methods in economics). Praha, Svoboda, 72, 283-5 p.

76 Terrail, J. P. "Notes sur les rapports entre économie politique et sociologie", *Pensée* 166, nov-dec 72 : 25-35.

77 Van Rompuy, V. "De huidige stand van de economische wetenschap" (The actual state of economic science), *Tijds. Econ.* 17(4), 1972 : 403-415.

78 Van Zuthem, H. J. *Inleiding in de economische sociologie. Mensen en machten in het economische leven* (Introduction to economic sociology. Men and powers in economic life). Amsterdam, De Bussy; Utrecht, Oosthoek, 73, xii-250 p.

79 Bibl. xxi-81. Ward, B. *What's wrong with economics?* CR: R. I. Downing, *J. econ. Liter.* 11(2), jun 73 : 539-540.

80 Wehler, H. U. (comp.). *Geschichte und Ökonomie* (History and economy). Köln, Kiepenheur und Witsch, 73, 397 p.

81 Weiskopf, W. A. "Economics and meaninglessness", *Nebraska J. Econ. Busin.* 11(4) 1972 : 67-77.

82 Worswick, G. D. N. (ed.). *Uses of economics.* New York, Barnes and Noble Books, 72, viii-227 p.

83 Zwintz, R. "Zur Theorie der ökonomisch-relevanten aussermarktmässigen Beziehungen" (On the theory of economically relevant non-economic relations), *Z. Wirtsch u. soz.-Wiss.* 92(2), 1972 : 129-153.


## B.12 Micro-economic and macro-economic approaches
## Approches micro-économiques et macro-économiques

[See also / Voir aussi: **B.32; F.23;** 3995, 4371, 4804, 5281, 5730]

84 Andersen, B. N. *Noter til makroteori* (Notes on macrotheory). København, Universitetsforlaget Gad, 72, 134 p.

**B.32**    **Model method**
             **Méthode des modèles**

[See also / Voir aussi: **B.12; F.23; F.25;** 1648, 1952, 2150, 2201, 2343, 2542, 2547, 2866, 3367, 3385, 3900, 3950, 4055, 4058, 4318, 4344, 4374, 4397, 4631, 4917, 5199, 5371, 5400, 6492]

188   ALCAIDE INCHAUSTI, A. (ed.). *Lecturas de econometría* (Readings on econometrics). Madrid, Gredos, 72, 402 p.

189   ALLINGHAM, M. G. "Tatonnement stability: an econometric approach", *Econometrica* 40(1), jan 72 : 27-41.

190   AMEMIYA, T.; WU, R. Y. "The effect of aggregation on prediction in the autoregressive model", *J. Amer. statist. Assoc.* 67(339), sep 72 : 626-632.

191   ANDERSIN, H. E.; SULONEN, R. *Simuleringsteknik* (Simulation technique). Lund, Studentlitteratur, 72, 368 p.

192   BARRADOS, J. P. "A solution to the problem of the inconsistency of the classical exchange model", *Kyklos* 25(4), 1972 : 825-828.

193   BOJARSKI, R. (ed.). *Modele matematyczne i identyfikacja procesów* (Mathematical models and process identification. (I). Wrocław, Zakł., Nar. im Ossoliń, 72, 274 + 234 p.

194   BOWDEN, R. J. "More stochastic properties of the Klein-Goldberger model", *Econometrica* 40(1), jan 72 : 87-98.

195   BRUNNER, K. (ed.). *Problems and issues in current econometric practice*. Columbus, College of Administrative Science, Ohio State University, 72, vii-284 p.

196   BYRON, R. P. "Testing for misspecification in econometric systems using full information", *Int. econ. R.* 13(3), oct 72 : 745-756.

197   CAO-PINNA, V. *Econometria e pianificazione* (Econometrics and planning). Milano, ETAS Kompass, 72, 2 v.

198   Bibl. XXI-245. CHRYMES, P. J. *Distributed lags. Problems of estimation and formulation*. CR: C. A. SIMS, *J. econ. Liter.* 11(1), mar 73 : 107-109.

199   CZERWIŃSKI, Z. "O klasycznych modelach ekonometrycznych" (On classical econometric models), *Ekonomista* (1), 1973 : 39-52.

200   CZERWIŃSKI, Z. *Podstawy matematycznych modeli wzrostu gospodarczego* (Foundations of mathematical models of economic growth). Warszawa, Państwowe Wydawnictwo Ekonomiczne, 73, 189 p.

201   DAY, G. S. "Evaluating models of attitude structure", *J. Mkting Res.* 9(3), aug 72 : 279-286.

202   DENTON, F. T.; OKSANEN, E. H. "A multi-country analysis of the effects of data revisions on an econometric model", *J. Amer. statist. Assoc.* 67(338), jun 72 : 286-291.

203   DRHYMES, P. J. "Asymptotic properties of simultaneous least squares estimators", *Int. econ. R.* 13(2), jun 72 : 201-211.

204   DRHYMES, P. J. *et al.* "Criteria for evaluation of econometric models", *A. econ. soc. Measurement* 1(2), apr 72 : 291-324.

205   "Econometric models", *Amer. econ. R.* 63(2), mai 73 *Pap. and Proc.*: 385-411. With contributions by G. FROMM, L. R. KLEIN, H. TSURUMI, C. MORIGUCHI and R. G. BODKIN.

206   EDGERTON, D. L. "Some properties of two stage least squares as applied to nonlinear models", *Int. econ. R.* 13(1), feb 72 : 26-32.

207   FERNÁNDEZ DIAZ, A. "Sull' uso dei modelli nell'analisi economica e nella politica economica" (On the use of models in economic analysis and economic policy), *Riv. Polit. econ.* 62(10), oct 72 : 1263-1296.

208   GESSNER, P.; WACKER, H. *Dynamische Optimierung; Einführung, Modelle, Computerprogramme* (Dynamic optimization; methods, models, computer programs). München, C. Hanser, 72, 204 p.

209   GLYCOPANTIS, D. "Optimality conditions in certain models with intertemporally dependent states", *West. econ. J.* 10(2), jun 72 : 139-155.

210   GOLDFELD, S. M.; QUANDT, R. E. *Nonlinear methods in econometrics*. Amsterdam, North-Holland Publishing Co., 72, xi-280 p. CR: T. AMEMIYA, *J. econ. Liter.* 11(3), sep 73 : 924-925.

211   GOODMAN, S. R. *Successful use of new mathematical models*. Englewood Cliffs, N. J., Prentice-Hall, 72, 38 p.

212 GORIS, H. *Inleiding in de econometrie* (Introduction to econometrics). Amsterdam, J. H. de Bussy, 72, xii-236 p.

213 GRABOWSKI, W. *Elementy ekonometrii i programowania matematycznego. II. Deterministyczne modele optymalizacyjne* (Elements of econometrics and of mathematical programming. II. Deterministic optimizing models). Warszawa, Szkoła Główna Planowania i Statystyki, 73, 288 p.

214 GREŃ, J.; GRUSZCZYŃSKI, M.; KANTON, M. *Elementy ekonometrii i programowania matematycznego. I. Modele ekonometryczne* (Elements of econometrics and of mathematical programming. I. Econometric models). Warzawa, Szkoła Główna Planowania i Statystyki, 73, 143 p.

215 HABIBAGAHI, H.; KLEIN, L. R. "Analog solution of econometric models", *Engin. Economist* 17(2), jan-feb 72 : 115-133.

216 HARTLEY, M. J. "Optimum simulation path estimators", *Int. econ. R.* 13 (3), oct 72 : 711-727.

217 Bibl. xxi-251. HICKMAN, B. G. (ed.). *Econometric models of cyclical behavior.* CR: K. BRUNNER, J. *econ. Liter.* 11(3), sep 73 : 926-933.

218 HOWREY, E. P.; KLEIN, L. R. "Dynamic properties of nonlinear econometric models", *Int. econ. R.* 13(3), oct 72 : 599-618.

219 HU, T. W. *Econometrics: an introductory analysis.* Baltimore, University Park Press, 73, viii-172 p.

220 IANCU, A. *Eficienta economică maximă. Metode de modelare* (Maximum economic efficiency. Model method). Bucuresti Editura politică, 72, 431 p.

221 JOHANSEN, L. "Simple and general nonsubstitution theorems for input-output models", *J. econ. Theory* 5(3), dec 72 : 383-394.

222 JUJA, T. "Optymalizacyjny wielogałęziowy model wzrostu gospodarki narodowej w układzie przestrzennym (The optimization of a multibranch model of national economy growth), *Zesz. nauk. wyzsz. Szkoły ekon. w Poznan.* 43, 1972 : 25-42.

223 KEELER, E. B. "A twisted turnpike", *Int. econ. R.* 13(1), feb 72 : 160-166.

224 KELEJIAN, H. H. "Information lost in aggregation: a Bayesian approach", *Econometrica* 40(1), jan 72 : 19-26.

225 KENDRICK, D. "On the Leontief dynamic inverse", *Quart. J. Econ.* 86(4), nov 72 : 693-696.

226 KLEMM, H.; MIKUT, M. *Lagerhaltungsmodelle; Theorie und Anwendung* (Inventory models; theory and utilization). Berlin, Verlag Die Wirtschaft, 72, 268 p.

227 KONDRATOWICZ, L. *Synteza procesów modelowania i symulacji systemów dyskretnych* (Synthesis of modelling and simulating processes of discrete systems). Gdańsk, Wydawnictwo Instytutu Morskiego, 73, 62 p.

228 MAKI, D. P.; THOMPSON, M. *Mathematical models and applications, with emphasis on the social, life, and management sciences.* Englewood Cliffs, N. J. Prentice-Hall, 73, xv-492 p.

229 MIKHALEVSKIJ, B. N. "Mechanical-organic economic models and models of an open multistage dynamic system", *Matekon* 9(1), 1972 : 3-32.

230 MIRMAN, L. J. "On the existence of steady state measures for one sector growth models with uncertain technology", *Int. econ. R.* 13(2), jun 72 : 271-286.

231 MORISHIMA, M. et al. *The working of econometric models.* Cambridge, University Press, 72, ix-339 p.

232 MUCKL, W. J. "Eine Verallgemeinerung des Wachstumsmodells von Solow und ihre Anwendung auf das neo-klassische Theorem" (A generalization of Solow's growth model and its application to the neo-classical theorem) *Kyklos* 25(4), 1972 : 771-790.

233 MURPHY, J. L. *Introductory econometrics.* Homewood, Ill., R. D. Irwin, 73, xii-524 p.

234 NASIŁOWSKI, M. "Rozwinięta formuła M. Kaleckiego a idea modelu pracy" (M. Kalecki's formula developed and the concept of a labour model of growth), *Ekonomista* (4), 1973 : 863-879.

235 NEWBURY, D. "The importance of malleable capital in optimal growth models", *J. econ. Theory* 5(1), aug 72 : 21-41.

236 NORDBERG, L. "Om möjligheterna att utnyttja data från flera länder vid konstruktion av ekonometriska modeller" (The possibilities of using data from several countries in the construction of econometric models) *Ekon. Samfund. Ts.* 26(2), 1973 : 105-116.

237   ROZIN, B. B.; ŽURAVEL', N. U. *Raspoznavanie obrazov i regressionnyj analiz i ėkonomičeskih issledovanijah* (Recognition of models and regressive analysis in economic researches), Novosibirsk, 1972, 282 p.

238   RYVKIN, A.; AMITOV, I. *Problemy ėkonometričeskogo modelirovanija* (Problems of econometric model building). Moskva, 72, 299 p.

239   SECCHI, C. "L'uso dei modelli econometrici per lo studio di situazioni alternative" (The use of econometric models for the study of alternative situations), *Riv. Polit. econ.* 62(10), oct 72 : 1297-1318.

240   SHANIN, T. (ed.). *The rules of the game. Cross-disciplinary essays on models in scholarly thought.* London, Tavistock, 72, XVI-391 p.

241   SIWOŃ, B. *Współczesne tendencje rozwoju rachunku kosztów i wyników* (Contemporary trends in the development of input-output calculus). Warszawa, Państwowe Wydawnictwo Ekonomiczne, 72, 279 p.

242   SWAMY, P. A. V. B.; ACORA, S. S. "The exact finite sample properties of the estimators coefficients in the error components regression models", *Econometrica* 40(2), mar 72 : 261-275.

243   TOKOYAMA, K.; MURAKAMI, Y. "Relative stability in two types of dynamic Leontief models", *Int. econ. R.* 13(2), jun 72 : 408-415.

244   TREYZ, G. I. "An econometric procedure for ex post policy evaluation", *Int. econ. R.* 13(2), jun 72 : 212-222.

245   VANGREVELINGHE, G. *Économétrie.* Paris, Hermann, 73, 204 p.

246   WALLIS, K. G. *Introductory econometrics.* Chicago, Aldine; London, Gray-Mills Publishing Ltd, 72, 6-124 p.

247   WILLIAMS, R. L.; CROUCH, R. L. "The adjustment speed of neoclassical growth models", *J. econ. Theory* 4(3), jun 72 : 552-586.

248   Bibl. XXI-399. ZELLNER, A. *An introduction to Bayesian inference in econometrics.* CR: E. E. LEAMER, *J. econ. Liter.* 10(4), dec 72 : 1232-1234.

## B.33      Linear programming
             Modèles linéaires

[See also / Voir aussi: 2806, 4790]

249   ADAMS, F. G.; GRIFFIN, J. M. "An econometric-linear programming model of the US petroleum refining industry", *J. Amer. statist. Assoc.* 67(339), sep 72 : 542-551.

250   ALHO, K. "On estimation of linear distribution models", *Kansantalous* 68(3), 1972 : 240-245.

251   BARBIROLI, G.; DONINI, B. R. "La programmazione lineare come metodo per l'ottimazzione dei consumi e delle spese alimentari" (Linear programming as a method for optimization of consumption and food expenditures) *Statistica (Bologna)* 33(1), jan-mar 73 : 123-138. [Italy.]

252   BOWDEN, R. "The generalised characteristic equation of a linear dynamic system", *Econometrica* 40(1), jan 72 : 201-203.

253   CHOW, G. C. "Optimal control of linear econometric systems with finite time horizon" *Int. econ. R.* 13(1), feb 72 : 16-25.

254   COOPER, J. P. "Asymptotic covariance matrix of procedures for linear regression in the presence of first order serially correlated disturbances", *Econometrica* 40(2), mar 72 : 305-310.

255   HANNAN, E. J.; TERRELL, R. D. "Time series regression with linear constraints", *Int. econ. R.* 13(2), jun 72 : 189-200.

256   HUGHES, A.; GRAWIOG, D. E. *Linear programming: an emphasis on decisionmaking.* Reading, Mass., Addison-Wesley Publishing Co., 73, xv-414 p.

257   Bibl. XXI-303. LEMPERS, F. B. *Posterior probabilities of alternative linear models. Some theoretical considerations and empirical experiments.* CR: M. S. GEISEL, *J. econ. Liter.* 11(1), mar 73 : 109-110.

258   LUTJOHANN, H. "Another note on linear aggregation of economic relations" *Int. econ. R.* 13(2), jun 72 : 426-428.

259   OTSUKI, M. "Oscillations in stochastic simulation of linear systems", *Econ. Stud. Quart.* 22(3), dec 71 : 54-71.

260  SIMONNARD, M.; CHOUTET, X. *Programmation linéaire; technique du calcul économique.* 2e éd. rev. et augm. Paris, Dunod, 72. [Vol. I. *Fondements*].

261  THOMPSON, G. E. "Linear programming and microeconomic analysis", *Nebraska J. Econ. Busin.* 11(4), 1972 : 25-36.

262  TURNOVSKY, S. J. "Optimal stabilization policies for deterministic and stochastic linear systems", *R. econ. Stud.* 40(1), jan 73 : 79-95.

## B.4    ACCOUNTING METHOD AND THEORY
## MÉTHODE ET THÉORIE COMPTABLES

263  BUCKLEY, J. W.; LIGHTNER, K. M. *Accounting: an information systems approach.* Encino, Calif., Dickenson Publishing Co., 73, xxviii-1308 p.

264  COLDITZ, B. T.; GIBBINS, R. W. (eds.). *Accounting perspectives.* Sydney-New York, McGraw-Hill, 72, 208 p.

265  ESTES, R. W. *Accounting and society.* Los Angeles, Melville Publishing Co., 73, xiii-411 p.

266  ESTRADA, S. N. *Depreciaciones, previsiones y reservas: teoría y práctica contable* (Depreciation, forecasts and reserves; accounting theory and practice). Mendoza, Argentina, Universidad Nacional de Cuyo, Facultad de Ciencias Económicas, 72, 34-5 p.

267  FOKIN, A. I. *Nekotorye problemy hozjajstvennogo rašěeta v sovremmenyh uslovijah* (Some problems of economic accounting under contemporary conditions). Voronež, Izdatel'stvo voronežskogo Universiteta, 72, 280 p.

268  GIBSON, C. J.; MEREDITH, G. G.; PETERSON, R. (eds.). *Accounting concepts; readings.* Melbourne, Cassell Australia, 72, viii-398 p.

269  LANDA GARAMENDI, J. M. *Cómo implantar la contabilidad analítica* (How to set up analytical accounting). Madrid, Ibérico Europea de Ediciones 72, 121 p.

270  LAZZATI, S. C. *Ensayos sobre teoría contable* (Essays on accounting theory). Buenos Aires, Ediciones Macchi, 72, 103 p.

271  MARGOLIS, N.; HARMON, N. P.; SIMINI, J. P. *Accounting essentials.* New York, Wiley, 72, xi-308 p.

272  MAUTZ, R. K. *Effect of circumstances on the application of accounting principles: a research study prepared for Financial Executives Research Foundation.* New York, Financial Executives Research Foundation, 72, vii-188 p.

273  McDONALD, D. L. *Comparative accounting theory.* Reading, Mass., Addison-Wesley Publishing Co., 72, xii-112 p.

274  POPOV, Z. "Demografsko ražunovodstvo—problemi integrisanja društvenih statistika" (Economic accounting—the problems of the integration of demographic and social statistics), *Ekon. Misao* 6(2), jun 73 : 141-158.

275  SALMONSON, R. F.; HERMANSON, R. H.; EDWARDS, J. D. *A survey of basic accounting.* Homewood, Ill., R. D. Irwin, 73, xi-411 p.

276  SKINNER, R. M. *Accounting principles.* Toronto, Canadian Institute of Chartered Accountants, 72, 483 p.

277  SOBIS, H. "Rachunkowosc i informatyka w systemie informacji ekonomicznej" (Accounting and EDP in the system of economic information), *Prace nauk. wyzsz. Szkoły ekon. Wrocław.* 41, 1973 : 5-42.

278  STERLING, R. R. (ed.). *Research methodology in accounting; papers and responses.* Lawrence, Kan., Scholars Book Co., vii-163 p.

279  VANGERMEERSCH, R. G. J. (ed.). *Accounting: socially responsible and socially relevant.* New York, Harper and Row, 72, xi-363 p.

280  WALGENBACH, P. H.; DITTRICH, N. E. *Accounting: an introduction.* New York, Harcourt Brace Jovanovich, 73, xv-575 p.

281  WALKER, R. C. (ed.). *An introduction to accounting; selected readings.* New York, MSS Information Corp., 72, 93 p.

# C  GENERAL AND BASIC WORKS
## OUVRAGES GÉNÉRAUX ET OUVRAGES DE BASE

### C.1  COMPREHENSIVE TREATISES AND TEXTBOOKS
### TRAITÉS D'ÉCONOMIE GÉNÉRALE. MANUELS

282  AL-FANJARI, M. Sh. *al-Madhal ilá al-iqtiśâd al-Islâmî* (Introduction to Islamic economics). al-Qâhiraf, Dâr al-Nahḍaf al-'Arabi, 72, n.p.

283  AULD, D. A. L.; GRANT, E. K. *Macroeconomics: a programmed book for Canadian students.* Scarborough, Ont., Prentice-Hall of Canada, 72, 128 p.

284  BANGS, R. B. *Men, money and markets; an introduction to economic reasoning.* Pacific Grove, Calif., Boxwood Press, 72, vii-307 p.

285  CAPODAGLIO, G. *Manuale di economica* (Manual of economics). Bari, F. Cacucci, 72, xii-520 p.

286  DAYAN, A. *Manuel de la distribution: fonctions, structures, évolution.* Paris, Éditions d'organisation, 72, 206 p.

287  ECONOMIST INTELLIGENCE UNIT. *Key issues in applied economics, 1947-1997.* London, Longman, 72, x-166 p.

288  LEVY, F. D. Jr., SUFRIN, S. C. *Basic economics; analysis of contemporary problems and policies.* New York, Harper and Raw, 73, xxiii-483 p.

289  LIPSEY, R. G.; SPARKS, G. R.; STEINER, P. O. *Economics.* New York, Harper and Row, 73, xvii-789 p.

290  MARZANO, A. *Politica economica dei grandi aggregati* (Economic policy of large aggregates). Bari, F. Cacucci, 72, 605 p.

291  MOMIGLIANO, F. *Lezioni di economia industriale e teoria dell'impresa* (Lessons of industrial economics and theory of the firm). Torino, G. Giappichelli, 72, v.

292  MOORE, B. J. *An introduction to modern economic theory.* New York, Free Press, 73, xxiii-551 p.

293  MORRICE, A. *The fundamentals of economics.* London, Heinemann, 72, xv-238 p.

294  NAPOLEONI, C.; ANTINOLFI, R. *Lezioni di macroeconomia* (Lessons of macroeconomics). Napoli, De Simone, 72, 270 p.

295  NORTON, H. S. "Reviewing economics textbooks: some comments on the process", *J. econ. Liter.* 11(3), sep 73 : 889-897.

296  PEROVIĆ, M. *Politička ekonomija* (Political economy). Beograd, Službeni list SFRJ, 72, 512 p.

297  PERRIN, M. S. *Comprendre les mécanismes actuels de l'économie.* Paris, Entreprise moderne d'éditions, 72, 279 p.

298  PETERSON, W. C. *Elements of economics.* New York, Norton, 73, xiv-542 p.

299  PHILLIPS, J.; PEARL, C. *Elements of economics.* New York, Macmillan, 73, ix-260 p.

300  POWICKE, J. C.; ILES, D. J.; DAVIES, B. *Applied economics.* London, Edward Arnold, 72, vi-239 p.

301  SALAMA, P.; VALIER, J. *Une introduction à l'économie politique.* Paris, F. Maspéro, 73, 209 p.

302  SCHMALENSEE, R. *Applied microeconomics; problems in estimation, forecasting and decision-making.* San Francisco, Holden-Day, 73, ix-118 p.

303  SEDDON, E.; APPLETON, J. D. S. *Applied economics.* London, Macdonald and Evans, 72, xii-348 p.

304  SEIDMAN, A. W. *An economics textbook for Africa.* 2nd ed. rev. enl. London, Methuen; New York, Harper and Row Publ. inc., 72, xvii-333 p.

305  SLESINGER, R. E.; OSMAN, J. W. *Basic economics; problems, principles, policy.* Berkeley, Calif., McCutchan Publishing Corp., 72, ix-714 p.

306  TSCHOPP, P. *Éléments d'économie politique* Genève, Georg, 72, 241 p.

307 UEBELE, H.; ZÖLLER, W. *Arbeitsbuch Kostenrechnung* (A cost accounting manual). Berlin-New York, Springer-Verlag, 72, viii-153 p.

308 WOLOZIN, H. *Introduction to economics: an interdisciplinary approach.* Boston, Holbrook Press, 73, xvi-262 p.

## C.2 FUNDAMENTAL PRINCIPLES OF ECONOMIC THEORY PRINCIPES FONDAMENTAUX DE LA THÉORIE ÉCONOMIQUE

### C.21 Theory of general economic behaviour Théorie du comportement économique en général

309 BECKMANN, M. J.; KAPUR, K. C. "Conjugate duality: some applications to economic theory", *J. econ. Theory* 5(2), oct 72 : 292-302.

310 BROCK, W. A. "On models of expectations that arise from maximizing behavior of economic agents over time", *J. econ. Theory* 5(3), dec 72 : 348-376.

311 JACOBSEN, S. E. "On Shephard's duality theorem", *J. econ. Theory* 4(3), jun 72 : 458-464.

312 KAMIEN, M. I.; SCHWARTZ, N. L. "Exclusion costs and the provision of public goods", *Publ. Choice* 12, apr 72 : 43-55.

313 MISZEWSKI, M. "Teoria motywacji Johna K. Galbraitha" (J. K. Galbraith's theory of motivation), *Zesz. nauk. wyzsz. Szkoły ekon. w Katowic.* 45 1972 : 183-208.

314 PARVIN, M. "Economic determinants of political unrest: an econometric approach", *J. Conflict Resol.* 17(2), jun 73 : 271-296.

### C.22 Decision and game theory Décision et théorie des jeux

[See also / Voir aussi: **G.3351**; 3617]

315 AGRAWAL, R. C.; HEADY, E. O. *Operations research methods for agricultural decisions.* Ames, Iowa State University Press, 72, x-303 p.

316 AZEVEDO, H. DE O. "Notas sobre o problema da decisão: um levantamento exploratório" (Notes on a decision problem: an exploratory survey), *R. brasil. Estud. polít.* 36, jul 73 : 7-36.

317 BOLDUR, G. *Fundamentarea complexă a procesului decizional economic* (Complex bases of the economic decision-making process). Bucureşti, Editura ştiinţifică, 73, 212 p.

318 CARLSON, C. E. "Om företagsekonomiska beslut" (Decision in business economics), *Ekon. Samfund. Ts.* 26(1), 1973 : 21-31.

319 DAVIS, O. A.; DeGROOT, M. H.; HINICH, M. J. "Social preference orderings and majority rule", *Econometrica* 40(1), jan 72 : 147-157.

320 DREZE, J. H. "Econometrics and decision theory", *Econometrica* 40(1), jun 72 : 1-17.

321 ELIASON, A. L. "A closed model approach to business gaming", *Simul. and Games* 4(1), mar 73 : 3-17.

322 FALCIGLIA, A. "L'approcio della teoria dei giochi allo studio dei problemi economici: note critiche" (Game theory approach to the study of economic problems: critical notes), *Ric. econ.* 26(1-2), jan-jun 72 : 114-163.

323 FANDEL, G. *Optimale Entscheidung bei mehrfacher Zielsetzung* (Optimal decision-making in the case of multiple objectives). Berlin-New York, Springer-Verlag, 72, 121 p.

324 GRUBBSTRÖM, R. W. *Economic decisions in space and time; theoretical and experimental inquiries into the cause of economic motion.* Gothenburg, University of Gothenburg, 73, 379 p.

325 HAEHLING VON LANZENAUER, C. *Operations Research und betriebliche Entscheidungsprobleme* (Operational research and decisional research in the firm). Frankfurt-am-Main, F. Knapp, 72, 188 p.

326 KALUZA, B. *Spieltheoretische Modelle und ihre Anwendungsmöglichkeiten im Versicherungswesen* (Game theory, models and possibilities of using them in an insurance system). Berlin, Duncker und Humblot, 72, 137 p.

327 KANTOROVIĆ, L. V.; GORSTKO, A. B. *Optimal'nye rešenija v ěkonomike* (Optimal decisions in economics). Moskva, Nauka, 72, 231 p.

328 KAU, P.; HILL, L. "A threshold model of purchasing decisions", *J. Mkting Res.* 9(3), aug 72 : 264-270.

329    LEE, S. M. *Goal programming for decision analysis.* Philadelphia, Auerbach Publishers, 72, xiv-387 p.

330    LEONARDZ, B. *To stop or not to stop. Some elementary optimal stopping problems with economic interpretations.* Stockholm, Almqvist und Wiksell, 73, 178 p.

331    MOSKOWITZ, H. *A dynamic programming approach for finding pure admissible decision functions in statistical decisions.* West Lafayette, Ind., Krannert Graduate School of Industrial Administration, 73, 27 p.

332    PLOTT, C. R. "Ethics, social choice theory and the theory of economic policy", *J. math. Sociol.* 2(2), jul 72 : 181-208.

333    RENAUD, J. P. "Situation de dépendance et modèles de prise de décisions" *Canad. R. Sociol. Anthropol.* 10(1), feb 73 : 44-61.

334    RIEPER, B. *Entscheidungsmodelle zur integrierten Absatz- und Produktionsprogrammplanung für ein Mehrprodukt-Unternehmen* (Decision models for a programed and integrated planning of sales and of production). Wiesbaden, Dr. Gabler, 73, 300 p.

335    RIVETT, P. *Principles of model building: the construction of models for decision analysis.* London-New York, Wiley, 72, 10-141 p.

336    ROLSHAUSEN, C. *Rationalität und Herrschaft; zum Verhältnis von Marktsoziologie und Entscheidungslogik* (Rationality and power: on the link between market sociology and decisional logic). Frankfurt, Europäische Verlagsanstalt, 72, 115-1 p.

337    ROSENTHAL, R. W. "Cooperative games in effectiveness form", *J. econ. Theory* 5(1), aug 72 : 88-101.

338    STÅHL, I. *Bargaining theory.* Stockholm, Ekonomiska forsknings-institutet vid Handels-högskolan i Stockholm, EFI, 72, 11-313 p.

339    THOMAS, H. *Decision theory and the manager.* London, Pitman, 72, x-137 p.

340    WILSON, R. "Social choice theory without the Pareto principle", *J. econ. Theory* 5(3), dec 72 : 478-486.

### C.23    Risk and uncertainty
### Risque et incertitude

[See also / Voir aussi: 3880]

341    BÁCKSAI, T.; HUSZTI, E. "A gazdasági kockázatról" (On economic risk) *Közgazd. Szle* 20(1), jan 73 : 32-47.

342    BORCH, K. "Uncertainty and indifference curves", *R. econ. Stud.* 40(1), jan 73 : 141.

343    BROCK, W. A.; MIRMAN, L. J. "Optimal economic growth and uncertainty: the discounted case", *J. econ. Theory* 4(3), jun 72 : 479-513.

344    CAFFE, F. "La strategia dell'allarmismo economico" (The strategy of economic alarmism), *G. Economisti* 31(9-10), sep-oct 72 : 692-699.

345    "Decision-making under uncertainty", *Amer. econ. R.* 63(2), mai 73 *Pap. and Proc.:* 129-144. With contributions by: A. J. DOUGLAS, S. A. ROSS, J. L. BICKSLER, A. BARNEA, J. BABAD.

346    KORTEWEG, P. "Uncertainty and the behaviour of wealth-owner and policymaker: the cases of the optimum portfolio-mix and the optimum policy-mix", *Economist (Haarlem)* 120(4), jul-aug 72 : 367-377.

347    MALINVAUD, E. "The allocation of individual risks in large markets", *J. econ. Theory* 4(2), apr 72 : 312-328.

348    POULIQUEN, L. Y. *L'appréciation du risque dans l'évaluation des projets.* Paris, Dunod, 72 xii-102 p. [Issued also in English under title: *Risk analysis in project appraisal.*]

349    SIEGEL, J. J. "Risk, interest, and forward exchange", *Quart. J. Econ.* 86(2), mai 72 : 303-309.

350    STARR, R. M. "Optimal production and allocation under uncertainty", *Quart. J. Econ.* 87(1), feb 73 : 81-95.

351    STIGUM, B. P. "Resource allocation under uncertainty", *Int. econ. R.* 13(3), oct 72 : 431-459.

352    TARASCIO, V. J.; MURPHY, J. L. "Uncertainty, learning, and dynamic utility theory", *Quart. R. Econ. Busin.* 12(3), 1972 : 19-33.

# D HISTORY OF ECONOMIC THOUGHT
## HISTOIRE DE LA PENSÉE ÉCONOMIQUE

### D.0 GENERAL STUDIES
### ÉTUDES GÉNÉRALES

[See also / Voir aussi:

353 CEDRAS, J. *Histoire de la pensée économique, des origines à la révolution marginaliste.* Paris, Dalloz, 73, 177 p.

354 FINKELSTEIN, J.; THIMM, A. L. *Economists and society; the development of economic thought from Aquinas to Keynes.* New York, Harper and Row, 73, xvi-366 p.

355 FUNDABURK, E. L. *Development of economic thought and analysis.* Metuchen, N. J., Scarecrow Press, 73, lvi-875 p.

356 FUNDABURK, E. L. *The history of economic thought and analysis: a selective international bibliography.* Metuchen, N. J., Scarecrow Press, 73, s.p.

357 "Radical economics and the history of economic thought", *Amer. econ. R.* 63(2), mai 73 *Pap. and Proc.*: 145-159. With contributions by D. R. FUSFELD and E. NELL.

358 RIJNVOS, C. J. *Waardering van het economisch denken* (Evaluation of economic thought). Leiden, Stenfert Kroese, 72, 136 p.

359 SABOLOVIĆ, D. *Historija političke ekonomije* (History of political economy). Zagreb, Sveučilište; "Informator", 72, xi-142-2 p.

360 SHACKLE, G. L. S. *Epistemics and economics: a critique of economic doctrines.* Cambridge, Eng., University Press, 72, 482 p.

361 ZURAWICKI, S. *Historia myśli ekonomicznej* (History of economic thought). Wrocław, Wysza Szkoła Ekonomiczna we Wrocławiu, 73, 187 p.

### D.2 MERCANTILISTS, PHYSIOCRATS
### LES MERCANTILISTES ET LES PHYSIOCRATES

362 ANSPACH, T. "The implications of the theory of moral sentiments for Adam Smith's economic thought", *Hist. polit. Econ.* 4(1), 1972 : 176-206.

363 CZARKOWSKI, J. "Poglądy monetarne Nikołaja Kopernika" (Nicolas Copernicus' views on money), *Ekonomista* 4, 1973 : 825-851.

364 GÔRSKI, J. "Teoria ekonomiczna Nikołaja Kopernika" (Nicolas Copernicus's economic theory), *Ekonomista* 4, 1973 : 803-823.

365 HOLLANDER, S. *The economics of Adam Smith.* London, Heinemann Educational; Toronto-Buffalo, University of Toronto Press, 73, x-351 p.

366 KAUSHIL, S. "The case of Adam Smith's value analysis", *Oxford econ. Pap.* 25(1), mar 73 : 60-71.

367 NORD, W. "Adam Smith and contemporary social exchange theory", *Amer. J. Econ. Sociol.* 32(4), oct 73 : 421-436.

368 PALMADA, R. *Mercantilismo, un sistema de interpretación* (Mercantilism: a system of interpretation). Mendoza, Universidad Nacional de Cuyo, Facultad de Ciencias Económicas, 72, 40-6-4-3 p.

369 ZAJDA, J. "Kopernikowska teoria pieniądza" (Copernican theory of money), *Ruch prawn. ekon. socjol.* 4, 1973 : 17-40.

### D.3 LIBERALISM (PIONEERS AND CLASSICS)
### LE LIBÉRALISME DES FONDATEURS ET DES CLASSIQUES

370 GROENEWEGEN, P. D. "Three notes on Ricardo's theory of value and distribution", *Austral. econ. Pap.* 11(18), jun 72 : 53-64.

371     KITTRELL, E. R. "Wakefield's scheme of systematic colonization and classical economics", *Amer. J. Econ. Sociol.* 32(1), jan 73 : 87-111.

372     MYERS, M. L. "Philosophical anticipations of laissez-faire", *Hist. polit. Econ.* 4(1) 1972 : 163-175.

373     SOWELL, T. *Say's law: an historical analysis.* Princeton, N. J., Princeton University Press, 72, 247 p. CR: H. W. SPIEGEL, *J. econ. Liter.* 11(2), jun 73 : 537-538.

374     SOWELL, T. "Sismondi: a neglected pioneer", *Hist. polit. Econ.* 4(1), 1972 : 62-88.


**D.4     SOCIALISM**
         **SOCIALISME**

**D.41     Non-Marxian socialism**
         Socialisme non-marxiste

375     ENGELHARDT, W. W. *Robert Owen und die sozialen Reformbestrebungen seit Beginn der Industrialisierung* (Robert Owen and social reform aspirations since the beginning of industrialization). Bonn, Domus-Verlag, 72, 44 p.

376     GRUNER, S. M. *Economic materialism and social moralism. A study in the history of ideas in France from the latter part of the 18th century to the middle of the 19th century.* The Hague, Mouton, 73, 213 p.

377     NOVE, A.; NUTI, D. M. (eds.). *Socialist economics: selected readings.* Harmondsworth, Penguin, 72, 526 p.


**D.42     Marxism**
         Marxisme

[See also / Voir aussi: **N.120;** 1838, 2167, 3786, 4136]

378     BAUER, R. *et al. Ekonomia polityczna socjalizmu* (Political economy and socialism). Warszawa, Państwowe Wydawnictwo Naukowe, 72, 403-1 p.

379     BOTTA, F. "Marx, Keynes e i limiti della economia mista" (Marx, Keynes and the limits of mixed economy), *Polit. ed Econ.* 4(1-2), jan-apr 73 : 124-135.

380     BRESS, L. *Kommunismus bei Karl Marx; von der spekulativen zur ökonomischen Konzeption* (Communism in Karl Marx: the passage from a speculative conception to an economic conception). Stuttgart, G. Fischer, 72, viii-245 p.

381     FAZIK, A. "Marxovo pojetí odcizené práce a cesty humanizace práce v podmínkách socialistické společnosti" (Marx's conception of alienated labour and ways of humanization of labour in a socialist society), *Sociol Čas.* 9(2), 1973 : 161-171.

382     GOUX, J. J. *Economie et symbolique: Freud, Marx.* Paris, Éditions du Seuil, 73, 278 p.

383     GREM, J. *Karl Marx, capitalist.* Oak Park, Ill., Enterprise Publications, 72, 126 p.

384     HARRIS, D. J. "On Marx's scheme of reproduction and accumulation", *J. polit. Econ.* 80(3), mai-jun 72 : 505-522.

385     KOSTA, J.; MEYER, J.; WEBER, S. *Warenproduktion im Sozialismus; Überlegungen zur Theorie von Marx und zur Praxis in Osteuropa* (Merchandise production in socialism; reflections on Marx's theory and practice in Eastern Europe). Frankfurt-am-Main, Fischer Taschenbuch Verlag, 73, 237 p.

386     KÜHNE, K. *Ökonomie und Marxismus* (Economics and marxism). Neuwied, Luchterhand, 72. [Vol. I. *Zur Renaissance des Marxschen Systems.*]

387     LEMMNITZ, A. *Gegenstand und Methode der marxistisch-leninistischen politischen Ökonomie* (Object and method of Marxist-Leninist political economy). Berlin, Dietz, 72, 79 p.

388     MAITAL, S. "Is Marxian growth crisis-ridden ?", *Hist. polit. Econ.* 4(1), 1972 : 113-126.

389     MORISHIMA, M. *Marx's economics; a dual theory of value and growth.* Cambridge, Eng., University Press, 73, viii-198 p.

390     ROTH, O.; JAKS, J. *Náčrt teórie hospodárskej politiky* (Communist theory of economic policy). Bratislava, Pravda, Žilina, Pravda, 72, 240-3 p.

391     ŠIK, O. *Der dritte Weg; die marxistisch-leninistische Theorie und die moderne Industriegesellschaft* (The third way; Marxist-Leninist theory and modern industrial society). Hamburg, Hoffmann und Campe, 72, 450 p.

392     SLOAN, P. *Marx and the orthodox economists.* Oxford, Blackwell, 73, viii-181 p.

393 TULLIO-ALTAN, C. "La teoria del valore-lavori di K. Marx nel quadro dei problemi attuali dell'antropologia economica" (K. Marx's labour theory of value in the framework of the present problems of economic anthropology), *Crit. sociol. (Roma)* 23, 1972 : 5-23; 24, 1972-73 : 10-58.

**D.5 OTHER DOCTRINES**
**AUTRES DOCTRINES**

**D.51 Christian doctrine**
**Christianisme**

394 ALBERICO, A. "La doctrina económica de la Iglesia" (The economic doctrine of the Church), *Lecciones y Ensayos* 42, 1970 : 125-131.

**D.52 Co-operative doctrine**
**Coopératisme**

395 KLEER, J. "Z zagadnień myśli spółdzielczej w Polsce Ludowej, 1944-1949" (Co-operative thought in People's Poland 1944-1949), *Spóld. Kwartal. Nauk.* 4, 1973 : 23-45.

**D.56 Other diverse or individual trends**
**Autres tendances diverses ou individuelles**

[See also / Voir aussi:

396 MILLER, W. L. "Herbert Spencer's theory of welfare and public policy", *Hist. polit. Econ.* 4(1), 1972 : 207-231.

**D.6 HISTORICISM AND INSTITUTIONALISM**
**HISTORICISME ET INSTITUTIONALISME**

397 TILMAN, R. "Thorstein Veblen: incrementalist and utopian", *Amer. J. Econ. Sociol.* 32(2), apr 73 : 155-169.

**D.7 MARGINALISM AND NEO-LIBERALISM**
**MARGINALISME ET NÉO-LIBÉRALISME**

398 FINIS, G. DE. "L'equazione walrasiana: note di teoria monetaria" (The Walrasian equation: notes on monetary theory), *Risparmio* 21(5), mai 73 : 807-823.

399 MATSUURA, T. "L'importanza delle ricerche paretiane nel Giappone odierno" (The importance of research on Pareto in Japan today), *G. Economisti* 31(7-8), jul-aug 72 : 485-502.

400 MOORE, J. C. *Pareto optimal allocations as competitive equilibria.* West Lafayette, Ind., Krannert Graduate School of Industrial Administration, Purdue University, 73, 70-9 p.

401 PEACOCK, A. T.; ROWLEY, C. K. "Pareto optimality and the political economy of liberalism", *J. polit. Econ.* 80(3), mai-jun 72 : 476-490.

402 TOMMISSEN, P. "Pareto's bijdrage tot de economische wetenschap" (Pareto's contribution to economics), *Econ. soc. Tijds.* 26(5), oct 72 : 383-402.

**D.8 RECENT TRENDS**
**TENDANCES RÉCENTES**

**D.80 General studies**
**Études générales**

403 GRUCHY, A. G. *Contemporary economic thought: the contribution of neo-institutional economics.* London, Macmillan, 73, 4-ix-360 p.

404    Hromušin, G. B. *Buržuaznye teorii političeskoj ekonomii* (Bourgeois theories of political economy). Moskva, Politizdat, 72, 296 p.

405    Bibl. xxi-477. Lindbeck, A. *The political economy of the New Left: an outsider's view.* CR: J. Tobin, *J. econ. Liter.* 10(4), dec 72 : 1216-1218.

406    Rau, E. *Der Verfall des Fortschrittsgedankens in der ökonomischen Theorie zum Irrationalismus in der bürgerlichen Ökonomie* (The decline of the idea of progress in economic theory, on irrationalism in bourgeois economy). Köln, Pahl-Rugenstein, 72, 280 p.

### D.81    Local studies
### Études localisées

[See also / Voir aussi: 5295]

407    Bibl. xxi-472. Breit, W.; Ransom, R. L. *The academic scribblers. American economists in collision.* CR: W. D. Grampp, *Amer. polit. Sci. R.* 67(3), sep 73 : 984-985.

408    Hicks, J. R. *Capital and time; a neo-Austrian theory.* Oxford, Clarendon Press, 73, xi-213 p.

409    Inglot, S. *et al. Zarys polskiej myśli ekonomicznorolniczej do drugiej wojny światowej* (Outline of Polish economic-agricultural thought after World War II). Wrocław, Zakład Narodowy im. Ossolińskich, 73, 449 p.

410    Schwertfeger, R. *Politische Ökonomie in Polen; zur Entwicklung des nationalökonomischen Denkens in Polen während der sechziger Jahre* (Political economy in Poland; on the development of national economic thought in Poland during the 1960's). Bern, P. Haupt, 73, 224 p.

411    Stojanović, I. "Marginalizam u savremenoj francuskoj socialistickoj ekonomskoj misli" (Marginalism in the contemporary socialist economic thought in France), *Ekon. Misao* 6(2), jun 73 : 49-64.

### D.82    Individual contributions
### Contributions individuelles

[See also / Voir aussi: 2153, 3031, 3784, 3853, 3873, 4005-4008, 4016, 4020, 4033, 4136, 4325, 4608, 4619, 5161, 5217, 5219, 5316, 6431, 6433, 6443, 6563]

412    Barcelo, A. "El desplante teórico de Piero Sraffa" (Piero Sraffa's theoretical provocation), *A. Econ. (Madrid)* 15, jul-sep 72 : 29-52.

413    Bentin, L. A. *Johannes Popitz und Carl Schmitt; zur wirtschaftlichen Theorie des totalen Staates in Deutschland* (Johannes Popitz and Carl Schmitt: on the economic theory of the totalitarian State in Germany) München, Beck, 72, ix-186 p.

414    Burger, D. H. "In memoriam: C. E. Ayres", *Amer. J. Econ. Sociol.* 32(3), jul 73 : 335-336.

415    *Collected writings of John Maynard Keynes (The).* IX. *Essays in persuasion* X. *Essays in biography.* 2nd and 3rd ed. New York, St Martin's Press, 72, xix-451 p., xix-460 p. CR: R. Lekachman, *J. econ. Liter.* 11(3), sep 73 : 902-904.

416    Cumes, J. W. C. *The indigent rich; a theory of general equilibrium in a Keynesian system.* Potts Point, Pergamon Press Australia, 71, 218 p.

417    Deans, R. H.; Deans, J. S. "John Rae and the problems of economic development", *R. soc. Econ.* 30(1), mar 72 : 97-111.

418    Hess, E. R. *Rodrigo Facio; el economista* (Rodrigo Facio: economist). Costa Rica, Universidad, San Pedro, 72, 223 p.

419    Heyel, C. *John Diebold on management.* Englewood Cliffs, N. J., Prentice-Hall, 72, ix-282 p.

420    Koshal, R. K.; Koshal, M. "Gandhian economic philosophy", *Amer. J. Econ. Sociol.* 32(2), apr 73 : 191-209.

421    Landau, Z. "Feliks Młynarski (1884-1972)". Zarys zycia i działalnosci na polu finansów (Felix Młynarski, 1884-1972. Outline of life and activities in the field of finance), *Finanse* 11, 1973 : 58-69.

422    Marjanović, G. "Ekonomist dr Mihailo Vujić" (Dr. Mihailo Vujić, economist), *Ekon. Misao* 6(1), mar 73 : 71-93. [1853-1913.]

423 SÁNCHEZ TARNIELLA, A. *Myrdal y la economía del siglo XX. Hacia un nuevo concepto del problema económico* (Myrdal and XXth century economics. Towards a new concept of the economic problem). Madrid, Afrodisio Aguado, 72, 125 p.

424 SHACKLE, G. L. S. "Keynes and today's establishment in economic theory: a view", *J. econ. Liter.* 11(2), jun 73 : 516-519.

425 SMITHIES, A. "Keynes revisited", *Quart. J. Econ.* 86(3), aug 72 : 463-473.

426 TOBIN, J. "Friedman's theoretical framework", *J. polit. Econ.* 80(5), sep-oct 72 : 852-863.

427 VICTOR, R. F. *John Maynard Keynes, father of modern economics.* Charlotteville, N. Y., SamHar Press, 72, 31 p.

428 VISSER, H. "Keynes en de neoklassieken: een herinterpretatie" (Keynes and the neo-classics), *Economist (Haarlem)* 120(1), jan-feb 72 : 27-51.

429 WEINTRAUB, S. *et al. Keynes and the Monetarists, and other essays.* New Brunswick, N. J., Rutgers University Press, 73, xi-227 p.

430 WHITAKER, J. K. "Alfred Marshall: the years 1877 to 1885", *Hist. polit. Econ.* 4(1), 1972 : 1-61.

431 WONG, S. "The 'F-Twits' and the methodology of Paul Samuelson", *Amer. econ. R.* jun 73 : 312-325.

# E ECONOMIC HISTORY
# HISTOIRE ÉCONOMIQUE

## E.0 GENERAL STUDIES
## ÉTUDES GÉNÉRALES

[See also / Voir aussi: 4002]

432  CONSEJO LATINO AMERICANO DE CIENCIAS SOCIALES. Comisíon de Historia Económico. *La historia económica en América Latina* (Economic history in Latin America). México, [XXXIX Congreso Internacional de Americanistas, Lima, Perú, agosto, 1970], 2 vols.

433  CRISTÓBAL, R. *Nombres de la historia económica* (Names from economic history). Madrid, Editiones Gráficas Espejo, 72, 319 p.

434  DIAMOND, D. E.; GUILFOIL, J. D. *United States economic history*. Morristown, N. J., General Learning Press, 73, xviii-712 p.

435  FOGEL, R. W. "Current directions in economic history", *J. econ. Hist.* 32(1), mar 72 : 1-2.

436  FUSCO, A. M. *Sulla storiografia dell'economica* (On economic historiography). Napoli, Giannini, 72, xi-271 p.

437  INSTITUT DE SOCIOLOGIE SOLVAY. Centre d'histoire économique et sociale. *Contributions à l'histoire économique et sociale*. VI. 1970-71. Bruxelles, Éditions de l'Université de Bruxelles, 72, 239 p.

438  LUNDEN, K. *Økonomi og samfund. Synspunkt på økonomisk historie* (Economy and society. Point of view on economic history). Oslo, Universitetsforlaget, 72, 105 p.

439  MAURO, F. *Des produits et des hommes; essais historiques latino-américains XVIe-XXe siècles*. Paris, Mouton, 72, viii-174 p.

440  McCLELLAND, P. D. "Model-building in the New Economic History", *Amer. behav. Scientist* 16(5), mai 73 : 631-651.

441  MURPHY, E. *A history of the British economy, 1086-1970*. London, Longman, 73, 819-xiii p.

442  ROSA, L. DE; ROMEO, R.; ZANGHERI, R. *La storiografia economica italiana degli ultimi vent'anni in alcuni recenti contributi* (Italian economic historiography during the last twenty years in some recent contributions). Milano, Celuc, 72, 124 p.

443  TEMIN, P. (ed.). *New economic history: selected readings*. Harmondsworth, Penguin, 73, 445 p.

444  TRASSELLI, C. *Appunti per una introduzione alla storia economica* (Notes for an introduction to economic history). Messina, Peloritana, 73, 91 p.

445  VAN DER WEE, H. *Historische aspecten van de economische groei* (Historical aspects of economic growth). Antwerpen-Utrecht, Uitgeverij De Nederlandsche Boekhandel, 72, 245 p.

446  VOLTES BOU, P. *Historia de la economía española hasta 1800* (History of the Spanish economy till 1800). Madrid, Editora Nacional, 72, 379 p.

## E.1 PREHISTORY. ANTIQUITY
## PRÉHISTOIRE. ANTIQUITÉ

447  AUSTIN, M.; VIDAL-NAQUET, P *Economies et sociétés en Grèce ancienne (périodes archaïque et classique)*. Paris, A. Colin, 72, 416 p.

448  BONNEAU, D. *Le fisc et le Nil; incidences des irrégularités de la crue du Nil sur la fiscalité foncière dans l'Egypte grecque et romaine*. Paris, Cujas, 71, 286 p.

449  KHER, N. N. *Agrarian and fiscal economy in the Mauryan and post Mauryan age (cir. 324 B.C.-320 A.D.)*. Delhi, Motilal Banarsidass, 73, xxxiii-468 p. [India].

## E.2 MIDDLE AGES
## MOYEN ÂGE

450 BOLENS, L. "Engrais et protection de la fertilité dans l'agronomie hispano-arabe. XIe-XIIe siècles", *Et. rur.* 46, apr-jun 72 : 34-60.

451 COSTE, P. "La vie pastorale en Provence au milieu du XIVe siècle", *Et. rur.* 46, apr-jun 72 : 61-75.

452 DUBY, G. *Guerriers et paysans, VII-XIIe siècle; premier essor de l'économie européenne.* Paris, Gallimard, 73, 308 p.

453 GENNARO, G. DE. *Saggi di storia economica (Sec. X-XVII)* (Essays on economic history : from the 10th century to the 17th century). Bari, F. Cacucci, 72, 209 p. [Italy.]

454 HODGETT, G. A. J. *A social and economic history of medieval Europe.* London Methuen, 72, 10-246 p.

455 LLOYD, T. H. *The movement of wool prices in medieval England.* Cambridge, Eng., Published for the Economic history review at the University Press, 73, vi-75 p.

456 MAZZAOUI, M. F. "The cotton industry of Northern Italy in the late Middle Ages: 1150-1450", *J. econ. Hist.* 32(1), mar 72 : 262-286.

457 POSTAN, M. M. *Essays on medieval agriculture and general problems of the medieval economy.* Cambridge, Eng., University Press, 73, 302 p.

458 POSTAN, M. M. *Medieval trade and finance.* Cambridge, Eng., University Press, 73, vi-382 p.

459 POSTAN, M. M. *The medieval economy and society; an economic history of Britain, 1100-1500.* Berkeley, University of California Press; London, Weidenfeld and Nicolson, 73, viii-261 p.

460 TANGHERONI, M. *Politica, commercio, agricoltura a Pisa nel Trecento* (Politics, trade agriculture in Pisa in the 14th century). Pisa, Pacini, 73, 242 p.

461 ZORN, W. *Einführung in die Wirtschafts- und Sozialgeschichte des Mittelalters und der Neuzeit: Probleme und Methoden* (Introduction to the economic and social history of the Middle Ages and recent times: problems and methods). München, C. H. Beck, 72, 110 p.

## E.3 XVIth, XVIIth, XVIIIth CENTURIES
## XVIe, XVIIe et XVIIIe SIÈCLES

462 ANNANEPESOV, M. *Hozjajstvo turkmen v XVIII-XIXvv.* (The Turkmen economy in the XVIIIth-XIXth centuries). Ašhabad, Ilym, 72, 283 p.

463 BOSSIS, P. "Le milieu paysan aux confins de l'Anjou, du Poitou et de la Bretagne, 1771-1789", *Et. rur.* 47, jul-sep 72 : 122-147.

464 CHAMBERS, J. D. *Population, economy, and society in pre-industrial England.* Ed. by W. A. ARMSTRONG, London-New York, Oxford University, 72, xiv-162 p.

465 CHAUSSINAND-NOGARET, G. *Gens de finance au XVIIIe siècle.* Paris, Bordas, 72, 159 p.

466 Bibl. XXI-576. CLARKSON, L. A. *The pre-industrial economy in England, 1500-1750.* CR: G. R. ELTON, *J. econ. Liter.* 11(3), sep 73 : 906-907.

467 DAVICO, R. "Baux, exploitations, techniques agricoles en Piémont dans la deuxième moitié du XVIIIe siècle", *Et. rur.* 46, apr-jun 72 : 76-101.

468 DENT, J. *Crisis in finance: crown, financiers and society in seventeeth century France.* Newton Abbot, David and Charles, 73, 288 p.

469 HILDEBRANDT, R. "Augsburger und Nürnberger Kupferhandel 1500-1619" (Copper trade in Augsburg and Nürnberg 1500-1619), *Z. Wirtsch.-u. soz. Wiss.* 92(1), 1972 : 1-31.

470 LÓPEZ SEGRERA, F. *Cuba; capitalismo dependiente y subdesarrollo (1510-1959)* (Cuba: dependent capitalism and underdevelopment, 1510-1959). La Habana, Casa de las Américas, 72, 400 p.

471 SHEPHERD, J. F.; WALTON, G. M. *Shipping, maritime trade, and the economic development of North America.* London-New York, Cambridge University Press, 72, ix-255 p. CR: P. TEMIN, *J. econ. Liter.* 11(3), sep 73 : 908-909.

472 SHEPHERD, J. F.; WALTON, G. M. "Trade, distribution, and economic growth in colonial America", *J. econ. Hist.* 32(1), mar 72 : 128-145.

473 *Sur la population française au XVIIIe et au XIXe siècles.* Paris, Société de démographie historique, 73, 507 p.

E.4      **DEVELOPMENT OF INDUSTRIALIZATION AND CAPITALISM**
         **(SINCE 1750)**
         **DÉVELOPPEMENT DE L'INDUSTRIALISATION ET DU**
         **CAPITALISME (DEPUIS 1750)**

E.41     Industrial revolution
         Révolution industrielle

474      ARFÉ, G. *et al. L'Età della rivoluzione industriale* (The period of the industrial revolution).
         Torino, Unione tipografico-editrice torinese, 72, 919 p.

475      HENNING, F. W. *Die Industrialisierung in Deutschland 1800 bis 1914* (Industrialization
         in Germany, 1800-1914). Paderborn, Schöningh, 73, 304 p.

476      HOHENBERG, P. "Change in rural France in the period of industrialization 1830-1914",
         *J. econ. Hist.* 32(1), mar 72 : 219-240.

477      LANE, P. *The Industrial Revolution, 1750-1830.* London, Batsford, 72, 96 p.

478      LÉON, P.; CROUZET, F.; GASCON, R. (eds.). *L'industrialisation en Europe au XIXe siècle;
         cartographie et typologie, Lyon, 7-10 octobre 1970.* Paris, Éditions du Centre national
         de la recherche scientifique, 72, 619 p.

479      LIEBERMAN, S. (ed.). *Europe and the industrial revolution.* Cambridge, Mass., Schenkman
         Pub. Co.; Morristown, N. J., General Learning Press, 72, xi-475 p.

480      MENDELS, F. F. "Proto-industrialization: the first phase of the industrialization process",
         *J. econ. Hist.* 32(1), mar 72 : 241-261.

481      MORI, G. *La rivoluzione industriale. Economia e società in Gran Bretagna nella seconda
         metà del secolo XVIII* (The industrial revolution. Economy and society in Great
         Britain in the second half of the 18th century). Milano, Mursia, 72, 238 p.

482      SHEEHAN, J. J. (ed.). *Industrialization and industrial labor in nineteenth-century Europe.*
         New York, Wiley, 73, 173 p.

483      STAMP, A. H. *The agricultural and industrial revolutions.* London-New York, Regency
         Press, 72, 159-8 p.

484      WALTON, J. R. *A study in the diffusion of agricultural machinery in the nineteenth century.*
         Oxford, University of Oxford, School of Geography, 73, 45 p. [UK].


E.42     History of capitalism
         Histoire du capitalisme

         [See also / Voir aussi: N.110]

485      Bibl. XXI-606. PAPANDREOU, A. G. *Paternalistic capitalism.* CR: H. K. BETZ, *J. econ.
         Liter.* 11(2), jun 73 : 556-558.

486      TORTELLA CASARES, G. *Los orígenes del capitalismo en España; banca, industria y ferro-
         carriles en el siglo XIX* (Origins of Spanish capitalism; bank; industry and railroads
         in the 19th century). Madrid, Tecnos, 73, xxii-407 p.


E.43     National and continental economies
         Économies nationales et continentales

         [See also / Voir aussi: 1940, 4352]

487      ASHER, E. "Industrial efficiency and biased technical change in American and British
         manufacturing: the case of textiles in the nineteenth century", *J. econ. Hist.* 32(2),
         jun 72 : 431-442.

488      BARTH, E. *Entwicklungslinien der deutschen Maschinenbauindustrie von 1870 bis 1914*
         (Development lines of German machine-building industry 1870-1914). Berlin,
         Akademie-Verlag, 73, xvi-212 p. [Based on *Die deutsche Maschinenbauindustrie in der
         industriellen Revolution,* by A. SCHRÖTER.]

489      BREACH, R. W.; HARTWELL, R. M. (eds.). *British economy and society, 1870-1970;
         documents, descriptions, statistics.* London, Oxford University Press, 72, xviii-406 p.

490      FRIEDLANDER, D. "Demographic patterns and socioeconomic characteristics of the coal-
         mining population in England and Wales in the nineteenth century", *Econ. Develop.
         cult. Change* 22(1), oct 73 : 39-51.

491 GIRAULT, R. *Emprunts russes et investissements français en Russie, 1887-1914. Recherches sur l'investissement international.* Paris, A. Colin, 73, 624 p.

492 GUILLAUME, P. *La population de Bordeaux au XIXe siècle; essai d'histoire sociale.* Paris, A. Colin, 72, 304 p.

493 HYDE, F. E. *Far Eastern trade, 1860-1914.* London, A. and C. Black, 73, xii-229 p.

494 Bibl. XXI-627. ISSAWI, C. (ed.). *The economic history of Iran: 1800-1914.* CR: S. ZABIH, *Amer. polit. Sci. R.* 66(4), dec 72 : 1383-1384.

495 JOHNSON, E. A. J. *The foundations of American economic freedom; government and enterprise in the age of Washington.* Minneapolis, University of Minnesota Press, 73, ix-335 p.

496 MAYHEW, A. "A reappraisal of the causes of farm protest in the United States, 1870-1900", *J. econ. Hist.* 32(2), jun 72 : 464-475.

497 Bibl. XXI-636. McCLOSKEY, D. N. (ed.). *Essays on a mature economy: Britain after 1840.* CR: P. DEANE, *J. econ. Liter.* 11(3), sep 73 : 907-908.

498 PORTER, G. *The rise of big business, 1860-1910.* New York, Crowell, 73, vi-119 p. [USA].

499 ROVERI, A. *Dal sindacalismo rivoluzionario al fascismo. Capitalismo agrario e socialismo nel Ferrarese (1870-1920)* (From revolutionary trade unionism to fascism. Agrarian capitalism and socialism in Ferrara Province, 1870-1920). Firenze, La nuova Italia, 72, xiii-397 p.

500 SANDERSON, M. *The universities and British industry, 1850-1970.* London, Routledge and Kegan Paul, 72, x-436 p.

501 TAYLOR, A. J. *Laissez-faire and state intervention in nineteenth-century Britain; prepared for the Economic History Society.* London, Macmillan, 72, 80 p.

502 USELDING, P. J. "Factor substitution and labor productivity growth in American manufacturing, 1839-1899", *J. econ. Hist.* 32(3), sep 72 : 670-681.

## E.44 History of colonization
### Histoire de la colonisation

[See also / Voir aussi:

503 GENOVESE, E. D. *The slave economies.* New York, Wiley, 73. [Contents: Vol. 1. *Historical and theoretical perspectives.* Vol. 2. *Slavery in the international economy.*]

504 MARTIN, P. *The external trade of the Loango Coast, 1576-1870; the effects of changing commercial relations on the Vili Kingdom of Loango.* Oxford, Clarendon Press, 72, ix-193 p.

505 RENAULT, F. *L'abolition de l'esclavage au Sénégal, l'attitude de l'administration française, 1848-1905.* Paris, P. Geuthner, 72, 109 p.

## E.5 RECENT ECONOMIC HISTORY (FROM 1914 TO 1945)
### HISTOIRE ÉCONOMIQUE RÉCENTE (DE 1914 À 1945)

[See also / Voir aussi:

506 AUERBACH, R. D. "An estimation procedure for the federal cash deficit applied to the United States interwar period, 1920-1941", *West. econ. J.* 10(4), dec 72 : 474-476.

507 BENAVIDES, L. *Política económica en la II República española* (Economic policy in the Second Spanish Republic). Madrid, Guadiana de Publicaciones, 72, 279 p.

508 DOKUČAEV, G. A. *Rabočij klass Sibiri i Dal'nego Vostoka poslevoennye gody 1946-1950* (Siberia and the Far East working class during the postwar years, 1946-1950). Novosibirsk, Nauka, 72, 212 p.

509 GRAMM, W. P. "The real-balance effect in the great depression", *J. econ. Hist.* 32(2), jun 72 : 499-519.

510 HIRATA, Y. *Prosperity, Great Depression and New Deal; a bibliography of American economy during the interwar period.* Tokyo, Yushodo Booksellers, 72, xv-262 p.

511 KENNEDY, D. M. (ed.). *The American people in the depression.* West Haven, Conn., Pendulum Press, 73, 176 p.

512 KINDLEBERGER, C. P. *The world in depression, 1929-1939.* London, Allen Lane, 73, 336 p.

513    KIRKWOOD, J. B. "The great depression: a structural analysis", *J. Money Cred. Bank.*
       4(4), nov 72 : 811-837.

514    LUCAS, R. E.; RAPPING, L. A. "Unemployment in the great depression: is there a full
       explanation ?", *J. polit. Econ.* 80(1), jan-feb 72 : 186-191.

515    SCHNEIDER, H. *Das sowjetische Aussenhandelsmonopol 1920-1925* (The Soviet foreign
       trade monopoly between 1920 and 1925). Köln, Verlag Wissenschaft und Politik, 73,
       214 p.

516    SOBEL, R. *The age of giant corporations; a microeconomic history of American business,*
       *1914-1970.* Westport, Conn., Greenwood Press, 72, xiii-257 p.

517    SWATEK, D. *Unternehmenskonzentration als Ergebnis und Mittel nationalsozialistischer*
       *Wirtschaftspolitik* (Enterprise concentration, results and means of National-Socialist
       economic policy). Berlin, Duncker und Humblot, 72, 172 p.

518    WATEN, J. L. *The depression years, 1929-1939.* Melbourne, Cheshire, 72, 60 p. [Aus-
       tralia.]

519    WOŹNA, B. "Specyfika wymiany towarowej miedzy Polską a Związkiem Radzieckim w
       latach 1921-1939" (Characteristic features of goods exchange between Poland and the
       Soviet Union in the years 1921-1939), *Zesz. nauk. wyzsz. Szkol. ekon. Katowic.* 45,
       1972 : 49-78.

# F ECONOMIC ACTIVITY
# ACTIVITÉ ÉCONOMIQUE

### F.1 PRESENT ECONOMIC CONDITIONS (SINCE 1945) BY AREAS
### CONDITIONS ÉCONOMIQUES ACTUELLES (DEPUIS 1945) PAR RÉGIONS

[See also / Voir aussi:

520   Pócs, E. "A fejlett tökesországok gazdasági helyzete" (Economic situation of developed capitalist countries in 1972 : forecast for 1973), *Közgazd. Szle* 20(5), mai 73 : 599-612.
521   Vanoli, A. *L'économie mondiale*. Paris, Hachette, 73, 510 p.

### F.1(1) Africa
### Afrique

[See also / Voir aussi:

522   Brown, T. M. "Macroeconomic data of Ghana", *Econ. B. Ghana* 2(1), 1972 : 25-53; 2(2), 1972 : 61-79.
523   Duggan, W. R. *A socioeconomic profile of South Africa*. New York, Praeger 73, xviii-181 p.
524   *Économie des pays d'Afrique noire (L')*. Cameroun, RCA, Congo, Cote d'Ivoire, Dahomey, Gabon, Haute-Volta, Mali, Mauritanie, Niger, Sénégal, Tchad, Togo. Paris, Ediafric-Service, 73, 330 p. [Numéro spécial du *Bulletin de l'Afrique noire*.]
525   "Indicateurs économiques dahomiens", *Notes Inform. Statist. Banque centr. Etats Afr. Ouest* 207, jun 73 : 32 p.
526   "Indicateurs économiques nigériens", *Notes Inform. Statist. Banque centr. Afr. Ouest* 207, jun 73 : 24 p.
527   "Indicateurs économiques sénégalais", *Notes Inform. Statist. Banque centr. Afr. Ouest* 209, aug-sep 73 : 32 p.
528   "Indicateurs togolais", *Notes Inform. Statist. Banque centr. Afr. Ouest* 208, jul 73 : 32 p.
529   O'Loughlin, C.; Ewusi, K. "Social matrices and indicators in the traditional African economy", *R. Income Wealth* 18(4), dec 72 : 377-391.
530   Rubio Garcia, L. "Características económicas y sociales del 'poder' del mundo africano" (Economic and social characteristics of the African world's "power"), *Africa (Madrid)* 24(371), nov 72 : 6-10; 24(372), dec 72 : 6-11.
531   Schaetzen, Y. de. "L'économie gabonaise", *R. franç. Et. polit. afr.* 8 (90), jun 73 : 67-94.
532   Schaetzen, Y. de. "Notes sur l'économie du Zaire", *R. franç. Ét. polit. afr.* 91, jul 73 : 88-109.
533   "Senegal : de grandes transformations", *Europe-France O.-Mer* 50(518), mar 73 : 6-56.
534   Stallings, B. *Economic dependency in Africa and Latin America*. Beverly, Hills, Sage Publications, 72, 60 p.

### F.1(2) America
### Amérique

*Latin America / Amérique Latine*

535   Azcurra, F. H. "La situación económica argentina" (Economic situation in Argentina), *Crist. y Soc.* 11(34-35), 1973 : 59-72.

536    BLEDEL, R. *La economía argentina (1952-1972); aplicación constante de la política de "libre empresa", la confesión de Prebisch* (The Argentine economy, 1952-1972 : a constant application of "free enterprise" policy, the Prebisch's credo). Buenos Aires, Juarez Editor, 72, 123 p.

537    "Brésil : situation économique et financière", *Bol. econ. financ.* (3), 1972 : 83 p.

538    "Economia brasileira em 1972(A) (The Brazilian economy in 1972), *Conjunt econ.* 27(2), feb 73 : 6-120.

539    "Économie de la République de Panama (L')", *B. franç. ital. Amér. Sud. Ét. écon.* (4), jul-sep 73 : 33 p.

540    FARLEY, R. *The economics of Latin America; development problems in perspective.* New York, Harper and Row, 73, x-400 p.

541    FURTADO, C. *Análise de "modelo" brasileiro* (An analysis of the Brazilian model). Rio de Janeiro, Civilização Brasileira, 72, 122 p.

542    JAGUARIBE, H. *Crisis y alternativas de América Latina: reforma o revolución* (Crisis and alternatives in Latin America: reform or revolution). Buenos Aires, Editorial Paidós, 72, 211 p.

543    LENOIL, L. "La situación económica del país (The economic situation of the country), *Estudios (Montevideo)* 66, jan-mar 73 : 33-43. [Uruguay.]

544    MARTÍNEZ ALIER, J. *Cuba: economía y sociedad* (Cuba: economy and society). Paris, Ruedo Ibérico, 72, 254 p.

545    ODELL, P. R.; PRESTON, D. A. *Economies and societies in Latin America: a geographical interpretation.* London-New York, Wiley, 73, ix-265-8 p.

546    "Panorama de la economía venezolana en el segundo semestre del año 1971" (Panorama of the Venezuelan economy during the second semester of the year 1971), *R. Econ. latinoamer.* 9(33), 1972 : 7-43.

547    "Problèmes et évolution de l'économie des pays sud-américains en 1971 et au cours des premiers mois de 1972", *Banque franç. ital. Amér. Sud* nov-dec 72 : 3-168.

548    QUESADA, C. *Puerto Rico: la proletarización de una economía* (Puerto Rico: the proletarianization of an economy). Algorta, Zero; Madrid, ZYX, 72, 38 p.

549    RAMIL CEPEDA, C. *Crisis de una burguesía dependiente; balance económico de la "Revolución Argentina" 1966-1971* (Crisis of the dependent bourgeoisie; economic results of the "Argentine Revolution" 1966-1971). Buenos Aires, Ediciones La Rosa Blindada, 72, xiv-112 p.

550    RAMOS CORDOVA, S. *Chile: una economía de transicion ?* (Chile: an economy in transition ?). La Habana, Casa de las Américas, 72, 547 p.

551    Bibl. xxi-719. SAUNDERS, J. (ed.). *Modern Brazil: new patterns and development.* CR: R. M. SCHNEIDER, *Amer. polit. Sci. R.* 67(4), dec 73 : 1421-1424.

552    "Situación económica en 1972" (Economic situation in 1972), *Exam. Sit. econ. México* 49(566), jan 73 : 3-57. [Mexico.]

553    SMITH, C. A. "Market articulation and economic stratification in Western Guatemala", *Food Res. Inst. Stud.* 11(2), 1972 : 203-233.

*North America / Amérique du Nord*

[See also / Voir aussi: 2274, 4344]

554    AULD, D. A. L. (ed.). *Economics: contemporary issues in Canada.* Toronto, Hold, Rinehart and Winston of Canada, Minneapolis, Minn., Mine Publications, 72, ix-180 p.

555    BEACH, R. A. *Nixon's inheritance: a drunken economy.* Roslyn Heights, N. Y., Libra Publishers, 72, 143 p.

556    "Business outlook for 1973 (The)", *J. Busin.* 46(1), jan 73 : 1-102. [USA.]

557    CHANT, J. *et al.* (eds.). *Canadian perspectives in economics.* Don Mills, Ont., Collier-Macmillan Canada, 72, var. pag.

558    COCHRAN, T. C. *American business in the twentieth century.* Cambridge, Harvard University Press, 72, vi-259 p.

559    COOPER, J. C. *The recovery of America.* Philadelphia, Westminster Press, 73, 176 p.

560    DOREL, G.; RAYNAUD, A. *Les États-Unis en devenir; puissance et transformation d'une économie.* Paris, Doin, 73, 168 p.

561    HOCKIN, T. A. *et al. The Canadian condominium; domestic issues and external policy* Toronto, McClelland and Stewart, 72, 176 p.

562    OFFICER, L. H.; ANDERSEN, P. R.; WILTON, D. A. *Supply relationships in the Canadian economy; an industry comparison.* East Lansing, Michigan State University, 72, x-173 p.

563    PASSELL, P.; ROSS, L. *The retreat from riches; affluence and its enemies.* New York, Viking Press, 73, xiii-203 p. [USA.]

564    "U.S. economy in 1972 (The)", *Survey curr. Busin.* 53(1), jan 73 : 12-29.

## F.(1)    Asia
##        Asie

[See also / Voir aussi: 6581]

565    BOFFA, G. "L'economia cinese: valutazioni e problemi" (The Chinese economy: evaluations and problems), *Polit. ed Econ.* 4(1-2), jan-apr 73 : 77-90.

566    "Chinese economy at the present juncture (The)", *Amer. econ. R.* 63(2), mai 73 *Pap. and Proc.*: 215-235. With contributions by: T. C. LIU, K. C. YEH, D. H. PERKINS, R. S. ECKAUS and T. G. RAWSKI.

567    DAROESMAN, R. "An economic survey of West Java", *B. Indon. econ. Stud.* 8(2), jul 72 : 29-54.

568    DINKEVIČ, A. I. *Očerki ėkonomiki sovremnoj Japonii* (Characteristics of the contemporary Japanese economy). Moskva, Nauka, 72, 376 p.

569    DONNITHORNE, A. "China's cellular economy: some economic trends since the cultural revolution", *China Quart.* 52, oct-dec 72 : 605-619.

570    DUTT, A. K. (ed.). *India: resources, potentialities and planning.* Dubuque, Iowa, Kendall/Hunt Publishing Co., 72, xiii-138 p.

571    HLA MYINT, U. *Southeast Asia's economy: development policies in the 1970s.* Harmondsworth, Penguin, 72, 189 p.

572    JAIN, O. P. "Economy of Laos", *India Quart.* 28(3), jul-sep 72 : 236-254.

573    KHAN, A. R. *Economy of Bangladesh.* London, Macmillan, 72, xviii-196 p.

574    KHERA, H. S. *Problems and prospects of the Malaysian economy.* Petaling Jaya, Central News Agency, 72, v-134 p.

575    KOTOVSKIJ, G. G.; ČELYSEV, E. P. *Sovremennaja Indija: ėkonomika, politika, kul'tura* (Contemporary India: economy, politics, culture). Moskva Nauka, 72, 283 p.

576    LAVALLEE, L.; DIRER, F.; BOUCHE, E. *Problèmes économiques de la République démocratique du Viet-Nam.* Paris, Centre d'études et de recherches marxistes, 71, vii-160 p.

577    MONROE, W. F. "Japan's economy in the 1970's: implications for the world", *Pacific Aff.* 45(4), 1972-73 : 508-520.

578    RABUSHKA, A. *The changing face of Hong Kong: new departures in public policy.* Washington, American Enterprise Institute for Public Policy Research, 73, 79 p.

579    RAO, V. K. (ed.). *Bangla Desh economy: problems and prospects.* Delhi, Vikas Publications, 72, vi-199 p.

580    RAWSKI, T. G. "Recent trends in the Chinese economy", *China Quart.* 53, jan-mar 73 : 1-33.

581    SAUTTER, C. *Japon: le prix de la puissance.* Paris, Seuil, 73, 313 p.

582    SETH, K. L. *Economic prospects of Bangla Desh.* New Delhi, Trimurti Publications, 72, 103 p.

583    VEDOVATO, G. "Giappone 1972: economia del paese e relazioni commerciali con l'Europa" (Japan in 1972: the country's economy and trade relations with Europe), *Riv. Studi polit. int.* 40(1), jan-mar 73 : 69-92.

584    YAMAUCHI, K. *Chugoku shakaishugi keizai kenkyu jyosetsu* (An introduction to the socialist economy in China). Tokyo, Hosei Daigaku Shuppan-kyoku 72, 268 p.

## F.1(4)    Europe

[See also / Voir aussi: 3477, 5457]

585    Bibl. XXI-747. BECKERMAN, W. (ed.). *The Labour government's economic record, 1964-1970.* CR: P. B. MUSGRAVE, *J. econ. Liter.* 11(2), jun 73 : 559-561.

586    BERGERON, R. "L'évolution récente de l'économie sarde", *R. Géogr. Lyon* 48(1), 1973 : 61-97. [Italie.]

587    CONERT, H. *Einführung in die politische Ökonomie der Bundesrepublik* (Introduction to the political economy of the Federal Republic). (Frankfurt a. M.) Europäische Verl. Anst., 72, 102 p.

588    "Conjoncture en Belgique (La)", *Industrie* 26(12), dec 72 : 932-937.

589    DIRLAM, J. B.; PLUMMER, J. *An introduction to the Yugoslav economy*. Columbus, Ohio, C.E. Merrill Publishing Co., 73, ix-259 p.

590    "Economía española, 1973" (Spanish economy in 1973), *Nuestro Tiempo* 20(227), mai 73 : 73-143.

591    ESTAPE, F. *Ensayos sobre economía española* (Essays on the Spanish economy). Barcelona, Departamento de Teoría Económica, Facultad de Ciencias Económicas, Universidad de Barcelona, 72, 351 p.

592    "France économique en 1971-1972 (La)", *R. Écon. polit. (Paris)* 82(5), sep-oct 72 : 719-1068.

593    "Gesamtschau der österreichischen Wirtschaft im Jahre 1972" (An overview of the Austrian economy in 1972), *Osterr. Inst. Wirtsch.-Forsch. Mber.* 46(3), mar 73 : 97-165.

594    GIBSON, N. "Economic conditions and policy in Northern Ireland", *Econ. soc. R.* 4(3), apr 73 : 349-364.

595    GRAZIANI, A.; VIVO, G. DE. *L'economia italiana, 1945-1970* (The Italian economy, 1945-1970). Bologna, Il Mulino, 72, 396 p.

596    HEN, P. DE. *Over de financieel-economische machtsvorming in Nederland* (On the formation of financial-economic power in the Netherlands). Amsterdam, De Arbeiderspers, 72, 170 p.

597    JEDRZEJUK, R. "Gospodarka narodowa w roku 1972" (The national economy in 1972), *Finanse* 4, 1973 : 70-76. [Poland.]

598    KALIŃSKI, J.; KOSTROWICKA, I.; LANDAU, Z. *Gospodarka Polski Ludowej. I. 1944-1956* (Economy of the Polish People's Republic. I. 1944-1956). Warszawa, Szkoła Główna Planowania i Statystyki, 73, 210 p.

599    KORHONEN, T. "The Finnish economy in 1972 and the current outlook", *Bank Finland mthly B.* 47(5), mai 73 : 20-28.

600    KOZMA, F. "A magyar népgazdaság helye Európában" (The position of the Hungarian People's economy in Europe), *Közgazd. Szle* 20(9), sep 73 : 997-1010.

601    LENTI, L. *Grandeur et servitude de l'économie italienne*. Paris, Calmann-Levy, 73, 355 p.

602    LEVI, M. "L'Europe 1972-1980. Données et perspectives économiques", *Polit. étr.* 37(4), 1972 : 455-470.

603    MAHILLON, G. "La physionomie de l'économie tchècoslovaque, le tournant: 1968-1969", *Ét. slaves est-europ.* 17, 1972 : 98-106.

604    MILIĆEVIĆ, D. *Ekonomski položaj Jugoslavije* (The economic situation of Yugoslavian regions). Beograd, Institut društvenih' nauka, 72, 138 p.

605    OBST, W. *DDR-Wirtschaft; Modell und Wirklichkeit* (DDR economy. Model and reality). Hamburg, Hoffmann und Campe, 73, 279 p.

606    "Österreichische Wirtschaft nach Bundesländern 1969 bis 1972" (Austrian economy by region from 1969 to 1972), *Österr. Inst. Wirtsch. Forsch. Mber.* 46(10), oct 73 : 455-472.

607    PERPIÑA, Y.; GRAU, R. *De economía hispana, infraestructura, historia* (Spanish economy, infrastructure, history). Barcelona, Ediciones Ariel, 72, 368 p.

608    "Perspectives de l'économie régionale en 1973 (Les)", *R. Econ. mérid.* 19(79), jul-sep 72 : 1-44. [France.]

609    PRÖBSTING, K. "L'économie collective autrichienne et l'intégration européenne", *A. Écon. coll.* 61(3), jul-sep 73 : 279-286.

610    "Regards sur la vie économique en Grande-Bretagne", *R. écon. Banque nat. Paris* 24, oct 72 : 3-34.

611    RUPPERT, F. (ed.). *Die Wirtschaft. 1972* (The economy in 1972). München, Deutscher Taschenbuch Verlag, 72, 452 p. [Germany FR.]

612    SARNECKI, Z. "Niektóre elementy sytuacji ekonomicznofinansowej kraju w I półroczu 1973" (Selected issues of the economic and financial situation of the country in the first half of 1973), *Finanse* (10), 1973 : 61-72. [Poland.]

613    SCHNITZER, M. *East and West Germany: a comparative economic analysis*. New York, Praeger Publishers, 72, xxiii-446 p.

614    "Situation et perspectives de l'économie française à la fin décembre 1972", *Tendances Conjonct.* (1), 1973, *Suppl.:* 1-86.

615 URCIUOLI, C. "La situazione economic italiana" (The Italian economic situation), *Stato soc.* 16(11), nov 72 : 925-944.
616 VAES, E. "Hainaut d'hier et d'aujourd'hui", *Ét. écon. (Mons)* 3-4 (151-152), 1971 : 249-261.

### F.1(5)   Middle East
### Moyen Orient

[See also / Voir aussi:

617 "A.R.E. economy (The)", *Econ. B. (Cairo)* 25(4), 1972 : 237-252.
618 "Egyptian economy 1959-60-1969-70 (The)", *Econ. B. (Cairo)* 25(4), 1972 : 257-286.
619 "Egyptian economy, 1971 (The)", *Nat. Bank Egypt* 26(1), 1973 : 24-48.
620 FACCHINI, E. *Dipendenza economica e sviluppo capitalistico in Israele* (Economic dependence and capitalist development in Israel). Milano, F. Angeli, 72, 318 p.

### F.1(6)   Pacific
### Pacifique

621 ARNDT, H. W.; BOXER, A. H. (eds.). *The Australian economy: a second volume of readings.* Melbourne, Cheshire, 72, 587 p.
622 MOUNTAIN, G. R. "The Australian economy. Problems and new challenges" *R. Soc. Ét. Expans.* 72(254), jan-feb 73 : 9-15.

### F.1(7)   USSR
### URSS

[See also / Voir aussi:

623 CLARKE, R. A. *Soviet economic facts, 1917-1970.* London, Macmillan, 72, xi-151 p.
624 MALININ, S. N. *et al. Aktual'nye problemy političeskoj ėkonomii v svete rešenij XXIV s'ezda KPSS* (Topical problems of the political economy in light of the XXIVth CPSU Congress decisions). Minsk, Izdatel' stvo BGU, 72, 247 p.
625 MELKAZE, V. I. *et al. Ėkonomika sovetskoj Gruzii. Dostiženija, problemy, perspektivy* (The Soviet Georgian economy. Results, problems and forecasts). Tbilisi, Izdatel'stvo S. KP Gruzii, 72, 606 p.
626 PAVETTO, R. *L'economia comunista* (The communist economy). Firenze, Vallecchi, 72, 146 p.
627 UNITED STATES. Congress. Joint Economic Committee. *Soviet economic prospects for the seventies.* Washington, United States Government Printing Office, 73, xvii-776 p.

### F.2   NATIONAL INCOME AND CAPITAL (ESTIMATION AND FORECASTING)
### REVENU, CAPITAL NATIONAL (ÉVALUATION ET PRÉVISION)

### F.21   National income or product
### Revenu (ou produit) national

### F.211   *Concept*

[See also / Voir aussi: **K.1; K.20;** 3184, 6464]

628 BELIK, Ju. A. *Čto takoe nacional'nyj dohod i kak on ispol'zuetoja* (What national income is and how it is utilized). Moskva, Ekonomika, 72, 55 p.

### F.212   *Amount*
### *Volume*

[See also / Voir aussi: **K.21; K.322;** 4925]

629 BOUSE, V. "Dynamika a úroveň národniho duchodu v zemich RVHP v obdobi 1950-1970" (The dynamic and the national income level in the COMECON countries during the 1950-1970 period), *Plan. Hospod.* 24(11), nov 72 : 69-77.

630    CECONI, T. A. "Algunas consideraciones sobre el producto bruto interno argentino
       durante el periodo 1945-1970" (Some considerations on the internal gross product of
       Argentina during the 1945-1970 period), *Trim. econ.* 39(156), oct-dec 72 : 797-816.

631    DEANE, R. S.; GRINDELL, D.; LUMSDEN, M. A. *New data for economic research.* Wellington,
       Reserve Bank of New Zealand, 72, 35 p. [National income in New Zealand.]

632    JEGLITSCH, H. "Der Beitrag der Bundesländer zum Brutto-Nationalprodukt 1964 bis
       1970" (The contributions of "Länder" to the gross national product between 1964
       and 1970), *Österr. Inst. Wirtsch.-Forsch. Mber.* 46(1), jan 73 : 8-84. [Austria.]

633    KECK, A. *Leistung, Wachstum, Wohlstand; unser Nationaleinkommen, Quelle des gesell-
       schaftlichen Reichtums* (Efficiency, growth, welfare: our national income as a source of
       economic wealth). Berlin, Verlag Die Wirtschaft, 73, 152 p.

634    LEKACHMAN, R. *National income and the public welfare.* New York, Random House, 72,
       iv-149 p. [USA.]

635    ŁUKASZUK, A. "Dochöd narodowy w latach 1960-1970" (National income in the 1970's),
       *Prace nauk. wyzsz. Szkoły ekon. Wrocław.* 37, 1973 : 131-148. [Poland.]

636    PAULA, H. "Das Bruttoinlandprodukt 1972 nach Wirtschaftsbereichen" (The gross
       national product in 1972 by economic sector), *Bayern in Zahlen* 27(8), aug 73 : 283-286.
       [Germany, FR.]

637    SCHWEIGER, I. "1973 forecast of gross national product, consumer spending, saving,
       and housing", *J. Busin.* 48(1), jan 73 : 6-10.

638    SHEPPACH, R. C. Jr. *State projections of the gross national product, 1970, 1980.* Lexington,
       Mass., Lexington Books, 72, xvii-269 p. [USA.]

639    [ŠMAEV] SHMAEV, G. G.; KUPAEVA, L. M. "Modeling the dynamics of Soviet national
       income on analogue computers", *Matekon* 8(4), 1972 : 382-389.

640    "U.S. national income and product accounts 1969-72", *Survey curr. Busin.* 53(7), jul
       73 : 14-51.

641    WEINROBE, M. "Accounting for pollution: pollution abatement and the national pro-
       duct", *Land Econ.* 49(2), mai 73 : 115-121. [USA.]

642    YI, H. J. *A study of the structural change of expenditures on gross national product in the
       process of economic growth: with special reference to the Korean economy, as a case of a
       developing country in comparison with developed countries.* Pittsburgh, University
       Center for International Studies, University of Pittsburgh, 73, 40 p.

## F.22    National capital and wealth
##         Capital (ou richesse) national

[See also / Voir aussi: **G.332;** 4700, 5867]

643    BOR, M. Z.; JACKOV, V. A. *Upravlenie socialističeskim vosproizvodstvom* (Socialist
       reproduction management). Moskva, Mysl', 72, 286 p.

644    ČERNE, F. "Reprodukcijski mehanizen v ekonomski teoriji socializma" (The mechanism
       of reproduction in socialist economic theory), *Ekon. R. (Ljubljana)* 23(2-3), sep 72 :
       151-166.

645    EMEL'JANOV, A. M.; RADAEV, V. V. *Problemy socialističeskogo vosproizvodstva na so-
       vremennom ètape razvitija èkonomiki* (Problems of the socialist reproduction at the
       contemporary stage of economic development). Moskva, Moskovskij gosudarstvennyj
       Universitet, 72, 244 p.

646    IVANOV, N. I. *Problemy èkonomičeskoj èffektivnosti rasširennogo vosproizvodstva pri
       socialisme* (Problems of the enlarged reproduction economic efficiency under socialism).
       Kiev, Izdatel'stvo Kievskogo Universiteta, 72, 160 p.

647    JABŁOŃSKA-SKINDER, H. *Warunki procesu akumulacji w krajach afrykańskich* (Conditions
       of accumulation process in African countries). Szczecin, Wydawnictwo Politechniki
       Szczecińskiej, 72, 159 p.

648    MUSAKOZAEV, Š. (ed.). *Effektivnost' obščestvennogo proizvodstva v Kirgizskoj SSR* (Effi-
       ciency of social production in the SSR of Kirghiztan). Frunze, Ilim, 72, 133 p.

**F.23** **National economic accounting**
**Comptabilité économique nationale**

**F.230** *General studies*
*Études générales*

[See also / Voir aussi:

649  GLUŠČEVIĆ, B. "Sistem društvenih računa i programiranje razvoja" (The system of social accounts and the programming of development), *Ekon. Misao* 6(2), jun 73 : 98-112.

650  HEWINGS, G. J. "Input-output models aggregation for regional impact analysis", *Growth and Change* 3(1), jan 72 : 15-19. With a comment by R. B. WILLIAMSON : 20.

651  INSTITUTE OF SOCIAL STUDIES. "National accounting and development problems", *Develop. and Change* 4(2), 1972-73 : 1-91.

652  JOHANSEN, L. *Simple and general non-substitution theorems for input-output models.* Oslo, Institute of Economics, University of Oslo, 72, 13 p.

653  MAITAL, S. "The Tableau économique as a Leontief model", *Quart. J. Econ.* 86(3), aug 72 : 504-507.

654  RESZCZYŃSKI, Z. M. *Całosciowe bilansowanie procesu reprodukcji* (Comprehensive accounting of the reproduction process), Warszawa, Państwowe Wydawnictwo Naukowe, 73, 288 p.

655  RICHARDSON, H. W. *Input-output and regional economics.* New York, Wiley, 72, 294 p.

656  SANGAJŁO, R. "Metody konstrukcji regionalnych tablic przepływów miedzygaleziowych" (Methods of construction of the regional input-output tables) *Zesz. nauk. wyzsz. Szkoły ekon. w Poznan.* 43, 1972 : 87-105.

657  SEDELEV, B. V. *Ekonomiko-matematičeskoe modelirovanie processov rassirennogo vosproizvodstva* (Economic and mathematical models elaboration of the enlarged reproduction processes). Moskva, 72, 112 p.

659  VISINOIU, N. "Sistemul contabilit tii nationale" (The national accounting system), *Stud. Čerc. econ.* (4), 1971 : 209-214.

660  WIERZBICKI, J. *Rachunek usług niemateriainych w gospodarce narodowej* (Calculation of nonmaterial services in the national economy). Warszawa, Państwowe Wydawnictwo Naukowe, 73, 216 p.

**F.231** *Local studies*
*Études localisées*

[See also / Voir aussi: 3472, 6560]

661  ALMAEV, T. M. *et al. Mežotraslevye svjazi i proporcii narodnogo hozjajstva Kirgizii* (Inter-industry relations and proportions of the Kirghiz national economy). Frunze, Kyrgyzstan, 72, 139 p.

662  ARTEMOVA, L. *et al.* "Ekonomičeskij analiz obščestvennogo proizvodstva na osnove pokazatelej balansa narodnogo hozjajstva" (The economic analysis of social production based on the indexes of national economy equilibrium), *Plan. Hoz.* 50(10), oct 73 : 28-35. [USSR.]

663  BRENDER, A. "Un tableau économique pour la Chine en 1970", *Econ. et Soc.* 7(2-3), feb-mar 73 : 557-570.

664  CARNEIRO LEAO, A. S. *et al.* "Matriz de insumo-produto do Brasil" (Input-output matrix of Brasil), *R. brasil. Econ.* 27(3), jul-sep 73 : 3-10.

665  "Comptes de l'agriculture de l'année 1972 (Les)", *Écon. et Statist.* 45, mai 73 : 21-30. [France.]

666  "Comptes nationaux de la Belgique, 1963-1971 (Les)", *B. Statist. (Bruxelles)* 58(7-8), jul-aug 72 : 371-433.

667  FRANCE. Institut national de la statistique et des études économiques. *Les comptes de l'agriculture française de 1971.* Paris, INSEE, 72, 52 p.

668  FRANCE. Institut national de la statistique et des études économiques. *Les comptes des entreprises par secteurs. Séries 1962-1969.* Paris, INSEE, 72, 282 p. (Coll. de l'INSEE, Série C, n° 20).

669    FRANCE. Institut national de la statistique et des études économiques. *Tableaux écono-miques de la région parisienne*. Paris, INSÉE, 72, XI-412 p.

670    GIANNONE, A. "La contabilità nazionale e la programmazione economica in Italia" (National accounting and economic programming in Italy), *A. Fac. Econ. Com. (Messina)* 10(1), 1972 : 163-181.

671    GINSBURGH, V. "Un modèle trimestriel de l'économie belge", *C. écon. Bruxelles* 55, 3e trim. 72 : 321-358.

672    HALTTUNEN, H.; MOLANDER, A. "The input-output framework as a part of a macro-economic model: production, price, income block in the Bank of Finland quaterly econometric model", *Kansantalous* 68(3), 1972 : 219-239.

673    HENDERSON, J. Y. "The possible uses and scope of a national balance sheet for Aus-tralia", *Econ. Record* 48(123), sep 72 : 340-356.

674    KOROPECKYJ, I. S. "Methodological problems of calculating national income for Soviet republics", *J. region. Sci.* 12(3), dec 72 : 387-400.

675    LEE, T. H.; MOORE, J. R.; LEWIS, D. P. *Regional and interregional intersection flow analysis; the method and an application to the Tennessee economy*. Knoxville, University of Tennessee Press, 73, vii-164 p.

676    MENG, C. W. "An inter-industry analysis of the Singapore economy, 1967" *Malayan econ. R.* 17(1), apr 72 : 25-50.

677    NESTEROV, L. "National wealth estimation in socialist countries", *R. Income Wealth* 18(3), sep 72 : 287-301.

678    NIKOLIĆ, D.; MIJATOVIĆ, J. "Analitički globalni ekonometrijski model razvoja in-dustrije i rudarstva" (A global analytic econometric model of the growth of industry and mining), *Ekonomist (Zagreb)* 25(3-4) 1972 : 445-462. [Yugoslavia.]

679    OUSSET, J.; NEGRE, M. "Des comptes nationaux aux comptes régionaux. L'exemple des comptes de l'agriculture", *R. écon. (Paris)* 24(4), jul 73 : 549-576. [France.]

680    SCHAFFER, W. A. *et al. Interindustry study of the Hawaiian economy*. Honolulu, Research and Economic Analysis Division, Department of Planning and Economic Develop-ment, State of Hawaii, 72, 104 p.

681    SEMENOV, A. F. *Mežotraslevoj balans respubliki* (Intersector balance of a republic). Moskva, Statistika, 72, 103 p. [USSR.]

682    SERADZEDINOV, D. *Otčetnyj balans obščestvennogo produkta sojuznoj respubliki* (Metod-ologičeskie voprosy sostavlenija) (Balance sheet of a republic's-social production. Methodological questions of its elaboration) Taškent, Uzbekistan, 73, 173 p. [USSR.]

683    SINGH, P. "Input-output analysis—an appraisal in the context of as an yet unfinished experiment in Kenya", *R. Income Wealth* 18(4), dec 72 : 393-398.

684    TREML, V. G. *et al. The structure of the Soviet economy; analysis and reconstruction of the 1966 input-output table*. New York, Praeger Publishers, 72, xxiv-660 p.

685    TSURUMI, H. *A four-sector econometric model of the Canadian economy*. Kingston, Ont., Institute for Economic Research, Queen's University, 72, 49 p.

686    UNIONE ITALIANA DELLE CAMERE DI COMMERCIO, INDUSTRIA, ARTIGIANATO E AGRI-COLTURA. *I conti economici regionali, 1963-1971*. (Regional economic accounts, 1963-1971). Milano, F. Angeli, 73, 199 p. [Italy.]

687    VAL'TUH, K. K. (ed.). *Mežotraslevoj balans proizvodstvennyh moščnostej* (Intersector balance of productive capacities). Moskva, Ekonomika, 72, 183 p. [USSR.]

688    WOS, A. "Rolnictwo w bilansie przepływów mi dzygał ziowych" (Agriculture in the input-output balance), *Zagadn. Ekon. roln.* (1), 1973 : 3-20. [Poland.]

**F.24    National economic budget**
        **Budget économique national**

**F.240    *General studies***
           ***Études généralisées***

689    Bibl. XXI-905. BONESS, A. J. *Capital budgeting: the public and private sectors*. CR: J. C. MILLER, III. *J. econ. Liter.* 11(2), jun 73 : 579-580.

**F.25     Forecasting**
**Prévision**

**F.251     *Technique***

[See also / Voir aussi: **B.32; G.3351;** 1629, 1956, 2294, 2320, 2369, 2373, 2430, 3657, 3679, 4399, 4469, 4582, 4659, 4671, 4787, 4959, 5174, 5196, 5914, 6435]

690     AMBROZIAK, T.; SPRATEK, L.; WIAK, M. *Wybrane problemy i metody prognozowania* (Some selected problems and methods of forecasting). Warszawa, Osrodek Badawczo-Rozwojowy Informatyki, 73, 135 p.

691     DEMSKI, J. S.; FELTHAM, G. A. "Forecast evaluation", *Accting R.* 47(3), jul 72 : 533-548.

692     ELLIOTT, J. W. "A direct comparison of short-run GNP forecasting models", *J. Busin.* 46(1), jan 73 : 33-60.

693     FRANCHINI, R. *Teoria della previsione* (Forecasting theory). 2nd rev. ed. Napoli, Giannini, 72, 172 p.

694     HARBORDT, S. "Die Grenzen einer Prognose. Anmerkungen zur Simulationsstudie des Club of Rome" (The limits of a projection. Remarks on Club of Rome's simulation study), *Soz. Welt* 23(4), 1972 : 410-424.

695     KANTON, M. "Prognozy gospodarcze — cechy charakterystyczne i ich rola w gospodarkach kapitalistycznej i socjalistycznej" (Economic forecasting, its characteristic features and role in capitalist and socialist economies), *Zesz. nauk. Szkoły główn. Plan. Statyst.* 86, 1972 : 11-20.

696     KLEIN, D. (ed.). *Futurologie und Zukunftsforschung* (Futurology and research on the future). Berlin, Deutscher Verlag der Wissenschaften, 72, 283 p.

697     LIEBLING, H.; RUSSELL, J. "The econometrics of price expectations in short-term forecasting", *Amer. Economist* 16(1), 1972 : 102-111.

698     MANKEVIĆ, L. S. "Ispol'zovanie statističeskogo metoda integral'nyh ocenok pri prognozirovanii cen vo vnešnej torgovla" (Utilization of the integral estimations statistical method in forecasting foreign trade prices), in: *Problemy perspektivnogo narodnohozjajstvennogo planirovanija*. II. Moskva, 1972 : 119-133.

699     NYKOWSKI, I. "O mozliwosci uproszczeń w metodzie rzutu gradienta według Rosena przy jednym warunku ograniczającym" (On possible reductions in the Rosen gradient projection model with one restrictive condition), *Zesz. nauk. Szkoły główn. Plan. Statyst.* 86, 1972 : 81-104.

700     PADBURY, P.; WILKINS, D. *The future: a bibliography of issues and forecasting techniques.* Monticello, Ill., Council of Planning Librarians, 72, 102 p.

701     PAWŁOWSKI, Z. *Prognozy ekonometryczne* (Econometric forecasting). Warszawa, Państwowe Wydawnictwo Naukowe, 73, 285 p.

702     POLSZAKIEWICZ, B. "Ocena niektórych metod przewidywania koniunktury gospodarczej w krajach kapitalistycznych" (Evaluation of some methods of business forecasting in capitalist countries), *Zesz. nauk. wyzsz. Szkoły ekon. Poznan.* 44, 1972 : 7-26.

703     PRANDECKA, B. *et al. Metody prognozowania i zakres tresci prognoz długofalowych w róznych krajach za szczególnym uwzglednieniem aspektu przestrzennego* (Methods of forecasting and content of long-term forecasts in different countries, with particular emphasis on regional aspects). Warszawa, Instytut Geografii PAN, Instytut Ekonomiki Produkcji SGPIS, 72, 216 p.

704     STEWART, J. "Dummy variables, stochastic linear constraints and tests of prediction", *Manchester Sch. Econ. soc. Stud.* 40(4), dec 72 : 375-383.

705     SWEDEN. Statistika centralbyrån. *Trender och prognoser. Befolkning utbildning och arbetsmarknad | Trends and forecasts. Population, education and labour market.* Stockholm, Allmänna förlaget, 72, 179 p.

706     TEEKENS, R. *Prediction methods in multiplicative models.* Rotterdam, Universitaire Pers Rotterdam, 72, viii-124 p.

707     TUGWELL, F. (ed.). *Search for alternatives: public policy and the study of the future.* Cambridge, Mass., Withrop Publishers, 73, xvi-335 p.

708     VASIL'EV, Ju. N. *Prognozirovanie i perspektivnoe planirovanie v promyšlennosti* (Forecasting and perspective planning in industry). Leningrad, Lenizdat, 73, 195 p.

709     WHEELWRIGHT, S. C.; MAKRIDAKIS, S. G. *Forecasting methods for management.* New York, Wiley, 73, xiii-241 p.

35

**F.252**    *Particular studies*
             *Études particulières*

[See also / Voir aussi: 1706, 3425, 3751, 4711, 5759, 5814]

710    FEDORENKO, N. P. "Metodologičeskie problemy social'no-ekonomičeskogo prognozirovanija" (Methodological problems concerning socio-economic forecasting), *Ékon. matem. Metody* 9(2), mar-apr 73 : 195-203. [USSR.]

711    FLEISCHER, W. "Untersuchungen am Prognosesystem für die wirtschaftliche Entwicklung der Bundesrepublik Deutschland von M. Krelle" (W. Krelle's researches on a forecasting system for the Federal Republic of Germany), *Schweizer. Z. Volkswirtsch. Statist.* 108(4), dec 72 : 663-668.

712    GAJDA, J. "Rozwój przemysłu w systemie prognoz społeczno-gospodarczych" (Development of industry and the system of social and economic forecasting), *Fol. econ. cracov.* 13, 1973 : 47-85. [Poland.]

713    LESZ, M. "Les méthodes de la prévision économique en Pologne", *R. Est* 4(1), jan 73 : 5-26 ?

714    POKROVSKIJ, A. I. *Prognozy bez plana. O prognozirovanii v SŠA* (Forecasts without plan. About forecasting in the USA). Moskva, Znanie, 72, 47 p.

715    RATO, H. "La prévision technologique. Application de la méthode Delphi et de la méthode de l'arbre de décisions en Belgique", *C. Bruxelles* 58, 2e trim. 73: 271-303.

716    Bibl. XXI-962. SURREY, M. J. C. *The analysis and forecasting of the British economy*, CR: H. T. SHAPIRO, *J. econ. Liter.* 11(2), jun 73 : 564-567.

717    UNITED STATES. Bureau of Labor Statistics. *Projections of the post-Vietnam economy*, 1975. Washington, United States Government Printing Office, 72, iv-34 p.

718    ZELLENTIN, G.; KOHLER, B. *Europa 1985 neunzehnhundertfünfundachtzig: gesellschaft und politische Entwicklungen in Gesamteuropa* (Europe in 1985: social and economic evolution in the European ensemble). Bonn, Europa-Union-Verlag, 72, 173 p.


**F.3**      **STRUCTURES**

**F.30**     **General studies**
             **Études générales**

**F.301**    *Theory*
             *Théorie*

[See also / Voir aussi: **B.32; F.230; F.320; F.330; F.50;** 5216]

719    CHRISTIN, I. *Théorie des structures et des systèmes économiques.* Paris, Dalloz, 73, 154 p.
720    KRAINER, R. E. "Economic structure and the assignment problem: a contribution to the theory of macro-economic policy for net creditor countries", *Canad. J. Econ.* 6(2), mai 73 : 239-247.

721    SIMONIS, U. E. *Infrastruktur; Theorie und Praxis* (Infrastructure; theory and practice). Kiel, Institut für Weltwirtschaft an der Universität Kiel, 72, vii-354 p.

722    VISNJAKOVA, I. V. "Infrastruktura i razvoj proizvodnje" (Infrastructure and the development of production), *Ekon. Misao* 6(1), mar 73 : 40-51.


**F.302**    *Descriptive studies*
             *Études descriptives*

[See also / Voir aussi: **F.231; F.321; F.331; F.51;** 2738, 3195, 4099, 6613]

723    ARCANGELO, E. D'. *Le principali strutture del Mezzogiorno* (The main structures of the South). Napoli, Libreria scientifica, 72, 110 p. [Italy.]

724    ASKANAS, B. *Wirtschaftsstrukturen in Osteuropa. Ein Vergleich mit West-europa* (Economic structures of Eastern Europe. A comparison with Western Europe). Wien, Verrein Österreisches Institut für Wirtschaftsforschung, 72, 56 l.

725    BIANCHI, A. *Analisi evolutiva della struttura economica del Lazio. Ipotesi di sviluppo 1975-85...* (Evolution of the economic structure of Latium. Development hypothesis, 1975-85...). Roma, C.I.O.S., 72, 219 p. [Italy.]

726 JAROSEVSKIJ, B. E. "Strukturnye problemy peruanskoj ekonomiki" (Problems of the Peruvian economic structure), *Latin. Amer.* (2), mar-apr 73 : 27-39.

727 JOHNSON, S. R.; SMITH, P. E. "Structural aspects of the Phillips relation in the US economy", *Nebraska J. Econ. Busin.* 11(4), 1972 : 101-120.

728 JOHNSTON, T. L.; BUXTON, N. K.; MAIR, D. *Structure and growth of the Scottish economy.* London, Collins, 71, 356 p.

729 KOČETOV, A. A. "Strukturnye izmenenija v promyšlennosti i osobennosti tehničeskogo progressa v Anglii posle vtoroj mirovoj vojny" (Structural changes in industry and characteristics of the technical progress in England after the Second World War), in: *Problemy političeskoj ekonomii.* Moskva, 1972 : 277-312.

730 KRAUSE, E. A. *Structural changes in West German agriculture.* Washington, United States Department of Agriculture, Economic Research Service, 72 v-66 p.

731 LAMBERT, D. C. "Comment rompre le dualisme de structure en Amérique latine ? La solution de l'économie mixte", *Mondes en Dévelop.* 2, 1972 : 103-150.

732 MARTÍNEZ LE CLAINCHE, R. *México: elementos para el estudio estructural de su economía* (Mexico: elements for the structural study of its economy). México, Universidad Nacional Autónoma de México, Instituto de Investigaciones Económicas, 72, 136 p.

733 MOHR, H. J. *Economía colombiana: une estructura en crisis; análisis del proceso reciente y perspectivas* (Colombian economy: a structure in crisis; analysis of the recent process and perspectives). Bogotá, Centro de Investigación y Acción Social; Ediciones Tercer Mundo, 72, xviii-315 p.

734 SACKS, S. R. "Changes in industrial structure in Yugoslavia, 1959-1968" *J. polit. Econ.* 80(3), mai-jun 72 : 561-574.

735 SANTHANAM, K. V.; PATIL, R. H. "A study of the production structure of the Indian economy: an international comparison", *Econometrica* 40(1), jan 72 : 159-176 ?

736 STARCENKOV, G. I. "Strukturnye izmenenija i ekonomike Turcii" (Structural changes in the Turkish economy), *Narody Azii Afriki* (3), mai-jun 73 : 17-29.

737 STINGL, J. "Änderung der Wirtschaftsstruktur und Mobilität der Arbeitskräfte" (Modification of the economic structure and labour mobility), *Turzinger Stud.* (2), 1973 : 20-31. [Germany, F.R.]

738 TIMÁR, M. "Gazdaságunk szervezete — fejlesztési politikánk" (The structure of our economy. Our development policy), *Közgazd. Szle* 20(10), oct 73 : 1129-1151. [Hungary.]

739 WALESZKO, M. "Strukturalne przemiany gospodarcze" (Structural economic changes), *Prace nauk. wyžsz. Szkoły ekon. Wrocław.* 37, 1973 : 107-129.

740 WILLMOTT, W. E. *Economic organization in Chinese society.* Stanford, Cal. Stanford University Press, 72, xi-461 p.

### F.31 Specific aspects
### Aspects spécifiques

### F.311 *Geographical aspects*
### *Aspects géographiques*

### F.3110 *General studies*
### *Études générales*

[See also / Voir aussi: 2611, 3226, 3427]

741 ALONSO, W. "The economics of urban size", *Region. Sci. Assoc. Pap. and Proc.* 26, 1971 : 67-83.

742 CETINĂ, E. *Elemente de geografie economica a lumji. Resurse energetice, materii prime industriale si agricole* (Elements of economic geography. Energy resourses, industrial and agricultural raw materials). Bucuresti, Editura didactică si pedagogică, 72, 199 p.

743 CORNA PELLEGRINI, G. *La ricerca geografica urbana* (Urban geographic research). Milano, Vita e pensiero, 73, xxxvi-431 p.

744 DOZO, S. R. M.; GARCÍA FIRBEDA, M. *Tratado de geografía económica* (A treatise on economic geography). Buenos Aires, Ediciones Macchi, 72, v.

745 GOLDSTEIN, G. S.; MOSES, L. N. "A survey of urban economics", *J. econ. Liter.* 11(2), jun 73 : 471-515.

746 GOODALL, B. *The economics of urban areas.* Oxford-New York, Pergamon Press 72, xii-379 p.

747 GRIESON, R. E. (ed.). *Urban economics; readings and analysis.* Boston, Little, Brown, 73, x-453 p.

748 GUIGOU, J. L. *Théorie économique et transformation de l'espace agricole.* Paris, Gauthier-Villars, 72. 1. *Théorie spatiale et localisation agricole.* 2. *Méthodologie et analyse.*

749 HARRIS, C. C. Jr. *The urban economies, 1985: a multiregional, multi-industry forecasting model.* Lexington, Mass. Lexington Books, 73, xvi-230 p.

750 HERBERT, D. T. *Urban geography; a social perspective.* Newton Abbot, David, and Charles, 72, 320 p.

751 HIRSCH, W. Z. *Urban economic analysis.* New York, McGraw-Hill, 73, xviii-450 p.

752 HURST, M. E. E. *A geography of economic behavior; an introduction.* North Scituate, Mass., Duxbury Press, 72, x-427 p.

753 JAROSEVSKIJ, B. E. *Teorija periferijnoj ekonomiki* (Theory of the peripheral economy) Moskva, Mysl', 73, 214 p.

754 KOTTIS, G. C. "Problems of defining an urban economy", *Planning Outlook* 12, 1972 : 9-16.

755 LAMBOOY, J. G. *Economie en ruimte. Inleiding in de economische geografie en de regionale economie* (Space economies. Introduction to economic geography and regional economy). Assen, Van Gorcum, 72, viii-246 p.

756 MERA, K. "On the urban agglomeration and economic efficiency", *Econ. Develop. cult Change* 21(2), jan 73 : 309-324.

757 RASMUSSEN, D. W. *Urban economics.* New York, Harper and Row, 73, viii-196 p.

758 RASMUSSEN, D. W.; HAWORTH, C. T. (eds.). *The modern city; readings in urban economics.* New York, Harper and Row, 73, x-302 p.

759 SAUSKIN, Ju. G. *Ekonomičeskaja geografija: istorija, teorija, metody, praktika* (Economic geography: history, theory, methods, practice). Moskva, Mysl', 73, 559 p.

760 SCHMIDT, G. "Wanderings through the European geography", *Ind. J. soc. Res.* 14(1), apr 73 : 11-29.

761 "Spatial economics", *Amer. econ. R.* 63(2), mai 73 *Pap. and Proc:* 52-70. With contributions by: C. WOLF, Jr.; D. WEINSCHROTT, E. SHESHINSKI and J. ROTTENBERG.

762 *Villes (Les); contribution à l'étude de leur développement en fonction de l'évolution économique.* Reims, Université de Reims, 72, 295 p.

**F.3111** *Basic geographical data*
*Données géographiques de base*

[See also / Voir aussi: 2576, 3960, 4756, 4761]

763 BORCHERT, G. *Die Wirtschaftsräume der Elfenbeinküste* (Economic space of the Ivory Coast). Hamburg, Deutsches Institut für Afrika-Forschung, 72, 174 p.

764 BURLEY, T. M. *The Philippines: an economic and social geography.* London Bell, 73, xii-375 p.

765 CARVALHO FERREIRA, C. M. DE. "Uma metodologia para estudo de polarização e seleção de pólos de desenvolvimento em Minas Gerais" (A methodology for the study of polarization and selection of development poles in Minas Gerais), *R. geogr. (Rio de Janeiro)* 75, dec 71 : 127-153. [Brazil.]

766 "Croissance et planification urbaines", *R. écon. (Paris)* 23(6), nov 72 : 929-1101. [France.]

767 DALMASSO, E.; FILLON, P. "Aspectos de la organización espacial del Ecuador" (Aspects of the spatial organization of Ecuador), *R. mexic. Sociol.* 34(1), jan-mar 72 : 75-94.

768 DINEV, L. "Die wirtschaftsgeographische Entwicklung Bulgariens nach dem zweiten Weltkrieg" (The evolution of the economic geography of Bulgaria after the 2d World War), *Österr. Osth.* 15(2), mai 73 : 155-174.

769 DMITRIEVSKIJ, Ju. D.; ŠAHNOVIČ, K. A.; JAG'JA, V. S. *Ekonomičeskaja geografija stran Severo-Vostočnoj i vostočnoj Afriki* (The economic geography of the North Eastern and Eastern Africa countries). Leningrad, 72, 124 p.

770 DURIĆ, V. "Ekonomsko-geografski aspekti transformacije društva i njihov ntičaj na redistribuciju aktivnog stanovništva po delatnostima" (Economic and geographical

aspects of the transformation of society and their influence on the distribution of active population by branch of activity), *Stanovništvo* 10(1-2), jan-jun 72 : 30-43. [Yugoslavia.]

771  ESTALL, R. C. *A modern geography of the United States: aspects of life and economy.* Harmondsworth, Penguin, 72, xiii-401 p.

772  "Études d'économie urbaine", *A. Univ. Sci. soc. Toulouse* 20(1-2), 1972 : 221-437. [France.]

773  FREY, L. "Poli di sviluppo e politica dell'occupazione" (Poles of development and employment policy), *Riv. int. Sci. soc.* 80(5-6), sep-dec 72 : 518-534. [Italy.]

774  HARTWICK, J. M.; CROWLEY, R. W. *Urban economic growth; the Canadian case.* Ottawa, Information Canada, 72, xii-402 p.

775  HUSAYN, 'A. al-R.-'A. *Nashát mudun al-Irâq wa-tatawwuruhâ* (Growth of Iraqi cities and their development). al-Qâhiraf, Mu'ahad al-Buhuth waldirâsât al-'Arabîyaf, Qism al-Buhûth wal-dirâsât al-tarîhîyaf wal-giglnâfîyaf, 73, 114 p.

776  JARMUHAMEDOV, M. Š. *Geografija ėkonomičeskih rajonov Kazahstana* (Geography of Kazakhstan economic regions). Alma-Ata, Mektep, 72, 200 p.

777  LAVRISČEV, A. N. *Ekonomičeskaja geografija SSR;* (USSR economic geography). Moskva, Ekonomika, 72, 687 p.

778  MAURO, F. "El rol de las ciudades en el desarrollo regional en América Latina. Industrialización y urbanización" (The role of cities in regional development in Latin America. Industrialization and urbanization), *R. mexic. Sociol.* 34(1), jan-mar 72 : 65-73.

779  PAPA, O. "Sul grado di urbanizzazione delle regioni italiane" (On the rate of urbanization of the Italian regions), *Rass. econ. (Napoli)* 37(3) mai-jun 73 : 779-783.

780  QUELLENNEC, M. "Différences et ressemblances entre régions économiques", *Coll. INSÉÉ Sér. R.* 12, mai 73 : 33-49. [France.]

781  RITTER, U. P. *Siedlungsstruktur und wirtschaftliche Entwicklung* (Urban structure and economic development). Berlin, Duncker und Humblot, 72, 177 p. [Latin America.]

782  RUPPERT, K. (ed.). *Sozialgeographische Probleme Südosteuropas* (Social-geographic problems of Southeast Europe). Kallmünz, M. Lassleben, 73, 130 p.

783  SEMPLE, R. K.; GAUTHIER, H. L.; YOUNGMANN, C. E. "Growth poles in São Paulo, Brazil", *A. Assoc. Amer. Geogr.* 62(4), dec 72 : 591-598.

784  SERÓ, R.; MAYMÓ, J. *Les transformacions economiques al delta de l'Ebre* (Economic transformations of the Ebro Delta). Barcelona, Banca Catalana, Servei d'Estudis, 72, 164 p. [Spain.]

785  SOLER, C. M. *Geografía económica general y Argentina (síntesis panorámica de los factores económicos mundiales y argentinos)* (General economic geography and Argentina, a panoramic synthesis of world and Argentine economic factors). Buenos Aires, Editorial El Coloquio, 72, 163 p.

786  SUVOROVA, G. T.; STEPANOV, A. I. *Ėkonomičeskaja geografija SSSR* (Economic geography of the USSR.) Moskva, Ekonomika, 72, 311 p.

787  "Ville (La) et le développement économique", *Corresp. municip.* 142, jun 73 : 4-47. [France.]

788  "Villes moyennes", *R. Pyrénées* 44(4), oct 73 : 170 p. [France.]

789  VOLKOV, A. G. "Vlijanie urbanizacii na demografičeskie processy v SSSR" (The influence of urbanization on the USSR demographic processes), in: *Problemy sovremennoj urbanizacii.* Moskva, 1972 : 105-124.

**F.3112**  *The location of productive forces*
*Localisation des forces productives*

[See also / Voir aussi: 3174, 3198]

790  ALVENSLEBEN, R. VON. *Zur Theorie und Ermittlung optimaler Betriebsstandorte* (A contribution to the theory and research of optimal location of firms). Meisenheim-am-Glan, A. Hain, 73, 160 p.

791  BELL, T. *Industrial decentralisation in South Africa.* Cape Town, Oxford University Press, 73, xii-304 p.

792    BENCZE, I.; TAJTI, E. V. *Budapest; an industrial-geographical approach.* Budapest, Akadémiai Kiadó, 72, 168 p.

793    BLACKBORN, A. "The location of foreign-owned manufacturing plants in the Republic of Ireland", *Tijds. econ. soc. Geogr.* 63(6), 1972 : 438-443.

794    BOURRIERES, P.; DESTRIBATS, M. *Implantations industrielles dans le Tiers-monde; condition du succès.* Paris, Eyrolles, 73, 144 p.

795    CATERINA, G. "Il processo di localizzazione delle industrie manifatturiere" (The processus of location of manufacturing industries), *Nord e Sud* 20(161), mai 73 : 29-33.

796    DIENES, L. "The Budapest agglomeration and Hungarian industry: a spatial dilemma", *Geogr. R.* 63(3), jul 73 : 356-377.

797    DONOLO, C. *Stratégies de décentralisation et de localisation industrielle* Paris, Bordas, 72, 189 p.

798    DORE, A. "Problèmes de localisation industrielle et d'aménagement des zones industrielles en Bourgogne", *R. Écon. Centre-Est* 15(59), jan-mar 73 : 75-91.

799    DURAND, P. *Industrie et régions. L'aménagement industriel de la France.* Paris, La Documentation française, 72, 126 p.

800    EKELUND, R. B.; HOOKS, D. I. "Joint demand, discriminating two-part tariffs and location theory: an early American contribution", *West. econ. J.* 10(1), mar 72 : 84-94.

801    FERGUSON, D. C. *et al.* "Determining alternative locations for plant processing facilities: a method for guidance of policymakers", *R. Mkting agric. Econ.* 40(4), dec 72 : 155-169. [Australia.]

802    FIERLA, I. *Geografia przemysłu Polski | The geography of industry of Poland.* Warszawa, Państowe Wydawnictwo Ekonomiczne, 73, 222 p.

803    FROLOV, N. P. *Razvitie i razmeščenija proizvoditel'nyh sil Moldavskoj SSR* (Development and location of the SSR Moldavia's productive forces). Moskva, Nauka, 72, 174 p.

804    GAŁAJ, D. (ed.). *Rozwój społeczno-gospodarczy rejonu uprzemysławianego. Na przykładzie rejonu Płocka* (Socio-economic development of an industrialized region. An example of the Płock region). Warszawa, Państowe Wydawnictwo Naukowe, 73, 420 p.

805    GARCIA ECHEVARRIA, S. "Las decisiones de localización de la empresa" (Enterprise location decisions), *R. Econ. polít.* 63, jan-apr 73 : 51-101.

806    GARRISON, C. B. "The impact of new industry: an application of the economic base multiplier to small rural areas", *Land Econ.* 48(4), nov 72 : 329-337.

807    GHOSH, A.; CHAKRABARTI, A. *Programming and interregional input-output analysis; an application to the problem of industrial location in India.* Cambridge, Eng., University Press, 73, viii-104 p.

808    HAMER, A. M. *Industrial exodus from central city: public policy and the comparative costs of location.* Lexington, Mass., Lexington Books, 73, xiii-107 p.

809    HANSEN, N. M. *Location preferences, migration, and regional growth; a study of the South and Southwest United States.* New York, Praeger Publishers, 73, xv-186 p.

810    HARRIS, C. C. Jr.; HOPKINS, F. E. *Locational analysis: an interregional econometric model of agriculture, mining, manufacturing, and services.* Lexington, Mass., Lexington Books, 72, xov-303 p.

811    HOUSSEL, J. P. "Essor des villes manufacturières de l'habillement et industrialisation spontanée dans 'l'Italie du Milieu' ", *R. Géogr. Lyon* 47 (4), 1972 : 361-383.

812    IOVENKO, G. I. *Osobennosti kompleksnogo razvitija otraslej promyšlennosti v industrial'nyh rajonah* (Characteristics of the complex development of industry sectors in industrial regions). Kiev, 72, 52 p.

813    JAEGER, J. P. "Approche de la localisation industrielle en France à partir d'une analyse factorielle des structures régionales", *R. écon. Sud-Ouest* 21(4), 1972 : 633-685.

814    JENSEN, B. S. *Udflytning af statsinstitutioner. Et instrument i lokaliseringspolitikken* (The decentralization of state institutions. An instrument in location policy). København, Landsplanudvalget, 72, 218 p.

815    LEVIN, A. P. *Vodnyj faktor v razmeščenii promyšlennogo proizvodstva* (Water factor in industrial production location). Moskva, Strojizdat, 73, 167 p.

816    LONSDALE, R. E. "Manufacturing decentralization: the discouraging record in Australia", *Land Econ.* 48(4), nov 72 : 321-328.

817    MATLIN, I. S. "Modelirovanie razvitija sistemy rasselenija metodom statističeskih ispytanij" (Model elaboration of a location system by the method of statistical tests), in: *Problemy perspectivnogo narodnohozjajstvennogo planirovanija.* I. Moskva, 72: 144-163.

40

818 MONHEIM, H. *Zur Attraktivität deutscher Städte; Einflüsse von Ortspräferenzen aud der Standortwahl von Bürobetrieben* (Attraction potential of German cities; influence of geographical preferences on choice of a site for implantation of office firms). München, Geographische Buchhandlung in Komm., 72, x-125 p.

819 NIKODEMSKI, J.; ZIELIŃSKI, T. *Społeczno-ekonomiczne przeobrazenia okregów przemysło-wych województwa katowickiego* (Social and economic transformations of industrial areas of Katowice voivodship). Katowice, Slêski Instytut Naukowy, 72, 183 p.

820 NISHIOKA, H.; KRUMME, G. "Location conditions, factors and decisions: an evaluation of selected location surveys", *Land Econ.* 49(2), mai 73 : 195-205. [USA.]

821 NIVLET, J. M. "La décentralisation industrielle", *Indicateurs Écon. Centre* 1, apr 73 : 21 p. [France.]

822 OLOKO, O. "Influence of unplanned versus planned factory locations on worker commit-ment to industrial employment in Nigeria", *Socio-econ. Plan. Sci.* 7(2), apr 73 : 189-207.

823 OTTERBECK, L. *Location and strategic planning. Towards a contingency theory of industrial location.* Stockholm, Economic Research Institute, 73, 66-1 p.

824 POETZCH, R. "Una nota sulle situazioni di rischio nell'analisis della localizzazione industriale" (A note on the risk situation in the analysis of industrial location), *Ratio* 4(2), 2 sem. 71 : 282-292.

825 RILEY, R. C. *Industrial geography.* London, Chatto and Windus, 73, xii-228 p.

826 ROZENFEL'D, Š. L. *Territorial'naja differenciacija êdinovremennyh zatrat i êffektivnost' razmeščenija proizvodstva. Na primere zanadnyh i vostočnyh rajonov SSSR* (territorial differentiations of exeptional costs and efficiency of production location. On the example of the USSR Western and Eastern regions). Moskva, Nauka, 72, 296 p.

827 SAFAEV, A. S. *Optimizacija razvitija otrasli promyšlennosti v êkonomičeskom rajone* (Op-timization of industrial sector development in an economic region). Moskva, Nauka, 73, 263 p.

828 SINHA, B. *Industrial geography of India.* Calcutta, World Press, 72, xxiii-320 p.

829 STRUYK, R. J. "Evidence on the locational activity of manufacturing industries in metropolitan areas", *Land Econ.* 48(4), nov 72 : 377-382.

830 TUMERTEKIN, E. *Istanbul sanayiinde kurulus yeri / Analysis of the location of industry in Istanbul.* Istanbul, Baski Edebiyat Fakültesi Matbaasinda yapilmistir, 72, 133-2 p.

831 WARREN, K. "The location of British heavy industry. Problems and policies" *Geogr. J.* 139(1), feb 73 : 76-83.

832 WHEAT, L. F. *Regional growth and industrial location: an empirical viewpoint.* Lexington, Mass., Lexington Books, 73, xii-223 p.

833 ZASTAVNYJ, F. D. *Problemy razmeščenija promyšlennosti i formirovanija industrial'nyh kompleksov v SSSR. Faktornye issledovanija* (Problems of industry location and of industrial complexes formation in the USSR. Research factors). L'vov, Izdatel'stvo L'vovskogo Universiteta, 72, 159 p.

## F.3113 Regional planning
### Aménagement régional

[See also / Voir aussi: 3402, 5171, 6359]

834 ALAEV, E. B. *Regional'noe planirovanie v razvivajuščihsja stranah* (Regional planning in the developing countries). Moskva, Nauka, 73, 216 p.

835 ARNAUDO, A. A. "Desarrollo regional en el plan de desarrollo y seguridad 1971-75" (Regional development in the development and security plan), *Desarr. econ.* 12(47), oct-dec 72 : 495-517.

836 BARANOV, É. F. (ed.). *Dinamičeskie modeli territorial'nogo planirovanija* (Dynamic models of territorial planning). Moskva, Nauka, 72, 311 p.

837 BARON, P. "Probleme der japanischen Regionalpolitik" (Regional planning problems in Japan), *Int. Asien Forum* 3(4), oct 72 : 542-552.

838 BHAT, L. S. *Regional planning in India.* Calcutta, Statistical Publishing Society, 72, 153 p.

839 BOGOTA. Camara de Comercio. "Desarrollo regional" (Regional development) *R. Cam. Com. Bogota* 2(7), jun 72 : 1-196. [Colombia.]

840 BOUDEVILLE, J. R. *Aménagement du territoire et polarisation.* Paris, Editions M. Th. Génin, 72, 279 p. [France.]

841    BRÓSSE, U. *Ziele in der Regionalpolitik und in der Raumordnungspolitik; Zielforschung und Probleme der Realisierung von Zielen* (The objectives of regional policy and regional planning). Berlin, Duncker und Humbmot, 72, 181 p.

842    BROWN, A. J. *The framework of regional economics in the United Kingdom.* Cambridge University Press, 72, xvii-352 p.

843    BUCH, H. "La planification régionale et l'administration régionale en Belgique", *R. Inst. Cienc. soc.* 18, 1971 : 259-165.

844    BUCK, T. W.; LOWE, J. F. "Regional policy and the distribution of investment", *Scott. J. polit. Econ.* 19(3), nov 72 : 253-271. [UK.]

845    CENTRE FOR ENVIRONMENTAL STUDIES. *Urban and regional research in the United Kingdom, 1972: an annotated list.* London, Centre for Environmental Studies, 72, 125 p.

846    CHOJNICKI, Z.; CZYZ, T. *Zmiany struktury regionalnej Polski w swietle przepływów towarowych w latach 1958-1966* (Changes of the regional structure of Poland in the light of goods flows in the years 1958-1966). Warszawa, Państwowe Wydawnictwo Naukowe, 72, 159 p.

847    CIAMAGA, L. *Polityka przestrzennego zagospodarowania krajów Europy Zachodniej* (Politics of regional development of the West European countries) Warszawa, Państwowe Wydawnictwo Ekonomiczne, 72, 271 p.

848    COURBIS, R.; PRAGER, J. Cl. "Analyse régionale et planification nationale le projet de modèle 'Regina' ", *Coll. INSÉÉ Sér. R.* 12, mai 73 : 5-32.

849    DELORD, P. "L'aménagement de la région du Bas-Rhône et du Languedoc", *B. Inform. Comité Agence Bassin Rhône-Méditer.-Corse* 4, dec 72 : 16-34. [France].

850    "Desarrollo regional", *Bol. Estud. econ. (Bilbao)* 27(86), aug 72 : 305-793.

851    "Desarrollo regional, una problema de justicia" (Regional development, a problem of justice), *R. Fomento soc.* 28(108), oct-dec 72 : 353-409. [Spain.]

852    DURRIEU, Y. *L'impossible régionalisation capitaliste; témoignages de Fos et du Languedoc.* Paris, Anthropos, 73, 268 p. [France.]

853    ÉL'MEEV, V. Ja.; RJASČENKO, B. R.; JUDIN, È. P. *Kompleksnoe planirovanie ėkonomičeskogo i social'nogo razvitija rajona* (Complex planning of the region's economic and social development). Leningrad, Lenizdat, 72, 126 p. [USSR.]

854    FIOCCO, S. *Problemi di sviluppo della regione abruzzese* (Problems of the development of the Abruzzi region). L'Aquila, L.U. Japadre, 72, 149 p. [Italy.]

855    FISCHER, G. *Praxisorientierte Theorie der Regionalforschung* (Praxis oriented theory for regional research). Tübingen, Mohr, 73, x-300 p. [Switzerland.]

856    FISK, T.; JONES, K. *Regional development.* London, Fabian Society, 72, 2-36 p. [UK.]

857    GAUTHIER, H. L.; SEMPLE, R. K. "Tendências nas desigualdades regionais da economia brasileira" (Tendencies of regional inequalities of the Brazilian economy), *Dados* 9, 1972 : 103-113.

858    GEISENBERGER, S. "Raumordnungspolitik in der Marktwirtschaft" (Regional planning in a system of market economy), *Civitas (Mannheim)* (11), 1972 : 139-155. [Germany, FR.]

859    GEORGE, P. "La place de la région dans l'évolution des techniques de planification et de gestion socialistes", *Ét. int.* 3(4), dec 72 : 485-492.

860    GERSDORFF, R. VON. "General remarks on regional sociology and on the elaboration of 'profiles of types of regions' ", *Amér. lat.* 13(4), oct-dec 70 : 71-77.

861    GIOJA, R. I. *Planeamiento urbano y regional en Brasil* (Urban and regional planning in Brazil). Buenos Aires, Ediciones DRUSA, 72, 59 p.

862    HALLETT, G.; RANDALL, P. J.; WEST, E. G. *Regional policy forever? Essays on the history, theory and political economy of forty years of 'regionalism'.* London, Institute of Economic Affairs, 73, xii-152 p.

863    HAZELHOFF, D. *Over de samenhang tussen economische, sociaal-culturele en ruimtelijke planning in Nederland* (On the connection between economic, socio-cultural and spatial planning in the Netherlands). 's-Gravenhage, Staatsuitgeverij, 72, 24 p.

864    HILLS, G. A.; LOVE, D. V.; LACATE, D. S. *Developing a better environment: ecological land-use planning in Ontario; a study of methodology in the development of regional plans.* Toronto, Ontario Economic Council, 73, xi-175-7 p.

865    HOOSON, D. "The outlook for regional development in the Soviet Union", *Slavic R.* 31(3), sep 72 : 535-554.

866    ISARD, W. *et al. Ecologico-economic analysis for regional development. Some initial ex-*

*plorations with particular reference to recreational resource use and environmental planning.* New York, Free Press; London, Collier-Macmillan, 72, xviii-270 p.

867   ISTITUTO PER LA SCIENZA DELL'AMMINISTRAZIONE PUBBLICA. *La regione e il governo del territorio* (The region and regional planning). Milano, Giuffrè, 72, 156 p.

868   JAATINEN, S. "Aluesuunnittelun perusongelmat" (Basic problems of regional planning), *Terra* 85(1), 1973 : 4-11.

869   Bibl. XXI-1142. KAIN, J. F.; MEYER, J. R. (eds.). *Essays in regional economics.* CR: J. H. CUMBERLAND, *J. econ. Liter.* 11(2), jun 73 : 593-594.

870   KOŁODZIEJSKI, J. *Model planowania regionalnego* (Model of regional planning). Warszawa, Państwowe Wydawnictwo Naukowe, 72, 153 p.

871   KOVAĆ, B. "Model procesa reprodukcije malog područja" (A model for the process of small region reproduction), *Ekon. Misao* 6(2), jun 73 : 126-140.

872   KUKLINKI, A. R. (ed.). *Growth poles and growth centres in regional planning.* The Hague, Mouton, 72, x-306 p.

873   LACOUR, C. *Aménagement du territoire et développement régional.* Paris, Dalloz, 73, 115 p. [France.]

874   LEAHY, W. H.; McKEE, D. L. "A Schumpeterian view of the regional economy" *Growth and Change* 3(4), oct 72 : 23-25.

875   Bibl. XXI-1159. LEFEBER, L.; DATTA-CHAUDHURI, M. *Regional development: experiences and prospects in South and Southeast Asia.* CR: P. DESAI, *J. econ. Liter.* 11(1), mar 73 : 136-138.

876   LEVIN, M. R. *Community and regional planning; issues in public policy.* Rev. and updated ed. New York, Praeger, 72, xv-343 p.

877   LUTTRELL, W. L. "Location planning and regional development in Tanzania", *Develop. and Change* 4(1), 1972-73 : 17-38.

878   MALISZ, B. *Metody planowania regionalnego* (Methods of regional planning) Warszawa, Państwowe Wydawnictwo Naukowe, 72, 124 p.

879   MASSER, I. *Analytical models for urban and regional planning.* Newton Abbot, David and Charles; New York, Halsted Press Division, 72, 164 p.

880   MIHAILOVIĆ, K. *Regional development. Experiences and prospects in Eastern Europe.* The Hague, Mouton, 72, xiv-221 p.

881   MOORE, B.; RHODES, J. "Evaluating the effects of British regional economic policy", *Econ. J.* 83(329), mar 73 : 87-110.

882   MUSSATI, G. "La compatibilità delle decisioni fra pianificazione regionale e pianificazione nazionale" (Decision compatibility between regional planning and national planning), *Riv. Polit. econ.* 63(4), apr 73 : 435-463.

883   NÄSLUND, M.; PERSSON, S. *Regionalpolitik* (Regional policy). Stockholm, Norstedt, 72, 270 p. [Sweden.]

884   NEWMAN, M. *The political economy of Appalachia: a case study in regional integration.* London-Toronto-Lexington, Mass., Heath and Co., 72, xviii-192 p. CR: W. H. MIERNYK, *J. econ. Liter.* 11(3), sep 73 : 964-966.

885   OPAŁŁO, M. *Mierniki rozwoju regionów* (Measures of regional development). Warszawa, Państwowe Wydawnictwo Ekonomiczne, 72, 282 p.

886   ORTMANN, F. *Überlegungen zur regionalpolitischen Anwendbarkeit des Multiplikatorkonzeptes* (Reflections on the use of the multiplier concept in regional planning). Tübingen, Mohr, 73, v-184 p.

887   PLATT, R. H. *The open space decision process: spatial allocation of costs and benefits.* Chicago, University of Chicago, Department of Geography, 72, xi-189 p. [USA.]

888   POTZCH, R.; VOIGT, F. (eds.). *Le développement régional et les secteurs économiques. Résultats de la recherche comparative européenne sur les régions en retard des pays industrialisés.* La Haye-Paris, Mouton, 72, 273 p.

889   REY, V. "Organisation régionale et structure urbaine de la Roumanie, d'après la littérature géographique roumaine récente", *A. Géogr.* 81 (448), nov-dec 72 : 711-729.

890   REYE, U. "Teoria del desarrollo regional" (Regional development theory), *Adm. y Desar.* 12, 1973 : 113-183.

891   RICHARDSON, H. W. *Regional growth theory.* London, Macmillan; New York, Wiley, 73, viii-264 p.

892   ROSS, M. "Procedures for integrated regional planning: the background to decentralisation", *Econ. and soc. R.* 4(4), jul 73 : 523-542. [Ireland.]

893    ROUSSELOT, M. "La régionalisation du VIe Plan", *Aménag. Territ. Dévelop. région.* (6),
       1973 : 41-95. [France.]

894    SADLER, P.; ARCHER, B.; OWEN, C. *Regional income multipliers: the Anglesey study.*
       Cardiff, University of Wales Press, 73, xii-109 p.

895    SECOMSKI, K. (ed.). *Elementy teorii planowania przestrzennego* (Elements of regional
       planning theory). Warszawa, Państwowe Wydawnictwo Naukowe, 72, 221 p.

896    "Statistiques et indicateurs de régions françaises. Édition 1972", *Coll. INSÉÉ Sér. R.*
       (9); dec 72 : 1-336.

897    STOUSE, P. A. D. Jr. "Regional specialization in developing areas: the altiplano of
       Bolivia", *R. geogr. (Rio de Janeiro)* 74, jun 71 : 51-67.

898    TINDAL, C. R. "Regional development in Ontario", *Canad. publ. Adm.* 16(1), 1973 :
       110-123.

899    TOWN, G. A. (ed.). *Policies for regional development in New Zealand.* Wellington, New
       Zealand Institute of Public Administration, 72, 124 p.

900    TRIAS FARGAS, R. *Introducció a l'economia de Catalunya, un anàlisi regional* (Introduction
       to the economy of Catalonia, a regional analysis). Barcelona, Edicions 62, 72, 140 p.

901    VETTORI, P. *La programmazione economica regionale in Italia* (Italian regional economic
       planning). Pisa, Giardini, 72, 147 p.

### F.312    *Demographical aspects*
           *Aspects démographiques*

[See also / Voir aussi: **G.211**; **G.213**; **O.126**; 2564, 2577, 3164, 4448, 4743]

902    BAHR, H. M.; CHADWICK, B. A.; THOMAS, D. L. (eds.). *Population, resources, and the
       future; non-Malthusian perspectives.* Provo, Utah; Brigham Young University Press,
       72, vii-352 p.

903    BARKIN, D. "A Mexican case study: the demographic impact of regional development",
       *Growth and Change* 3(4), oct 72 : 15-22.

904    BEN-PORATH, Y. "Short-term fluctuations in fertility and economic activity in Israel",
       *Demography (Ann Arbor)* 10(2), mai 73 : 185-204.

905    BLANDY, R.; WERY, R. "Population and employment growth: Bachue-1", *Int. Lab. R.*
       107(5), mai 73 : 441-449.

906    BOROWSKI, S. "Differentiation of fertility in the conditions of progressing industrializa-
       tion and urbanization", *Stud. Demogr.* 34, 1973 : 13-33.

907    BOROWSKI, S. "Perspektywy badań demograficznych w Polsce" (The perspectives of
       demographic studies in Poland), *Ruch prawn. ekon. socjol.* 4, 1973 : 57-70.

908    BUTZ, W. P.; SCHULTZ, T. P. *An information strategy for improving population policy in
       low-income countries.* Santa Monica, Rand Corporation, 72, 19 p.

909    CAIN, G. G.; WEININGER, A. "Economic determinants of fertility: results from cross-
       sectional aggregate data", *Demography (Ann Arbor)* 10(2), mai 73 : 205-221.

910    CHIASSINO, G.; COMITE, L. DI. "Sulla struttura della mortalità in Italia e in Belgio"
       (On the structure of mortality in Italy and in Belgium), *G. Economisti* 31(7-8), jul-aug
       72 : 446-468.

911    CLARK, C. "Popolazione e sviluppo" (Population and development), *Riv. Polit. econ.*
       63(3), mar 73 : 307-322.

912    COCHRANE, S. H. "Population and development: a more general model", *Econ. Develop.
       cult. Change* 21(3), apr 73 : 409-422.

913    DENTON, F. T.; SPENCER, B. G. "A simulation analysis of the effects of population
       change on a neoclassical economy", *J. polit. Econ.* 81(2), mar-apr 73 : 356-375.

914    DJOKANOVIC, T. "La population et le développement économique des pays sous-
       développés", *Quest. act. Social.* 115, sep 73 : 91-106.

915    "Economics of population", *Amer. econ. R.* 63(2), mai 73 *Pap. and Proc.*: 71-89. With
       contributions by: T. P. SCHULTZ, J. L. FISHER, R. G. RIDKER and D. G. JOHNSON.

916    GALLAWAY, L. E. "The quality of life, population, and environment: the importance of
       historical perspective", *R. soc. Econ.* 30(1), mar 72 : 37-45.

917    GLASS, D. V.; REVELLE, R. (eds.). *Population and social change.* London, E. Arnold;
       New York, Crane, Russak, 72, vii-520 p.

918    JAEGER, K. *Altersstrukturveränderungen der Bevölkerung. Ersparnis und wirtschaftliches*

*Wachstum: eine theoretische Analyse* (Modification of population age structure. Savings on economic growth; a theoretical analysis). Berlin, Duncker und Humblot, 73, 293 p.

919 Jones, G. W.; Selvaratnam, S. *Population growth and economic development in Ceylon.* Colombo, Hansa Publishers, 72, xii-249 p.

920 Kitagawa, E. M.; Hauser, P. M. *Differential mortality in the United States: a study in socioeconomic epidemiology.* Cambridge, Mass., Harvard University Press, 73, xx-255 p.

921 Kleinman, D. S. "Fertility variation and ressources in rural India (1961)" *Econ. Develop. cult. Change* 21(4), *Part I* jul 73 : 679-696.

922 Leistner, G. M. E. *Population and resources in Southern Africa.* Pretoria, Africa Institute of South Africa, 72, 29 p.

923 McIntyre, R. J. "The fertility response to abortion reform in Eastern Europe: demographic and economic implications", *Amer. Economist* 16(2), 1972 : 64-65.

924 Morss, E. R.; Reed, R. H. (eds.). *Economic aspects of population change.* Washington, United States Government Printing Office, 73, xii-379 p.

925 "New economic approaches to fertility", *J. polit. Econ.* 81(2), mar-apr 73 : 2-299.

926 Ominde, S. H.; Ejiogu, C. N. *Population growth and economic development in Africa.* London, Heinemann, 72, xxii-421 p.

927 Patiño, R. E. "Presión demográfica, productividad agrícola y empleo" (Demographic pressure, agricultural productivity and employment), *R. Econ. latinoamer.* 9(36), 1973 : 159-181.

928 Peterhoff, R. "Demographische Probleme Polens unter dem Aspekt der Industrialisierung" (Poland's demographic problems concerning industrialization), *Osteuropa* 23(2), feb 73 : 128-136.

929 Pitchford, J. "Population and optimal growth", *Econometrica* 40(1), jan 72 : 109-136.

930 "Population des pays du Marché commun (La): problèmes économiques et sociaux", *Inform. soc. (Paris)* 26(11), nov 72 : 2-95.

931 Ridker, R. G. (ed.). *Population, resources and the environment.* Washington, United States Government Printing Office, 72, 377 p.

932 Roeske-Słomka, I. "Współzależność naturalnego rozwoju demograficznego i wzrostu gospodarczego regionów" (The interrelationship between natural demographic development and the economic growth of regions), *Stud. demogr.* 31, 1973 : 85-100.

933 "Série socio-démographique: activité sociale et économique de la population", *Indicateurs Écon. Centre* 1-2, jul 72 : 3-34. [France.]

934 Singh, I.; Srivastava, D.; Gupta, Y. P. "Impact of population growth on farm household incomes in Daryapur Kalan village of the union territory of Delhi", *Sociol. rur.* 12(3-4), 1972 : 450-456.

935 Sly, D. F.; Chi, P. "Economic development, modernization and demographic behavior: longitudinal analysis of mortality change", *Amer. J. Econ. Sociol.* 31(4), oct 72 ; 373-386.

936 Spengler, J. J. *Population economics: selected essays.* Compiled by R. S. Smith, et al. Durham, N. C., Duke University Press, 72, 536 p. CR: M. R. Haines, *Contemp. Sociol.* 2(5), sep 73 : 559-562

937 Stockwell, E. G. "Some observations on the relationship between population growth and economic development during the 1960s", *Rur. Sociol.* 37(4), dec 72 : 628-632.

938 Thirlwall, A. P. "A cross section study of population growth and the growth of output and per capita income in a production function framework", *Manchester Sch. Econ. soc. Stud.* 40(4), dec 72 : 339-356.

939 United States. Bureau of Economic Analysis. *Population and economic activity in the United States and standard metropolitan statistical areas, historical and projected, 1950-2020.* Washington, BEA, 72, ix-521 p.

940 Vaz da Costa, R. "Crescimento populacional e desenvolvimento econômico" (Population growth and economic development), *R. mexic. Sociol.* 34(2), apr-jun 72 : 317-334. [Brazil.]

941 Žučenko, V. S.; Ste enko, V. S. *Vlijanie social'no-ěkonomičeskih faktorov na demografičeskie processy* (The influence of socio-economic factors on demographic processes). Kiev, Naukova Dumka, 72, 238 p.

**F.313    *Sociological aspects***
**   *Aspects sociologiques***

[See also / Voir aussi: 1910, 2731, 4508, 4549, 4686, 5456, 6020]

942    Arskaja, L. P. *"Otrytaja ėkonomika" i rabočij klass Japonii* (The "open economy" and the working class in Japan). Moskva, Nauka, 72, 146 p.

943    Campo, E. del. "Estructura social del Ecuador" (Social structure of Ecuador), *Economía (Quito)* 8(57), jan 73 : 48-64.

944    Černjak, V. A.; Rozenberg, C. R. "Izmenenie social'noj struktury obščestva i proizvodstvennyj kollektiv" (Society's social structure changes and the productive collectivity), *Filos. Nauki* (2), 1973 : 51-62.

945    Chodak, S. "Brotherhood or otherhood ? Some aspects of societal change in modernizing rural Africa", *Sociol. rur.* 12(3-4), 1972 : 302-314.

946    Gonzalez Salazar, G. "Crecimiento económico y desigualdad social en México: una visión esquemática" (Economic growth and social inequality in Mexico: a schematic vision), *R. mexic. Sociol.* 33(3), jul-sep 71 : 541-562.

947    Goussault, Y. "Stratifications sociales et coopération agricole", *Tiers-Monde* 14(54), apr-jun 73 : 281-294.

948    Gueda, P. "A propos des soi-disant nouvelles 'couches moyennes' ", *Crit. Écon. polit.* (11-12), apr-sep 73 : 192-206. [France.]

949    Ianni, O. "La formación del proletariado rural en el Brasil" (The formation of the rural proletariat in Brazil), *R. mexic. Sociol.* 33(3), jul-sep 71 : 475-488.

950    Ionescu, C. "Economic factors of change in the social structure", *R. roum. Sci. soc. Sér. Sociol.* 16, 1972 : 17-28.

951    Klocke, H. "Zur Sozialstruktur der landwirtschaftlichen Bevölkerung Ungarns" (Social structure of the Hungarian agricultural population), *Osteuropa* 23(1), jan 73 : 29-42.

952    Mandić, I. "Ekonomski položaj radničke klase Jugoslavije" (Economic position of the working class in Yugoslavia), *Sociologija* 14(3), 1972 : 461-475.

953    Mines, M. *Muslim merchants; the economic behaviour of an Indian Muslim community.* New Delhi, Shri Ram Centre for Industrial Relations and Human Resources, 72, vi-136 p.

954    Peralta Ramos, M. *Etapas de acumulación y alianzas de clases en la Argentina (1930-1970)* (Stages of accumulation and class alliances in Argentina, 1930-1970). Buenos Aires, Siglo Veintiuno Argentina Editores, 72, 187 p.

955    Rjabova, I. A. *Rabočij klass i profojuzy Malajzii* (The Malaysian working class and trade unions). Moskva, Nauka, 72, 148 p.

956    Rouveyran, J. C. *La logique des agricultures de transition: l'exemple des sociétés paysannes malgaches.* Paris, G. P. Maisonneuve et Larose, 72, 277 p.

957    Smith, A. H.; Martin, W. E. "The socio-economic behavior of cattle ranchers, with implications for rural community development in the West", *Amer. J. agric. Econ.* 54(2), mai 72 : 217-225. [USA.]

958    "Social stratification and career mobility", *Soc. Sci. Inform./Inform. Sci. soc.* 11(5), oct 72 : 7-390.

958    *Struktura i ruchliwosc społeczna* (Social structure and mobility). Wrocław Zakład Narodowy im. Ossolińskich, 73, 271 p.

960    Sylos Labini, P. "Sviluppo economico e classi in Italia" (Economic development and social classes in Italy), *Quad. Sociol.* 21(4), oct-dec 72 : 371-443.

961    Widerszpil, S. *Przeobrazenia struktury społecznej w Polsce Ludowej* (Transformations of the social structure in the Polish People's Republic). Warszawa, Ksiażka i Wiedza, 73, 287 p.

962    Zorin, V. I.; Grivennaja, V. K. "Social'no-professional'naja struktura sel'skohozjajstvennoj intelligencii ee razvitija v uslovijah naučnotehničeskoj revoljucii" (The agricultural intelligentsia's socio-professional structure and trends of its development in the scientific and technical revolution conditions), *Filos. Nauki* (2), 1973 : 62-71.

**F.314**   *Legal aspects: property rights*
*Aspects juridiques: droits de propriété*

[See also / Voir aussi: **H.1123; 1823**]

963   EREMIN, A. M. *Otnošenija socialističeskoj sobstvennosti i ěkonomičeskoe upravlenie* (Relations between socialist property and economic management). Moskva, Ekonomika, 73, 119 p.

964   FURUBOTN, E.; PEJOVICH, S. "Property rights and economic theory: a survey of recent literature", *J. econ. Liter.* 10(4), dec 72 : 1137-1162.

965   HESSIN, N. V. "O dvuh osnovnyh napravlenijah analiza sobstvennosti i ego meste v sisteme socialističeskih proizvodstvennyh otnošenij" (The two main trends of the analysis of property and its place in the system of socialist production relations), *Vestn. Moskov. Univ. Ser. Ěkon.* 28(3), mai-jun 73 : 58-72.

966   IGNATOVSKIJ, P. A. "Razvitie osobščestvlenija proizvodstva i sbliženie dvuh form socialističeskoj sobstvennosti" (Development of production socialization and the bringing together of two forms of socialist property), in: *Ěkonomičeskie i social'no-političeskie problemy kommunističeskogo stroitel'stva v SSSR.* Moskva, 1972 : 48-60.

967   KARDELJ, E. "Les contradictions de la propriété sociale dans la pratique socialiste contemporaine", *Quest. act. Social.* 108, aug-dec 72 : 26-56. [Yougoslavia.]

968   KOSTA, J. "Über den Eigentumsbegriff im Sozialismus" (The concept of property under socialism), *Osteuropa* 23(7), jul 73 : 511-521.

969   MOLNÁR, E. "A tulajdon marxista értelmezése" (The marxist interpretation of property), *Közgazd. Szle* 20(5), mai 73 : 573-587.

970   NICOLAU, V. "Cocul şi rolul proprietătii personale în socialism" (Place and role of individual property under socialism), *Probl. econ. (Bucuresti)* 26(9), sep 73 : 29-37.

971   RUBANOV, A. A. "Social'nye aspekty prava licnoj sobstvennosti v SSSR" (Social aspects of personal property rights in the USSR), *Sov. Gos. Pravo* 46(9), sep 73 : 25-32.

972   SALZWEDEL, J. "Verfassungsrechtlich geschützte Besitzstände und ihre "Uberleitung" in neues Recht — Zur Theorie der gesetzesfesten Rechtspositionen" (The right of property provided by the Constitution and its "transposition" in the new legislation. On the theory of juridical positions rooted in the law), *Verwaltung* 5(1), 1972 : 11-36. [Germany FR.]

973   SIRJAEV, Ju. "Socialističeskaja sobstvennost' v uslovijah ěkonomičeskoj integracii stran-členov SEV" (Socialist property in the conditions of economic integration of CAEM countries), *Vopr. Liter.* 17(7), jul 73 : 94-102.

974   SPOO, E. (ed.). *Fetisch Eigentum: wie privat sind Grund und Boden?* (The property fetish: to what point is land a private good?). München, Hanser, 72, 94 p.

**F.32**   **Underdevelopment**
**Sous-développement**

**F.320**   *General studies*
*Études générales*

[See also / Voir aussi: **F.330;** 2212, 2389, 2578, 2585, 2753, 3238, 3885, 3992, 4095, 4321, 4409, 4410, 4414, 4481, 4748, 5156, 5359, 5473, 5514, 5817, 5845, 6325, 6331, 6498]

975   AFXENTIOU, P. "Underdevelopment and government intervention", *Riv. int. Sci. econ. com.* 19(10), oct 72 : 954-970.

976   AGBODAN, M. T. *Die Imitation als Phase in Entwicklungsprozess und ihre Rückwirkung auf den technischen Fortschritt* (Imitation: a phase of the development process and its retroaction on technical progress). Meisenheim-am-Glan, A. Hain, 73, x-172 p.

977   ALPERT, P. *Partnership or confrontation? Poor lands and rich.* New York, The Free Press; London, Collier-Macmillan, 73, xiv-269 p.

978   BANERJI, R.; DONGES, J. B. *Economic development and the patterns of manufactured exports.* Kiel, Institut für Weltwirtschaft, 72, 24 p.

979   BEHRMAN, J. R. "Short-run flexibility in a developing economy", *J. polit. Econ.* 80(2), mar-apr 72 : 292-313.

980   BENOT, Y. *Qu'est-ce que le développement?* Paris, F. Maspéro, 73, 185 p.

981    BERGMANN, H. "Einige Anwendungsmöglichkeiten der Entwicklungsskalierung von Leik und Matthews" (Some possible applications of Leik's and Matthew's development scale), *Z. Soziol.* 2(3), jul 73 : 207-226.

982    BERNSTEIN, H. (ed.). *Underdevelopment and development: the Third World today: selected readings.* Harmondsworth, Penguin, 73, 384 p.

983    BLARDONE, G. *Progrès économique dans le Tiers-monde, environnement socio-politique, croissance démographique et urbanisation.* Paris, Librairie sociale et économique, 72, 237 p.

984    BURNET, I. D. "An interpretation of take-off", *Econ. Rural* 48(123), sep 72 : 424-428.

985    CHALMERS, D. A. "Demystification of development", *Changing Latin Amer.* 30(4), aug 72 : 109-122.

986    ELKAN, W. *An introduction to development economics.* Harmondsworth, Penguin, 73, 155 p.

987    EVERS, T. T.; WOGAU, P. VON. "Dependencia': lateinamerikanische Beiträge zur Theorie der Unterentwicklung" ('Dependency': Latin American contributions to the theory of underdevelopment), *Argument* 15(4-6), jul 73 : 404-454.

988    "Experience of development (The)", *Amer. econ. R.* 63(2), mai 73, *Pap. and Proc.*: 450-468. With contributions by: A. C. KELLEY, J. WILLIAMSON, H. B. CHENERY and N. G. CARTER.

989    FARKAS, P. et al. *The economic situation of developing countries in 1971.* Budapest, Hungarian Academy of Sciences, 72, 44 p.

990    FARMER, R. N. *Benevolent aggression; the necessary impact of the advanced nations on indigenous peoples.* New York, David McKay Co., 72, xiv-337 p.

991    FINKSTERBUSCH, K. "Recent rank ordering of nations on terms of level and rate of development", *Stud. comp. int. Develop.* 8(1), print 73 : 52-70.

992    FURTADO, C. "Il mito dello sviluppo e il futuro del Terzo Mondo" (The myth of development and the future of the Third World), *Aff. est.* 5(19), jul 73 : 130-141.

993    GARZOUZI, E. *Economic growth and development: the less developed countries.* New York, Vantage Press, 72, 359 p.

994    GOH, K. S. *The economics of modernization and other essays.* Singapore, Asia Pacific Press, 72, x-294 p.

995    GRANAHAM, D. V. et al. *Contents and measurement of socioeconomic development; a staff study.* New York, Praeger, 72, xiv-161 p.

996    GRANIER, R. "Essai sur la nature de la croissance rapide des pays moins développés (1950-1969)," *Ét. int.* 3(4), dec 72 : 516-557.

997    HERMANN, H. H. *Wettlauf mit dem Chaos. Eine Sozialökonomie der Dritten Welt* (Race against chaos. A social economy of the Third World). Rowohlt (Tashenbuch-Verlag), 72, 122 p.

998    HOLLIMAN, J. *The ecology of world development.* London, Voluntary Committee on Overseas Development, 72, 32 p.

999    "Inégal développement (L')", *Mondes en Dévelop.* (1), 1973 : 21-193.

1000   JAFFE, A. J. "Notes on developing countries and their statistics", *R. Income Wealth* 18(3), sep 72 : 313-326.

1001   JAYARAMAN, R. "Some theoretical considerations in the study of social development in the Third World", *Sociol. rur.* 13(3-4), 1973 : 237-254.

1002   KASDAN, A. R. *The third world; a new focus for development.* Cambridge, Mass., Schenkman Pub. Co., Morristown, N. J., General Learning Press, 73, xi-127 p.

1003   KELLEY, A. C.; WILLIAMSON, G.; CHEETHAM, R. J. *Dualistic economic development: theory and history.* Chicago, University of Chicago Press, 72, xi-399 p.

1004   KHALATBARI, P. "Zu den demographisch-ökonomischen Hemmnissen der Wirtschaftswachstums in den Entwicklungsländern" (Demographic and economic obstacles to the growth of developing countries), *Wirtsch.-Wiss.* 21(1), jan 73 : 62-79.

1005   KUZ'MIN, S. A. *Sistemnyj analiz ėkonomiki razvivajuščihsja stran (Problemy metodologii)* (Systems analysis of the developing countries economy. Methodological problems). Moskva, Nauka, 72, 317 p.

1006   McNAMARA, R. S. *One hundred countries, two billion people; the dimensions of development.* London, Pall Mall Press; New York, Praeger Publishers, 73, 140 p.

1007   MEIRA PENNA, J. O. DE. *Psicologia do subdesenvolvimento* (Psychology of underdevelopment). Rio de Janeiro, APEC Editora, 72, 231 p.

1008 PAPIC, A. "Les pays non-alignés et le développement économique", *Quest. act. Social.* 114, aug 73 : 3-28.

1009 PASINETTI, L. "I problemi dello sviluppo economico e i paesi del 'Terzo Mondo' " (The problems of economic development and the Third World countries), *Riv. int. Sci. soc.* 80(5-6), sep-dec 72 : 599-616.

1010 PETRALIAS, N. S. *Kritische Beiträge zur Theorie der dualistischen Entwicklung* (Critical contributions to the theory of dualist development) Meisenheim-am-Glan, A. Hain, 73, v-325-viii p.

1011 Bibl. XXI-1364. POWELSON, J. *Institutions of economic growth. A theory of conflict management in developing countries.* CR: R. HOLLEY, *J. econ. Liter.* 11(1), mar 73 : 95-96; D. NACHMIAS, *Amer. polit. Sci. R.* 67(3), sep 73 : 1085-1086.

1012 PRIEBE, H. (ed.). *Das Eigenpotential im Entwicklungsprozess* (Self-potential in the development process). Berlin, Duncker und Humblot, 72, 110 p.

1013 RAO, M. S. A. *Tradition, rationality, and change; essays in sociology of economic development and social change.* Bombay, Popular Prakashan, 72, 182 p.

1014 Bibl. XXI-1367. SACHS, I. *La découverte du Tiers-Monde.* CR: C. BRAULT, *R. franç. Sociol.* 13, 1972 *Suppl.:* 733-734.

1015 SELLEKAERTS, W.; SELLEKAERTS, B. "Les réserves optimales pour les pays développés et en voie de développement", *Ét. int.* 3(3), sep 72 : 318-329.

1016 SIMHA, S. L. N. (ed.). *Economic and social development.* Bombay, Vora, 72, xix-492 p.

1017 SOARES, G. A. D. "Desarrollo económico y estructura de clases" (Economic development and class structure), *R. mexic. Sociol.* 33(3), jul-sep 71 : 437-474.

1018 STEIN, L. *Economic realities in poor countries.* Sydney, Angus and Robertson Education, 72, 199 p.

1019 Bibl. XXI-1373. SZENTES, T. *The political economy of underdevelopment.* CR: W.W. ROSTOW, *Amer. polit. Sci. R.* 67(3), sep 73 : 1091-1093.

1020 THIRLWALL, A. P. *Growth and development: with special reference to developing economies.* London, Macmillan, 72, xiv-322 p.

1021 UVALIĆ, R. *Nerazvijena područja u razvijenim zapadnim zemljama* (Underdeveloped areas in Western developed countries: a comparative study). Beograd, Srpska akademija nauka i umetnosti, Ekonomski institut, 72, 244 p.

1022 VAN NIEUWENHUIJZE, C. A. O. (ed.). *Development: the Western view | La perspective occidentale du développement.* The Hague, Mouton, 72, 295 p.

1023 VERWEY, W. D. *Economic development, peace, and international law.* Assen, Van Gorcum, 72, xx-362 p.

1024 WALESZKO, M. *Elementy teorii rozwoju gospodarki socjalistycznej* (Elements of the theory of the development of the socialist economy). Katowice, Wydawnictwo Uniwersytetu Saskiego, 72, 109 p.

## F.321 *Local studies*
### *Études localisées*

[See also / Voir aussi: **O.134;** 2372, 2751, 2928, 3153, 3181, 3429, 4105, 4113, 4346, 4838, 4981, 5081, 5286, 5335, 5701, 5769, 7313, 6358, 6561]

1025 ALLEN, C.; KING, K. (eds.). *Developmental trends in Kenya; proceedings of a seminar.* Edinburgh, Centre of African Studies, University of Edinburgh 73, 337 p.

1026 "Amérique latine. Faits et doctrines du développement", *Mondes en Dévelop.* (3), 1973 : 9-162.

1027 AMIN, C. A. "Arab economic growth and imbalances 1945-1970", *Égypte contemp.* 63(350), oct 72 : 257-295.

1028 AMIN, S. "Développement et transformations structurelles: l'expérience de l'Afrique, 1950-1970", *R. Tiers-Monde* 13(51), jul-sep 72 : 467-490.

1029 AMIN, S. "Underdevelopment and dependence in Black Africa: origins and contemporary forms", *J. mod. Afr. Stud.* 10(4), dec 72 : 503-524.

1030 ASHCRAFT, N. *Colonialism and underdevelopment: processes of political economic change in British Honduras.* New York, Teachers College Press, 73, ix-180 p.

1031 BELEKY, L. P. "Development of Liberia", *J. mod. Afr. Stud.* 11(1), mar 73 : 43-60.

49

1032    BONONO D'AMICO, S. "Una aproximación al desarrollo político y económico de Vene-
        zuela" (An approach to the political and economic development of Venezuela),
        *Amér. lat.* 13(4), oct-dec 70 : 18-32.

1033    BRAVO BRESANI, J.; SAGASTI, F. "Elementos para una estrategia del desarrollo en el
        contexto del sistema global" (Elements for a development strategy in the global
        system context), *Mondes en Dévelop.* 1, 1973 : 47-92 [Peru.]

1034    BUNEGINA, I. "Tendencii razvitija brazilskoj ěkonomiki" (Tendencies of Brazilian
        economic development), *Mir. Ékon. meždun. Otnoš.* 16(6), jun 73 : 125-132.

1035    CAMILLERI, C. *Jeunesse, famille et développement. Essai sur le changement socio-culturel
        dans un pays du Tiers-Monde (Tunisie)*. Paris, Editions du CNRS, 73, viii-507 p.

1036    CAMPBELL, G. *Brazil struggles for development.* London, Charles Knight, 72, ix-206 p.

1037    CARDOSO, F. H. "Dependency and development in Latin America", *New Left R.* 74,
        jul-aug. 72 : 83-95.

1038    CHALMERS, D. A. "The demystification of development", *Proc. Acad. polit. Sci.* 30(4),
        aug 72 : 109-122. [Latin America.]

1039    "China's developmental experience", *Proc. Acad. polit. Sci.* 31(1), mar 73 : 1-227.

1040    Bibl. XXI-1394. COOPER, C. A.; ALEXANDER, S. S. (eds.). *Economic development and
        population growth in the Middle East.* CR: H. S. ATESOGLU, *J. econ. Liter.* 11(3), sep
        73 : 917-918.

1041    CORONA RENTERIA, A. "El comercio exterior y el crecimiento económico de México"
        (Foreign trade and the economic growth of Mexico), *Investig. econ.* 31(122), apr-
        jun 71 : 265-304.

1042    "Côte d'Ivoire: la poursuite de l'expansion et ses nouvelles bases", *Europe France
        O.-Mer (Paris)* 50(516), jan 73 : 8-60.

1043    DAMACHI, U. G.; SEIBEL, H. D. (eds.). *Social change and economic development in Nigeria.*
        New York, Praeger, 73, xxiii-252 p.

1044    DEHAVEN, R. K. "Economic development policy in Peron's Argentina", *Econ. Aff.*
        17(1-2), jan-feb 72 : 83-91.

1045    DESHMUKH, C. D. *Aspects of development.* New Delhi, Young Asia Publication 72,
        300-2 p. [India.]

1046    DIBB, P. *Siberia and the Pacific: a study of economic development and trade prospects.*
        New York, Praeger Publishers, 72, xxii-288 p.

1047    DORTICOS, D. "Análisis y perspectivas del desarrollo de la economía cubana" (Analysis
        and perspectives of development of the Cuban economy), *Econ. e Desarr.* 12, jul-aug
        72 : 28-61.

1048    DUQUE, H. *As contradições no desenvolvimento brasileiro* (Contradictions of Brazilian
        development). Rio de Janeiro, Editora Paralelo, 72, 220 p.

1049    ECKSTEIN, A. "Economic growth and change in China: a twenty-year perspective",
        *China Quart.* 54, apr-jun 73 : 211-241.

1050    ESTÉVEZ, A. (ed.). *Desarrollo económico y planificación en la República Argentina: selección
        bibliográfica, 1930-1972* (Economic development and planning in the Argentine
        Republic: a bibliographical selection, 1930-1972) Buenos Aires, Consejo Federal de
        Inversiones, 72, 394 p.

1051    FERRARI BRAVO, L. *Stato e sottosviluppo. Il caso del Mezzogiorno italiano* (State and
        underdevelopment. The case of the Italian South). Milano, Feltrinelli, 72, 177 p.

1052    FERREIRA, C. N.; FERREIRA, L. DOM; MOLETTA, E. T. *Bibliografia seletiva sobre desen-
        volvimento econômico no Brasil* (A selective bibliography on economic development
        in Brazil). Rio de Janeiro, IPEA/Doc., 72, 96 p.

1053    FRISS, I. "Underdevelopment and experiences of East-European socialist countries",
        *Acta oecon.* 9(3-4), 1972 : 359-364.

1054    FURTADO, C. "The post 1964 Brazilian model of development", *Stud. comp. int. Develop.*
        8(2), 1973 : 115-127.

1055    GALLARDO, J. "Financial structure and the direction of economic development in the
        Philippines", *Philippine econ. J.* 10(2), 2 sem. 72 : 215-240.

1056    GOERING, J. M. "Social effects and limitations of development planning: the case of
        Indonesia and Singapore", *Hum. Org.* 31(4), hiv 72 : 385-393.

1057    GRACIARENA, J. "La dinámica del capitalismo subdesarrollado en América Latina"
        (The dynamics of underdeveloped capitalism in Latin America), *Foro int.* 13(4),
        apr-jun 73 : 427-441.

1058 GUZMAN FERRER, M. L.; AGUILAR ALVAREZ, I.; LAMADRID IBARRA, A. "México: desarrollo de las distintas entidades territoriales del país (1940-1970)" (Mexico: development of distinct territorial entities in the context of the global system), *Mondes en Dévelop.* (1), 1973 : 165-193.

1059 IOANESJAN, S. I. *Laos: social'no-èkonomičeskoe razvitie* (Laos: socio-economic development). Moskva, Nauka, 72, 184 p.

1060 KOMOROŰSKI, S. M. "Development-for whom ? A preliminary inquiry into African realities", *Africana B.* 17, 1972 : 125-191.

1061 KUITENBROUWER, J. B. W. *Growth and equality in India and China: a historical comparative analysis.* The Hague, Institute of Social Studies, 73, iii-42 p.

1062 LEFF, N. "Economic development and regional inequality: origins of the Brazilian case", *Quart. J. Econ.* 86(2), mai 72 : 243-262.

1063 LIERDEMAN, J. L. *Planification de la croissance et organisation de l'espace en Côte d'Ivoire.* Abidjan, Office de la recherche scientifique et technique d'Outre-Mer, 72, iv-126 ff.

1064 MAAS, J. "Un modèle de croissance des pays exportateurs de pétrole", *C. écon. Bruxelles* 55, 3 trim. 72 : 423-440.

1065 MARINI, R. M. *Sous-développement et révolution en Amérique latine.* Paris, F. Maspéro, 72, 199 p. CR: I. S. WIARDA, *Amer. polit. Sci. R.* 67(4), dec 73 : 1406-1407.

1066 MARQUARDT, W. "Madagaskar. Zur wirtschaftlichen Entwicklung, 1971-72" (The economic development of Madagascar, 1971-72), *Int. Afr. Forum* 8 (11-12), nov-dec 72 : 623-630.

1067 MARZOUK, G. A. *Economic development and policies: case study of Thailand.* Rotterdam, Rotterdam University Press, 72, 473 p. CR: J. L. ENOS, *J. econ. Liter.* 11(3), sep 73 : 918-919.

1068 "Méditerranée et le développement (La)", *Mondes en Dévelop.* 2, 1973 : 5-234.

1069 M. RUSHDI, M. *al-Taṭawwur al-iqtiṣâdi fi Miṣr* (Economic development of Egypt). Misr, Dâr al-Ma'ârif, 72, 2 v.

1070 MUNDIGO, A. I. *Elites, economic development, and population in Honduras.* Cornell, N. Y., Cornell University, 72, xii-310 p.

1071 NOWLAN, D. M. "The formation of development strategy in tropical Africa", *Co-existence* 10(1), mar 73 : 34-56.

1072 OKSENBERG, M. "China's developmental experience", *Proc. Acad. polit. Sci.* 31(1), mar 73 : 1-227.

1073 OMO-FADAKA, J. "La voie tanzanienne du développement", *Impact* 23(2), apr-jun 73 : 115-126.

1074 PARKER, "Ideological and economic development in Tanzania", *Afr. Stud. R.* 15(1), apr 72 : 43-78.

1075 POPPINO, R. E. "Brasil: novo modelo para o desenvolvimento nacional" (Brazil: a new model for national development), *R. brasil. Estud. polít.* 36, jul 73 : 105-114.

1076 PRADO, C. *História e desenvolvimento; a contribuição da historiografia para a teoria e pratica do desenvolvimento brasileiro* (History and development: a contribution to historiography for theory and practice of Brazilian development). Sao Paulo, Editora Brasiliense, 72, 92 p.

1077 RAY, D. "The dependency model of Latin American underdevelopment", *J. interamer. Stud.* 15(1), feb 73 : 4-20.

1078 RENAUD, B. M. "Conflict between national growth and regional income equality in a rapidly growing economy: the case of Korea", *Econ. Develop. cult. Change* 21(3), apr 73 : 429-445.

1079 "Republic of Korea: economic development and major policy issues", *Econ. B. Asia Far East* 23(1), jun 72 : 37-60.

1080 RITTER, A. P. M. "Growth strategy and economic performance in revolutionary Cuba: past, present and prospective", *Soc. Econ. Stud.* 21(3), sep 72 : 313-337.

1081 SANTIAGO, Z. "A arrancada econômica do Brasil: custos sociais e instrumentalidade" (The economic take off of Brazil: social costs and instrumentality), *Dados* (9), 1972 : 7-20.

1082 SCHATZ, S. P. (ed.). *South of the Sahara: development in African economies.* London, Macmillan, 72, vii-363 p.

1083 SECHI, S. (ed.). *Dipendenza e sottosviluppo in America Latina* (Dependence and underdevelopment in Latin America). Torino, Fondazione Luigi Einaudi, 72, 418 p.

1084    SERRA, J. "El milagro económico brasileño: realidad o mito ?" (The Brazilian economic
        miracle: reality or myth ?), *R. mexic. Sociol.* 34(2), apr-jun 72 : 245-292.

1085    SINGH, V. B. (ed). *Studies in African economic development.* New Delhi, Impex India, 72,
        xii-299 p.

1086    ŠIROKOV, G. K. (ed.). *Ekonomika sovremennoj Indii. Problemy rosta* (The contemporary
        Indian economy. Problems of growth). Moskva, Nauka, 72, 178 p.

1087    STEVENSON, P. "External economic variables influencing the economic growth rate of
        seven major Latin American nations", *Canad. R. Sociol. Anthropol.* 9(4), nov 72 :
        347-356.

1088    SWAMY, S. "Economic growth in China and India, 1952-70. A comparative appraisal",
        *B. econ. Develop. cult. Change* 21(4) *Part II* jul 73 : 1-84.

1089    TERRADAS, J. "Las lineas del desarrollo socio-político en la América Latina" (Axes of
        politico-social development in Latin America), *R. Inst. Cienc. soc.* 21, 1973 : 229-240.

1090    TORRES, J. F. "Concentration of political power and levels of economic development in
        Latin American countries", *J. Develop. Areas* 7(3), apr 73 : 397-410.

1091    TURQUIEH, A. "Développement économique et planification au Liban: 1958-1970",
        *Maghreb-Machrek* 57, mai-jun 73 : 72-80.

1092    UPPAL, J. S.; SALKEUER, L. R. (eds.). *Africa: problems in economic development.* New
        York, Free Press, 72, ix-353 p.

1093    VEJSNER, L. I.; ŠIROKOV, G. K. (eds.). *Teorija ėkonomičeskogo rosta razvivajuščihsja stran
        Azii* (Theory of economic growth in the Asian developing countries). Moskva, Nauka,
        73, 284 p.

1094    WEINAND, H. C. "Some spatial aspects of economic development in Nigeria", *J. develop.
        Areas* 7(2), jan 73 : 247-264.

### F.33    Growth, maturity, stagnation
          Croissance, maturité, stagnation

### F.330    *General studies*
            *Études générales*

[See also / Voir aussi: **F.320; G.111; L.123;** 2120, 2122, 2549, 2569, 3182, 3236, 3994,
3999, 4021, 4322, 4621, 4668, 5039, 6052, 6436, 6439, 6445, 6453, 6459, 6465, 6488]

1095    ADISESHIAH, M. S. *It is time to begin; the human role in development: some further re-
        flections for the seventies.* Paris, Unesco, 72, 182 p.

1096    ANDERSON, K. P. "Optimal growth when the stock of resources is finite and depletable",
        *J. econ. Theory* 4(2), apr 72 : 256-267.

1097    AREILZA, J. M. DE. "Los límites del crecimiento" (The limits of growth), *R. Estud. soc.*
        (6), sep-dec 72 : 47-56.

1098    ARGE, R. C. D'; KOGIKU, K. C. "Economic growth and the environment", *R. econ.
        Stud.* 40(1), jan 73 : 61-77.

1099    AYAL, E. B. (ed.). *Micro aspects of development.* New York, Praeger Publishers, 73,
        xxxi-311 p.

1100    BAGNASCO, A. "Lo sviluppo disuguale" (Unequal growth), *Impresa* 14(3), mai-jun 73 :
        169-175.

1101    BHAGWATI, J.; ECKAUS, R. S. (eds.). *Development and planning: essays in honour of Paul
        Rosenstein Rodan.* London, Allen and Unwin, 72, 343 p.

1102    BREMS, H. *Labor, capital and growth.* Lexington, Mass., Lexington Books, 73, xvii-188 p.

1103    BUDZIŃSKI, F. "Współczynnik kapitału w modelach wrostu gospodarczego" (Capital
        coefficient in the models of economic growth), *Fol. oecon. cracov.* 14, 1973 : 45-60.

1104    CASAS, F. R. "The theory of intermediate products, technical change and growth",
        *J. int. Econ.* 2(2), mai 72 : 189-200.

1105    CHESNAIS, J. C.; SAUVY, A. "Progrès économique et accroissement de la population: une
        expérience commentée", *Population* 28(4-5), jul-oct 73 : 843-857.

1106    COLE, H. S. D. *et al.* (eds.). *Models of doom; a critique of The Limits to growth.* New York
        Universe Books, 73, 244 p.

1107    CORNWALL, J. *Growth and stability in a mature economy.* London, Martin Robertson;
        New York, Wiley, 72, 287 p.

1108 "Coûts de la croissance (Les)", *R. Écon. polit. (Paris)* 83(1), jan-feb 73 : 1-204.

1109 COZZI, T. *Teoria dello sviluppo economico. Le grandi teorie e i modelli aggregati di crescita* (Theory of economic development. The major theories and aggregate growth models). Bologna, Il Mulino, 72, 319 p.

1110 DASMANN, R. F.; MILTON, J. P.; FREEMAN, P. H. *Ecological principles for economic development.* London-New York-Morges-Washington, D.C., John Wiley, 73, vii-252 p.

1111 DEAN, W. "Economic development and environmental deterioration", *Stud. comp. int. Develop.* 7(3), aut 72 : 278-287.

1112 *Economic growth.* New York, Columbia University Press, 72, xx-92 p.

1113 ELLIOT, C. *The development debate.* New York, Friendship Press, 71, 128 p.

1114 ELTIS, W. A. *Growth and distribution.* New York, Wiley, 73, xi-364 p.

1115 FELIX, F. *World markets of tomorrow: economic growth, population trends, electricity and energy, quality of life.* London, New York, Harper and Row, 72, xxv-364-9 p.

1116 FREY, B. S. "Interactions between preferences and consumption in economic development", *Scott. J. polit. Econ.* 20(1), feb 73 : 53-64.

1117 GAHLEN, B. *Der Informationsgehalt der neoklassischen Wachstumstheorie für die Wirtschaftspolitik* (Informative content of the neo-classical theory of growth for economic policy). Tübingen, Mohr, 72, xix-437 p.

1118 GAHLEN, B.; OTT, A. E. (eds.). *Probleme der Wachstumstheorie* (Problems of growth theory). Tübingen, Mohr, 72, viii-463 p.

1119 GILL, R. T. *Economic development: past and present.* Englewood Cliffs, N. J. Prentice-Hall, 73, viii-143 p.

1120 GLASTETTER, W. "Quantitatives oder qualitatives Wachstum?" (Quantitative or qualitative growth?), *Gegenwartskunde* 21(4), 1972 : 405-417.

1121 GOULD, J. D. *Economic growth in history: survey and analysis.* London, Methuen; New York, Hirper and Row, 72, xx-460 p.

1122 GUHA, A. "Two-class neoclassical growth", *Quart. J. Econ.* 86(4), nov 72 : 687-690.

1123 HAVENS, A. E. "Methodological issues in the study of development", *Sociol rur.* 12(3-4), 1972 : 252-272.

1124 HEILBRONER, R. L. "Growth and survival", *For. Aff.* 51(1), oct 72 : 139-153.

1125 HEMMER, H. R. *Strukturprobleme des Wirtschaftswachstums. Zur Theorie der Zwei-Sektoren-Modelle mit limitationalen Produktionsfaktoren* (Structural problems of economic growth. On the theory of two sector models with limitational growth factors). Freiburg i. Br., Rombach, 72, 228 p.

1126 HENRICHSMEYER, W. "Economic growth and agriculture: a two-sector analysis", *German econ. R.* 10(4), 1972 : 310-326.

1127 HODSON, H. V. *The diseconomics of growth.* London, Angus and Robertson; New York, Ballantine Books, 72, 239 p.

1128 HUISMAN, S. *Economische groei en economie* (Economic growth and economics). Assen, Van Gorcum; Amsterdam, Openbare les-Vrije Universiteit, 72, 25 p.

1129 INFNATE, E. F.; STEIN, J. L. "Optimal growth with robust feedback control" *R. econ. Stud.* 40(1), jan 73 : 47-60.

1130 "Interpretations of economic growth", *Amer. econ. R.* 63(2), mai 73 *Pap. and Proc.*: 428-449. With contributions by: M. ABRAMOWITZ, P. A. DAVID, R. R. NELSON and S. G. WINTER.

1131 IWAI, K. "Optimal economic growth and stationary ordinal utility—a Fisherian approach", *J. econ. Theory* 5(1), aug 72 : 121-151.

1132 JAMES, F. J.; HUGHES, J. W. *Economic growth and residential patterns: a methodological investigation.* New Brunswick, N. J., Rutgers University, 72, 211 p.

1133 JHA, L. K. *Economic development: ends and means.* Bombay, Vora, 73, viii-208.

1134 JÖHR, A. "Die Grenzen des Wachstums" (The limits of growth), *WIST* 2(6), jun 73 : 261-266.

1135 KALMBACH, P. *Wachstum und Verteilung in neoklassischer und postkeynesianischer Sicht* (Growth and interactions in a neo-classical and post-keynesian view). Berlin, Duncker und Humblot, 72, 232 p.

1136 KAMRANY, N. M. "Economic growth and environmental impact: evaluating alternatives", *Socio-econ. plan. Sci.* 7(1), feb 73 : 37-53.

1137 KEMP, A. "Growth and development. A contrary view of the economic factor" *Politico* 37(4), dec 72 : 793-803.

1138   KREGEL, J. A. *The theory of economic growth.* London, Macmillan, 72, 96 p.

1139   KROMPHARDT, J. *Wachstum und Konjunktur: Grundlagen ihrer theoretischen Analyse und wirtschaftpolitische Steuerung* (Growth and conjuncture: bases of its theoretical analysis and economic policy management). Göttingen, Vandenhoeck und Ruprecht, 72, 284 p.

1140   KUZNETS, S. "Innovations and adjustments in economic growth", *Swedish J. Econ.* 74(4), dec 72 : 431-451.

1141   KUZNETS, S. "Modern economic growth: findings and reflections", *Amer. econ. R.* 63(3), jun 73 : 247-258.

1142   LATTES, R. *Pour une autre croissance.* Paris, Editions du Seuil, 72, 159 p.

1143   LEFEBVRE, H. "Les idéologies de la croissance", *Homme et Soc.* 27, jan-mar 73 : 3-17.

1144   LEFRINGHAUSEN, K. "Der Zielkonflikt zwischen ökonomischen Wachstum und sozialem Fortschritt in der Entwicklungspolitik" (The conflict of goals between economic growth and social progress in development policy), *Vierteljahresberichte* 45, sep 71 : 241-251.

1145   "Limits of growth controversy (The)", *Futures (Guildford)* 5(1), feb 73 : 4-152.

1146   LIS, S. "Analityczne mierniki rozwoju gospadarczego" (Analytical indices of economic growth), *Fol. oecon. Cracov.* 12, 1972 : 109-122.

1147   LIS, S. "Czynniki ograniczające dokładność międzynarodowych porównań poziomu wzrostu gospodarczego za pomocą dochodu narodowego" (Factors limiting the exactitude of international comparisons of economic growth using national income), *Gosp. plan.* 1, 1973 : 26-39.

1148   MAITRA, P. "Concept of economic development—reexamined", *Econ. Aff.* 17(1-2), jan-feb 72 : 37-48.

1149   MARCINIAK, S. *Struktura i efektywność wzrostu gospodarki socjalistycznej* (Structure and efficiency of the growth of the socialist economy). Warszawa, Państwowe Wydawnictwo Naukowe, 73, 212 p.

1150   MASSE, P. *La crise du développement.* Paris, Gallimard, 73, 183 p.

1151   McGRANAHAN, D. V. *et al. Contents and measurement of socio-economic development.* New York, F. A. Praeger, 72, xiv-161 p. CR: R. S. THORN, *J. econ. Liter.* 11(3), sep 73 : 920-921.

1152   Bibl. XXI-1500. MEADOWS, D. H. *et al. The limits to growth.* CR: R. M. WARE, *J. econ. Liter.* 10(4), dec 72 : 1256-1258.

1153   MEISSNER, H. *Theorie des Wirtschaftwachstums. Hoffnung und Dilemma der bürgerlichen Ökonomie* (Economic growth theory. Hope and dilemma of bourgeois economy). Berlin, Akademie-Verlag, 72, 75 p.

1154   MORICE, G. *La croissance économique: une illusion comptable.* Paris, J. J. Pauvert, 72, 92 p.

1155   NATIONS UNIES. Bureau économique et social de Beirut. "Croissance économique et le niveau de qualification de la population active dans divers pays du Moyen-Orient", *Proche-Orient. Ét. écon.* 73, mai-aug 72 : 155-200.

1156   NEKOLA, J.; VERBA, J. "K otázce vztahu nákladu na vyzkumnou a vyvojovou činnost a nekterych charakteristik sociálné ekonomického rozvoje" (A contribution to the problem of relations between R and D activity and some indicators of socio-economic development), *Ekon-matem. Obzor.* 8(1), 1972 : 40-57.

1157   "No-growth society (The)", *Daedalus* 102(4), aut 73 : 1-241.

1158   "Objecteurs de croissance (Les)", *Nef* 52, sep-oct 73 : 1-149.

1159   PAJESTKA, J. "Ogólne współzaleănosci rozwojowe i społeczne czynniki postępu" (General development and the social factors of progress), *Ekonomista* (1), 1973 : 9-38.

1160   PALLOIX, C. *Problèmes de la croissance en économie ouverte.* 2e éd. rev. Paris, F. Maspéro, 73, 211 p.

1161   PENOUIL, M. *Economie du développement.* Paris, Dalloz, 72, 118 p.

1162   PULLIAINEN, K. "Taloudellisen kasvun ekologinen kritiikki" (An ecological critique of economic growth), *Kansantal. Aikakausk.* 68(2), 1972 : 111-123.

1163   RIMMER, D. *Macromancy. The ideology of 'development economics'.* London, Institute of Economic Affairs, 73, 64 p.

1164   RYDER, H. E.; HEAL, G. M. "Optimum growth with intertemporally dependent preferences", *R. econ. Stud.* 40(1), jan 73 : 1-33.

1165   SADOWSKI, Z. "Granice wzrostu gospodarczego" (The problem of limits of economic growth), *Ekonomista* 3, 1973 : 537-554.

1166 SAUVY, A. *Croissance zéro ?* Paris, Calmann-Lévy, 73, 331 p.

1167 SCHRÖDER, J. "Neo-classical growth in an open economy: a note", *Economica (London)* 39(156), nov 72 : 447-449.

1168 SEGURA, J. "En torno al crecimiento económico" (About economic growth), *Inform. com. esp.* 477, mai 73 : 157-162.

1169 SPRINKEL, B. W. "Continued expansion in 1973 amid growing prosperity", *J. Busin.* 46(1), jan 73 : 1-5.

1170 STREETEN, P. *The frontiers of development studies.* London, Macmillan; New York, Wiley, 72, xv-498 p.

1171 TIMOFIEJUK, I. *Mierniki wzrostu gospodarczego* (Measures of economic growth) 2e ed. rev. enl. Warszawa, Państwowe Wydawnictwo Ekonomiczne, 73, 196 p.

1172 TIMOFIEJUK, I. *Stopa wzrostu gospodarczego. Metody liczenia* (Rate of economic growth. Methods of calculation). Warszawa, Państwowe Wydawnictwo Ekonomiczne, 73, 128 p.

1173 TREMOLIERES, M. *Les facteurs institutionnels du développement.* Neuchâtel (Editions de) la Baconnière; Lausanne, Paris, Payot, 72, 199 p.

1174 Ul HAG, M. "The limits to growth: a critique", *Finance and Develop.* 9(4), dec 72 : 2-8.

1175 UNITED NATIONS. Centre for Economic and Social Information. *The case for development; six studies.* New York, Praeger Publishers, 73, ix-302 p.

1176 VAL'TUH, K. K. *Problemy narodnohozjajstvennogo optimuma* (Problems of the national economy optimum). Novosibirsk, Nauka, 73, 384 p.

1177 WALL, D. (ed.). *Chicago essays in economic development.* Chicago, University of Chicago Press, 72, xvi-370 p.

1178 WILKINSON, R. G. *Poverty and progress; an ecological model of economic development.* London, Methuen; New York, Praeger, 73, xi-225 p.

1179 YOUNGSON, A. J. (ed.). *Economic development in the long run.* London, Allen and Unwin, 72, 3-256 p.

1180 ZAREMBKA, P. *Toward a theory of economic development.* San Francisco, Holden-Day, 72, xii-249 p.

### F.331 Local studies
### Études localisées

[See also / Voir aussi: 2628, 3744, 3750, 4102, 4441, 6522]

1181 BERNOS, R. "Les rapports États-Unis Europe — un conflit pour la croissance", *R. écon. (Paris)* 24(5), sep 73 : 867-878.

1182 BLUMENFELD, H. "Growth rate comparisons: Soviet Union and German Democratic Republic", *Land Econ.* 49(2), mai 73 : 122-132.

1183 CAZES, G.; REYNAUD, A. *Les mutations récentes de l'économie française: de la croissance à l'aménagement.* Paris, Doin, 73, 215 p.

1184 CREȚOIU, R. "Ritmurile cresteril economice si eficienta acumulării in unele tări socialiste" (Economic growth rythms and efficiency of accumulation in some socialist countries), *Finante și Cred.* 18(10), oct 72 : 11-21.

1185 Bibl. XXI-1534. DAVIS, L. E. *et al. American economic growth: an economist's history of the United States.* CR: R. M. ROBERTSON, *J. econ. Liter* 10(4), dec 72 : 1210-1212.

1186 Bibl. XXI-1533. DAVIS, L. E.; NORTH, D. C. *Institutional change and American economic growth.* CR: R. M. ROBERTSON, *J. econ. Liter.* 10(4), dec 72 : 1210-1212.

1187 DOBRIN, B. *Bulgarian economic development since World War II.* New York, Praeger Publishers, 73, xv-185 p.

1188 DUNAJEWSKI, H. "Les taux de croissance des pays socialistes", *R. Est* 4(1) jan 73 : 47-72.

1189 "Economic development in Finland in 1972", *Econ. R. (Helsinki)* (1), 1973 : 9-43.

1190 FALLENBUCHL, Z. M. "Croissance économique et echanges extérieurs de L'Union Soviétique et de l'Europe de l'Est, 1971-1975", *R. Est* 4(1), jan 73 : 27-45.

1191 FIRESTONE, O. J. "Innovations and economic development — the Canadian case", *R. Income Wealth* 18(4), dec 72 : 399-419.

1192 GORZIG, B. *Die Entwicklung des Wachstumspotentials in den Wirtschaftsbereichen der Bundesrepublik Deutschland. Analyse und Projektion bis 1980* (The development of growth potential in the German Federal Republic. Analysis and projects for 1980). Berlin, Duncker und Humblot, 72, 148 p.

1193    HOROWITZ, D. *The enigma of economic growth; a case study of Israel.* New York, Praeger, 72, xiv-157 p.

1194    INSTITUTUL CENTRAL DE DOCUMENTARE TEHNICĂ. *Bezvoltarea economică a R. S. Cehoslovace* (Economic development of Czechoslovakia). București, Consiliul Național pentru Știință și Tehnologie, Institutul central de documentare tehnică, 72, 95 p.

1195    INSTITUTL CENTRAL DE DOCUMENTARE TEHNICĂ. *Dezvoltarea economică a R. S. F. Iugoslavia* (Economic development in Yugoslavia). București, Consiliul National pentru Stiință si Tehnologie, Institutul central de documentare tehnică, 72, 88 p.

1196    KANAMORI, H. "What accounts for Japan's high rate of growth", *R. Income Wealth* 18(2), jun 72 : 155-171.

1197    LAGASSE, C. E. "Accumulation et consommation dans la croissance stalinienne", *A. Écon. coll.* 61(3), jul-sep 73 : 303-345. [USSR.]

1198    LI, W. L. "Japanese immigration and economic growth in Taiwan", *Migr. int.* 10(4), 1972 : 188-197.

1199    MILLS, J. *Growth and welfare: a new policy for Britain.* London, Martin Robertson and Co. Ltd, New York, Barnes and Noble, 72, xiii-206 p.

1200    MINABE, S. "Capital-output ratios, technical changes and the patterns of economic growth in the United States and Canada", *Amer. Economist* 16(2), 1972 : 157-161.

1201    MINAMI, R. *The turning point in economic development; Japan's experience.* Tokyo, Kinokuniya Bookstore Co., 73, xix-330 p.

1202    MOISUC, C. *Coordonate principale ale dezvoltării economice (1971-1990)* (Major coordinates of economic development, 1971-1990). București, Editura politică, 72, 81 p. [Rumania.]

1203    Bibl. XXI-1548. MORLEY, J. W. (ed.). *Dilemmas of growth in prewar Japan.* CR: H. D. SMITH, II. *Amer. polit. Sci. R.* 67(4), dec 73 : 1408-1410.

1204    NASILOWSKI, M. "Le développement économique de la Pologne au cours des années 1950-1970", *R. Est* 4(3), jul 73 : 27-47.

1205    OHKAWA, K.; HAYAMI, Y. *Economic growth: the Japanese experience since the Meiji era.* Tokyo, Japan Economic Research Center, 73, 2 vols.

1206    OKAWA, K.; ROSOVSKY, H. *Japanese economic growth; trend acceleration in the twentieth century.* Stanford, Calif., Stanford University Press, 73, xvi-327 p.

1207    OKITA, S. *Economic development in the 1970's; Japan and Asia.* Tokyo, Japan Economic Research Center, 72, 56 p.

1208    PAYNE, S. G. "Political ideology and economic modernization in Spain", *Wld Polit.* 25(1), oct 72 : 155-181.

1209    PRODI, R. "Sistema industriale e sviluppo economico in Italia" (Industrial system and economic development in Italy), *Mulino* 22(226), mar-apr 73 : 197-229.

1210    QUIJADA, J.; RACHDORF, H. W. "Zur sozio-ökonomischen Entwicklung Spaniens" (Social economic development of Spain), *Sozial. Polit.* 5(23), apr 73 : 1-35.

1211    SAUTTER, C. "L'expansion japonaise", *Écon. et Statist.* 45, mai 73 : 3-20.

1212    SUHAREVSKIJ, B. M. *O sovremennom etape razvitija ekonomiki socializma v SSSR* (On the contemporary stage of the socialist economic development in the USSR). Moskva, Ekonomika, 72, 173 p.

1213    TAIT, A. A.; BRISTOW, J. A. (eds.). *Ireland. Some problems of a developing economy.* New York, Barnes and Noble, 72, ix-239 p. CR: N. J. J. FARLEY, *J. econ. Liter.* 11(3), sep 73 : 921-923.

1214    TOMINAGA, K. "Développement et changement social au Japon. Une analyse parsonienne", *Sociol. Trav.* 15(3), jul-sep 73 : 269-292.

1215    TONIOLO, G. *Lo sviluppo economico italiano, 1861-1940.* (Italian economic development, 1961-1940). Roma-Bari, Laterza, 73, xi-413 p.

1216    TSURUMI, H. "Effects of wage-parity and price synchronization between Canada and the United States on Canadian economic growth: simulation experiments with a macro-model", *Int. econ. R.* 13(3), oct 72 : 644-678.

1217    UENO, H. "A long-term model of economic growth of Japan, 1906-1968", *Int. econ. R.* 13(3), oct 72 : 619-643.

1218    UJIIE, J.; YEUNG, P. "Japan's economic growth and balance of trade", *Amer. Economist* 16(2), 1972 : 106-122.

1219    'UTHMĂN, 'U. M. *Numûw al-iqtišăd al-Isră'îlî* (Israeli economic growth). al-Qâḥiraṭ, Markaz al-Dirâsât al-Siyâsiyaṭ wal-istratîjîyaṭ, 72, 198 p.

1220 "Zur Wirtschaftsentwicklung der Bundesrepublik Deutschland in den Jahren 1972 und 1973" (Economic growth of the German Federal Republic in 1972 and 1973), *WSI Mitt.* 25(11), nov 72 : 333-363.

## F.4 ECONOMIC EQUILIBRIUM AND EVOLUTION : MECHANISMS MÉCANISMES DE L'ÉQUILIBRE ET DE L'ÉVOLUTION ÉCONOMIQUES

[See also / Voir aussi: **B.32; F.330; F.50;** 3855, 3861, 4320, 6378]

1221 BENAVIE, A. "Disequilibrium static analysis", *West. econ. J.* 10(1), mar 72 : 76-83.

1222 BEWLEY, T. F. "Existence of equilibrium in economies with infinitely many commodities", *J. econ. Theory* 4(3), jun 72 : 514-540.

1223 BROOME, J. "Approximate equilibrium in economies with indivisible commodities", *J. econ. Theory* 5(2), oct 72 : 224-249.

1224 CEBULA, R. "A reconsideration of the diagramatics of voluntary exchange in a general equilibrium context", *Amer. Economist* 16(1), 1972 : 148-151.

1225 CHANG, W. W.; SMYTH, D. J. "Stability and instability of IS-LM equilibrium" *Oxford econ. Pap.* 24(3), nov 72 : 372-384.

1226 HAY, G. A.; McGOWAN, J. J. "External economies and competitive equilibrium", *Canad. J. Econ.* 5(4), nov 72 : 562-564.

1227 HILDENBRAND, K. "Continuity of the equilibrium-set correspondence", *J. econ. Theory* 5(1), aug 72 : 152-162.

1228 HILDENBRAND, W.; MERTENS, J. F. "Upper hemi-continuity of the equilibrium set correspondence for pure exchange economies", *Econometrica* 40(1), jan 72 : 99-108.

1229 Bibl. XXI-1577. JOHNSON, H. G. *The two-sector model of general equilibrium.* CR: R. SATO, *J. econ. Liter.* 10(4), dec 72 : 1206-1207.

1230 KÁLDOR, N. "The irrelevance of equilibrium economics", *Econ. J.* 82(328), dec 72 : 1237-1255.

1231 KORLIRAS, P. G. "A note on the disequilibrium method in macroeconomics", *Amer. Economist* 16(2), 1972 : 79-82.

1232 LIBURA, U. "Równowaga gospodarcza a jakość produkcji i innowacje" (Economic equilibrium and the quality of production), *Zesz. nauk. Szkoły główn. Plan. Statyst.* 89, 1972 : 7-30.

1233 MUENCH, T. J. "The core and the Lindahl equilibrium of an economy with the public good: an example", *J. econ. Theory* 4(2), apr 72 : 241-255.

1234 MUKHERJI, A. "On complementarity and stability", *J. econ. Theory* 4(3), jun 72 : 442-457.

1235 Bibl. XXI-1580. NEGISHI, T. *General equilibrium theory and international trade.* CR: J. N. BHAGWATI, *J. econ. Liter.* 11(2), jun 73 : 573-574.

1236 NICOLA, P. C. *Equilibrio generale e crescita economica* (General equilibrium and economic growth). Bologna, Il Mulino, 73, 167 p.

1237 NICOLA, P. C. "Soluzioni stazionarie e semistazionarie nello equilibrio economico generale" (Stationary and quasi-stationary solutions in general economic equilibrium), *Industria* (1-2), jan-mar 72 : 3-16.

1238 NIEDUSZYŃSKI, M. *Dynamiczna równowaga gospodarcza* (Dynamic economic equilibrium) Warszawa, Państwowe Wydawnictwo Ekonomiczne, 73, 214 p.

1239 MINDYCK, R. S. *Optimal planning for economic stabilization; the application of control theory to stabilization policy.* Amsterdam, North-Holland Publishing, 73, xii-167 p.

1240 PRESTON, A. J. "A paradox in the theory of optimal stabilization", *R. econ. Stud.* 39(4), oct 72 : 423-432.

1241 RADER, T. "General equilibrium theory with complementary factors", *J. econ. Theory* 4(3), jun 72 : 372-380.

1242 SAMUELSON, P. A. "The general saddlepoint property of optimal-control motions", *J. econ. Theory* 5(1), aug 72 : 102-120.

1243 SOFRANKO, A. J.; BEALER, R. C. "Modernization balance, imbalance, and domestic instability", *Econ. Develop. cult. Change* 22(1), oct 73 : 52-72.

1244 ZELDER, R. E.; ROSS, M. H.; COLLERY, A. "Internal and external balance in an 'almost classical' world", *West. econ. J.* 10(3), sep 72 : 346-351.

## F.5      FLUCTUATIONS, CYCLES AND TRENDS
##          FLUCTUATIONS, CYCLES ET TENDANCES

### F.50     General studies
####         Études générales

[See also / Voir aussi: 4530]

1245    DRAGILEV, M. "Sovremennyj cikl: nekotorye teoretičeskie aspekty" (The contemporary cycle: some theoretical aspects), *Mir. Ekon. meždun. Otnoš* 16(6), jun 73 : 73-81.

1246    HEUBES, J. "Zyklisches Wachstum" (Cyclical growth), *Z. ges. Staatswiss.* 129(1), feb 73 : 62-87.

1247    KRÜGER, R. "Einige kritische Gedanken zur wirtschaftspolitischen Relevanz konjunktur- und wachstumstheoretischer Aussätze" (Some critical remarks on the political relevance of business cycles and economic growth models), *Z. Wirtsch.-u. soz.-Wiss.* 92(1), 1972 : 33-49.

1248    LAIDLER, D. "Simultaneous fluctuations in prices and output. A business cycles approach", *Economica (London)* 40(157), feb 73 : 60-72.

1249    NEUMANN, K. *Konjunktur und Konjunkturpolitik. Möglichkeiten und Grenzen der Konjunkturpolitik* (Business cycles and related policy. Possibilities and limits of economic policy). Frankfurt am Main, Europäische Verlag Anstalt, 72, 159 p.

1250    OLIVERA, J. H. "Gradualismo, ineficacia a estabilidad cíclica" (Gradualism, inefficiency and cyclical instability), *Económica (La Plata)* 18(1), jul-aug 72 : 45-53.

1251    OTT, A. E. (ed.). *Wachstumszyklen. Über die neue Form der Konjunkturschwankungen* (Growth cycles. On a new form of economic fluctuations). Berlin, Duncker und Humblot, 73, 269 p.

1252    RÖMHELD, D. *Das Hickssche Konjunkturmodell und seine monetäre Problematik* (Hick's business cycles model and its monetary problematic). Berlin, Duncker und Humblot, 72, 90 p.

1253    SENN, L. "The transmission of business cycles from a national to a regional system", *Industria* (1-2), jan-mar 72 : 101-114.

1254    TEICHMANN, U. *Konjunktur- und Wachstumspolitik, Konflikt oder Konnex* (Business cycles and growth policy, conflict or connection). Wiesbaden, Betriebswirtschaftlicher Verlag Gabler, 72, 151 p.


### F.51     Local studies
####         Études localisées

1255    ECONTEL RESEARCH. *The business cycle in Australia, 1950-1971.* London, ER, 72, 20 p.

1256    FRANCO, G. "Crisi strutturale" (Structural crisis), *Riv. int. Sci. econ. com.* 19(11), nov 72 : 1029-1039. [Italy.]

1257    KUDO, A. "L'economia giapponese nell'analisi del ciclo economico" (The Japanese economy in economic cycle analysis), *Polit. ed Econ.* 4(1-2), jan-apr 73 : 71-76.

1258    LA MALFA, G. *Crisi economica e politica dei redditi* (Economic crisis and incomes policy). Roma, Edizioni della Voce, 72, 180 p. [Italy.]

1259    LENTI, L. "Business cycles and price trend in Italy", *R. econ. Condit. Italy* 27(3), mai 73 : 113-126.

1260    PERLO, V. *The unstable economy: booms and recessions in the United States since 1945.* London, Lawrence and Wishart; New York, International Publishers, 73, 238 p.

1261    PEVZNER, Ja. "Cikly v poslevoennoj Japonii" (Cycles in Japan since the war), *Mir. Ekon. meždun. Otnoš.* 16(7), jul 73 : 91-95.

1262    POKATAEV, Ju. "Poslevoennye cikly i krizisy v SŠA" (Cycles and crisis in the United States after the war), *Mir. Ekon. meždun. Otnoš.* 16(6), jun 73 : 81-88.

1263    WAGNER, A. *Die Wachstumszyklen in der Bundesrepublik Deutschland: eine komparativ-dynamische Komponenteanalyse für die Jahre 1951-1970* (Growth cycles in the German Federal Republic: a comparative-dynamic analysis of components for the year 1951-1970). Tübingen, Mohr, 72, xx-435 p.

1264    WATERMAN, A. M. C. *Economic fluctuations in Australia, 1948 to 1964.* Canberra, Australian National University Press, 72, xvi-227 p.

# G  ORGANISATION OF PRODUCTION
# ORGANISATION DE LA PRODUCTION

## G.1  PRODUCTIVITY, OUTPUT, TECHNOLOGICAL PROGRESS
## PRODUCTIVITÉ, RENDEMENT, PROGRÈS TECHNIQUE

### G.10  General studies
### Études générales

#### G.101  *Concepts*

[See also / Voir aussi: 2192, 3178, 3519]

1265   ABAD ARANGO, D. "Tecnología y dependencia" (Technology and dependence), *Trim. econ.* 40(158), apr-jun 73 : 371-392.

1266   AFANAS, Ev, V. G. *Naučno-tehničeskaja revoljucija, upravlenie, obrazovanie* (The scientific and technical revolution, management, education). Moskva, Politizdat, 72, 431 p.

1267   AHRAMOVIČ, R. T. *et al. Naučno-tehničeskaja revoljucija i razvivajuščiesja strany* (The scientific and technical revolution and the developing countries). Moskva, Nauka, 73, 224 p.

1268   ALFVEN, H. "Science, technocratie et le pouvoir politico-économique", *Impact* 22(1-2), jan-jun 72 : 91-99.

1269   BAHR, H.-D. *et al. Technologie und Kapital* (Technology and capital). Frankfurt-am-Main, Suhrkamp, 73, 234 p.

1270   BHALLA, A. S. "Implications of technological choice in African countries" *Afr. Spectrum* 8(1), 1973 : 18-28.

1271   BLAGOJEVIČ, S. "Tehničko-tehnološki progres i dugoročne strukturne promene u privredi SFRJ" (Technical and technological progress and long-term structural changes in the Yugoslav economy), *Ekon. Misão* 6(2), jun 73 : 33-48.

1272   BROWN, L. A.; LENTNEK, B. "Innovation diffusion in a developing economy: a mesoscale view", *Econ. Develop. cult. Change* 21(2), jan 73 : 274-292.

1273   BUCHHOLZ, A. *Bericht über eine Tagung zum Thema Wissenschaftlich-technische Revolution und Wettbewerb der Systeme.* (Report on a congress with the theme of the scientific and technological revolution and systems competition). Köln, Bundesinstitut für Ostwissenschaftliche und Internationale Studien, 72, 43 p.

1274   CACICI, V. "Sul tema del progresso tecnico in Italia" (On the subject of technical progress), *Rass. econ. (Napoli)* 37(4), jul-aug 73 : 927-939.

1275   CETRON, M. J.; BARTOCHA, B. *The methodology of technology assessment.* New York, Gordon and Breach, 72, viii-235 p.

1276   CETRON, M. J.; BARTOCHA, B. (eds.). *Technology assessment in a dynamic environment.* London-New York, Gordon and Breach Science Publishers, 73, xiv-1036 p.

1277   COLIN, R. "Politique de participation et développement technologique", *Dévelop. et Civilis.* 49-50, sep-dec 72 : 11-18.

1278   COOPER, C. "Science and technology in development", *J. Develop. Stud.* 9 (1), oct 72 : 1-199.

1279   "Évolution sociale de la technologie (L')", *R. int. Sci. soc.* 25(3), 1973 : 271-424.

1280   FIEDOR, B. "Nauka jako czynnik rozwoju gospodarczego" (Science as a factor of economic development), *Prace nauk. wyssz. Szkoły ekon. Wrockaw.* 37, 1973 : 47-79.

1281   FIORAVANTI, E. *El concepto de modo de producción* (The mode of production concept). Barcelona, Ediciones Península, 72, 284 p.

1282   FLECK, F. H. *Die ökonomische Theorie des technischen Fortschritts und seine Identifikation* (Economic theory of technical progress and its identification). Meisenheim-am-Glan, A. Hain, 73, 253 p.

1283    GATOVSKIJ, L. M. "Ob organičeskom soedinenii dostiženij naučno-tehničeskoj revoljucii s preimuščestvami socialističeskoj sistemy hozjajstva" (On the organic union between the scientific and technical revolution results and the socialist economic system's advantages), in: *Ėkonomičeskie i social'na političeskie problemy kommunističeskogo stroitel'stva v SSSR.* Moskva, 1972 : 136-158.

1284    GATOVSKIJ, L. M. *et al. Planirovanie i stimulirovanie naučno-tehničeskogo progressa* (Planning and stimulation of scientific and technical progress). Moskva, Ekonomika 72, 239 p.

1285    HAMILTON, D. R. L. *Technology, man and the environment.* London, Faber, 73, 3-357 p.

1286    HANOCH, G.; ROTHSCHILD, M. "Testing the assumptions of production theory: a non-parametric approach", *J. polit. Econ.* 80(2), mar-apr 72 : 256-275.

1287    HERMANOWSKI, H. "Nauka jako podstawowa sila wytwórcza" (Science as a basic productive force), *Zesz. nauk. wyzsz. Szkoły ekon. Katowic.* 45, 1972 : 5-28.

1288    HETZLER, S. A. *Applied measures for promoting technological growth.* London, Boston, Routledge and Kegan Paul, 73, xiii-337 p.

1289    HILHORST, J. G. M. "Development axes and the diffusion of innovation", *Develop. and Change* 4(1), 1972-73 : 1-16.

1290    KAMAEV, V. D. *Sovremennaja naučno-tehničeskaja revoljucija: ekonomičeskie formy i zakonomernosti* (The contemporary scientific and technical revolution: economic forms and laws). Moskva, Nysl', 72, 274 p.

1291    KAMIEN, M. I.; SCHWARTZ, N. L. "Some economic consequences of anticipating technical advance", *West. econ. J.* 10(2), jun 72 : 123-138.

1292    KAMIEN, M. I.; SCHWARTZ, N. L. "Timing of innovations under rivalry", *Econometrica* 40(1), jan 72 : 43-60.

1293    KELLEY, A. C.; WILLIAMSON, J. G.; CHEETHAM, R. J. "Biased technological progress and labor force growth", *Quart. J. Econ.* 86(3), aug 72 : 426-447.

1294    KOSOV, Ė. V.; POPOV, G. H. *Upravlenie mežotraslevymi naučno-tehničeskimi programmami* (Inter-sectoral scientific and technical program management) Moskva, Ėkonomika, 72, 151 p.

1295    KOZIKOV, I. A. *Problemy sootnošenija naučno-tehničeskoj social'noj revoljucii* (The correlation problems between the scientific and technical revolutions and the social revolution). Moskva, Izdatel'stvo moskovskogo universiteta, 72, 111 p.

1296    KOZLOV, Ju. K. *Organizacionnye problemy naučno-tehničeskogo progressa* (Organizational problems of scientific and technical progress). Moskva, Mysl', 72, 436 p.

1297    KRAJUHIN, G. A. *Ėffektivnost' proizvodstva tehničeskij progress* (Production efficiency and technical progress). Leningrad, Lenizdat, 73, 199 p.

1298    KUDJASOV, A. H. *Naučno-tehničeskaja revoljucija i ee social'no-ekonomičeskie posledstvija* (The scientific and technical revolution and its socio-economic consequences). Sverdlovsk, Sredno-Ural'skoe knižnoe Izdatel'stvo, 72, 200 p.

1299    KUZNECOV, I. V. *Rassirenie proizvodstva tovarov narodnogo potreblenija* (The increase in national consumer goods production). Moskva, Profizdat, 72, 48 p.

1300    LANE, J. S. "The implications of steady state growth for endogenous and embodied technological change", *Int. econ. R.* 13(2), jun 72 : 342-358.

1301    LEBEDEV, V. G.; PLEHOC, G. G. *Rol'nauki v razvitii proizvodstva* (Role of science in production development). Moskva, Ėkonomika, 72, 53 p.

1302    LOKIEC, M. *Technology and labor in the postwar era.* Columbia, S. C., Bobbin Publications, 72, xxx-140 p.

1303    MAJER, H. *Die technologische Lücke zwischen der Bundesrepublik Deutschland und den Vereinigten Staaten von Amerika; eine empirische Analyse* (The technological gap between the German Federal Republic and the United States of America: an empirical analysis). Tübingen, Mohr, 73, xx-438 p.

1304    MARTINO, J. P. (ed.). *An introduction to technological forecasting.* London, Gordon and Breach, 72, x-108 p.

1305    MOLINS CODINA, J. "Progreso tecnologico, progreso técnico y desarrollo. Una aplicación al caso español" (Technological progress, technical progress and development. An application to the Spanish case), *Cuad. Econ.* 1(l1), jan-jun 73 : 76-112.

1306    NOVAES, P. *Tecnología e recursos humanos* (Technology and human resources). Rio de Janeiro, Editôra Renes, 72, 145 p.

1307 PAVITT, K. "Technology, international competition and economic growth: some lessons and perspectives", *Wld Polit.* 25(2), jan 73 : 183-206.

1308 PIEL, E. J.; TRUXAL, J. G. *Man and his technology: problems and issues.* New York, McGraw-Hill, 73, 261 p.

1309 PLOTNIKOV, K. N. *Problemy upravlenija naučnymi issledovanijami* (Scientific research management problems). Moskva, Nauka, 73, 285 p.

1310 "Política científica e tecnológica" (Scientific and technological policy) *R. Adm. públ. (Rio de Janeiro)* 7(2), apr-jun 73 : 3-202. [Brazil.]

1311 PROSTJAKOV, I. I. *Uskorenie tehničeskogo progressa v uslovijah hozjajstvennoj reformy* (Technical progress acceleration under the economic reform conditions). Moskva, Mysl', 73, 158 p.

1312 RAHLIN, I. V. *Naučno-tehničeskij progresi ēffektivnost' novyh materialov* (Scientific and technical progress and new materials efficiency). Moskva, Nauka, 73, 352 p.

1313 ROSE, J. (ed.). *Technological injury; the effect of technological advances on environment, life, and society.* London-New York, Gordon and Breach Science, 73, xx-224 p.

1314 ROSEN, S. "Learning by experience as joint production", *Quart. J. Econ.* 86(3), aug 72 : 366-382.

1315 ROSENBERG, N. "Factors affecting the diffusion of technology", *Explor. econ. Hist.* 10(1), 1972 : 3-33.

1316 SABATIER, A. *Les chemins de l'innovation.* Paris, Chotard, 73, 203 p.

1317 SAGASTI, F. R. "Towards a new approach for scientific and technological planning", *Soc. Sci. Inform./Inform. Sci. soc.* 12(2), apr 73 : 67-95.

1318 SHERMAN, R.; TOLLIXON, R. "Technology, profit, risk, and assessments of market performance", *Quart. J. Econ.* 86(3), aug 72 : 448-462.

1319 SKLAIR, L. *Organized knowledge: a sociological view of science and technology.* St. Albans, Hart-Davis MacGibbon, 73, 284 p.

1320 SOLO, R. A.; ROGERS, E. M. (eds.). *Inducing technological change for economic growth and development.* Ann Arbor (Mich.), Michigan State University Press, 72, xvi-238 p.

1321 ŠPIRT, A. Ju. *Naučno-tehničeskaja revoljucija i razvivajuščiesja strany* (The scientific and technical revolution and the developing countries). Moskva, Izdatel'stvo APN, 72, 160 p.

1322 SPRUCH, W. *Strategia postępu technicznego. Wstęp do teorii* (Strategy of technological progress. Introduction to the theory). Warszawa, Państwowe Wydawnictwo Naukowe, 73, 486 p.

1323 STREETEN, P. "Technology gaps between rich and poor countries", *Scott. J. polit. Econ.* 19(3), nov 72 : 213-230.

1324 TEITEL, S. "Tecnología, industrialización y dependencia" (Technology, industrialisation and dependance), *Trim. econ.* 40(159), jul-sep 73 : 601-625.

1325 THRING, M. W.; BLAKE, A. *Man. machines and tomorrow.* London-Boston, Routledge and Kegan Paul, 73, xiii-127-8 p.

1326 Bibl. XXI-1660. TILTON, J. E. *International diffusion of technology: the case of semiconductors.* CR: W. H. GRUBER, *J. econ. Liter.* 11(1), mar 73 : 130-131.

1327 TRAPEZNIKOV, S. P. *et al. Naučno-tehničeskaja revoljucija i social'nyj progress* (The scientific and technical revolution and social progress). Moskva, Politizdat, 72, 367 p.

1328 VOLKOV, O. I. "Problemy planovogo upravlenija naučno-tehničeskim progressom" (Problems of planned management of scientific and technical progress), in: *Planirovanie i stimulirovanie naučno-tehničeskogo progress.* Moskva, 73 : 1-29.

1329 WILLIAMS, B. R. (ed.). *Science and technology in economic growth.* London, Macmillan; New York, Wiley, 73, xviii-446 p.

1330 WITTE, E. *Organisation für Innovationsentscheidnungen: das Promotoren-Modell* (Organization for innovation decision: the model of promotors). Göttingen, O. Schwartz, 73, viii-74 p.

## G.102 *Automation*

[See also / Voir aussi: 2477]

1331 FEDORENKO, N. G. (ed.). *Avtomatizironayye sistemy upravlenija predprijatijami* (Automated systems of enterprise management). Moskva, Nauka, 72, 214 p.

1332 INTERNATIONAL LABOR OFFICE. *Automation in developing countries*. Geneva, ILO, 72, x-246 p.

1333 INTERNATIONAL LABOR OFFICE. *Labour and social implications of automation and other technological developments*. Sixth item on the agenda. Geneva, ILO, 72, 75 p.

1334 KRUČININ, I. A. *Ėkonomičeskaja ėffektivnost' ASU* (Economic efficiency of automated systems). Moskva, Znanie, 72, 48 p.

1335 LUKE, H. D. *Automation for productivity*. New York, Becker and Hayes, 72, vii-290 p.

1336 MAJZEL', I. A. *Nauka, avtomatizacija, obščestvo* (Science, automation, society). Leningrad, Nauka, 72, 280 p.

1337 VELES'KO, Ė. I. *et al. Planovye rasčety v uslovijah ASU* (Planned estimation under automated system conditions). Moskva, Ėkonomika, 72, 239 p.

## G.11 Productivity : functions and measurement
## Productivité : fonctions et mesure

### G.111 *Output functions (increasing, constant, decreasing returns)*
### *Fonctions de rendement (croissantes, stables, décroissantes)*

[See also / Voir aussi: 2670]

1338 AFRIAT, S. N. "Efficiency estimation of production function", *Int. econ. R.* 13(3), oct 72 : 568-598.

1339 ARDENTI, J.; REICHENBACH, J. "Estimation de la fonction de production CES pour la Suisse", *Schweizer. Z. Volkswirtsch. Statist.* 108(4), dec 72 : 575-590.

1340 BECKMAN, M. J.; SATO, R.; SCHUPACK, M. "Alternative approaches to the estimation of production functions and of technical change", *Int. econ. R.* 13(1), feb 72 : 33-52.

1341 BIOLLEY, T. DE. *A new class of neo-classical production functions with corresponding investment behaviour*. Namur, CERUNA; Gembloux, Éditions Duculot, 72, xii-154 p.

1342 BITROS, G. "Replacement of the durable inputs of production", *Amer. Economist* 15(1), 1972 : 36-56.

1343 BRITVIN, V. G. "Ob usložnenii funkcii upravlenija socialističeskim proizvodstvom" (About the complexity of the socialist management production function), in: *Aktual' nye problemy upravlenija social'nymi processami pri socializnie*. Moskva, 1972 : 17-34.

1344 CANDELA, G. *La funzione della produzione in agricoltura* (Production function in agriculture). Milano, A. Giuffrè, 72, 65 p.

1245 CLUFF, A. T. "The cyclical behavior of labor productivity: implications for an incomes policy", *Quart. R. Econ. Busin.* 12(3), 1972 : 35-43.

1346 DIAMOND, P. A.; MIRRLEES, J. A. "Aggregate production with consumption externalities", *Quart. J. Econ.* 87(1), feb 73 : 1-24.

1347 FROHN, J. "Estimation of CES production functions with neutral technical change for industrial sectors in the Federal Republic of Germany, 1958-1968", *R. Income and Wealth* 18(2), jun 72 : 185-199.

1348 GOLOBORD'KO A. N. *Obščestvennyj kontrol'nad proizvodstvom i raspredeleniem pri socializme* (Social control of production and distribution under socialism). Kiev, Izdatel'stvo kievskogo Universiteta, 73, 295 p.

1349 Bibl. XXI-1694. GRILICHES, Z.; RINGSTAD, V. *Economies of scale and the form of the production function: an econometric study of Norwegian manufacturing establishment data*. CR: E. HOPE, *J. econ. Liter.* 10(4), dec 72 : 1204-1206.

1350 GUERBEROFF, S. L. "Sobre la aplicabilidad del análisis por función de producción para Argentina: análisis de un caso" (On the applicability of production function analysis in Argentina: a case analysis), *Económica (La Plata)* 18(1), jan-apr 72 : 23-44.

1351 GUHA, A. "CES production functions à la Samuelson", *R. econ. Stud.* 39(4), oct 72 : 501-503.

1352 GUJARATI, D.; FABOZZI, F. "Partial elasticities of factor substitution based on the CES production function: some empirical evidence", *B. econ. Res.* 24(1), mai 72 : 3-12.

1353 HARRIS, D. J. "Capital, distribution, and the aggregate production function", *Amer. econ. R.* 63(1), mar 73 : 100-113.

1354 HARRIS, D. J. "Feasible growth with specificity of capital and surplus labor", *West. econ. J.* 10(1), mar 72 : 65-75.

1355 HEIDRICH Z. *Rezerwy produkcyjne i ich wykorzystanie* (Productive capacity reserves and their utilization). Warszawa, Państowe Wydawnictwo Ekonomiczne, 73, 227 p.

1356 HEUBES, J. "Elasticity of substitution and growth rate of output", *German econ. R.* 10(2), 1972 : 170-175.

1357 ISAEVA, M. G. *Formy otraslevoj organizacii i effektivnost' proizvodstva* (Forms of sectoral organization and production efficiency). Alma-Ata, Nauka, 73, 256 p.

1358 JANVRY, A. DE. "The class of generalized power production functions", *Amer. J. agric. Econ.* 54(2), mai 72 : 234-237.

1359 JONES, R. W. "Activity analysis and real incomes: analogies with production models", *J. int. Econ.* 2(3), aug 72 : 277-302.

1360 KELEJIAN, H. H. "The estimation of Cobb-Douglas type functions with multiplicative and additive errors: a further analysis", *Int. econ. R.* 13(1), feb 72 : 179-182.

1361 KOCKELKORN, G. *Zweistufige Produktionsfunktionen mit konstanten Substitutionselastizitäten* (Two-tiered production functions with constant substitution elasticities). Würzburg, Physica-Verlag, 72, 157 p.

1362 KOT, S. M. "Funkcja produkcji z uwzględnieniem zmian parametrów strukturalnych w czasie" (The production function and the chronological changes in its parameters), *Zesz. nauk. wyższ. Szkoły ekon. w Krakow.* 51, 1972 : 155-170.

1363 KRENGEL, R. "Measurement of total factor input, technical change and output by industry in the Federal Republic of Germany, 1958-1968", *R. Income Wealth* 18(2), jun 72 : 173-183.

1364 MAGYIR, J. "A termelésnövekedés forrasainak kvantitativ tényezöi" (Quantitative factors of the sources of production growth), *Közgazd. Szle* 20(6), jun 73 : 715-725. [Hungary.]

1365 MAKAROV, S. P. *Centralizovannoe upravlenie proizvodstvom v uslovijah reformy* (Centralized planning of production under reform conditions) Moskva, Mysl', 72, 175 p.

1366 MARTYNIAK, Z. "Zastosowanie modeli i algorytmów optymalizacyjnych w organizowaniu procesów produkcyjnych" (The use of optimizing algorithms and models in organization of production processes), *Zesz. nauk. wyższ. Szkoły ekon. Krakow.* 56, 1973 : 39-57.

1367 McINTOSH, J. "Some notes on the surrogate production function", *R. econ. Stud.* 39(4), oct 72 : 505-510.

1368 MERA, K. "Regional production functions and social overhead capital: an analysis of the Japanese case", *Region. urb. Econ.* 3(2), mai 73 : 157-186.

1369 MEYER, R. A.; KADIYALA, K. R. *Linear and nonlinear estimation of production functions.* Lafayette, Ind., Herman C. Krannert Graduate School of Industrial Administration, Purdue University, 72, 22 l. — 9 p.

1370 MOSKOWITZ, H. *The value of information in aggregate production planning: a behavioral experiment.* Lafayette, Ind., Herman C. Krannert Graduate School of Industrial Administration, Purdue University, 72, 31-11 p.

1371 POL, J. E. "A note on the generalized production function", *R. econ. Stud.* 40(1), jan 73 : 139-140.

1372 ROODMAN, G. M. "The fixed coefficients production process under production uncertainty", *J. industr. Econ.* 20(3), jul 72 : 273-286.

1373 SCHRADER, H. *Produktionsfunktionen des Agrarsektors; Konzept, Schätzung und Anwendung* (The production function of the agricultural sector: concept, evaluation and utilization). Meisenheim-am-Glan, A. Hain, 73, 217 p.

1374 STERNAD, V. "Metody odvozeni jednotlivych typu produkčních funkci" (Alternative types of production functions), *Ékon.-matem. Obzor* 8(1), 1972 : 1-18.

1375 TOLKAČEV, A. S. *Problemy teorii i analiza effektivnosti obščestvennogo proizvodstva* (Social production efficiency theory and analysis problems) Moskva, Ekonomika, 72, 335 p.

1376 VAZQUEZ, A. "Input demand functions in the theory of production", *Riv. int. Sci. econ. com.* 19(10), oct 72 : 931-953.

1377 VAZQUEZ PEREZ, A. "Las demandas de los factores en la teoría de la producción: el equilibrio a largo plazo" (Factor demands in the production theory: long-term equilibrium), *A. Econ. (Madrid)* 8(13), jan-mar 72 : 197-227.

1378 VIHLJAEV, A. V. *Rost effektivnosti proizvodstva i izmenenie proporcij* (Growth of production efficiency and proportions change). Moskva, Izdatel'stvo Moskovskogo Universiteta, 73, 168 p.

63

1379    WEINTRAUB, S. "Marginal productivity and macrodistribution theory", *West. econ. J.* 10(1), mar 72 : 45-56.
1380    WYDYMUS, S. "Ekonometryczny model funkcji produkcji i wydajnosci pracy w przedsiębiorstwie przemysłowym" (Econometric model of production function and labour productivity in industrial enterprises), *Zesz. nauk. wyższ. Szkoły ekon. Krakow.* 51, 1972 : 115-142.
1381    YEUNG, P.; TSANG, H. "Generalized production function and factor-intensity crossovers: an empirical analysis", *Econ. Record* 48(123), sep 72 : 387-399.


### G.112    Measurement: principles and techniques
         Principes et techniques de mesure

[See also / Voir aussi:

1382    AGAPOVA, V. "Uzaimosvjaz' pokazatelej proizvoditel' nosti truda i pribyli" (The interrelation between labour productivity and profit indexes), *Ėkon. Nauki* 16(9), sep 73 : 45-52.
1383    GAVRILOV, R. V. *Izmerenie proizvoditel'nosti truda* (Labour productivity measurement). Iževsk, Udmurtija, 72, 123 p.
1384    GREENBERG, L. *A practical guide to productivity measurement.* Washington, Bureau of National Affairs, 73, vi-71 p.
1385    GRIFFIN, J. M. "An economic measure of capacity in a joint product, multiprocess industry", *J. polit. Econ.* 80(4), jul-aug 72 : 703-723.
1386    KULIK, C. "Propozycja sporzadzania pewnych schematów postępowania przy szacowaniu parametrów modeli matematycznych procesów technologicznych" (A proposal for the construction of certain procedural schemes for estimating parameters of mathematical models of the technological process) *Zesz. nauk. wyższ. Szkoły ekon. Krakow.* 51, 1972 : 1911-199.
1387    MEGYERI, E. "A vallalati alapok optimalis kihasznalasa és a hatékonyság mérés néhány problémaja" (The optimal utilization of basic enterprise data and the problems of productivity measurement), *Közgazd. Szle* 20(10), oct 73 : 1169-1185. [Hungary.]
1388    NADIRI, M. I. "International studies of factor inputs and total factor productivity; a brief survey", *R. Income Wealth* 18(2), jun 72 : 129-154.
1389    NORMAN, R. G.; BAHIRI, S. *Productivity measurement and incentives.* London Butterworths, 72, 10-181 p.
1390    O'HERLIHY, C. S. J. "Capital/labour substitution and the developing countries: a problem of measurement", *Oxford Univ. Inst. econ. Statist.* 34(3), aug 72 : 269-280.
1391    TABAČNIKAS, B. I. "Kategorija effektivnosti obščestvennogo proizvodstva i e pokazateli" (Category of social production efficiency and its indexes), in: *Sovremennye problemy ėkonomiki i narodonaselenija SSSR* Leningrad, 72 : 306-319.


### G.12    Productivity : descriptive studies
         Productivité : études descriptives

[See also / Voir aussi: **H.1116; H.2113; H.411;** 1908, 4102, 4506, 4521]

1392    ABERG, T. "Regional productivity differences in Swedish manufacturing", *Region. urb. Econ.* 3(2), mai 73 : 131-156.
1393    BROWN, E. H. P. "Levels and movements of industrial productivity and real wages internationally compared, 1860-1970", *Econ. J.* 83(329), mar 73 : 58-71.
1394    BYRSKI, B.; LUCHTER, E. "Produktywnosc srodków trwałych w przemysle a decyzje inwestycyjne" (Productivity of capital goods in industry and investment decisions), *Zesz. nauk. wyzsz. Szkoły ekon. Krakow* 50, 1972 : 51-69. [Poland.]
1395    DIENES, L. "Regional variations of capital and labor productivity in Soviet industry", *J. region. Sci.* 12(3), 1972 : 401-406.
1396    "Évolution de la productivité", *Statist. Ét. financ. Sér. orange* 3(12), 4 trim. 73 : 3-11. [France.]
1397    KALISIAK, J. *Badanie efektywności ekonomicznej postępu techniczno-organizacyjnego na przykładzie przemysłu przetwórczego Japonii, Niemieckiej Republiki Federalnej,*

*Polski i Stanów Zjednoczonych* (Research on economic efficiency of technological and organizational progress, on the example of the manufacturing industries of Japan, the GFR, Poland and the USA), Warszawa, Państwowe Wydawnictwo Naukowe, 73, 227 p.

1398 KARPOHIN, D. N. *Proizvoditel'nost' obščestvennogo truda i narodnohozjajstvennye proporcii* (Social labour productivity and the national economy proportions). Moskva, Msyl', 72, 317 p. [USSR.]

1399 LENGELLE, M. "Réflexions sur la productivité du travail dans l'agriculture et l'équilibre entre les trois grands secteurs de l'économie dans les pays en voie de développement", *Mondes en Dévelop.* (2), 1972 : 223-237.

1400 McKERSIE, R. B.: HUNTER, L. C. *Pay, productivity and collective bargaining* London, Macmillan; New York, St Martin's Press, 73, xvii-389 p. [UK.]

1401 MIKUL'SKIJ, K. I. *Problemy ěffektivnosti socialističeskoj ěkonomiki iz opyta hozjajstvennogo sotrudničestva v stranah SEV* (Problems of socialist economy efficiency. From the experiment of the Comecon countries economic cooperation). Moskva, Nauka, 72, 283 p.

1402 NORDHAUS, W. D. "The recent productivity slowdown", *Brookings Pap. econ. Activity* (3), 1972 : 493-535.

1403 TRIPATHI, K. M. "Higher productivity in a developing economy: an urgent need", *Ind. Lab. (Delhi)* 13(6), jun 72 : 809-830. [India.]

1404 VALKOV, I. *Proizvoditelnost na truda i rabotna zaplata v promišlenostta na NRB* (Labour productivity and wages in the Bulgarian PR's industry). Sofija, Partizdat, 73, 231 p.

1405 VARZIN, N. "Rost proizvoditel'nosti truda v stranah SEV" (The increase of labor productivity in COMECON member countries), *Vopr. Ěkon.* 25(1), jan 73 : 72-78. [Also published in Hungarian, *Közgazd. Szle* 20(4), apr 73 : 471-479.]

## G.13 Productivity policy
## Politique de productivité

[See also / Voir aussi: **H.1116; H.2113; H.511; 3234**]

1406 ANIKIN, B. A. *Metody povyšenija proizvoditel'nosti truda inženerno-techničeskih rabotniko* (Methods for increasing labour productivity of scientific and technical workers). Moskva, Znanie, 72, 32 p.

1407 ARTEMOV, Ju. M.; PARASOČKA, V. T. *Fond material'nogo pooščrenija i rost proizvoditel'nosti truda* (Material stimulation funds and labour productivity growth). Moskva, Finansy, 72, 64 p.

1408 BOR, M. Z. *Ěffektivnost'obščestvennogo proizvodstva i problemy optimal'nogo planirovanija* (Efficiency of social production and problems of optimal planning). Moskva, Mysl', 72, 336 p.

1409 ČERKASOV, V. Ě. *Ěkonomičeskie stimuly proizvodstva* (Economic incentives for production). Alma-Ata, Kazahstan, 72, 156 p.

1410 CUBAROF, Ju. V. "Stimulirovanie proizvoditel'nosti truda" (Stimulation of labour productivity), *Finansy SSSR* 47(6), jun 73 : 31-35. [USSR.]

1411 EGIAZARJAN, G. "Razvitie hozjajstvennogo rasčeta i stimulizovanije proizvodstva" (The development of financial autonomy and the stimulation of production), *Kommunist Ěstonii* 29(2), feb 73 : 57-72.

1412 KAPESOV, N. "Značenie moral'nyh stimulov k trudu pri socialisme" (The meaning of moral incentives for labour under socialism), *Filos. Nauki* (1), 1971 : 106-116.

1413 KAZAČENOK, A. G. *Problemy proizvoditel'nosti truda* (Labour productivity problems). Minsk, Nauka i tehnika, 73, 192 p.

1414 LEVITIN, L. I. *Trudovoj kollektiv i socialističeskoe sorevnovanie* (Labour collectivity and socialist stimulation). Frunze, Kyrgyzstan, 72, 86 p.

1415 MANZA, A. P. *Proizvoditel'nost' truda i stimuly eě rosta. Voprosy teorii i metodiki* (Labour productivity and incentives for its growth. Theoretical and methodoligical questions). Kišinev, Štiinca, 72, 99 p.

1416 SOLOV'EV, P. F. *Socialističeskoe sorevnovanie—metod kommunističeskogo stroitel'stva* (Socialist stimulation in the method of communist edification). Frunze, Kyrgyzstan, 72, 104 p.

1417    Turčins, Ja. B. *Optimizacija socialističeskogo proizvodstva* (Optimization of socialist production). Riga, Zinatne, 72, 340 p.

1418    Włodarczyk, M. "Metody optymalizacji okresu użytkowania srodków produkcji" (Optimization methods for the period of maintenance of means of production), *Przegl. statyst.* 3, 1973 : 351-362.

## G.2    LABOUR PROBLEMS
## PROBLÈMES DU TRAVAIL

### G.20    General studies
### Études générales

1419    Barzel, Y.; McDonald, R. J. "Assets, subsistence, and the supply curve of labor", *Amer. econ. R.* 63(4), sep 73 : 621-633.

1420    Bujan, I. V. *Social'no-ěkonomičeskie osnovy truda pri socializme* (Socio-economic bases of labour under socialism). Kiev, Naukova Dunka, 73, 191 p.

1421    Cartter, A. M.; Marshall, F. R. *Labor economics; wages, employment, and trade unionism.* Rev. ed. Homewood, Ill., R. D. Irwin, 72, xiv-584 p.

1422    Dougherty, C. R. "Estimates of labor aggregation functions", *J. polit. Econ.* 80(6), nov-dec 72 : 1101-1119.

1423    Gin, L. T.; Baskatov, V. D. "O soderžanii truda v uslovijah naučno-tehničeskoj revoljucii pri socializme" (On the labour content in the scientific and technical revolution conditions under socialism), *Nauk. Dokl. vysš. Školy nauč. Kommunizm* (4), 1973 : 20-27.

1424    Ivanova, Z. B. *Psihologija na truda* (The psychology of work). Sofija, Nauka i izkustvo, 72, 360 p.

1425    King, J. E. *Labour economics.* London, Macmillan, 72, 76 p.

1426    Knjazev, B. V. et al. *Voprosy razvitija trudovogo kollektiva pri socializme* (Questions on the development of the labour collective under socialism). Moskva, 72, 236 p.

1427    Kuz'menkov, V. P. *Kibernetika i trud* (Cybernetics and labour). Minsk, Nauka tehnika, 72, 168 p.

1428    Martin, R.; Fryer, R. H. *Redundancy and paternalist capitalism: a study in the sociology of work.* London, Allen and Unwin, 73, 3-278 p.

1429    Michón, F. "Miejsce ekonomiki pracy w naukach ekonomicznych i perspektywy jej rozwoju" (The role of labour economics in economic sciences and its prospect of development), *Fol. oecon. cracov.* 14, 1973 : 9-25.

1430    Perez Luno, A. E. "El trabajo como problema filosófico (Work as a philosophical problem), *R. Estud. polit.* 183-184, mai-aug 72 : 257-266.

1431    Pfaller, A. "Organized labour, income distribution and the conditions for economic development. A framework for comparative research", *Vierteljahresberichte* 53, sep 73 : 265-288.

1432    Rees, A. *The economics of work and pay.* New York, Harper and Row, 73, ix-247 p.

1433    Tomcuk, P. V. *Obščestvennaja forma truda pri socializme (Voprosy metodologii i teorii)* (The social form of labour under socialism. Methodological and theoretical questions). L'vov, L'vovskij Universitet, 72, 204 p.

1434    Tovmasjan, S. S. *Filosofskie problemy truda i tehniki* (Philosophical problems of work labour and techniques). Moskva, Mysl', 72, 279 p.

1435    Vernieres, M. *Travail et croissance; essai sur le role du facteur travail au cours du processus de croissance.* Paris, Éditions Cujas, 72, 204 p.

1436    Zinn, K. G. *Arbeitswerttheorie; zum heutigen Verständnis der positiven Wirtschaftstheorie von Karl Marx* (The theory of labor value: for the present comprehension of Karl Marx's positive economic theory). Herne, Verlag Neue Wirtschafts-Briefe 72, 147 p.

**G.21    Labour force and labour market
Main-d'œuvre et marché du travail**

**G.210    *General studies
Études générales***

[See also / Voir aussi: 4017, 5121]

1437   BULOCNIKOVA, L. *et al. Socialno-ěkonomičeskie problemy ispol'zovahija rabočej šily* (Socio-economic problems of labour force utilization). Moskva, Mysl', 73, 208 p.

1438   ČEMBROVSKIJ, V. V. "Sovremennaja naučnaja revoljucija i trudovye resursy" (The contemporary scientific revolution and labour resources), in: *Trudovye resursy.* Kišinev, 1972 : 3-20.

1439   COEN, R. M. "Labour force and unemployment in the 1920's and 1930's: a re-examination based on postwar experience", *R. Econ. Statist.* 55(1), feb 73 : 46-55.

1440   CORINA, J. *Labour market economics: a short survey of recent theory.* London, Heinemann Educational, 72, 7-81 p.

1441   DENISOV, A. A. *et al. Rabočaja sila y sistema socialističeskih proizvodstvennyh otnosenij* (Labour force in the socialist production relations system). Jaroslavl', 73, 164 p.

1442   "Dual labor markets", *Amer. econ. R.* 63(2), mai 73 *Pap. and Proc.*: 359-384. With contributions by: M. REICH, D. M. GORDON, R. C. EDWARDS, T. VIETORISZ, B. HARRISON and M. J. PIORE.

1443   FLAMHOLTZ, E. "Human resource accounting: its role in management planning and control", *Econ. soc. Tijds.* 26(5), oct 72 : 3-22.

1444   FLAMHOLTZ, E. "Toward a theory of human resource value in formal organizations", *Accting R.* 47(4), oct 72 : 666-678.

1445   HALEY, W. J. "Human capital: the choice between investment and income", *Amer. econ. R.* 63(5), dec 73 : 929-944.

1446   HOLMES, J. M. "The Keynesian aggregate supply function of labour", *J. Amer. Statist. Assoc.* 67(340), dec 72 : 797-802.

1447   JAKIMOV, V. N. "Zakonomernosti vosproizvodstva rabočej sily pri socializme" (Laws of labour force reproduction under socialism), in: *Vosproizvodstvo rabočej sily v uslovijah tehničeskogo progressa.* Čeboksary, 1972 : 6-78.

1448   JAKUBAUSKAS, E. B.; PALOMBA, N. A. *Manpower economics.* Reading, Mass., Addison-Wesley Publishing Co., 73, xi-301 p.

1449   KALACHEK, E. D. *Labor markets and unemployment.* Belmont, Calif., Wadsworth Publishing Co., 73, 146 p.

1450   LJUL'ČENKO, G. *et al. Voprosy vosproizvodstva i racional'nogo ispol'zovanija trudovyh resursov* (Questions of labour resources reproduction and rational utilization). Kaunas, 72, 197 p.

1451   LUNDE, J. *Menneskelig kapital* (Human capital). København K, Studenterradet ved Københavns Universitet, 72, 5-145 p.

1452   MABRY, B. DuP. *Economics of manpower and the labor market.* New York, Intext Educational Publishers, 73, xiv-682 p.

1453   MAJKOV, A. Z. (ed.). *Problemy racional'nogo ispol'zovanija trudovyh resursov* (Problems of labour resources rational utilization). Moskva, Ěkonomika, 73, 527 p.

1454   NOVIKOV, K. A.; MAJKOV, A. Z. *Normativnye akty po ispol'zovaniju trudovyh resurso v* (Normative acts in labour resources utilization). Moskva, Juridičeskaja Literature, 72, 943 p.

1455   PARSONS, D. O. "Specific human capital: an application to quit rates and lay off rates", *J. polit. Econ.* 80(6), nov-dec 72 : 1120-1143.

1456   PHILLIPS, L.; VOTEY, H. L.; MAXWELL, D. "Crime, youth, and the labour market", *J. polit. Econ.* 80(3), mai-jun 72 : 491-504.

1457   PSACHAROPOULOS, G.; HINCHLIFFE, K. "Further evidence on the elasticity of substitution among different types of educated labor", *J. polit. Econ* 80(4), jul-aug 72 : 786-792.

1458   RAJKIEWICZ, A. "Czynniki kształtujace sytuację na rynku pracy" (Social and economic factors affecting labour market), *Probl. Ekon. (Warszawa)* 2, 1973 : 7-14.

1459   RAZIN, A. "Investment in human capital and economic growth", *Metroeconomica* 24(2), mai-aug 73 : 101-116.

67

1507  CHANDAVARKAR, A. G. "More growth—more employment? A challenge for the less-developed countries", *Finance and Develop.* 9(2), jun 72 : 28-35.

1508  CORBILLE, F. "Chômage et réserves de main-d'œuvre: une gestion impérialiste des excédents?", *Crit. Écon. polit.* 10, jan-mar 73 : 4-29.

1509  ELOY, J. Y.; VANDERPOTTE, G. "Ambiguïtés des définitions du chômage", *Sociol. Trav.* 15(3), jul-sep 73 : 293-306.

1510  FLANAGAN, R. J. "The US Phillips curve and international unemployment rate differentials", *Amer. econ. R.* 63(1), mar 73 : 114-131.

1511  GHOSH, B. N. "Note on 'work-making' and 'work-stretching': aspects of disguised unemployment", *Ind. econ. J.* 19(3), jan-mar 72 : 377-386.

1512  HAMAKER, H. G. "Over werkloosheid. Bespreking van enige recente literatuur" (About unemployment. A review of some recent literature), *Sociol. Gids* 20(5), sep-oct 73 : 369-385.

1513  HSIEH, C. "Measuring the effects of trade expansion on employment; a review of some research", *Int. Lab. R.* 107(1), jan 73 : 1-29.

1514  KURMAN, M. V. "Optimal'naja zanjatost' naselenija v socialističeskom obščestve. Količestvennyj aspekt" (Optimal employment of populations in the socialist society. A quantitative aspect), *Demogr. Tetrady* (6-7), 1972 : 185-198.

1515  LEIGH, D. E. "An empirical investigation of the determinants of the level of unemployment in six major occupations", *West. econ. J.* 10(4), dec 72 : 384-395.

1516  LOGVINOV, L. D. *Vseobščaja zanjatost' i razdelenie truda pri socializme* (General employment and labour distribution under socialism). Moskva, Mysl', 72, 239 p.

1517  MacRAE, C. D. "The relation between unemployment and inflation in the Laffer-Ransom model", *J. Busin.* 45(4), oct 72 N: 513-518.

1518  MADAIAH, M. "Disguised unemployment and economic growth: a duagrammatic representation", *Ind. econ. J.* 19(1), jul-sep 71 : 74-84.

1519  MATON, J. "Employment, output, income distribution and technical progress a theoretical model", *Tijds. Econ.* 17(4), 1972 : 417-426.

1520  POLEMAN, T. T. "Employment, population and food: the new hierarchy of development problems", *Food Res. Int. Stud.* 11(1), 1972 : 11-27.

1521  POST, J. G. "Werkloosheid, inflatie en rentevorming" (Unemployment, inflation and income for a nation), *Economie (Tilburg)* 37(6), mar 73 : 229-242.

1522  VERMA, P. "Employment effects of technological change", *Manpower J.* 8(4), jan-mar 73 : 9-17.

### G.2121    *Aggregate level*
         *Niveau global*

[See also / Voir aussi: 2845, 3184, 4106, 4108, 4120, 4530, 5635]

1523  BAIROCH, P. *Urban unemployment in developing countries; the nature of the problem and proposals for its solution.* Geneva, International Labour Office, 73, v-99 p.

1524  BANERJEE, R. M. "Employment in small industry in West Bengal", *Manpower J.* 8(1), apr-jun 72 : 100-119.

1525  BAXTER, J. L. "Long-term unemployment in Great Britain, 1953-1917", *B. Oxford Univ. Inst. Econ. Statist.* 34(4), nov 72 : 329-344.

1526  BEAUCOURT, C. "Le plein emploi en U.R.S.S.", *Projet* 72, feb 73 : 204-211.

1527  BHAGWAT, A. "Main features of the employment problem in developing countries", *Staff Pap.* 20(1), mar 73 : 78-99.

1528  BOWERS, J. K. *et al.* "Some aspects of unemployment and the labour market, 1966-71", *Nat. Inst. econ. R.* 62(4), nov 72 : 75-88. [UK.]

1529  CAFFE, F. "Considerazioni sul problema della disoccupazione in Italia" (Considerations on the unemployment problem in Italy), *Riv. int. Sci. econ. com.* 20(1), jan 73 : 6-17.

1530  CANADA. Department of Labour. Economics and Research Branch. *Employment, wages and working conditions in industries under federal jurisdiction,* 1965-1970. Ottawa, Information Canada, 72, xiii-202 p. [Canada.]

1531  DESTEFANIS, M. *et al. L'analyse de l'emploi par région et département.* Paris, Presses universitaires de France, 73, 216 p. [France.]

1532    DREKONJA, G. "Employment problems in Latin America: the Colombian and Cuban cases compared", *Stud. comp. int. Develop.* 8(2), été 73 : 162-182.

1533    EHRENBERG, R. G. "The demand for State and local government employees", *Amer. econ. R.* 63(3), jun 73 : 366-379.

1534    *Employment and earnings. United States, 1909-1971.* Washington (D.C.), United States Government Printing Office, 72, xlviii-688 p.

1535    FERNANDEZ GASCON, E. "Subempleo en América latina" (Underemployment in Latin America), *R. mexic. Trab.* 20(1), jan-mar 73 : 32-45.

1536    FINDIA, M. "L'occupazione in Italie e nel Mezzogiorno secondo i tre ultimi censimenti" (Employment in Italy and in the South according to the last censuses), *Rass. econ. (Napoli)* 37(4), jul-aug 73 : 951-969.

1537    FRANCE. Institut national de la statistique et des études économiques. *Structures des emplois en 1971.* Paris, INSEE, 72, 68 p.

1538    GELDNER, I. *Berechnung von Arbeitslosenzahlen nach Branchen* (Evaluation of the number of unemployed by branch), Linz, Österreichisches für Arbeitsmarktpolitik, 72, 51 p. [Austria.]

1539    GONZÁLEZ SALAZAR, G. *Subocupacion y estructura de clases sociales en México* (Underemployment and class structure in Mexico). México, Universidad Nacional Autónoma de México, Facultad de Ciencias Políticas y Sociales, 72, 162 p.

1540    GORDON, R. J. "The welfare cost of higher unemployment", *Brookings Pap. econ. Activity* (1), 1973 : 133-205. [USA.]

1541    HART, K. "Informal income opportunities and urban employment in Ghana", *J. mod. Afr. Stud.* 11(1), mar 73 : 61-89.

1542    HASSAN, M. "Unemployment in Latin America: causes and remedies", *Amer. J. Econ. Sociol.* 32(2), apr 73 : 179-190.

1543    HILL, M. J. et al. *Men out of work; a study of unemployment in three English towns.* Cambridge, Eng., University Press, 73, 193 p.

1544    HUGON, P. "La planification de l'enseignement et de l'emploi en Afrique noire et à Madagascar", *R. écon. Madagascar* 6, jan-dec 71 : 265-315.

1545    JACKSON, M. "Unemployment and occupational wage changes in local labor markets", *Industr. Lab. Relat. R.* 26(4), jul 73 : 1135-1145. [USA.]

1546    KJELD, P. "Sysselsättningsproblem i U-land" (Employment problems in underdeveloped countries), *Int. Stud. (Stockholm)* (5), mai 72 : 4-18.

1547    LEIGH, D. E. "Short-run analysis of the occupational structure of unemployment in the United States", *J. econ. Busin.* 25(1), 1972 : 35-38.

1548    MacKAY, R. P. "Employment creation in the development areas", *Scott. J. polit. econ.* 19(3), nov 72 : 287-296. [UK.]

1549    OFFICE NATIONAL D'INFORMATION SUR LES ENSEIGNEMENTS ET LES PROFESSIONS. *Tendances d'évolution de l'emploi en France jusqu'en 1975.* Paris, ONISEP, 72, 48 p.

1550    PERRY, G. "Unemployment flows in the US labor market", *Brookings Pap. econ. Activity* (2), 1972 ; 245-292.

1551    POHL, R.; LAVILHE, P.; LIONNET, R. "Enquête sur l'emploi de 1970", *Coll. INSÉÉ. Sér. D* 20, feb 73 : 109 p. [France.]

1552    POHL, R. et al. "Enquête sur l'emploi de 1971 et 1972", *Coll. INSÉÉ Sér. D* 12, mai 72 : 1-77; 19, feb 73 : 111 p. [France.]

1553    SALAIS, R. "L'évolution de l'emploi dans les pays du Marché commun de 1958 à 1970", *Écon. et Statist.* 41, jan 73 : 3-16.

1554    SALAIS, R.; LIONNET, R. *Enquêtes sur l'emploi de 1968 et 1969: résultats détaillés.* Paris, Institut national de la statistique et des études économiques, 73, 143 p. [France.]

1555    SCULLY, G. W.; GALLAWAY, L. E. "A spectral analysis of the demographic structure of American unemployment", *J. Busin.* 46(1), jan 73 : 87-102. [USA.]

1556    SHECK, R. C.; BROWN, L. A.; HORTON, F. E. "Employment structure as an indicator of shifts in the space economy: the case of the Central American Common Market region", *R. geogr. (Rio de Janeiro)* 75, dec 72 : 49-72.

1557    SMITH, L. D. "Aspects of the employment problem: a case study of Kenya", *Round Table* 249, jan 73 : 105-114.

1558    STEWART, M. *Employment, conditions in Europe.* Eppings, Gower Press; London, Employment Conditions Abroad Ltd, 72, xviii-206 p.

1650    GOLDSTEIN, J. H. *The effectiveness of manpower training programs: a review of research on the impact on the poor.* Washington, United States Government Printing Office, 72, vii-70 p. [USA.]

1651    GREEN, R. "Manpower planning in New Zealand", *New Zealand J. publ. Adm.* 35(2), mar 73 : 39-47.

1652    HAIDARI, I. (ed.). *The new labour policy: impact and implications.* Karachi, Economic and Industrial Publications, 72, 95 p. [Pakistan.]

1653    HALLMAN, H. W.; CRAWFORD, E.; BRISCOE, A. F. *Jobs for all: employment and manpower programs for the seventies.* Washington, Center for Governmental Studies, 72, v-199 p. [USA.]

1654    HIRSCH, E. *Employment and income policies for Iran.* Geneva, International Labour Office, 73, vi-100 p.

1655    HUSZÁR, I. *et al.* "Fundamental problems in the long-range manpower planning and living standard policies", *Acta oecon.* 9(2), 1972 : 137-151. [Hungary.]

1656    INTERNATIONAL LABOUR OFFICE. *Employment, incomes and equality; a strategy for increasing productive employment in Kenya.* Geneva, I.L.O., 72, xx-600 p.

1657    KIDDER, D. E. *Education and manpower planning in India.* Bombay, Progressive Corporation, 73, ix-182 p.

1658    KIRSCHEN, E. S. "La flexibilité de l'offre de travail en Belgique; rôle de la politique économique", *C. écon.* Bruxelles 55, 3e trim. 72 : 403-410.

1659    MACKAY, D. I.; REID, G. L. "Redundancy, unemployment and manpower policy", *Econ. J.* 82(328), dec 72 : 1256-1272. [UK.]

1660    MUKHERJEE, S. *Making labour markets work; a comparison of the U.K. and Swedish systems.* London, Political and Economic Planning, 72, x-153 p.

1661    NABI, M. "Éléments d'introduction à une politique de l'emploi", *R. algér. Trav.* (10) sep 71 : 37-49. [Algérie.]

1662    ORGANIZATION FOR ECONOMIC COOPERATION AND DEVELOPMENT. *Manpower policy in Japan.* Paris, OECD, 73, 169 p.

1663    ORGANIZATION FOR ECONOMIC COOPERATION AND DEVELOPMENT. *Manpower policy in Norway.* Paris, Washington, D.C., OECD Publications Center, 72, 241 p.

1664    PIERSON, J. H. G. *Essays on full employment, 1942-1972.* Metuchen, N. J., Scarecrow Press, 72, xxiii-362 p. [USA.]

1665    RUDNER, M. "Malayan labor in transition: labor policy and trade unionism, 1955-1963", *Mod. Asian Stud.* 7(1), jan 73 : 21-45.

1666    SHAEFFER, R. G. *Nondiscrimination in employment: changing perspectives, 1963-1972.* New York, Conference Board, 73, iii-100 p.

1667    SOLOW, R. M. "What happened to full employment ?", *Quart. R. Econ. Busin.* 13(2), été 73 : 7-20. [USA.]

1668    TAIGAR, S. "Quelques aspects de la politique d'emploi en Roumanie", *Inst. int. Ét. soc. B.* (9), 1972 : 107-117.

1669    ULMAN, L. (ed.). *Manpower programs in the policy mix.* Baltimore, Johns Hopkins University Press, 73, viii-165 p. [USA.]

1670    WOLFBEIN, S. L. *Manpower policy: perspectives and prospects.* Philadelphia, Temple University, School of Business Administration, 73, xxii-220 p. [USA.]

1671    ZAK, S. I. *Planirovanie truda i zarahotnoj platy v stroitel'nyh organizacijah* (Labour and wages planning in construction organizations). Moskva, Strojizdat, 72, 95 p.

### G.224    Employment policy: special classes of labour
###          Politique d'emploi: secteurs particuliers

#### G.2241    Children and juveniles
####          Enfants et jeunes gens

[See also / Voir aussi: 1702, 2062]

1672    ADIE, D. K. "Teen-age unemployment and real federal minimum wages", *J. polit. Econ.* 81(2), mar-apr 73 : 435-441. [USA.]

1673    AHIER, V. "Young unemployed, who are they and why ?", *B.A.C.I.E. J.* 27(1), mar 73 : 8-14. [UK.]

1674   BOGDANOVA, T. P. *Trud i social'naja aktivnost' molodeži* (Labour and youth social activity). Minsk, Belorusskij Universitet, 72, 240 p.

1675   *Emplois tenus par les jeunes de 17 ans (Les)*. Paris, La Documentation française, 73, 127 p. [France.]

1676   JURRIENS, R. "Bedrijfsleven en werkende jeugd in Nederland" (Companies and young employees in the Netherlands), *Econ. soc. Tijds.* 26(5), oct 72 : 507-516.

1677   KALAŠNIKOVA, R. I. "Socialističeskoe sorevnovanievaznyj faktor povyšenija trudovoj aktivnosti molodezi" (Socialist emulation is an essential factor for the elevation of youth labour activity), in: *Voprosy naučnogo kommunizma*. II. Moskva, 1972 : 110-131.

1678   MEL'NOV, M. A. (ed.). *Osnovy ėkonomiki truda i proizvodstva dlja molodyh rabočih* (Economy of labour and production bases for young workers). Moskva, Politizdat, 72, 272 p.

1679   RAWLINS, V. L. "Manpower programs for disadvantaged youths", *Indus. Relat. (Berkeley)* 11(2), mai 72 : 184-197.

1680   SRIVASTAVA, R. K.; SELVARATNAM, S. "Youth employment in Ceylon: problems and prospects", *Marga* 1(4), 1972 : 27-59.

1681   TAYLOR, R. B. *Sweatshops in the sun; child labor on the farm*. Boston, Beacon Press, 73 xvii-216 p.

### G.2242   Women
Femmes

1682   ANGRIST, S. S. "Measuring women's career commitment", *Sociol. Focus* 5(2), 1972-1972 : 29-39.

1683   BLITS, R. C.; OW, C. H. "A cross-sectional analysis of women's participation in the professions", *J. polit. Econ.* 81(1), jan-feb 73 : 131-144.

1684   BOESJES-HOMMES, R. W. "Overheids-beleid ten aanzien van de inschakeling van de vrouw in het arbeidsproces. Het Zweedse model" (Authority functions regarding the integration of woman in the work process. The Swedish example), *Soc. Maandbl. Art.* 28(4), apr 73 : 213-225.

1685   BORRIES, H. J. "Die Entwicklung der Erwerbstätigkeit der Frauen und ihre Einfluss-faktoren" (The evolution of woman's job and its determinig factors), *Wirtsch. u. Statist.* (3), mai 73 : 149-154. [Germany, FR.]

1686   BRANDT, G.; KOOTZ, J.; STEPPKE, G. *Zur Frauenfrage im Kapitalismus* (The feminíst question in capitalism). Frankfurt-am-Main, Suhrkamp, 73, 254 p.

1687   BULWIK, H. C.; ELICKS, S. R. *Affirmative action for women: myth and reality*. Berkeley, Institute of Business and Economic Research, University of California, 72, vi-69 p.

1688   DREHER, R. "Aspekte der Frauenarbeit in Japan" (Aspects of woman's labor in Japan), *Int. Asian Forum* 4(3), jul 73 : 455-464.

1689   "Emploi féminin (L'). Recherches pour une problématique", *Bull. CERP* 20(3-4), jul-dec 71 : 451 p. [France.]

1690   ESCALERE, B. "Place de la femme dans le droit du travail", *Vie soc.* (12), dec 72 : 655-662.

1691   EVANS, D. R. "Image and reality: career goals of educated Ugandan women", *Canad. J. Afr. Stud.* 6(2), 1972 : 213-232.

1692   FONTENEAU, G. "Analysis of the causes of the restricted participation of women in trade union life", *Labor* 45(5), 1972 : 193-203.

1693   FURNARI, M. "Occupazione femminile in agricoltura e mercato del lavoro" (Female labour in agriculture and labour market), *Riv. Econ. agr.* 28(1), jan-feb 73 : 19-39. [Italy.]

1694   GALENSON, M. *Women and work; an international comparison*. Ithaca, N. Y. State School of Industrial and Labor Relations, Cornell University, 73, viii-120 p.

1695   GARANCSY, G. "Situation juridique de la femme qui travaille en Hongrie", *R. Pays Est* 13(1), 1972 : 85-98.

1696   HABER, S. "Trends in work rates of white females, 1890 to 1950", *Industr. Lab. Relat. R.* 26(4), jul 73 : 1122-1134. [USA.]

1697   HANQUET, H. *Travail professionnel des femmes et mutations sociales*. Bruxelles, Éditions "Vie ouvrière", 72, 405 p.

1698   HAYGHE, H. "Labor force activity of married women", *Mthly Lab. R.* 96(4), apr 73 : 31-36.

1699    LANTIER, F. *Le travail et la formation des femmes en Europe; incidences de la planification de l'éducation et du changement technologique sur l'accès aux emplois et aux carrières.* Paris, La Documentation française, 72, 67 p.

1700    LEPARO, R. "Capitalisme et patriarcat à travers l'analyse économique du travail féminin", *Crit. Écon. polit.* (11-12), apr-sep 73 : 164-191. [France.]

1701    LORING, R.; WELLS, T. *Breakthrough; women into management.* New York, Van Nostrand Reinhold Co., 72, xi-202 p.

1702    MAFFEI, M.; VESSIA, A. *La tutela del lavoro delle donne e dei fanciulli* (The protection of female and child labour). Novara-Roma, PEM, 72, vii-398 p. [Italy.]

1703    MARCHAK, P. "Women workers and white-collar unions", *Canad. R. Sociol. Anthropol.* 10(2), mai 73 : 134-147.

1704    OPPENHEIMER, V. "Demographic influence on female employment and the status of women", *Amer. J. Sociol.* 78(4), jan 73 : 946-961.

1705    PERRICONE, R. A. *L'inserimento della donna nelle attività economiche in Italia* (The woman's insertion in Italian economic activity). Roma, Società italiana di economia, demografia e statistica, 72, 96 p.

1706    POTET KERGOAT, M. "L'emploi féminin en Bretagne. Analyse de l'évolution et prévisions", *B. Conjonct. région. (Rennes)* 17(4), 1972 : 30 p.

1707    SCHEURINGER, B. *Die Berufsmobilität von Frauen* (Professional mobility of women). Linz, Österreichisches Institut für Arbeitsmarktpolitik, 72, 295 p.

1708    SCHWARZ, A. "Illusion d'une émancipation et aliénation réelle de l'ouvrière zairoise", *Canad. J. Afr. Stud.* 6(2), 1972 : 183-212.

1709    SILVER, C. B. "Salon, foyer, bureau; women and the professions in France", *Amer. J. sociol.* 78(4), jan 73 : 836-851.

1710    SORKIN, A. L. "On the occupational status of women, 1870-1970", *Amer. J. Econ. Sociol.* 32(3), jul 73 : 235-243. [USA.]

1711    SPENCER, B. G. "Determinants of the labour force participation of married women: a micro-study of Toronto households", *Canad. J. Econ.* 6(2), mai 73 : 222-238.

1712    SULLEROT, E. *L'emploi des femmes et ses problèmes dans les États membres de la Communauté.* Luxembourg, Office des publications officielles des Communautés européennes, 72, 50 p.

1713    SWEET, J. A. "Employment of rural farm wives", *Rur. Sociol.* 37(4), dec 72 : 553-577.

1714    SZTOKMAN, N. "Tendances récentes de l'activité professionnelle des Parisiennes", *Ét. Région. paris.* 46(36), oct 72 : 10-20.

1715    TRAXLER, G. *Zwischen Tradition und Emanzipation. Probleme der Frauenarbeit in Österreich* (Between tradition and emancipation. Problems raised by female work in Austria). Wien, W. Braumüller, 73, 195 p.

1716    WOODHALL, M. "Investment in women; a reappraisal of the concept of human capital", *Int. R. Educ.* 19(1), 1973 : 9-29.

1717    YOUSSEF, N. H. "Differential labor force participation of women in Latin American and Middle Eastern countries: the influence of family characteristics", *Soc. Forces* 51(2), dec 72 : 135-153.

### G.2243    The older workers
### Travailleurs âgés

1718    ILLES, Gy. "A nyugíjasok foglalkoztatása 1970-ben" (The employment of retired persons in 1970), *Statiszt. Szle* 50(11), nov 72 : 1142-1154. [Hungary.]

1719    NATIONAL COUNCIL ON THE AGING. "Studies on problems of work and age", *Industr. Gerontol.* 16, 1973 : 1-98.

1720    SHATTO, G. M. (ed.). *Employment of the middle-aged; papers from industrial gerontology seminars.* Springfield, Ill., C. C. Thomas, 72, xvi-215 p.

1721    SLATER, R. "Age discrimination in Great Britain", *Industr. Gerontol.* 15, 1972 : 12-19.

### G.2244    The handicapped
### Les invalides

1722    HYMAN, H. H.; STOKES, J.; STRAUSS, H. M. "Occupational aspirations among the totally blind", *Soc. Forces* 51(4), jun 73 : 403-416.

1723 LEHTO, M.; RUUSKA, T. "Vajaakuntoisten työhönsijoittuminen" (Employment of handicapped), *Sos. Aikakausk.* 66(6), 1972 : 609-624.

1724 PIERSON, F. C. *Community manpower services for the disadvantaged.* Kalamazoo, Mich., W. E. Upjohn Institute for Employment Research, 72, x-86 p.

### G.2245 *Minority groups*
*Minorités*

[See also / Voir aussi: 1666, 1771, 2175, 2186, 2191, 2195]

1725 ADALS, A. V. "Black-white occupational differentials in Southern metropolitan employment", *J. hum. Resources* 7(4), 1972 : 500-517.

1726 AGOSTINI; BONNAUD. "Étude sur les travailleurs immigrés", *R. franç. Aff. soc.* 26(4), oct-dec 72 : 10-30.

1727 ALDRICH, H. E. "Employment opportunities for Blacks in Black ghettos: the role of White-owned business", *Amer. J. Sociol.* 78(6), mai 73 : 1403-1425. [USA.]

1728 ASHENFELTER, O. "Racial discrimination and trade unionism", *J. polit. Econ.* 80(3), mai-jun 72 : 435-464.

1729 BAIN, T.; PAUGA, A. "Foreign workers and the intra-industry wage structure in West Germany", *Kyklos* 25(4), 1972 : 820-824.

1730 BARONTINI, C. "Les travailleurs immigrés et les luttes de classe en France", *C. Communisme* 49(5), mai 73 : 35-44.

1731 BONAĆ, V. "Jugoslovenski radnici u SR Nemačkoj" (Yugoslav workers in GFR), *Sociologija* 15(2), 1973 : 313-326.

1732 CASTLES, S.; KOSACK, G. *Immigrant workers and class structure in Western Europe.* London, New York, London Oxford University Press, 73, xiv-514 p.

1733 COOMBS, H. C. "The employment status of aborigines", *Austral. econ. Pap.* 11(18), jun 72 : 8-18.

1734 DAOUD, Z. "Les travailleurs maghrébins en Europe", *Remarques afr.* 15(420), apr 73 : 15-20.

1735 "Étrangers dans les conflits du travail (Les)", *Hommes et Migr. Doc.* 23(832-833), oct 72 : 3-31. [France.]

1736 FIETKAU, W. *Sogenannte Gastarbeiter* (Foreign workers). Wuppertal, Jugenddienst-Verlag, 72, 230 p. [Germany FR.]

1737 GLEBER, S. M. *Business values and Black employment; a case study in cultural adaptation.* Reading, Mass., Addison-Wesley Publishing Co., 73, 26 p.

1738 HODGE, R. W. "Toward a theory of racial differences in employment", *Soc. Forces* 52(1), sep 73 : 16-31.

1739 JACKSON, R. "Job-discrimination and the use of bonuses", *Amer. J. Econ. Sociol.* 32(4), oct 73 : 351-366.

1740 KAN, A. G. "Inostrannye rabočie v skandinavii" (Foreign workers in Scandinavia), *Rasy i Nar.* (2), 1972 : 176-190.

1741 KAYSER, B. *Les retours conjoncturels de travailleurs migrants et les effets de l'émigration.* Paris, O.C.D.E., 72, 59 p.

1742 KLEE, E. (ed.). *Gastarbeiter* (Foreign workers). Frankfurt-am-Main, Suhrkamp, 72, 266 p. [Germany, FR.]

1743 KNEZEVIĆ, R. "Neki problemi jugoslvenskih radnika zaposlenih u SR Nemačkoj" (Some problems of Yugoslav workers employed in GFR), *Sociologija* 15(2), 1973 : 289-311.

1744 KOOYMAN, J.; VAN DE PAS, J. *The economic effects on the Netherlands of recruiting foreign labour.* The Hague, Central Planning Bureau, 72, 53 p.

1745 LEVINE, M. *The untapped human resource: the urban Negro and employment equality.* Morristown, N. J., General Learning Press, 72, xiv-237 p.

1746 MILLER, D. R. "Emigrant Turkish workers—a framework for analysis", *Mid. East. techn. Univ. Stud. Develop.* (3), 1971 : 529-540.

1747 MOGULL, R. G. "Discrimination in the labor market", *J. Black Stud.* 3(2), dec 72 : 237-249. [USA.]

1748 NAGEL, T. "Equal treatment and compensatory discrimination", *Philos. publ. Aff.* 2(4), été 73 : 348-363. [USA.]

1749    NOTTER, N. "Statut des travailleurs étrangers en Allemagne fédérale", *Dr. soc.* 36(4), apr 73 : 223-230.

1750    OFFNER, P. "Labor force participation in the ghetto", *J. hum. Resources* 7(4), aut 72 : 460-481. [USA.]

1751    PAPYLE, H. "Travailleurs étrangers en France: essai d'une bibliographie en langue française", *Hommes et Migr.* 120, 1973 : 1-196.

1752    PETER, A. *Die Beschäftigung ausländischer Arbeitskräfte in Österreich* (Employment of foreign manpower in Austria). Linz, Österr. Inst. für Arbeitsmarktpolitik, 72, 11 p.

1753    ROSENBLUM, G. *Immigrant workers; their impact on American labor radicalism.* New York, Basic Books, 73, vi-189 p.

1754    SMITH, P. "The problem of migrant workers", *Contemp. R.* 223(1291), aug 73 : 57-62.

1755    VALABREGUE, C. *L'homme déraciné; le livre noir des travailleurs étrangers.* Paris, Mercure de France, 73, 204 p.

1756    VERKOREN, N. "Foreign workers in Western Europe. A regional approach", *Europ. demogr. Inform. B.* 4(3), 1973 : 129-134.

1757    VÖLKER, G. E. "Impact of Turkish labour migration on the economy of the Federal Republic of Germany", *Grman econ. R.* 11(1), 1973 : 61-77.

1758    VON FURSTENBER, G. M.; CARTWRIGHT, W. S.; VANCE, M. (eds.). *Discrimination in employment: a selected bibliography.* Monticello, Ill., Council of Planning Librarians, 72, 24 p.

1759    WENK, M.; TOMASI, S. M.; BARONI, G. (eds.). *Pieces of a dream; the ethnic worker's crisis with America.* New York, Center for Migration Studies, 72, vii-212 p.

1760    WILLIAMS, D. L. *Some political and economic aspects of Mexican immigration into the United States since* 1941*; with particular reference to this immigration into the State of California.* San Francisco, R. and E Research Associates, 73, v-74 p.

## G.23      Working conditions
Conditions de travail

[See also / Voir aussi: **G.252; M.22**]

1761    ALLEGRO, J. T. *Socio-technische organisatieontwikkeling* (Development of socio-technical organization). Leiden, Stenfert Kroese, 73, 278 p. [Job satisfaction.]

1762    BARZEL, Y. "The determination of daily hours and wages", *Quart. J. Econ.* 87(2), mai 73 : 220-238.

1763    BEAUCHESNE, M. N. "Lutte ouvrière et conditions du travail en Italie", *Écon. et Hum* 213, oct-dec 73 : 3-14.

1764    BIENEFELD, M. A. *Working hours in British industry: an economic history.* London, London School of Economics and Political Science; Weidenfeld and Nicolson, 72, 293 p.

1765    BÖHLE, F.; ALTMANN, N. *Industrielle Arbeit und soziale Sicherheit; eine Studie über Risiken im Arbeitsprozess und auf dem Arbeitsmarkt* (Industrial work and social security; a study of risks in the work process and on the labour market). Frankfurt-am-Main, Athenäum, 72, 273 p. [Germany, FR.]

1766    BRUYNS, R. A. C. *De invloed van werk en milieu op arbeidsmotivatie* (The influence of work and environment on motivation to work). Assen, Van Gorcum, 72, 257 p.

1767    ČERNJAVSKIJ, Ja. *Puti ulučšenija ispol'zovanija rabočego vremeni (Balans zatrat rabočesko vremeni na predprijatii* (Ways to improve labour time utilization. Balance of labour-time costs in an enterprise). Moskva, Ekonomika, 72, 141 p.

1768    GALLAIS-HAMONNO, G. *Des loisirs; analyse économique de la demande de loisir en France.* Paris, S.E.D.E.I.S., 72, xii-601 p.

1769    GOODING, J. *The job revolution.* New York, Walker, 72, 213 p.

1770    GREENE, C. N.; ORGAN, D. W. "An evaluation of causal models linking the received role with job satisfaction", *Adm. Sci. Quart.* 18(1), mai 73 : 95-103.

1771    GREENSTREET, M. "Labour conditions in the Gold Coast during the 1930's with particular reference to migrant labour and the mines", *Econ. B.* 2(2), 1972 : 32-46; 2(3), 1972 : 30-40.

1772    GRISET, A. "Les conditions de travail des O.S.", *Sociol. Trav.* 15(2), apr-jun 73 : 226-230. [France.]

1773    "Job satisfaction and productivity", *Gallup Opin. Index* 94, apr 73 : 1-40.

1774 KRZYKALA, F. "Zmianowosc w pracy w przemysle polskim a problemy humanizacji pracy" (Shiftwork in labour in Polish industry and the problem of work humanization), *Probl. Org.* (2), 1973 : 127-134.

1775 KUROVSKIJ, K. I. "Voprosy redukcii truda" (Questions of labour reduction), *Izv. Akad. Nauk SSSR Ser. ekon.* 4(1), 1973 : 103-114.

1776 LACHAUD, J. P. "Les premières expériences de travail temporaire dans les entreprises industrielles et commerciales de l'agglomération bordelaise", *R. écon. Sud-Ouest* 21(3), 1972 : 415-463.

1777 LAROUCHE, V.; LEVESQUE, A.; DELORME, F. "Satisfaction au travail ? Problèmes associés à la mesure", *Relat. industr.* 28(1), 1973 : 76-109.

1778 LIS, J. *Praca wielozmianowa w przemysle* (Multishift work in industry). Warszawa, Państwowe Wydawnictwo Ekonomiczne, 73, 229 p.

1779 MULFORD, E. "Job satisfaction: a method of analysis", *Personnel Manag. (Epping)* 1(3), 1972 : 48-57.

1780 MULFORD, E. *Job satisfaction: a study of computer specialists.* Harlow, Longman, 72, xii-242 p.

1781 MUSZALSKI, W. *Skracanie czasu pracy* (Shortening of work time). Warszawa, Centralna Rada Związków Zawodowych, 73, 179 p.

1782 PESTONJEE, D. M.; BASU, G. "Study of job motivations of Indian executives", *Ind. J. Industr. Relat.* 8(1), jul 72 : 3-16.

1783 PRYBIL, L. D. "Job satisfaction in relation to job performance and occupational level", *Personnel J.* 52(2), feb 73 : 94-100.

1784 RÖHSLER, W.; SCHMIDT, G. *Die Arbeitszeit* (Working time). Berlin, E. Schmidt, 73, 352 p.

1785 SARAPATA, A. (ed.). *Problematyka i metody badan nad zadowoleniem z pracy. Materialy z konferencji 24-26 marca 1972* (Problems and methods of research on work satisfaction. Materials of the Conference 24-26 March 1972). Wrocław, Zakład Narodowy im. Ossolińskich, 73, 130 p.

1786 SARTIN, P. *La réussite professionnelle.* Verviers, Gérard and Co., 72, 315 p.

1787 SCHNORR, G. "Le travail temporaire", *C. Dr. europ.* 9(2), 1973 : 131-183.

1788 SINGHAL, S.; UPADHYAYA, H. S. "Psychology of men at work; employee perception of job incentives", *Ind. J. industr. Relat.* 8(1), jul 72 : 17-30.

1789 SLUZALEC, A.; GRABARA, A. "Organizacyjny aspekt humanizacji warunków pracy w przedsiebiorstwach przemysłowych" (Organizational aspects of humanization of working conditions), *Hum. Pracy* (4), 1973 : 41-49.

1790 SUSMAN, G. I. "Job enlargment; effects of culture on worker responses", *Industr. Relat. (Berkeley)* 12(1), feb 73 : 1-15.

1791 WILKINSON, A. "Motivation des travailleurs en Europe", *Synopsis* 12(5), sep-oct 72 : 1-10.

1792 ZIN'KOVSKIJ, M. M. *Ėkonomičeskie voprosy obrany truda v černoj petallurgii* (Economic conditions of labour safety in the iron industry). Moskva, Metallurgija, 72, 73 p.

## G.24 Labour relations
Relations de travail

### G.240 *General studies*
*Études générales*

[See also / Voir aussi: 1690, 1950, 1959, 1984, 1993]

1793 BAKELS, H. L. *Schets van het Nederlands arbeidsrecht* (Sketch of Dutch labour law). Deventer, Kluwer, 72, xii-211 p.

1794 BLEECKER, T. *Labor law and practice in the Republic of China (Taiwan).* Washington, United States, Government Printing Office, Bureau of Labor Statistics, 72, viii-72 p.

1795 BROWN, E. C. "Fondamental Soviet labor legislation", *Industr. Lab. Relat. R.* 26(2), jan 73 : 778-792.

1796 DESOLRE, G. "Introduction au nouveau droit du travail soviétique", *R. Trav. (Bruxelles)* 73(6-7), jun-jul 72 : 631-651.

1797 GHIMPU, S. "Principes fondamentaux du nouveau code du travail", *R. roum. Sci. soc. Sér. Sci. jur.* 17(1), 1973 : 33-46.

2171    VELARDE FUERTES, J. "La reforma de la empresa en la Comunidad económica europea" (The reform of the enterprise in the European Economic Community), *R. Estud. soc.* (6), sep-dec 72 : 27-45.

2172    Bibl. XXI-2368. WIEDEMANN, H. *Das Unternehmen in der Evolution. Soziologische Studie zu Organization, Automation, Führung, Konkurrenz und Kooperation im Unternehmen* (Enterprise evolution: a sociological study on the organization, automation, leadership, competition and co-operation of entrepreneurs). CR: G. BUSCHGES, *Kölner Z. Soziol. u. soz.-Psychol.* 24(4), dec 72 : 875-882.

2173    WÓJCIK, P. "Burżuazyjno-technokratyczny a socjalistyczny model prsedsiębiorstwa" (The bourgeois technocratic and social model of the enterprise), *Stud. socjol.* 44(1), 1972 : 183-212.

### G.331    *Entrepreneurship*
####         *L'entrepreneur, théorie et fonction*

[See also / Voir aussi: 2287, 2293]

2174    BRYANT, W. R. "Japanese businessman and private economic diplomacy", *Japan Interpreter* 6(2), été 70 : 220-231.

2175    COLES, F. "Financial institutions and black entrepreneurship", *J. Black Stud.* 3(3), mar 73 : 329-349. [USA.]

2176    DAEMS, H. "Réflexion théorique sur les aspects quantitatifs de la stratégie des entrepreneurs", *R. Inst. Sociol.* 45(2), 1972 : 245-257.

2177    DRESSANG, D. L. "Entrepreneurialism and development administration", *Adm. Sci. Quart.* 18(1), mar 73 : 76-85.

2178    ELLIS, T.; CHILD, J. "Placing stereotypes of the manager into perspective", *J. Manag. Stud.* 10(3), oct 73 : 233-255.

2179    ERNST, H.; MEISTERT, H. *Regenten der Wirtschaft; Arbeits- und Führungsstile deutscher Chefs* (Those who manage society; work and leadership style of German managers), München, Verlag Moderne Industrie, 73, 319 p.

2180    EŠIN, P. S. "Vlija ie stilja raboty rukovoditelja na formirovanie vzaimootnošenij v kollektive" (Influence of the manager's activity style on the formation of interrelations in a collectivity), *Čelovek i Obšč.* (11), 1973 : 182-187.

2181    GASSER, C. *Unternehmensführung im Strukturwandel; Krise der Dynamik* (Enterprise management in structural change; crisis of the dynamic). Düsseldorf, Econ Verlag, 72, 209 p.

2182    HART, G. P. *Some socio-economic aspects of African entrepreneurship with particular reference to the Transkei and Ciskei.* Grahamstown S. A., Institute of Social and Economic Research, Rhodes University, 72, xvi-237 p.

2183    HARTMANN, B. *et al. Unternehmensführung und Organisation* (Entrepreneurship and organization). Wiesbaden, Betriebswirtschaftlicher Verlag T. Gabler, 73, 277 p.

2184    HERMANS, A. "Leiders van de industrie; persoonlijkheid, waadensysteem, visie" (Industrial leaders; personality, value system, ideas), *Tijds. soc. Wetensch.* 17(4), 1972 : 419-435.

2185    JAVILLONAR, G. V.; PETERS, G. R. "Sociological and social psychological aspects of Indian entrepreneurship", *Brit. J. Sociol.* 24(3), sep 73 : 314-328.

2186    LEE, R. F. *The setting for Black business development: a study in sociology and political economy.* Ithaca, New York State School of Industrial and Labor Relations Cornell University, 73, xvii-249 p.

2187    LEGGATT, T. W. *The training of British managers; a study of need and demand.* London H. M.S.Q., 72, 209 p.

2188    LOUIS, P. P. *Success unlimited: great industrialists of the world.* Centerville, Ohio, Orient House Publications, 73, vi-276 p.

2189    MOŠNA, Z. *O socialistické vychove k rízení* (The socialist training of executives). Praha, Svoboda, 72, 239-3 p.

2190    PAPANEK, H. "Pakistan's big businessmen: Muslim separatism, entrepreneurship, and partial modernization", *Econ. Develop. cult. Change* 21(1), oct 72 : 1-32.

2191    PURYEAR, A. N.; WEST, C. A. *Black enterprise, inc.; case studies of a new experiment in Black business development.* Garden City, N.Y., Anchor Press, 73, xii-462 p.

2192 SAUTU, R.; WAINERMAN, C. *El empresario y la innovación: un estudio de las disposiciones de un grupo de dirigentes de empresas argentinas hacia el cambio tecnológico* (The entrepreneur and innovation; a study of the attitudes of a group of firm managers in Argentina towards technological change). Buenos Aires, Editorial del Instituto, 71, xx-306 p.

2193 SWAYNE, C. B.; TUCKER, W. R. *The effective entrepreneur.* Morristown, N.J., General Learning Press, 73, xv-181 p.

2194 TOURRAIN, R. *Le chef d'entreprise face à ses responsabilités.* Besançon, l'auteur, 72, viii-384 p.

2195 VENABLE, A. S. *Building Black business; an analysis and a plan.* New York, Crowell, 72, xi-132 p.

2196 ZĄBKOWICZ, L. *Kierownik w przemyśle* (Manager in industry). Warszawa, Państwowe Wydawnictwo Ekonomiczne, 73, 274 p.

### G.332 Capital and capital formation
### Le capital et sa formation

[See also / Voir aussi: **F.22**; 5514]

2197 AMENDOLA, M. "Thrift, economic life of capital, and productivity in a model with heterogeneous capital", *Oxford econ. Pap.* 24(3), nov 72 : 345-356.

2198 BABKINA, Z. "Izmenenie organičeskogo stroenija kapitala SSA v uslovijah naučno-tehničeskoj revoljucii" (The modification of the organic composition of capital in the United States within the conditions of the scientific and technical revolution), *Ekon. Nauki* 16(9), sep 73 : 85-94.

2199 BONESS, A. J.; CHEN. A. H.; JATUSIPITAK, S. "On relations among stock price behavior and changes in the capital structure of the firm", *J. financ. quant. Anal.* 7(4), sep 72 : 1967-1982.

2200 CASS, D. "Distinguishing inefficient competitive growth paths: a note on capital overaccumulation and rapidly diminishing future value of consumption in a fairly general model of capitalistic production", *J. econ. Theory* 4(2), apr 72 : 224-240.

2201 CASS, D. "On the Wicksellian point-input, point-output model of capital accumulation: a modern view (or, neoclassicism slightly vindicated)", *J. polit. Econ.* (1), jan-feb 73 : 71-97.

2202 CHIAMPARINO, S. "Capitale, lavoro e curva di Philipps" (Capital, labour and Phillipps curve), *Rass. sind. Quad.* 11(42), mai-jun 73 : 65-78.

2203 HANSEN, T.; KOOPMANS, T. C. "On the definition and computation of a capital stock invariant under optimization", *J. econ. Theory* 5(3), dec 72 : 487-522.

2204 Bibl. XXI-2409. HARCOURT, G. C. *Some Cambridge controversies in the theory of capital.* CR: D. L. HOOKS, *J. econ. Liter.* 11(1), mar 73 : 75-77.

2205 KOLTUNOV, V. M. "Vseobščij zakon kapitalističeskogo nakoplenija v uslovijah sovremennogo gosudarstvenno-monopolističeskogo kapitalizma" (The general law of capitalist accumulation in the contemporary state monopolist capitalism conditions), *Trudy Gor'k. vysš. part. Školy* (10), 1972 : 3-218.

2206 MAIRESSE, J. *L'évaluation du capital fixe productif; méthodes et résultats.* Paris, Institut national de la statistique et des études économiques, 72, 268 p.

2207 MERVILLE, L. J.; TAVIS, L. A. "Optimal working capital policies: a chance-constrained programming approach", *J. financ. Quant. Anal.* 8(1), jan 73 : 47-59.

2208 MONT'ALEGRE, O. *Capital e capitalismo no Brasil* (Capital and capitalism in Brazil) Rio de Janeiro, Editora Expresso e Cultura, 72, 437 p.

2209 MORRIS, R. D. *An examination of cut-off rates for capital expenditure analysis under capital rationing.* St. Lucia, University of Queensland Press, 72, 77-138 p.

2210 NEELSEN, K. *Kapital und Mehrwert* (Capital and surplus). Berlin, Dietz Verlag, 73, 109 p.

2211 ÖHQUIST, H. "Kapitalets produktivitet i industriföretag" (Capital productivity in industrial enterprise), *Ekon. Samfund. Ts.* 26(3), 1973 : 159-166.

2212 ONOH, J. K. *Strategic approaches to crucial policies in economic development. A macro link study in capital formation, technology and money.* Rotterdam, Rotterdam University Press, 72, xiii-236 p.

99

2213    OYEJIDE, T. A. "Deficit financing, inflation and capital formation: an analysis of the Nigerian experience, 1957-1970", *Niger. J. econ. soc. Stud.* 14(1), mar 72 : 27-43.

2214    ROGOVSKIJ, I. T. *Vseobščij zakon kapitalističeskogo nakoplenija* (The general law of capitalist accumulation). Minsk, Izdatel'stvo BGU, 73, 64 p.

2215    SALANA, P. *Le procès de "sous-développement". Essai sur les limites de l'accumulation nationale du capital dans les économies semi-industrialisées.* Paris, F. Maspéro, 72, 183 p.

2216    ŠERMENEV, M. K. *Finansovye reservy v rasširennom vosproizvodstva* (Financial reserves in enlarged reproduction). Moskva, Finansy, 73, 207 p.

2217    WEIZSACKER, C. C. VON. "The temporal structure of the production process and the problem of the distribution of income between capital and labour", *German econ. R.* 10(4), 1972 : 289-309.

**G.333    Financement methods**
**Méthodes de financement**

**G.3330    General studies**
**Études générales**

[See also / Voir aussi: **L.30; 2258**]

2218    AGOSTINI, J. M. *Le choix des investissements: programmation mathématique.* Paris, Dunod, 72, vi-113-7 p.

2219    BAJMURATOV, U. B. *Metody analiza i očenki ekonomičeskoj effektivnosti kapital'nyh vloženij* (Methods of capital investment economic efficiency analysis and estimation). Alma-Ata, Nauka, 72, 319 p.

2220    BIRMAN, A. M. "Kredit i finansy predprijatij" (Credit and the financing of the firm), *Den'gi i Kred.* 31(4), apr 73 : 37-43. [USSR.]

2221    BRUMELLE, S. L.; SCHWAB, B. "Capital budgeting with uncertain future opportunities; a Markovian approach", *J. financ. quant. Anal.* 8(1), jan 73 : 111-122.

2222    BUNIN, P. G.; PERLAMUTROV, V. L.; SOKOLOVSKIJ, L. H. *Ekonomiko-matematičeskie metody upravlenija oborotnymi sredstvami* (Economic and mathematical methods of circulating assets management). Moskva, Finansy, 73, 240 p.

2223    CARRAN, R. D. *Financing business and industry.* Newton Abbot, David and Charles, 71, ix-179 p.

2224    DIMAN, D.; KELLER, C.; SERUZIER, H. *Dossier statistique sur le financement des entreprises.* Paris, chez les auteurs, 72, 60 p.

2225    GAVALDA, C.; BOULOC, B. *Le financement des entreprises; circuits bancaires et extra-bancaires.* Paris, Dalloz, 73, vi-273 p.

2226    GIRAULT, F.; ZISSWILLER, R. *Finances modernes; théorie et pratique.* Paris, Dunod, 73, v.

2227    GIRAULT, F.; ZISSWILLER, R. *Gestion des capitaux circulants et choix des investissements.* Paris, Dunod, 73, xxxii-307 p.

2228    GRANELLE, J. J. "L'incertitude et la décision d'investissement dans l'entreprise", *A. Sci. écon. appl.* 30(2), oct 72 : 97-143.

2229    HALEY, C. W.; SCHALL, L. D. *The theory of financial decisions.* New York, Mc-Graw-Hill, 73, xviii-383 p.

2230    JEAN, W. H. *Finance.* New York, Dryden Press, 73, viii-360 p.

2231    KROUSE, C. G. "On the theory of optimal investment, dividends, and growth in the firm", *Amer. econ. R.* 63(3), jun 73 : 269-279.

2232    KROUSE, C. G. "Optimal financing and capital structure programs for the firm", *J. Finance* 27(5), dec 72 : 1057-1071.

2233    LACHET, P. A. (ed.). *La politique de financement des entreprises.* Paris, Presses universitaires de France, 72, 94-2 p.

2234    LANGGUTH, R.; RAUTENBERG, H. G. *Finanzierung und Investitionsrechnung* (Financing and investment accounting). Düsseldorf, VDI-Verlag, 73, x-89 p.

2235    LASSAK, H. P. *Kapitalbudget, Unsicherheit und Finanzierungsentscheidung* (The capital budget, insecurity and financing decision). Meisenheim-am-Glan, Hain, 73, iv-180 p.

2236    MULFORD, M. J. "Raising the capital budgeting hurdle", *J. industr. Econ.* 20(3), jul 72 : 287-290.

2237    NAPIÓRKOWSKI, R. *Instrumenty finansowe w gospodarce zapasami* (Financial instruments in stock management). Warszawa, Państwowe Wydawnictwo Ekonomiczne, 73, 214 p.

2238 PHILIPPATOS, G. C. *Financial management: theory and techniques.* San Francisco, Holden-Day, 73, xix-661 p.

2239 QUAST, D. *Steuerbegünstigte Kapitalanlagen in betriebswirtschaftlicher, steuerlicher und zivilrechtlicher Sicht* (Capital investments with fiscal advantages from the viewpoint of entreprise economy and fiscal and civil law). Köln-Bonn, Hanstein, 73, 32 p.

2240 RÄDLER, A. J.; RAUPACH, A. *Handbuch der steuerbegünstigten Kapitalanlagen* (Handbook of capital investments benefiting from fiscal advantages). Köln-Marienburg, O. Schmidt, 73, xvi-668 p.

2241 RIEMENSCHNITTER, A. *Die Kreditfinanzierung im Modell der flexiblen Planung* (Credit financing in the flexible planning model). Berlin, Duncker und Hubmlot, 72, 107 p.

2242 WISSENBACH, H. *Finanzierungskonzepte zur Absatzsteigerung* (Concepts of financing for growth of outlets). Frankfurt-am-Main, Verlag Arbeitsgemeinschaft Wirtschaft 72, 79 p.

2243 ZAHAROV, A. K. *Kapital'nye vloženija i tovarno-denežnyj mehanizm* (Capital investments and the commercial and monetary mechanism). Moskva, Nauka, 73, 180 p.

### G.3331 *Cost of capital*
*Coût du capital*

2244 STAPLETON, R. C. "Taxes, the cost of capital and the theory of investment", *Econ. J.* 82(328), dec 72 : 1273-1292.

### G.3332 *Self-financing*
*Autofinancement*

2245 BLAGOJEVIĆ, S. "Problemi investicionog samofinansiranja" (The problems of self-financing investments), *Ekon. Misão* 6(1), mar 73 : 7-23.

2246 WIATR, M. S. "Samofinansowanie a samospłacanie inwestycji" (Self-financing and investment self-payment), *Finanse* (11), 1973 : 29-41.

### G.3333 *Depreciation, revaluation, amortization*
*Dépréciation, réévaluation, amortissement*

[See also / Voir aussi: **K.321**]

2247 FEDAK, Z. "Nowe stawki i zasady amortyzacji" (New rates and principles of depreciation), *Finanse* (6), 1973 : 1-12.

2248 GORDON, J. "Niektóre problemy teorii i praktyki amortyzacji" (Some problems of the theory and depreciation practice), *Finanse* (1), 1973 : 18-28.

2249 LJUBIMCEV, Ju. I. *Cikl vosproizvodstva i amortizacija osnovnyh fondov (Voprosy teorii i metodologii)* (Reproduction cycle and fixed assets amortization. Theoretical and methodological questions). Moskva, Ekonomika, 73, 175 p.

2250 MATĚJA, M.; VEJMOLA, S. "Ekonomická critéria v teorii osnovy" (Economic criteria of replacement theory), *Ekon.-matem. Obzor* 8(3), 1972 : 253-268.

2251 "Régime fiscal de l'amortissement dans la C.E.E. (Le)", *Fiscalité europ.* (1), 1973 : 9-20.

2252 TOMOVSKI, S. "Amortizacija i proširena reprodukcija" (Amortization and enlarged reproduction), *Gediš. ekon. Fak. (Skopje)* 15, 1971 : 267-283. [Yugoslavia.]

### G.334 *Size*
*Dimension de l'entreprise*

### G.3341 *General studies*
*Études générales*

[See also / Voir aussi: **G.320;** 3096, 4212, 4565]

2253 ARDURA CALLEJA, M. L. *et al. La pequeña y media industria en Espana.* (Small and medium-sized industry in Spain). Madrid, Aguilar, S.A. de Ediciones, 72, xii-322 p.

2254    BALTENSPERGER, E. "Economies of scale, firm size, and concentration in banking", *J. Money Cred. Bank.* 4(3), aug 72 : 467-488.

2255    BRITTO, A. J.; LATIFF, T. A. A. "Small scale industry: profile of urban entrepreneurs", *Soc. Action* 23(3), jul-sep 73 : 290-297. [India.]

2256    CLARKE, P. *Small businesses; how they survive and succeed.* Newton Abbot, Eng., David and Charles; New York, Barnes and Noble, 72, 395 p.

2257    COESTER, F. "Die Zukunft der kleinen und mittleren Selbstandigen" (The future of small and medium-sized independent enterprises), *Civitas (Mannheim)* (11), 1972 : 186-203. [Germany FR.]

2258    CUERVO, A. "La dimensión de la empresa y la financiación" (The size of the enterprise and its financing), *R. Econ. polít.* 63, jan-apr 73 : 25-49.

2259    DEEKS, J. "The small firm. Asset or liability ?", *J. Manag. Stud.* 10(1), feb 73 : 25-47.

2260    "Dimensión empresarial (La)" (The dimension of the enterprise), *Bol. Estud. econ. (Bilbão)* 27(87), dec 72 : 801-1291. [Spain.]

2261    DUHAMEL, H. *Physiologie d'une grande entreprise.* Paris, Flammarion, 72, 188 p.

2262    ITOH, T. *Structural analysis of the problem of medium and small enterprises in contemporary Japan.* Tokyo, Institute of Management and Labor Studies, Keio University, 72, 25 p.

2263    KOZLOWSKI, T. B. *Optymalne wielkosci przedsiebiorstw przemyslowych* (Optimal size of industrial enterprises). Warszawa, Państwowe Wydawnictwo Ekonomiczne, 73, 200 p.

2264    KRUBER, K. P. *Unternehmensgrössen und Wettbewerb auf wachsenden Märkten* (The size of the enterprise and the dimension of competition on expanding markets). Baden-Baden, Nomos Verlagsgesellschaft, 73, 254 p.

2265    LIM, R. *What you should know about scientific management for small business.* Dobbs Ferry, N.Y., Oceana Publications, 73, vii-116 p.

2266    LINDSTRÖM, C. "Om assymetrisk konkurrenz mellan stora och sma företag" (The assymetric competition between small and big enterprises), *Ekon. Samfund. Ts.* 25(4), 1972 : 221-226.

2267    MASON, R. S. "Product diversification and the small firm", *J. Busin. Pol.* 3(3), print 73 : 28-39.

2268    METZNER, R. "Klein- und Mittelunternehmen im Monopolisierungsprozess" (Small and medium-sized enterprises in the process of monopolization), *IPW Ber.* 2(1), jan 73 : 29-37.

2269    NATIONS UNIES. Organisation des Nations Unies pour le développement industriel. *La petite industrie dans les pays arabes du Moyen-Orient.* New York, NU, 72, x-102 p.

2270    OOMMEN, M. A. *Small industry in Indian economic growth; a case study of Kerala.* Delhi, Research Publications in Social Sciences, 72, 193, vp.

2271    SCHWAMM, H. "Small firms in Europe", *J. Wld Trade Law* 6(6), nov-dec 72 : 648-660.

2272    SLATER, D. "Small-scale industries in the Indian economy", *South Asian R.* 7(1), oct 73 : 31-42.

2273    WAITE, D. "The economic significance of small firms", *J. industr. Econ.* 21(2), apr 73 : 154-166. [UK.]

2274    WESTON, J. F.; ORNSTEIN, S. I. (eds.). *The impact of large firms on the U.S. economy.* Lexington, Mass., Lexington Books, 73, xxi-306 p.

2275    WILD, R. "The small company, profitability, management resources and management techniques", *J. Busin. Pol.* 3(1), aut 72 : 10-21.


**G.3342**    *Handicrafts, and handicraft policy*
              *Artisanat et politique de l'artisanat*

2276    "Artisanat et le secteur des métiers (L')", *R. écon. Banque nat. Paris* 26, apr 73 : 12-21. [France.]

2277    CHOLAJ, H. *W cieniu wielkiego przemysłu. O socjalistycznej spółdzielczosci pracy* (In the shadow of big industry. On socialist handicrafts co-operatives). Warszawa, Wiedza Powszechna, 73, 286 p.

2278    ESPEJEL, C. *Las artesanías tradicionales en México* (Traditional handicrafts in Mexico). México, Secretaría de Educación Pública, 72, 158 p.

2279    JENKINS, J. G. *The craft industries.* London, Longman, 72, xxi-128-16 p. [UK.]

2280 PARYCZKO, L. *Spółdzielczosc pracy w Polsce w latach* 1945-1955 (Handicraft co-operatives in Poland in the years 1945-1955). Warszawa, Centralna Rolniczych Spółdzielni, 73, 306 p.

### G.335 Technical management
### Organisation technique

**G.3351** *Administrative methods*
*Méthodes administratives*

[See also / Voir aussi: **H.1130; H.2130;** 2067, 2137]

2281 ABAD, A. *Management and organization development; a behavioural science approach.* New Delhi, Rachna Prakashan, 72, xii-148 p.

2282 ABDURAHMANOV, S. A.; LAPŠIN,ʲ Ju. P.; JAKOVENKO, Ė. G. *Avtomatizirovannye sistemy upravlenija v narodnom hozjajstve SSSR* (Automated management systems in the USSR national economy). Moskva, Ekonomika, 72, 45 p.

2283 ALBRECHT, L. K. *Organization and management of information processing systems.* New York, Macmillan, 72, xiii-383 p.

2284 ALLEN, L. A. *Professional management: new concepts and proven practices.* London-New York, McGraw-Hill, 73. xi-235 p.

2285 AL-SALMI, 'A.; NEHRT, L. C. *Siyâsâṭ wa-estirâtijiyâṭ al-idârat fil-duwal al-nâmiyat* (Managerial policy and strategy for developing countries). Mišr, Dar al Ma'arif, 72, 447 p.

2286 ANDERSON, J. R.; MARDAKER, J. B. "An appreciation of decision analysis in management", *R. Mkting agric. Econ.* 40(4), dec 72 : 170-184.

2287 ANYON, G. J. *Entrepreneurial dimensions of management.* Wynnewood, Pa. Livingston Publishing Co., 73, xiii-217 p.

2288 ASTEN, K. J.; REYNOLDS, R. W. (eds.). *Data communications for business information systems.* New York, Macmillan, 73, xiv-359 p.

2289 BABEAU, A.; DESPLAS, M. *Analyse quantitative des décisions de l'entreprise; la décision de production.* Paris, Bordas, 73, 199 p.

2290 BAKER, F. (ed.). *Organizational systems; general systems approaches to complex organizations.* Homewood, Ill., R. D. Irwin, 73, xv-584 p.

2291 BALLE, C.; PEAUCELLE, J. L. *Le pouvoir informatique dans l'entreprise.* Paris, Éditions d'organisation, 72, 168 p.

2292 BARTLETT, A. C.; KAYSER, T. A. (eds.). *Changing organizational behavior.* Englewood Cliffs, N.J., Prentice-Hall, 73, xiii-434 p.

2293 BEDFORD, N. M. "The concept of management information systems for managers", *Manag. int. R.* 12(2-3), 1972 : 25-34.

2294 BENTON, W. K. *Forecasting for management.* Reading, Mass., Addison-Wesley Publishing Co., 72, x-209 p.

2295 BERRETTA, J. C.; MOBASHERI, F. "An optimal strategy for capacity expansion", *Engin. Economist* 17(2), jan-feb 72 : 79-98.

2296 BIELSKI, M. *Formalne i rzeczywista struktura organizacyjna* (Formal and real structure of organization). Warszawa, Państwowe Wydawnictwo Ekonomiczne, 73, 169 p.

2297 Bibl. XXI-2520. BLEICHER, K. *Perspektiven für die Organisation und Führung von Unternehmungen* (Perspectives for business organization and management). CR: G. BUSCHGES *Kölner Z. Soziol. u. soz.-Psychol.* 24(4), dec 72 : 875-882.

2298 BOURDIN, J. *Contrôle de gestion.* Paris, Dalloz, 72, 130 p.

2299 BRONNIKOV, Ju. N. *Racionalizacija processov upravlenija na predprijatii* (Management processes rationalization in an enterprise). Moskva, Ekonomika, 72, 69 p.

2300 BROSTER, E. J. *Management statistics.* London, Longman, 72, xv-333 p.

2301 BRUNEAU, J. M. *La gestion des entreprises d'après le recensement de la distribution de 1966.* Paris, Institut national de la statistique et des études économiques, 72, 131 p.

2302 BURSK, E. C.; DARLING, C. M.; SMITH, T. A. (eds.). *Challenge to leadership; managing in a changing world.* New York, Free Press, 73, x-372 p.

2303 BYRNES, W. G.; CHESTERTON, B. K. *Decisions, strategies and new ventures; modern tools for top management.* London, Allen and Unwin, 73, 3-195 p.

2304    CARDULA, I.; MICU, I. *Gestiunea întreprinderii moderne. Economie aplicată* (Modern enterprise management, applied economics). Bucuresti, Editura didactica si pedagogica, 72, 132 p.

2305    CARNAROLI, S. *Tecnica della programmazione aziendale a lungo termine* (Technique of long-term firm planning). Milano, F. Angeli, 72, 295 p.

2306    CARROLL, S. J. Jr.; TOSI, H. L. Jr. *Management by objectives: applications and research.* New York, Macmillan, 73, viii-216 p.

2307    CLARK, P. A. *Action research and organizational change.* London, Harper and Row, 72, xii-172 p.

2308    COLEMAN, R. J.; RILEY, M. J. (eds.). *MIS: management dimensions.* San Francisco, Holden-Day, 73, xii-703 p.

2309    CZERMIŃSKI, A.; TRZCIENIECKI, J. *Elementy teorii organizacji i zarządzania* (Elements of the theory of organization and management). Warszawa, Państwowe Wydawnictwo Naukowe, 73, 175 p.

2310    DACCO, G. *L'organizzazione aziendale. Analisi introduttiva* (Firm management. Introductive analysis). Parma, Studium Parmense società cooperativa editrice libraria, 72, 385-xii p.

2311    DEBICKÉ VAN DER NOOT, R. *La dinamica della struttura aziendale* (The dynamics of firm structure). Milano, Celuc, 72, 259 p.

2312    DENNING, B. W. (e.d). *Corporate planning: selected concepts.* London-New York, McGraw-Hill, 72, 373 p.

2313    DEW, R. B.; KENNETH, P. G. *Management control and information; studies in the use of control information by middle management in manufacturing companies.* London, Macmillan; New York, Wiley, 73, xiii-120 p.

2314    DIEBOLD, J. *Rethinking the practice of management: the impact of data processing, management information systems, and communications.* New York, Praeger, 73, xvii-324 p.

2315    DRĄG, M. "Planowanie w przedsiębiorstwach zintegrowanych" (Planning in integrated enterprises), *Roczniki Inst. Handlu wewn* (2), 1973 : 105-131.

2316    DROZD, S. (ed.). *Problemy wdrażania teorii gospodarowania do praktycznej działalności przedsiębiorstw* (Problems of introducing management theory into the practice of enterprises activity). Szczecin, Instytutu Ekonomiki Przemysłu Politechniki Szczecińskiej, 72, 202 p.

2317    DWORAK, W *Moderne Unternehmensorganisation in der Praxis* (Modern organization of enterprises in practice). München, Verlag Moderne Industrie, 72, 309 p.

2318    EBELTOFT, A. *Organisasjonsutvikling* (Organizational development). Oslo, Tanum, 72, 159 p.

2319    ELLIOTT, J. W. *Economic analysis for management decisions.* Homewood, Ill., R. D. Irwin, 73, xi-378 p.

2320    ELLIOTT-JONES, M. F. *Economic forecasting and corporate planning.* New York, Conference Board, 73, iii-75 p.

2321    ELM, W. A. *Das Management-Informationssystem als Mittel der Unternehmensführung* (The management information system as a tool of enterprise management). Berlin-New York, De Gruyter, 72, 214 p.

2322    ESTAFEN, B. D. *The comparative management of firms in Chile.* Bloomington, Graduate School of Business, Division of Research, Indiana University, 73, xii-217 p.

2323    FIRNBERG, D. *Computers, management and information.* London, Allen and Unwin, 73, 3-136, 6 p.

2324    FLAKIEWICZ, W. *Podejmowanie decyzji kierowniczych* (Managerial decision making). Warszawa, Państwowe Wydawnictwo Ekonomiczne, 73, 175 p.

2325    FRĄCKIEWICZ, J. *Nowoczesne metody kierowania przedsiębiorstwem* (Modern methods of enterprise management). Warszawa, Państwowe Wydawnictwo Naukowe, 73, 384 p.

2326    FRANK, M. *Kierowanie aktywizujące w przedsiębiorstwie* (Activating management in enterprises). Warszawa, Centralna Rada Związków Zawodowych, 73, 406 p.

2327    "Future of computers in business organizations (The)", *J. contemp. Busin.* 1(2), print 72 : 1-71.

2328    GEDYMIN, O. "Metody cybernetyczne w zarządzaniu" (Cybernetic methods in management) *Probl. Org.* (2), 1973 : 111-125.

2329 GIFFLER, B. *Production management models and systems.* Caldwell, N.J., Management Seminars Institute, 72, xvi-528 p.

2330 GRAHAM, J. *Systems analysis in business.* London, Allen and Unwin, 72, 3-209 p.

2331 GROSSACK, I. M.; MARTIN, D. D. *Managerial economics; microtheory and the firm's decisions.* Boston, Little, Brown, 73, xiii-480 p.

2332 GUILLAUMES. *Vers une politique de gestion concertée; élaboration d'un modèle pratique.* Paris, Éditions d'organisations, 73, 124 p.

2333 GVISHIANI, D. *Organisation and management; a sociological analysis of Western theories.* Moscow, Progress Publishers, 72, 461 p.

2334 HANER, F. T.; FORD, J. C. *Contemporary management.* Columbus, Ohio, Merrill, 73, xii-420 p.

2335 HARRY, M. J.S. *Production management.* London, Hutchinson Educational Ltd, 72, 77 p.

2336 HAYNES, W. W.; COYNE, T. J.; OSBORNE, D. K. (eds.). *Readings in managerial economics.* Dallas, Business Publications, 73, xii-438 p.

2337 HODGETTS, R. M.; ALBERS, H. H. *Cases and incidents on the basic concepts of management.* New York, Wiley, 72, ix-124 p.

2338 HORWITZ, R. *Realities of profitability; an analysis of managerial action.* London, Pan Books, 73, 6-153 p.

2339 HUNT, J. W. *The restless organisation.* Sydney, New York, Wiley, 72, xi-460 p.

2340 HUSE, E. F.; BOWDITCH, J. L. *Behavior in organizations: a systems approach to managing.* Reading, Mass., Addison-Wesley Publishing Co., 73, xi-500 p.

2341 JACOB, H. *Elektronische Datenverarbeitung als Instrument der Unternehmensführung* (EDP as an instrument for firm management). Wiesbaden, Betriebswirtschaftlicher Verlag Gabler, 72, 393 p.

2342 JANAKIEV, R. *Naučno-tehničeskata revoljucija i avtomatiziranite sistemi i za upravlenie i informacija* (The scientific and technical revolution and the automated system in management and information). Sofija, Partizdat, 72, 269 p.

2343 JONES, G. T. *Simulation and business decisions.* Harmondsworth, Penguin, 72, 172 p.

2344 JUN, J. S.; STORM, W. B. *Tomorrow's organizations: challenges and strategies.* Glenview, Ill., Scott, Foresman, 73, 450 p.

2345 KANTER, J. *Management-oriented management information systems.* Englewood Cliffs, N.J., Prentice-Hall, 72, xiv-270 p.

2346 KAST, F. E.; ROSENZWEIG, J. E. (eds.). *Contingency views of organization and management.* Chicago, Science Research Associates, 73, xi-355 p.

2347 KIEZUN, W. "Oceana stanu badań i dorobku, oraz dalsze zadania i kierunki rozwoju nauk o organizacji i zarządzaniu" (Present state, achievements, further objectives and directions of development of organization and management sciences: review and appraisal), *Ekonomista* (2), 1973 : 391-415.

2348 KIEZUN, W. "Stan aktualny i perspektywy rozwoju nauki organizacji i zarządzania" (Present condition and prospective development of organization and management science), *Probl. Org.* (2), 1973 : 3-30.

2349 KINGDOM, D. R. *Matrix organization: managing information technologies.* London, Tavistock Publications; New York, Harper and Row Publishers Inc., 73, xx-227 p.

2350 KLEIN, W. H.; MURPHY, D. C. (eds.). *Policy: concepts in organizational guidance; a book of readings.* Boston, Little, Brown, 73, ix-340 p.

2351 KNUDSON, H. R.; WOODWORTH, R. T.; BELL, C. H. *Management; an experiential approach.* New York, McGraw-Hill, 73, xvii-442 p.

2352 LATINI, F. *Il sistema informativo di gestione* (Management information system). Milano, F. Angeli, 72, 190 p.

2353 LAUZEL, P. *Gestion rationnelle de l'entreprise.* Paris, Entreprise moderne d'édition 72, T. 1 et T. 2.

2354 LEAVITT, H. J.; DILL, W. R.; EYRING, H. B. *The organizational world.* New York, Harcourt Brace Jovanovich, 73, xvi-335 p.

2355 Bibl. XXI-2569. LEVINSON, H.; MOLINARI, J.; SPOHN, A. G. *Organizational diagnosis.* CR: J. PFEFFER, *Contemp. Sociol.* 2(5), sep 73 : 516-517.

2356 LINDEMANN, P.; NAGEL, K. (eds.). *Management-Informatijnssysteme* (Management information systems). Neuwied, Lutchterhand, 72, 323 p.

2357 LOBESTEIN, J. *Organiser, commander, structurer; les trois impératifs du gouvernement de l'entreprise.* 2 ed. rev. et augm. Paris, Éditions d'organisation, 73, 335 p.

2358    LODI, J. B. *A diretoria da empresa; estratégia e estrutura (Firm management; strategy and structure)*. Petrópolis, Editôra Vozes, 72, 168 p.

2359    LONGENECKER, J. G.; PRINGLE, C. *Principles of management and organizational behavior: selected readings*. Columbus, Merrill, 73, viii-375 p.

2360    LORSCH, J. W.; LAWRENCE, P. R. (eds.). *Organization planning; cases and concepts*. Homewood, Ill., R. D. Irwin Inc., 72, x-341 p.

2361    LUSSATO, B. *Introduction critique aux théories des organisations*. Paris, Dunod, 72, xxii-192 p.

2362    LUTHANS, G. *Organizational behavior: a modern behavioral approach to management*. New York, McGraw-Hill, 73, xiv-562 p.

2363    MESCON, M. H. *et al. The management of enterprise*. New York, Macmillan, 73, x-245 p.

2364    MEYER, J. *Objectifs et stratégies de l'entreprise*. Paris, Dunod, 72, ix-307 p.

2365    MICHAEL, S. R.; JONES, H. R. *Organizational management: concepts and practice*. New York, Intext Educational Publishers, 73, viii-632 p.

2366    MICHELON, L. C. *The myths and realities of management*. Cleveland, Republic Education Institute, 72, viii-199 p.

2367    MINER, J. B. *The management process; theory, research and practice*. New York, Macmillan, 73, xi-559 p.

2368    MINTZBERG, H. *The nature of managerial work*. New York, Harper and Row, 73, xiii-298 p.

2369    MORRELL, J. (ed.). *Management decisions and the role of forecasting*. Harmondsworth, Penguin, 72, 377 p.

2370    MURRAY, J. V.; DER EMBSE, T. J. VON. *Organizational behavior: critical incidents and analysis*. Columbus, Ohio, Merrill, 73, xii-305 p.

2371    MUSIOŁ, M. "Analiza ekonomiczna narzedziem skutecznego zarządzania" (Economic analysis as an instrument of effective management), *Zesz. nauk. wyzsz. Szkoły ekon. Katowic.* 45, 1972 : 231-255.

2372    NEGANDHI, A. R. *Management and economic development. The case of Taiwan*. The Hague, Martinus Nijhoff, 73, xi-176 p.

2373    NELSON, C. R. *Applied time series analysis for managerial forecasting*. San Francisco, Holden-Day, 73, xiv-231 p.

2374    NEWMAN, D. *Organization design; an analytical approach to the structuring of organizations*. London, Edward Arnold, 73, xv-136 p.

2375    NEWPORT, M. G. *The tools of managing; functions, techniques and skills* Reading, Mass., Addison-Wesley Publishing Co., 72, xiii-193 p.

2376    NIELEN, G. C. J. F. *Information systems in a management structure*. Tilburg, University Press, Rotterdam, Rotterdam University Press, 72, vi-88 p.

2377    NIGGEMANN, W. *Optimale Informationsprozesse in betriebswirtschaftlichen Entscheidungssituationen* (Optimal processes of information in enterprise decision making situations). Wiesbaden, Betriebswirtschaftlicher Verlag T. Gabler, 73, 170 p.

2378    "Organization development: an overview", *J. contemp. Busin.* 1(3), été 72 : 1-73.

2379    "Organizational forms and internal efficiency", *Amer. econ. R.* 63(2), mai 73 *Pap. and Proc.*: 316-334. With contributions by: O. E. WILLIAMSON and D. L. MARTIN.

2380    PINOTEAU, C. *Les risques de la gestion des entreprises*. Paris, Librairie générale de droit et de jurisprudence, 73, 453 p.

2381    POLI, O. C. "La gestione delle imprese nel mondo" (Firm management in the world), *A. Sociol. (Milano)* (9), 1972 : 24-31.

2382    PRICE, J. L. *Handbook of organizational measurement*. Lexington, Mass., Heath, 72, 210 p.

2383    RADFORD, K. J. *Information systems in management*. Reston, Va., Reston Publishing Co., 73, viii-181 p.

2384    REESER, C. *Management: functions and modern concepts*. Glenview, Ill., Scott, Foresman, 73, xv-524 p.

2385    RÖMHELD, D. *Informationssysteme und Management Funktionen* (Information systems and management functions). Wiesbaden, Betriebswirtschatlicher Verlag Gabler, 73, 182 p.

2386    ROODMAN, H. S.; ROODMAN, Z. *Management by communication*. Toronto, Methuen Publications, 73, xii-340 p.

2387    ROSENBLATT, S. B.; BONNINGTON, R. L.; NEEDLES, B. E. Jr. *Modern business; a systems approach*. Boston, Houghton Mifflin, 73, vii-542 p.

2388 Ross, J. E.; Kami, M. J. *Corporate management in crisis; why the mighty fall.* Englewood Cliffs, N.J., Prentice-Hall, 73, 268 p.

2389 Rothwell, K. J. *The scope of management and administration problems in development.* The Hague, Institute of Social Studies, 73, 60 p.

2390 Rudelius, W.; Erickson, W. B.; Bakula, W. J. Jr. *An introductory to contempory business.* New York, Harcourt Brace Jovanovich, 73, xvii-588 p.

2391 Sarien, R. G. (ed.). *Managerial styles in India.* Agra, Raim Prasad, 73, vii-247 p.

2392 Scanlan, B. K. *Principles of management and organizational behavior.* New York, Wiley, 73, xv-512 p.

2393 Schiemenz, B. *Regelungstheorie und Entscheidungsprozesse: ein Beitrag zur Betriebskybernetik* (Regulation theory and decision process; a contribution to enterprise cybernetics). Wiesbaden, Gabler, 72, 199 p.

2394 Schmitz, H. *Projektplanung; ein Beitrag zur Planung und Überwachung von komplexen Entwicklungsvorhaben* (Project planning; a contribution to the planning and supervision of complex development projects). Düsseldorf, VDI-Verlag, 72, 93 p.

2395 Sethi, N. K. *Social sciences in management. An environmental view.* The Hague, Nijhoff, 72, x-107 p.

2396 Shore, B. *Operations management.* New York, McGraw-Hill, 73, xvi-550 p.

2397 Sikula, A. F. (ed.). *Essays in management and administration.* Columbus, Ohio, Merrill, 73, xi-385 p.

2398 Sikula, A. F. *Management and administration.* Columbus, Ohio, C. E. Merrill Publishing Co., 73, x-364 p.

2399 Stamper, R. *Information in business and administrative systems.* London, B. T. Batsford, 73, 362 p.

2400 Stępowski, M. Projektowanie przedsiębiorstwa" (Designing the organisation of an enterprise), *Probl. Org.* (3), 1973 : 55-73.

2401 Sutton, C. J. "Management behaviour and a theory of diversification" *Scott. J. polit Econ.* 20(1), feb 73 : 27-42.

2402 Taylor, B.; Hawkins, K. (eds.). *A handbook of strategic planning.* London, Longman, 72, xxii-456 p.

2403 Taylor, B.; MacMillan, K. (eds.). *Business policy; teaching and research.* New York, Wiley; Bradford, Bradford University Press; Lockwood, 73, x-429 p.

2404 Taylor, W. J.; Watling, T. F. *The basic arts of management.* London, Business Books, 72, xvi-207 p.

2405 Teglovic, S.; Lynch, R. (eds.). *Topics in management information systems.* New York MSS Information Corporation, 73, 295 p.

2406 Thierauf, R. J. *Data processing for business and management.* Ed. Daniel W. Geeding. New York, Wiley, 73, xiii-693 p.

2407 Thomas, J. M.; Bennis, W. G. (eds.). *The management of change and conflict; selected readings.* Harmondsworth, Penguin, 72, 507 p.

2408 Thompson, A. A. Jr. *Economics of the firm; theory and practice.* Englewood Cliffs, N.J., Prentice-Hall, 73, xvi-591 p.

2409 Tihomirov, Ju. A. *Upravlenčeskoe rešenie* (Management decision making). Moskva, Nauka, 72, 288 p.

2410 Uyterhoeven, H.; Ackerman, R. W.; Rosenblum, J. W. *Strategy and organization text and cases in general management.* Homewood, Ill., R. D. Irwin 73, xii-856 p.

2411 Vardaman, G. T. *Dynamics of managerial leadership.* Philadelphia, Auerbach Publishers, 73, viii-151 p.

2412 Varga, Gy. "Adalékok a vezetés és a vallalkozás Kérdéseihez" (Contributions to the problem of firm management), *Közgazd. Szle* 20(5), mai 73 : 505-519; 20(6), jun 73, 633-648.

2413 Wheeler, B. O.; Adams, T. J. *The business of business; an introduction.* San Francisco Canfield Press, 73, viii-403 p.

2414 Wild, R. *Management and production.* Harmondsworth, Penguin, 72, 250 p.

2415 Wild, R. *Mass-production management, the design and operation of production flow-line systems.* London-New York, John Wiley and Sons, 72, x-237 p.

1416 Wilson, C. L. *Case studies in quantitative management.* London, Intertext, 72, iii-106 p.

2417 Bibl. xxi-2613. Wren, D. A. *The evolution of management thought.* CR: W. H. Knowles, *J. econ. Liter.* 11(2), jun 73 : 577-579.

**G.3352**   *Financial management*
            *Organisation financière*

[See also / Voir aussi: **G.333**; 3140, 4137]

2418    ABAD, A. *Gestión financiera en la empresa española* (Financial management in the Spanish firm). Madrid, Index, 72, 352 p.

2419    ANGERMANN, A.; BARTELS, H. G. *Haushaltskonsolidierung und Finanzierungsrechnung* (Budget calculation and financial accounting). Weinheim-Basel, Beltz, 72, 250 p.

2420    ATGÉ, G.; ROCHÉ, C. *Comptabilité des sociétés commerciales.* Paris, Masson, 72, iv-156 p.

2421    BARNEA, A. "A note on the cash-flow approach to valuation and depreciation of productive assets", *J. financ. quant. Anal.* 7(3), jun 72 : 1841-1846.

2422    BILAT, J. "Rola rachunkowosci w integracji systemu informacji ekonomicznej w przedsiebiorstwie" (The role of accounting in the integration of an economic information system in enterprises), *Prace nauk. wyzsz. Szkoly ekon. Wrockaw.* 41, 1973 : 43-55.

2423    BISCHOFF, W. *Cash flow und working capital: Schlüssel zur finanzwirtschaftler Unternehmensanalyse* (Cash flow and working capital: key to a financial and economic analysis of the firm). Wiesbaden, Betriebswirtschaftlicher Verlag Gabler, 72, 195 p.

2424    BLAKE, R. R.; MOUTON, J. S. *How to assess the strengths and weaknesses of financial management.* Austin, Tex., Scientific Methods, 72, iv-124 p.

2425    BRANDT, L. K. *Analysis for financial management.* Englewood Cliffs, N.J., Prentice-Hall, 72, xii-542 p.

2426    BUSCHGEN, H. E. *Grundlagen betrieblicher Finanzwirtschaft* (Bases of financial economy of the enterprise). Frankfurt-am-Main, Knapp, 73, 128 p.

2427    CAO-PINNA, V. *Bilanci aziendali e contabilità nazionale* (Balance-sheets of the firm and national accounting). Milano, F. Angeli, 73, 221 p.

2428    CEBROWSKA, T. "Rola analizy bilansu w kompleksowej ocenie działalnosci przedsiębiorstwa" (The role of budget analysis in the aggregated rating of the activity of an enterprise), *Prace Nauk. wyzsz. Szkoły ekon. Wrocław.* 39, 1973 : 5-13.

2429    CHRISTY, G. A.; RODEN, P. F. *Finance: environment and decisions.* San Francisco, Canfield Press, 73, xv-432 p.

2430    CLARK, J.; ELGERS, P. "Forecasted data in financial statements: disclosure format and attestation", *Riv. int. Sci. econ. com.* 19(12), dec 72 : 1135-1159.

2431    CZERMIŃSKI, A.; SZAJOWSKI, J. *Rozrachunek wewnatrzzakłdowy. Metoda zarządzania w przedsiębiorstwie socjalistycznym* (Self-accounting internal plant system. Method of management in socialist enterprises). Warszawa, Państwowe Wydawnictwo Ekonomiczne, 73, 253 p.

2432    CZERMIŃSKA, E. "Znaczenie systemu finansowego dla sprawnego przetwarzania zasobów w przedsiębiorstwie" (The influence of the financial system on the efficiency of transformation processes in the firm), *Zesz. nauk. wyzsz. Sskoły ekon. Poznan.* 42, 1972 : 7-34.

2433    FEDOROWICZ, Z. "Ewolucja systemy finansowego przedsiębiorstwa" (Evolution of the financial system in enterprises), *Probl. Org.* (3), 1973 : 35-54.

2434    FÖSTER,. W, *Die Liquidationsbilanz* (The liquidation balance-sheet). Köln, Dr. O. Schmidt, 72, xix-223 p.

2435    FRANZ, K. P. *Bilanzierung und Erfolgsrechnung* (Balance-sheet and accounting results). Düsseldorf, VDI-Verlag, 73, x-90 p.

2436    GAJL, N. (ed.). *Zagadnienia kontroli finansowo-gospodarczej przedsiębiorstw i zjednoczeń* (Problems of financial-economic control of enterprises and industrial associations). Wrocław, Zakład Narodowy im Ossolińskich, 73, 303 p.

2437    GAL, G. *La comptabilité dans les P.M.E.; base d'une gestion dynamique.* Paris, Éditions d'organisation, 73, 181 p.

2438    GRAPPIN, M. *Comptabilité et gestion.* Paris, Sirey, 72, 246 p.

2439    GRAY, J. C.; JOHNSTON, K. S. *Accounting and management action.* New York, McGraw-Hill, 73, xvi-574 p.

2440    HARTMANN, B. *Bilanzen* (Financial statements). Stuttgart, C. E. Poeschel, 73, 104 p.

2441    JONES, R. L.; TRENTIN, H. G. *Budgeting, key to planning and control; practical guidelines for managers.* Rev. ed. New York, American management association, 71, xii-308 p.

2442    KALETA, J. "Planowanie akumulacji finansowej przedsiebiorstw" (Planning of the financial accumulation of enterprises), *Prace nauk. wyzsz. Szkoł ekon. Wrocķaw.* 36, 1973 : 13-38.

2443  KELLOCK, J. *Company accounts*. London, Heinemann, 72, x-205 p.

2444  KELLOCK, J. *Fundamentals and preparation of accounts*. London, Heinemann, 72, x-182 p.

2445  KERPPOLA, K. "Kirjanpitoinformaatio yrityksen intressenteille" (Book-keeping for interested parties of an enterprise), *Liiketal. Aikakausk.* 22(1), 1973 : 43-62.

2446  KUOSA, A. *Budjetointi liikeyrityksessä* (Budget in business). Provoo-Helsinki, W. Söderström, 72, 180-1 p.

2447  LAGHET, P. A. (ed.). *Le controle financier de l'entreprise*. Paris, Presses universitaires de France, 73, 93 p.

2448  LARCON, J. P.; LISIMACHIO, J. L. *Stratégie et politique financière; études de cas et commentaires*. Paris, Dunod, 72, xi-216 p.

2449  LEMBRE, E. DE. "De cash-flow" (Cash flow), *Econ. soc. Tijds.* 26(5), oct 72 : 28-38.

2450  LEPICARD, A.; ZISSWILLER, R. *Cas de finance d'entreprise*. Paris, Dunod, 73, x-537 p.

2451  LOTZE, H. J.; REUSS, K. H. *Informationen für Bilanzen und Modelle; Nomenklaturen, Koeffizienten, Aggregation* (Information for financial statements and models: nomenclature, coefficients and aggregation). Berlin, Verlag Die Wirtschaft, 72, 254, 254 p.

2452  "Mathematical models as a tool for financial management", *A. Sci. econ. appl.* 30(3), dec 72 : 273-298.

2453  MOROSINI, F. *I budget di sviluppo nell'impresa industriale* (The development budgets in the industrial enterprise). Milano, F. Angeli, 72, 418 p.

2454  NECKEBROEK, M. "Consolidatie in boekhoudkundig verband" (Consolidation and accountancy), *Econ. soc. Tijds.* 26(5), oct 72 : 493-505.

2455  PISKORSKI, J. "System finansowy organizacji spółdzielczych i kierunki dalszego jego usprawnienia" (Financial system of co-operative organizations and orientations of its improvement), *Finanse* (1), 1973 : 29-41.

2456  PUTZ, D. *Une modélisation de la gestion de trésorerie*. Bruxelles, La Renaissance du livre, 72, 291 p.

2457  PYHRR, P. A. *Zero-base budgeting; a practical management tool for evaluating expenses*. New York, Wiley, 73, xv-231 p.

2458  RABE, B. "Financiele modellen als beleidsinstrument in de onderneming" (Financial models as an instrument of enterprise management), *Econ. soc. Tijds.* 27(2), apr 73 : 173-180.

2459  RABINOVIČ, H. A. *Učet osnovnyh fondov v novyh uslovijah* (Fixed assets accounting under the new conditions). Moskva, Finansy, 72, 126 p. [USSR.]

2460  RAJZER, K. *Podstawy rachunkowości przedsiębiorstw* (Principles of accounting in enterprises). Kraków, Wyzsza Szkoła Ekonomiczna w Krakowie, 73, 151 p.

2461  RAMBOZ, A. *La comptabilité au service de la gestion industrielle*. Paris, Entreprise moderne d'édition, 72, 181 p.

2462  ROGGE, H. J. *Methoden und Modelle der Prognose aus absatzwirtschaftlicher Sicht; ein Beitrag zur Prognoseforschung im Unternehmensbereich* (Methods and models of forecasting from the viewpoint of outlets. A contribution to forecasting research on the enterprise). Berlin, Duncker und Humblot, 72, 200 p.

2463  ŠČENKOV, S. A. *Sistema ščetov i buhgalterksij balans predprijatija* (Accounting system and accounting balance sheet of an enterprise). Moskva, Finansy, 73, 142 p.

2464  SHUCKETT, D. H.; MOCK, E. J. *Decision strategies in financial management*. New York, AMA COM, 73, 243 p.

2465  "Stratégie financière de l'entreprise", *Anal. financ.* 14, 3 trim. 73 : 27-76.

2466  THIEBEN, E. *Budgetierung* (Budget establishment). München, Verlag Modern Industrie, 73, 160 p.

2467  THOMAS, A. L.; BASU, S. *Basic financial accounting*. Belmont, Calif., Wadsworth Publishing Co., 72, 790 p.

2468  TOMASCH, R. *Von der Buchhaltung zur Bilanz* (From accounting to financial statement). Graz-Wien, Leykam, 72, 164 p.

2469  TUNG, N. H. *Controladoria financeira das emprêsas* (Financial control of firms). Sao Paulo, Edições Universidade Emprêsa, 72, 435-4 p.

2470  VATTEVILLE, É. *Introduction à l'analyse financière de la croissance de la firme*. Paris, Cujas, 72, 128 p.

2471  VIGNERON, J. M. *Introduction au contrôle de gestion*. Paris, Dunod, 72, xiii-367 p.

2472　WAJCHMAN, M. *Balance general; una aplicación de la programación por camino crítico* (General balance-sheet: an application of critical path analysis). Mendoza, Argentina, Universidad Nacional de Cuyo, Facultad de Ciencias Económicas, 72, 12 l.

2473　WALSH, F. J. Jr. *Planning corporate capital structures.* New York, The Conference Board, 72, ii, ii-41 p.

2474　WEISS, H. *Die Finanzplanung der Unternehmung* (Financial planning of the enterprise). Winterthur, Hans Schellenberg, 72, xii-102 p.

2475　Bibl. XXI-2674. WHITTINGTON, G. *The prediction of profitability and other studies of company behaviour.* CR: M. A. CREW, *J. econ. Liter.* 11(2), jun 73 : 574-576.

### G.3353　*Economic calculation, production costs and functions*　*Calcul économique, coûts et fonctions de production*

[See also / Voir aussi: C.22; H.1131; H.2131; H.4131; 2298, 2438]

2476　BARON, D. P. "Limit pricing and models of potential entry", *West. econ. J.* 10(3), sep 72 : 298-307.

2477　BELUHA, N. T. *Hozjajstvennyj učet i ego rol' v ASU* (Cost accounting and its role in the automated system). Moskva, Finansy, 72, 72 p.

2478　BUDDE, R. *Strategische Plan- und Standardkostenrechnung; die Technik der Budgetierung und Kostenkontrolle* (Strategic forecasting of cost calculation and of standard costs techniques of budgeting and cost control) Berlin, E. Schmidt, 73, 214 p.

2479　DASGUPTA, A. K.; PEARCE, D. W. *Cost-benefit analysis: theory and practice.* London, Macmillan, 72, 270 p.

2480　DEARDEN, J. *Cost accounting and financial control systems.* Reading, Mass., Addison-Wesley Publishing Co., 73, xv-539 p.

2481　DEWHURST, R. F. J. *Business cost-benefit analysis.* London-New York, McGraw-Hill, 72, x-287 p.

2482　FRIEDMAN, J. W. "Duality principles in the theory of cost and production revisited", *Int. econ. R.* 13(1), feb 72 : 167-170.

2483　GELLEIN, O. S.; NEWMAN, M. S. *Accounting for research and development expenditures.* New York, American Institute of Certified Public Accountants 73, xii-117 p.

2484　GOULD, J. R. "Externalities, factor proportions and the level of exploitation of free access resources", *Economica (London)* 39(156), nov 72 : 383-402.

2485　GREENHUT, M. L.; OHTA, H.; SCHEIDELL, J. "A model of market areas under discriminatory pricing", *West. econ. J.* 10(4), dec 72 : 402-413.

2486　HELLER, W. P. "Transactions with set-up costs", *J. econ. Theory* 4(3), jun 72 : 465-478.

2487　HINRICHS, H. H.; TAYLOR, G. M. *Systematic analysis; a primer on benefit-cost analysis, and program evaluation.* Pacific Palisades, Calif., Goodyear Publishing Co., 72, vi-152 p.

2488　HOULTON, M. L. *An introduction to cost and management accounting.* London, Heinemann, 73, xv-261 p.

2489　JARZEMBOWSKI, A. "Rachunek kosztów normatywnych jako zródło informacji dla potrzeb zarzadzania w warunkach nowoczesnego przetwarzania danych" (Standard costs accounting as an information source for management—under modern data processing conditions), *Zesz. nauk. wyzwz. Szkoły ekon. Poznan.* 42, 1972 : 69-100.

2490　LAYARD, R. (ed.). *Cost-benefit analysis; selected readings.* Harmondsworth Penguin, 72, 496 p.

2491　LELAND, H. E. "The dynamics of a revenue maximizing firm", *Int. econ. R.* 13(2), jun 72 : 376-385.

2492　LEONTARES, M. K. *Organosis kostologiou* (Elements of cost accounting). 'Athênai, Pámisos, 72, 311 p.

2493　MARCHAND, J. R.; RUSSELL, K. P. "Externalities, liability, separability and resource allocation", *Amer. econ. R.* 63(4), sep 73 : 611-620.

2494　MARGULIS, A. Š. *Buhgalterskij učet |v otrasljah narodnogo hozjajstva* (Cost accounting in the national economy sectors). Moskva, Finansy, 73, 456 p.

2495　MIGEAL, I. "Étude par modèle de simulation des effets de l'inflation par les coûts sur l'évolution des résultats des entreprises", *A. Sci. écon. appl.* 30(3), dec 72 : 221-242.

2496　MISHAN, E. J. *Elements of cost-benefit analysis.* London, Allen and Unwin, 72, 3-151 p. [American ed. published under title: *Economics of social decision.*]

2497   NICHOLS, G. E. *Programmed cost accounting; a participative approach.* Homewood, Ill., R. D. Irwin, 73, xiv-471 p.

2498   NORSTROM, C. J. "A sufficient condition for a unique nonnegative internal rate of return", *J. financ. quant. Anal.* 7(3), jun 72 : 1835-1839.

2499   REVSINE, L. *Replacement cost accounting.* Englewood Cliffs, N.J., Prentice-Hall, 73, xiii-194 p.

2500   RYBIN, V. I. *Razvitie upravlenija i hozrasčet* (Management development and cost-accounting). Moskva, Ekonomika, 72, 144 p.

2501   SAWICKI, K. *Analiza kosztów w przedsiebiorstwie przemysłowym* (Cost analysis in industrial enterprises). Warszawa, Państwowe Wydawnictwo Ekonomiczne, 73, 259 p.

2502   SOLTYS, D. "Metodologiczne aspekty prac przygotowaxczych nad usprawnieniem systemu rachunku kosztów w przedsiebiorstwie" (Methodological aspects of preliminary works on improvement of the costs calculation system in an enterprise), *Prace nauk. wyzsz. Szkoły ekon. Wrocĸaw.* 42, 1973 : 99-130.

2503   SOWELL, E. M. *The evolution of the theories and techniques of standard costs.* University, University of Alabama Press, 73, x-539-1 p.

2504   STALLMAN, J. C. "A framework for evaluating cost control procedures for a process", *Accting R.* 47(4), oct 72 : 774-790.

2505   STARRETT, D. A. "Fundamental nonconvexities in the theory of externalities" *J. econ. Theory* 4(2), apr 72 : 180-199.

2506   WESTON, J. F. "Pricing behavior of large firms", *West. econ. J.* 10(1), mar 72 : 1-18.

2507   ZALEWSKI, S. "Ewidencyjny model procesu integracji kontroli i analizy kosztów" (An evidential model of the process of costs analysis and control), *Prace nauk. wyzsz. Szkoły ekon. Wrocĸaw* 42, 1973 : 131-142.

# H PRODUCTION (GOODS AND SERVICES)
# PRODUCTION (BIENS ET SERVICES)

## H.0 PRODUCTION AND CONSERVATION, GENERAL STUDIES
## PRODUCTION ET CONSERVATION, ÉTUDES GÉNÉRALES

[See also / Voir aussi: 2854, 3368, 3502, 3814, 3906, 4377, 5250, 5835]

2508 ALESSIO, F. J. "Environmental quality control: social rules and economic problems", *R. soc. Econ.* 30(3), sep 73 : 340-351.

2509 BAIN, J. S. *Environmental decay; economic causes and remedies.* Boston, Little, Brown, 73, ix-253 p.

2510 BALTENSPERGER, M. "Die volkswirtschaftliche Quantifizierung des Umweltkostes" (The measurement of environment protection costs), *Schweizer. Z. Volkswirtsch. Statist.* 108(3), sep 72 : 405-423.

2511 BARTKOWSKI, T. *Ochrona zasobów przyrody i zagospodarowanie środowiska geograficznego* (Protection of natural resources and development of geographic environment). Warszawa, Państwowe Wydawnictwo Naukowe, 73, 340 p.

2512 BECKERMAN, W. "Economists, scientists and environmental catastrophe", *Oxford econ. Pap.* 24(3), nov 72 : 327-344.

2513 BERRY, L.; KATES, R. W. 3 views on environmental problems, in East Africa", *Afr. R.* 2(3), jan 72 : 299-314.

2514 BINSWANGER, H. C. "Ökonomie und Ökologie—neue Dimensionen der Wirtschaftstheorie" (Economy and ecology—new dimensions of economic theory), *Schweizer. Z. Volkswirtsch. Statist.* 108(3), sep 72 : 251-281.

2515 BURTON, T. L. *Natural resource policy in Canada; issues and perspectives.* Toronto, McVlelland and Stewart, 72, 174 p.

2516 CARTER, W. "Teaching environmental economics", *J. econ. Educ.* 4(1), 1972 : 36-42.

2517 COOMBER, N. H.; BISWAS, A. K. *Evaluation of environmental intangibles.* New York, Genera Press, 73, 77 p.

2518 CURRY-LINDAHL, K. *Conservation for survival: an ecological strategy.* London, Gollancz, 72, xv-335 p.

2519 DORFMAN, R.; DORFMAN, N. (eds.). *Economics of the environment; selected readings.* New York, Norton, 72, xl-426 p.

2520 "Economics of pollution", *Amer. econ. R.* 63(2), mai 73 *Pap. and Proc.:* 236-256. With contributions by C. S. RUSSELL, M. K. EVANS and R. DORFMAN.

2521 EDEL, M. *Economics and the environment.* Englewood Cliffs, N.J., Prentice-Hall, 73, viii-162 p.

2522 EHRLICH, P. R.; EHRLICH, A. H., HOLDREN, J. P. *Human ecology; problems and solutions.* San Francisco, W. H. Freeman, 73, xi-304 p.

2523 EMERSON, F. C. (ed.). *The economics of environmental problems.* Ann Arbor, Division of Research, Graduate School of Business Administration, University of Michigan, 73, xvi-98 p.

2524 FIFE, W. C. "The management of resources", *Publ. Adm. (Sudney)* 32(2), jun 73 : 131-154. [Australia.]

2525 FORSTER, B. A. "A note on the optimal control of pollution", *J. econ. Theory* 5(3), dec 72 : 537-539.

2526 FREEMAN, A. M.; HAUEMAN, R. H.; KNEESE, A. V. *The economics of environmental policy.* New York, Wiley, 73, xii-184 p.

2527 FREY, B. S. *Umweltökonomie* (Economics of environment). Göttingen, Vandenhoeck und Ruprecht, 72, 142 p.

2528   FREY, R. L. "Umweltschutz als wirtschaftspolitische Aufgabe" (Environmental protection as a task of economic policy), *Schweizer. Z. Volkswirtsch. Statist.* 108(3), sep 72 : 453-477.

2529   GARVEY, G. *Energy, ecology, economy.* New York, Norton, 72, 235 p.

2530   GREENWOOD, N. H.; EDWARDS, J. M. B. *Human environments and natural systems; a conflict of dominion.* North Scituate, Mass., Duxbury Press, 73, xii-429 p.

2531   HARROY, P. "L'environnement et l'économie", *Soc. roy. Écon. polit. Belgique* 362, jun 72 : 3-27.

2532   HITE, J. C.; LAURENT, E. A. *Environmental planning: an economic analysis; applications for the coastal zone.* New York, Praeger, 72, xiv-155 p.

2533   HITE, J. C. et al. *The economics of environmental quality.* Washington, American Enterprise Institute for Public Policy Research, 72, 113 p.

2534   INSTITUT DE SOCIOLOGIE. Centre d'écologie humaine. *Pour une conservation efficace de l'environnement. Aspects sociaux, politiques et administratifs.* Bruxelles, ISS, 72, 142 p.

2535   JÖHR, W. A. "Zur Frage der Berücksichtigung der Umweltproblematik in der volkswirtschaftlichen Gesamtrechnung" (On the problem of integrating environmental deterioration into national accounting), *Schweizer. Z. Volkswirtsch. Statist.* 108(3), sep 72 : 425-437.

2536   KOLM, S. "Introduction à l'économie de l'environnement", *Schweizer. Z. Volkswirtsch. Statist.* 108(3), sep 72 : 329-346.

2537   KRJUĆKOV V. V. *Krajnij sever: problemy racional'nogo ispol'zovanija prirodnyh resursov* (Far North: problems of the rational utilization of natural resources). Moskva, Mysl', 73, 184 p.

2538   LOWENTHAL, D., RIEL, M. *Environmental structures: semantic and experiential components.* New York, American Geographical Soviety, 72, iv-48 p.

2539   MAISON DES SCIENCES DE L'HOMME. *Political economy of environment. Problems of method.* Papers presented at the symposium held at the Maison des Sciences de l'Homme, Paris, 5-8 July, 1971. The Hague, Mouton, 72, 237 p.

2540   MANSHARD, W. "Umweltbelastung in Entwicklungsländern. Gegenwärtige und zukünftige Perspectiven" (Environment problems in developing countries. Present and future prospects), *Vierteljahresberichte* 52, jun 73 : 117-126.

2541   MASON, W. H.; FOLKERTS, G. W. *Environmental problems; principles, readings, and comments.* Dubuque, Iowa, W. C. Brown, 73, x-399 p.

2542   MAY, R. M. *Stability and complexity in model ecosystems.* Princeton, N.J., Princeton University Press, 73, ix-235 p.

2543   McCAMY, J. L. *The quality of the environment.* New York, Free Press, 72, viii-276 p.

2544   MINC, A. A. *Ékonomičeskaja ocenka estestvennyh resursov (naučno, metodičeskie problemy učeta geografičeskih različij v effektivnosti ispol'zovanija)* (Economic estimation of natural resources. Scientific and methodological problems of the estimation of geographic differences in their utilization efficiency). Moskva, Mysl', 72, 303 p.

2545   MONSEN, R. J. *Business and the changing environment.* New York, McGraw-Hill, 73, x-290 p.

2546   MONTGOMERY, W. D. "Markets in licenses and efficient pollution control programs", *J. econ. Theory* 5(3), dec 72 : 395-418.

2547   MULLER, F. "An operational mathematical programming model for the planning of economic activities in relation to the environment", *Socio-econ. plan. Sci.* 7(2), apr 73 : 123-138.

2549   "Natural resources as a contraint on economic growth", *Amer. econ. R.* 63(2), mai 73 *Pap. and Proc.*: 106-128. With contributions by: S. GORDON, N. ROSENBERG, P. G. BRADLEY, C. MORSE.

2550   ORGANIZATION FOR ECONOMIC CO-OPERATION AND DEVELOPMENT. *Problems of environmental economics;* record of the Seminar held at the OECD in Summer 1971. Paris, OECD, 72, 278 p.

2551   PAGE, T. *Economics of involuntary transfers; a unified approach to pollution and congestion externalities.* Berlin-New York, Springer, 73, viii-159 p.

2552   PARISH, R. M. "Economic aspects of pollution control", *Austral. econ. Pap.* 11(18), jun 72 : 32-43.

2553   POLE, N. (ed.). *Environmental solutions.* Cambridge, Eco-Publications, 72, 136 p.

2554   *Pollution and conservation; selected papers.* Adelaide, University of Adelaide, Department of Adult Education, 72, v-106 p.

2555   "Problèmes de l'environnement (Les)", *R. écon. Sud-Ouest* 22(1), 1973 : 13-86.

2556   RICH, P. E.; TUSSING, A. R. *The national park system in Alaska; an economic impact study.* College, University of Washington Press, 73, 88 p.

2557   SERDITYH, B. G. *Ėkonomija material'nyh resursov* (The material resources economy) Moskva, Profizdat, 72, 32 p.

2558   THOMPSON, D. N. *The economics of environmental protection.* Cambridge, Mass., Winthrop Publishers, 73, x-278 p.

2559   TOSI, H.; ALDAG, R.; STOREY, R. "On the measurement of the environment: an assessment of the Lawrence and Lorsch environmental uncertainty subscale", *Adm. Sci. Quart.* 18(1), mar 73 : 27-36.

2560   UTTON, A. E.; HENNING, D. H. (eds.). *Environmental policy; concepts and international implications.* New York, Praeger, 73, ix-266 p. [Reprints from two issues of *Natural Resources Journal* 11(3), jul 71, 12(2), apr 72.]

2561   VICTOR, P. A. *Economics of pollution.* London, Macmillan, 72, 87 p.

2562   VICTOR, P. A. *Pollution: economy and environment.* London, Allen and Unwin, 72, 3-247 p.

2563   VIEILLE, P. "Dégradation de l'environnement et économie de marché", *Diogène* 84, oct-dec 73 : 68-93.

2564   WALDRON, I.; RICKLEFS, R. E. *Environment and population; problems and solutions.* New York, Holt, Rinehart and Winston, 73, viii-232 p.

2565   WALTER, I. *Environmental management and the international economic order.* New York, New York University Center for International Studies, 73, iii-85 p.

2566   WATSON, W. D. "Costs of air pollution control in the coal-fired electric power industry", *Quart. R. Econ. Busin.* 12(3), 1972 : 63-85.

2567   WATT, K. E. F. *Principles of environmental science.* New York, McGraw-Hill, 73, xiv-319 p.

2568   WENDERS, J. T. "Profit maximization, pollution abatement, and corrective pollution taxes", *J. econ. Issues* 6(2-3), sep 72 : 137-140.

2569   WERNER, J. "Umweltschutz und Wachstumsproblematik" (The protection of environment and the growth problem), *Ordo* 24, 1973 : 157-177.

2570   WINTHROP, H. "The environmental dilemma: possible steps toward its dissolution", *Amer. J. Econ. Sociol.* 31(4), oct 72 : 387-396.

## H.1    AGRICULTURE

### H.11    Agricultural economics
Économie agricole

#### H.110    *General studies*
*Études générales*

[See also / Voir aussi: 2743]

2571   AUBAKIROV, Ja. A. *Ispol'zovanie ėkonomičeskih zakonov socializma v sel'skom hozjajstve* (Utilizations of socialist economic laws in agriculture). Alma-Ata, Kazahstan, 72, 212 p.

2572   AUSTRUY, I. "Révolution agricole et développement", *R. écon. Madagascar* (7), jan-dec 72 : 11-25.

2573   BROWN, J. "Agricultural economics in the decade ahead", *Canad. J. agric. Econ.* 20(3), nov 72 : 1-8.

2574   DILLON, J. L. "The outlook for agricultural economics", *Austral. J. agric. Econ.* 16(2), aug 72 : 73-81.

2575   GITTINGER, J. P. *Economic analysis of agricultural projects.* Baltimore, Johns Hopkins University Press, 72, viii-221 p.

2576   KOSTROWICKI, J. *Zarys geografii rolnictwa* (Outline of agricultural geography). Warszawa, Państwowe Wydawnictwo Naukowe, 73, 631 p.

2577   KUMAR, J. *Population and land in world agriculture; recent trends and relationships.* Berkeley, Institute of International Studies, University of California, 73, xiv-318 p.

2578 LEDUC, G. "Le rôle de l'agriculture dans le développement économique", *Ét. Statist. Cameroun Afr. équat. Banque centr.* 180, jan 73 : 5-16.

2579 MANETSCH, T. J. *et al. A generalized simulation approach to agricultural sector analysis; with special reference to Nigeria.* East Lansing, Michigan State University, 71, xvii-362 p.

2580 MELLOR, J. W. "Accelerated growth in agricultural production and the intersectoral transfer of resources", *Econ. Develop. cult. Change* 22(1), oct 73 : 1-16.

2581 ÔKAWA, K. *Differential structure and agriculture: essays on dualistic growth.* Tokyo, Kinokuniya Bookstore Co., 72, xi-298 p. CR: V. W. RUTTAN, *J. econ. Liter.* 11(3), sep 73 : 912-914.

2582 ROGAČEV, S. V. *Ėkonomičeskie zakony i razvitie sel'skogo hozjajstva* (Economic laws and agricultural development). Moskva, Ėkonomika, 73, 231 p.

2583 THOMAS, W. J. "Looking at the future of agriculture", *J. agr. Econ.* 24(3), sep 73 : 443-464.

2584 THORBECKE, E. "Sector analysis and models of agriculture in developing countries", *Food Res. Inst. Stud.* 12(1), 1973 : 73-89.

2585 THORNTON, D. S. "Agriculture in economic development", *J. agr. Econ.* 24(2), mai 73 : 225-287.

2586 TOMCZAK, F.; RAJTAR, J. *Ekonomika rolnictwa. Zarys teorii* (Economics of agriculture. Outline of the theory). 2nd ed. rev. enl. Warszawa, Szkoła Główna Planowania i Statystyki, 73, 337 p.

2587 VEDOVATO, G. "L'agricoltura nella strategia internazionale dello sviluppo" (Agriculture in the international strategy of development), *Riv. Studi polit. int.* 39(3), jul-sep 72 : 355-371.

2588 WOS, A. "Materiałochłonnosc i pracochłonnosc produkcji rolniczej" (Material and labour consumption of agricultural production), *Zagadn. Ekon. rolnej* (2), 1973 : 21-37.

## H.111 *Technical factors of agricultural productivity* *Facteurs techniques de la productivité agricole*

### H.1110 *General studies: farming methods* *Études générales: méthodes d'exploitation*

[See also / Voir aussi: 2631, 2669, 3374, 3548, 6022]

2589 AL-BUȚAYĤÎ, 'A. al-R. M. *Dirâsaṭ fî jughrâfiyaṭ al-Irâq al-zirâ'îyaṭ* (Studies on agricultural geography of Iraq). Baghdâd, Maṭba'aṭ al-Irshâd, 72, 208 p.

2590 BARBAŠIN, A. I. *Ėkonomičeskoe osobnovanie i organizacionnye formy specializacii sel'skogo hozjajstva* (Economic basis and organizational forms of agricultural specialization). Moskva, Ėkonomika, 73, 199 p.

2591 BECKFORD, G. L. "Economic organization of plantations in the Third World", *Stud. comp. int. Develop.* 7(3), 1972 : 243-263.

2592 CESARINI, G. *Mezzogiorno contadino. Progresso tecnologico e strutture tradizionali* (Rural South. Technological progress and traditional structures). Bologna, Edagricole, 72, v-135 p. [Italy.]

2593 FLORENT'EV, L. Ja. *Opyt specializacii sel'skohozjajstvennogo proizvodstva RSFSR* (Experiment of Russian agricultural production specialization). Moskva, Rossel'-hozizdat, 72, 481 p.

2594 FLOYD, B. *Some spatial aspects of rural land use in tropical Africa: typologies, models, and case studies.* Mona, Department of Geography, University of the West Indies, 72, 89-xiv p.

2595 FUSSELL, G. E. *The classical tradition in West European farming.* Rutherford, N. J., Fairleigh Dickinson University Press, 72, 237 p.

2596 GARNER, F. H. *Modern British farming systems: an introduction.* London, Elek; New York, Barnes and Noble, 72, x-246-12 p.

2597 JONES, J. O. (ed.). *Land use planning, the methodology of choice: a compilation of review articles and annotated bibliography.* Slough, Commonwealth Agricultural Bureaux, 72, 3-1-47 p.

2645    STEINWENDTNER, P. *Die Mechanisierung in der Tiroler Landwirtschaft* (The mechaniza-
        tion of Tyrolian agriculture). Innsbruck, Wagner's Universitätsbuchhandlung in
        Komm., 72, 128 p.

**H.1114**    *Fertilizers*
              *Engrais*

2646    DOLL, J. P. "A comparison of annual versus average optima for fertilizer experiments",
        *Amer. J. agric. Econ.* 54(2), mai 72 : 226-233.
2647    HANSEL, H. "Zu Fragen der Wirtschaftlichkeit bei der Übernahme neuer Verfahren.
        Mineraldüngung in Ghana" (The problem of the profitability of the adoption of new
        process: mineral manure in Ghana), *Afr. Spectrum* 7(2), 1972 : 15-31.

**H.1115**    *Other factors*
              *Autres facteurs*

2648    BARRACLOUCH, S.; SCHATAN, J. "Technological policy and agricultural development",
        *Land Econ.* 49(2), mai 73 : 175-194.
2649    CROUCH, B. R. "Innovation and farm development, a multidimensional model"
        *Sociol. rur.* 12(3-4), 1972 : 431-449.
2650    ÉGOROVA, A. S. *Organizacija mašinnoj obrabotki ekonomičeskoj informacii v sel'skom
        hozjajstve* (Mechanical organization of economic information processing in agricul-
        ture). Moskva, Statistika, 73, 316 p.
2651    ERNY, P. "Expériences d'enseignement rural en Afrique noire", *Probl. soc. zaïr*
        96-97, mar-jun 72 : 41-52.
2652    FAILLY, D. DE. "Agricultural education in Zaire: an essay in the methodology of
        analysis and evaluation", *Sociol. rur.* 12(3-4), 1972 : 457-473.
2653    "Formation en milieu rural (La)", *Éduc. perm.* 16, oct-dec 72 : 3-116. [France.]
2654    HAYWARD, F. M.; INGLE, C. R. (eds.). *African rural development: the political dimension.*
        East Lansing, African Studies Center, Michigan State University, 72, iv-105 p.
2655    HÖGNER, R. "Die Entwicklung des landwirtschaftlichen Schulwesens" (The develop-
        ment of agricultural education), *Bayern in Zahlen* 26(11), nov 72 : 411-413.
2656    HOUÉE, P. *Les étapes du développement rural.* Paris, Éditions Économie et humanisme,
        72, 2 vols.
2657    JANVRY, A. DE. "A socio-economic model of induced innovations for Argentine
        agricultural development", *Quart. J. Econ.* 87(3), aug 73 : 410-435.
2658    JANVRY, A. DE; MARTINEZ, J. C. "Induccion de innovaciones y desarrollo agropecuario
        argentino" (Induction of innovations and Argentina agricultural development),
        *Economica (La Plata)* 18(2), mai-aug 72 : 179-213.
2659    KAUSHAL, M. R. "African rural development", *Ind. coop. R.* 9(4), jul 73 : 429-439.
2660    MENANTEAU-HORTA, D. *Aspectos sociológicos en el desarrollo técnico de la agricultura en
        Chile: la aplicación de un modelo de difusión de innovaciones* (Sociological aspects in the
        technical development of Chilean agriculture: application of an innovation diffusion
        model). Asunción, Centro Paraguayo de Estudios Sociológicos, 72, 14 p.
2661    SACHCHIDANANDA. *Social dimensions of agricultural development.* Delhi, National
        Publishing House, 72, x-197 p.
2662    TIHONOV, V. A. *Ėkonomika i organizacija primenenija tehniki v sel'skom hozjajstva*
        (Economics and organization of use of techniques in agriculture). Moskva, Kolos, 72,
        242 p.
2663    VIAL, A. "Formation permanente et agriculture", *Paysans* 17(99), apr-mai 73 : 45-53.
        [France.]

**H.1116**    *Productivity policy in agriculture*
              *Politique de productivité en agriculture*

[See also / Voir aussi: 2598, 3974]

2664    ANDREEV, A. N. "V bor'be za povyšenie effektivnosti sel'skohozjajstvennogo proiz-
        vodstva" (The struggle to increase agricultural production efficiency), *Kommunist
        Ukr.* 47(11), nov 72 : 35-42.

2665   BADCZEWSKI, J. *Produkcyjnosc gospodarstw chłopówrobotników* (Productivity of farms owned by peasant-factory workmen). Warszawa, Ludowa Spółdzielnia Wydawnicza, 72, 150 p. [Poland.]

2666   BARRY, A. M. "Consideraciones sobre la productividad y la transformación agraria" (Thoughts on productivity and agrarian transformation), *Lecciones y Ensayos* 42, 1970 : 9-24. [Argentina.]

2667   BUNNIES, H. "Beiträge zur Quantifizierung des Ertragszuwachses von Getreide" (Contributions to the quantification of the increase in grains profitability), *Agrarwirtschaft* 22(8), aug 73 : 283-296.

2668   FARKOWSKI, C. *Zróznicowanie produkcyjnosci gospodarst w indywidualnych w Polsce* (Productivity differentiation of individual farms in Poland). Warszawa, Ludowa Spółdzielnia Wydawnicza, 73, 232 p.

2669   GHOSH, A. "Size-structure, productivity and growth: a case study of West Bengal agriculture", *Bangladesh econ. R.* 1(1), jan 73 : 59-70.

2670   IHAMUOTILA, R. *Productivity and aggregate production functions in the Finnish agricultural sector*, 1950-1969. Helsinki, Valtion painatuskeskus, 72, 87 p.

2671   LAJLIEV, D. S. *Puti povyšenija ēffektivnosti sel'skohozjajstvennogo proizvodstva Kirgizi*, (Means of elevation of Kirghiz agricultural production). Frunze, Kyrgyzstan, 72, 171 p.

2672   LAZAR, T. "Stimularea prin pret a rutroducerii technicii noi in agricultura" (Stimulation of the introduction of modern techniques in agriculture by means of prices), *Probl. econ. (Bucuresti)* 26(6), jun 73 : 43-49.

2673   PRASAD, K. "Employment potential of higher productivity. The case of Indian agriculture", *Soc. Action* 23(2), apr-jun 73 : 117-136.

2674   PYTKOWSKI, W. "Postep a prawa produkcji w rolnictwie" (Progress and production rules in agriculture), *Zagadn. Ekon. rolnej* (4), 1973 : 87-100.

2675   RAJ VIR SINGH. "Labour productivity and size of farm", *Ind. J. industr. Relat.* 8(2), oct 72 : 245-253. [India.]

2676   RUSONOV, I. V. *Intensifikacija sel'skogo hozjajstva. Zonal'nye osobennosti* (Agricultural intensification. Zonal characteristics). Moskva, Ēkonomika, 72, 230 p.

2677   RYCHLIK, T. "Postep techniczny a organizacja rolnictwa" (Technical progress and organization of agriculture). *Zagadn. Ekon. rolnej* (3), 1973 : 17-35.

2678   VORONCOV, A. P. *Proizvoditel'nost' truda i zarabotnaja plata v sovhozah* (Labour productivity and wages in state farms). Moskva, Kolos, 73, 231 p.

2679   WATTS, E. R. "Reaching East Africa's farmers—a survey of recent efforts to increase the effectiveness of agricultural extension in Kenya, Uganda and Tanzania", *J. Adm. Overseas* 12(2), apr 73 : 112-124.

2680   WIELBURSKI, R. "Rozwazania na tle badań produktywności rolnictwa Polski i innych krajów" (Considerations based on research work on agricultural productivity in Poland and other countries), *Zagadn. Ekon. rolnej* (2), 1973 : 39-51.

### H.112   Forms of agricultural enterprise and land tenure
### Formes d'entreprise agricole et de tenure du sol

### H.1121   Private forms of agricultural enterprise
### Entreprises privées

[See also / Voir aussi: 2665, 2668, 2696, 2747]

2681   BURZESKI, V. "Sitnoto selsko stopantsvo vo denešni uslovi" (The small agricultural enterprise under present conditions), *Godiš. ekon. Fak. (Skopje)* 15, 1971 : 105-129.

2682   GRAHAM, J. R.; REDFERN, J. M.; MEENEN, H. J. *Estate planning: problems, tools, and case studies of Arkansas farm estates*. Fayetteville, Agricultural Experiment Station, 72, 118 p.

2683   GROCHOWSKI, Z. "Sytuacja ekonomiczna gospodarki chłopskiej w roku 1972 i perspektywy na przyszłość" (Economic situation in peasant farming in 1972 and its future perspectives), *Zagadn. Ekon. rolnej* (4), 1973 : 23-38.

2684   KHAN, W.; TRIPATHY, R. N. *Intensive agriculture and modern inputs prospects of small farmers; a study in West Godavari District*. Hyderabad, National Institute of Community Development, 72, viii-124 p. [India.]

2729    Barraclough, S. L.; Collarte, J. C. (eds.). *Agrarian structure in Latin America; a resume of the CIDA land tenure studies of: Argentina, Brazil, Chile, Colombia, Ecuador, Guatemala, Peru.* Lexington, Mass., Lexington Books, 73, xxvi-351 p. [Slightly altered version of *Tenencia de la tierra y reforma agraria en América latina*, published by CIDA in 1971.]

2730    Bride, A. "Migrations, colonisations et modifications des structures agraires sur la côte équatorienne", *R. mexic. Sociol.* 33(4), oct-dec 71 : 803-829.

2731    Brzoza, A. *Zastosowanie łańcuchów Markowa do analizy ewolucji struktury agrarnej i struktury społecznej wsi w Polsce* (Application of Markov chains to the analysis of agrarian structure and rural social structure in Poland). Warszawa, Instytut Ekonomiki Rolnej, 73, 38 p.

2732    Chiffelle, F. "Le remembrement parcellaire au service de l'aménagement régionale. Le cas de la Suisse", *A. Géogr.* 82(449), jan-feb 73 : 28-41.

2733    Famoriyo, S. "Elements in developing land tenure policies for Nigeria", *Quart. J Adm.* 7(1), oct 72 : 55-67.

2734    Bibl. xxi-2898. Feder, E. *The rape of the peasantry: Latin America's landholding system.* CR: M. Kling, *Amer. polit. Sci. R.* 67(1), mar 73 : 246-247.

2735    Gates, P. W. *Landlords and tenants on the prairie frontier; studies in American land policy.* Ithaca, N.Y., Cornell University Press, 73, vii-333 p.

2736    Gresham, C. A. *Eifionydd: a study in landownership from the medieval period to the present day.* Cardiff, University of Wales Press, 73, xix-419-5 p.

2737    Guyot, D. "The politics of land: comparative development in two states of Malaysia", *Pacific Aff.* 44(3), 1971 : 368-389.

2738    Heffernan, W. D. "Sociological dimensions of agricultural structures in the United States", *Sociol. rur.* 12(3-4), 1972 : 481-499.

2739    Horii, K. "The land tenure system of Malay Padi farmers", *Develop. Econ.* 10(1), mar 72 : 45-73.

2740    Johnson, O. E. "Economic analysis, the legal framework and land tenure systems", *J. Law Econ.* 15(1), apr 72 : 259-276.

2741    Kimani, S. M. "The structure of land ownership in Nairobi", *Canad. J. Afr. Stud.* 6(3), 1972 : 379-402.

2742    Lamps, M. "L'évolution des structures agraires et de la politique agricole en République Démocratique Allemande", *R. Est* 3(4), oct 72 : 51-61.

2743    Lebeau, R. *Les grands types de structures agraires dans le monde.* Paris, Masson et Cie, 72, 120 p.

2744    Podedworny, M. "The customary land tenure; selected problems of agrarian reforms and agricultural development in countries of Africa South of the Sahara", *Africana B.* 15, 1971 : 95-122.

2745    Ruiz-Maya, C. "Los regímenes de tenencia de la tierra en España" (Land tenure systems in Spain), *A. Econ. (Madrid)* 8(13), jan-mar 72 : 125-196.

2746    "Structures foncières (Les)", *Paysans* 17(98), feb-mar 73 : 7-43. [France.]

2747    Szemberg, A. "Dzierzawa ziemi w gospodarce indywidualnej w Polsce" (Land tenure in private farming in Poland), *Zagadn. Ekon. rolnej* (3), 1973 : 57-68.

2748    Trivedi, K. D.; Trivedi, K. "Consolidation of holdings in Uttar Pradesh", *J. Adm. Overseas* 12(3), jul 73 : 179-189. [India.]

2749    Viana, J. "Características de la propiedad de la tierra en Colombia" (Characteristics of land tenure in Colombia), *Doc. polít.* 100, jul-aug 72 : 8-41.

2750    West, H. W. *Land policy in Buganda.* Cambridge, Eng., University Press, 72, xiv-244 p.

2751    Williams, J. C. *Lesotho land tenure and economic development.* Pretoria, Africa Institute, 72, 52 p.

**H.1124**   *Land and real estate reforms*
             *Réformes agraires et foncières*

**H.11240**  General studies
             Études générales

2752    Brzoza, A. "Ewolucja struktura agrarnej jako proces stochastyczny" (Agrarian structure evolution as a stochastic process), *Zagadn. Ekon. rolnej* (1), 1973 : 81-105.

2753    DORNER, P. *Land reform and economic development.* Harmondsworth, Eng., Penguin Books, 72, 167 p.

2754    GARCIA, A. "¿Reforma agraria o modernización tecnológica? La crisis del modelo tecnocrático de cambio" (Agrarian reform or technological modernization? The crisis of the technocratic model of change), *Trim. econ.* 39(156), oct-dec 72 : 771-782.

#### H.11241    Local studies
####              Études localisées

[See also / Voir aussi: 2720, 2744]

2755    ACOSTA, J. "Leyes de reforma agraria en Cuba y el sector privado campesino" (Agrarian reform legislation in Cuba and the private peasant sector), *Econ. y Desarr.* (12), jul-aug 72 : 84-115.

2756    BARRACLOUCH, S.; AFFONSO, A. "Diagnóstico de la reforma agraria chilena, novembre 1970-junio 1972" (Diagnostic of the Chilean agrarian reform, November 1970-June 1972), *Cuad. Real. nac.* 16, apr 73 : 71-123.

2657    BILLAZ, R.; MAFFEI, E. "La reforma agraria chilena y el camino hacia el socialismo" (The Chilean agrarian reform and the road towards socialism), *Cuad. Real. nac.* (11), jan 72 : 45-79.

2758    BLANKENSTEIN, C. S.; ZUKEVAS, C. "Agrarian reform in Ecuador: an evaluation of past efforts and the development of a new approach", *Econ. Develop. cult. Change* 22(1), oct 73 : 73-94.

2759    BROKENSHA, D.; GLAZIER, J. "Land reform among the Mbeere of Central Kenya" *Africa (London)* 43(3), jul 73 : 182-206.

2760    CHATANAY, J. N. "Nécessité historique, la révolution agraire en Algérie est d'abord un instrument de justice sociale", *Paysans* 17(98), feb-mar 73 : 45-54.

2761    ESTRELLA, C. F. "Philippine agrarian reform policies: a survey", *Spectrum* 1(3), apr 73 : 1-7.

2762    GAITZSCH, A. "Hemmende Faktoren bei der Modernisierung der peruanischen Agrarstruktur. Ergebnisse einer Fallstudie in der Pampa de Anta, Cuzco" (The obstacles to modernization in the agrarian structure of Peru. Results of a case study in the Pampa de Anta, Cuzco), *Dritte Welt* 2(2), 1973 : 235-250.

2763    GALINA, A. D. *Čili: bor'ba za agrarnuju reformu* (Chile, the struggle for the agrarian reform). Moskva, Nauka, 72, 215 p.

2764    GOMEZ HURTADO, A. "El problema agrario en Colombia" (The agrarian problem in Colombia), *Universitas (Bogotà)* 43, nov 72 : 291-302.

2765    HARBESON, J. W. *Nation-building in Kenya; the role of land reform.* Evanston, Ill., Northwestern University Press, 73, xxi-367 p.

2766    HOBEN, A. "Social anthropology and development planning; a case study in Ethiopian land reform policy", *J. mod. Afr. Stud.* 10(4), dec 72 : 561-582.

2767    HUIZER, G. *Peasant mobilisation and land reform in Indonesia.* The Hague, Institute of Social Studies, 54 p. multigr.

2768    KARIM, A. "Agrarian changes in Algeria", *Wld marx. R.* 16(1), jan 73 : 89-95. [Also published in *Nouv. R. int.* 16(2), feb 73 : 90-100.]

2769    KIRBY, J. "Venezuela's land reform: progress and change", *J. interamer. Stud.* 15(2) mai 73 : 205-220.

2770    LEHMANN, D. "Peasant consciousness and agrarian reform in Chile", *Archiv. europ. Sociol.* 13(2), 1972 : 296-325.

2771    LUCAS, P. "La réforme agraire en Algérie", *Homme et Soc.* 27, jan-mar 73 : 131-142.

2772    MAFEJE, A. *Agrarian revolution and the land question in Buganda.* The Hague, Institute of Social Studies, 73, 27 p.

2773    MANZANILLA SCHAFFER, V. "México: la entrega de la tierra y la reforma agraria integral" (Mexico: land remittance and total agrarian reform), *R. Cienc. soc. (Puerto Rico)* 16(2), jun 72 : 187-211.

2774    MORTIMER, R. A. *The Indonesian Communist Party and land reform, 1959-1965.* Clayton, Vic., Centre of Southeast Asian Studies, Monash University, 72, vi-73 p.

2775    PANGANIBAN, L. C. *Land reform administrative procedures in the Philippines; a critical analysis.* Madison, Land Tenure Center, University of Wisconsin-Madison, 72, ii-42 l.

2822    LAMYKIN, I. A. *Isčislenie i analiz sebestoimosti sel'skohozjajstvennoj produkcii* (Calculation and analysis of the agricultural production cost prices). Moskva, Ėkonomika, 72, 305 p.

2823    LIBKIND, A. S. *Nakoplenie, kapital'nye vloženija i fondootdača v kolhozah* (Accumulation, capital investments and efficiency in collective farms). Moskva, Ėkonomika, 73, 192 p.

2824    PENSON, J. E. "Demand for financial assets in the farm sector: a portfolio balance approach", *Amer. J. agric. Econ.* 54(2), mai 72 : 163-174.

2825    POKIN'ČEREDA, A. P. *Ėkonomiko-statističeskoe izučenie proizvodstvennyh fondov kolhozov i sovhozov* (Economic and statistical study of collective and state farms productive funds). Moskva, Statistika, 72, 151 p.

2826    POLETAEV, P. "Osnovnye fondy v sel'skom hozjajstve i pokazateli effektivnosti thispol'zovanija" (Fixed stocks in agriculture and profitability indexes of their utilisation). *Plan. Hoz.* 50(8), aug 73 : 84-90.

2827    SKALOZUBOVA, N. A.; STEJNMAN, M. Ja. *Finansovoe planirovanie v sovhozah* (Financial planning in state farms). Moskva, Finansy, 73, 143 p.

2828    TUMANOVA, M. D. *Rasširennoe vosproizvodstvo v sovhozah pri polnom hozrasčete* (Enlarged reproduction in state farms under a complete cost accounting system). Moskva, Kolos, 73, 119 p.


**H.1132**    *Agricultural bookkeeping*
              *Comptabilité agricole*

2829    FILIPIAK, B. *Finansowe mierniki pracy w rolnictwie panstwowym* (Financial measures of work in State agriculture). Warszawa, Państwowe Wydawnictwo Ekonomiczne 73, 262 p. [Poland.]

2830    LECHI, F. *Contabilità agraria* (Agricultural accounting). Padova, CEDAM, 72, 133 p.


**H.114**    **Agricultural policy**
             **Politique agricole**

         [See also / Voir aussi: 2742, 4668]

2831    ADDY, J. *The agrarian revolution.* London, Longman, 72, vii-104 p. [UK.]

2832    "Agricultural policy in the countries signatory to the Andean subregional integration agreement", *Econ. B. Latin Amer.* 16(2), jul-dec 71 : 91-119.

2833    ANDREWS, S. *Agriculture and the Common Market.* Ames, Iowa State University Press, 73, xiii-183 p.

2834    BAUDIN, P. "Crises monétaires et politique agricole commune", *R. Marché commun* 167, aug-sep 73 : 309-318.

2835    BELAL, A. A.; AGOURRAM, A. J. "Les problèmes posés par la politique agricole dans une économie 'dualiste': les leçons d'une expérience, le cas marocain", *B. écon. soc. Maroc* 33(122), jul-sep 71 : 1-36.

2836    BERGMANN, T. "Die Agrarpolitik der Bundesrepublik. Ergebnisse und Aussichten" (Agrarian policy of Germany FR. Results and perspectives), *WSI Mitt.* 26(9), sep 73 : 253-360.

2837    BLUM, R. "Grüne Revolution als entwicklungspolitische Strategie" (Green revolution as a development policy strategy), *Z. Wirtsch.-u. soz.-Wiss.* 92(2), 1972 : 169-183.

2838    BORER, M. A. *Sozialethische Wertüberlegungen in der Agrarpolitik* (Reflections concerning social and ethnic values in agricultural policy). Heidelberg, F. H. Kerle, 72, 174 p. [Switzerland.]

2839    CHIAROMONTE, G. *Agricoltura. Mercato Comune e regioni* (Agriculture. Common Market and regions). Roma, Editori riuniti, 73, 136 p. [Italy.]

2840    CHIAROMONTE, G. *Agricoltura, sviluppo economico, democrazia. La politica agraria e contadina dei comunisti, 1965-1972* (Agriculture, economic development, democracy. Agricultural and land policy of the Communists, 1965-1972). Bari, De Donato, 73, 269 p. [India.]

2841    CHOŁAJ, H. *Budowa socjalizmu na wsi a polityka rolna* (The building of socialism in the country and agricultural policy). Warszawa, Wiedza Powszechna, 73, 128 p.

2842 ESPOSTO, A. *Politica agraria e unità contadina* (Agrarian policy and peasant unity). Roma, Editori riuniti, 72, 342 p. [Italy.]

2843 GAETANI D'ARAGONA, G. "Il futuro della politica agricola della Comunità" (The future of Community agricultural policy), *Rass. econ. (Napoli)* 36(5), sep-oct 72 : 1257-1272.

2844 GAWRON, W. *Metodyka programowania sieciowego w rolnictwie* (Methods of network programming in agriculture). Warszawa, Instytut Ekonomiki Rolnej, 72, 57 p.

2845 GRISSA, A. *Politiques agricoles et emploi. Étude de cas: la Tunisie.* Paris, OCDE, 73, 237 p.

2846 HARRISON, A. "L'agricoltura e la politica agricola della Gran-Bretagna" (Great Britain's agriculture and agricultural policy), *Riv. Polit. agr.* 19(4), dec 72 : 21-29.

2847 HARTMANN, A. "Sozialökonomische und agrartechnische Aspekte der 'Grünen Revolution' Indonesiens" (Socio-economic and agronomic aspects of the "Green Revolution" in Indonesia), *Vierteljahresberichte* 51, mar 73 : 61-76.

2848 Bibl. XXI-3034. HEADY, E. O.; MAYIS, L. V.; MADSEN, H. C. *Future farm programs: comparative costs and consequences.* CR: K. H. PARSONS, *J. econ. Liter.* 11(2), jun 73 : 585-586.

2849 JOHNS, I. B. "Agricultural sector planning in New Zealand", *Polit. Sci. (Wellington)* 24(1), apr 72 : 2-14.

2850 JOHNSTON, B. F.; PAGE, J. M.; WARR, P. "Criteria for the design of agricultural development strategies", *Food Res. Inst. Stud.* 11(1), 1972 : 27-57.

2851 KENZEGUZIN, M. B. *Optimal'noe planirovanie sel'skogo hozjajstva* (Optimal planning of agriculture). Alma-Ata, Kajnar, 72, 191 p.

2852 KIENE, W. "Zölle oder Verlustausgleichezahlungen ? Eine Wohlfahrtskosten-Analyse der österreichischen Agrarpolitik" (Tariffs or deficiency payments ? A welfare-costs analysis of Austria's agricultural policy), *Z. Wirtsch.-u. soz.-Wiss.* 92(4), 1972 : 405-419.

2853 KILBY, P.; JOHNSTON, B. F. "The choice of agricultural strategy and the development of manufacturing", *Food Res. Inst. Stud.* 11(2), 1972 : 155-175.

2854 KLEINEWEFERS, H. "Wirtschaftspolitische Konzeption und Umweltproblematik: das Beispiel der Agrarpolitik" (Economic policy and environmental problems: the example of agricultural policy), *Schweizer. Z. Volkswirtsch. Statist.* 108(3), sep 72 : 283-328.

2855 KLJUKIN, B. D. *SŠA: pravovoe regulirovanie sel'skogo hozjajstva* (USA: the legal regulation of agriculture). Moskva, Nauka, 72, 295 p.

2856 LEWANDOWSKI, J. *Zagadnienia rozwoju rolnictwa w socjalizmie* (Problems of development of agriculture in socialism). Warszawa, Państwowe Wydawnictwo Ekonomiczne, 72, 202 p.

2857 LOUWES, S. L. "Landbouwpolitiek. Failliet van een 'monodisciplinaire' landbouw-economische benadering" (Agricultural policy. Bankruptcy of a monodisciplinary agricultural-economic approach), *Economist (Haarlem)* 120(3), mai-jun 72 : 217-240.

2858 MALVE, P. "A European approach to agricultural cooperation", *Atlantic Community Quart.* 10(2), 1972 : 203-214.

2859 MANEGOLD, D. "Agrarpolitische Entwicklungen in der EWG" (The evolution of EEC agricultural policy), *Agrarwirtschaft* 21(12), dec 72 : 419-430.

2860 McHENRY, D. E. Jr. "The utility of compulsion in the implementation of agricultural policies: a case study from Tanzania", *Canad. J. Afr. Stud.* 7(2), 1973 : 305-316.

2861 MEGRET, C. "L'élargissement des Communautés européennes et la politique agricole commune", *R. trim. Dr. europ.* 8(4), oct-dec 72 : 752-765.

2862 ORGANIZATION FOR ECONOMIC COOPERATION AND DEVELOPMENT. Committee of Agriculture. *Structural reform measures in agriculture.* Paris, OECD, 72, 286 p.

2863 PANT, Y. P.; JAIN, S. C. *Long term planning for agriculture in Nepal.* Delhi, Vikas Publications, 72, vii-182 p.

2864 POELMANS, J.; LECOMTE, J. *L'agriculture européenne et les pays tiers.* Bruxelles, Presses universitaires de Bruxelles, 72, x-185 p.

2865 POPP, H. W. "Die schweizerische Landwirtschaft und die EWG" (Swiss agriculture and the EEC), *Aussenwirtschaft (St Gallen)* 27(3), 1972 : 104-119.

2866 RAY, D. E.; O'HEADY, E. "Government farm programs and commodity interaction: a simulation analysis", *Amer. J. agric. Econ.* 54(4), nov 72 : 578-590. [USA.]

2867  RECHTZIEGIER, E. "'Grüne Revolution' in Entwicklungsländern—Realitäten und Widersprüche" (The "Green Revolution" in developing countries: realities and contradictions), *IPW Ber.* 2(5), mai 73 : 24-36.

2868  RECHTZIEGLER, E. "Mythos und Wirklichkeit der 'grünen Revolution'" (Myth and reality of the "green revolution"), *Z. Erdkundeunterricht* 25(3), 1973 : 91-103.

2869  ROGERS, S. J.; DAVEY, B. H. *Common agricultural policy and Britain.* Westhead, Saxon House, 73, x-158 p.

2870  RÖSSING, R.-B. *Die agrarpolitischen Konzeptionen der Schweiz, Grossbritanniens, der EWG und der USA* (Agricultural policy conceptions of Switzerland, Great Britain, the EEC and the USA). Bern, H. Lang, 72, vii-291 p.

2871  RUTHENBERG, H. *Landwirtschaftliche Entwicklungspolitik; ein Überblick über die Instrumente zur Steigerung der landwirtschaftlichen Produkten in Entwicklungsländern* (Agricultural development policy; a panorama of instruments to increase agricultural production in developing countires). Frankfurt-am-Main, DLG-Verlag, 72, xii-308 p.

2872  RUTTAN, V. W.; HAYAMI, Y. "Strategies for agricultural development", *Food Res. Inst. Stud.* 11(2), 1972 : 129-148.

2873  SOURD, L. J. *Agriculture et croissance économique: politique agricole.* Paris, J.-B. Baillière, 72, 248 p.

2874  "Strategies for agricultural development in the 1970s", *Food Res. Inst. Stud.* 12(1), 1973 : 9-72.

2875  TEWARI, R. N. *Agricultural planning and co-operatives.* Delhi, Sultan Chand, 72, vi-100 p.


## H.12      Agricultural production
Production agricole

### H.121      *General and local studies*
*Études générales et localisées*

[See also / Voir aussi: 3212, 4745]

2876  ALLAN, J. A.; MCLACHLAN, K. S.; PENROSE, E. (eds.). *Libya: agriculture and economic development.* London, F. Cass, 73, xxii-214 p.

2877  BANDYOPADHYAYA, K. "Agricultural production in China and India: a comparison," *China Rep.* 9(2), mar-apr 83 : 31-39.

2878  BANDYOPADHYAYA, K. "Land yields and agricultural inputs in China and India during 1950s and 1960s", *China Rep.* 9(3), mai-jun 73 : 41-52.

2879  BRANDKAMP, F.; LOHMANN, B. "Produktion und Wertschöpfung der Landwirtschaft in der Bundesrepublik" (Production and added value in agriculture in the Federal Republic), *Agrarwirtschaft* 22(2), feb 73 : 41-57. [Germany, FR.]

2880  CHAUDHURI, P. (ed.). *Readings in Indian agricultural development.* London, Allen and Unwin, 72, 3-192 p.

2881  CRISOSTOME, C.; BARKER, R. "Growth rates of Philippine agriculture: 1948-1969", *Philippine econ. J.* 11(1), 1 sem 72 : 88-148.

2882  DANEO, C. *Agricultura e sviluppo capitalistico in Italia* (Agriculture and capitalist development in Italy). Torino, G. Einaudi, 72, 244 p.

2883  DORNER, P.; QUIROS, R. "Institutional dualism in Central America's agricultural development", *J. Latin Amer. Stud.* 5(2), nov 73 : 217-232.

2884  ETIENNE, G. "India's new agriculture; a survey of the evidence", *South Asian R.* 6(3), apr 73 : 197-213.

2885  FIGUEROA MARTINEZ, E. "La agricultura y el desarrollo económico" (Agriculture and economic development), *R. Econ. polit.* 63, jan-apr 73 : 7-24. [Spain.]

2886  FRUCK, H.; DRAEGER, W. "Zur Entwicklung der Landwirtschaft in den Mitgliedsländern der RGW" (The development of agriculture in the Comecon member countries), *Jb. Wirtsch.-Gesch.* (4), 1972 : 197-201.

2887  HOUILLER, F. "L'économie agricole en 1971", *R. Écon. polit. (Paris)* 82(5), sep-oct 72 : 952-965. [France.]

2888  JOHNSON, D. G. *World agriculture in disarray.* London, Macmillan; New York, St Martin's Press, Trade Policy Research Centre, 73, 304 p.

2889 KLINKIEWIXZ, K. "Rozwój produkcji rolnej w krajach RWPG" (Advance of agricultural production in member-countries of the Council of Mutual Economic Assistance), *Zagadn. Ekon. rolnej* (5-6), 1973 : 123-137.

2890 KOLBUSZ, F. "Rozwój rolnictwa krajów członkowskich RWPG w latach 1966-1970" (Development of agriculture in the CMEA countries, 1966-1970), *Zagadn. Ekon. rolnej* (1), 1973 : 107-123.

2891 LOUVEL, B. "Agriculture et socialisme en Bulgarie", *Écon. et Polit.* 220, nov 72 : 121-138.

2892 MAY, B. "Die Entwicklung der Landwirtschaft in Bangladesh und Pakistan" (Agricultural development in the Bangladesh and Pakistan), *Int. Asien Forum* 4(2), apr 73 : 279-305.

2893 MERKEL, K.; IMMLER, H. (eds.). *DDR, Landwirtschaft in der Diskussion* (Discussion on the DDR agricultural economy). Köln, Verlag Wissenschaft und Politik, 72, 126 p.

2894 MUNDLAK, Y.; AVNI, G. *Hašpa'at sahar hofši 'im ha-šetahim ha-munzaqim 'al ha-haqlaût be-Yisrael* (The effect of free trade with the administered territories on Israel's agriculture). Rehôvôt Ha-merkaz le-mehqor be-Kalkala haqlait, 72, 119 p.

2895 MUTAUX-DESAI, V. "Agriculture in Africa: its role, problems and prospects", *Afr. Quart.* 12(1), apr-jun 72 : 24-40.

2896 NORMAN, D. W. *Economic analysis of agricultural production and labour utilisation among the Hausa in the North of Nigeria.* East Lansing, Department of Agricultural Economics, Michigan State University, 73, 48 p.

2897 PATRICK, G. F. *Desenvolvimento agrícola do nordeste* (Agricultural development in the Northeast). Rio de Janeiro, IPEA/INPES, 72, 319 p. [Brazil.]

2898 "Production agricole en 1972 (La)", *B. mens. Écon. Statist. agric.* 21, nov 72 : 1-21.

2899 QUANCE, I.; TWEETEN, L. "Excess capacity and adjustment potential in US agriculture", *Agric. Econ. Res.* 24(3), jul 73 : 57-66.

2900 RADIĆ, M. "Ekonomski položaj agrarna proizvodnje" (Economic situation of agricultural production), *Socijalizam* 15(11-12), nov-dec 72 : 1309-1317. [Yugoslavia.]

2901 RUNOWICZ, A. Z. "Some problems of agricultural development in Africa (South of the Sahara)", *Africana B.* 14, 1971 : 95-118.

2902 STAUB, W. J. *Agricultural development and farm employment in India.* Washington Economic Research Service, United States Department of Agriculture, 73, x-109 p.

2903 VERHAEGEN, G. "Le développement de l'agriculture paysanne au Zaïre", *Zaïre-Afr.* 13(76), jun-jul 73 : 345-360.

2904 VERHAEGEN, G. "Le rôle de l'agriculture dans le développement économique du Zaïre", *Zaïre-Afr.* 13(74), apr 73 : 205-220.

2905 ZENI, E. R. *El destino de la agricultura argentina* (The destiny of Argentine agriculture). Buenos Aires, Editorial La Pléyade, 72, 172 p.

**H.122** **Studies on the various products**
**Études par produits**

**H.1221** *Grains*
*Céréales*

[See also / Voir aussi: 3971]

2906 BARANKIEWICZ, M.; PIERŠCIONEK, Z. "Rozwiązanie zadania optymalizacji planów krótkookresowych w przemyśle zbożowo-młynarskim" (Solutions for the problem of optimization of short-term planning in the wheat and flour industry), *Przegl. statyst.* (4), 1973 : 393-403.

2907 BELOZERCEV, A. G. *Tehničeskij progress v zernovom hozjajstve* (Technical progress in the grain economy). Moskva, Kolos, 72, 270 p.

2908 BERQUE, A. "Une mutation des campagnes japonaises: la riziculture à Hokkaido", *A. Géogr.* 82(451), mai-jun 73 : 291-315.

2909 CONNORS, T. *The Australian wheat industry: its economics and politics.* Armindale, N. S. W., Gill Publications, 72, ix-157 p.

2910 DESIRE, E. P. "La culture du maïs aux États-Unis", *Inform. géogr.* 36(5), nov-dec 72 : 220-232.

2911    DMITRIEV, V. S. *Ėkonomika proizvostva zerna na orošaemyh zemljah* (Economics of grain production in irrigated soils). Moskva, Kolos, 73, 288 p.

2912    DUE, J. M.; KARR, G. L. "Strategies for increasing rice production in Sierra-Leone", *Afr. Stud. B.* 16(1), apr 73 : 23-72.

2913    ESPOSITO DE FALCO, V. "La coltura del grano in Italia e nel Mezzogiorno" (Corn culture in Italy and in the South), *Rass. econ. (Napoli)* 36(6), nov-dec 72 : 1651-1671.

2914    FEDORUK, P. S. *Zernovoe hozjajstvo osnovnyh zernoproizvodjaščih stran mira* (The corn economy of essential corn-producing countries in the world). Kiev, Urozaj, 72, 203 p.

2915    GHOSH, R. "A note on availability of foodgrains in India", *Econ. Aff.* 17(8), aug 72 : 373-385.

2916    LONGWORTH, J. W.; McLELAND, W. J. "Economies of size in wheat production", *R. Mkting agric. Econ.* 40(2), jun 72 : 53-66.

2917    MISIUNA, W. "Produkcja zbózw krajach RWPG" (Grain production in the countries of the Council of Mutual Economic Assistance), *Zagadn. Ekon. rolnej* (3), 1973 : 88-99.

2918    MOREAU, J. "Perspectives offertes par la riziculture à Madagascar", *Terre malgache/Tany malagasy* 14, dec 72-jan 73 : 227-242.

2919    RILEY, R. A. "Distribución del maíz al Oeste de Guatemala: algunas consideraciones metodológicas" (Distribution of corn in the West of Guatamala: some methodological considerations), *Amér. indíg.* 33(2), apr-jun 73 : 471-493.

### H.1222    *Other foodstuffs and beverages*
### *Autres denrées alimentaires et boissons*

2920    ALVIM, P. de T.; ROSÁRIO, M. *Cacau ontem e hoje* (Cocoa, yesterday and today). Itabuna, CEPLAC, 72, 83 p. [Brazil.]

2921    ANDERSON, A. G. "Plantation and Petani: problems of the Javanese sugar industry", *Pacific Viewpoint* 13(2), sep 72 : 127-154.

2922    BOUJADI, L. "La betterave et le Tiers-Monde", *Paysans* 17(101), aug-sep 73 : 45-50.

2923    CANITROT, A.; SOMMER, J. "Productividad y ocupación en la producción de azucar en Tucumán" (Productivity and occupation in Tucuman sugar production), *Económica (La Plata)* 18(3), sep-ced 72 : 251-278. [Argentina.]

2924    COULET, L.; TIRONE, L. "Les cultures fruitières en Italie, production et débouchés", *Méditerranée* 13(2), 1972 :104-118; 13(3-4), 1972 : 177-185.

2925    LAGADIN, N. *Eficienta economică iu viticultură* (Economic efficiency in viticulture). Bucureşti, Ceres, 72, 131 p.

2926    LEZZI-SANTORO, C. "L'evoluzione della coltura degli agrumi in Puglia" (The evolution of citrus fruit in Puglia), *Nord e Sud* 20(160), apr 73 : 78-87.

2927    LITTLE, I. M. D.; TIPPING, D. G. *A social cost benefit analysis of the Kulai Oil Palm Estate: West Malaysia.* Paris, Development Centre of the Organisation for Economic Cooperation and Development, 72, 95 p.

2928    LLORENTE MARTINEZ. et al. *La cana de azucar y el desarrollo nacional* (Sugar cane and national development). Cali, Asociacióà Nacional de Cultivadores de Caña de Azúr, 72, 35 p. [Colombia.]

2929    LOPEZ GOMEZ, A. "El cultivo del plátano en Canarias" (Banana cultivation in the Canary Islands), *Estud. geogr.* 33(126), feb 72 : 5-68. [Spain.]

2930    MAILLARD, J. C. "Bilan et problèmes actuels de l'économie bananière de la Colombie", *C. O.-Mer* 25(100), oct-dec 72 : 390-417.

2931    MAURICE, P. "Situation et perspectives de l'activité sucrière à la Réunion", *R. écon. Madagascar* (6), jan-dec 71 : 185-243.

2932    MELE, R. *L'industria enologica nel Mezzogiorno* (Wine industry in the South). Napoli, Centro di studi aziendali Giuseppe Cenzato, 72, vi-273 p. [Italy.]

2933    OLAYEMI, J. K. "Technology in the Western Nigeria cocoa industry: an empirical study", *Econ. B. Ghana* 2(2), 1972 : 47-60.

2934    ŠORNIKOV, A. M. *Ėkonomika kormoproizvodstva* (Economics of fodder plants production). Čeboksary, Čuvašknigoizdat, 73, 127 p.

2935    "Structures du vignoble de Champagne (Les)", *Note Écon. région. Champagne-Ardenne* 40, 2 trim 73 : 61-88. [France.]

2936    VAN DER WEL, P. P. *The development of the Ghana sugar industry 1960-1970. An exercise in ex-post evaluation.* The Hague, Institute of Social Studies, 73, 31 p. multigr.

**H.1223**   *Other vegetable products*
            *Autres productions végétales*

[See also / Voir aussi: 3970]

2937   BRYAN, P. "Le problème des fourrages en Union Soviétique", *R. Est* 3(4), oct 72 : 29-49.
2938   COLLIER, W. WERDAJA, S. T. "Smallhoder rubber production and marketing", *B. Indones. econ. Stud.* 8(2), jul 72 : 67-92. [Indonesia.]
2939   "Culture du coton en République centrafricaine (La)", *Banque États Afr. centr. Ét. Statist.* (4), aug-sep 73 : 441-453.
2940   EMMRICH, C. O. "L'économie mondiale du tabac: tendances et problèmes", *B. mens. Écon. Statist. agric.* 22(5), mai 73 : 1-48.
2941   FALLAS, M. A. *La factoría de tabacos de Costa Rica* (Tobacco manufacture in Costa Rica). San José, Editorial Costa Rica, 72, 249 p.
2942   MULLER, D. O. "Die Entwicklung der kommerziellen Baumwollkultur in Uganda und Kenya" (The development and commercialization of cotton production in Uganda and Kenya), *Afr. Spectrum* 7(3), 1972 : 62-82.

**H.1224**   *Animal products: cattle raising, meat, milk and derived products, poultry, fishing*
            *Productions animales: élevage, viande, lait et dérivés, volailles, pêche*

[See also / Voir aussi: 2817]

2943   BUCK, A. "La production porcine à Madagascar", *Terre malgache / Tany malagasy* 14, dec 72-jan 73 : 193-217.
2944   CHAUSSADE, J. "La pêche artisanale vendéenne et ses problèmes", *Noirois* 20(78), apr-jun 73 : 279-299.
2945   COLMAN, D. R.; MIAH, H. "On some estimates of price flexibilities for meat and their interpretation", *J. agr. Econ.* 24(2), mai 73 : 353-368.
2946   DESIRE, E. "La disparition de l'élevage ovin en Beauce, élément de la transformation d'un système agricole", *Ét. Région paris.* 47(37), jan 73 : 1-28. [France.]
2947   DIETRICH, G. "L'élevage bovin et le lait dans le département des Vosges", *Acta geogr.* 4(10-11), apr-sep 72 : 79-114.
2948   FARSTAD, N. *Fisheries development in Newfoundland. Aspects of development, location and infrastructure.* Bergen Universitetsforlaget, 72, 124 p.
2949   FOOD AND AGRICULTURE ORGANIZATION OF THE UNITED NATIONS. *Near East regional study; animal husbandry, production and health, fodder production and range management in the Near East and FAO's policies and plans for promoting the animal industry.* Rome, FAO, 72, iv-312 p.
2950   GASOLIBA, C. A. *Estudio económico de las industrias cárnicas* (An economic study of meat industries). Barcelona, Banca catalana, 72, 249 p. [Spain.]
2951   GIRDLESTONE, J. "The regional supply pattern of beef cattle for slaughter in Queensland", *Quart. R. agric. Econ.* 26(1), jan 73 : 44-60. [Australia.]
2952   GUELLEC, J. "Notes sur la production et la transformation de la viande", *Ét. région. Suppl. B. Conjonct. écon. Bretagne* 21, 4 trim 72 : 18 p. [France.]
2953   HATFIELD, C. R. Jr. "Livestock development in Sukumaland: the constituents of communication", *Sociol. rur.* 12(3-4), 1972 : 361-383.
2954   KALMANOVITZ, S. "El desarrollo de la ganadería en Colombia, 1950-1972" (The development of cattle raising in Colombia), *Bol. mens. Estadíst.* 21(253-254), aug-sep 72 : 193-238.
2955   KOŽOKARU, É. V.; POJAG, M. A. *Rybohozjajstvennoe ispol'zovanie vodyh resursov Moldavii* (Fish industry utilization of Moldavian water resources). Kišinev, Izdatel'-stvo CK KP Moldavii, 73, 208 p.
2956   KURTA, J. S. *Beef production: an economic report.* Ed. by F. G. STURROCK. Cambridge, University of Cambridge, Department of Land Economy, Agricultural Economics Unit, 72, 40 p.
2957   LUX, W. R. "The Peruvian fishing industry: a case study in capitalism at work", *R. Hist. Amér.* 71, jan-jun 71 : 137-146.

131

2958    MAYER, A. *Die Molkereiwirtschaft in Südtirol* (The economic situation of dairies in the South Tyrol). Insbruck, H. Kowatsch, 72, 131 p. [Austria.]

2959    MAYRHOFER, K. *Probleme der österreichischen Landwirtschaft—der milchwirtschaftliche Aussenhandel* (Problems of Austrian agricultural economy—foreign trade in malk) Wien, Verlag des Österreichischen Gewerkschaftsbundes, 72, 83 p.

2960    McCoy, J. H. *Livestock and meat marketing.* Westport, Conn., AVI Publications Co., 72, ix-465 p.

2961    MICHALCZEWSKA, A. "Ekonometryczna analiza długofalowych tendencji produkcji żywca w Polsce" (Econometric analysis of long-range trends in cattle production in Poland), *Zagadn. Ekon. rolnej* (5-6), 1973 : 91-104.

2962    MISIUNA, W. "Produkcja zwierzęca w krajach RWPG" (Animal production in member countries of the Council for Mutual Economic Aid), *Zagadn. Ekon. rolnej* (4), 1973 : 101-117.

2963    O'MARY, C. C.; DYER, I. A. (eds.). *Commercial beef cattle production.* Philadelphia, Lea and Febiger, 72, ix-393 p.

2964    PAGOT, J. "Le développement d'une production animale: l'élevage bovin en zone tropicale", *Tech. et Dévelop.* (7), mai 73 : 10-17.

2965    "Pêche maritime à Madagascar (La)", *Terre malgache / Tany malagasy* 14, dec-jan 73 : 219-226.

2966    "Pêche maritime belge de 1960 à 1971 (La)", *B. Statist. (Bruxelles)* 58(12), dec 72 : 730-735.

2967    PIZZARO VILLANUEVA, J. B. *Análisis económico de los costos y retornos en la producción del cerdo parrillero* (An economic analysis of costs and returns in grilling swine production). Pergamino, Estación Experimental Regional Agropecuaria Pergamino, 72, 32 p.

2968    POWELL, B. J.; MACFARLANE, I. "The changing structure and economic situation of the Australian dairy industry", *Quart. R. Econ. Busin.* 25(4), oct 72 : 255-278.

2969    "Produits avicoles (Les)", *Doss. Polit. agric. commune* (10), nov 72 : 16 p. [CEE.]

2970    "Produits laitiers (Les)", *Doss. Polit. agric. commune* (12-13), jan-feb 73 : 16 p. [CEE.]

2971    RAMAROSON, S.; RAZAFINDRAKOTO, D. "L'élevage à Madagascar: situation actuelle et perspectives d'avenir", *Terre malgache / Tany malagasy* 14, dec 72-jan 73 : 1-21.

2972    RAVOAJARISON, M.; SCHREDER, A.; SIMEON, M. "Inventaire commenté des études récentes sur l'élevage à Madagascar", *Terre malgache / Tany malagasy* 14, dec 72-jan 73 : 23-38.

2973    "Recent developments in the Australian sheep industry", *Quart. R. Econ. Busin.* 25(4), oct 72 : 245-254.

2974    RICHEZ, P. "Les difficultés de l'élevage porcin traditionnel à Madagascar", *Terre malgache / Tany malagasy* 14, dec 72-jan 73 : 59-75.

2975    ROTHSCHILD, B. J. (ed.). *World fisheries policy; multidisciplinary views.* Seattle, University of Washington Press, 72, xix-272 p.

2976    ROZSAVÖLGYI, H. *La empresa y el desarrollo agro-pecuario en América latina* (The firm and cattle development in Latin America). Buenos Aires, Paidos, 72, 109 p.

2977    SAARINEN, P. "Prospects for the development of milk production in Finland", *Econ. R. (Helsinki)* (2), 1973 : 47-51.

2978    SERRES, H. "Le zébu malgache face aux besoins en viande: intérêt et limites des croisements", *Terre malgache / Tany malagasy* 14, dec 72-jan 73 : 39-57.

2979    SMETHERMAN, B. B.; SMETHERMAN, R. M. "Peruvian fisheries conservation and development", *Econ. Develop. cult. Change* 21(2), jan 73 : 338-351.

2980    STARKOV, A. "Ékonomičeskie problemy zivotnovodčeskih kompleksov" (Economic problems concerning cattle raising enterprises), *Vopr. Ékon.* 25(9), sep 73 : 53-63.

2981    "Symposium on commercial fishing", *J. polit. Econ.* 80(4), jul-aug 72 : 761-778. [USA.]

2982    TUSSING, A. R.; MOREHOUSE, T. A.; BABB, J. D. Jr (eds.). *Alaska fisheries policy: economics, resources, and management.* Fairbanks, Institute of Social, Economic and Government Research, University of Alaska, 72, ix-470 p.

2983    VAN ARSDALL, R. N.; SKOLD, M. D. *Cattle raising in the United States.* Washington, Economic Research Service, United States Department of Agriculture, 73, iv-88 p.

2984    "Viande bovine (La)", *Doss. Polit. agric. commune* (9), oct 72 : 16 p. [CEE.]

2985    "Viande porcine (La)", *Doss. Polit. agric. commune* (1), nov 71 : 11 p. [CEE.]

2986 WHITE, B. J. "Supply projections for the Australian beef industry", *R. Mkting agric. Econ.* 40(1), mar 72 : 3-14.

**H.1225** *Forest and forestry: timber, wood and related industries*
*Production forestière et industrie du bois*

[See also / Voir aussi: 2098, 2548]

2987 AGUERA FERNANDEZ, F. "Nuestra industria maderera. Supervivencia y auge de la madera" (Our wood industry. Survival and boom in wood), *R. sind. Estadíst.* 27(107), 3 trim 72 : 18-36. [Spain.]
2988 "Bois en Côte d'Ivoire (Le)", *Note Inform. Statist. Banque centr. Afr. Ouest* 206, mai 73 : 16 p.
2989 BOUSSARD, C. "Les industries forestières en République centrafricaine", *Ét. Statist. Cameroun Afr. équat. Banque centr.* 178, nov 72 : 676-683.
2990 CEHMISTRNKO, A. F. (ed.). *Problemy ekonomičeskoj effektivnosti v lesnom hozjajstve* (Problems of economic efficiency in the forestry industry). Moskva, Lesnaja Promyš- lennost', 72, 167 p.
2991 MARSZAŁEK, T. *Zagadnienia ekonomiki gospodarstwa leśnego* (Problems of forestry economics). Kraków, Towarzystwo Naukowe Organizacji i Kierownictwa, 72, 100 p.
2992 MEDVEDEV, N. "Lesnaja industrija i eě zadači" (Forestry industry and its aims), *Plan. Hoz.* 50(10), oct 73 : 17-27.
2993 ŠLYKOV, V. M. *Problemy razvitija lesopromyšlennogo proizvodstva* (Problems of forestry industry production development). Moskva, Lesnaja promyšlennost', 73, 136 p.
2994 VOROB'EV, G. "Racional'noe ispol'zovanie i ohrana lesov" (Rational use and conserva- tion of forests), *Plan. Hoz.* 50(6), jun 73 : 19-24.

**H.2** **INDUSTRY**
**INDUSTRIE**

**H.21** **Industrial economics**
**Économie industrielle**

**H.210** *General studies*
*Études générales*

[See also / Voir aussi: 2153, 4491]

2996 BARROWS, D. S.; DUTTA, A. K.; MASKILL, R. "A model for industrial identification", *Econ. Aff.* 17(1-2), jan-feb 72 : 25-36.
2997 GISBERT, P. *Fundamentals of industrial sociology.* Bombay, Tata McGraw-Hill Publishing Co., 72, x-369 p.
2998 HASAN, 'A. al-B. M. *'Ilm al-ijtimâ'aṭ sinâ-i* (Industrial sociology). al-Qâhirat, Makṭabaṭ al-anjlu al-Misriyaṭ, 72, 619 p.
2999 HERMAN, B. "On the choice of the optimal industry", *Weltwirtsch. Archiv* 109(1), 1973 : 70-85.
3000 HERMANOWSKI, H. (ed.). *Ekonomika i programowanie przemysłu* (Economics and programming of industry). Warszawa, Państwowe Wydawnictwo Naukowe, 73, 305 p.
3001 "Industrie et société: défis et réponses. L'Europe à la recherche d'un nouveau visage", *France-Forum* 119-121, nov-dec 72 : 2-111.
3002 JEROVŠEK, J. *Industrijska sociologija* (Industrial sociology). Maribor, Obzorja, Visoka komercialna šola, 72, 284-1 p.
3003 JOHNSEN, Y. *Industri og samfunn* (Industry and society). Oslo, Universitetsforlaget, 73, 67 p.
3004 JULIENNE, R. *Économie industrielle.* Paris, 72, 188 ff. multigr.
3005 KANTOR, L. M.; GRUNKIN, M. N. *Ěkonomika, organizacija i planirovanie promyš- lennogo proizvodstva* (Industrial production economics, organization and planning). Moskva, Ěkonomika, 72, 423 p.

3006  KRZYSZTOFIAK, M.; PARADYSZ, S.; ZYSNARSKI, J. *Statystyka w przedsiebiorstwach przemysłowych* (Statistics in industrial enterprises). Warszawa, Państwowe Wydawnictwo Ekonomiczne, 73, 375 p.

3007  LAMBERTON, D. M. (ed.). *Industrial economics; selected readings.* Ringwood, Vic., Penguin Books, 72, 264 p.

3008  PARKER, S. R. *et al. The sociology of industry.* 2nd rev ed. London, Allen and Unwin, 72, 200 p.

3009  PICHŇA, J. A. *Sociológica podniku* (Industrial sociology). Bratislava, Práca; Nitra, Nitrianske tlač., 72, 151-2 p.

### H.211  Technical factors of industrial productivity
### Facteurs techniques de la productivité dans l'industrie

#### H.2111  Industrial concentration: horizontal, vertical
#### Concentration industrielle: horizontale, verticale

[See also / Voir aussi: **G.321; 2094**]

3010  BEHRMAN, J. N. "Industrial integration and the multinational enterprise", *A. Amer. Acad. polit. soc. Sci.* 403, sep 72 : 46-57.

3011  BORYSIUK, W. "Proces koncentracji produkcji w polskim przemysle hutnicta zelaza w latach 1950-1970" (Concentration of production in Polish ferrous metallurgy, 1950-1970), *Zesz. nauk. Szkoły główn. Plan. Statyst.* 87, 1972 : 65-85.

3012  "Concentration industrielle en Grande-Bretagne (La)", *Oxford econ. Pap.* 24(3), nov 72 : 432-451.

3013  GABRUSEWICZ, W. "Istota i proces integracji przedsiebiorstw przemysłowych" (The nature and process of integration of industrial enterprises), *Zesz. nauk. wyzsz. Szkoły ekon. Poznan.* 41, 1972 : 139-151.

3014  GOULENE, P. "Les conglomérats: phénomène transitoire ou nouveau type de concentration industrielle ?", *Tiers-Monde* 13(52), oct-dec 72 : 779-789. [États-Unis.]

3015  GROSSACK, I. M. "The concept and measurement of permanent industrial concentration", *J. polit. Econ.* 80(4), jul-aug 72 : 745-760.

3016  MANCKE, R. B. "Iron ore and steel: a case study of the economic causes and consequences of vertical integration", *J. industr. Econ.* 20(3), jul 72 : 220-229.

3017  MARFELS, C. "Concentration in petroleum refining in the European Community: an entropy approach", *Econ. int. (Genova)* 25(4), nov 72 : 721-730.

3018  Bibl. XXI-3186. PRATTEN, C. F. *Economies of scale in manufacturing industry.* CR: M. A. CREW, *J. econ. Liter.* 10(4), dec 72 : 1255-1256.

3019  RYDÉN, B. *Mergers in Swedish industry. An empirical analysis of corporate mergers in Swedish industry,* 1946-1969. Stockholm, Almquist och Wiksell, 72, ix-323 p. CR: F. WEDERWANG, *J. econ. Liter.* 11(2), jun 73 : 580-581.

3020  ŠILIN, I. G. *Optimizacija razmirov proizvodstva v promyšlennosti* (Optimization of production size in industry). Moskva, Izdatel'stvo Moskovskogo Universiteta, 73, 214 p.

3021  ŠIM, P. S. *Problemy koncentracii promyšlennogo proizvodstva (Na materialah Kazahstana)* (Problems of industrial production concentration. From Kazahstan materials). Alma-Ata, Nauka, 72, 127 p.

#### H.2112  Other facteurs
#### Autres facteurs

[See also / Voir aussi: **G.102; 3306**]

3022  ANGLADE, B.; CUKIER, H. (eds.). *Innovation et produits nouveaux.* Paris, Dunod, 73, 223 p.

3023  BEITEL, W. *Ökonomische Probleme der Realisierung des technischen Fortschritts in der sowjetischen Industrie* (Economic problems caused by the realization of technical progress in Soviet industry). Berlin, Duncker und Humblot, 72, 132 p.

3024  BERTUZZI, B.; GALLI, F. *La spesa dell'industria privata per la ricerca scientifica, 1970-1972* (The expenditure of private industry for scientific research 1970-1972). Roma, Confederazione generale dell'industria italiana, 72, x-124 p. [Italy.]

3025  BIEDA, W. "Rozwój specjalizacji w przemyśle wysoko rozwinietych krajów kapitalisic-znych" (Increase in specialization in the industry of highly developed capitalist countries). *Zesz. nauk. wyzsz. Szkoly ekon. Krakow.* 58, 1973 : 77-91.

3026  BLAKE, R. R.; MOUTON, J. S. *How to assess the strengths and weaknesses of research and development.* Austin, Tex., Scientific Methods, 72, iv-128 p.

3027  CETRON, M. J.; DAVIDSON, H.; RUBENSTEIN, A. H. (eds.). *Quantitative decision aiding techniques for research and development management.* New York, Gordon and Breach, 72, ix-205 p.

3028  CORIGLIANO, G. "Il lancio di nuovi prodotti: necessità di un approccio professionale" (The launching of new products: the need for a professional approach), *Impresa* 14(2), mar-apr 72 : 105-111.

3029  DONINI, P. G. "Sviluppo industriale e ricerca scientifica in Israele" (Industrial development and scientific research in Israel), *Oriente mod.* 53(1), jan 73 : 1-28.

3030  FIGUEIREDO, N. F. DE *A transferencia de tecnologia no desenvolvimento industrial no Brasil* (Technology transfer in industrial development of Brazil). Rio de Janeiro, IPEA/INPES, 72, 360 p.

3031  FISHER, F. M.; TEMIN, P. "Returns to scale in research and development: what does the Schumpeterian hypothesis imply ?", *J. polit. Econ.* 81(1), jan-feb 73 : 56-70.

3032  GAIBISSO, A. M. "La ricerca scientifica in Italia: la gestione dei fondi stanziati del settore pubblico" (Scientific research in Italy: management of state sector budgetary funds), *Impresa* 14(5), sep-oct 72 : 363-365.

3033  HERMANOWSKI, H. *Funkcje i organizacja zaplecza naukowo-technicznego w przemysle* (Functions and organization of scientific and technological background in industry). Warszawa, Państwowe Wydawnictwo Ekonomiczne, 73, 278 p.

3034  HOSTETTLER, W. F. *Bestimmungsfaktoren der industriellen Forschung und Entwicklung* (Determination factors in industrial research and development). Zürich, Schulthess Polygraphischer Verlag, 72, x-140 p.

3035  JOHNSON, P. S. *Co-operative research in industry; an economic study.* New York, Wiley, 73, 216 p.

3036  Bibl. xxi-3215. MANSFIELD, E. *et al. Research and innovation in the modern corporation.* CR: F. M. SCHERER, *J. econ. Liter.* 11(2), jun 73 : 583-585.

3037  PASCHEN, H.; KRAUCH, H. (eds.). *Methoden und Probleme der Forschungs- und Entwicklungsplanung* (Methods and problems of research and development planning). München-Wien, Oldenbourg, 72, 235 p.

3038  RISPOLI, M. *La politica dei nuovi prodotti* (New products policy). Milano, ISEDI, 72, 173 p.

3039  SABIN, C. *Organizarea cercetării stiintifice* (Organization of scientific research). Bucuresti, Consiliul National pentry Stiinta si Tehnologie, Institutul central de documentare tehnica, 72, 115 p.

3040  SCIENCE COUNCIL OF CANADA. *Policy objectives for basic research in Canada.* Ottawa, Information Canada, 72, 75 p.

3041  SELLSTEDT, B. *Selection [of product development projects under uncertainty.* Stockholm, Bonnier, 72, 230 p.

3042  SKINNER, R. N. *Launching new products in competitive markets.* London, Associated Business Programmes, Cassell; New York, Wiley, 72, vii-184 p.

3043  SLOCUM, D. H. *New venture methodology.* New York, American Management Association, 72, viii-208 p.

3044  TARAPORE, S. S. "Transferring industrial technology", *Finance and Develop.* 9(2), jun 72 : 16-21.

3045  TREILLE, J. M. *Progrès technique et stratégie industrielle.* Paris, Éditions Économie et humanisme, 73, 143 p.

3046  VRCELJ, D. "Uticaj tehnicko-tehnoloških promena na konstituisanje sektora u industriji Srbije" (The influence of technical and technological progress on the development of the leading sectors of Serbian industry), *Ekon. Misao* 6(1), mar 73 : 24-39.

3047  ZAMPETTI, S. "La sous-traitance industrielle internationale et les pays en voie de développement", *Reflets Perspect. Vie écon.* 12(1), 1973 : 17-30.

**H.2113**   *Productivity policy in industry*
             *Politique de productivité dans l'industrie*

[See also / Voir aussi: **G.13**]

3048   BURNHAM, D. C. *Productivity improvement.* Pittsburgh-New York, Columbia University Press, 73, 73 p. [Industrial productivity.]

3049   BYRSKI, B.; LUCHTER, E. "Productywnosc srodków trwałych w przemysle—czynniki kształtujace, interpretacja pomiarów)" (Productivity of fixed assets in industry—generating factors, interpretation of results), *Fol. oecon. cracov.* 13, 1973 : 87-118.

3050   CHANDRASEKAR, K. "US and French productivity in 19 manufacturing industries", *J. industr. Econ.* 21(2), apr 73 : 110-125.

3051   CHOWDHURY, A.; AHMAD, Q. K. "Productivity trends in the manufacturing sector of Bangladesh: a case study of selected industries", *Bangladesh econ. R.* 1(2), apr 73 : 119-148.

3052   FILIPPOVA, G. D. *Planirovanie proizviditel'nosti truda v promyšlennosti* (Labour productivity planning in industry). Moskva, Ėkonomika, 73, 152 p.

3053   GLINKOWSKI, C. "Warunki optymalizacji wykorzystania zdolnosci produkcyjnej w przemysle" (Optimization conditions for production capacities in industry), *Zesz. nauk. wyzsz. Szkoły ekon. Poznan.* 41, 1972 : 153-165.

3054   KÁLDOR, M.; RÉDEI, L. "A teljes termékenység alakulása a koho és gépiparban" (The development of global productivity in the metal and mechanical industry), *Statiszt. Szle* 50(11), nov 72 : 1108-1119.

3055   KALJAKIN, P. V.; KOVALERČUK, Ja. V.; MASEVIČ, M. G. *Povyšenie effektivnosti promyšlennogo proizvodstva* (Industrial production efficiency elevation). Moskva, Juridičeskaja Literatura, 72, 199 p.

3056   LESZCZYŃSKI, K. *Rachunek ekonomiczny efektywnosci podnoszenia jakosci produkcji* (Economic calculation of efficiency of improving production quality). Warszawa, Polskie Towarzystwo Ekonomiczne, 73, 98 p.

3057   MAJ, H. "Zgodnosc bodzców materialnych w działalnosci biezacej i rozwojowej" (Problems of compatibility of economic incentives to promote both the current and development activity of industrial enterprises), *Ekonomista* (3), 1973 : 555-574.

3058   POLJAK, A. M. *Intensifikacija proizvodstva i problemy sniženija materialoemkosti* (Production intensification and problems of reducing material costs). Moskva, Ėkonomika, 73, 143 p.

3059   TEMPLE, P.; BRANCY, J.-J. "Industries allemandes et francaises: charges d'exploitation et productivités semblables", *Écon. et Statist.* 48, sep 73 : 3-15.

3060   TEREHOV, V. F. *Intensifikacija proizvodstva v evropejskih stranah SEV* (Production intensification in the Comecon European countries). Moskva, Nauka, 72, 224 p.

3061   TIŠČENKOV, I. A.; FATUEV, A. A. *Pravovye voprosy material'nogo stimulirovanija rabotnikov promyšlennosti* (Legal questions of industrial workers material stimulation), Moskva, Juridičeskaja literatura, 72, 215 p.

3062   VJAL'JATAGA, Ju. "Kak lučše stimulirovat' povyšenie proizviditel'nosti truda v promyšlennosti" (How to better stimulate the increase of labour productivity in industry), *Kommunist Ėstonii* 29(1), jan 73 : 46-53. [USSR.]

3063   VOJTOLOVSKIJ, V. N. *Plan povyšenija effektivnosti proizvodstva* (The production efficiency elevation plan). Moskva, Ėkonomika, 72, 55 p.

**H.212**   **Forms of industrial enterprise (legal status)**
            **Formes d'entreprise industrielle (statut légal)**

[See also / Voir aussi: **N.31; N.32**]

**H.2122**   *Co-operative and community enterprise*
             *Entreprises coopératives et communautaires*

3064   WALTHER, U. *Finanzierung und Wachstum von Genossenschaftsbetrieben* (Financing and growth of co-operative enterprises). Tübingen, Mohr, 72, 201 p.

3065   ZEPF, G. *Kooperativer Führungsstil und Organisation* (Cooperative style of management and organization). Wiesbaden, Betriebswirtschaftlicher Verlag T. Gabler, 72, 231 p.

**H.2123** *Mixed enterprise*
*Entreprises mixtes*

3066 EYSKENS, M. "Le rôle de l'État dans l'économie mixte", *Soc. roy. Écon. polit. Belgique* 366, nov 72 : 31 p.

3067 MUSOLF, L. D. *Mixed enterprise; a developmental perspective.* Lexington, Mass., Lexington Books, 72, xiv-172 p.

**H.2124** *Industrial property*
*Propriété industrielle*

3068 ABERNATHY, D.; KNIPE, W. *Ideas, inventions and patents; an introduction to patent information.* Atlanta, Ga., Pioneer Press, 73, x-118 p.

3069 HIANCE, M.; PLASSAERAUD, Y. *Brevets et sous-développement; la protection des inventions dans le Tiers-monde.* Paris, Libraries techniques, 72, ix-323 p.

3070 PALMER, J. P. "The separation of ownership from control in large US industrial corporations", *Quart. R. Econ. Busin.* 12(3), 1972 : 55-62.

3071 PLAISANT, R. "La règlementation des brevets d'invention et son unification mondiale", *R. int. Dr. comp.* 24(3), jul-sep 72 : 533-550.

3072 SCHMOOKLER, J.; HURWICZ, L. (eds.). *Patents, invention, and economic change; data and selected essays.* Cambridge, Mass., Harvard University Press, 72, xvii-292 p.

**H.213** **Management of the industrial firm**
**Gestion de la firme industrielle**

**H.2130** *General studies*
*Études générales*

[See also / Voir aussi: **G.3351; 2300**]

3073 AURICH, W.; SCHROEDER, H.-U. *System der Wachstumsplanung im Unternehmen* (The system of growth planning in the firm). München, Verlag Moderne Industrie, 72, 608 p.

3074 BEDWORTH, D. D. *Industrial systems: planning, analysis, control.* New York, Ronald Press, 73, x-504 p.

3075 BEHARA, D. N. *Mathematical methods for industrial management.* Hamilton, Ont., University Press of Canada, 72, s.p.

3076 BETHUNE, A. DE. "Contrôle de gestion et système d'information dans l'entreprise industrielle. Une esquisse théorique", *Rech. écon. Louvain* 38(2), jul 72 : 175-205.

3077 BRECH, E. F. L. *Managing for revival: a plan of action towards effective management through marketing.* London, Management Publications Ltd., 72, x-292 p. [Industrial management in Great Britain.]

3078 BYRSKI, B. "Założenia zmian w systemie zarzadzania przemysłem" (Prerequisites of changes in the system of industrial management), *Probl. Ekon. (Warszawa)* (4), 1973 : 15-26. [Poland.]

3079 CARLSSON, B. "The measurement of efficiency in production: an application to Swedish manufacturing industries 1968", *Swedish J. Econ.* 74(4), dec 72 : 468-485.

3080 CHASE, R. B.; AQUILANO, N. J. *Production and operations management; a life cycle approach.* Homewood, Ill., R. D. Irwin, 73, xii-691 p.

3081 CONYNGHAM, W. J. *Industrial management in the Soviet Union; the role of the CPSU in industrial decision-making,* 1917-1970. Stanford, Calif., Hoover Institution Press. Stanford University, 73, xxxvi-378 p.

3082 ČURKIN, A. N. *Ulučšenie raboty s kadrami-nadeznaja garantija effektivnosti našej ekonomiki* (The improvement of the managers' activity is a sure guarantee for our economic efficiency). Tbilisi, Izdatel'stvo CK KP Gruzii, 72, 80 p.

3083 DOKTOR, R. H.; MOSES, M. A. (eds.). *Managerial insights: analysis, decisions, and implementation.* Englewood Cliffs, N. J., Prentice-Hall, 73, ix-437 p.

3084 Bibl. XXI-2541. DULLIEN, M. *Flexible Organisation. Praxis, Theorie und Konsequenzen des Projekt- und Matrix-Management* (Flexible organization. Practice, theory and consequences of project and matrix management). CR: G. BUSCHGES, *Kölner Z. Soziol. u. soz.-Psychol.* 24(4), dec 72 : 875-882.

3085    DZAVADOV, G. A.; POPOV, V. V. "Sistema ekonomičeskih metodov upravlenija socialis-
        tičeskim proizvodstvom" (System of economic methods of socialist production
        management), in: *Ėkonomičeskie problemy naučno-tehničeskogo progressa v socialisti-
        českih i kapitalističeskih stranah.* Moskva, 1972 : 112-126.

3086    ELLINGER, J.; SCHOLZ, W. *Sozialistische Demokratie im Industriebetrieb; Bedingungen,
        Methoden, Erfahrungen* (Socialist democracy in the industrial enterprise; conditions,
        methods, experiments). Berlin, Staatsverlag der Deutschen Demokratischen Republik,
        72, 149 p.

3087    FOSTER, D. W. *Managing for growth.* London, Longman, 72, xi-113 p.

3088    FREUND, K. P. *Auslese von Unternehmensleitern; ein internationaler Vergleich* (Selected
        enterprise heads; an international comparison). Meisenheim-am-Glan, A. Hain, 72,
        184-xii p.

3089    FROLOV, A. A. *Planirovanie na socialističeskih promyšlennyh predprijatijah* (Planning
        in socialist industrial enterprises). Moskva, Profizdat, 72, 48 p.

3090    GACKOWSKI, Z. *Informatyka w zarzadzaniu przesiebiorstwem przemysłowym* (EDP in
        industrial enterprise management). Warszawa, Państwowe Wydawnictwo Ekono-
        miczne, 73, 410 p.

3091    GEJFMAN, R. S.; PODOL'NYJ, I. B.; ŠUBIK, V. B. *Upravlenie vspomogatel'nym proiz-
        vodstvom promyšlennogo predprijatija* (Management of an industrial enterprise auxiliary
        production). Doneck, Donbass, 72, 112 p.

3092    GLASER, W. A. "Der Industriebetrieb im interkulturellen Vergleich" (The industrial
        enterprise, a cross-cultural comparison), *Soz. Welt* 23(3), 1972 : 293-318.

3093    GUR'JANOV, S. T. *Social'nye metody upravlenija proizvodstvom* (Social methods of
        production management). Saransk, Mordknigoizdat, 72, 571 p.

3094    HANES, N. *Organizarea centralelor industriale* (Centralized industrial organization).
        Bucuresti, Consiliul National petru Stiinta si Tehnologie, Institutul central de
        documentare tehnica, 72, 112 p.

3095    HANUSZ, T. *Planowanie wykonawcze produkcji w przedsiebiorstwie przemysłowym*
        (Executive planning of production in industrial enterprise). Warszawa, Państwowe
        Wydawnictwo Ekonomiczne, 72, 218 p.

3096    IYENGAR, K. S. *The philosophy of small scale industrial management.* New Delhi, Today
        and Tomorrow's Printers and Publishers, 72, xix-195 p.

3097    JOVANOVIĆ, N. *Organizacija i poslovanje preduzeca* (Industrial organization and
        management). Beograd, Savremena administracija, 72, xii-306-1 p.

3098    KOZLOVA, O. V. *Metody upravlenija promyšlennym predprijatiem* (Methods of in-
        dustrial enterprise management). Moskva, Ėkonomika, 73, 127 p.

3099    LESKIEWICZ, Z. *Zarzadzanie w przemysle zachodnio-europejskim. Kierunki i tendencje*
        (Management in West European industry. Directions and trends). Warszawa,
        Państwowe Wydawnictwo Ekonomiczne, 73, 247 p.

3100    LUKATIS, I. *Organisationsstrukturen und Führungsstile 'in Wirtschaftsunternehmen*
        (Organization structure and leadership style in economic firms). Frankfurt-am-Main,
        Akademische Verlagsanstalt, 72, x-328 p. [Industrial organization in Germany FR.]

3101    MIL'NER, B. Z. et al. *SŠA: organizacionnye formy i metody upravlenija promyšlennymi
        korporacijami* (The USA: organizational forms and methods of industrial corporation
        management). Moskva, Nauka, 72, 381 p.

3102    MISIŃSKA, D. "Niektóre problemy teorii i praktyki panowego zarzadzania przemysłem"
        (Some problems of the theory and practice of planned industrial management),
        *Prace nauk. wyzsz. Szkoły ekon. Wrocław* 37, 1973 : 5-23.

3103    MUJZEL, J. "The economic system of management of industrial organizations",
        *East. Europ. Econ.* 11(1), 1972 : 18-57.

3104    MURAV'EV, Ė. P. *Zadači i osnovnye principy perspektivnogo planirovanija na pred-
        prijatii* (Objectives and essential principles of prospective planning in an enterprise).
        Moskva, Ėkonomika, 72, 39 p.

3105    OLESNEVIĆ, L. A. (ed.). *Problemy social'nogo upravlenija na promyšlennom predprijatii*
        (Problems of social management in an industrial enterprise). Kiev, 72, 142 p.

3106    PETUHOV, R. M.; LAZUTKIN, Ė. S. *Ėkonomičeskaja effektivnost' i organizacij proizvodst-
        va* (Economic efficiency and production management). Moskva, Ėkonomika, 72, 223 p.

3107    REZNIČEK, J. *Rizeni prumyslovych podniku* (The management of industrial enterprise),
        Praha, Svoboda, 72, 374-5 p.

3108 SILBERSTON, A.; SETON, F. (eds.). *Industrial management: East and West*. New York, Praeger, 73, xvi-260 p.

3110 ŠKIREDOV, V. P. *Rol' ob"ektivnogo v upravlenii proizvodstvom* (The role of objective and subjective in production management). Moskva, Ékonomika, 72, 140 p.

3111 SOROČKIN, I. M.; GRIŠIN, L. I. *Naučnaja organizacija truda i upravlenija na predprijatijah mjasnoj promyšlennosti* (Scientific organization of labour and management in the meat industry enterprises). Moskva, Piščevaja promyšlennost', 73, 248 p.

3112 SYTNIK, V. F. *Optimal'nye i statističeskie modeli planirovanija proizvodstva* (Optimal and statistical models of production planning). Kiev, Izdatel'stvo Kievskogo Universiteta, 72, 294 p.

3113 VENU, S. "Corporate planning in a developing economy; Indian experience", *Long Range Planning* 5(3), sep 72 : 29-35.

3114 VLADIMIRSKIJ, B. D. *Ékonomičeskie zadaci promyšlennyh predprijatij i pervičnyh proforganizacij v novyh uslovijah* (Economic objectives of industrial enterprises and grassroots professional organizations under the new conditions). Érevan, Ajastan, 72, 127 p.

3115 WEIDAUER, R.; WETZEL, A. *Sozialistische Leitung im Betrieb und Kombinat* (Socialist management of the firm and the corporation). Berlin, Die Wirtschaft, 72, 336 p.

3116 WISZNIEWSKI, Z. *Zarzadzanie przedsiebiorstwem przemysłowym* (Management of an industrial enterprise). Warszawa, Państwowe Wydawnictwo Ekonomiczne, 73, 194 p.

3117 WURL, H.-J. *Die Anwendung der Simulationstechnik zur betriebswirtschaftlichen Beurteilung industrieller Projekte in Entwicklungsländern* (The utilization of simulation techniques to test industrial projects in developing countries). Berlin, Ducker und Humblot, 71, 140 p.

3118 ZBICHORSKI, Z. "Gospodarka srodkami produkcji w przedsiebiorstwie" (Industrial goods management in the enterprise), *Probl. Org.* (3), 1973 : 107-123.

## H.2131 *Economic calculation and production costs*
### *Calcul économique et coûts de production*

[See also / Voir aussi: **G.3353**; 2211, 2453, 3898]

3119 AFREMOV, V. M. *Fiksirovannye platezi v promyšlennosti* (Fixed payments in industry). Moskva, Finansy, 73, 128 p.

3120 AHLERT, D.; FRANZ, K. P. *Industrielle Kostenrechnung* (Industrial cost accounting). Düsseldorf, VDI-Verlag, 73, xi-127 p.

3121 ALYMOV, A. N.; FEDORIŠČEVA, A. N. *Vosproizvodstvo i ispol'zovanie proizvodstvennyh fondov v ugol'noj promyšlennosti* (Reproduction and utilization of productive funds in the coal industry). Kiev, Naukowa Dumka, 72, 292 p.

3122 BAZAROVA, G. V. "O nekotoryh napravlenijah dal'nejšego soveršenstvovanija sistemy raspredelenija pribyli v promyšlennosti" (Some orientations of the future reinforcement of the profit distribution system in industry), *Finansy SSSR* 46(12), dec 72 : 61-67.

3123 BITTNEROWA, E.; GLINKOWSKI, C. "Mierniki makro-ekonomicznej analizy wykorzystania srodków trwałych w przemysle" (Macroeconomic measures analysing the use of fixed assets in industry), *Ruch prawn. ekon. socjol.* (1), 1973 : 159-177.

3124 BOROVIK, F. V.; PLAŠČINSKIJ, N. A. *Obrazovanie fonda proizvodstvennogo nakoplenija v promyšldnnoxgi* (Formation of the productive accumulation fund in industry). Minsk, Nauka i Tehnika, 72, 320 p.

3125 CICHOWSKI, E. "System ekonomiczno-finansowy państwowych przedsiebiorstw przemysłowych w Bułgarskiej Republice Ludowej" (Economic and financial system of the State industrial enterprise of the Bulgarian Democratic Republic), *Finanse* (11), 1973 : 47-57.

3126 DUDICK, T. S. *Profile for profitability: using cost control and profitability analysis*. New York, Wiley-Interscience, 72, xvii-253 p.

3127 DUMAČEV, A. P. *Hozrasčetnye ob'edinenija v promyšlennosti* (Cost accounting unions in industry). Leningrad, Lenizdat, 72, 195 p.

3128   ISAEV, V. A. "Ispol'zovanie osnovnogo kapitala v promyšlennosti Anglii" (The utilisa-
       tion of fixed assets in English industry), *Vestn. Moskov. Univ. Ser. Ėkon.* 28(4),
       jul-aug 73 : 82-90.

3129   JAMPOL'SKIJ, S. M. *Hozrasčetnye faktory uskorenija tehničeskogo progressa v promyš-
       lennosti* (Cost accounting factors of technical progress acceleration in industry). Kiev,
       Naukova Dumka, 73, 255 p.

3130   JEDRYCHOWSKI, S. "Kierunki doskonalenia systemu finansowego w przemysle kluc-
       zowym" (Lines of improvement in the financial system of key industries), *Finanse* (4),
       1973 : 1-12.

3131   KALAŠNIKOVA, L. M. *Soveršenstvovanie upravlenija i hozrasčeta na tekstil'nyh pred-
       prijatijah* (Management and cost accounting improvement in textile enterprises).
       Moskva, Legkaja industrija, 72, 303 p.

3132   KOCEV, G. N. *Problemi sebestojnostta v premislenostta* (Cost price problems in industry).
       Sofija, Partizdat, 73, 184 p.

3134   KOVALEVSKIJ, A. M. *Perspektivnoe planorovanie na promyšlennyh predprijatijah i v
       proizvodstvennyh ob'edinenijah* (Prospective planning in industrial enterprises and
       productive unions). Moskva, Ėkonomika, 73, 318 p. [USSR.]

3135   KRAVCOV, I. I. *Polnye kapital'nye vlozenija v otrasli promyšlennosti* (Global capital
       investments in industrial sectors). Moskva, Nauka, 73, 132 p. [USSR.]

3136   MOREJNIS, J. I. "Metodika opredelenija i analiza oboračivaemosti oborotnyh sredst
       promyšlennogo predprijatija" (The method of determination and the analysis of the
       circulation of working capital in the industrial enterprise), *Finansy SSSR* 47(2),
       feb 73 : 76-84.

3137   NEILD, P. G. "Financial planning in British industry", *J. Busin. Pol.* 3(3), 1973 : 11-18.

3138   PAŁASZWSKI, T. *Rachunek cen i kosztów w budownictwie* (Price and cost calculation in
       the building industry). Warszawa, Arkady, 73, 255 p. [Poland.]

3139   PANIĆ, M.; CLOSE, R. E. "Profitability of British manufacturing industry", *Lloyds
       Bank R.* 109, jul 73 : 17-30.

3140   PAVLOV, V. S. "Oborotnye sredstva promyšlennosti i effektovnost' obščestvennogo
       proizvodstva" (Working capital in industry and the efficiency of social production),
       *Finansy SSSR* 47(8), aug 73 : 13-22.

3141   POPOV, D. I.; MITJAEV, N. I. *Ispol'zovanie osnovnyh fondov metallurgičeskih pred-
       prijatij* (Fixed assets utilization in metallurgy enterprises). Moskva, Metallurgija,
       72, 104 p. [USSR.]

3142   RYŽKOV, I. I. *Naučno-tehničeskij progress i effektovnost' osnovnyh fondov v legkoj
       promyšlennosti* (Scientific and technical progress and fixed assets efficiency in light
       industry). Kiev, Naukova Dumka, 73, 239 p. [USSR.]

3143   SARNECKI, Z. "Oddziaływanie instrumentów finansowych na zagospodarowanie
       zapasów nieprawidłowych w 1972 roku" (Influence of financial tools on utilization of
       abnormal stocks in 1972), *Finanse* (9), 1973 : 17-31. [Poland.]

3144   SOŁTYS, D. "Rachunek materialnych kosztów bezpośrednich produkcji organicznej w
       systemie wewnatrzzakładowego rozrachunku gospodarczego" (Calculation of material
       direct costs of organic production in the system of an internal plant self-accounting
       system), *Prace nauk. wyzsz. Szkoły ekon. Wrocław.* 39, 1973 : 77-97.

3145   SUDOŁ, S. *Rachunek kosztów w zarzadzaniu przedsiebiorstwem przemysłowym* (Costs
       calculation in the management of an industrial enterprise). Warszawa, Państwowe
       Wydawnictwo Ekonomiczne, 72, 187 p.

3146   SWATLER, L. *Bodzce finansowe w gospodarce srodkami trwałymi* (Financial incentives
       in fixed assets management). Warszawa, Państwowe Wydawnictwo Ekonomiczne, 73,
       287 p.

3147   SWATLER, L. *System finansowy przedsiebiorstw przemysłowych* (Financial system of
       industrial enterprises). Szczecin, Politechnika Szczecińska, 73, 151 p.

       **H.2132**   *Industrial bookkeeping*
                    *Comptabilité industrielle*

3148   JAGIELIŃSKI, M.; NISENGOLC, S. *Ksiegowosc i kalkulacja w przedsiebiorstwie przemys-
       łowym* (Bookkeeping and calculation in industrial enterprises). Warszawa, Państwowe
       Wydawnictwo Ekonomiczne, 73, 579 p.

3149 Płoszajski, T. *Rachunkowosc przedsiebiorstw budownictwa* (Accounting of building enterprises). Warszawa, Państwowe Wydawnictwo Ekonomiczne, 73, 439 p.

3150 Sarocchi, P. *De la comptabilité analytique au controle budgétaire. Initiation à la comptabilité industrielle.* Paris, Éditions d'organisation, 72, 229 p.

## H.214 Industrial policy
### Politique industrielle

[See also / Voir aussi: 1969, 3081, 4228, 4527, 4924, 5246, 5318]

3151 Antal, Z. "Probleme und Fortschritt der industriellen Entwicklung in Sibirien" (Problems and perspectives of industrial development in Siberia), *A. Univ. Sci. budapest. Sect. geogr.* (7), 1971 : 115-126.

3152 Armengaud, A. "Difficultés actuelles de la politique industrielle", *R. polit. parl.* 74(837), dec 72 : 17-26. [France.]

3153 Baer, W.; Villela, A. V. "Industrial growth and industrialization: revisions in the stages of Brazil's economic development", *J. develop. Areas* 7(2), jan 73 : 217-234. [Also published in Portugese in *Dados* (9), 1972 : 114-134.]

3154 Bagdasarov, V. Š. *Iz istorii industrial'nogo razvitija Uzbekistana*, 1959-1965 *gg.* (From Uzbekistan's industrial development history, 1959-1965). Taškent, Fan, 72, 148 p.

3155 Cardoso, F. H. "Industrialization, dependency and power in Latin America", *Berkeley J. Sociol.* 17, 1972-1973 : 79-95.

3156 Bibl. xxi-3333. Carnoy, M. *Industrialization in a Latin American common market* CR: R. D. Hansen, *Amer. polit. Sci. R.* 67(3), sep 73 : 1111-1113.

3157 Casas Gonzalez, A. "Industrialización e integración" (Industrialization and integration), *R. Econ. latinoamer.* 9(35), 1973 : 43-54. [Latin America.]

3158 Charbonneau, B. "À la recherche d'une politique de développement industriel des pays du Tiers-Monde", *Industr. Trav. O.-Mer* 21(230), jan 73 : 15-22.

3159 Cohn, G. "La industrialización en Brazil: proceso y perspectivas" (Industrialization in Brazil: process and prospects), *R. mexic. Sociol.* 33(3), jul-sep 71 : 489-516.

3160 Dadrian, V. N. "Nationalism, communism and Soviet industrialization. A theoretical exposition", *Sociol. int. (Berlin)* 10(2), 1972 : 183-212.

3161 Dragan, I. "Aspects sociaux de l'industrialisation des zones rurales en Roumanie", *R. roum. Sci. soc. Sér. Sociol.* 17, 1973 : 77-100.

3162 Farley, N. J. J. "Outward looking policies and industrialization in a small economy: some notes on the Irish case", *Econ. Develop. cult. Change* 21(4), *Part I* jul 73 : 610-628.

3163 Fiallo, F. R. "Alternativas de política industrial en la República Dominicana" (Industrial policy alternatives in the Dominican Republic), *Trim. econ.* 40(157), jan-mar 73 : 159-172.

3164 Fischer, W. "Rural industrialization and population change", *Comp. Stud. Soc. Hist.* 15(2), mar 73 : 158-170.

3165 Fischer, W. *Wirtschaft und Gesellschaft im Zeitalter der Industrialisierung* (Economy and society in the era of industrialization). Göttingen, Vandenhoeck und Ruprecht, 72, 547 p.

3166 Fornari, M. "Industrialization without development: a comment on an Italian case study", *Sociol. rur.* 13(1), 1973 : 15-26.

3167 Granick, D. "La planification centrale de l'industrie en Roumanie", *R. Est* 4(2), apr 73 : 5-65.

3168 Halpar, P. "Problemas del desarrollo de la estructura industrial en los países latinoamericanos de orientación capitalista" (Problems of development of the industrial structure in Latin American countries of capitalist orientation), *Desarr. indoamer.* 6(19), oct 72 : 47-54.

3169 Hollingsworth, J. R. "Perspectives on industrializing societies", *Amer. behav. Scientist* 16(5), mai-jun 73 : 715-739.

3170 Kaynor, R. S.; Schultz, K. F. *Industrial development; a practical handbook for planning and implementing development programs.* New York, Praeger, 73, xvii-185 p.

3171 Klatzmann, J. "L'industrialisation rurale est-elle possible ? L'exemple de la région de Brive", *Sociol. rur.* 12(3-4), 1972 : 474-480.

3172   Komló, L. "The industrialization and integration of agriculture in a socialist country", *Acta oecon.* 10(1), 1973 : 67-79.

3173   Lafferty, W. M. "Industrialization and labor radicalism in Norway: an ecological analysis", *Scand. polit. Stud.* (7), 1972 : 157-175.

3174   Lavell, A. M. "Regional industrialization in Mexico; some policy considerations", *Region. Stud.* 6(3), sep 72 : 343-362.

3175   Lee, S. Y. "Some basic problems of industrialization in Singapore", *J. develop. Areas* 7(2), jan 73 : 185-216.

3176   Lim, C. P. "Need for greater emphasis on industrialization in Malaysian economic development strategy", *Ekon. J.* 12(2), 1972 : 44-60.

3177   Link, M. *Stand und Zukunftsperspektiven der Industrialisierung Brasiliens* (Present state and prospects for the industrialization of Brazil). Bern-Stuttgart, Paul Haupt, 72, 158 p.

3178   Lisikiewicz, J. "Postep techniczny w poszczególnych stadiach industrializacji" (Technical progress in different stages of industrialization), *Zesz. nauk. Szkoły głównź. Plan. Statyst.* 87, 1972 : 87-107.

3179   Maltzahn, D. "Industrial policy in the EEC", *Busin. Economist* 4(2), 1972 : 55-61.

3180   Miller, F. C. *Industrialization in Mexico; old villages and a new town.* Menlo Park, Calif., Cummings Publishing Co., 73, 161 p.

3181   Muñoz, G. O. "Industrialización y subdesarrollo" (Industrialization and underdevelopment), *Cuad. Real. nac.* (12), apr 72 : 26-48.

3182   Muns Albuixech, J. *Industrialización y crecimiento de los países en desarrollo* (Industrialization and growth in developing countries). Esplugues de Llobregat, Ediciones Ariel, 72, 312 p.

3183   Nandi, K. L. *Growth in selected Indian industries; some facets of industrial planning in a growing democracy.* Calcutta, World Press, 72, xxv-146 p.

3184   Negreponti-Delivanis, M. "Les conséquences de l'industrialisation dans les pays en voie de développement sur l'emploi et sur la répartition du revenu national", *R. Écon. polit. (Paris)* 83(1), jan-feb 73 : 76-107.

3185   Organization for Economic Cooperation and Development. *The industrial policy of Japan.* Paris, OECD, 72, 195 p.

3186   Ossa, C. "Estrategía de desarrollo industrial. Algunos resultados empíricos" (Industrial development strategy: some empirical results), *Trim. econ.* 39(156), oct-dec 72 : 753-769. [Chile.]

3187   Peláez, C. M. *História da industrializacão brasileira; crítica à teoria estruturalista no Brasil* (History of Brazilian industrialization; critique of structuralist theory in Brazil). Rio de Janeiro, APEC, 72, 241 p.

3188   Pinard, J. *Les industries du Poitou et des Charentes; étude de l'industrialisation d'un milieu rural et de ses villes.* Poitiers, SFIL, 72, 515 p. [France.]

3189   Power, J. H. "The role of protection in industrialization policy with particular reference to Kenya", *East. Afr. econ. R.* 4(1), jun 72 : 1-20.

3190   Román, Z. (ed.). *Progress and planning in industry.* Budapest, Akadémiai Kiadó, 72, 417 p.

3191   Rotstein, A. (ed.). *An industrial strategy for Canada.* Toronto, New Press, 72, 130 p.

3192   Rull Sabater, A. "Processus d'industrialisation latino-américain: directives fondamentales", *Mondes en Dévelop.* (2), 1972 : 87-102.

3193   Toniolo, G. "Le fasi dell' industrializzazione italiana e la crisi del 1971-1972" (The stages of Italian industrialization and the 1971-1972 crisis), *Riv. int. Sci. econ. com.* 19(11), nov 72 : 1040-1053.

3194   Toulemon, R. "Perspectives communautaires dans le domaine de la politique industrielle, technologique et scientifique", *Ét. écon. (Mons)* 3-4(151-152), 1971 : 263-281.

3195   Van Rhijn, T. "Les Pays-Bas et la politique de structure industrielle", *Reflets Perspect. Vie écon.* 12(2), 1973 : 149-164.

3196   Warren, B. "Imperialism and capitalist industrialization", *New Left R.* 81, sep-oct 73 : 3-53.

3197   Younctil, L. "Social and economic costs of industrialization in Korea", *Korea J.* 13(10), oct 73 : 18-28.

### H.22 Industrial production
### Production industrielle

### H.221 *General and local studies*
*Études générales et localisées*

[See also / Voir aussi: 2169, 3701]

3198 BARBOUR, K. M. *The growth, location, and structure of industry in Egypt.* New York, Praeger, 72, xiv-222 p.

3199 BEGALIEV, S.; SOODANBEKOV, K. *Promyšlennost Kirgizstana v devjatoj pjatiletke* (Kirgizstan industry in the ninth five-year plan). Frunze, Kyrgyzstan, 72, 159 p.

3200 CYRON, E. *Przemiany w strukturze współczesnego przemysłu Stanów Zjednoczonych* (Changes in the structure of contemporary industry in the USA). Warszawa, Państwowe Wydawnictwo Naukowe, 73, 286 p.

3201 DEVICHI, J. P. "La situation de l'industrie française en 1972", *Écon. et Statist.* 48, sep 73 : 17-31.

3202 ERSON, G. "Les industries de croissance en Suède", *R. écon. Sud-Ouest* 22(2), 1973 : 313-330.

3203 ESPOSITO, L.; PERSICO, P. "L'industria manufatturiera in Campania, 1961-1971" (Manufacturing industries in Campania, 1961-1971), *Nord e Sud* 20(164-165), aug-sep 73 : 154-166. [Italy.]

3204 "Évolution de la production industrielle en 1972 (L')", *B. Statist.* 59(3), mar 73 : 178-182. [Belgique.]

3205 FRANCE. Institut national de la statistique et des études économiques. *Situation de l'industrie française en 1971.* Paris, INSÉÉ, 73, 215 p.

3206 GERBI, M. "Modalità di sviluppo dell'industria italiana nell'economia internazionale" (The modality of the development of Italian industry in the international economy), *Impresa* 14(4), jul-aug 72 : 273-281.

3207 GIRGIS, M. "Determinanten der industriellen Entwicklung in Ägypten" (Determinants of industrial development in Egypt), *Weltwirtschaft* (1), 1973 : 113-140.

3208 GORDAN, S. "Análisis crítico del crecimiento industrial argentino" (Critical analysis of Argentine industrial growth), *Investig. econ.* 31(123), jul-sep 71 : 619-632.

3209 JEZOWSKI, K. "Rozwój przemysłu dolnoslaskiego w latach 1945-1970" (Development of Lower Silesia industry in the years 1945-1970), *Prace nauk. wyzsz. Szkoły ekon. Wrocław.* 40, 1973 : 5-17.

3210 MACEDO SOARES E SILVA, E. DE. *As instituiçoes de industria e comércio do Brasil / Industrial and commercial institutions in Brazil.* Rio de Janeiro, Crown, 72, 799 p.

3211 MALBOGUNJE, A. L. "Manufacturing and the geography of development in tropical Africa", *Econ. Geogr. (Worcester)* 49(1), jan 73 : 1-20.

3212 MARTYNOV, V. A.; MOROZOV, V. A. (eds.). *SŠA: sovremennye ěkonomičeskie svjazi promyšlennosti s sel'skim hozjajstvom* (The USA: contemporary economic relations between industry and agriculture). Moskva, Nauka, 72, 267 p.

3213 MATTEI, F. "Situation and prospects of Italian industry", *R. econ. Condit. Italy* 26(5), sep 72 : 349-361.

3214 MILLAN, H. "Industria manufacturera, 1958-1969" (The manufacturing industry, 1958-1969), *Bol. mens. Estadíst.* 21(250-251). mai-jun 72 : 195-244. [Colombia.]

3215 MOLLE, W. "Les industries de croissance aux Pays-Bas", *R. écon. Sud-Ouest* 22(2), 1973 : 331-364.

3216 MORONEY, J. R. *The structure of production in American manufacturing.* Chapel Hill, North Carolina, University of North Carolina Press, 72, xiii-174 p. CR: P. ZAREMBKA, *J. econ. Liter.* 11(3), sep 73 : 900-902.

3217 O'MALLEY, P. *Irish industry: structure and performance.* Dublin, Gill and MacMillan; New York, Barnes and Noble, 72, ix-141 p. CR: N. J. J. FARLEY, *J. econ. Liter.* 11(3), sep 73 : 921-923.

3218 Bibl. XXI-3368. REVENKO, A. F. *Promyšlennaja statistika SŠA* (US industrial statistics). CR: V. HOLUBNYCHY, *J. econ. Liter.* 11(3), sep 73 : 933-935.

3219 SHEPERD, W. G. "Structure and behavior in British industries, with US comparisons", *J. industr. Econ.* 21(1), nov 72 : 35-54.

3220 "Situation de l'industrie française en 1971", *Coll. INSÉÉ Sér. E* 18, feb 73 : 215 p.

3221   "Situation et perspectives dans l'industrie. Novembre 1972", *Point écon. Auvergne* (10)
       dec 72 : 1-16. [France.]

3222   SZYBKOWSKI, M. "Produkcja przemysłowa Polski na tle niektórych krajów" (Industrial
       production in Poland as compared with other countries), *Wiadom. statyst.* (1), 1973 :
       8-11.

3223   TONCRE, J. E. *Industrial development in a rapidly growing community.* Boston, Financial
       Publishing Co., 72, ix-115 p.

3224   VAYSSIERE, J. (éd.). *La industria española* (Spanish industry). Paris, Masson, 72, 120 p.

3225   VENTESOL, G. "Le développement industriel de la Communauté européenne", *France-
       Forum* 122-123, jan-feb 73 : 2-12.


**H.222**   *Specific industries*
           *Industries particulières*


**H.2221**   *Energy: sources, consumption*
            *Énergie: sources et consommation*

**H.22210**   General studies
             Études générales

3226   CURRAN, D. *Géographie mondiale de l'énergie.* Paris, Masson, 73, 254 p.

3227   "Europe de l'énergie (L')", *Synthèses* 27(311-312), mai-jun 72 : 7-125.

3228   GIRAUD, A. "Réflexions sur l'évolution de la demande d'énergie en Europe et le rôle
       possible de l'énergie nucléaire", *R. écon. fr.-suisse* 53(2), 1973 : 1017.

3229   GRENON, E. *Pour une politique de l'énergie. Charbon ? Pétrole ? Atome ?* Verviers, Éditions
       Gérard, 72, 352 p.

3230   GROOTE, P. DE "Quelques éléments d'appréciation socio-économique de l'évolution
       énergétique", *R. Inst. Sociol.* 45(4), 1972 : 615-627.

3231   KÄHR, W. "Die Entwicklung des Energieverbrauchs der Schweiz im Zeitraum 1950 bis
       1970 und Vorschau auf das Jahr 2000" (The development of energy consumption in
       Switzerland from 1950 to 1970 and its perspectives for the year 2000), *Schweizer. Z.
       Volkswirtsch. Statist.* 109(3), sep 73 : 385-405.

3232   KIM, K. M. *Soveršenstvovanie struktury toplivno-ėnergetičeskogo balansa Srednej Azii*
       (The improvement of the Central Asian energy balance structure). Taškent, Fan, 73,
       220 p.

3233   PADALKO, L. P. *Matematičeskie metody optimal'nogo planirovanija razvitija i ėksploatacii
       ėnergosistem* (Mathematical methods for the optimal planning of the energy systems
       development and exploitation). Minsk, Vyšejšaja Škola, 72, 200 p.

3234   POLEŠČUK, N. G. *Ėnergoorużennost' i proizvoditel'nost' truda* (Energy utilization and
       labour productivity). Moskva, Ėkonomika, 73, 175 p.

3235   RIDGEWAY, J. *The last play; the struggle to monopolize the world's energy resources.* New
       York, E. P. Dutton, 73, 446 p.

3236   Bibl. XXI-3387. SCHURR, S. H. (ed.). *Energy, economic growth, and the environment.*
       CR: F. FORSCHER, *J. econ. Liter.* 11(3), sep 73 : 955-957.

3237   SCHWEIKERT, H. "Zur Planung der Energieversorgung in stadtischen Agglomerationen"
       (The planning of energy supply in urban agglomerations), *Schweizer. Z. Volkswirtsch.
       Statist.* 109(3), sep 73 : 421-437.

3238   SEIFERT, W. W.; BAKR, M. A.; KETTANI, M. A. (eds.). *Energy and development: a case
       study.* Cambridge, Mass., MIT Press, 73, xix-300 p.

3239   SURREY, A. J.; BROMLEY, A. J. "Energy resources", *Futures (Guildford)* 5(1), feb 73 :
       90-107.

3240   THERING, M. W. "Why the world urgently needs an energy policy", *Int. Relat. (London)*
       4(3), mai 73 : 225-239.

3241   "US Canadian energy resource development", *Case West. J. int. Law* 5(1), 1972 : 36-86.

3242   VAILLAUD, M. "Énergie et croissance", *Nef* 30(52), sep-nov 73 : 99-111.

3243   WEERTS, P. "L'approvisionnement de la Belgique en énergie au cours de la période
       1950-1970", *Bénélux B. trim. écon. statist.* (4), nov 72 : 18-31.

3244   ZLATOPOL'SKIJ, A. N.; PRUZNER, S. L. *Organizacija i planirovanie teploėnergetiki* (Organi-
       zation and planning of thermic energy). Moskva, Vysšaja škola, 72, 335 p.

**H.22211** Coal, lignites, etc.
Charbons, lignites, etc.

[See also / Voir aussi: 3121]

3245 DJADYK, V. N.; BRATKOV, Ė. N.; GIMETNERMAN, L. D. *Novye formy hozjajstvovanija v ugol'noj promyšlennosti* (New forms of economic management in the coal industry). Kiev, Tehnika, 72, 230 p.

3246 GLEBOVA, L. I. "O nekotoryh ėlementah ėkonomičeskoj ocenko nedr i cenoobrazovanija v gornoj promyšlennosti" (On some elements of the coal beds economic efficiency and the fixation of prices in mining industry), *Vopr. Ėkon. Dal'n. Vost.* (3), 1972 : 11-124.

**H.22212** Coal gas
Gaz

[See also / Voir aussi: 3251, 3274]

**H.22213** Electricity: production, distribution
Électricité : production, distribution

3247 BULAVIN, V. I. "Ėlektroenergetika Latinskoj Ameriki" (Electric energy in Latin America), *Latin. Amer.* (2), mar-apr 73 : 12-26.

3248 ELIOSIDA, C. T.; VILLENA, R. S. "Some economic aspects of electric energy in the Philippines", *Philippine Econ. B.* 9(1-3), jan-sep 72 : 30-38.

3249 ĖROFEEV, I. A. *Ėlektroenergetika SSSR v novoj pjatiletke, 1971-1975* (USSR electric energy in the new five-year plan, 1971-1975). Moskva, Prosveščenie, 72, 112 p.

3250 FERNANDEZ, G. "Presente y futuro de la industria eléctrica española" (Present and future of the Spanish electric industry), *Inform. comp. esp.* 474, feb 73 : 155-161.

3251 LANEON, H. H. "Electric and gas combination and economic performance", *J. Econ. Busin.* 25(1), 1972 : 1-13.

**H.22214** Oil and by-products, refining
Pétroles et dérivés, raffinage

[See also / Voir aussi: 3017, 3951, 4874]

3252 ALONSO GONZÁLEZ, F. *Historia y petróleo: México en su lucha por la independencia económica; el problema del petróleo* (History and oil: Mexico in its struggle for economic independence; the problem of petroleum). México, Ediciones El Caballito, 72, 322 p.

3253 'ATÎQAH, 'A. A. *Athar al-batrûl'alá al-iqtišâd al-Lîbî 1956-1969* (The influence of petroleum on the Libyan economy, 1956-1969). Bayrût, Dar al-Tali'at lil-Taba'a/t wal-Nashr, 72, 224 p.

3254 BARGER, T. G. "Middle Eastern oil since the Second World War", *A. Amer. Acad. polit. soc. Sci.* 401, mai 72 : 31-44.

3255 BENCHIKH, M. *Les instruments juridiques de la politique algérienne des hydrocarbures.* Paris, Librarie générale de droit et de jurisprudence, 73, viii-344 p.

3256 BREYERS, S.; MACAVOY, P. W. "The natural gas shortage and the regulation of natural gas producers", *Harvard Law R.* 86(6), apr 73 : 941-987.

3257 BRUCE, C. J. "The open petroleum economy: a comparison of Keynesian and alternative formulations", *Soc. econ. Stud.* 21(2), jun 72 : 125-152.

3258 BURRELL, R. M.; COTTRELL, A. J. *Politics, oil and the Western Mediterranean.* Beverly Hills, Calif., Sage Publications, 73, ii-80 p.

3259 CARMOY, G. DE. "Énergie, pétrole et politique", *Études (Paris)* oct 72 : 363-378.

3260 CASAL, H. N. *El petróleo* (Petroleum). Buenos Aires, Centro Editor de América Latina, 72, 110 p.

3261 CICCHETTI, C. J. *Alaskan oil: alternative routes and markets.* Washington-Baltimore, Johns Hopkins University Press, 72, xvii-142 p.

3262 DORSEY, J. J. "The petrochemical industry of Taiwan: raw materials", *Industry free China* 39(1), jan 73 : 13-27.

3302    "Situation der österreichischen Aluminiumindustrie und die Aussichten bis 1975. (Die)" (The situation of the aluminium industry and its future to 1975), *Österr. Inst. Wirtsch.-Forsch. Mber.* 46(4), apr 73 : 184-192. [Austria.]

### H.2224    Mechanical industry
### Industries mécaniques

### H.22240    General studies
### Études générales

3303    DRAPEZO, P. A. *et al. Ékonomika v spomogatel'nyh proizvodstv na mašinostroitel'nom predprijatii* (Economics of auxiliary production in mechanical enterprises). Minsk, Belarus', 73, 167 p.

3304    GÁBOR, O.; GEDE, M. "A gépipar szerepe a magyar népgazdaság fejlödésében és a gazdasági struktura változásában" (The role of the machine industry in the development of the Hungarian People's economy and the transformation of economic structures), *Közgazd. Szle* 20(4), apr 73 : 405-418.

3305    MORAND, J. C. "Les industries mécaniques en Lorraine: 13.000 emplois créés entre 1962 et 1972", *Doss. Écon. lorraine* (11), dec 72 : 32 p. [France.]

3306    POPP, G. *Die Organisation des Forschungs- und Entwicklungsbereichs in der schweizerischen Maschinenindustrie* (The organization of the research and development field in the Swiss machine industry). Aarau, Keller, 72, xii-255 p.

3307    VARGA, Gy.; PÓCS, E. "A gépipar fejlödésének nemzetközi tendenciái" (The international trends of machine industry development), *Közgazd. Szle* 20(2), feb 73 : 158-173.

### H.22241    Machine tools
### Machine-outils

3308    ANDREEV, A. M. *et al. Ékonomika stankoinstrumental'noj promyšlennosti* (Economics of the machine-tool industry). Moskva, Mašinostroenie, 72, 279 p.

3309    Bibl. XXI-3448. CHENG, C.-Y. *The machine-building industry in Communist China.* CR: T. G. RAWSKI, *Amer. polit. Sci. R.* 67(2), jun 73 : 649-650; S. H. CHOU, *J. econ. Liter.* 11(1), mar 73 : 98-100.

3310    FIELD, R. M. "The Chinese machine-building industry: a reappraisal", *China Quart.* 54, apr-jun 73 : 308-320.

### H.22242    Car industry; agricultural machines; rolling stock...
### Industrie automobile; machines agricoles; matériel roulant pour chemins de fer

3311    BAXTER, W. P. "The Soviet passenger car industry", *Survey* 19(3), 1973 : 218-240.

3312    BISCARETTI DI RUFFIA, R. "Situation and prospects of the motor industry in Italy", *R. econ. Condit. Italy* 27(1-2), jan-mar 73 : 43-52.

3313    BORISOVA, K. "Avtomobil'naja promyšlennost' zapadnoj Évropy" (The car industry in Western Europe), *Mir. Ékon. mezdun. Otnoš.* 16(6), jun 73 : 132-139.

3314    MACIEJEWSKI, I. "Rozwój produkcji samochodów ciezarowych w Polsce" (The growth of motor-truck production in Poland), *Zesz. nauk. Szkoly główn. Plan. Statyst.* 87, 1972 : 109-124.

3315    MERCER, L. J.; MORGAN, W. D. "The American automobile industry: investment demand, capacity, and capacity utilization, 1921-1940", *J. polit. Econ.* 80(6), nov-dec 72 : 1214-1231.

3316    "Perspectives de l'industrie automobile dans le Tiers-Monde", *Industr. Trav. O.-Mer* 21(236), jul 73 : 595-602.

3317    RADDAVERO, B. C. "Análisis de la transferencia de la tecnológia externa a la industria argentina: el caso de la industria automotriz" (Analysis of the transfer of foreign technology to Argentine industry: the case of the auto industry), *Económica (La Plata)* 18(3), sep-dec 72 : 367-388.

3318    RHYS, D. C. *The motor industry. An economic survey.* London, Butterworths, 72, 475 p.

3319    SZÉPLAKI, L. "Structure, conduct and performance in modern American automobile manufacturing", *South Afr. J. Econ.* 40(3), sep 72 : 216-234.

**H.22243**  Electrical appliances, electronic industries
Matériel électro-mécanique, industrie électronique

3320  DARJES, P. C.; TAAKE, H.-H. "Die Eletronikindustrie Süd-Koreas. Bisherige Entwicklung und volkswirtschaftliche Bedeutung" (The electronic industry in South Korea. Past development and its economic meaning), *Int. Asien Forum* 3(4), oct 72 : 553-559.

**H.22244**  Shipbuilding
Constructions navales

3321  GOMEZ Y ALONSO DE CELADA, J. M. "La concentración de empresas navieras" (Concentration of shipbuilding enterprises), *Bol. Estud. econ. (Bilbao)* 28(88), apr 73 : 209-223.

3322  RYDYGIER, W. "Funkcjonowanie systemu ekonomiczno-finansowege przemysłu okretowego. Wazniejsze doswiadczenia w latach 1971-1972" (Major experiences of the economic and financial system's functioning in the shipbuilding industry, 1971-1972), *Finanse* (9), 1973 : 1-16.

**H.22245**  Aircraft industry
Construction aéronautique

3323  HARTLEY, K. "The export performance of the British aircraft industry", *Yorkshire B. econ. soc. Res.* 24(2), nov 72 : 81-86.

**H.2225**  *Textile industry, clothes, leather goods, shoes*
*Textiles et habillement, cuir, chaussures*

[See also / Voir aussi: 3131, 3638]

3324  BIEGANSKI, M. *L'industrie textile du Nord de la France; structure, emploi, marché du travail. Direction régionale du travail et de la main-d'œuvre du Nord, échelon régional de l'emploi de Lille.* Ministère d'État chargé des affaires sociales, 72, various pagings.

3325  GARZÓN PAREJA, M. *La industria sedera en España* (The silk industry in Spain). Granada, Archivo de la Real Chancillería, 72, 6-521 p.

3326  HUFFMIRE, D. W. "Strategies of the United States textile industry in the post World War II period", *J. Busin. Pol.* 3(1), 1972 : 31-36.

3327  "Industria textil colombiana (La)" (The textile Colombian industry), *Bol. mens. Estadíst.* 21(255-256), oct-nov 72 : 171-199.

3328  KALTENECKER, M. "A világ textiliparának várható fejlödése a hetvenes években" (The foreseeable development of the world textile industry during the 1970's), *Statiszt. Szle* 50(11), nov 72 : 1120-1141.

3329  NARAYANSWAMY, M.; SRI RAM, V. *Garment industry in India; economics of a labour-intensive industry.* New Delhi, Economic and Scientific Research Foundation, 72, viii-251 p.

3330  ORGANISATION DES NATIONS UNIES POUR LE DÉVELOPPEMENT INDUSTRIEL. *L'industrie textile.* New York, NU, 72, viii-52 p.

3331  PRIESTLAND, C. H. (ed.). *Focus; economic profile of the apparel industry, with extensive comparative data on the American textile industry.* Arlington, Va., American Apparel Manufacturers Association, 72, 65 p.

3332  THERY, P. "La restructuration de l'industrie belge de la chaussure", *Reflets Perspect. Vie éxon.* 12(2), 1973 : 135-148.

**H.2226**  *Building and building materials industry*
*Construction et matériaux de construction*

[See also / Voir aussi: 3138, 3149]

3333  AMINOV, Š. A. *Kompleksnoe razvitie promyšlennosti stroitel'nyh materialov Srednej Azii* (Complex development of the Central Asian building materials industry). Dušanbe, Doniš, 73, 234 p.

3334 BABEV, N. *Reforma v stroitel'stve* (Reform in the construction industry). Ashabad, Turkmenistan, 72, 132 p.

3335 BOGACEV, V. N. "Problemy razvitija stroitel'noj industrii Sibiri" (Development problems of the building industry in Siberia), *Izv. Sib. Otdel. Akad. Nauk SSSR Ser. obšč. Nauk* 10(2), 1973 : 34-47.

3336 ČERNIKOV, I. S. *Analiz hozjajstvennoj dejatel'nosti upravlenij mehanizacii stroitel'stva* (Analysis of the economic activity of construction mechanization organizations). Moskva, Finansy, 73, 112 p.

3337 DANNER, P. "Baupreise und Baukonjunktur in Bayern seit 1958" (Price and economic situation in the building sector in Baviaria since 1958), *Bayern in Zahlen* 27(8), aug 73 : 271-267.

3338 GERMINIDS, D. A. *The construction industry in Mexico*. Paris, Organisation for Economic Cooperation and Development, Development Centre, 72, 91 p. [Also published in French.]

3339 GNIEWASZEWSKI, J. "Budownictwo na półmetku pieciolatki" (The building industry halfway through the 5-year plan), *Invest. i Budown.* (10), 1973 : 8-13. [Poland.]

3340 HOŁDOWSKA, E. "Problematyka prognozowania i planowania długookresowego zwiazanego z budownictwem" (The problems of forecasting and long-term planning in the building industry), *Zesz. nauk. wyzsz. Szkoły ekon. Poznan.* 41, 1972 : 69-82.

3341 "Industria del cemento en España (La)" (Cement industry in Spain), *R. Inform. econ. mund.* 249, apr-jun 73 : 3-28.

3342 KAŁKOWSKI, L. "Rola budownictwa w makroregionie południowym" (Building industry in the Southern macro-region), *Probl. Ekon. (Warszawa)* (4), 1973 : 42-50. [Poland.]

3343 MATJUŠIN, V. N. *Planirovanie izderžek stroitel'nogo proizvodstva v uslovijah hozjajstvennoj reformy* (Planning construction industry costs under the economic reform conditions). Moskva, Strojizdat, 73, 145 p.

3344 NATIONS UNIES. Département des affaires économiques et sociales. *Tendances dans l'industrialisation de la construction*. New York, NU, 72, iv-66 p.

3345 NIECIUŃSKI, W. "Prognoza rozwoju budownictwa mieszkaniowego do 1990 r." (Forecast of construction development till 1990), *Miasto* (7), 1973 : 1-6.

3346 RING, P. *Tendenzen der bauwirtschaftlichen Entwicklung in Berlin (West) bis zum Jahre 1976* (Development trends of the building industry [West] Berlin until 1976). Berlin, Duncker und Hubmot, 73, 47 p.

3347 ROWIŃSKI, L. "Specjalizacja przedsiebiorstw budowlanych a koordynacja inwestycji" (Building enterprise specialization and investment coordination), *Invest. i Budown.* (2), 1973 : 14-20. [Poland.]

3348 ŠER, I. D. *Finansovo-kretidnye problemy ekonomičeskoj reformy v stroitel'stve* (Financial and credit problems of the economic reform in the construction industry). Moskva, Finansy, 73, 191 p. [USSR.]

### H.2227 Chemical industry
### Industrie chimique

3349 "Economics of heroin", *Amer. econ. R.* 63(2), mai 73 *Pap. and Proc.*: 257-279. With contributions by P. A. FERNANDEZ, C. CLAGUE, M. H. MOORE and J. A. SEAGRAVES.

3350 MICHEL, D. "L'industrie pharmaceutique française et Roussel-Uclaf", *Écon. et Polit.* 224, mar 73 : 29-49.

3351 MORETTI, G. "The Italian plastic materials industry", *R. econ. Condit. Italy* 27(3), mai 73 : 162-177.

3352 NATALE, G. *L'industria chimica in Italia* (The chemical industry in Italy). Napoli, Guida, 72, 116 p.

3353 "Plastics industry in Taiwan (The)", *Industry free China* 38(3), sep 72 : 24-40.

3354 RUSHING, F. W. "Growth, capital-output ratios and the Soviet chemical industry", *Econ. int. (Genova)* 25(4), nov 72 : 731-743.

3355 SAVINSKIJ, Ě. S. *Himizacija narodnogo hozjajstva i proporcii razvitija himičeskoj promyšlennosti* (Chemical utilization in the national economy and the chemical industry proportions). Moskva, Himija, 72, 311 p. [USSR.]

3356 ŠKARENKOV, Ju. S. *Sotrudničestvo stran SEV v razvitii himičeskoj promyšlennosti* (The Comecon countries co-operation in the chemical industry development). Moskva, Nauka, 72, 183 p.

H.2228    *Other industries*
          *Autres industries*

[See also / Voir aussi: 5347]

3357  Burris G. *Unternehmungsplanung in der Papierindustrie* (Enterprise planning in the paper industry). Bern, Herbert Lang; Frankfurt-am-Main, Peter Lang, 72, 223 p. [Switzerland.]

3358  Cabanne, C. "Les industries agricoles et alimentaires dans la France de l'Ouest", *Norois* 20(78), apr-jun 73 : 322-335.

3359  "Industrie alimentaire en Tunisie (L')", *Syrie Monde arabe* 20(233), jun 73 : 11-27.

3360  Niculescu, N. I. *Metodologie şi strategie în organizare, posibilităţi şi experienţe în aplicarea lor în industria alimentară* (Methodology and strategy in the organization, possibilities and experiences in the food industry). Bucureşti, Consiliul Naţional pentry Ştiinţa şi Tehnologie, Institutul central de documentare tehnică, 72, 108 p.

3361  Niculescu, I. N. *Tehnici si metode moderne în diversificarea produselor alimentare* (Modern techniques and methods for diversification of food production). Bucuresti, Ceres, 72, 280 p.

3362  Puhal'skij, I. M. *Konservnaja promyšlennost' severnogo Kavkaza. Sostojanie i problemy razvitija* (Canned foods industry in Northern Caucasia. Study and problems of its development). Rostov, Kniznoe izdatel'stvo, 72, 158 p.

3363  Skalik, J. "Rozwój przemysłu spozywczego" (Development of the food industry), *Prace nauk. wyzsz. Szkoły ekon. Wrocław.* 37, 1973 : 149-164.


H.3    TRANSPORTATION AND COMMUNICATION
       TRANSPORTS ET COMMUNICATIONS

H.31   Transportation economics and policy
       Économie et politique des transports

H.310  *General studies*
       *Études générales*

[See also / Voir aussi: 3518]

3364  Aberle, G. "Die Abgabenpolitik bei öffentlich angebotenen Gütern: das Beispiel der Verkehrsinfrastruktur" (Duty policy in the case of public goods: the traffic infrastructure example), *Z. Wirtsch.-u. soz.-Wiss.* 92(1), 1972 : 57-77.

3365  Attar, H.; Ghaussy, A. G.; Tuchtfeldt, E. *Verkehrsprobleme in Entwicklungsländern.* (Transport problems in developing countries). Bern-Suttgart, Paul Haupt, 72, 156 p.

3366  Azar, V. I.; Poljak, S. V. *Transport i turizm* (Transport and tourism). Moskva, Transport, 73, 159 p.

3367  Bakaev, A. A. *Ėkonomiko-matematičeskie modeli planirovanija i proektirovanija transportnyh sistem* (Economic and mathematical models for planning and forecasting of transport systems). Kiev, Tehnika, 73, 220 p.

3368  Barat, J. "Transporte e ecologia" (Transport and ecology), *R. Adm. municip. (Rio de Janeiro)* 20(119), jul-aug 73 : 19-34.

3369  Becker, J. *Probleme regionaler Güterfernverkehrsprognosen* (Problems posed by the forecasting of regional circulation of merchandise over long distances). Göttingen, Vandenhoeck und Ruprecht, 72, 304 p.

3370  Blauwens, G. "The optimal output of transport in an imperfect economic environment", *J. Transport Econ. Pol.* 6(3), sep 73 : 285-293.

3371  Drake, J. W. *The administration of transportation modeling projects.* Lexington, Mass., Lexington Books, 73, xvii-246 p.

3372  France. Commissariat général du plan d'équipement et de productivité. *Les transports.* Paris, A. Colin, 72, 352 p.

3373  Georgano, G. N. (ed.). *Transportation through the ages.* New York, McGraw-Hill, 72 xii-311 p.

3374  Goldberg, M. A. "An evaluation of the interaction between urban transport and land use systems", *Land Econ.* 48(4), nov 72 : 338-346.

3375    GRZYWACZ, W. *Infrastruktura transportu* (Transport infrastructure). Warszawa, Wydawnictwo Komunikacji i Łacznosci, 72, 255 p.

3376    GUNSTON, B. *Transportation; problems and prospects.* London, Thames and Hudson; New York, Dutton, 72, 216 p.

3377    HELDMANN, H. "The role of transport in the national economy", *Almanach* 1970 : 36-96.

3378    KOLESOV, L. I. "Nekotorye voprosy opredelenija valovoj produkcii transporta" (Some definition problems of transport gross production), *Izv. Sib. Otdel. Akad. Nauk SSSR Ser. obšč. Nauk* 10(2), 1973 : 48-55.

3379    KOPOCIŃSKI, B. "O pewnym systemie transportu jako systemie obsługi masovej" (On a type of transport system as a queueing system), *Przegl. statyst.* (2), 1973 : 193-200.

3380    KUZNECOV, V. N. (ed.). *Voprosy povyšenija effektivnosti transportno-ekonomičeskih svjazej* (Problems of increasing the efficiency of the relations between transport and economy). Ufa, 72, 124 p.

3381    McLAREN, W. S.; MYERS, B. B. *Guided ground transportation; a review and bibliography of advanced systems.* Ottowa, Information Canada, 72, xiii-515 p.

3382    MIRON, J. R. *Regional transportation systems and population impact modelling: a theoretical development.* Toronto, University of Toronto-York University Joint Program im Transportation, 72, 25-1 l.

3383    OFFICER, L. H. "Discrimination in the international transportation industry", *West. econ. J.* 10(2), jun 72 : 170-181.

3384    ORGANISATION DE COOPÉRATION ET DE DÉVELOPPEMENT ÉCONOMIQUES. *Quatrième Symposium international sur la théorie et la pratique dans l'économie des transports; compte rendu des débats / Fourth International Symposium on Theory and Practice in Transport Economics / Viertes internationales Symposium über Theorie und Praxis in der Verkehrswirtschaft. La Haye, 5-7 octobre 1971.* Paris, OCDÉ, 72, 182 p.

3385    POTTS, R. B.; OLIVER, R. M. *Flows in transportation networks.* New York, Academic Press, 72, xi-192 p.

3386    RAKOWSKI, M.; WITKOWSKI, T. "Rachunek efektywnosci ekonomicznej w prognozowaniu rozwoju transportu" (Account of economic efficiency in transport development forecasting), *Przegl. komunik.* (3), 1973 : 11-16.

3387    RODIERE, R. *Les transports.* Paris, Dalloz, 73, viii-215 p.

3388    RODIERE, R.; CHEMEL, A. "Transports. Mise en place générale du droit communautaire des transports (années 1970 et 1971)", *R. trim. Dr. europ.* 8(4), oct-dec 72 : 766-775.

3389    SCHAEFER, H. (ed.). *Étude méthodologique pour l'établissement à l'échelle nationale et régionale de plans d'ensemble pour les transports.* Paris, CEMT, 72, iv-54 p.

3390    SENECA, R. S. "Inherent advantage, costs, and resource allocation in the transportation industry", *Amer. econ. R.* 63(5), dec 73 : 945-956.

3391    TARSKI, I. *Ekonomika i organizacja transportu miedzynarodowego* (Economics and organization of international transport). Warszawa, Państwowe Wydawnictwo Ekonomiczne, 73, 456 p.

3392    VICKERMAN, R. "The demand for non-work travel", *J. Transport Econ. Pol.* 6(2), mai 72 : 176-210.

3393    WOHL, M. *Transporation investment planning; an introduction for engineers and planners.* Lexington, Mass., Lexington Books, 72, xv-155 p.

3394    ZIELIŃSKI, Z. *Zastosowanie metod matematycznych w planowaniu i zarzadzaniu w przedsiebiorstwie transportowym* (Application of mathematical methods in the planning and management of a transport enterprise). Szczecin, Towarzystwo Naukowe, Organizacji i Kierownictwa, 73, 252 p.

### H.311    *Local studies*
         *Études localisées*

[See also / Voir aussi: 4518, 4863]

3395    BADACH, K. "Ekonometryczna prognoza przewozów ładunków do roku 1990" (Econometric forecast of goods transportation up to 1990), *Przegl. komunik.* (4), 1973 : 1-9. [Poland.]

3396  BARAT, J. "O planejamento dos transportes nas áreas metropolitanas" (Planning of transportation in metropolitan areas), *R. Adm. municip. (Rio de Janeiro)* 19(114), sep-dec 72 : 5-28. [Brazil.]

3397  BAUER, K. *Die Gleichbehandlung der Verkehrsträger durch den Staat* (State application of equal treatment to transport means). Bern-Stuttgart, Paul Haupt, 72, 158 p. [Switzerland.]

3398  BRONŠTEJN Ja. T. *Perspektivy razvitija transporta Tadzikskoj SSR (Metody i rezul'taty prognoza)* (Development prospects of Tadjik transportation. Forecast methods and results). Dušanbe, Duniš, 73, 221 p.

3399  CRVCANIN, M. "Application de modèles intégrés à la planification des systèmes de transports de la région lausannoise", *Schweizer. Z. Volkswirtsch Statist.* 109(3), sep 73 : 357-374. [Suisse.]

3400  FANO, P. L. *Il traffico urbano in Italia* (Urban traffic in Italy). Milano, F. Angeli, 72, 199 p.

3401  FARZA, A. "La situation des transports en Tunisie", *R. tunis. Sci. soc.* 9(30-31), 2-3 trim 72 : 73-101.

3402  GIANFRANCESCO, M. DI. "Politica dei transporti e sviluppo economico regionale: aspetti storici del disquilibrio italiano" (Transportation policy and regional economic development: historical aspects of the Italian imbalance), *Riv. Polit. econ.* 62(12), dec 72 : 1499-1541.

3403  GRAF, H. -G. "Zukünftige Verkehresentwicklung in der Schweiz" (The future evolution of transport in Switzerland), *Schweizer. Z. Volkswirtsch. Statist.* 109(3), sep 73 : 341-354.

3404  HEINZE, G. W.; KYPKE-BURCHARDI B. U. "Regionalstruktur und Verkahrsaufkommen Eine empirische Untersuchung" (Regional structure and development of transport. An empirical study). *Jb. soz.-Wiss.* 23(3), 1972 : 321-341. [Germany, FR.]

3405  JAROCKIJ, A. S. (ed.). *Ėkonomičeskie problemy transporta Moldavii* (Economic problems of transportation in Moldavia). Kišinev, Štiinca, 73, 148 p.

3406  JATOSTI, A. "Containers, a technological revolution in transport", *R. econ. Condit. Italy* 26(6), nov 72 : 472-489.

3407  KAIN, J. F. "How to improve urban transportation at practically no cost", *Publ. Pol.* 20(3), 1972 : 335-358. [USA.]

3408  KASPAR, J. "Dlouhodobá koncepce rozvoje dopravy" (The long term conception of the development of transportation), *Plán. Hospod.* 25(7), jul 73 : 74-82. [Czechoslovakia.]

3409  KENDALL, S. "The development of transport in Brazil", *Bank London South Amer. R.* 6(70), oct 72 : 540-550.

3410  MADEYSKI M. "Ogólnikrajowy system transportowy jako podstawa polityki i prognozy rozwojowej transportu" (The transport system), *Zesz. nauk.* 85, 1971 : 9-58. [Poland.]

3411  MEDVEDEV, V. F. "Transport v sisteme hozjajstvennogo kompleksa Belorusskoj SSR" (Transport in the Belorussian economic complex system), *Vopr. Geogr. Belorus.* (3), 1972 : 165-181.

3412  MERTINS, H. *National transportation policy in transition.* Lexington, Mass., Lexington Books, 72, xvii-224 p. [USA.]

3413  MEYER, A. "Die Eigenarten der öffentlichen Verkehrsbedienung der Stadt Tananarive" (Characteristics of public transport in Tananarive), *Schweizer. Archiv. Verkehrswiss. u. -Polit.* 28(3), sep 73 : 225-233.

3414  MILLER, D. R. (ed.). *Urban transportation policy: new perspectives.* Lexington, Mass., Lexington Books, 72, xiv-209 p.

3415  MILLS, N. B. "A look at the transportation system in the United States", *Soc. Sci. (Winfield)* 48(3), 1973 : 160-166.

3416  NENDIGUI, J. "Les problèmes des transports au Tchad", *Ét. Statist. Cameroun Afr. équat. Banque centr.* 182, mar 73 : 151-166.

3417  NORADOUNGUIAN, G. *Les entreprises de transports fluviaux, maritimes et aériens en 1969, enquête de 1970.* Paris, Institut national de la statistique et des études économiques, 72, 67 p. [France.]

3418  OLCOTT, E. "Innovative approaches to urban transportation planning", *Publ. Adm. R.* 33(3), mai-jun 73 : 215-224. [USA.]

3419  "Personal mobility and transport policy", *PEP Broadsheet* 39(542), jun 73 : 1-134. [UK.]

3420  Bibl. XXI-3570. PRUDY, H. L. *Transport competition and public policy in Canada.* CR: J. F. DUE, *J. econ. Liter.* 11(1), mar 73 : 127-129.

3511   Turczyńska, T. "Marketing w transporcie lotniczym" (Marketing in air transport), *Przegl. komunik.* (7), 1973 : 24-30.

3512   Wolley, P. K. "A cost-benefit analysis of the Concorde Project", *J. Transport Econ. Pol.* 6(3), sep 72 : 225-239. [UK—France.]

### H.38    Mass communications (economic problems and policy)
###         Moyens de communication (problèmes économiques et politiques)

#### H.380   *General studies*
####          *Études générales*

3513   "Comunità e comunicazione" (Community and communication), *Futuribili* 6(49-50), aug-sep 72 : 8-144.

3514   "Economics of information", *Amer. econ. R.* 63(2), mai 73 *Pap. and Proc.:* 31-51. With contributions by J. Hirshleifer, J. G. Telser and P. Nelson.

3515   *Économie et moyens de diffusion.* Paris, Institut de science économique appliquée, 72 702-993 p. *(Économies et Sociétés).*

3516   Fjaestad, B.; Nowak, K. *Massmedia och företagen* (Mass media and enterprises). Stockholm, Forum, 72, 395 p.

3517   Muller-Doohm, S. *Medienindustrie und Demokratie; verfassungspolitische Interpretation, sozioökonomische Analyse* (The media industry and democracy; constitutional policy interpretation and socio-economic analysis). Frankfurt-am-Main, Athenaum, 72, 278 p. [Germany, FR.]

3518   "Networks: information, communication and transportation", *Ekistics* 35(211), jun 73 : 318-384.

3519   Ruggles, R.; Ruggles, N. "Communication in economics: the media and technology", *A. econ. soc. Measurement* 1(2), apr 72 : 217-231.

#### H.381   *Radio, television*
####          *Radio, télévision*

3520   Besen, S. M.; Soligo, R. "The economics of the network-affiliate relationship in the television broadcasting industry", *Amer. econ. R.* 63(3), jun 73 : 259-268.

3521   Kieve, J. *The electric telegraphy: a social and economic history.* Newton Abbot, David and Charles, 73, 310 p.

3522   Webbink, D. "Population profits and entry in the television broadcasting industry", *J. industr. Econ.* 21(2), apr 73 : 167-176.

#### H.382   *Press and book industry*
####          *Presse et industrie du livre*

3523   Bagdikian, B. H. "The myth of newspaper poverty", *Columbia J-ism R.* mar-apr 73 : 19-25. [USA.]

3524   Brodbeck, H. *Ökonomische Wirkungen des technischen Fortschritts in der westdeutschen Druck-Industrie,* 1951-1967 (Economic repercussions of technical progress in the West German printing industry, 1951-1967). Freiburg/Schweiz, Universitatsverlag, 72, 250 p.

3525   Ossorio-Capella, C. *Der Zeitungsmarkt in der Bundesrepublik Deutschland* (The press market in the German Federal Republic). Frankfurt-am-Main, Athenaum, 72, 356 p.

#### H.383   *Entertainment industry and other pastimes*
####          *Industrie des spectacles et autres divertissements*

3526   Demmert, H. G. *The economics of professional team sports.* Lexington, Mass., Lexington Books, 73, ix-106 p.

3527   Dost, M.; Hopf, F.; Kluge, A. *Filmwirtschaft in der BRD und in Europa: Götterdämmerung in Raten* (The film industry in the German Federal Republic and in Europe; twilight of the gods on credit). München, Hanser, 73, 208 p.

3528 GARCIA MARTIN, F. "Notas sobre política económica de la cinematografía española" (Notes on the economic policy of the Spanish film industry), *Inform. com. esp.* 473, jan 73 : 95-123.

3529 JESSUA, O. "Le film au service de l'entreprise", *Hommes et Techn.* 29(339), jan 73 : 28-82.

## H.39 Domestic tourist trade, hotel business
## Tourisme intérieur, industrie hôtelière

[See also / Voir aussi: **O.323**; 3366, 4867]

3530 ADAMOWICZ, A.; BOSIAKOWSKI, Z. *Ekonomika turystyki* (Economics of tourism). Warszawa, Szkoła Główna Planowania i Statystyki, 73, 112 p.

3531 ARRIA, D. "El turismo en el marco general de la integración de América latina y sus vinculaciones con Centroamérica y el Caribe" (Tourism within the general framework of the integration of Latin America and its ties with Central America and the Carribean), *R. Integr.* 14, sep 73 : 177-188.

3532 BARETJE, R.; DEFERT, P. P. *Aspects économiques du tourisme.* Paris, Berger-Levrault, 72, 356 p.

3533 BOYER, M. *Le tourisme.* Paris, Éditions du Seuil, 72, 261 p.

3534 BRYDEN, J. M. *Tourism and development: a case study of the Commonwealth Caribbean.* Cambridge, Eng., University Press, 73, xii-236 p.

3535 CASTEX, F. *L'équipement touristique de la France.* Paris, France-Empire, 72, 604 p.

3536 DENARINIS, F. "Tourism in Italy on the eve of the expansion of the EEC", *R. econ. Condit. Italy* 26(5), sep 72 : 379-396.

3537 DESPLANQUES, H. "Une nouvelle utilisation de l'espace rural en Italie: l'agritourisme", *A. Géogr.* 82(450), mar-apr 73 : 151-164.

3538 DOVER, M. "Recreation, tourism and the farmer", *J. agric. Econ.* 24(3), sep 73 : 465-477.

3539 "Dynamique et contrainte du tourisme social", *Confronter* 14-15, sep-nov 72 : 122 p. [France.]

3540 "Hôtellerie en Normandie (L')", *Statist. Écon. normande* (4), 1972 : 30 p. [France.]

3541 KORNAK, A. *Społeczno-ekonomiczne funkcje usług turystycznych. Na przykładzie województwa bydgoskiego* (Social and economic function of tourist services. On the example of Bydgoszcz voivodship). Warszawa, Państwowe Wydawnictwo Naukowe, 72, 144 p.

3542 KRYNICKI, J. *Krajowy i zagraniczny ruch turystyczny* (Internal and foreign tourist traffic). Wrocław, Wyzsza Szkoła Ekonomiczna we Wrocławiu, 73, 246 p.

3543 LIMA FILHO, A. DE O. "O marketing de turismo: planejamento e análise sistêmica" (Tourism marketing: planning and systematic analysis), *R. Adm. Emprêsas* 13(3), sep 73 : 77-88.

3544 MARTINEZ TERRERO, J. "Futuro del turismo en América latina" (Future of tourism in Latin America), *R. Econ. latinoamer.* 9(33), 1972 : 121-141.

3545 NICOLARDI, E. "Note e considerazioni sull'ordinamento regionale del turismo" (Notes and considerations on the regional organization of tourism), *Realtà econ.* 4(7-8), jul-aug 72 : 47-52. [Italy.]

3546 OSTROWSKI, S. *Ruch turystyczny w Polsce* (Tourist traffic in Poland). 2nd rev. ed. enl. Warszawa, Sport i Turystyka, 72, 318 p.

3547 PERRIN, H. "La promotion des équipement touristiques en montagne", *Aménag. Territ. Dévelop. région.* (6), 1973 : 231-241. [France.]

3548 ROSSI, R.; BARTOLELLI, M. *Ambiente rurale. Una nuova risorsa per il turismo* (Rural environment: a new resource for tourism). Roma, Agriturist, 72, 247 p.

3549 SAINDON, J. *Recensement de la distribution de 1966: hotels, cafés, restaurants autres services.* Paris, Institut national de la statistique et des études économiques, 72, 108 p.

3550 SESSA, A. *Turismo e terzo mondo* (Tourism and Third World). Cagliari, Editrice sarda Fossataro, 72, 644 p.

3551 STRAHL, A. *Aspects économiques, sociaux et politiques du phénomçne touristique; le cas d'Israel.* Genève, Université de Genève, Faculté des sciences économiques et sociales, 72, 255 p.

3552 SURÓWKA, D. "Wpływ ruchu turystycznego na obroty jednostek handlowych w miejscowosciach turystycznych" (Influence of tourism on trade turnover in the tourist centres), *Probl. ekon.* (1), 1973 : 108-116. [Poland.]

3553 Tomati, M. *I fabbricanti di vacanze. La rivoluzione nel turismo* (The vacation merchants. Tourism revolution). Milano, F. Angeli, 73, 125 p.

3554 "Tourisme en Autriche (Le)", *Espaces* 2(8), apr-jun 72 : 5-122.

3555 "Tourisme et emploi dans les Alpes", *R. Géogr. alpine* 61(4), 1973 : 509-570.

3556 Wahab, S.-E. A. "Elements of macro-planning in tourism development", *R. Tourisme* 28(2), apr-jun 73 : 50-58.

3557 Wassé, M. "La théorie du développement de l'industrie touristique dans les pays sous-développés", *A. afr.* 1971-1972 : 53-72.


## H.4      TRADE AND DISTRIBUTION
##          COMMERCE ET DISTRIBUTION

### H.41    Economics of distribution
###         Économie de la distribution

#### H.410   *General studies*
####         *Études générales*

[See also / Voir aussi: 3643]

3558 Andrieux, P. *Distribution: le commerce indépendant.* Paris, Dunod, 72, vii-134 p.

3559 Bereznicki, M. "Tyzyko handlowe- analiza kompleksowa" (Trade risk-complex analysis), *Handel wewn.* (3), 1973 : 32-44.

3560 Cagolov, N. A. (ed.). *Tovarno-deneznye otnošenija v sisteme planomerno organizovannogo socialističeskogo proizvodstva* (Commercial and monetary relations in the socialist planned production system). Moskva, Izdatel'stvo Moskovskogo Universiteta, 71, 373 p.

3561 Cusin, G. "Alcuni aspetti della controversia sulla teoria neoclassica aggregata della distribuzione" (Some aspects of the controversy on the aggregated neoclassical theory of distribution), *Ric. econ.* 26(1-2), jan-jun 72 : 59-113.

3562 Głowacki, R. "Model nowoczesnego handlu w swietle badań nad problemem wez-łowym" (The model of modern trade in the light of research work on the basic problem), *Handel wewn.* (4), 1973 : 4-11.

3563 Gresle, F. "Éléments pour une sociologie du commerce", *R. franç. Sociol.* 13(4), oct-dec 72 : 569-576.

3564 Karpov, P. P. *Raspredelenie sredstv proizvodstva v uslovijah hozjajstvovanija* (Means of production distribution in the new economic conditions). Moskva, Ėkonomika, 72, 159 p.

3565 Klee, J.; Wendt, P. D. (eds.). *Physical Distribution im modernen Management* (Physical distribution in modern management). München, Verlag Moderne Industrie, 72, 371 p.

3566 Levin, A. I. *Socialističeskij vnutrennij rynok (Zakonomernosti i problemy razvitija)* (Socialist home market. Laws and development problems). Moskva, Mysl', 73, 270 p.

3567 Osipenkov, P. S. *Problemy socialističeskogo raspredelenija. Zakon raspredelija po trudu i mehanizm ego ispol'zovanija* (Problems of socialist distribution. The distribution law according to labour and the mechanism of its utilization). Moskva, Mysl', 72, 159 p.

3568 Pravdin, D. I. *Neproizvodstvennaja sfera: effektivnost' i stimulirovanie* (The non-productive sphere: efficiency and stimulation). Moskva, Mysl', 73, 302 p.

3569 Rama Das, R. *Introduction to physical distribution.* New Delhi, S. Chand, 73, 173 p.

3570 Saval, G. A. *Der Bertriebsweg für Konsumgüter* (The distribution network of consumer goods). Berlin, Duncker und Humblot, 72, 227 p.

3571 Smirnova, K. V. *Stimulirovanie truda v sluzbe byta* (Labour stimulations in the service industries). Moskva, Ėkonomika, 72, 64 p.

3572 Solodkov, M. V.; Poljakova, T. D.; Ovsjannikov, L. N. *Teoretičeskie problemy uslug i neproizvodstvennoj sfery pri socializme* (The services and theoretical problems of the non-productive sphere under socialism). Moskva, Izdatel'stvo moskovskogo universi-teta, 72, 348 p.

3573 Stein, H. *Arbeitsfeld Handel, Berufe zwischen Produzent und Konsument* (The field of activity of commerce, the trades between producers and consumers). Frankfurt-am-Main, Aspekte-Verlag, 72, 119 p.

3574 TRACOL, P. C. *Les canaux de distribution; le commerce indépendant isolé.* Paris, Dunod, 72, 294 p.

3575 VERBER, V. L. *Ėkonomika mehanizacii truda v torgovle* (Economics of the labour mechanization in trade). Moskva, Ėkonomika, 73, 151 p.

**H.411** *Productivity factors in commercial enterprise*
*Facteurs de productivité dans l'entreprise commerciale*

**H.4112** *Commercial techniques*
*Techniques commerciales*

**H.41121** Marketing research and studies (methodology)
Recherches et études de marché (méthodologie)

[See also / Voir aussi: 2462, 2960, 3028, 3077, 3511, 3658, 3666]

3576 ANDREASEN, A. R. (ed.). *Improving inner-city marketing.* Chicago, American Marketing Association, 72, viii-278 p.

3577 ARIOTTI, R. "Il marketing in Italia" (Marketing in Italy), *Mulino* 22(226), mar-apr 73 : 301-322.

3578 AUDY, R. *Stratégie publicitaire et marketing.* Paris, Dunod, 71, vi-118 p.

3579 BARNETT, J. (ed.). *Paths to profit; case studies in marketing success—and failure.* Princeton, Dow Jones Books, 73, 131 p.

3580 BERENSON, C.; EILBIRT, H. (eds.). *The social dynamics of marketing.* New York, Random House, 73, xiii-409 p.

3581 BIEDERMANN, E. A. *Marketing als Unternehmensstrategie eine programmierte Einführung* (Marketing as an enterprise strategy. A programmed initiation). Düsseldorf, Droste, 72, 163 p.

3582 BLAKE, R. R. *How to assess the strengths and weaknesses of marketing and sales.* Austin, Tex., Scientific Methods, 72, iv-160 p.

3583 BÖCKER, F. *Der Distributionsweg einer Unternehmung; eine Marketing-Entscheidung* (The distribution circuit of a firm: a marketing decision). Berlin, Duncker und Humblot, 72, 210 p.

3584 BOLT, G. J. *Marketing in the EEC.* London, Kogan Page, 73, 127 p.

3585 BRAND, G. T. *The industrial buying decision: implications for the sales approach in industrial marketing.* London, Cassell; New York, Wiley, 72, 134 p.

3586 BUCHMANN, K.-H. *Quantitative Planung des Marketing-Mix auf der Grundlage empirisch verfügbarer Informationen* (Quantitative planning of marketing mix on the basis of available empirical information). Berlin-New York, De Gruyter, 73, 186 p.

3587 CARLI, C. *Marketing e market research. Teoria, metodi e tecniche, strategie* (Marketing and market research. Theory, methods and techniques, strategies). Milano, F. Angeli, 72, 397 p.

3588 CHRISTOPHER, M.; WILLS, G. (eds.). *Marketing logistics and distribution planning.* London, G. Allen and Unwin, 72, 392 p.

3589 "Costs and pricing in market research", *J. Market Res. Soc.* 14(4), oct 72 : 195-241.

3590 COX, K. K.; ENIS, B. M. *The marketing research process; a managerial approach to purchasing relevant information for decision making.* Pacific Palisades, Calif., Goodyear Publishing Co., 72, xiv-622 p.

3591 CUNDIFF, E. W.; STILL, R. R.; GOVONI, N. A. P. *Fundamentals of modern marketing.* Englewood Cliffs, N. J., Prentice-Hall, 73, xii-419 p.

3592 DAVIDSON, J. H. *Offensive marketing: or how to make your competitors followers.* London, Cassell, 72, xii-308 p.

3593 DEVELEY, D. "Analyse du reproduit et politiques de marketing", *Dir. Gestion Entr.* (3), mai-jun 73 : 59-62.

3594 DIAMOND, J.; PINTEL, G. *Principles of marketing.* Englewood Cliffs, N. J., Prentice-Hall, 72, ix-402 p.

3595 DORN, D. "Marketing in der Staatswirtschaft" (Marketing and public economy), *Z. Wirtsch. u. soz.-Wiss.* 93(1), 1973 : 21-23.

3596 DRAGAN, J. C. *Marketing for Africa's development; building the peace.* Milan, Nagard, 72, 87 p.

3597   DRIHEN, E.; ISRAEL, D. *Le prix de vente d'un produit nouveau + méthodes de détermination + stratégies impliquées*. Paris, Dalloz, 72, viii-87-3 p.

3598   DUBLINIEC, E. "Techniki ankietowe w badaniach marketingowych" (Survey techniques in marketing research), *Zesz. nauk. Szkoły Plan. Statyst.* 88, 1972 : 119-144.

3599   el-ANSARY, A. I. *On the measurement of power in distribution channels*. Baton Rouge, Division of Research, College of Business Administration, Ouisiana State University, 73, iv-84 p.

3600   EVANS, R. H.; BECKMAN, M. D. (eds.). *Cases in marketing: a Canadian perspective*. Scarborough, Ont., Prdentice-Hall of Canada, 72, xiii-174 p.

3601   FISERA, J. "Le marketing en Tchécoslovaquie et dans les autres pays de l'Est", *R. Est* 3(3), jul 72 : 177-185.

3602   FISCHER-WINKELMANN, W. F. *Marketing: Ideologie oder operable Wissenschaft ?* (Marketing: ideology or operational science ?). München, Goldmann, 72, 152 p.

3603   FOGELBERG, G.; BRIDGES, J. S. *New Zealand case studies in marketing*. Wellington, Hicks, Smith, 72, 162 p.

3604   FOSTER, D. W. *Planning for products and markets*. London, Longman, 72, xx-352 p.

3605   FRYE, R. W. *Introduction to the marketing system*. San Francisco, Canfield Press, 73, xii-340 p.

3606   GOLDSTUCKER, J. L.; LA TORRE, J. R. DE. (eds.). *International marketing*. Chicago, American Marketing Association, 72, vi-117 p.

3607   GOVONI, N. A. P. (ed.). *Contemporary marketing research; perspectives and applications*. Morristown, N. J., General Learning Press, 72, xi-538 p.

3608   GRASHOF, J. F.; KELMAN, A. P. *Introduction to macro-marketing*. Columbus, Ohio, Grid, 73, 94 p.

3609   GUIRDHAM, M. *Marketing: the management of distribution channels*. Oxford-New York, Pergamon Press, 72, xvi-206 p.

3610   HANAFY, A. A. "Approaches for marketing systems development", *Égypte contemp.* 64(351), jan 73 : 79-95.

3611   HAYHURST, R. *et al. Organizational design for marketing futures*. London, Allen and Unwin, 72, 3-217 p.

3612   HILL, R. W. *Marketing technological products to industry*. Oxford-New York, Pergamon Press, 73, xii-221 p.

3613   HOPKINS, D. S. *The short-term marketing plan*. New York, Conference Board, 72, 94 p.

3614   HUGHES, G. D. *Demand analysis for marketing decisions*. Homewood, Ill., R. D. Irwin, 73, xiii-306 p.

3615   JOLSON, M. A.; HISE, R. T. *Quantitative techniques for marketing decisions*. New York, Macmillan, 73, xi-238 p.

3616   KELLEY, E. J.; LAZER, W. (eds.). *Managerial marketing; policies, strategies, and decisions*. Homewood, Ill., R. D. Irwin, 73, xiv-490 p. [Evolved from previous editions of *Managerial marketing; perspectives and viewpoints*.]

3617   KRAUTTER, J. *Marketing-Entscheidungsmodelle* (Decision models in marketing). Wiesbaden, Betriebswirtschaftlicher Verlag, 73, 197 p.

3618   KROEBER-RIEL, W. (ed.). *Marketingtheorie; verhaltensorientierte Erklärungen von Marktreaktionen* (Marketing theory; explanations oriented towards market reaction behavior). Köln, Kiepenheuer und Witsch, 72, 412 p.

3619   LAZER, W.; KELLEY, J. *Social marketing; perspectives and viewpoints*. Homewood, Ill., R. D. Irwin, 73, xiii-505 p.

3620   LEBEL, B. *Les études de marché, outil du marketing*. Paris, Éditions d'organisation, 72, 244 p.

3621   LEVY, J. "Le marketing implique-t-il une traduction fidèle des besoins du consommateur ?", *Human. et Entr.* 78, apr 73 : 25-38.

3622   LÖBER, W. *Marktommunikation; ein interdisciplinäres Modell* (Market communication: an interdisciplinary model). Wiesbaden, T. Gabler, 73, 226 p.

3623   MAKIEŁA, M. "Czy marketing jest nauka ?" (Is marketing a science ?), *Ekonomista* (3), 1973 : 677-684.

3624   MALLEN, B. E.; KIRPALANI, V.; LANE, G. *Marketing in the Canadian environment*. Scarborough, Ont., Prentice-Hall of Canada, 73, vii-296 p.

3625   MARAK, J. "Analiza korelacyjna jako metoda badania rynku wiejskiego" (Correlation analysis as a method of rural market research), *Prace nauk wyzsz. Szkoły ekon. Wrocław.* 38, 1973 : 73-91.

3626 *Marketing in a changing world; the role of market research.* Amsterdam, Esomar, 72 x-454 p.

3627 MARTIN, C. *Gestion du produit et stratégie des débouchés.* Paris, Bordas, 72, 256 p.

3628 MEINERS, D. *Einführung ins Marketing* (Introduction to marketing). München, List 72, 175 p.-1 l.

3629 MORRIS, G. P.; FRYE, R. W. (eds.). *Current marketing views.* San Francisco Canfield Press, 73, ix-374 p.

3630 NATIONAL COUNCIL OF APPLIED ECONOMIC RESEARCH. *New perspectives in marketing.* New Delhi, NCAER, 72, xii-204 p.

3631 PAŁASZEWSKA-REINDL, T.; WISNIEWSKI, A. *Organizacja badan rynku w wybranych przedsiebiorstwach handlowych* (Organization of market research in selected commercial enterprises). Warszawa, Instŝtut Handlu Wewnetrznego, 73, 188 p.

3632 REVZAN, D. A. *The marketing significance of geographical variations in wholesale-retail sales ratios: 1972 perspective.* Berkeley, Institute of Business and Economic Research, University of California, 73, viii-143 l.

3633 REMIJSEN, A. C. "De levenscyclus van het produkt en de marketingpolitiek" (Products life-cycle and marketing strategy), *Econ. soc. Tijds.* 26(5), oct 72 : 517-525.

3634 RIBAS MUNTÁN, R. *Técnicas de marketing* (Marketing techniques). Madrid, Editorial Index, 72, 781 p.

3635 RIMMER, J. O. (ed.). *Marketing in New Zealand.* Wellington, Hicks Smith, 72, xii-308 p.

3636 RISLEY, G. *Modern industrial marketing.* New York, McGraw-Hill, 72, xiv-363 p.

3637 RODGER, L. W. (ed.). *Marketing concepts and strategies in the next decade.* New York, Wiley, 73, 248 p.

3638 ROSS, D. A. *Marketing for manufacture; a study of the marketing for manufacture of New Zealand crossbred wool.* Christchurch, Wool Research Organisation of New Zealand, 71, 111 p.

3639 SCHAFFIR, K. H.; TRENTIN, H. G. *Marketing information systems.* New York, AMACOM, 73, vii-327 p.

3640 SCHRÖDER, H. J. *Grundlagen und Grundbegriffe des Marketing* (Bases and fundamental concepts of marketing). Düsseldorf, VDI-Verlag, 73, xi-127 p.

3641 SCHWARTZ, D. J. *Marketing today; a basic approach.* New York, Harcourt Brace Jovanovich, 73, sis-716 p.

3642 SEIBERT, J. C. *Concepts of marketing management.* New York, Harper and Row, 72, x-566 p.

3643 SICCA, L. *Ricerche di marketing e distribuzione commerciale* (Marketing research and trade distribution). Padova, CEDAM, 72, xii-562 p.

3644 SITTIG, C. A. *Marketing Management Informations- und Entscheidungssysteme* (Marketing management informational decision system). Neuwied, Luchterhand, 72, 205 p.

3645 STIDSEN, B.; SCHUTTE, T. F. "Marketing as a communication system: the marketing concept revisited", *J. Mkting* 36(4), oct 72 : 22-27.

3646 SZYMCZAK, J. "Miejsce i rola sales promotion w systemie marketingowym" (The place and the role of sales promotion in marketing system), *Roczn. Inst. Handlu wewn.* (4) 1973 : 79-88.

3647 THUMMEL, D. *Entwicklung einer Konzeption zur Bestimmung des langfristigstrategischen Marketing-Mix* (Development of a strategy making it possible to develop a long-term marketing-mix strategy). Bern-Stuttgart, Paul Haupt, 72, x-151 p.

3648 TULL, D. S.; ALBAUM, G. S. *Survey research: a decisional approach.* New York, Intext Educational Publishers, 73, x-244 p.

3649 TURNER, H. M. Jr. *The people motivators; consumer and sales incentives in modern marketing.* New York, McGraw-Hill, 73, ix-269 p.

3650 UHR, E. B. *Marketing problems; situations for analysis.* New York, Wiley, 73, ix-195 p.

3651 VAINER, A. *Marketingul produselor noi* (New product marketing). București, Consiliul Național pentru Știință si Tehnologie, Institutul de documentare tehnică, 72, 92 p.

3652 WALKER, B. J.; HAYNES, J. B. (eds.). *Marketing channels and institutions; readings in distribution concepts and practices.* Columbus, Ohio, Grid, 73, v-438 p.

3653 WILKIE, W. L.; PESSEMIER, E. A. *Issues in marketing's use o j multi-attribute attitude models*. Lafayette, Ind., Herman C. Krannert Graduate School of Industrial Administration, Purdue University, 72, 60-5 p.

3654    WINKLER, J. *Winkler on marketing planning*. New York, Wiley, 73, xii-291 p.

3655    WIŚNIEWSKI, A. "Organizacja i warunki sprawnego funkcjonowania analizy rynku w przedsiebiorstwie" (Organization and conditions of efficient functioning of market analysis in an enterprise), *Handel wewn.* (2), 1973 : 18-24.

3656    WIŚNIEWSKI, A. "Stan analizy rynku w przedsiębiorstwach handlowych" (Status of market research in trade enterprises), *Roczn. Handlu wewn.* (3), 1973 : 83-95.

3657    ZAGO, R. "Previsione e programmazione nel marketing dei beni strumentali" (Forecast and programming in the marketing of consumer goods), *Impresa* 14(4), jul-aug 72 : 255-261.

**H.41122**   Advertising, commercial services
           Publicité, services commerciaux

3658    BRIOSCHI, E. T. "Situazione e prospettive della publicità" (Situation and prospects of advertising), *Vita e Pensiero* 55(3), mai-jun 72 : 30-38.

3659    BUELL, V. P. *Changing practices in advertising decision-making and control*. New York, Association of National Advertisers, 73, ix-114 p.

3660    BURKE, J. D. *Advertising in the marketplace*. New York, Gregg Division, McGraw-Hill, 73, 440 p.

3661    COHEN, M. "La publicité en question", *Hum. et Entr.* 78, apr 73 : 65-88.

3662    COHEN, M. *Vers un nouveau style de publicité*. Paris, Dunod, 73, iv-117 p.

3663    DUBOIS, M. *La publicité en question*. Paris, Bordas, 72, 223 p.

3664    ELKIN, F. *Rebels and colleagues; advertising and social change in French Canada*. Montreal, McGill-Queen's University Press, 73, xii-227 p.

3665    ESNAOLA, J. R. "La publicidad en 1972" (Advertising in 1972), *Estud. empresar.* 24(3), dec 72 : 45-63.

3666    GÉRARD, A. B. L. *La publicité; branche-clé du marketing*. Paris, Dunod, 72, xii-204 p.

3667    GROSSE, W. H. *How industrial advertising and promotion can increase marketing power*. New York, AMACOM, 73, xi-141 p.

3668    HERMANNS, A. *Sozialisation durch Werbung; Sozialisationswirkung von Werbeaussagen in Massenmedien* (Socialization through advertising; the socializing effect of advertising methods in the mass media). Düsseldorf, Bertelsmann Universitatsverlag, 72, 140 p.

3669    HOFMANN, H. J. *Oligopolistische Werbepolitik unter dem Einfluss potentieller Konkurrenz* (Oligopolistic advertising policy under the influence of potential competition). Göttingen, Vandenhoeck und Ruprecht, 72, ix-133 p.

3670    HURWOOD, D. L.; BROWN, J. K. *Some guidelines for advertising budgeting*. New York, The Conference Board, 72, iii-65 p.

3671    INGLIS, F. *The imagery of power: a critique of advertising*. London, Heinemann, 72, x-139-10 p.

3672    MILLER, R. A. "Advertising and competition: some neglected aspects", *Antitrust B.* 17(2), 1972 : 467-478.

3673    PENINOU, G. *Intelligence de la publicité. Étude sémiotique*. Paris, R. Laffont, 72, 303 p.

3674    RENNER, J. *Werbung bei Jugendlichen* (Advertising among the young). Wiesbaden, Betriebswirtschaftlicher Verlag, 72, 178 p.

3675    SARGENT, H. W. (ed.). *Frontiers of advertising theory and research*. Palo Alto, Calif., Pacific Books, 72, 191 p.

3676    SOROKINA, R. I. *Planirovanie i effektivnost' torgovoj reklamy* (Commercial advertising planning and efficiency). Moskva, Ėkonomika, 72, 77 p.

3677    SZTUCKI, T. "System reklamy—jego elementy i struktura" (Publicity system—its components and structure), *Roczn. Handlu wewn.* (3), 1973 : 60-77.

3678    UNWIN, S. "A synchronistic theory of advertising", *J. Mkting* 36(4), oct 72 : 16-21.

**H.41123**   Salesmanship, sales techniques
           Techniques de vente

        [See also / Voir aussi: 3573, 3582]

3679    BOLT, G. J. *Market and sales forecasting—a total approach*. London, Kegan Page Ltd; New York, Halsted Press Division, 72, 359 p.

3680 BROWNE, J. *The used-car game: a sociology of the bargain.* Lexington, Mass., Lexington Books, 73, xvii-184 p.

3681 CASTAGNOL, Y. *Principes et pratique de la promotion des ventes.* Paris, J. Delmas, 72, pagination multiple.

3682 CHRISTENSEN, N. C. *The magic power of command selling: how to take charge of the sale.* West Nyack, N. Y., Parker Publishing Co., 73, 204 p.

3683 DODGE, H. R. *Field sales management; text and cases.* Dallas, Business Publications, 73, xii-355 p.

3684 DUMONT, G. F. *La force de vente de l'entreprise; statut, formation, et rémunération des représentants.* Paris, Les Éditions d'organisation, 73, 114 p.

3685 DUNN, A. H.; JOHNSON, E. M. *Managing the sales force.* Morristown, N. J., General Learning Press, 73, viii-225 p.

3686 EISEMANN, F. *Usages de la vente commerciale internationale (incoterms).* Paris, Éditions Jupiter, 72, 318 p.

3687 MATOSSIAN, P. D. *Pronósticos de ventas* (Sales forecasting). Buenos Aires, Centro Internacional de Información Económica, 72, vii-216 p.

3688 MAUSER, F. F. *Salesmanship: a contemporary approach.* New York, Harcourt Brace Jovanovich, 73, xi-287 p.

3689 POKEMPNER, S. J. *Information systems for sales and marketing management.* New York, The Conference Board, 73, v-81 p.

3690 ULLRICH, L. *Verkaufsförderung für Investitionsgüter* (Sales promotion for investment goods). Wiesbaden, Betriebswirtschaftlicher Verlag Gabler, 72, 188 p.

3691 ZIMMERLI, H. *Verkaufsplanung. Eine modelltheoretische Betrachtung* (Sales planning. A theoretical model study). Winterthur, Hans Schellenberg, 72, xxviii-282 p.

### H.412 *Forms of commercial enterprise (legal status)*
*Formes d'entreprise commerciale (status légal)*

### H.4122 *Consumer co-operatives*
*Coopératives de consommation*

[See also / Voir aussi: 3725, 4567]

3692 ABDURAHIMOV, I. T. *Pribyl' i rentabel'nost' i kooperativnoj torgovle* (Profit and efficiency in cooperative trade). Moskva, Ėkonomika, 73, 143 p.

3693 BOCZAR K. *Spółdzielczosc zaopatrzenia i zbytu jako cznynnik rozwoju ekonomicznego i społecznego wsi polskiej* (Supply and marketing co-operatives as a factor of economic and social development of Poland). Warszawa, Centrala Rolniczych Spółdzielni, 73, 62 p.

3694 "Consumer's co-operation", *Maharashtra co-op. Quart.* 56(1-2), oct 72-jan 73 : 135-173. [India.]

3695 GARBACIK, E. *Spółdzielczošč spožywców w Polsce Ludowej* (Consumers' co-operatives in the Polish People's Republic). Warszawa, Centrala Rolnicza Spółdzielni, 73, 149 p.

3696 GOYAL, S. K. *Consumers' cooperative movement in India.* Meerut, Meenakshi Prakashan, 72, xi-228 p.

3697 MARECKI, J. (ed.). *Kierowanie działalnością spółdzielni spozywców* (Management of the activity of consumers co-operatives). Warszawa, Społem, 73, 195 p.

3698 MARECKI, J. (ed.). *Kierunki działalności spółdzielczości spožywców* (Trends in activity of consumers co-operatives). Warszawa, Centrala Rolniczych Spółdzielni, 72, 285 p.

3699 NOAWCKI, S. "Problemy zarządzania handlem spółdzielczym" (Problems of co-operative trade management), *Spółd. Kwartal. Nauk.* (3), 1973 : 51-67.

3700 PANKRATOV, F. G. *Povyšenie ėffektivnosti optovoj torgovli potrebitel'skoj kooperacii* (Elevation of efficiency of consumer co-operative wholesale trade). Moskva, Ėkonomika, 72, 143 p.

3701 PUTINCEV, A. I. *Kooperativnaja torgovlja promyšlennymi tovarami* (Cooperative trade of industrial goods). Moskva, Ėkonomika, 73, 96 p.

3702 RUWWE, H.-F. *Die Stellung der Konsumgenossenschaften im Sozialismus Osteuropas.* (Position of consumer co-operatives in Eastern European socialism). Tübingen, Mohr, 72, viii-206 p.

3703  SOLOMAHA, L. K. *Problemy razvitija i soveršentvovanija material'no-tehničeskoj bazy kooperativnoj torgovli* (Problems of development and improvement of the material and technical basis of co-operative trade). Moskva, Ékonomika, 72, 134 p.

3704  Bibl. XXI-3805. TEUBER, H. *Führungsgrundlagen in einer Einkaufsgenossenschaft* (Bases for operating in a purchasing co-operative). CR: W.W. ENGELHARDT, *Kölner Z. Soziol. u. soz.-Psychol.* 25(3), sep 73 : 665-666.

### H.413    Management of the commercial enterprise
### Gestion de l'entreprise commerciale

#### H.4130    General studies
#### Études générales

3705  BORZĘCKI, M. *et al.* "Próba oceny przydatności systemu informatycznego dla kierowania i zarzadzania przedsiębiorstvem handlowym" (Evaluation of the information system in the management of a trade enterprise), *Roczn. Inst. Handlu wewn.* (4), 1972 : 23-47.

3706  DRAG, M. *Planowanie w przedsiębiorstwach handlowych* (Planning in commercial enterprises). Warszawa, Państwowe Wydawnictwo Ekonomiczne, 73, 250 p.

3707  GRYZANOV, Ju. P.; FANICKIJ, A. I. *Upravlenie tovarnymi zapasami v torgovle* ((Management of commercial stores in trade). Moskva, Ékonomika, 73, 215 p.

3708  KLOG, M. "Aspekty metodologiczne oceny wydajnosci sklepów" (Methodological aspects of the evaluation of shop efficiency), *Handel wewn.* (4), 1973 : 29-39.

3709  MICHALSKI, E. "Podejmowanie decyzji w przedsiębiorstwie handlowym" (Decision making in commercial enterprises), *Prace nauk. wyższ. Szkoly ekon. Wrocław.* 38, 1973 : 121-137.

3710  MISIAG, F. "Koncepcja integrowanego przedsiębiorstwa handlowego" (Conception of an integrated trade enterprise), *Roczn. Inst. Handlu wewn.* (2), 1973 : 57-80.

3711  NOWACKI, S. "System zarządzania przedsiębiorstwami handlu państwowego" (Management system of state trade enterprises), *Handel wewn.* (5), 1973 : 1-13.

3712  NUROWSKI, H. *Analiza gospodarki przedsiębiorstw handlowych* (Analysis of the activity of commercial enterprise). 2nd enl. ed. Warszawa, Państwowe Wydawnictwo Ekonomiczne, 73, 326 p.

3713  PAŃKÓW, W. "Procesy organizačjne i kierownicze w zintegrowanych przedsiębiorstwach handlowych" (Organization and management process in an integrated trade enterprise), *Roczn. Inst. Handlu wewn.* (2), 1973 : 81-104.

3714  SKOVORODA, K. M. *Ékonomičeskie metody upravlenija torgovlej* (Economic methods of trade management). Moskva, Ékonomika, 73, 118 p.

3715  SZCZEPAŃSKI, J.; SZYSZKO, L. "Rola marży w parametrycznym systemie zarządzania handlem" (The role of margin in the parametric system of trade management), *Finanse* (4), 1973 : 58-62.

3716  ŻAKOWSKI, W. "Nowy system zarządzania w przedsiębiorstwach handlowych" (A new system of management in commercial enterprises), *Probl. Ekon. (Warszawa)* (4), 1973 : 27-39.

#### H.4131    Economic calculation, costs of distribution, profit margins
#### Calcul économique, coûts de distribution, marges bénéficiaires

[See also / Voir aussi: 3700, 3774]

3717  BOGACKA-KISIEL, E. "Wpływ marży na rentowność przedsiębiorstwa handlowego" (Impact of margin on the profitability of a commercial enterprise), *Prace nauk. wyższ. Szkoły ekon. Wrocław.* 36, 1973 : 53-69.

3718  BOGUSŁAWSKI, M. "Kompleksowe zmiany systemu ekonomiczno-finansowego w handlu wewnętrznym" (Complex changes of the economic-financial system in home trade), *Handel wewn.* (3), 1973 : 1-22.

3719  BUDZICH, E. *Efektywność wykorzystania środków gospodarczych w przedsiębiorstwie handlowym* (Efficiency of economic means in commercial enterprises). Warszawa, Biblioteka Instytutu Handlu Wewnętrznego, 72, 169 p.

3720 ČEKALIN, A. H.; MORGUN, S. F.; GRIŠČENKO, G. A. *Material'noe stimulirovanie na predprijatijah bytovogo obluživanija* (Material incentives in services enterprises). Moskva, Legkaja industrija, 73, 160 p.

3721 CHIPMAN, J. S.; MOORE, J. C. "Social utility and the gains from trade", *J. int. Econ.* 2(2), mai 72 : 157-172.

3722 FONAREV, É. N. *Finansovye problemy gosudarstvennoj torgovli* (Financial problems of State trade). Moskva, Finansy, 72, 176 p.

3723 GRANDMONT, J. M.; MCFADDEN, D. "A technical note on classical gains from trade", *J. int. Econ.* 2(2), mai 72 : 109-125.

3724 IVANYTS'KYJ, V. I.; UŠANKOVA, N. N. *Planirovanie kapital'nyh vloženij v torgovle* (Capital investments planning in trade). Moskva, Ékonomika, 72, 71 p.

3725 KOROPOV, L. S.; PINIŠKO, V. S. *Normirovanie oborotnyh sredstv v potrebitel'skoj kooperacii* (Norms elaboration of circulating assets in a consumer cooperative). Moskva, Ékonomika, 73, 120 p.

3726 LOKŠIN, R. A. *O povyšenii ekonomičeskoj effektivnosti torgovli* (On trade economic efficiency elevation). Moskva, Ékonomika, 72, 80 p.

3727 ŚLEDZIŃSKI, A. "Kierunki doskonalenia systemu finansowego przedsiębiorstw handlu srodkami produkcji" (Lines of improvement in the financial system of means of production in trade enterprises), *Finanse* (4), 1973 : 13-28.

3728 SZCZEPAŃSKI, J.; SZYSZKO, L. "Przedmiot i zadania gospodarki finansowej przedsiębiorstw handlowych" (Scope and goals of financial economy of trade enterprises), *Finanse* (2), 1973 : 1-8.

3729 WAN, H. Y. "A note on trading gains and externalities", *J. int. Econ.* 2(2), mai 72 : 173-180.

### H.4132  Procurement and stocks
*Achat et stocks*

3730 CAŁCZYŃSKI, A. "Metody ustalania poziomu zapasów w przedsiębiorstwie handlowym" (Methods of modelling the stock level in a trade enterprise), *Handel wewn.* (4), 1973 : 12-21; (5), 1973 : 31-41.

3731 HAGIAC, R.; GEORGESCU, I. *Mecanizarea si automatizarea depozitelor industriale si comerciale* (Mechanization and automation of the warehouse industry and trade). Bucuresti, Consiliul National pentru Stiinta si Tehnologie, Institutul central de documentare tehnica, 72, 120 p.

3732 KEMPLIŃSKI, A. *Zapasy nieprawidłowe* (Excessive stocks). Warszawa, Państwowe Wydawnictwo Ekonomiczne, 73, 209 p.

3733 THURSTON, P. H. "Les plans de besoins dans la gestion des stocks", *Dir. Gestion Entr.* (3), mai-jun 73 : 25-30.

3734 ZIEG, K. C. Jr.; ZIEG, S. H. *Profile of a growth stock; a method of security selection for large capital appreciation.* Larchmont, N. Y., Investors Intelligence, 72, 111 p.

### H.4133  Commercial bookkeeping
*Comptabilité commerciale*

[See also / Voir aussi: 3765]

3735 BURZYM, E. et al. *Rachunkowość przedsiebiorstw handlowych* (Accounting of commercial enterprises). Warszawa, Państwowe Wydawnitwo Naukowe, 73, 283 p.

### H.414  **Internal trade policy**
**Politique du commerce intérieur**

[See also / Voir aussi: 3749]

3736 DANECKI, J. "Przesłanki i założenia perspektywicznej polityki podziału" (Premises and assumptions of the prospective policy of distribution), *Stud. socjol.* 48(1), 1973 : 5-48.

3737 GREGOR, B. *Rynek artykułów do produkcji rolnej w warunkach szybkiej industrializacji* (Market of articles for agricultural production under conditions of rapid industrialization). Warszawa, Centrala Rolniczych Spółdzielni, 72, 230 p.

3738  SZTUCKI, T. "Model organizacji zintegrowanego przedsiębiorstwa handlowegi i jego usytuowania w branżowym systemie handlowym" (Model of organization of an integrated commercial enterprise and its place in a trade system based on fragmentation according to product lines), *Roczn. Inst. Handlu wewn.* (2), 1973 : 4-55.

3739  WRZOSEK, W. "Przemiany strukturalne w handlu" (Structural changes in trade), *Zesz. nauk. Szkoły główn. Plan. Statyst.* 89, 1972 : 31-56.

### H.4141    *Problem of the cost of distribution*
###             *Problème du coût de la distribution*

3740  NOWAKOWSKA, A. "Analiza porównawcza kosztów handlu państwowego i spółdzielczego" (Comparative analysis of costs in socialized and co-operative trade), *Zesz. nauk. wyzsz. Szkoły ekon. Krakow.* 53, 1972 : 67-90.

### H.42    Internal trade, descriptive studies
###         Commerce intérieur, études déscriptives

### H.420    *General studies*
###          *Études générales*

3741  BÖDECKER, W. *Allokations- und Distributionsprobleme bei Kollektivgütern* (Problems posed by allocation and distribution of collective goods). Meisenheim-am-Glan, A. Hain, 72, 190 p.

3742  "Commerce intérieur français (Le)", *Docum. franç. illustr.* 275, oct 72 : 5-95.

3743  DESPAX, A. "Les sociétés françaises de distribution en 1971", *Coopération* 42(10-11), oct-nov 72 : 23-51.

3744  EISLER, P. "The tertiary sphere and economic growth in the USA", *East. Europ. Econ.* 10(3), 1972 : 277-362.

3745  FABIUNKE, G.; MANN, P.; UHLIG, K.-H. *Der Binnenhandel im staatsmonopolistischen Kapitalismus der BRD* (Internal trade in the framework of state monopoly capitalism in the German Federal Republic). Berlin, Verlag Die Wirtschaft, 72, 208 p.

3746  FANSTEN, M. *L'évolution du commerce français depuis 1962 d'après l'opinion des commerçants.* Paris, Institut national de la statistique et des études économiques, 72, 212 p.

3747  HODOLY, A. "Funkcjonowanie, organizacja i kierunki rozwoju handlu wewnętrznego w Polsce" (Performance, organization and lines of development of internal trade in Poland), *Roczn. Inst. Handlu wewn.* (3), 1973 : 5-10.

3748  JAMPEL, W. "Le commerce intérieur de la Pologne", *R. Est* 4(1), jan 73 : 73-117.

3749  KAZARSKAJA, N. I.; LOBOVIKOV, Ju. V.; ČISTOV, G. Ja. *Ėkonomika i planirovanie sovetskoj torgovli* (Economics and planning of Soviet trade). Moskva, Ėkonomika, 73, 320 p.

3750  OFER, G. *The service sector in Soviet economic growth; a comparative study.* Cambridge, Mass., Harvard University Press, 73, xi-202 p.

3751  QUIN, C. "Le commerce en France à l'horizon 1980", *Coopération* 42(10-11), oct-nov 72 : 7-15.

3752  SOROKINA, V. F. *Vnutrennjaja torgovlja Anglii* (England's interior trade). Moskva, Nauka, 72, 188 p.

3753  ZALA, F. "A fogyasztói piac és a belkereskedelem" (The consumption market and home trade), *Közgazd. Szle* 20(7-8), jul-aug 73 : 919-933. [Hungary.]

### H.421    *Wholesale trade*
###          *Commerce de gros*

[See / Voir: 3632, 3700]

### H.422    *Retail trade*
###          *Commerce de détail*

[See also / Voir aussi: 3632]

3754  ARNDT, J. "Temporal lags in comparative retailing", *J. Mkting* 36(4), oct 72 : 40-45.

3755  BESNARD, M. *De la boutique au supermarché: pâtir ou prospérer.* Niort, Nicolas-Imbert, 72, 95-1 p.

3756 BODEWYN, J. J.; HOLLANDER, S. C. (eds.). *Public policy toward retailing: an international symposium.* Lexington, Mass., Lexington Books, 72, vii-482 p.

3757 BÖTTCHER, H.-J. *Kreditierung als Instrument der Absatzsicherung im Einzelhandel* (The credit card; an instrument making it possible to consolidate outlets in retail trade). Berlin, Duncker und Humblot, 73, 182 p.

3758 FRANCE. Commission des comptes commerciaux de la nation. *Le commerce de détail dans la distribution.* Paris, Institut national de la statistique et des études économiques, 71, 93 p.

3759 GREIPL, E. *Einkaufszentren in der Bundesrepublik Deutschland; Bedeutung sowie Grundlagen und Methoden ihrer ökonomischen Planung* (Shopping centers in the German Federal Republic; bases and methods of their economic planning). Berlin, Duncker und Humblot, 72, 210 p.

3760 HAUBOLD, O. "Kierunki rozwoju domów towarowych w wybranych krajach kapitalistycznych" (Development directions of department stores in selected capitalist countries), *Roczn. Inst. Handlu wewn.* (4), 1972 : 3-13.

3761 HAUBOLD, O.; OLESIŃSKA, I. "Domy towarowa w Polsce jako przodująca forma handlu detalicznego" (Department stores in Poland—a leading form of retailing), *Roczn. Inst. Handlu wewn.* (3), 1973 : 11-32.

3762 HAVENGA, J. J. D. *Retailing: competition and trade practices.* Leiden, A. W. Sijthoff, 73, viii-254 p.

3763 JANKE, D.; FRÖBRICH, H. *Technologie und Arbeitsorganisation im Einzelhandel* (Technology and work organization in retail trade). Berlin, Verlag Die Wirtschaft, 72, 132 p. [Germany, DR.]

3764 JOHANSEN, H. E.; FUGUITT, G. V. "Changing retail activity in Wisconsin villages: 1939-1954-1970", *Rur. Sociol.* 39(2), 1973 : 207-218. [USA.]

3765 JURICH, W.; STÖCKL, B.; GRASOWSKI, H. *Wirtschaftliche Rechnungsführung im Konsumgüterbinnenhandel* (Economic accounting in internal trade of consumer goods). Berlin, Verlag Die Wirtschaft, 72, 136 p.

3766 KARSTEN, H.; PETERS, H. *Die Kaufhalle; Entwicklung, Leitung, Organisation, Technologie* (The department store; development, management, organization and technology). Berlin, Verlag Die Wirtschaft, 72, 197 p.

3767 KOPYŚ, U. "Analiza wielkosci i stopnia wykorzystania powierzchni wiejskich sklepów samoobsługowych" (Analysis of the size and degree of utilisation of the rural self-service stores), *Roczn. Inst. Handlu wewn.* (4), 1972 : 72-81.

3768 KRASIŃSKI, Z. "Zróżnicowanie w stanie zapasów i cyklu dostaw towarowych w sieci detalicznej handlu wiejskiego i miejskiego" (Differentiation in the stockpiling and goods supply cycle of the retail trade network in the country and in towns), *Zesz. nauk. wyzsz. Szkoły ekon. Poznan.* 45, 1973 : 43-58.

3769 KRAUSE, E.; POHLHAUS, J. *Sortimentsbestimmung im Einzelhandelsbetrieb* (Determination of merchandise assortment in retail trade). Berlin, Verlag Die Wirtschaft, 72, 157 p.

3770 LUNI, P. *L'impermercato* (The supermarket). Milano, F. Angeli, 72, 260 p.

3771 MERCIOIU, V. "Čai privind modernizarea retelei comerciale cu amanuntul" (Ways of modernizing the retail trade network), *Stud. Čerc. econ.* (4), 1971 : 103-113. [Rumania.]

3772 NIKITIN, V. M. *Planirovanie rozničnogo tovarooborota* (Retail trade planning). Moskva, Ėkonomika, 72, 80 p.

3773 ORGEIG, H. D. *Der Einzelhandel in den Cities von Duisburg, Düsseldorf, Köln und Bonn* (Retail trade in the cities of Duisburg, Düsseldorf, Köln and Bonn). Wiesbaden, F. Steiner, 72, ix-164 p.

3774 PETROV, G. V. *Tovarooborot i pribyl'. Puti povyšenija rentabel'nosti rozničnoj torgovli* (Trade and profit. Means of retail trade efficiency elevation). Leningrad, Lenizdat, 73, 216 p.

3775 STAUCH, B. *Langfritige Entwicklungstendenzen im Einzelhandel* (Long-term development trends in retail trade). Winterthur, Hans Schellenberg, 72, xvi-174 p. [Switzerland.]

3776 TANBURN, J. *Superstores in the 70's: a comparison of shopping developments in Britain and the Common Market.* London, Lintas, 72, x-42 p.

3777 WADINAMBIARATCHI, G. H. "Theories of retail development", *Soc. econ. Stud.* 21(4), dec 72 : 391-403.

3778 WALUDA, B. "Doskonalenie lokalizacji i asortymentacji detalu wiejskiego" (Improvement of country retail trade localization and assortment of goods), *Handel wewn.* (5), 1973 : 42-49.

# I PRICE AND MARKETS
# PRIX ET MARCHÉS

## I.1 BASIC CONCEPTS
## CONCEPTS DE BASE

### I.11 Value
### Valeur

[See also / Voir aussi: 4464, 5476]

3779 AMIN, S. *La fin d'un débat, l'échange inégal et la loi de la valeur*. Paris, Anthropos, 73, 190 p.

3780 DOBB, M. H. *Theories of value and distribution since Adam Smith; ideology and economic theory*. Cambridge, Eng., University Press, 293 p.

3781 HUDOKORMOV, G. N. *Obščestvennaja stoimost' i zakupočnye ceny* (Social value and purchase prices). Moskva, Mys'l, 73, 263 p.

3782 INAMOV, M. "Obščestvennaja potrebitel'naja stoimost' i socialističeskaja rentabel'nost' " (The social use value and the socialist efficiency), *Nauč. Zap. Taškent. Inst. nar. Hoz.* (3), 1972 : 113-125.

3783 MANFRA, L. "La teoria del valore e lo 'scambio ineguale' " (The theory of value and the 'unequal exchange'), *Crit. sociol. (Roma)* 23, 1972 : 151-173.

3784 NEILL, R. *A new theory of value: the Canadian economics of H. A. Innis*. Toronto-Buffalo, University of Toronto Press, 72, viii-159 p. CR: W. J. SAMUELS, *J. econ. Liter.* 11(3), sep 73 : 904-906.

3785 STEPHENSON, M. A. "The paradox of value: a suggested interpretation", *Hist. polit. Econ.* 4(1), 1972 : 127-139.

3786 VECCHIS, F. DE. "Un articolo di Bortkiewicz sul metodo marxiano di trasformazione dei valori in prezzi" (An article by Bortkiewicz on Marxian method of the transformation of values into prices), *R. int. Sociol. (Roma)* 8(2-3), 1972 : 77-88.

3787 WALTON, P.; GAMBLE, A. *From alienation to surplus value*. London, Sheed and Ward, 72, xii-241 p.

3788 WISWEDE, G. "Rationalität und soziales Wertsystem" (Rationality and social value system), *Z. Wirtsch.- u. soz.-Wiss.* 92(4), 1972 : 385-392.

### I.12 Price
### Prix

[See also / Voir aussi: 3786, 4465]

3789 BEAR, R. M. "Margin levels and the behavior of futures prices", *J. financ. quant. Anal.* 7(4), sep 72 : 1907-1930.

3790 BRUTUS, L. "O dialektičeskoj prirode cen. Zavisimost' cen ot tempov vosproizvodstva" (About the dialectic nature of prices. Dependence of prices from the reproduction rates), *Trudy Tallinsk. politehn. Inst.* (9), 1972 : 29-50.

3891 CHACKO, D. *Price*. New York, St Martin's Press, 73, 279 p.

3792 COLLARD, D. A. *Prices, markets and welfare*. London, Faber; New York, Crane, Russak, 72, viii-210 p.

3793 GALATIN, M. "A true price index when the consumer saves", *Amer. econ. R.* 63(1), mar 73 : 185-194.

3794 GAL'PERIN, V. M. "Concerning certain properties of prices", *Matekon* 8(4), 1972 : 339-354.

3795    MAJUMDAR, M. "Some general theorems on efficiency prices with an infinite-dimensional commodity space", *J. econ. Theory* 5(1), aug 72 : 1-13.

3796    MALINVAUD, E. "Prices for individual consumption, quantity indicators for collective consumption", *R. econ. Stud.* 39(4), oct 72 : 385-405.

3797    MARIN, E. *La teoría de precios en los sistemas económicos capitalista y socialista* (Price theory in capitalist and socialist economic systems). Mendoza, Universidad Nacional de Cuyo, Facultad de Ciencias Económicas, 72, 41-3 p.

3798    MOORE, M. "Stigler on inflexible prices", *Canad. J. Econ.* 5(4), nov 72 : 486-493.

3799    NEEL, R. E. (ed.). *Readings in price theory.* Cincinnati, South-Western Publishing Co., 73, vi-554 p.

3800    PRESCOTT, E. C.; LUCAS, R. E. "A note on price systems in finite dimensional space", *Int. econ. R.* 13(2), jun 72 : 416-422.

## I.13    Exchange
##        Échange

[See also / Voir aussi: 3783]

3801    JACOBS, P.; ZABALZA, A. "Conducta individual y mercado. Una nueva aproximación a la teoría del intercambio" (Industrial behaviour and market. A new approach to the theory of exchange), *Moneda y Créd.* 121, jun 72 : 3-22.

## I.2    MARKETS AND PRICE FORMATION
##      MARCHÉS ET FORMATION DU PRIX

### I.21    Theory
###       Théorie

### I.211    *Market*
###        *Le marché*

### I.2111    *Supply and demand*
###         *Offre et demande*

[See also / Voir aussi: 3792, 3840]

3802    GLAIS, M. *La notion de demande à l'entreprise.* Tours, Mame, 72, 142 p.

3803    KRUTIKOV, F. A. (ed.). *Izučenia sprosa v socialističeskih stranah* (Demand study in socialist countries). Moskva, Ékonomika, 72, 136 p.

3804    McCALLUM, B. T. "Inventory holdings, rational expectations, and the law of supply and demand", *J. polit. Econ.* 80(2), mar-apr 72 : 386-393.

3805    MOSENSON, R.; DROR, E. "A solution to the qualitative substitution problem in demand theory", *R. econ. Stud.* 39(4), oct 72 : 433-441.

3806    NEFEDOV, V. K. *Statističeskoe nabljudenie sprosa* (The statistical study of demand) Moskva, Ékonomika, 72, 72 p.

3807    PERIMAN, R. *Theory of markets.* Hindsdale, Ill., Dryden Press, 72, viii-124 p.

3808    TAYLOR, L. D.; WEISERBS, D. "On the estimation of dynamic demand functions", *R. Econ. Statist.* 54(4), nov 72 : 459-465.

3809    WOLFFRAM, R. *Die Irreversibilität von Angebots- und Nachfragefunktionen* (The irreversibility of supply and demand functions). Hamburg, P. Parey, 72, 86 p.

3810    YEUNG, P. "A note on the rules of derived demand", *Quart. J. Econ.* 86(3), aug 72 : 511-517.

### I.2112    *Techniques of analysis: indifference, preference, substitution, complementarity,*
###         *elasticity*
###         *Techniques d'analyse: indifférence, préférence, substitution, complémentarité,*
###         *élasticité*

[See also / Voir aussi: **L.211**; 3805]

3811    BEHRMAN, J. R. "Sectoral elasticities of substitution between capital and labor in a developing economy: time series analysis in the case of postwar Chile", *Econometrica* 40(2), mar 72 : 311-326.

3812    Bose, S. "A new proof of the non-substitution theorem", *Int. econ. R.* 13(1), feb 72 :
        183-186.

3813    Graham, D. A.; Jacobson, E.; Weintraub, E. R. "Transactions costs and the conver-
        gence of a 'trade out of equilibrium' adjustment process", *Int. econ. R.* 13(1), feb 72 :
        123-131.

3814    Kohn, R. E. "Price elasticities of demand and air pollution control", *R. Econ. Statist.*
        54(4), nov 72 : 392-400.

3815    Koo, A. Y.; Hasenkamp, G. "Structure of revealed preference: some preliminary
        evidence", *J. polit. Econ.* 80(4), jul-aug 72 : 724-744.

3816    Lackman, C. L. "A note on the derivation of price elasticity from the response of total
        revenue to price changes", *Amer. Economist* 16(2), 1972 : 175.

3817    Manera, G. *Analisi della domanda. Teoria e metodi* (Demand analysis. Theory and
        methods). Milano, A. Giuffre, 72, 308 p.

3818    Noe, N. N.; Furstenberg, G. M. "The upward bias in the consumer price index due to
        substitution", *J. polit. Econ.* 80(6), nov-dec 72 : 1280-1286.

3819    Sato, R.; Koizumi, T. "On the elasticities of substitution and complementarity",
        *Oxford econ. Pap.* 25(1), mar 73 : 44-56.


**I.212    Forms of market and patterns of price formation**
           *Formes de marché et modes de formation du prix*

        **I.2120    General studies**
                    *Études générales*

        [See also / Voir aussi: 4594]

3820    Abt, S. *Matematyczno-statystyczne podstawy analizy rynku* (Mathematical-statistical
        basis of market analysis). Warszawa, Państwowe Wydawnictwo Ekonomiczne, 72,
        298 p.

3821    Baron, D. P. "Limit pricing, potential entry, and barriers to entry", *Amer. econ. R.*
        63(4), sep 73 : 666-674.

3822    Bollobás, B.; Stern, N. "The optimal structure of market areas", *J. econ. Theory* 4(2),
        apr 72 : 174-179.

3823    Cartell, J.; Cossé, P.-T. *La concurrence capitaliste*. Paris, Éditions du Seuil, 73, 179 p.

3824    Castellino, O. (ed.). *Economie di mercato ed economie socialiste* (Market economy and
        socialist economies). Torino, G. Giappichelli, 72, 167 p.

3825    Ehrlich, I.; Becker, G. S. "Market insurance, self-insurance, and self-protection",
        *J. polit. Econ.* 80(4), jul-aug 72 : 623-648.

3826    Emmerson, R. D. "Optima and market equilibria with indivisible commodities", *J.
        econ. Theory* 5(2), oct 72 : 177-188.

3827    Hebert, R. F. "History of the law of market area", *Quart. J. Econ.* 86(4), nov 72 : 563-
        571.

3828    Herdzina, K. "Marktstruktur und Wettbewerb" (Market structure and competition),
        *Z. Wirtsch.- u. soz.-Wiss.* 93(3), 1973 : 267-283.

3829    Hess, A. C. "Experimental evidence on price formation in competitive markets", *J.
        polit. Econ.* 80(2), mar-par 72 : 375-385.

3830    Ireland, N. J. "Concentration and the growth of market demand: a comment on
        Gaskins' limit pricing model", *J. econ. Theory* 5(2), oct 72 : 303-305.

3831    Laden, B. E. "Excess demand and average cost explanations for price change", *Quart.
        R. Econ. Busin.* 12(4), 1972 : 7-18.

3832    Lange, M. *Preisbildung bei neuen Produkten* (Price formation with new products). Berlin,
        Duncker und Humblot, 72, 199 p.

3833    Magee, S. P. "Factor market distortions, production, and trade: a survey", *Oxford
        econ. Pap.* 25(1), mar 73 : 1-43.

3834    Mynarski, S. *Cybernetyczne aspekty analizy rynku* (Cybernetic aspects of market ana-
        lysis). Warszawa, Państwowe Wydawnictwo Naukowe, 73, 223 p.

3835    Mynarski, S. *Metody analizy rynku* (Methods of market analysis). Warszawa, Państ-
        wowe Wydawnitcwo Naukowe, 73, 113 p.

3836    Nieuwenhuysen, J. P. "Incomes, prices and competition policy in Australia", *Austral.
        econ. R.* 18(2), 1972 : 9-16.

3837   NIKAIDO, H. "Relative shares and factor price equalization", *J. int. Econ.* 2(3), aug 72 : 257-263.

3838   NIKITIN, S. M. *Problemy cenoobrazovanija v uslovijah sovremennogo* (Fixation of prices problems under the contemporary capitalist conditions). Moskva, Nauka, 73, 383 p.

3839   OBST, N. P. "On organized markets under uncertainty", *West. econ. J.* 10(2), jun 72 : 182-192.

3840   RADNER, R. "Existence of equilibrium of plans, prices and price expectations in a sequence of markets", *Econometrica* 40(2), mar 72 : 289-303.

3841   RAMSEY, J. B. "Limiting functional forms for market demand curves", *Econometrica* 40(2), mar 72 : 327-341.

3842   RANDALL, A. "Market solutions to externality problems: theory and practice", *Amer. J. agric. Econ.* 54(2), mai 72 : 175-183.

3843   SAMUELSON, P. A. "The consumer does benefit from feasible price stability", *Quart. J. Econ.* 86(3), aug 72 : 476-493. Followed by a rejoinder by the author: 500-503.

3844   SATO, R. "The stability of the competitive system which contains gross complementary goods", *R. econ. Stud.* 39(4), oct 72 : 495-499.

3845   SCOTT, R. H. *The pricing system.* San Francisco, Holden-Day, 73, xv-293 p.

3846   SIK, O. *Economia di mercato con o senza capitalismo ?* (Market economy with or without capitalism ?). Roma-Milano, Unione italiana per il progresso della cultura, 72, 77 p.

3847   STERN, N. "The optimal size of market areas", *J. econ. Theory* 4(2), apr 72 : 154-173.

3848   TARR, D. G. "Stability in a Cournot market characterized by uncertainty", *West. econ. J.* 10(3), sep 72 : 330-336.

3849   WHEATON, W. C. "On the possibility of a market for externalities", *J. polit. Econ.* 80(5), sep-oct 72 : 1039-1044.

3850   WILLIAMS, F. E. "The effect of market organization on competitive equilibrium: the multi-unit case", *R. econ. Stud.* 40(1), jan 73 : 97-113.

3851   ZANETTI, G.; DONNA, G. "Formazione del prezzo in una struttura di mercato differenziata" (Price formation in a differentiated market structure), *Ratio* 4(2), 2 sem 71 : 177-215.

### I.2121   Perfect competition
### Concurrence parfaite

3852   MAURICE, S. C. "Long-run factor demand in a perfectly competitive industry", *J. polit. Econ.* 80(6), nov-dec 72 : 1271-1279.

### I.2122   Imperfect competition, monopoly
### Concurrence imparfaite, monopole

[See also / Voir aussi: **G.321; H.2111; O.122; 2105**]

3853   ATKINSON, P. E. "Comments on Chamberlin's analysis of monopolistic competition", *Amer. Economist* 16(1), 1972 : 152-165.

3854   BARRO, R. J. "Monopoly and contrived depreciation", *J. polit. Econ.* 80(3), mai-jun 72 : 598-602.

3855   BATRA, R. N. "Monopoly theory in general equilibrium and the two-sector model of economic growth", *J. econ. Theory* 4(3), jun 72 : 355-371.

3856   BERGSON, A. "On monopoly welfare losses", *Amer. econ. R.* 63(5), dec 73 : 853-870.

3857   BIERSMANN, H. "Ein dynamischer Ansatz zur Oligopoltheorie (ein Beitrag zur Wahl der optimalen Strategien in Oligopolsituationen)" (Dynamics in the theory of oligopoly. A contribution to the choice of optimal strategies in oligopolies), *Schweizer. Z. Volkswirtsch. Statist.* 108(4), dec 72 : 555-573.

3858   BISH, R. L.; O'DONOGHUE, P. D. "Public goods, increasing cost, and monopsony: reply", *J. polit. Econ.* 81(1), jan-feb 73 : 231-236.

3859   COASE, R. H. "Durability and monopoly", *J. Law Econ.* 15(1), apr 72 : 143-149.

3860   CYERT, R. M.; DeGROOT, M. H. "An analysis of cooperation and learning in a duopoly context", *Amer. econ. R.* 63(1), mar 73 : 24-37.

3861   GABSZEWICZ, J. J.; VIAL, J. "Oligopoly 'à la Cournot' in general equilibrium analysis", *J. econ. Theory* 4(3), jun 72 : 381-400.

3862     GEFFROY, C.; LOASBY, B. J. *La portée de la théorie de la concurrence monopolistique*, par C. GEFFROY. *Hypothèse et paradigme dans la théorie de la firme*, par B. J. LOASBY. Paris, Mame, 72, 126 p.

3863     HERDZINA, K. "Oligopolistische Interdependenz, funktionsfahiger Wettbewerb und Wettbewerbsvoraussetzungen" (Oligopolistic interdependence, efficient competition and competition forecasting), *Jb. soz.-Wiss.* 24(1), 1973 : 55-84.

3864     HOWE, W. S. "Bilateral oligopoly and competition in the UK food trades", *Busin. Economist* 5(2), 1973 : 77-87.

3865     JIPE, G. "Le développement des monopoles et la tendance à la stagnation: éléments pour une critique des theses 'stagnationnistes' américaines", *Crit. Écon. polit.* (11-12), apr-sep 73 : 94-123.

3866     KAMERSCHEN, D. R.; SMITH, P. E. "Stability in duopoly models", *Econ. Stud. Quart.* 22(3), dec 71 : 39-49.

3867     KAMERSCHEN, D. R.; WALLACE, R. L. "The costs of monopoly", *Antitrust B.* 17(2), 1972 : 485-496.

3868     KONSTANTINOVIĆ, G. *Teorija monopolističke konkurencija gradanskih ekonomista* (The theory of monopolistic competition of western economists). Beograd, Institut za ekonomska istrazivanja, Savremena administracija, 73, viii-138-2 p.

3869     LEVITAN, R.; SHUBIK, M. "Price duopoly and capacity constraints", *Int. econ. R.* 13(1), feb 72 : 111-122.

3870     McCARTHY, J. T. *Trademarks and unfair competition.* Rochester, N. Y., Lawyers Co-operative Publishing Co., 73, 2 vols.

3871     Bibl. XXI-3966. NICHOLSON, M. *Oligopoly and conflict: a dynamic approach.* CR: M. SHUBIK, *J. econ. Liter.* 11(3), sep 73 : 900.

3872     OKUGUCHI, K. "Quasi-competitiveness and Cournot oligopoly", *R. econ. Stud.* 40(1), jan 73 : 145-148.

3873     OKUGUCHI, K. "The stability of the Stackelberg duopoly solutions: extensions of Kamerschen-Smith's results", *Econ. Stud. Quart.* 22(3), dec 71 : 50-55.

3874     PATEL, M. A.; MENON, A. G. *The law of monopolies and restrictive trade practices.* Karachi, August Publications, 72, 48-xi p.

3875     PERKINS, W. C. "A note on the nature of equilibrium in monopolistic competition", *J. polit. Econ.* 80(2), mar-apr 72 : 394-402.

3876     PERRAKIS, S.; SAHIN, I. "Resource allocation and scale of operations in a monopoly firm: a dynamic analysis", *Int. econ. R.* 13(2), jun 72 : 399-407.

3877     SHERMAN, R. *Oligopoly: an empirical approach.* Lexington, Mass., Lexington Books, 72, xviii-192 p.

3878     SIEPER, E.; SWAN, P. L. "Monopoly and competition in the market for durable goods", *R. econ. Stud.* 40(3), jul 73 : 333-351.

3879     VAN DER WEEL, H. "Een dynamisch duopoli-model II" (A dynamic duopoly model II), *Economist (Haarlem)* 120(4), jul-aug 72 : 353-366.

3880     ZABEL, E. "Multiperiod monopoly under uncertainty", *J. econ. Theory* 5(3), dec 72 : 524-536.

### I.2123    Price policy and control
           *Politique et contrôle du prix*

3881     BAILEY, E. E. "Peak-load pricing under regulatory constraint", *J. polit. Econ.* 80(4), jul-aug 72 : 662-679.

3882     CHARPY, J. *La politique des prix; comment stabiliser les prix dans les économies industrielles ?* Paris, Calmann-Lévy, 73, xvi-308 p.

3883     FRANKEL, M. "Pricing decisions under unknown demand", *Kyklos* 26(1), 1973 : 1-24.

3884     GORDON, R. J. "Wage-price controls and the shifting Phillips curve", *Brookings Pap. econ. Activity* (2), 1972 : 385-421.

3885     HOFFMANN, H. "O planejamento e o mecanismo de preços" (Planning and price mechanism), *R. Adm. Empresas* 13(1), jan-mar 73 : 29-39.

3886     SELOWSKY, M. "Cost of price stabilization in an inflationary economy", *Quart. J. Econ.* 87(1), feb 73 : 44-59.

3887     SILBERSTON, A. "Should prices be controlled ?", *Austral. econ. R.* 18(3), 1972 : 41-43.

3888  UNITED STATES. Board of Governors of the Federal Reserve System. Social Science Research Council. *The econometrics of price determination.* Washington, Publications Services, Division of Administrative Services, Board of Governors, Federal Reserve System, 72, 397 p.

3889  VASIL'EV, P. P. "The problem of establishing a price policy in a stock control system", *Matekon* 8(4), 1972 : 374-381.

3890  VAYRYNEN, O. "Priskontrollen in samhallspolitiken" (Price control in public policy), *Ekon. Samfund. Ts.* 26(2), 1973 : 75-86.

3891  WILCZYŃSKI, W. "Teoria i polityka cen a ekonomika jakosci" (Theoretical price policy and quality economics), *Ruch prawn. ekon. socjol.* (1), 1973 : 121-134.

3892  WILLIAMS, H. R.; BENNETT, R. E. "Wage and price controls efficiency, equity, and decontrol", *Nebraska J. Econ. Busin.* 11(4), 1972 : 87-100.

### I.2124  Price formation under planning
Formation du prix en système planifié

[See also / Voir aussi: 3133, 3753]

3893  BRENDEL, G.; FAUDE, E. "Wesenszüge und Entwicklungstendenzen des RGW-Preisbildungssystems" (Characteristics and tendencies of the evolution of the price system in the CAEM), *Wirtsch.-Wiss.* 21(9), sep 73 : 1283-1297.

3894  HABART, B. "Cenová kontrola jako součašt plánovitého řizení cen" (Price control as an integral part of methodical price policy), *Plán. Hospod.* 25(6), jun 73 : 10-20. [Czechoslovakia.]

3895  IONETE, C. *Comportamentul procesului de formare a preturilor* (Behavioral process of price formation). Bucureşti, Editura Academiei Republicii Socialiste România, 72, 180 p. [Rumania.]

3896  KARPIUK, P. *Aktualne problemy polityki cen* (Present problems of price policy). Warszawa, Państwowe Wydawnictwo Ekonomiczne, 72, 286 p. [Eastern Europe.]

3897  KISS, T. "La formazione dei prezzi nell'area del Comecon" (Price formation in the Comecon area), *Polit. Econ.* 3(6), nov-dec 72 : 92-100.

3898  KOSMINSKIJ, B. M. *Sebestoimost' v planovom cenoobrazovanii* (Cost prices in planned price establishing). Moskva, Nauka, 72, 183 p.

3899  MARER, P. *Postwar pricing and price patterns in socialist foreign trade, 1946-1971.* Bloomington, International Development Research Center, Indiana University, 72, iv-102 p.

3900  MIHAJLUŠKIN, V.; ZVEREV, V. "Ispol'zovanie mezotraslevyh i mnogoproduktovyh modelej dlja planirovanija i prognozirovanija cen" (Utilization of intersector and multi-product models for prices planning and forecasting), *Vopr. Cenoobraz.* (11), 1972 : 30-49.

3901  POPKIEWICZ, J. "Le système des prix en économie socialiste" *R. Est* 4(3), jul 73 : 49-63. [Pologne.]

3902  "Problemy cenoblazovanija" (Problems concerning the formation of prices), *Plan. Hoz.* 50(8), aug 73 : 43-71. [USSR.]

3903  SZTYBER, W. B. *Teoria i polityka cen w gospodarce socjalistycznej* (Theory and policy of prices in the socialist economy). 2nd ed. rev. Warszawa, Państwowe Wydannictwo Naukowe, 73, 455 p.

3904  WROŃSKI, J. *Prezentacja niektórych pogladów na zasady kształtowania cen w gospodarce socjalistycznej* (Presentation of some opinions about principles of price formation in the socialist economy). Warszawa, Instytut Finansów, 73, 95 p.

### I.22  Price levels, markets, price policies (descriptive studies)
Niveau des prix, marchés, politiques des prix (études déscriptives)

### I.221  General studies
Études générales

3905  HANSEN, B.; TOURK, K. "Three papers on price and trade indices for Afghanistan", *Econ. B. Asia Far East* 22(1-2), jun-sep 71 : 13-24.

3906 KRAMER, J. H. "Prices and the conservation of natural resources in the Soviet Union", *Sov. Stud.* 24(3), jan 73 : 364-373.

3907 MARTON, Á. "A fogyasztói árak változásai Magyarországon a második világháború útán"(The evolution of consumption prices in Hungary after the Second World War), *Statiszt. Szle* 51(6), jun 73 : 619-639.

3908 PICCOLO, D. "L'evoluzione dei prezzi al consumo in Italia, 1956-1972" (The evolution of consumption prices in Italy, 1956-1972), *Rass. econ. (Napoli)* 37(2), mar-apr 73 : 449-486.

3909 "Prezzi nell'economia italiana (I)" (Prices in the Italian economy), *Nord e Sud* 20(162), jun 73 : 17-24.

3910 RAVALLI, S. "L'aumento dei prezzi: cause, prospettive, rimedi" (Price increase: causes, prospects, remedies), *Realtà econ.* 4(7-8), jul-aug 72 : 5-15. Italy.

### I.222     Price policies and controls
Politiques et contrôles des prix

[See also / Voir aussi: **I.2124; I.2311**]

3911 ARNDT, H. "Competition, price and wage flexibility, and inflation: the German experience", *Antitrust B.* 17(3), 1972 : 859-883.

3912 BOURGOIGNIE, T. "La réglementation des prix en Belgique", *Econ. soc. Tijds.* 27(4). aug 73 : 387-400.

3913 CAMY, P. "Le contrôle des prix au Luxembourg", *Bull. Statec* 18(6), 1972 : 173-175,

3914 Bibl. XXI-4012. FELS, A. *The British Prices and Incomes Board.* CR: D. WHITEHEAD, *J. econ. Liter.* 11(2), jun 73 : 561-562.

3915 KELLENBERGER, E. *Gescheiterte Teuerungs- und Konjunkturpolitik* (The failure of anti-price increase policy and conjunctural policy). Bern, Stämpfli, 72, 143 p. [Switzerland.]

3916 MARTON, Á. "Az osztrák fogyasztó árpolitika és áralakulás néhány jellegzetessége" (Some characteristics of price policy and formation of consumption prices in Austria). *Statiszt. Szle* 51(2), feb 73 : 160-172.

3917 TYAMANS, A. L. "The use of productivity gains in the price control program of the United States", *Econ. soc. Tijds.* 27(2), apr 73 : 181-191.

### I.223     Comparative studies
Études comparatives

3918 AGMON, T. "Country risk: the significance of the country factor for share-price movements in the United Kingdom, Germany, and Japan", *J. Busin.* 46(1), jan 73 : 24-32.

### I.23     Specific prices and markets
Prix et marchés de produits particuliers

### I.231     Agricultural products
Produits agricoles

### I.2310     General studies
Études générales

[See also / Voir aussi: **L.231; 2942, 2945**]

3919 ABBOTT, J. C. *et al. Rice marketing.* Rome, FAO; London, HMSO; New York, UNIPUB, 72, x-189 p.

3920 ANGELINI, T. "Möglichkeiten zur Verbesserung der Funktionsfähigkeit des Bodenmarktes" (Possibilites of improving the functioning capacity of the agricultural market), *Wirtsch. u. Recht* 24(4), 1972 : 269-286. [Switzerland.]

3921 ATKINS, M. H. "Price-quantity relationships within the British butter market", *J. agr. Econ.* 24(2), mai 73 : 369-380. [UK.]

3922 BÖCKENHOFF, E. "Vorausschau auf den Schweinemarkt" (Perspectives of the swine market), *Agrarwirtschaft* 22(10), oct 73 : 352-357. [Germany, FR.]

3923    GOUYON, H. DE. "Prix agricoles et mouvement général des prix dans les différents pays de la CÉÉ", *B. Liaison Inform. Adm. Centr. Écon. Finances* 62, jan-feb 73 : 31-47.

3924    KRUSZE, N. "Układ i poziom cen owoców w Polsce na tle innych krajow" (Price system and level for fruits in Poland compared with those of other countries), *Zagadn. Ekon., rolnej* (3), 1973 : 69-82.

3925    HOUCK, J. P.; RYAN, M. E. "Supply analysis for corn in the United States: impact of changing government programs", *Amer. J. agric. Econ.* 54(2), mai 72 : 184-191.

3926    "Landwirtschaftliche Märkte an der Jahreswende 1972-1973 (Die)" (The agricultural markets at the end of 1972 and the beginning of 1973), *Agrarwirtschaft* 21(12), dec 72 : 417-470. [Germany, FR.]

3927    MALHOMME, C. "Les prix agricoles dans l'inflation", *Écon. et Statist.* 40, dec 72 : 15-24 [France.]

3928    MASSON, P. "L'évolution des prix et l'agriculture", *Écon. rur.* 95, jan-mar 73 : 43-59. [France.]

3929    MILLER, G. L.; ROBERTS, I. M. "The effect of price change on wine sales in Australia", *Quart. R. agric. Econ.* 25(3), jul 72 : 231-239.

3930    MOHAMMAD, T. *Price movements of agricultural commodities in Mardan, 1961-1970.* Peshawar, Board of Economic Enquiry, North West Frontier Province, University of Peshawar, 72, vi-128 p.

3931    MOHAMMAD, T. *Prices of agricultural commodities in Chitral, 1961-1970.* Peshawar, Board of Economic Enquiry, North West Frontier Province, University of Peshawar, 72, iii-58 l.

3932    MULES, T. J. "A supply function for dairy products", *Austral. J. agric. Econ.* 16(3), dec 72 : 195-203.

3933    POHORILLE, M. *Ceny i dochody w rolnictwie* (Prices and income in agriculture). Warszawa, Państwowe Wydawnictwo Rolnicze i Lesne, 72, 262 p.

3934    ROGERS, K. D.; SRIVASTAVA, U. K.; HEADY, E. O. "Modified price, production, and income impacts of food aid under market differentiated distribution", *Amer. J. agric. Econ.* 54(2), mai 72 : 201-208.

3935    RUNOWICZ, A. "Rynek wewnętrzny a tempo utowarowienia rolnictwa" (Internal market and the rate of commercialization of agriculture), *Ekonomista* (1), 1973 : 117-135.

3936    SÁNDOR, I. "Piackutatás a mezögazdasági és élelmiszeripari termékek piacán" (Market prospection on the agricultural and food products market), *Közgazd. Szle* 20(6), jun 73 : 726-732. [Hungary.]

3937    TOMIĆ, C. "Cene poljoprivrednih proizvoda" (Prices of agricultural products), *Jugosl. Pregl.* 16(11-12), nov-dec 72 : 411-416. [Yugoslavia.]

3938    VIAL, E. E. *Prices and consumption of dairy products with price supports and milk orders.* Washington, United States Government Printing Office, 72, v-81 p.

3939    WARRACK, A. "A conceptual framework for analysis of market efficiency", *Canad. J. agric. Econ.* 20(3), nov 72 : 9-22. [Agricultural market in Canada.]

3940    WHETHAM, E. H. *Agricultural marketing in Africa.* London, Oxford University Press, 72, xi-240 p.

**I.2311**    *Agricultural prices policy*
        *Politique des prix agricoles*

[See also / Voir aussi: **I.234**; 5959]

3941    ALAMGIR, M.; BERLAGE, L. J. J. B. "Foodgrain (rice and wheat) demand, import and price policy for Bangladesh", *Bangladesh econ. R.* 1(1), jan 73 : 25-58.

3942    BERTHOLD, T. *Die Agrarpriespolitik der DDR* (The DDR's agricultural prices policy). Berlin, Duncker und Humblot, 72, 295 p.

3943    CSEPELY-KNORR, A. *et al.* "Az élelmiszergazdaság árszínvonalának vizsgálata" (The consideration of the price level in the food sector), *Közgazd. Szle* 20(9), sep 73 : 1037-1046. [Hungary.]

3944    HATCH, J. H. "The implications of the frozen vegetables case for Australian trade practices legislation", *Econ. Record* 38(123), sep 72 : 374-386.

3945    MORIAK, T. F. "A comparison of three tools for analyzing price policy in agricultural development", *Amer. Economist* 16(2), 1972 : 162-165.

### I.232    Industrial products
####         Produits industriels

[See also / Voir aussi: **L.233;** 2938, 3337]

3946  BARANOWSKA, Z. "Reforma cen zbytu w przemysle w latach 60" (The reform of selling prices in industry in the 1960's), *Prace nauk. wyzsz. Szkoły ekon. Wrocław.* 37, 1973 : 25-45.

3947  BRAUN, W. *Der Arzneimittelmarkt in der BDR* (The pharmaceutical market in the German Federal Republic). Köln, Deutsche Industrieverlags-GmbH, 72, 95 p.

3948  BROWN, C. P. "Some implications of tin price stabilisation", *Malayan econ. R.* 17(1), apr 72 : 99-118.

3949  FRANKENA, M. "Marketing characteristics and prices of exports of engineering goods from India", *Oxford econ. Pap.* 25(1), mar 73 : 127-132.

3950  LEWIS, K. A. "An econometric analysis of the markets for textile fibers", *Amer. J. agric Econ.* 54(2), mai 72 : 238-244.

3951  "Marché des hydrocarbures au Sénégal (Le)", *Notes Inform. Statist. Banque centr. Afr Ouest* 199, oct 72 : 1-58.

3952  ORTEGA, R. "Precios y salarios industriales en España: un intento de aproximacion" (Industrial prices and wages in Spain: a tentative approach), *Moneda y Créd.* 123, dec 72 : 3-37.

3953  POHL, R. *Lohnkosten und Preisentwicklung in der Industrie der Bundesrepublik Deutschland* (Wage costs and price development in industry in the German Federal Republic). Berlin, Duncker und Humblot, 72, 39 p.

3954  VAN VRE, E. "Inleiding tot de farmaceutische marketing" (An introduction to pharmaceutical marketing), *Econ. soc. Tijds.* 26(5), oct 72 : 375-382.

### I.233    Other goods and services
####         Autres biens et services

[See also / Voir aussi: 3246, 4602]

3955  AMENDT, G. *Sucht, Profit, Sucht; politische Ökonomie des Drogenhandels* (Need, profit, need; political economy of the drug trade). Frankfurt-am-Main, März Verlag, 72, 187 p.

3956  ARCELUS, F.; MELTZER, A. H. "The markets for housing and housing services", *J. Money Cred. Bank.* 5(1), feb 73 *Part I:* 78-99.

3957  BENET, I.; GOCZÁN, L. "Kisérlet új földértékelésre" (Essay on a new evaluation of land), *Közgazd. Szle* 20(6), jun 73 : 699-714. [Hungary.]

3958  BERGSON, A. "Optimal pricing for a public enterprise", *Quart. J. Econ.* 86(4), nov 72 : 520-544 [USA.]

3959  BRUN, A. "L'évolution du prix de la terre et de la répartition de la propriété foncière agricole", *Écon. rur.* 95, jan-mar 73 : 3-22.

3960  DERYCKE, P. H. "Les coúts de la croissance urbaine", *R. Écon. polit. (Paris)* 83(1), jan-feb 73 : 121-170. [France.]

3961  DOUGLAS, G. W. "Price regulation and optimal service standards: the taxicab industry", *J. Transport Econ. Pol.* 6(2), mai 72 : 112-127.

3962  FELDSTEIN, M. "Equity and efficiency in public sector pricing: the optimal two-part tariff", *Quart. J. Econ.* 86(2), mai 72 : 175-187.

3963  GEE, J. M.; LAMBERT, J. D. "Transport costs and the location of firms", *B. econ. Res.* 24(1), mai 72 : 13-22.

3964  KING, A. T.; MIESZKOWSKI, P. "Racial discrimination, segregation and the price of housing", *J. polit. Econ.* 81(3), mai-jun 73 : 590-606.

3965  KIRKPATRICK, C. H. "The relevance of road-pricing in developing countries: some results for Tanzania", *Manchester Sch. Econ. soc. Stud.* 40(4), dec 72 : 357-374.

3966  LITTLE, I. M.; McLEOD, K. M. "The new pricing policy of the British airports authority", *J. Transport Econ. Pol.* 6(2), mai 72 : 101-115.

3967  LLUCH, E.; GASPAR, J. *Preus del sol a Catalunya* (Price of land in Catalonia). Barcelona, Banca Catalana, 72, 332 p.

3968    MAURIZI, A. R. "The effect of laws against price advertising: the case of retail gasoline", *West. econ. J.* 10(3), sep 72 : 321-329.

3969    NEUTZE, M. "The cost of housing", *Econ. Record* 48(123), sep 72 : 357-373. [Australia.]

3970    "Organisation commune des marchés: le tabac (L')", *Doss. Polit. agric. commune* 17, jun-jul 73 : 12 p.

3971    PRIEBE, H. "Agrarmarkt und Währungspolitik" (The agrarian market and monetary policy), *Wirtsch.-Dienst* 51(12), dec 72 : 639-646.

3972    "Prix des terres agricoles (Le)", *Note Écon. région. Champagne-Ardenne* 37, 3 trim 72 : 21-30. [France.]

3973    TIMMER, C. P. "Employment aspects of investment in rice marketing in Indonesia", *Food Res. Inst. Stud.* 11(1), 1972 : 59-85.

3974    WEBER, A. "Faktorpreise, Faktorproduktivität und Technologie in der amerikanischen, europäischen und japanischen Landwirtschaft von 1880 bis 1964" (Factor prices, factor productivity factors and technology in American, Japanese and European agriculture, 1880-1965), *Z. Wirtsch.-u. soz.-Wiss.* 93(2), 1973 : 197-223.

## I.234    *Price subsidies*
### *Subventions*

3975    ENGERMAN, S. L. "Some economic issues relating to railroad subsidies and the evaluation of land grants", *J. econ. Hist.* 32(2), jun 72 : 443-463.

3976    JOHNSON, D. G. *Farm commodity programs; an opportunity for change.* Washington, American Enterprise Institute for Public Policy Research, 73, 114 p. [Agricultural price supports in the USA.]

3977    LIND, T.; SERCK-HANSSEN, J. "Regional subsidies on labour and capital", *Swedish J. Econ.* 74(1), mar 72 : 68-83.

3978    SCHETTING, G. *Rechtspraxis der Subventionierung; eine Untersuchung zur normativen Subventionspraxis in der Bundesrepublik Deutschland* (Legal practice of subsidy allocation. A study of normative subsidy practice in the GFR). Berlin, Duncker und Humblot, 73, xx-349 p.

# J MONEY AND FINANCE
# MONNAIE ET FINANCE

## J.0 GENERAL WORKS
## OUVRAGES GÉNÉRAUX

### J.01 Theoretical studies
### Études théoriques

3979 AUBOIN, R. *Les vraies questions monétaires à l'épreuve des faits.* Paris, Hachette, 73, 373 p.

3980 BJORNSEN, M. K.; BOGAN, E. (eds.). *Penge* (Money). Kobenhavn, Politiken, 72, 432 p.

3981 BRUNNER, K.; MELTZER, A. H. "Money, debt, and economic activity", *J. polit. Econ.* 80(5), sep-oct 72 : 951-977.

3982 DAVIDSON, P. *Money and the real world.* London, Macmillan; New York, Wiley, 72, xv-369 p.

3983 DRAGHI, P. "Struttura monetaria e occupazione" (Monetary structure and employment) *Ric. econ.* 26(1-2), jan-jun 72 : 3-58.

3984 FISCHER, S. "Money, income, wealth, and welfare", *J. econ. Theory* 4(2), apr 72 : 289-311.

3985 FRIEDMAN, M. *Money and economic development.* New York, Praeger, 73, x-67 p.

3986 JOHNSON, H. G. *Further essays in monetary economics.* London, Allen and Unwin; Cambridge, Mass., Jarvard University Press, 73, 366 p.

3987 JONES, J. P. *The money story.* Newton Abbott, Eng., David and Charles; New York, Drake Publishers, 72, 152 p.

3988 KAUFMAN, G. G. *Money, the financial system, and the economy.* Chicago, Rand McNally, 73, xix-499 p.

3989 LEWIN, P. "The essential role of money in the economy", *South Afr. J. Econ.* 40(3), sep 72 : 268-274.

3990 MARTIN, D. A. "The medium is not the money", *J. econ. Issues* 6(2-3), sep 72 : 67-74.

3991 McCARTHY, M. J. "Money as net wealth", *Oxford econ. Pap.* 24(3), nov 72 : 413-416.

3992 McKINNON, R. I. *Money and capital in economic development.* Washington, Brookings Institution, 73, xii-184 p.

3993 NEWLYN, W. T. "The essential qualities of money: a note", *Manchester Sch. Econ. soc. Stud.* 40(4), dec 72 : 419-421.

3994 PIERSON, G. "The role of money in economic growth", *Quart. J. Econ.* 86(3), aug 72 : 383-395.

3995 POWELL, A. A.; WILLIAMS, R. A. (eds.). *Econometric studies of macro and monetary relations.* Amsterdam, North-Holland Publishing Co.; New York, American Elsevier Publishing Co., 73, viii-358 p.

3996 RIBOUD, J. *La vraie nature de la monnaie.* Paris, Éditions de la RPP, 73, 236 p.

3997 SAINT MARC, M. *Monnaie, espace, incertitude, théorie de la monétarisation.* Paris, Dunod, 72, xii-126 p.

3998 STANFORD, J. D. *Money, banking and economic activity.* Sydney-New York, J. Wiley and Sons Australasia, 73, x-130 p.

3999 Bibl. XXI-4095. STEIN, J. J. *Money and capacity growth.* CR: D. CASS, *J. econ. Theory* 11(1), mar 72 : 115-116.

### J.02 Monetary situation: descriptive studies
### Situation monétaire: études déscriptives

[See also / Voir aussi: O.2321; 5486]

4000 DIMITRIJEVIĆ, D. "Računi novčanih tokova Narodne banke Jugoslavije" (Accounts of monetary trends from the Yugoslav National Bank), *Ekon. Misao* 6(2), jun 73 : 113-125.

4001 FRIEDMAN, M. "Monetary trends in the United Kingdom", *Amer. Economist* 16(1), 1972 : 4-18.
4002 PELAEZ, C. M.; SUZIGAN, W. "Bases para a interpretaçao monetaria da historia econômica brasileira" (Basis for a monetary interpretation of Brasilian economic history), *R. brasil. Econ.* 26(4), oct-dec 72 : 57-93.
4003 RENIEWSKI, M. "Kształtowania się sytuacji pieniężno-rynkowej w latach 1971-1972" (Money and market development in 1971-1972), *Finanse* (4), 1973 : 63-70. [Poland.]
4004 STAJIĆ, S. "Neke ocene stepena razvijenosti Jugoslavije putem sintetičkih monetarnih agregata" (An appraisal of Yugoslavia's degree of development through synthetic monetary aggregates), *Ekon. Misao* 6(2), jun 73 : 76-97.

## J.1 MONEY
## MONNAIE

### J.11 General monetary theory
### Théorie monétaire générale

[See also / Voir aussi: **J.1510**; 4029, 4030, 4319]

4005 BRUNNER, K.; MELTZER, A. H. "Friedman's monetary theory", *J. polit. Econ.* 80(5), sep-oct 72 : 837-851.
4006 BRUNNER, K.; MELTZER, A. H. "Mr Hicks and the 'monetarists' ", *Economica (London)* 40(157), feb 73 : 44-59.
4007 DAVIDSON, P. "A Keynesian view of Friedman's theoretical framework for monetary analysis", *J. polit. Econ.* 80(5), sep-oct 72 : 864-882.
4008 DELLA CASA, G. "Teoria e politica monetaria nel pensiero di Milton Friedman" (Monetary theory and policy in Milton Friedman's thought), *Econ. int. (Genova)* 25(4), nov 72 : 663-682.
4009 EDWARDS, F. R. "More on substitutability between money and near monies", *J. Money Cred. Bank.* 4(3), aug 72 : 551-571.
4010 FLEMING, M. *Monetary theory.* London, Macmillan, 72, 63 p.
4011 GRANDMONT, J.-M.; YOUNES, Y. *On the efficiency of a monetary equilibrium...* Paris, chez les auteurs, 72, 38 ff. multigr.
4012 KALMBACH, P. (ed.). *Der neue Monetarismus; zwölf Aufsätze* (The new monetarism; twelve texts). München, Nymphenburger Verlagshandlung, 73, 303 p.
4013 KETTERER, K.-H.; SIMMERT, D.-B. "Moderne Quantitätstheorie und new liberalism" (Modern quantity theory and the new liberalism), *Wirtsch.-Dienst* 53(5), mai 73 : 261-266.
4014 NIEUWENBURG, C. K. F. "Een vorm van modern monetarisme" (A form of modern monetarism), *Economie (Tilburg)* 37(12), sep 73 : 537-569.
4015 LUCAS, R. E. "Expectations and the neutrality of money", *J. econ. Theory* 4(2), apr 72 : 103-124.
4016 PATINKIN, D. "Friedman on the quantity theory and Keynesian economics", *J. polit. Econ.* 80(5), sep-oct 72 : 883-905.
4017 PHELPS, E. S. "Money, public expenditure and labor supply", *J. econ. Theory* 5(1), aug 72 : 69-78.
4018 SAVING, T. R. "On the neutrality of money", *J. polit. Econ.* 81(1), jan-feb 73 : 98-119.
4019 STARR, R. M. "Exchange in barter and monetary economics", *Quart. J. Econ.* 86(2), mai 72 : 290-302.
4020 WOOD, J. H. *Money and output: Keynes and Friedman in historical perspective.* Birmingham, University of Birmingham, 72, 2-18 p.

### J.12 Monetary systems and standards
### Systèmes et standards monétaires

4021 HOLZHEU, F. "Das Geld- und Kreditsystem als Varibale im Wachstumsprozess" (The monetary and credit system as a variable of the growth process), *Jb-r nat.-Ökon. u. Statist.* 187(2), jan 73 : 97-106.

### J.13        Issue of money
           Émission de monnaie

4022    KOMAZEC, S. "Kritika savremene koncepcije emisije novca i novčane mase" (Critical
           view on the present conception of monetary issue and of monetary quantity), *Gledišta*
           13(10), oct 72 : 1314-1328.

### J.14        Quantity of money
           Volume de la monnaie

           [See also / Voir aussi: 4063, 4463]

4023    "Évolution des moyens monétaires et financiers mis à la disposition de l'économie
           pendant le premier trimestre 1972", *Statist. Ét. financ. Sér. rouge* 24(287), nov 72 :
           18-80. [France.]
4024    GILBERT, G. G. "Estimation of liquidity functions in the US economy", *Riv. int. Sci.
           econ. com.* 20(2), feb 73 : 107-129.
4025    MELITZ, J. "Une tentative d'explication de l'offre de monnaie en France" *R. écon.
           (Paris)* 24(5), sep 73 : 761-800.
4026    ROUSSEAUX, R. "De liquiditeitenmassa in Belgie en Nederland" (Mass liquidity in
           Belgium and the Netherlands), *Econ. soc. Tijds.* 26(5), oct 72 : 73-89.
4027    SAVIN, D. "Ekonomska politika i problemi likvidnosti u jugoslovenskoj privredi"
           (Economic policy and liquidity problems in the Yugoslav economy), *Ekonomist
           (Zagreb)* 25(3-4), 1972 : 543-562.
4028    TURNER, T. L. "A multivariate spectral analysis of the supply of money and credit",
           *J. Money Cred. Bank.* 4(4), nov 72 : 848-876.
4029    TYLER, J. R. "The optimum quantity of money", *Amer. Economist* 16(1), 1972 : 57-66.
4030    WEINTRAUB, S.; HABIBAGAHI, H. "Money supplies and price-output intermediateness:
           the Friedman puzzle", *J. econ. Issues* 6(2-3), sep 72 : 1-13.
4031    WIECZOREK, E. "Szybkosc oraz niezbędna ilosc pieniądza w obiegu" (The necessary
           amount of money in circulation and its rate of circulation), *Zesz. nauk. wyzsz. Szkoły
           ekon. Katow.* 44, 1972 : 9-39.

### J.15        Monetary dynamics
           Dynamique monétaire

### J.151       *Theory*
           *Théorie*

### J.1510      *General studies*
           *Études générales*

           [See also / Voir aussi: **J.14**]

4032    AKERLOF, G. A. "The demand for money: a general equilibrium inventory-theoretic
           approach", *R. econ. Stud.* 40(1), jan 73 : 115-130.
4033    BOHI, D. R. "Tobin vs. Keynes on liquidity preference", *R. Econ. Statist.* 54(4), nov 72 :
           479.
4034    BREGEL', Ě. Ja. *Denežnoe obraščenie i kredit kapitalističeskih stran* (Monetary circulation
           and credit of the capitalist countries). Moskva, Finansy, 73, 376 p.
4035    CHITRE, V. "A dynamic programming model of demand for money with a planned
           total expenditure", *Int. econ. R.* 13(2), jun 72 : 303-323.
4036    CLARK, C. "The demand for money and the choice for a permanent income estimate:
           some Canadian evidence, 1926-1965", *J. Money, Cred. Bank.* 5(3), aug 73 : 773-793.
4037    "Demande de monnaie en France (La): tentative d'explication", *Statist. Ét. financ. Sér.
           orange* 3(11), 3 trim 73 : 22-48.
4038    DICKSON, H. D.; STARLEAF, D. R. "Polynomial distributed lag structures in the demand
           function for money", *J. Finance* 27(5), dec 72 : 1035-1043.
4039    DINKEVIČ, A. I. *et al. Obščie problemy denežnogo obraščenija stran Azii* (General problems
           of Asian countries monetary circulation). Moskva, Nauka, 72, 286 p.

4040   GIBSON, W. E. "Demand and supply functions for money in the United States: theory and measurement", *Econometrica* 40(2), mar 72 : 361-370.

4041   HOLMES, J. M.; SMYTH, D. J. "The specification of the demand for money and the tax multiplier", *J. polit. Econ.* 80(1), jan-feb 72 : 179-185.

4042   KHATKHATE, D. R.; VILLANUEVA, D. P. "A behavioral theory of the money multiplier in the United States: an empirical test", *IMF Staff Pap.* 19(1), mar 72 : 125-144.

4043   LEVČUK, I. V. (ed.). *Denežnoe obraščenie i kredit* (Monetary circulation and credit). Moskva, Finansy, 72, 191 p.

4044   LYBECK, J. A. "A note on the short-run demand for money in Sweden", *Swedish J. Econ.* 74(4), dec 72 : 459-467.

4045   PETERSON, R. E. "A test of the permanent-income hypothesis of the demand for money using grouping as an instrumental variable", *J. polit. Econ.* 80(2), mar-apr 72 : 403-408.

4046   PETERSON, R. E. "The permanent-income hypothesis of the demand for money", *R. Econ. Statist.* 54(4), nov 72 : 364-373.

4047   SHORT, B. K. "The demand for money in Canada: a comment", *Economica (London)* 39(156), nov 72 : 442-446.

4048   SILVEIRA, A. M. "The demand for money. The evidence from the Brazilian economy", *J. Money Cred. Bank.* 5(1), feb 73 *Part I:* 113-140.

4049   SPRENKLE, C. M. "On the observed transactions demand for money", *Manchester Sch. Econ. soc. Stud.* 40(3), sep 72 : 261-267.

4050   WHITE, K. J. "Estimation of the liquidity trap with a generalized functional comparison", *Econometrica* 40(1), jan 72 : 193-199.


### J.1511   *Inflation-deflation*
         *Inflation-déflation*

[See also / Voir aussi: 1904, 4270, 4330, 4491, 5039, 6169, 6452]

4051   BALL, R. J.; DOYLE, P. (eds.). *Inflation. Selected readings.* Harmondsworth, Middlesex, Penguin Books, 72, 392 p.

4052   BARRO, R. J. "Inflationary finance and the welfare cost of inflation", *J. polit. Econ.* 80(5), sep-oct 72 : 978-1001.

4053   BULAT, S. "Antiinflaciona politika i njena efikasnost" (Anti-inflationist policy and its efficiency), *Gledišta* 13(10), oct 72 : 1343-1356.

4054   CARLI, G. "L'inflazione da costi e l'esigenza di una politica dei redditi" (Cost inflation and the need for an incomes policy), *Bancaria* 28(10), oct 72 : 1236-1240.

4055   COCHRANE, S. N. "Structural inflation and the two-gap model of economic development", *Oxford econ. Pap.* 24(3), nov 72 : 385-398.

4056   "Conference on secular inflation", *J. Money Cred. Bank.* 5(1), feb 73 *Part II:* 237-583.

4057   COSTE, R. "Inflation et processus de décision", *Consommation* 19(2), apr-jun 73 : 95-116.

4058   DAGUN, C. "La inflación estructural: un modelo econométrico" (Structural inflation: an econometric model), *Investig. econ.* 31(123), jul-sep 71 : 513-530.

4059   DONGILI, P. "Il problema dell'inflazione e la curva di Philipps" (The problem of inflation and the Philipps curve), *Riv. Polit. econ.* 63(1), jan 73 : 44-73.

4060   ĚNTON, R. "Infljacija v uslovijah monopolistčeskogo kapitalizma" (Inflation within monopoly capitalism conditions), *Mir. Ěkon. meždun. Otnoš.* 15(12), dec 72 : 56-73.

4061   FOSTER, E. *Cost and benefits of inflation.* Minneapolis, Minn., Federal Reserve Bank of Minneapolis, 72, 30 p.

4062   FRIEDMAN, I.S. *Inflation, a world-wide disaster.* Boston, Houghton Mifflin, 73, xiv-304 p.

4063   GOLDMAN, S. M. "Hyperinflation and the rate of growth in the money supply", *J. econ. Theory* 5(2), oct 72 : 250-257.

4064   GOLDSTEIN, M. "The trade-off between inflation and unemployment: a survey of the econometric evidence for selected countries", *Staff Pap.* 19(3), nov 72 : 647-698.

4065   GOMEZ CAMACHO, F. "La inflación, el gran fraude de la sociedad actual" (Inflation, the great fraud of present society), *R. Fomento soc.* 28(109), jan-mar 73 : 69-86.

4066   HENDERSHOTT, P. H.; VAN HORNE, J. S. "Expected inflation implied by capital market rates", *J. Finance* 28(2), mai 73 : 301-314.

4067    HENNEBERRY, B.; WITTE, J. G. "On the enigma of inflationary gaps", *J. polit. Econ.* 80(4), jul-aug 72 : 818-821.

4068    HINSHAW, R. (ed.). *Inflation as a global problem.* Baltimore, Johns Hopkins University Press, 72, x-163 p.

4069    Bibl. XXI-4158. *Inflation policy and unemployment theory. The cost benefit approach to monetary planning.* CR: R. EISNER, *J. econ. Liter.* 11(2), jun 73 : 562-564.

4070    JENSEN, W. "Stagflation, das grosse Dilemma der Wirtschaftspolitik" (Stagflation, great dilemma of economic policy), *Gegenwartskunde* 22(1), 1973 : 18-28.

4071    JOHNSON, H. G. *Inflation and the monetarist controversy.* Amsterdam-London, North Holland, 72, viii-108 p. CR: K. BRUNNER, *J. econ. Liter.* 11(1), mar 72 : 113-115.

4072    JONES, A. *The new inflation: the politics of prices and incomes.* London, Deutsch, 73, xi-228 p.

4073    JUSTER, F. P.; WACHTEL, P. "A note on inflation and the saving rate", *Brookings Pap. econ. Activity* (3), 1972 : 765-778.

4074    KARNI, E. "Inflation and real interest rate: a long-term analysis", *J. polit. Econ.* 80(2), mar-apr 72 : 365-374.

4075    KERSCHAGL, R. *Die Inflation* (Inflation). Wien, Verbund der wissenschaftlichen Gesellschaften Österreichs, 73, 179 p.

4076    LAIDLER, D. "The current inflation-explanation and policies", *Nat. Westminster Bank quart. R.* nov 72 : 6-20.

4077    LEVINSON, C. *Capital, inflation, and multinationals.* New York, Macmillan, 72, 306 p.

4078    MAKSIMOVA, L. "Otrazenienie specifiki ekonomičeskogo razvitija v burzuaznyh teorijah infljacii" (Reflection of the specificity of economic development in the bourgeois theories on inflation), *Ėkon. Nauki* 16(8), aug 73 : 95-104.

4079    MAURY, R. *La société d'inflation.* Paris, Éditions du Seuil, 73, 234 p.

4080    MODIGLIANI, F.; SHILLER, R. J. "Inflation, rational expectations and the term structure of interest rates", *Economica (London)* 40(157), feb 73 : 12-43.

4081    MORRIS, J. "The crisis of inflation", *Mthly R.* 25(4), sep 73 : 1-22.

4082    NEVILLE, J. W.; STAMMER, D. W. (eds.). *Inflation and unemployment; selected readings.* Ringwood, Vic., Penguin Books, 72, 245 p.

4083    RAU, E. "Die Ursachen der säkularen Inflation" (The causes of secular inflation), *Blätt. dtsche u. int. Polit.* 18(8), aug 73 : 818-840; 18(10), oct 73 : 1094-1106.

4084    ROBBINS, L. et al. *Inflation: economy and society; twelve papers by economists, businessmen and politicians on causes, consequences, cures.* London, Institute of Economic Affairs, 72, ix-136 p.

4085    ROSAS, L. E. "Demanda por dinero, demanda por cuentas de ahorro a inflación" (Demand for money, demand for saving accounts and inflation), *R. Planeación Desar. (Bogotá)* 4(2), apr-jun 72 : 25-33.

4086    ROTSCHILD, K. W. "Stagflation and intensified inflation. A primitive hypothesis", *Econ. J.* 82(328), dec 72 : 1383-1387.

4087    SARGENT, T. "Anticipated inflation and the nominal rate of interest", *Quart. J. Econ.* 86(2), mai 72 : 212-225.

4088    SCARFE, B. L. "A model of the inflation circle in a small open economy", *Oxford econ. Pap.* 25(2), jul 73 : 192-203.

4089    TARAFÁS, I. "Az infláció monetáris elméletéhez" (Contributions to the monetary theory of inflation), *Közgazd. Szle* 20(10), oct 73 : 1186-1199.

4090    TARR, R.; PATTILLIO, M.; COWLING, (eds.). *L'inflation.* 2 vols. Paris, Organisation de coopération et de développement économiques, 72, vi-115 p.; viii-262 p. CR

4091    TOBIN, J. "Inflazione e disoccupazione" (Inflation and unemployment), *Econ. int. (Genova)* 25(4), nov 72 : 591-622.

4092    "Transmission internationale de l'inflation (La)", *Perspect. écon. OCDE* 13, jul 73 : 89-106.

4093    VAN HORNE, J. C.; GLASSMIRE, W. F. "The impact of unanticipated changes in inflation on the value of common stocks", *J. Finance* 27(5), dec 72 : 1081-1092.

4094    VILLANUEVA, D. P.; ARYA, N. S. "Time deposits in the definition of money: further cross country inflation evidence", *Econ. Record* 48(123), sep 72 : 437-439.

**J.152** *Descriptive studies: inflation-deflation, anti-inflationary policies*
*Études déscriptives: inflation-déflation, politiques anti-inflationnistes*

[See also / Voir aussi: 1908, 3911, 3927, 4286, 4429, 4443, 4502, 4577, 5257, 5544, 5635, 5637]

4095 AME, M. "Inflation and 'openness' in less developed economies: a cross-country analysis", *Econ. Develop. cult. Change* 22(1), oct 73 : 31-37.

4096 ARNAUDO, A. A. *Un estudio sobre la velocidad de la inflación en Argentina, 1958-1966* (A study on the velocity of inflation in Argentina, 1958-1966). Buenos Aires, Ediciones Macchi, 72, 96 p.

4097 ARNDT, E. *Währungsstabilität und Lohnpolitik über die wirtschaftlichen und sozialen Folgen von Inflationen* (Monetary stability and wage policy; the economic and social policies of inflation). Tübingen, Mohr, 73, 60 p. [Germany, FR.]

4098 ASCHINGER, F. E. "Les mesures monétaires de lutte contre l'inflation en Suisse", *Soc. Banque suisse B.* (1), 1973 : 1-10.

4099 BORCHARDT, K. *Strukturwirkungen des Inflationsprozesses* (Structural effects of the inflation process). Berlin, Duncker und Humblot, 72, 22 p. [Germany, FR.]

4100 BOWEN, J.; HINSHAW, E. "Inflation and stagnation in Brazil: comment", *Econ. Develop. cult. Change* 21(3), apr 73 : 522-525.

4101 BURNS, A. "The problem of inflation", *Soc. Sci. (Winfield)* 48(2), 1973 : 67-74. [USA.]

4102 DESCAMPS, R. "Inflation, croissance et productivité", *Assoc. Cadres dir. Industr. B.* 279, nov-dec 72 : 587-595. [USA.]

4103 FASE, M. M. G. "Bond yields and expected inflation: a quantitative analysis of the Dutch experience", *Econ. quart. R.* 30, sep 72 : 5-10.

4104 HABERLER, G.; PARKIN, M.; SMITH, H. *Inflation and the unions: three studies in the effects of labour monopoly power on inflation in Britain and the USA.* London, Institute of Economic Affairs, 72, xii-88 p.

4105 KAHIL, R. *Inflation and economic development in Brazil, 1946-1963.* Oxford, Clarendon Press, 73, xvi-357 p.

4106 KALISKI, S. F. *The trade-off between inflation and unemployment: some explorations of the recent evidence for Canada.* Ottawa, Information Canada, 72, ix-114 p.

4107 KAU, R. K. C.; SCHULLER, M. L. "Inflation and the federal income tax", *Yale Law J.* 82(4), mar 73 : 716-744. [USA.]

4108 LECAILLON, J.; BOTALLA-GAMBETTA, B. "Inflation, répartition et chômage dans le France contemporaine", *R. écon. (Paris)* 24(3), mai 73 : 373-400.

4109 NEVILE, J. W. "Inflation and budgetary policy in Australia", *Bankers' Mag.* 216(1555), oct 73 : 165-169.

4110 PABLO, J. C. DE. *Política antiinflacionaria en la Argentina, 1967-1970* (Anti-inflationary policy in Argentina, 1967-1970). Buenos Aires, Amorrortu Editores, 72, 135 p.

4111 POBLACION BERNARDO, J. I. "La inflación en las economías occidentales" (Inflation in the Western economies), *Bol. Docum. Fondo Investig. econ. soc.* 5(1), jan-mar 73 : 5-13.

4112 PREST, A. R. "Inflation and the public finances", *Three Banks R.* 96, mar 73 : 3-29. [UK.]

4113 RANDALL, L. "Inflation and economic development in Latin America: some new evidence", *J. Develop. Stud.* 9(2), jan 73 : 317-322.

4114 SANDERS, P. G. "The current inflation: an academic view", *Bankers Mag.* 215(1550), mai 73 : 225-231. [UK.]

4115 SIEBKE, J.; WILLMS, M. "Inflation und Zinsniveau" (Inflation and the interest rate), *Wirtsch.-Dienst* 52(11), nov 72 : 577-582. [Germany, FR.]

4116 SIMKIN, C. G. F. "Inflation in Australia and New Zealand: 1953-1971", *Econ. Record* 48(124), dec 72 : 465-482.

4117 SIMONSEN, M. H. "O modelo da realimentaçao inflacionaria e as experiencias de esta-bilizaçao" (A model of inflationist realimentation and the stabilization experiences), *R. brasil. Econ.* 26(4), oct-dec 72 : 227-239. [Brazil.]

4118 SOUSA, A. DE. "Inflaçao e desenvolvimento en Portugal" (Inflation and development in Portugal), *Anál. soc.* 9(34), 1972 : 317-369.

4119 SZEGÖ, S. "The effects of Western inflation on the Hungarian monetary equilibrium", *Acta oecon.* 9(2), 1972 : 167-179.

4120 THIRSK, W. R. *Regional dimensions of inflation and unemployment;* a research report prepared for the Prices and Incomes Commission. Ottawa, Information Canada, 73, vii-155-165-ix p.

4121    VINCI, S. "Inflazione, politica dei redditi e politica meridionalista" (Inflation, incomes policy and Southern policy), *Rass. econ. (Napoli)* 36(5), sep-oct 72 : 1383-1397. [Italy.]

4122    WARNKE, B. "Preissteigerungen und inflationäre Entwicklung in der BRD" (The price increase and the inflationist revolution in the GFR), *IPW Ber.* 2(7), jul 73 : 15-25.

4123    ZANELETTI, R. "Inflazione, consumi sociali e politica fiscale" (Inflation, social consumption and fiscal policy), *Riv. Polit. econ.* 63(5), mai 73 : 567-578. [Italy.]

### J.16     Money market
          Marché monétaire

4124    EINZIG, P. *Parallel money markets.* 2 vols. London, Macmillan; New York, St Martin's Press, 72, viii-256 p.

4125    OSTROY, J. M. "The informational efficiency of monetary exchange", *Amer. econ. R.* 63(4), sep 73 : 597-610.

4126    PENGLAOU, C. "L'open-market en 1971", *R. Écon. polit. (Paris)* 82(5), sep-oct 72 : 925-938. [France.]

4127    SONTHEIMER, K. "On the determination of money prices", *J. Money Cred. Bank.* 4(3), aug 72 : 489-508.

4128    WILSON, J. S. G. "The Australian money market", *Banca naz. Lav. Quart. R.* 104, mar 73 : 46-69. [Also published in Italian in *Moneta e Cred.* 25(100), 4 trim 72 : 437-453.]

### J.161    *Discount rate*
          *Taux d'escompte*

[See also / Voir aussi: 4192]

4129    BURNS, J. M. "Academic views on improving the Federal Reserve discount mechanism", *J. Money Cred. Bank.* 5(1), feb 73 *Part I:* 47-60.

4130    HIGGINS, R. C. "Dividend policy and increasing discount rates: a clarification", *J. financ. quant. Anal.* 7(3), jun 72 : 1757-1762.

4131    SANDMO, A. "Discount rates for public investment under uncertainty", *Int. econ. R.* 13(2), jun 72 : 287-302.

### J.2      CREDIT
          CRÉDIT

### J.21     Bank structure
          Structure bancaire

### J.210    *General studies*
          *Études générales*

[See also / Voir aussi: 2254, 3998, 5585, 6200]

4132    ANTHONY, V. S. *Banks and markets.* London, Heinemann Educational, 72, x-130 p.

4133    CHALMERS, R. B. *Marketing bancário; os princípios básicos da economía e administração bancária* (Bank marketing; basic principles of bank economy and administration). Sao Paulo, Bestseller, 72, 159 p.

4134    EILON, S.; FOWKES, T. R. (ess.). *Applications of management science and finance.* London, Gower Press, 72, viii-286 p.

4135    FRANCE. Délégation à l'aménagement du territoire et action régionale. *La décentralisation du tertiaire. Les banques et les assurances.* Paris, DATAR, 73, 57 p.

4136    GAVRY, G. "The origin of Lenin's views on the role of banks in the socialist transformation of society", *Hist. polit. Econ.* 4(1), 1972 : 252-263.

4137    LORDAN, J. F. *The banking side of corporate cash management.* Boston, Financial Publishing Co., 73, x-114 p.

4138 RHOADES, S. A.; YEATS, A. J. "An analysis of entry and expansion conditions in bank acquisition and merger cases", *West. econ. J.* 10(3), sep 72 : 337-345.

## J.211    Bank systems
## Systèmes bancaires

[See also / Voir aussi: 4336, 4347]

4139 AMORE, G. DELL'. "La riforma del sistema bancario in rapporto alle esigenze dell'-agricoltura nazionale" (The reform of the banking system in relation to the demands of national agriculture), *Riv. Econ. agr.* 28(1), jan-feb 73 : 7-17. [Italy.]

4140 "Banques en Afrique (Les)", *R. franç. Ét. polit. afr.* 92, aug 73 : 25-76.

4141 BERNARD, H. P. "La evolucion del sistema bancario francés de 1965 a 1971" (The evolution of the French banking system from 1965 to 1971), *Moneda y Créd.* 124, mar 73 : 3-26.

4142 BLETON, P. *La banque et les affaires.* Paris, Bordas, 72, 205 p. [France.]

4143 CARDINALI, G. "L'evoluzione della banca italiana dalla riforma del 1936" (The evolution of Italian banking since the 1936 reform), *Risparmio* 21(3), mar 73 : 409-421.

4144 FALK-BJERKE, H. *Die Veränderungen im Bankwesen der EWG unter besonderer Berück-sichtigung der zunehmenden EWG-Integration* (Modification of the EEC banking system with particular attention to growing EEC integration). Wien, Manz, 72, 139 p.

4145 GOLAY, J. "Le système des banques en Suisse et leur structure", *R. écon. soc.* 30(4), dec 72 : 289-307.

4146 HOTTINGUER, B. "Les mutations récentes dans le système bancaire français", *R. Soc. Ét. Éxpans.* 71(253), nov-dec 72 : 834-838.

4147 JONES, J. C. H.; LAUDADIO, J. "Canadian bank mergers, the public interest and public policy", *Banca naz. Lav. Quart. R.* 105, jun 73 : 109-140.

4148 JONES, J. C. H.; LAUDADIO, L. "Economics of scale in Australian banking; a comment", *Econ. Record* 48(124), dec 72 : 570-574.

4149 JUNCKER, G. R.; OLDFIELD, G. S. "Projecting market structure by Monte-Carlo simulation: a study of bank expansion in New Jersey", *J. Finance* 27(5), dec 72 : 1101-1026.

4150 LE BESNERAIS, P. "L'évolution du système bancaire français à l'égard des financements immobiliers", *Banque* 48(315), feb 73 : 142-149.

4151 MOTTURA, P. *Il sistema bancario della Tunisia, 1956-1970* (The Tunisian banking system, 1956-1970). Milano, Cassa di risparmio delle provincie lombarde, 72, ix-324 p.

4152 ODLE, M. A. *The significance of non-bank financial intermediaries in the Caribbean; an analysis of patterns of financial structure and development.* Mona, Institute of Social and Economic Research, University of the West Indies, 72, xiv-212 p.

4153 PEREZ DE ARMINNAN, G. "Le système bancaire espagnol dix ans après la réforme de 1962", *Banque* 48(314), jan 73 : 32-42.

4154 PINDAK, E. "Tendances d'après-guerre dans les systèmes bancaires de l'Europe de l'Est", *Banque* 48(322), oct 73 : 888-903.

4155 PODOLSKI, T. M. *Socialist banking and monetary control; the experience of Poland.* Cambridge, Eng., University Press, 73, xiii-392 p.

4156 POTÁČ, S. "Die Rolle des Banksystems in der Volkswirtschaft der CSSR" (The role of the bank system in the people's economy of Czechoslovakia), *Österr. Osth.* 14(4), oct 72 : 349-356.

4157 RENDA, B. "Credito, risparmio e banche nelle prospettive dell' integrazione europea" (Credit, savings and banking in the European integration prospect), *Mondo aperto* 27(1), feb 73 : 9-23.

4158 RJABININA, É. D. *Kreditno-bankovskaja sistema sovremennoj Indii* (Credit and banking system in contemporary India). Moskva, Nauka, 72, 304 p.

4159 ROBINSON, S. W. *Multinational banking. A study of certain legal and financial aspects of the postwar operations of the US branch banks in Western Europe.* Leiden, Sijthoff, 72, xix-316 p.

4160 SARACENO, P. "Un secolo di attività bancaria nell'economia valtellinese" (A century of banking in the Valtellina economy), *Bancaria* 28(10), oct 72 : 1248-1263. [Italy.]

4161 "Sistema bancário" (Bank system), *Conjunt. econ.* 27(1), jan 73 : 46-87. [Brazil.]

4162 "Système bancaire japonais (Le)", *Japon Écon.* 50, jan 73 : 2-19.

4163   TAMAGNA, F. "L'evoluzione della struttura bancaria nell' esperienza degli Stati Uniti"
       (The evolution of the banking structure in the American experience), *Bancaria* 28(11),
       nov 72 : 1363-1369.

4164   WADSWORTH, J. E. (ed.). *The banks and the monetary system in the UK, 1959-1971.*
       London, Methuen; New York, Harper and Row, 73, x-527 p.

4165   YEATS, A. "An analysis of the effect of mergers on the banking market structure",
       *J. Money Cred. Bank.* 5(2), mai 73 : 623-636. [USA.]


       **J.212    Central banks**
       **Banques centrales**

       [See also / Voir aussi: 4319]

4166   ACHESON, K.; CHANT, J. F. "Bureaucratic theory and the choice of central bank goals:
       the case of the Bank of Canada", *J. Money Cred. Bank.* 5(2), mai 73 : 637-655.

4167   BARANNIKOV, A. I. "Rol'gosbanka v razvitii narodnogo hozjajstva" (The role of the
       Gosbank in the national economy), *Den'gi i Kred.* 31(2), feb 73 : 14-18. [USSR.]

4168   KROC, R. "Management strategy of a central bank in a developing country", *Finance
       and Develop.* 9(2), jun 72 : 42-47.

4169   LASO, L. E. *La banca central* (The Central Bank). Guayaquil, Impreso en Almacenes
       Editorial Colón, 72, 81 p.

4170   MAYER, T. "The Federal Reserve's policy procedures", *J. Money Cred. Bank.* 4(3),
       aug 72 : 529-550. [USA.]

4171   OSSOLA, R. "Il ruolo delle banche centrali nel funzionamento e nella regolazione del
       mercato delle eurovalute" (Central bank interventions and Euro currency markets),
       *Moneta e Cred.* 25(100), 4 trim 72 : 367-384. Also published in English in *Banca
       naz. Lav. Quart. R.* 104, mar 73 : 29-45.

4172   PATAT, J. P. *Les banques centrales.* Paris, Sirey, 72, vi-232 p.


       **J.213    Other public banking establishments, nationalized banks**
       **Autres institutions bancaires publiques, banques nationalisées**

4173   BARATTIERI, V. *Le banche di sviluppo nei paesi emergenti* (Development banks in develop-
       ing countries). Milano, A. Giuffrè, 72, vii-86 p.

4174   BOUZAN, A. "Concetraçao e economias de escala nos bancos comerciais brasileiros"
       (Concentration and economies of scale in Brazilian commercial banks), *R. Adm.
       Emprêsas* 13(3), sep 73 : 9-25.

4175   BRÄUTIGAM, J. *Kostenfunktionen in Kreditinstituten;* (The cost function in commercial
       banks). Wiesbaden, Betriebswirtschaftlicher Verlag T. Gabler, 72, 218 p.

4176   GHOSH, A.; BANERJEE, A. C. "Public sector banks: a balance sheet of their growth and
       performance", *Econ. Aff.* 17(9-10), sep-oct 72 : 463-469.

4177   SAKSENA, R. M. *Regional development banking.* Bombay, Somaiya Publications, 72, x-
       124 p.


       **J.214    Private banks**
       **Banques privées**

4178   MELITZ, J.; PARDUE, M. "The demand and supply of commercial bank loans", *J. Money
       Cred. Bank.* 5(2), mai 73 : 669-692.

4179   STULTS, A. "Il ruolo delle banche commerciali nel mercato del credito al consumo negli
       USA" (The role of the commercial banks in the consumer credit market in the USA),
       *Bancaria* 28(11), nov 72 : 1370-1380.


       **J.215    Savings banks**
       **Caisses d'épargne**

       [See also / Voir aussi: 4628]

4180   AMORE, G. DELL'. "Le casse di risparmio mondiali nel 1972" (World savings banks in
       1972), *Risparmio* 21(5), mai 73 : 743-755.

4181　Amore, G. Dell'. "Le casse di risparmio nell' evoluzione del sistema bancario italiano" (Savings banks in the evolution of the Italian banking system), *Risparmio* 20(10), oct 72 : 1597-1623.

4182　Avancini, P. *Das Sparbuch im österreichischen Recht* (The savings book in Austrian law). Wien, Manz, 73, 131 p.

4183　"Caisses d'épargne ordinaires en 1971 (Les)", *Statist. Ét. financ. Sér. bleue* 25(289), jan 73 : 64 p. [France.]

4184　Garcia Villarejo, A. "Una nueva estructura para las operaciones activas de las cajas de ahorros. Comentarios al reciente decreto de 31 de enero de 1973 sobre inversiones obligatorias de las cajas de ahorros" (A new structure for active operations of saving banks. Comments about the recent decree of the 31st of January 1973 on compulsory investments of the saving banks), *Moneda y Créd.* 123, dec 72 : 105-116.

4185　Guemas, B. "Évolution et fiscalité des Caisses d'Épargne", *J. Caisses Épargne* 92(4), apr 73 : 193-216. [France.]

4186　Last, B. *Die Zinspolitik der Sparkassen in der Bundesrepublik Deutschland unter wirtschafts-politischen Gesichtspunkten* (Interest policy of savings banks in the German Federal Republic from a political economy viewpoint). Berlin, Duncker und Humblot, 73, 135 p.

4187　Röper, B. *Die Wettbewerbsfunktion der deutschen Sparkassen und das Subsidiaritäts-prinzip; eine wettbewerbspolitische Analyse* (The competition policy of German savings banks and the principle of subsidiarity: a competition policy analysis). Berlin, Duncker und Humblot, 73, 200 p.

4188　Steiner, H. *Lebensgestaltung in Konsum und Arbeit. Zur Zielbestimmung der Sparkassen* (Life form in consumption and work. For a determination of objectives of savings banks). Wien, Sparkassenverlag, 207 p.

## J.216　Bank operations
### Technique bancaire

4189　Amore, G. Dell'. "I rapporti fra il risparmio nazionale e i depositi bancari" (Relations between national saving and bank deposits), *Bancaria* 28(10), oct 72 : 1228-1235.

4190　Ballerini, F. *Aspetti tecnici ed organizzativi della banca di credito ordinario* (Technical and organizational aspects of common credit banking). Milano, Celuc, 72, 353 p.

4191　Baltensperger, E. "Cost of banking activities: interactions between risk and operating costs", *J. Money Cred. Bank.* 4(3), aug 72 : 595-611.

4192　Brimmer, A. F. "Member bank borrowing, portfolio reserve discount policy", *West. econ. J.* 10(3), sep 72 : 243-297.

4193　Brown, G. R. "Optimal management of bank reserves", *J. financ. quant. Anal.* 7(5), dec 72 : 2031-2054.

4194　Kaufman, G. G. "Deposit variability and bank size", *J. financ. quant. Anal.* 7(5), dec 72 : 2087-2096.

4195　Martinez Cerezo, A. *Cómo estudia la banca a las empresas* (How the bank studies enterprises). Salamanca, Anaya, 72, 220 p.-1 l.

4196　Pye, G.; Young, I. "The effect of deposit rate ceilings on aggregate income", *J. Finance* 27(5), dec 72 : 1023-1034.

4197　Saraceno, P. *Le operazioni bancarie* (Banking operations). Milano, Vita e pensiero, 72, vi-217 p.

4198　Stevenson, H. *Informationssysteme für Kreditinstitute* (Information systems for credit institutes). Berlin-New York, De Gruyter, 73, 158 p.

4199　Stone, B. K. "The cost of bank loans", *J. financ. quant. Anal.* 7(5), dec 72 : 2077-2086.

4200　Walker, D. A. "A recursive programming approach to bank asset management", *J. financ. quant. Anal.* 7(5), dec 72 : 2055-2075.

4201　Wieczorek, E. "Oszczędnosci i metody oddziaływania na wzrost wkładów w państwach kapitalistycznych i socjalistycznych" (Savings and methods of influencing deposit growth in capitalist and socialist countries), *Finanse* (10), 1973 : 1-12.

**J.22 Credit: theory and operations**
**Le crédit: théorie et opérations de crédit**

**J.220** *General studies*
*Études générales*

[See also / Voir aussi: 4034, 4043]

4202 ORNSTIEN, E. J. *The marketing of money.* Epping, Gower Press, 72, x-254 p.

4203 POGODIN, Ju. N. "Kredit i ego effektivnost' v uslovijah socializma" (Credit and its efficiency in socialist society), *Den'gi i Kred.* 31(10), oct 73 : 37-43.

**J.221** *Evolution of credit: local studies*
*Évolution de crédit: études localisées*

4204 ALHADEFF, D. "Prosposte di riforma della struttura e della disciplina del sistema creditizio degli Stati Uniti" (Reform proposals for the structure and discipline of the American credit system), *Moneta e Cred.* 25(99), 3 trim 72 : 291-313.

4205 BREDEMEIER, S. *Erfahrungen mit der Kreditplafondierung* (Experiences concerning credit ceilings). Berlin, Duncker und Hubmot, 72, 191 p. [Europe.]

4206 MANIATIS, G. "The propensity to use bank credit: the case of industrial corporate entities in Greece", *Riv. int. Sci. econ. com.* 19(10), oct 72 : 986-998.

4207 PENNER, R. G.; SILBER, W. L. "The interaction between federal credit programs and the impact on the allocation of credit", *Amer. econ. R.* 63(5), dec 73 : 838-852. [USA.]

4208 POTAČ, S. "Le rôle du crédit dans la gestion planifiée de l'économie tchécoslovaque", *Aperçus Écon. tchécosl.* (6), sep 73 : 62-108.

4209 RIESZ, M. "A hitelelmélet központi kérdései az elmult 25 évben" (Central matters of the theory of credit during the past 25 years), *Közgazd. Szle* 20(1), jan 73 : 18-31. [Hungary.]

4210 SYROEZKI, G. "Kredit, ego effektivnost' i granicy" (Credit, its efficiency and its limits), *Den'gi i Kred.* 30(11), nov 72 : 41-54. [USSR.]

**J.222** *Short-term credit, discount*
*Crédit à court terme, opérations d'escompte*

4211 KROL, I. M. "K voprosy ob issledovanii effektivnosti kratkosročnogo kredita" (The problem of finding short term credit efficiency), *Den'gi i Kred.* 31(6), jun 73 : 46-56. [USSR.]

4212 TITTA, A. "Il credito bancario a breve e la piccola e media industria" (Short-term banking credit and small and medium-sized industry), *Risparmio* 21(2), feb 73 : 289-326.

**J.23 Specialized credit agencies and operations**
**Organismes et opérations de crédit spécialisés**

**J.231** *Consumer credit. Pawn houses*
*Crédit à la consommation. Crédit municipal*

4213 BRASCH, J. J.; CURTIS, W. W. *The consumer and option terms revolving credit.* St. Louis, Society of Certified Consumer Credit Executives, 72, xi-68 p. [USA.]

4214 CHARPENTIER, C. "Konsumtionskrediterna i Sverige" (Consumer credit in Sweden), *Ekon. R. (Stockholm)* 29(7), sep 72 : 314-318.

4215 DHONTE, P. "Le crédit à la consommation et l'épargne des ménages américains", *J. Caisses Épargne* 91(11), nov 72 : 722-732.

4216 MANDELL, L. "Consumer knowledge and understanding of consumer credit", *J. Consumer Aff.* 7(1), 1973 : 23-36. [USA.]

4217 MORGANSTERN, S. *Legal regulation of consumer credit.* Dobbs Ferry, N. Y., Oceana Publications, 72, ix-116 p.

4218 WALLACE, G. J. "The logic of consumer credit reform", *Yale Law J.* 82(3), jan 73 : 461-482.

4219 ZIEGEL, J. S. "Recent development in Canadian consumer credit law", *Mod. Law R.* 36(5), sep 73 : 479-495.

## J.232 Agricultural credit
## Crédit agricole

4220 BALZANI, A. "Contributo ed uno studio per la riforma del credito agrario" (Contribution and study for the reform of agricultural credit), *Riv. Dir. agr.* 51(3), jul-sep 72 : 1110-1127. [Italy.]

4221 BHATNAGAR, G. S.; JAIN, S. L. "Socio-economic aspects of rural credit patterns", *Ind. J. soc. Res.* 14(1), apr 73 : 40-43.

4222 COUTINHO DOS SANTOS, M. *Crédito investimento e financiamentos rurais* (Rural credit, investments and financing). Rio de Janeiro, Livraria Freitas Bastos, 72, viii-425 p.

4223 HOPKIN, J. A.; BARRY, P. J.; BAKER, C. B. *Financial management in agriculture*. Danville, Ill., Interstate Printers and Publishers, 73, 459 p.

4224 KÖKSAL, E. "Türkiye'de Tarimsal Kredi Sorunu" (Agricultural credit in Turkey), *Mid. East. techn. Univ. Stud. Develop.* (3), 1971 : 499-528.

4225 KOLYČEV, L. I. *Kredit i ĕffektivnost' kolhoznogo proizvodstva. Rol' kredita v rasvitii ekonomiki kolhozov* (Credit and collective farm production efficiency. The role of credit in the collective farm's economic development). Moskva, Finansy, 72, 256 p.

4226 KUCHS, W. *Geld und Kapital im landwirtschaftlichen Betrieb; Finanzierung und Finanzplanung* (Money and capital in the agricultural enterprise; financing and financial planning). Stuttgart, Deutscher Sparkassenverlag, 72, 79 p.

4227 RODERO FRANGANILLO, A. "El crédito al sector agrario" (Credit for the agrarian sector), *R. Fomento soc.* 28(110), apr-jun 73 : 191-197. [Spain.]

## J.233 Industrial and commercial credit
## Crédit industriel et commercial

[See also / Voir aussi: 3348]

4228 GRAYSON, L. E. "The role of suppliers credit in the industrialization of Ghana", *Econ. Develop. cult. Change* 21(3), apr 73 : 477-499.

4229 WIECZOREK, E. *Efektywność kretytu bankowego w finansowaniu zapasow przedsiębiorstwa* (Efficiency of bank credit in financing the stocks of enterprises). Warszawa, Instytut Fiansówsów, 72, 111 p.

## J.24 Credit control and policy
## Contrôle et politique du crédit

[See also / Voir aussi: **J.152; J.161; J.5;** 4217-4219]

4230 BRUNI, F. "Nota sul razionamento del credito e la neutralità della moneta" (A note on credit rationing and neutrality of money), *Industria* (1-2), jan-mar 72 : 76-81.

4231 BRUNI, F. "Sul razionamento di equilibrio del credito" (On the rationing of credit equilibrium), *Riv. int. Sci. econ. com.* 19(12), dec 72 : 1170-1183.

4232 FABRIZI, P. L. *L'evoluzione del controllo del credito in Gran Bretagna* (The evolution of credit control in Great Britain). Milano, Giuffrè, 73, 64 p.

4233 KLAUHS, H. *Zur Neuregelung des Kreditwesenrechtes* (For a new legal regulation of the credit system). Wien, Jupiter-Verlag, 72, 304 p. [Austria.]

4234 MIRAGLIA, G. "La politica del credito nel 1972" (Credit policy in 1972), *Rass. econ. (Napoli)* 37(3), mai-jun 73 : 721-742. [Italy.]

4235 WARIS, K. "Styrningen av kreditströmmarna" (Directing credit flows), *Ekon. Samfund. Ts.* 26(2), 1973 : 87-94.

## J.3 INSURANCE
## ASSURANCES

[See also / Voir aussi: 4135]

4236 ADDARIO, R. D'. *Fluttuazioni monetarie e loro influenza nel campo assicurativo* (Monetary fluctuations and their influence in the insurance domain). Roma, Tipo-litografia Bimospa, 72, 106 p.

4237 CARTER, R. L. *Economics and insurance: an introduction to the economic aspects of insurance.* Stockport, PH Press Ltd, 72, 7-157 p.

4238 JADOT, P. "Réassurance en excédent de sinistres, inflation, clause de stabilité et partage du sort", *A. Sci. écon. appl. A. Sci. écon. appl.* 30(4-5), 1973 : 389-457.

4239 KAMERSCHEN, D. R. "A note on economies of scale in life insurance", *J. Risk Insurance* 39(3), sep 72 : 473-474.

4240 LONG, J. D. Insurance subsidies and welfare economics", *J. Risk Insurance* 39(3), sep 72 : 341-350.

4241 NEUDIN, G. "L'évolution des assurances au cours de l'exercice 1970", *R. gén. Assur. terr.* 43(3), jul-sep 72 : 329-359. [France.]

4242 NEUDIN, G. "L'évolution des assurances au cours de l'exercice 1971", *R. gén. Assur. terr.* 44(3), jul-sep 73 : 313-343. [France.]

4243 PAAL, E. *Entwicklung und Entwicklungstendenzen in der Kreditsicherung* (Development and development trends in credit insurance). Wiesbaden, Betriebswirtschaftlicher Verlag, 73, 333 p. [Germany, FR.]

4244 "Sociétés d'assurances et de capitalisation en 1971 (Les)", *Statist. Ét. financ.* 25(294), jun 73 : 195 p. [France.]

4245 TROSPER, J. F. *The status of insurance in Afghanistan.* Bloomington, Indiana University, 72, vi-142 l.


## J.4 STOCK MARKET
## MARCHÉ FINANCIER

### J.41 Institutions, legislation and policy
### Institutions, législation et politique

#### J.411 *Investment trusts*
#### *Sociétés d'investissement*

4246 BAUM, D. J. *The investment function of Canadian financial institutions.* New York, Praeger, 73, xxii-264 p.

4247 LOREZ, M. *Das Fondsreglement nach dem Bundesgesetz über die Anlagefonds (vom 1. Juli 1966)* (Fund regulation according to the Federal law on investment funds of 1st July 1966). Zürich, Schulthess Polygraphischer Verlag, 72, xviii-90 p. [Switzerland.]

4248 OETINGER, N.-A. VON. *Amerikanische Investmentgesellschaften: eine Erfolgsanalyse* (American investment corporations: analysis of their success). Wiesbaden, Betriebswirtschaftlicher Verlag Gabler, 72, 270 p. [USA.]

4249 SPRINGER, J. L. *The mutual fund trap.* Chicago, Regnery, 73, 209 p.

4250 WATKINS, A. M. *Making money in mutual funds.* New York, Hawthorn Books, 73, x-181 p. [USA.]


#### J.412 *Securities: legislation*
#### *Régime des valeurs mobilières*

4251 BENSTON, G. J. "Required disclosure and the stock market: an evaluation of the Securities Exchange Act of 1934", *Amer. econ. R.* 63(1), mar 73 : 132-155. [USA.]

4252 BRETZ, W. G. *Juncture recognition in the stock market.* New York, Vantage Press, 72, xx-244 p.

## J.42 Economic functions and equilibrium
### Fonctions économiques et équilibre

### J.421 *Economic functions*
#### *Fonctions économiques*

4253 FOGLER, H. R. *Analyzing the stock market: a quantitative approach.* Columbus, Ohio, Grid, 73, 290 p.

4254 GOODMAN, G. J. W. *Supermoney.* New York, Random House, 72, x-301 p.

4255 JENSEN, M. C. (ed.) *Studies in the theory of capital markets.* New York, Praeger, 72, viii-376 p.

4256 JONES, C. P.; SIMKOWITZ, M. A. "The simultaneous nature of a capital market", *West. econ. J.* 10(4), dec 72 : 396-401.

4257 LORIE, J. H.; HAMILTON, M. T. *The stock market: theories and evidence.* Homewood, Ill., R. D. Irwin, 73, xiii-304 p.

4258 MOSSIN, J. *Theory of financial markets.* Englewood Cliffs, N. J., Prentice-Hall, 73, xiii-171 p.

4259 PIVATO, G. (ed.). *La borsa valori* (The stock exchange). Milano, A. Giuffrè, 72, xv-513 p.

### J.422 *Equilibrium, interest rate (and related policy)*
#### *Équilibre, taux d'intérêt (et politique)*

### J.4220 General studies
#### Études générales

[See also / Voir aussi: 4066, 4074, 4080, 4823]

4260 BIERMAN, H. J.; DOWNES, D. H.; HASS, J. E. "Closed-form stock price models", *J. financ. quant. Anal.* 7(3), jun 72 : 1797-1808.

4261 BOLTEN, S. E. *Cases in security analysis and portfolio management.* New York, Holt, Rinehart and Winston, 73, vii-194 p.

4262 CAGAN, P. *The channels of monetary effects on interest rates.* New York, Columbia University Press, 72, xvi-127 p.

4263 CARGILL. T. F.; MEYER, R. A. "A spectral approach to estimating the distributed lag relationship between long and short term interest rates", *Int. econ. R.* 13(2), jun 72 : 223-238.

4264 CARR, J.; SMITH, L. B. "Money supply, interest rates, and the yield curve", *J. Money Cred. Bank.* 4(3), aug 72 : 582-594.

4265 FUCHS, K. D. *Ertrag von Kapitalanlagen in Aktien. Eine methodisch-empirische Analyse* (Efficiency of investments in stocks. An empirical-methodological analysis). Wien, Manz, 72, 111 p.

4266 GALE, B. T. "Market share and rate of return", *R. Econ. Statist.* 54(4), nov 72 : 412-423.

4267 GARCIA, G. "Olech's theorem and the dynamic stability of theories of the rate of interest", *J. econ. Theory* 4(3), jun 72 : 541-544.

4268 GHOSH, D.; PARKIN, M. "A theoretical and empirical analysis of the portfolio debt, and interest rate behaviour of building societies", *Manchester Sch. Econ. soc. Stud.* 40(3), sep 72 : 231-244.

4269 Bibl. XXI-4411. GUTTENTAG, J. M. (ed.). *Essays on interest rates.* CR: E. J. KANE, *J. econ. Liter.* 10(4), dec 72 : 1234-1236.

4270 HARVEY, C. E. "On the cost-inflationary impact of high interest rates", *J. econ. Issues* 6(2-3), sep 72 : 97-105.

4271 HORVAT, B. "Fixed capital cost, depreciation multiplier and the rate of interest", *Europ. econ. R.* 4(2), jun 73 : 163-179.

4272 KAREKEN, J. H.; MUENCH, T.; WALLACE, N. "Optimal open market strategy: the use of information variables", *Amer. econ. R.* 63(1), mar 73 : 156-172.

4273 McGUIGAN, J. R.; KING, W. R. "Security option strategy under risk aversion, an analysis", *J. financ. quant. Anal.* 8(1), jan 73 : 1-15.

4274 NELSON, C. R. "Estimation of term premiums for average yield differentials in the term structure of interest rates", *Econometrica* 40(2), mar 72 : 277-287.

4275    NELSON, C. R. "Testing a model of term structure of interest rates in an error-learning framework", *J. polit. Econ.* 80(6), nov-dec 72 : 1259-1270.

4276    Bibl. XXI-4421. NELSON, C. R. *The term structure of interest rates.* CR: W. T. TERRELL, *J. econ. Liter.* 11(2), jun 73 : 569-571.

4277    PETTIT, P. R. "Dividend announcements, security performance, and capital market efficiency", *J. Finance* 27(5), dec 72 : 993-1007.

4278    PYLE, D. H. "Descriptive theories of financial institutions under uncertainty", *J. financ. quant. Anal.* 7(5), dec 72 : 2009-2029.

4279    ROSENFELD, F. *Analyse financière et gestion des portefeuilles.* Paris, Dunod, 72, xi-385 p. [Le présent ouvrage est une nouvelle version entièrement remaniée et mise à jour du livre publié en 1963 ... sous le titre: *Analyse des valeurs mobilières.*]

4280    Bibl. XXI-4428. SINGH, A. *Take-overs: their relevance to the stock market and the theory of the firm.* CR: M. A. CREW, *J. econ. Liter.* 11(2), jun 73 : 574-576.

4281    STARRETT, D. A. "On golden rules, the 'biological theory of interest', and competitive inefficiency", *J. polit. Econ.* 80(2), mar-apr 72 : 276-291.

4282    TWARK, A. J.; DUKES, W. P.; BOWLIN, O. D. *Security analysis and portfolio management; a casebook.* San Francisco, Holden-Day, 73, x-321 p.

4283    WAUD, R. N. "Monetary reform and the payment of interest on money", *J. polit. Econ.* 80(1), jan-feb 72 : 159-170.

4284    WILBUR, W. L. "Return and risk characteristics of high-grade bonds", *Quart. R. Econ. Busin.* 12(3), 1972 : 45-54.

### J.4221    *Local studies*
               *Études localisées*

[See also / Voir aussi: 4115]

4285    ASAMI, T. "Japan's capital market: recent developments", *Finance and Develop.* 9(4), dec 72 : 50-54.

4286    BETHLEHEM, G. "An investigation of the return on ordinary shares quoted on the Johannesburg Stock Exchange with reference to hedging against inflation", *South Afr. J. Econ.* 40(3), sep 72 : 254-267.

4287    DAVIS, E. W.; GRANT, A. T. K. "Small business and the capital market: reflections on the report on the Bolton Committee", *Moorgate and Wall Street* (3), 1972 : 48-62. [UK.]

4288    FASE, M. M. G. "A principal components analysis of market interest rates in the Netherlands, 1962-1970", *Europ. econ. R.* 4(2), jun 73 : 107-134.

4289    GLYN, A. "The stock market valuation of British companies and the cost of capital, 1955-1969", *Oxford econ. Pap.* 25(2), jul 73 : 213-240. [UK.]

4290    GUPTA, U. L. *Working of stock exchanges in India.* New Delhi, Thomson Press, 72, xi-335 p.

4291    HAWKINS, B. S. "Towards a European capital market", *R. Soc. Ét. Expans.* 72(254), jan-feb 73 : 81-87.

4292    ISAZA, B. R.; PRIETO, D. R.; GOMEZ, R. A. "Algunos aspectos de las tasas de interés en Colombia" (Some aspects of interest rates in Colombia), *R. Banco Republ.* 45(358), aug 72 : 1374-1387.

4293    KENT, C. H. *European stock exchange handbook.* Park Ridge, N. J., Noyes Data Corporation, 73, xvii-567 p.

4294    KING, J. L. *Human behavior and Wall Street.* Chicago, Swallow Press, 73, 226 p.

4295    KORSVOLD, P. E. "Price behaviour of new debt issues and channelling efficiency in three European capital markets", *J. Busin. Finance* 4(4), 1972 : 1-9.

4296    LAZZARINI, H. J. "El mercado de capitales argentino: una visión heterodoxa de su funcionamiento" (The Argentina stock market: a heterodox vision of its functioning), *R. Econ. latinoamer.* 9(36), 1973 : 137-157.

4297    LUTFALLA, M. "L'économie et la bourse américaine en 1972", *R. Sci. écon.* 48(175), sep 73 : 111-127.

4298    LUTFALLA, M. "Le marché financier", *R. Écon. polit. (Paris)* 82(5), sep-oct 72 : 939-951. [France.]

4299    MARNATA, F. *La Bourse et le financement des investissements.* Paris, A. Colin, 73, 122-5 p.

4300 MASERA, R. S. *The term structure of interest rates: an expections model tested on post-war Italian data.* London-New York-Tokyo-Toronto, Oxford University Press, 72, ix-211 p. CR: J. M. MASON, *J. econ. Liter.* 11(3), sep 73 : 935-936.

4301 MONROE, W. F. *Japan: financial markets and the world economy.* New York, Praeger, 73, xxix-217 p.

4302 PARES, I. "El mercado de valores español y la dicotomia invalida: unas consideraciones sobre la política bursatil" (The Spanish stock market and the invalid dichotomy: some considerations on stock exchange policy), *Moneda y Créd.* 121, jun 72 : 119-141. [Spain.]

4303 PELLERI, P. "Le borse estere nel 1972" (Foreign stock markets in 1972), *Bancaria* 29(2), feb 73 : 164-188.

4304 REINARDT, E. "Betrachtungen zur schweizerischen Zinspolitik" (Thoughts on Swiss interest rate policy), *Schweiz. Mh.* 53(8), nov 73 : 549-555.

4305 ROSA, J. J. "Equilibre et prix du risque sur le marché à terme de la Bourse de Paris", *J. Soc. Statist. Paris* 113(3), jul-sep 72 : 198-214.

4306 SAVING, T. R. "Toward a competitive financial sector", *J. Money Cred. Bank.* 4(4), nov 72 : 897-914. [USA.]

4307 SCHACHTER, G.; COHEN, B. "Influenze interne sui mercati dei capitali degli Stati Uniti" (Internal influences on capital markets in the United States), *Bancaria* 29(2), feb 73 : 156-163.

4308 SILVEIRA, A. M. "Interest rates and rapid inflation: the evidence from the Brazilian economy", *J. Money Cred. Bank.* 5(3), aug 73 : 794-805.

4309 SOLNICK, B. H. *European capital markets: towards a general theory of international investment.* Lexington, Mass., Lexington Books, 73, xii-114 p.

4310 THUNHOLM, L. E. "The capital market and economic progress", *Skand. Ensk. Bank. quart. R.* (1), 1973 : 2-12. [Sweden.]

4311 TUN WAI, U.; PATRICK, H. T. "Stock and bond issues and capital markets in less developed countries", *Staff Pap.* 20(2), jul 73 : 253-317.

4312 VITAL, S. M.; NESS, W. L. Jr. "O progresso do mercado brasileiro de capitais: una avaliaçao crítica" (Progress of the Brazilian capital market: a critical point of view), *R. Adm. Empresas* 13(1), jan-mar 73 : 7-17.

4313 WYCKOFF, P. *Wall Street and the stock markets: a chronology,* 1644-1971. Philadelphia, Chilton Book Co., 72, xiv-304 p.

## J.5 MONETARY POLICY
## POLITIQUE MONÉTAIRE

### J.50 General studies
### Études générales

[See also / Voir aussi: 4008, 4020, 5607, 5608, 5822, 6199, 6206, 6223]

4314 BRUNHOFF, S. DE; BRUINI, P. *La politique monétaire; un essai d'interprétation marxiste.* Paris, Presses universitaires de France, 73, 200 p.

4315 COURAKIS, A. S. "Monetary policy: old wisdom behind a new facade", *Economica (London)* 40(157), feb 73 : 73-86.

4316 HAVRILESKY, T. "Finding the optimal monetary strategy with information contraints", *J. Finance* 27(5), dec 72 : 1045-1056.

4317 HAVRILESKY, T. "A new program for more monetary stability", *J. polit. Econ.* 80(1), jan-feb 72 : 171-175.

4318 HENDERSON, D. W.; SARGENT, T. J. "Monetary and fiscal policy in a two-sector aggregative model", *Amer. econ. R.* 63(3), jun 73 : 345-365.

4319 HOLTROP, M. W. *Money in an open economy. Selected papers on monetary policy, monetary analysis and central banking.* Leiden, Stenfert Kroese, 72, xlvi-380 p.

4320 HOSEK, W. R. "Alternative monetary policies and the stability of equilibrium", *Econ. int. (Genova)* 25(4), nov 72 : 683-696.

4321 LAMPREAVE, J. L. "Política monetaria y política fiscal: contraste en un país desarrollado" (Monetary policy and fiscal policy: a contrast in a developed country), *Moneda y Créd.* 122, sep 72 : 13-64.

195

4322   MACKAY, R. "Monetary policy in a disequilibrium model of growth", *Amer. Economist* 16(1), 1972 : 77-101.

4323   MASERA, R. S. "Politica monetaria e politica finanziara in un economia aperta" (Monetary and financial policy in an open economy), *Riv. Polit. econ.* 63(2), feb 73 : 255-258.

4324   MINSKY, H. P. "An evaluation of recent monetary policy", *Nebraska J. Econ. Busin.* 11(4), 1972 : 37-56.

4325   MONISSEN, H. G. "Some theoretical issues in Keynesian stabilization policy", *Schweizer. Z. Volkswirtsch. Statist.* 108(4), dec 72 : 523-554.

4326   MOSSÉ, R. *Politique monétaire.* Paris, Payot, 72, 264 p.

4327   PARK, Y. C. "Some current issues in the transmission process of monetary policy", *IMF Staff Pap.* 19(1), mar 72 : 1-45.

4328   POOLE, W.; LIEBERMAN, C. "Improving monetary control", *Brookings Pap. econ. Activity* (2), 1972 : 293-335.

4329   SIJBEN, J. J. "Near-banking and monetary policy", *Econ. quart. R.* 31, dec 72 : 5-14.

4330   SIMONE, D. "Sobre política monetaria en alta inflación" (On monetary policy in intense inflation), *Económica (La Plata)* 18(1), jan-apr 72 : 55-118.

4331   SOCHER, K. *Koordination des Einsatzes geld- und finanzpolitischer Instrumente* (Coordination of intervention instruments of monetary and financial policy). Berlin, Duncker und Humblot, 71, 140 p.

4332   SWOBODA, A. K. "Monetary policy under fixed exchange rates: effectiveness, the speed of adjustment and proper use", *Economica (London)* 40(158), mai 73 : 136-154.

4333   TANNER, J. E. "Indicators of monetary policy: an evaluation of five", *Banca naz. Lav. quart. R.* 103, dec 72 : 413-427.

4334   TOWER, E. "Monetary and fiscal policy under fixed and flexible exchange rates in the inter-run", *J. Money Cred. Bank.* 4(4), nov 72 : 877-896.

4335   VACIAGO, G. "Politica monetaria: previsione e programmazione e breve" (Monetary policy: short-term forecasting and planning), *Moneta e Cred.* 25(99), 3 trim 72 : 314-340.

## J.51   Local studies
## Études localisées

[See also / Voir aussi: **J.152; J.161; J.24;** 3971, 4110, 4119, 4155, 5633, 6270]

4336   ARCUCCI, F. *La politica della liquidità nel sistema bancario svizzero* (Liquidity policy in the Swiss banking system). Milano, A. Giuffrè, 72, xxv-401 p.

4337   ARTIS, M. J. "Monetary policy in the United Kingdom: the indicator problem", *Banker's Mag.* 214(1543), oct 72 : 145-152; 214(1544), nov 72 : 185-191.

4338   BIAGLIOLI, M.; BISOGNI, M. C. "Politica monetaria e investimenti industriali in Italia: 1959-1969" (Monetary policy and industrial investments in Italy: 1959-1969), *G. Economisti* 31(7-8), jul-aug 72 : 413-445.

4339   BLONDEL, D.; PARLY, J. M. "La politique monétaire en 1971", *R. Écon. polit. (Paris)* 82(5), sep-oct 72 : 896-924. [France.]

4340   BURGER, A. E.; STEVENS, N. A. "Monetary expansion and Federal Open Market Committee operating strategy in 1971", *Fed. Reserve Bank St-Louis* 54(3), mar 72 : 11-31. [USA.]

4341   DEANE, R. S. *Papers on monetary policy, credit creation, economic objectives and the Reserve Bank.* Wellington, Reserve Bank of New Zealand, 72, 35 p. [New Zealand.]

4342   DINGLE, J. F.; SPARKS, G. R.; WALKER, M. A. "Monetary policy and the adjustment of chartered bank assets", *Canad. J. Econ.* 5(2), nov 72 : 494-514. [Canada.]

4343   FERBER, R. E. *Die britische Währungspolitik nach dem Zweiten Weltkrieg* (British monetary policy after the Second World War). Zürich Schulthess Polygraphischer Verlag, 72, iv-184 p.

4344   FISHER, G.; SHEPPARD, D. *Effects of monetary policy on the United States economy; a survey of econometric evidence.* Paris, Organisation for Economic Co-operation and Development, 72, 128 p. [Also published in French.]

4345   GOISIS, G. "La funzione di reazione delle autorità monetarie italiane nel periodo 1960-1969" (The reaction function of the Italian monetary authorities during the 1960-1969 period), *Riv. int. Sci. soc.* 81(3), mai-jun 73 : 208-228.

4346 GRIFFITHS, M. *Mexican monetary policy and economic development.* New York-London, Praeger, 72, xii-161 p. CR: J. SHEAHAN, *J. econ. Liter.* 11(3), sep 73 : 918-919.

4347 GRIFFITHS, B. "Resource efficiency, monetary policy and the reform of the UK banking system", *J. Money Cred. Bank.* 5(1), feb 73 *Part I:* 61-77.

4348 HODGMAN, D. "The effectiveness of monetary policy in the EEC", *Bankers' Mag.* 216(1555), oct 73 : 147-153.

4349 IL'JASOV, V. A. *Valjutnye problemy SŠA* (USA monetary problems). Moskva, Finansy, 72, 120 p.

4350 KHATKHATE, D. R. "Analytic basis of the working of monetary policy in less developed countries", *Staff Pap.* 19(3), nov 72 : 533-558.

4351 KIYĀNI, M. *Ansätze und Möglichkeiten der Geld- und Fiskalpolitik als Finanzierungsinstrumente einer gesamtwirtschaftlichen Entwicklungspolitik, dargestellt am Beispiel Persiens* (Beginnings and possibilities of monetary and fiscal policy as an instrument of financing global development policy according to the Iran example). Berlin, Duncker und Humblot, 71, 146 p.

4352 KÖLLNER, L. *Chronik der deutschen Währungspolitik 1871-1971* (A chronicle of German monetary policy, 1871-1971). Frankfurt-am-Main, E. Knapp, 72, 175 p.

4353 KOLODZIEJ, E. A. "French monetary diplomacy in the sixties: background notes to the current monetary crisis", *Wld Aff.* 135(1), 1972 : 5-39.

4354 KOOT, R. S. "Price expectations and monetary adjustments in Uruguay", *Soc. econ. Stud.* 21(4), dec 72 : 474-480.

4355 KUKKONEN, P. "Features of the Finnish monetary relationships", *Ekon. Samfund. Ts.* 26(2), 1973 : 123-131.

4356 LEWIS, M. K.; WALLACE, R. H. "Current issues of monetary policy in Australia", *Bankers' Mag.* 216(1555), oct 73 : 160-164.

4357 LOSSER, A. "La politique monétaire de la RFA", *R. Quest. allem.* 28(5), sep-oct 73 : 22-53.

4358 MAISEL, S. J. *Managing the dollar.* New York, Norton, 73, xi-322 p. [USA.]

4359 MATIAS, J. R. *Correção monetária* (Monetary correction). Rio de Janeiro, Editora Espressao e Cultura, 72, 127 p. [Brazil.]

4360 MENGARELLI, G. "La politica monetaria componente della crisi italiana" (The monetary policy component of the Italian crisis), *Riv. int. Sci. econ. com.* 19(11), nov 72 : 1095-1104.

4361 MINSKY, H. P. "Problems of US monetary policy in 1973", *Banker's Mag.* 1553, aug 73 : 63-68. [USA.]

4362 MINSKY, H. S. "An evaluation of recent US monetary policy", *Banker's Mag.* 214(1543), oct 72 : 141-144; 214(1544), nov 72 : 181-185; 214(1545), dec 72 : 229-235.

4363 MITTRA, S. *Monetary politics in India.* Bombay, Vora, 72, xii-250 p.

4364 NASSEF, E. S. M. A. M. *Monetary policy in developing countries; the Mexican case.* Rotterdam, Universitaire Pers Rotterdam, 72, ix-256 p.

4365 NEUBAUER, W. *Strategien, Techniken und Wirkungen der Geld- und Kreditpolitik. Eine theoretische und empirische Untersuchung für die Bundesrepublik Deutschland* (Strategies, techniques and effects of monetary and credit policy. A theoretical and empirical analysis for the Federal Republic of Germany). Göttingen, Vandenhoeck und Ruprecht, 72, 337 p.

4366 ORGANIZATION FOR ECONOMIC CO-OPERATION AND DEVELOPMENT. *Monetary policy in Japan.* Paris, OECD, 105 p.

4367 PARK, Y. C. "The role of money in stabilization policy in developing countries", *Staff. Pap.* 20(2), jul 73 : 379-418.

4368 "Politica monetaria do Brasil, 1947-1972 (A)" (The monetary policy of Brazil, 1947-1972), *Conjunt. econ.* 27(7), jul 73 : 76-97; 27(8), aug 73 : 151-161.

4369 PORTER, M. G. "Capital flows as an offset to monetary policy: the German experience", *IMF Staff Pap.* 19(2), jul 72 : 395-424.

4370 RASCHE, R. H. "Simulations of stabilization policies for 1966-1970 *J. Money Cred. Bank.* 5(1), feb 73 *Part I:* 1-25. [USA.]

4371 SDRALEVICH, A.; MONTI, M. "I modelli macroeconomici per la politica monetaria in Italia" (Macro-economic models for the Italian monetary policy), *Industria* (1-2), jan-mar 73 : 36-58.

4372 SHRIVASTAVA, N. N. *Evolution of the techniques of monetary management in India.* Bombay, Somaiya Publications, 72, x-415 p.

4373  TOMORI, S. "Monetary policy in a war economy—the Nigerian experience", *Soc. econ. Stud.* 21(3), sep 72 : 338-347.

4374  VACIAGO, G. "Monetary analysis and policy: an aggregated model for the Italian economy", *Banca naz. Lav. quart. R.* 105, jun 73 : 84-108.

4375  WINTERBERGER, G. "Gedanken zur schweizerischen Währungs- und Konjunkturpolitik" (Thoughts on Switzerland's monetary and economic policy), *Schweiz. Mh.* 53(4), jul 73 : 233-244.

4376  YEAGER, L. B. *Monetary policy and economic performance; views before and after the freeze.* Washington, American Enterprise for Institute for Public Policy Research, 72, 35 p. [USA.]

# K INCOME AND INCOME DISTRIBUTION
# REVENU ET DISTRIBUTION DU REVENU

### K.1 INCOME: CONCEPT AND THEORY
### REVENU: CONCEPT ET THÉORIE

[See also / Voir aussi: **F.211**]

4377 BECKERMAN, W. "'Environments', 'needs' and real income comparisons'', *R. Income Wealth* 18(4), dec 72 : 333-339.

4378 BLANCO LOSADA, M. A. "Producción, distribución y equilibrio de la renta'' (Production, distribution and income equilibrium), *De Economía* 25(122), jul-sep 72 : 467-500.

4379 BOWDEN, R. "Some implications of the permanent income hypothesis'', *R. econ. Stud.* 40(1), jan 73 : 33-37.

4380 CIAVARELLA, D. "Considerazioni teoriche sul reddito nella concezione della finanza dinamica'' (Theoretical considerations on income in the conception of dynamic finance), *Stato soc.* 17(5), jun 73 : 402-415; 17(6), jun 73 : 470-492.

4381 "Intergenerational determinants of individual incomes'', *Amer. econ. R.* 63(2), mai 73 *Pap. and Proc.*: 335-358. With contributions by: J. A. BRITTAIN, S. BOWLES and A. LEIBOWITZ.

4382 LAUMAS, P. S.; LAUMAS, G. S. "On how to calculate permanent income'', *R. Income Wealth* 18(4), dec 72 : 435-438.

4383 MAYER, T. *Permanent income, wealth, and consumption: a critique of the permanent income theory, the life-cycle hypothesis, and related theories.* Berkeley, University of California Press, 72, xv-415 p.

4384 MAYER, T. "Tests of the permanent income theory with continuous budgets'', *J. Money Cred. Bank.* 4(4), nov 72 : 757-778.

4385 McKEAN, J. R. "A note on the concept of revenue elasticity'', *Intermountain econ. R.* 3(2), 1972 : 98-99.

4386 SALES, H. *La croissance des revenus.* Paris, Presses universitaires de France, 72, 95 p.

4387 SARKISJAN, G. S. *Uroven', tempy i proporcii rosta real'nyh dohodov pri socializme* (Level, rythms, and proportions of real income growth in socialism). Moskva, Ekonomika, 72, 215 p.

### K.2 DISTRIBUTION OF NATIONAL INCOME
### DISTRIBUTION DU REVENU NATIONAL

#### K.20 General studies
#### Études générales

[See also / Voir aussi: **M.431**; 2217, 3780, 4469, 4470, 4884, 5611, 5800]

4388 BARBASH, J. "Approaches to incomes policy: a review article'', *J. econ. Issues* 6(4), dec 72 : 61-67.

4389 BURROWS, P.; HITIRIS, T. "Estimating the impact of incomes policy'', *B. econ. Res.* 24(1), mai 72 : 42-51.

4390 DeLEON, R. E. "A note on the use of aggregate personal income data as a research tool'', *West. polit. Quart.* 26(1), mar 73 : 170-173.

4391 DOUBEN, N. H. "Herverdelingspolitiek. Van hoofdzaak naar bijzaak ?'' (Redistribution policy: from main issue to side-issue ?), *Economist (Haarlem)* 120(2), mar-apr 72 : 113-133.

4392 ENGLAND, R. "Ability, opportunity, and the distribution of income: a review of Becker and Mincer'', *Amer. Economist* 16(1), 1972 : 137-147.

investment efficiency in the Yugoslav economy), *Ekonomist (Zagreb)* 25(3-4), 1972 : 423-443.

4831    BEŠTER, M. "Viri financiranja investicij v negospodarski sferi" (Sources of investment financing in the non-economic sphere), *Ekon. R. (Ljubljana)* 23(2-3), sep 72 : 127-139. [Yugoslavia.]

4832    CHIANCONE, A. "Il sistema svedese dei fonti di riserva per gli investimenti come strumento di stabilizzazione economica" (The Swedish system of reserve funds for investments as an instrument of economic stabilization), *Riv. int. Sci.* econ. com. 20(3), mar 73 : 242-266.

4833    DURDAG, M. *Some problems of developing financing. A case study of the Turkish first five-year plan 1963-67.* Dordrecht, Reidel, 73, xiii-297 p.

4834    FINK, G. "Die Investitionspolitik in der UdSSR 1950-1969" (Investment policy in the USSR from 1950 to 1969), *Osteuropa Wirtsch.* 17(4), dec 72 : 261-271.

4835    FOURNIER, J. P. *Le financement extérieur des investissements publics à Madagascar (1963-1971).* Tananarive, ORSTOM, 72, 57 p.

4836    GORDON, J. "Niektóre elementy długoterminowej polityki inwestycyjnej" (Some elements of long-term investment policy), *Invest. i Budown.* (5), 1973 : 29-32. [Poland.]

4837    HAMDANI, D. H. "Investment incentives in the Canadian budget", *B. int. fisc. Docum.* 26(9), sep 72 : 311-314.

4838    KATANGA, T. "Évolution de la législation de la République démocratique du Congo en matière d'investissements privés et son incidence sur le développement", *Cah. zaïr. Rech. Dévelop.* 17, numéro spécial 1971 : 123-152.

4839    ŁĄCZKOWSKI, W. "Finansowanie inwestycji w Jugosławii" (Financing of investments in Yugoslavia), *Ruch prawn. ekon. socjol.* (2), 1973 : 211-217.

4840    LIDWIN-PIOTROWSKA, E. "Kształtowanie się efektywnosci inwestycji w krajach EWG i RWPG w latach 1959-1969" (Investment efficiency in the E.E.C. and COMECON countries in the years 1959-1969), *Fol. oecon. cracov.* 14, 1973 : 61-77.

4841    LUTIER, E. *Le choix des investissements publics dans la région.* Grenoble, CERAT, 72, 138 ff. [France.]

4842    MARAIS, J. S. "Investing in South Africa", *South Afr. int. Quart.* 3(4), apr 73 : 231-239.

4843    MITREGA, J. "Aktualne problemy polityki inwestycyjnej" (Present problems of investment policy), *Nowe Drogi* 27(9), mai 73 : 13-26. [Poland.]

4844    NATTIER, F. E. *Investment in developing countries.* New York, Practising Law Institute 72, 224 p.

4845    PATHAK, M. T. *Significance of public investment for backward regions; a case study of the fluorspar project in Gujarat.* Vallabh Vidhyanagar, Department of Economics, Sardar Patel University, 72, x-156 p. [India.]

4846    PŁOCICA, A. "Inwestycje w połowie planu 5-letniego—wyniki i wnioski" (Investment in the middle of the 5-year plan), *Invest. i Budown.* (10), 1973 : 1-8. [Poland.]

4847    PYKA, T. *Programowanie optymalnych podziałów inwestycyjnych* (Optimal programming of capital investments). Warszawa, Państwowe Wydawnictwo, Naukkwe, 72, 15 p. [Poland.]

4848    RADOCEA, A. "Investitiile si rolul lor in dezvoltarea economico-sociala a Romaniei socialiste" (Investments and their role in the social-economic development of socialist Rumania), *R. Statist. (Bucuresti)* 21(12), dec 72 : 32-41.

4849    ROCKLEY, L. E. *Investment for profitability: an analysis of the policies and practices of U.K. and international companies.* London, Business Books 73, xiv-320 p.

4850    SEIDENSTECHER, G. *Reformmassnahmen im Bereich der Planung und Finanzierung von Investitionen in Osteuropa* (Reforms in the area of planning and financing of investments in Eastern Europe). Köln, Bundesinstitut für Ostwissenschaftliche und Internationale Studien, 71, 60 p.

4851    SERGEEV, S. S.; HARITONOV, N. S. *Kapital'nye vloženija v sel'skoe hozhajstvo: planirovanie i effektivnost'* (Capital investments in agricultural planning and efficiency). Moskva, Ekonomika, 72, 247 p.

4852    SHAPIRO, D. "Can public investment have a positive rate of return ?", *J. polit. Econ.* 81(2), mar-apr 73 : 401-413. [USA.]

4853    SULKOWSKI, C. "Méthodes de calcul du taux d'efficacité des dépenses d'investissement", *R. Est* 4(3), jul 73 : 65-84. [Pologne.]

4854 Szarota, R. "Proces doskonalenia systemu finansowania inwestycji" (Process of improvements in the investment financing system), *Finanse* (5), 1973 : 8-23. [Poland.]

4855 Ujházy, K. "A beruházástervezés tökéletesitésének idöszerü kérdései Czehszlovákiában" (Actual matters concerning the perfecting of investment planning in Czechoslovakia), *Közgazd. Szle* 19(11), nov 72 : 1269-1286.

4856 Vassilev, V. *L'investissement en économie socialiste.* Paris, Presses universitaires de France, 72, 94-2 p.

4857 Waksmundzki, S. "Warunki skutecznosci działania systemu finansowania inwestycji" (Conditions for efficient functioning of the investment financing system), *Finanse* (6), 1973 : 26-39. [Poland.]

4858 Woodward, J. T. "Investment programs and sale expectations for 1973", *Survey curr. Busin.* 53(3), mar 73 : 16-21. [USA.]

4859 Zjalić, Lj. M. "Metodi finansiranja razvoja nedovoljno razvijenih prodručja na primerima italijanskog i jugoslovenskog iskustva" (Methods of financing the development of insufficiently developed regions following the Italian and Yugoslav examples), *Ekonomist (Zagreb)* 25(3-4), 1972 : 519-530.

### L.32 Investments, by sectors
### Investissements, par secteurs

[See also / Voir aussi: 2624, 2818, 2823, 3135, 3347, 3453, 3960, 4338, 5048]

4860 Aberle, G. *Verkehrsinfrastrukturinvestitionen im Wachstumsprozess entwickelter Volkswirtschaften* (Investments in road infrastructure and their place in the economic growth of developed countries). Düsseldorf, Handelsblatt GmbH, 72, 218 p.

4861 Asmankina, A. I.; Fomina, G. A. "Opyt i problemy finansirovanija kapital'nyh vloženij v sel'skoe hozjajstvo" (Experience and problems of the financing of investments in agriculture), *Den'gi i Kred.* 31(7), jul 72 : 38-43. [USSR.]

4862 Barat, J. et al. "Investimento rodoviário e padroes de uso do solo" (Road investments and patterns of land utilization), *R. Adm. publ. (Rio de Janeiro)* 7(1), jan-mar 73 : 49-70. [Brazil.]

4863 Bartholmai, B. *Analyse des Angebotspotentials und Projektion des Investitionsbedarfs im Verkehr in der Bundesrepublik Deutschland* (Analysis of potential supply and projection of needs in investments in transportation in the German Federal Republic). Berlin, Duncker und Hubmot, 72, 176 p.

4864 Boatwright, B. D.; Eaton, J. R. "The stimulation of investment functions for manufacturing industry in the United Kingdom", *Economica (London)* 39(156), nov 72 : 403-418.

4865 Buchholz, E. *Wohnungswirtschaftliche Investitionsdeterminanten; eine theoretisch-empirische Analyse* (Determining factors of housing investments: a theoretical empirical analysis). Münster, Institut für Siedlungs- und Wohnungswesen der Westfälischen Wilhelms-Universität, 72, x-250 p.

4866 Carsalade, Y.; Nicolas, F. "Filo: modèle de financement du logement", *Statist. Ét. financ. Sér. orange* 3(9), 1 trim. 73 : 3-23. [France.]

4867 Eliasiewicz, T. "Problemy programowania inwestycji turystycznych" (Problems in programming investments for tourism), *Probl. ekon. (Warszawa)* (1), 1973 : 49-61. [Poland.]

4868 Filippini, R.; Giovanelli, L.; Orlando, G. "Politica degli investimenti nelle zone rurali come strumento dello sviluppo delle economie dualistiche" (Investment policy in rural areas as an instrument of development of dualistic economies), *Riv. Econ. agr.* 27(6), 1972 : 61-86. [Italy.]

4869 Glanowski, M. "Usprawnienie procesu inwestycyjnego w górnictwie energetyce" (Improvement in the investment process in the mining and energy industries), *Invest. i Budown.* (5), 1973 : 20-35. [Poland.]

4870 Gutelman, M. "Le financement de la réforme agraire comme rapport de classes", *Ét. rur.* 48, oct-dec 72 : 7-38.

4871 Habiby, A. J. "Financing industrial development in the Arab States", *Industr. Egypt* 48(2), apr-jun 72 : 4-11.

4872 Jasińska, D. "Ulgi inwestycyjne dla gospodarstw rolnych" (Investment allowances for agricultural holdings), *Finanse* (8), 1973 : 34-43. [Poland.]

4873    JURGENSEN, H. "Problem of investment planning in the transport field", *German econ. R.* 11(1), 1973 : 1-13.

4874    RYZENKOV, I. I. *Ekonomičeskaja effektivnost' kapital'nyh vloženij v neftedobyvajuščuju promyslennost'* (Economic efficiency of capital investments in the petroleum industry). Moskva, Nedra, 72, 168 p. [USSR.]

4875    THOMAS, R. "The new fiscal incentives to invest: liquidity and profitability aspects", *Scott. J. polit. Econ.* 19(3), nov 72 : 273-286. [UK.]

4876    ZIMMERMAN, J. F. "Financing public transportation", *Nat. civic R.* 62(6), jun 73 : 301-305. [USA.]

# M SOCIAL ECONOMICS AND POLICY
## ÉCONOMIE ET POLITIQUE SOCIALES

**M.1    BASIC CONCEPTS : SOCIAL ECONOMICS, SOCIAL POLICY
AND JUSTICE, WELFARE
CONCEPTS DE BASE : ÉCONOMIE, POLITIQUE ET JUSTICE
SOCIALES, BIEN-ÊTRE**

[See also / Voir aussi: 3792, 3987, 4240]

4877    BERLINER, J. S. *Economy, society and welfare; a study in social economics*. New York, Praeger, 72, xvii-196 p.

4878    FORTE, F.; MOSSETTO, G. *Economia del benessere e democrazia* (Welfare economics and democracy). Milano, F. Angeli, 72, 86 p.

4879    GINTIS, H. "A radical analysis of welfare economics and individual development", *Quart. J. Econ.* 86(4), nov 72 : 572-599.

4880    GINTIS, H. "Welfare economics of individual development", *Quart. J. Econ.* 86(4), nov 72 : 572-599.

4881    GREEN, J. R. "On the inequitable nature of core allocations", *J. econ. Theory* 4(2), apr 72 : 132-143.

4882    HOCH, R.; GROĆ, I. "A jóléti gazdaságtanról" (An economic survey of welfare), *Közgazd Szle* 19(12), dec 72 : 1447-1458.

4883    HOMČENKO, A. G. *Ekonomika narodnogo blagosostojanija* (Welfare economics) Krasnodar, Kniznoe izdatel'stvo, 72, 65 p.

4884    KATS, A. "On the social welfare function and the parameters of income distribution", *J. econ. Theory* 5(3), dec 71 : 377-382.

4885    LA GORCE, P. DE. *Pour un nouveau partage des richesses*. Paris, Bernard Grasset, 72, 141 p.

4886    LEVITAN, S. A.; REIN, M.; MARWICK, D. *Work and welfare go together*. Baltimore (Md.), Johns Hopkins University Press, 72, xii-143 p.

4887    MICHALEWSKI, A. *Ekonomia dobrobytu* (Welfare economics). Warszawa, Państwowe Wydawnictwo Ekonomiczne, 72, 315 p.

4888    MUELLER, D. C. "Constitutional democracy and social welfare", *Quart. J. Econ.* 87(1), feb 73 : 60-80.

4889    OSANA, H. "Externalities and the basic theorems of welfare economics", *J. econ. Theory* 4(3), jun 72 : 401-414.

4890    PFAFFENBERGER, W. *Wohlstandskriterien für die Wirtschaftsplanung in entwickelten kapitalistischen Marktwirtschaften* (Wealth criteria for economic planning in capitalist market economies). Berlin, Duncker und Humblot, 72, 106 p.

4891    SCHAFER, M. *Marktwirtschaft für morgen; Wohlstand als Aufgabe* (Market economy for tomorrow; welfare as a duty). Stutt art, Seewald Verlag, 72, 134 p.

4892    SCHULZ, H. R. "Sicherheit als Bestandteil der Wohlfart. Eine ökonomische Betrachtung über gesellschaftliche Kosten der Kriminalität" (Security as a component of welfare: an economic investigation on social costs of criminality), *Schweizer. Z. Volkswirtsch. Statist.* 108(3), sep 73 : 377-403.

4893    STAPEL, J. "Welzijn is geen welvaart, maar wat dan wel ?" (Welfare is not happiness, but then what is it ?), *Acta polit.* 8(2), 1973 : 214-219.

4894    "Work and welfare", *J. hum. Resources* 8, 1973 *Suppl.* : 2-125.

**M.11     Welfare criteria and measurement**
**Critère et mesures du bien-être**

4895   CHATFIELD, W. "The influence of the individual's relative position on his utility",
       *Amer. Economist* 16(2), 1973 : 148-150.

4896   FOLDES, L. "Expected utility and continuity", *R. econ. Stud.* 39(4), oct 72 : 407-421.

4897   PASCALLON, P. *La théorie du "second best" en procès; un premier état de la question.* Paris,
       Institut de science économique appliquée, 72, 366-694.

4898   SANTONI, G.; CHURCH, A. "A comment on the general theorem of the second best",
       *R. econ. Stud.* 39(4), oct 72 : 527-530.

4899   STIGUM, B. P. "Finite state, space and expected utility maximization", *Econometrica*
       40(2), mar 72 : 253-259.

**M.2     STANDARD OF LIVING**
**STANDARD DE VIE**

**M.20     General studies**
**Études générales**

[See also / Voir aussi: 5589]

4900   GANS, H. J. "The positive functions of poverty", *Amer. J. Sociol.* 78(2), sep 72 : 275-289.

4901   IUGA, C. "Interdependenţâ dintre rezultatele dezvoltării economice şi creşterea nivelului
       de trai" (Interdependence between economic development and increase in the
       standard of living), *Probl. econ. (Bucureşti)* 26(4), apr 73 : 69-77.

4902   JACKSON, D. *Poverty.* London, Macmillan, 72, 95 p.

4903   KUITENBROUWER, J. *On the practice and theory of affluence and poverty: some reflections.*
       The Hague, Institute of Social Studies, 73, 26 p.

4904   LUSZNIEWICZ, A. "Metodologiczne problemy badania poziomu zycia ludności" (Metho-
       dological problems of investigation of living standard of population), *Przegl. statyst.*
       (2), 1973 : 117-130.

4905   MOORE, B. Jr. *Reflections on the causes of human misery; and upon certain proposals to
       eliminate them.* Boston, Beacon Press, 72, 193p. CR: E. W. LEHMAN, *Contemp. Sociol.*
       2(5), sep 73 : 468-473.

4906   PENNY, D. H.; SINGARIMBUN, M. "A case study of rural poverty", *m. Indones. econ.
       Stud.* 8(1), mar 72 : 79-88.

4907   SWOBODA, H. *Die Qualität des Lebens; vom Wohlstand zum Wohlbefinden* (The quality
       of life: from material welfare to total well-being). Stuttgary, Deutsche Verlags-
       Anstalt, 73, 168 p.

4908   UNITED NATIONS. Economic and Social Council. Committee for Development Planning.
       *Attack on mass poverty and unemployment; views and recommendations of the Com-
       mittee for Development Planning.* New York, UN, 72, v-34 p.

4909   VIBY MOGENSEN, G.; MØRKEBERG, H. "Measuring the standard of living of self-employed
       farmers", *Sociol. rur.* 13(3-4), 1973 : 275-288.

4910   WINTHROP, H. "Poverty, the standard of living, and hunger: how they are affected by
       inflation", *J. hum. Relat.* 20(3), 1972 : 235-265.

4911   ZIENKOWSKI L. "Czy potrafimy mierzyć "poziom zycia" (Can we measure the stand-
       ard of living ?), *Wiadom. statyst.* (11), 1973 : 1-5.

**M.21     Local studies**
**Études localisées**

[See also / Voir aussi: **L.22**; 1655, 4553, 4703, 4749, 4765]

4912   ALLARDT, E.; VUSITALO, H. "Dimensions of welfare in a comparative study of the
       Scandinavian societies", *Scan. polit. Stud.* (7), 1972 : 9-27.

4913   ATKINSON, A. B. *Unequal shares: wealth in Britain.* London, Allen Lane, 72, xx-279 p.

4914   BANGO, J. F. "Niveau de vie et revenu de la paysannerie en Europe du Sud-Est (1960-
       1970), *Docum. Europe centr.* 10(4), jul-aug 72 : 257-273.

4915   BELCHER, J. C.; CRADER, K. W.; VAZQUEZ-CALCERRADA, P. B. "Determinants of level
       of living in rural Puerto Rico", *Rur. Sociol.* 36(2), 1973 : 187-195.

4916 COHEN, H. "Poverty and welfare: a review essay", *Polit. Sci. Quart.* 87(4), dec 72 : 631-652. [USA.]

4917 DEPATIE, R. "La pauvreté au Québec: une analyse économétrique", *Actual. écon.* 48(3), oct-dec 72 : 431-460.

4918 "Dimensions of poverty in America (The)", *Carr. Hist.* 64(382), jun 73 : 241-278.

4919 "Extent of poverty in Ireland", *Soc. Stud.* 1(4), aug 72 : 381-400.

4920 FERRAROTTI, F. "I poveri di New York" (Poverty in New York), *Crit. sociol. (Roma)* 23, 1972 : 184-190; 26, 1973 : 110-118.

4921 GALLAWAY, L. E. *Poverty in America.* Columbus, Ohio, Grid, 73, 160 p.

4922 GLOSTER, J. E. *Economics of minority groups.* Houston, Premier Print. Co., 73, iv-216 p. [USA.]

4923 HARBURY, C. D.; MCMAHON, P. C. "Inheritance and the characteristics of top wealth leavers in Britain", *Econ. J.* 83(331), sep 73 : 810-833.

4924 HARTWELL, R. M. *et al. The long debate on poverty. Eight essays on industrialisation and "the condition of England".* London, Institute of Economic Affairs, 72, xvi-243 p.

4925 HAUSER, S.; LÖRCHER, S. " 'Lebenstandard' und 'Sozialprodukt' " (Standard of living and "social product"), *Konjunkt.-Polit.* 19(2), 1973 : 81-102.

4926 HOLLINGWORTH, P. J. *The powerless poor; a comprehensive guide to poverty in Australia.* North Melbourne, Stockland Press, 72, 220 p.

4927 KONINGS, M. "L'analyse de la pauvreté aux Etats-Unis", *C. écon. Bruxelles* 59, 3 trim. 73 : 443-476.

4928 LEDERER, K. M. *The nature of poverty; an interpretative review of poverty studies with special reference to Canada.* Edmonton, Alta., Human Resources Research Council, 72, ii-115 p.

4929 MATJUHA, I. "Povyšenie žiznennogo urovnija trudjaščihsja SSSR" (The development of workers' standard of living in the USSR), *Vestn. Statist.* (12), dec 72 : 44-50.

4930 MCCORMACK, T. "Poverty in Canada: the Croll Report and its critics", *Canad. R. Sociol. Anthropol.* 9(4), nov 72 : 366-372.

4931 MEADE, J. E. "Poverty in the welfare state", *Oxford econ. Pap.* 24(3), nov 72 : 289-326. [UK.]

4932 MORIN, C.; LESTERLIN, F. "Vivre en Chine: niveau de vie, niveau de contentement" *Projet* 71, jan 73 : 25-38.

4933 "Review symposium on the 1968 level of living survey in Sweden", *Acta sociol.* 16(3), 1973 : 211-239.

4934 SCHEER, L. *Quality of life; Versuch eines europäischen Vergleichs* (Quality of life: a tentative European comparison). Wien, Arbeitsgemeinschaft für Lebensniveau vergleiche, 72, 64 p.

4935 SCHILLER, B. R. *Economics of poverty and discrimination.* Englewood Cliffs, N. J., Prentice-Hall, 73, vii-199p. [USA.]

4936 THOMAS, G. "Regional migration patterns and poverty among the aged in the South" *J. hum. Resources* 8(1), 1973 : 73-84.

4937 THOMAS, G. R.; STEWART, M. *Poverty in the nonmetropolitan South.* Athens, Regional Institute for Social Welfare Research, University of Georgia, 72, viii-143 p.

4938 THURON, L. C. *The economics of poverty and racial discrimination.* New York, Joint Council on Economic Education, 72, 19 p.

4939 VALDE, G.; COPPEDGE, R. O. *Income and poverty data for racial groups; a compilation for Oregon census county divisions.* Corvallis, Cooperative Extension Service, Oregon State University, 72, x-125 p. [USA.]


**M.3    SOCIAL AND WELFARE POLICY (GENERAL AND DESCRIPTIVE STUDIES)**
**POLITIQUE SOCIALE ET POLITIQUE DE BIEN-ÊTRE (ÉTUDES GÉNÉRALES ET DESCRIPTIVES)**

[See also / Voir aussi: 4888, 5189, 5227, 5265, 5329, 5487, 5622]

4940 BOULDING, K. E. *The economy of love and fear: a preface to grants economics.* Belmont, Calif., Wadsworth Publishing Co., 73, 116 p.

4941    BOULDING, K. E.; PFAFF, M.; PFAFF, A. (eds.). *Transfers in an urbanized economy; theories and effects of the grants economy.* Belmont, Calif., Wadsworth Publishing Co., 73, vi-376 p.

4942    BROVKIN, N. A. *Pod'em blagosostojanija naroda-glavnaja zadača pjatiletki* (Elevation of the people's welfare in an essential objective of the five-year plan) Leningrad, Lenizdat, 72, 82 p. [USSR.]

4943    BRUCE, M. *Rise of the welfare state: English social policy* 1601-1971. London, Weidenfeld and Nicolson, 73, xxvii-299 p.

4944    CULYER, A. J. *Economics of social policy.* London, Martin Robertson, 73, xii-268 p.

4945    EPŠTEJN, L. F. *Social'no-ekonomičeskie problemy planirovanija* (Planning socio-economic problems). Čeljabinsk, 72, 132 p.

4946    FRASER, D. *The evolution of the British Welfare State: a history of social policy since the Industrial Revolution.* London, Macmillan, 73, xviii-299 p.

4947    GILL, D. G. "Theoretical perspectives on the analysis and development of social policies" *Int. Soc. Wk* 15(3), 1972 : 17-28.

4948    GILL, D. G. *Unravelling social policy; theory, analysis and political action towards social equality.* Cambridge, Mass., Schenkman Publishing Co., Morristown General Learning Press, 73, xvii-171 p.

4949    GROSSMAN, M. "On the concept of health capital and the demand for health", *J. polit. Econ.* 80(2), mar-apr 72 : 223-255.

4950    GUNTER, H. "Sozialpolitik und post-industrielle Gesellschaft" (Social policy and post industrial society), *Soz. Welt* 24(1), 1973 : 1-24.

4951    KAHN, A. J. *Social policy and social services.* New York, Random House, 73, xi-210 p. [USA.]

4952    KAPLAN, A. "On the strategy of social planning", *Pol. Sci.* 4(1), mar 73 : 41-61.

4953    KAPP, K. W.; VILMAR, F.; SCHMIDT, H. (eds.). *Sozialisierung der Verluste? Die sozialen Kosten eines privatwirtschaftlichen Systems* (Socialization of losses? The social costs of a private economic system). München, C. Hanser, 72, 243 p.

4954    KNOOP, C. T. "The development and application of social policy in the United States", *R. soc. Econ.* 30(1), mar 72 : 54-83.

4955    MALDAGUE, R. "Dimension sociale du plan 1971-75 : un plan d'un style nouveau", *R. belge Sécur. soc.* 15(2), feb 73 : 151-162.

4956    MOJICA DUARTE, G. "Desarrollo y politica social" (Development and social policy *R. Planeación Desar.* 4(2), apr-jun 72 : 34-54.

4957    OFFE, C. "Advanced capitalism and the welfare state", *Polit. and Soc.* 2(4), sum 72 : 479-488.

4958    PIETRUCHA, J. *Polityka społeczna w regionach przemysłowych* (Social policy in industrial regions). Katowice, Śląski Instytut Naukowy, 72, 88 p.

4959    PODOSKI, K. *Prognozy rozwoju społecznego* (Forecasts of social development). Warszawa, Państwowe Wydawnictwo Naukowe, 73, 334 p. [Poland.]

4960    RAJKIEWICZ, A. (ed.). *Polityka społeczna* (Social policy). Warszawa, Państwowe Wydawnictwo Ekonomiczne, 73, 524 p.

4961    ROHDE, H. *Sozialplanung* (Social planning). Bonn-Bad Godesberg, Verlag Neue Gesellschaft, 72, 72 p. [Germany BR.]

4962    SCHWEFEL, D. *Beiträge zur Sozialplanung im Entwicklungsländern* (Contributions to social planning in developing countries). Berlin, Hessling, 72, 104 p.

4963    SLEEMAN, J. F. *The welfare state: its aims, benefits and costs.* London, Allen and Unwin, 73, 8-199 p. [UK.]

4964    SROCZYNSKA, I. "Aktualne problemy polityki socjalnej" (Actual matters of social policy", *Nowe Drogi* 26(11), nov 72 : 17-26. [Poland.]

4965    STAROVEROV, V. I. *et al. Social'naja programma devjatoj pjatiletki* (The ninth plan's social program). Moskva, Politizdat, 72, 144 p. [USSR.]

4966    SZUBERT, W. *Studia z polityki społecznej* (Studies on social policy). Warszawa, Państwowe Wydawnictwo Ekonomiczne, 73, 422 p.

4967    ter-DAVTIAN, L. "The development and application of social policy", *R. soc. Econ.* 30(2), aug 72 : 232-242.

4968    Bibl. XXI-5127. TITMUSS, R. M. *The gift relationship: from human blood to social policy.* CR: J. MOGEY, *Contemp. Sociol.* 2(3), mai 73 : 333-334.

## M.4 SOCIAL SECURITY, SOCIAL ASSISTANCE, WORK SAFETY
## SÉCURITÉ SOCIAL, ASSISTANCE SOCIALE, PROTECTION DU TRAVAIL

### M.41 Systems
### Systèmes

#### M.410 *General studies*
#### *Études générales*

4969 AL-JAMMÂL, M.; ABD AL-RAÑMAN, Ñ. *Durûs fîl-taámînąt al-ijtimą'iyąí* (Studies on social insurance). al-Iskenderîyąí, Muásasat shabad al-Jami'ąí, 73, 248 p.

4970 BOULTON, A. H. *The law and practice of social security*. Bristol, Jordan, 72, xxv-285 p.

4971 MOLES, R. R. "Aspectos administrativos de la seguridad social" (Administrative aspects of social security), *Estud. Segur. soc.* (3), 1972 : 43-75.

4972 PERRIN, G. "Régimes complémentaires et la sécurité sociale", *R. franc. Aff. soc.* 26(2), apr-jun 72 : 35-53.

4973 "Seguridad social y convenios colectivos" (Social security and collective agreements), *Segur. soc. (México)* 20(70), jul-aug 70 : 1-339.

### M.411 *Local studies*
### *Études localisées*

[See also / Voir aussi: 5030]

4974 "A proteçã social no Brasil" (Social protection in Brazil), *R. brasil. Estud. polit.* 35, jan 73 : 1-96.

4975 BAKHOVEN, A. F. "De programmering van de sociale verzekeringen in de periode 1972-75" (Programming of social insurances during the period 1972-75), *Soc. Maandbl. Arb.* 28(1), jan 73 : 7-16. [Netherlands.]

4976 BRAUN, H. *Soziale Sicherung; System und Funktion* (Social security; system and function). Stuttgart, W. Kohlhammer, 72, 103p. [Germany BR.]

4977 BROWN, J. D. *An American philosophy of social security; evolution and issues*. Princeton, N. J., Princeton University Press, 72, x-244 p.

4978 BUTSCHEK, F. "Die österreichische Sozialversicherung im Jahre 1972" (Austrian social insurance in 1972), *Österr. Inst. Wirtsch. Forsch. Mber.* 46(5), mar 73 : 223-227.

4979 CORREIA, S. "Sociedade em movimento e segurança social (Changing society and social security), *Estud. soc. corpor.* 12(35), mar 73 : 5-22. [Portugal.]

4980 ESCALA, G. V. "La seguridad social panameña y su nueva dinámica" (The Panamanian social security and its new dynamics), *Segur. soc. (México)* 21(76), jul-aug 73 : 51-88.

4981 FAJARDO, M. "La seguridad social en relación con el desarrollo económico y social (Social security in relation with social and economic development), *R. iberoamer. Segur. soc.* 22(1), jan-feb 73 : 61-85. [Peru.]

4982 FISHER, P. "Major social security issues; Japan, 1972", *Soc. Secur. B.* 36(3), mar 73 : 26-38.

4983 HASAN, N. *The social security system of India*. New Delhi, S. Chand, 72, xii-252 p.

4984 HAUPTVERBAND DER ÖSTERREICHISCHEN SOZIALVERSICHERUNGSTRAGER. *Fünfundzwanzig Jahre Hauptverband der Osterreichischen Sozialversicherungstrager* (25 years of the principle of association of Austrian social security organisms). Wien, Hauptverlag der Osterreichischen Sozialversicherungsträger, 73, 208 p.

4985 LANTSEV, M. "Progress in social security for agricultural workers in the USSR", *Int. Lab. R.* 107(3), mar 73 : 239-252.

4986 PESO Y CALVO, C. DEL, "Experiencias españolas en la aplicacion de la seguridad social a los trabajadores del campo" (Spanish experiences of the application of social security to rural workers), *R. Polit. soc.* 97, jan-mar 73 : 5-21.

4987 SANDERS, D. S. *The impact of reform movements on social policy change: the case of social insurance*. Fair Lawn, N. J. R. E. Burdick; 73, 205 p. [USA.]

4988 UNITED KINGDOM. Department of health and social security. "Social security in Great Britain", *Int. soc. Secur. R.* 25(3), 1972 : 145-173.

4989 WALLEY, J. *Social security; another British failure?* London, C. Knight, 72, ix-289 p.

### M.412 Comparative studies
### Études comparatives

4990 ARROBA, G. "Social security planning and national planning in the developing countries", *Int. soc. Secur. R.* 25(3), 1972 : 215-242.

4991 HERVO-AKENDENGUE, A. "Social security as an instrument in economic and social development of African countries", *Int. soc. Secur.* R. 25(3), 1972 : 177-214.

4992 INTERNATIONAL LABOUR OFFICE. Social Security branch. "Social security in Latin America: evolution and prospects", *Int. soc. Secur.* R. 25(4), 1972 : 305-356.

4993 PANAYOTOPOULOS, M. *La sécurité sociale des travailleurs migrants; étude sur les règlements de la CEE et la situation de la Suisse.* Genève, Georg, 73, viii-518 p.

4994 VAN LANGENDONCK, J. "Social security legislation in the E. E. C.", *Industr. Law J.* 2(1), mar 73 : 17-27.

4995 WADHAWAN, S. K. "Development of social security in Asia and Oceania", *Int. Soc. Secur.* R. 25(4), 1972 : 395-424.

### M.42 Protection against specific social risks
### Protection contre les risques sociaux spécifiques

### M.421 Family allowances
### Allocations familiales

4996 ASSERBERGHS, L. "Gezinsvergoedingen in België. Ontstaan en evolutie" (Family allowances in Belgium. Origin and evolution), *Tijds. soc. Wetensch.* 18(2), 1973 : 172-194.

4997 DURBIN, E. "Work and welfare: the case of aid to families with dependent children" ,*J. hum. Resources* (8), Suppl. 73 : 103-125.

4998 HOCHARD, J. "Prestations familiales et activité professionnelle", *Dr. soc.* 36(3), jun 73 : 383-392. [France.]

4999 KLOBASA, H. "Tarifliche Sozialzulagen und gesetzliches Kindergeld" (Rate increases in social and family allowances), *Bayern in Zahlen* 27(8), aug 73: 274-283. [Germany FR.]

5000 "Lapsilisät v.1971" (Family allowances in 1971), *Sos. Aikakausk.* 66(6), 1972 : 689-691. [Finland.]

5001 LISEIN-NORMAN, M. "Analyse comparative des prestations familiales dans l'Europe des Six. Réflexions sur la situation actuelle et l'orientation future", *C. écon. Bruxelles* 58, 2 trim. 73 : 219-239.

5002 MAGREZ, M. "Les allocations familiales spéciales", *R. belge Sécur. soc.* 14(9), sep 72 : 1009-1099. [Belgique.]

5003 MAJEWSKA, M. "Ubezpieczenie rodzinne" (Family allowances), *Praca Zabezp. spolecz* 15(5), mai 73 : 59-65. [Poland.]

5004 MOYNIHAN, D. P. *The politics of a guaranteed income: the Nixon administration and the Family Assistance Plan.* New York, Random House, 73, xiii-579p. CR: A. REES, *J. econ. Liter.* 11(3), sep 73 : 963-964.

5005 OROZCO FARRERE, R. "La protección familiar en la nueva ley del seguro social" (Family protection according to the new social security law), *Segur. soc. (México)* 20(79), jan-feb 73 : 47-63. [Mexico.]

5006 RIPA KRAUSE, R. "Asignaciones familiares" (Family allowances), *Segur. soc. (México)* 20(79), jan-feb 73 : 25-45. [Argentina.]

5007 SPITAELS-EVRARD, A. "L'allocation de naissance", *R. belge Sécur. soc.* 14(11-12), nov-dec 72 : 1331-1390. [Belgique.]

5008 STEELS, A. "Perspectives de nouvelles prestations familiales", *R. belge Sécur. soc.* 14 (11-12), nov-dec 72 : 1391-1456. [Belgique.]

### M.422 Unemployment insurance
### Assurance-chômage

5009 BECKER, J. M. "An evaluation of unemployment insurance", *R. soc. Econ.* 30(1), mar 72 : 30-36.

5010 BECKER, J. M. *Experience rating in unemployment insurance: an experiment in competitive socialism.* Baltimore, Johns Hopkins University Press, 72, xvi-403 p.

5011  COVEY, R. C.; HOLMES, A. S. *The economic impact of extending unemployment insurance to agriculture in Maryland.* College Park Agricultural Experiment Station, University of Maryland, 72, xiii-107 p.

5012  HEUER, E.; LOMB, W. *Arbeitslosenversicherung und Arbeitslosenhilfe* (Social security and assistance to the unemployed). Stuttgart-Berlin-Köln, Mainz, Kohlhammer 72, 132 p.

5013  SAN MARTIN ECHEGARRETA, E. R. "Sistemas de seguro por desempleo en el Uruguay" (Unemployment insurance systems in Uruguay), *Segur. soc. (México)* 20(76), jul-aug 72 : 27-39.

## M.423  *Accident insurance, work safety*
## *Assurance-accident, sécurité du travail*

5014  ALONSO OLEA, M. "El aseguramiento de los accidentes de trabajo" (Work accident insurance), *R. Polít. soc.* 98, apr-jun 73 : 35-57. [Spain.]

5015  DILLEMANS, R. "Les allocations aux handicapés", *R. belge Sécur. soc.* 15(9), sep 73 : 923-945. [Belgique.]

5016  ETALA, J. J. "Contingencia social de accidentes del trabajo y enfermedades profesionales" (Social risks of work accidents and of occupational diseases), *R. Segur. soc.* 5(48), jun 72 : 487-532. [Chile.]

5017  JANISZEWSKI, K. "Spory o swiadczenia przyslugujace w razie wypadkow przy pracy" (Conflicts over allowances due to work injuries), *Praca Zabezp. spiecz.* 14(12), dec 72 : 16-26. [Poland.]

5018  LOGAN, J. E. *An analysis of workmen's compensation: South Carolina and the United States.* Columbia, Bureau of Business and Economic Research, University of South Carolina, 72, x-206 p.

5019  PRIETO ESCUDERO, G. "Principios sociológicos del seguro de accidentes del trabajo" (Sociological principles of work accident insurance), *R. Trab. (Madrid)* 34, 2 trim. 71 : 49-67. [Spain.]

5020  WISNIEWSKI, J. "Les accidents du travail", *Hommes et Migr. Doc.* 24(842), apr 73 : 3-13. [France.]

## M.424  *Health insurance*
## *Assurance-maladie*

5021  BERKI, S. E. "National health insurance: an idea whose time has come ?", *A. Amer. Acad. polit. soc. Sci.* 399, jan 72 : 125-144.

5022  DEJARDIN, J. "L'assurance maladie-invalidité et les handicapés", *R. belge Sécur. soc.* 15(9), sep 73 : 947-963. [Belgique.]

5023  EASTON, A. (ed.). *The design of a health maintenance organization.* Hempstead, N. Y. Hofstra University, 73, xviii-747 p.

5024  FELDSTEIN, M. "The welfare loss of excess / health insurance", *J. polit. Econ.* 81(2) mar-apr 73 : 251-280. [USA.]

5025  FELDSTEIN, M.; FRIEDMAN, B.; LUFT, H. "Distributional aspects of national health insurance benefits and finance", *Nat. Tax. J.* 25(4), dec 72 : 497-510. [USA.]

5026  FISHER, P. *Prescription for national health insurance; a proposal for the U.S. based on Canadian experience.* Croton-on-Hudson, N. Y., North River Press, 72, ix-158 p.

5027  LEUTHY, F. "Réforme de l'assurance-maladie", *R. synd. suisse* 65(1), jan 73 : 24-36.

5028  NAVARRO, V. "National health insurance and the strategy for change", *Milbank Memor. Quart.* 51(2), 1973 : 223-251.

5029  NEWMAN, H. N. "Medicare and medicaid", *A. Amer. Acad. polit. soc. Sci.* 399, jan 72 : 114-124.

5030  NIEDUSZYŃSKI, M. "Analiza spolecznej i ekonomicznej efektywnosci uslug zdrowia" (Analysis of the social and economic efficiency of health service), *Stud. finans.* 13, 1972 : 118-151.

5031  PRICE, J. R.; FURSTENBERG, F. F.; ROTH, R. B. *National health insurance.* Washington, American Enterprise Institute for Public Policy Research, 72, 92 p.

5032  ROSETT, R. "The effect of health insurance on the demand for medical care", *J. polit. Econ.* 81(2), mar-apr 73 : 281-305. [USA.]

5033    TAYLOR, M. G. "Quebec medicare: policy formulation in conflict and crisis", *Canad. pibl. Adm.* 15(2), sum 72 : 211-250.

M.425    *Old age: pensions, retirement plans*
         *Vieillesse: pensions, retraites*

5034    "Assurance vieillesse en Algérie(L')", *R. algér. Trav.* (10), sep 71 : 53-64.
5035    PERRIN, G. "Supplementary pension schemes in the Nordic countries", *Int. Soc. Secur. R.* 25(4), 1972 : 357-375.
5036    RHEE, H. A. "International social security association social security for older people", *Int. Soc. Secur. R.* 25(1-2), 1972 : 42-70.
5037    SCHMÄHL, W. "Zur Struktur von Rentenleistungen" (The structure of pensions), *Z. ges. Staatswiss.* 129(1), feb 73 : 123-149. [Germany FR.]
5038    WEISE, R. W. "Early retirement under public pension systems in Latin America", *Int. soc. Secur. R.* 25(3), 1972 : 255-265.
5039    WILSON, T. "Pensions, inflation and growth", *Lloyds Bank R.* 108, apr 73 : 1-17.

M.43    **Economics of social security**
        **Economie de la sécurité sociale**

M.431    *Social security and income redistribution*
         *Sécurité sociale et redistribution du revenu*

5040    GARCIA DE LEANIZ Y DE LA TORRE, P. "Seguridad social y redistribucíon de la renta" (Social security and income redistribution), *R. iberoamer. Segur. soc.* 22(3), mai-jun 73 : 503-520.
5041    LEAL DE ARAUJO, L. "Social security as an instrument of income redistribution in the developing countries", *Int. soc. Secur. R.* 25(3), 1972 : 243-254.

M.432    *Social security and social assistance: costs and financing*
         *Coût et financement de la sécurité et de l'assistance sociales*

M.4320    *General studies*
          *Études générales*

5042    KLAPKOWSKI, B. "Zagadnienie rachunkowości społecznej" (The problem of social accountancy), *Fol. oecon. cracov.* (12), 1972 : 7-34.
5043    LECOUBLET, D. et al. "Le coût social: proposition pour un modèle", *C. Sociol. Démogr. médic.* 12(2), apr-jun 72 : 67-71.
5044    POPPER, F. J. "The social meaning of social accounting", *Polity* 4(1), fall 71 : 76-90.
5045    REGAN, D. H. "The problem of social cost revisited", *J. Law Econ.* 15(2), oct 72 : 427-437.
5046    SCHÄFER, D. "Über die Anwendbarkeit des Konzepts des konjunkturneutralen Haushalts auf die soziale Sicherung" (On the applicability of the conception of a neutral budget on social security), *Z. Wirtsch.-u: soz.-Wiss.* 92(2), 1972 : 185-203.

M.4321    *By sectors and countries*
          *Études par secteurs et régions*

5047    AČARKAN, V. A.; KRJAŽEV, V. G. *Obščestvennye fondy potreblenija v SSSR* (Social consumption funds in the USSR). Moskva, Ekonomika, 72, 63 p. [USSR.]
5048    ADAM, W.; STIEFEL, K. H. *Krankenhausfinanzierungsgesetz* (The hospital finance law) Köln, Grote, 72, 280 p. [Germany FR.]
5049    ARRANZ ALVAREZ, L. "El presupuesto social en una sociedad en desarrollo" (Social budget in a developing society), *R. iberoamer. Segur. soc.* 21(5), sep-oct 72 : 1039-1055. [Spain.]
5050    BERKI, S. E. *Hospital economics. Lexington*, Mass., Lexington Books, 72, xxi-270 p.
5051    BRITTAIN, J. A. *The payroll tax for social security.* Washington, Brookings Institution, 72, xiv-285 p. [USA.]

5052 "Budget social de la Nation. Comptes 1971-1972-1973", *Statist. Ét. financ. Sér. rouge* 25(295-296) jul-aug 73 : 1-69. [France.]

5053 DEJARDIN, J. "Causas generales del incremento de los gastos del seguro de enfermedad" (General causes of increase of health insurance expenses), *Estud. Segur. soc.* (3), 1972 : 5-22. [Belgium.]

5054 DRAPERI, R.; RIBAS, J. J. "L'évolution et le financement du coût des soins de santé", *Dr. soc.* 36(2), feb 73 : 122-129.

5055 FREOUR, P. *et al.* "Le coût médical: application à l'étude du coût comparé de la tuberculose (chez les alcooliques et chez les non buveurs)", *C. Sociol. Démogr. médic.* 12(2), apr-jun 72 : 61-66.

5056 FUCHS, V. R. (ed.). *Essays in the economics of health and medical care.* New York, Columbia University Press, 72, xxii-239p. [USA.]

5057 HARDING, E.; BODENHEIMER, T.; CUMMINGS, S. (eds.). *Billions for band-aids; an analysis of the U. S. health care system and of proposals for its reform.* San Francisco, San Francisco Bay Area Chapter, Medical Committee for Human Rights, 72, 128 p.

5058 ILLUMINATI, F. "Le coût de la santé", *Inform. soc. (Paris)* 26(11), nov 72 : 34-46.

5059 LAURENT, A. "Leistungsniveau und Kosten der sozialen Sicherheit in der E. W. G." (Financing coverage level and costs of social security in E. E. C. countries), *Arbeit u. soz. Polit.* 26(7-8), jul-aug 72 : 251-254.

5060 NIEDUSZYŃSKI, M. *Analiza nakładów na usługi socjalne w krajach RWPG* (Analysis of expenditure on social services in CMEA countries). Warszawa, Państwowe Wydawnictwo Ekonomiczne, 73, 302 p.

5061 PAULY, M.; REDISCH, M. "The not-for-profit hospital as a physicians cooperative", *Amer. econ. R.* 53(1), mar 73 : 87-99.

5062 RIBAS, J. J.; HASSE, J. "Acciones de la comunidad en el campo de la seguridad social y el presupuesto social europeo" (Community actions in the field of social security and the European social budget), *R. mexic. Segur. soc.* 1(4), 1972 : 23-65.

5063 SALKEVER, D. S. "A microeconometric study of hospital cost inflation", *J. polit. Econ.* 80(6), nov-dec 72 : 1144-1166.

5064 "Santé coût cher (La)", *Projet* 75, mai 73 : 495-618. [France.]

5065 TESSIER, J. F. *et al.* "Le coût de la maladie", *R. franç. Aff. soc.* 27(2), apr-jun 73 : 31-58. [France.]

5066 WARD, J. T.; TATCHELL, P. M. "Health expenditure in New Zealand", *Econ. Rec.* 48(124) dec 72 : 500-516.

## M.5 ECONOMICS OF EDUCATION
## ÉCONOMIE DE L'ÉDUCATION

5067 ALBRECHT, M.; KAISER, H. R. "Zur bildungspolitischen Situation in der BRD" (The situation of educational policy in West Germany), *Blatt. dtsche. u. int. Polit.* 17(12), dec 72 : 1297-1314.

5068 ALEXANDER, K.; JORDAN, K. F. (eds.). *Constitutional reform of school finance.* Lexington, Mass., Lexington Books, 73, 228 p. [USA.]

5069 ANDERSON, J. E. *Organization and financing of self-help education in Kenya.* Paris, Unesco; New York, UNIPUB Inc., 73, 70 p.

5070 ARTHUR, W. J. *A financial planning model for private colleges; a research report.* Charlottesville, University Press of Virginia, 73, xii-118 p.

5071 BARR, W. M.; WILKERSON, W. R. *Innovative financing of public school facilities.* Danville, Ill., Interstate Printers and Publishers, 73, 177 p.

5072 BARRO, S. M. *Theoretical models of school district expenditure determination and the impact of grants-in-aid.* Santa Monica, Rand, 72, ix-76 p. [USA.]

5073 BARZEL, Y. "Private schools and public school finance", *J. polit. Econ.* 81(1), jan-feb 73 : 174-186.

5074 BERKE, J. S. *et al. Financing equal education opportunity: alternatives for state finance: a background report originally prepared for the Fleischmann Commission.* Berkeley, Calif., McCutchan Publishing Corporation, 72, xiv-234 p.

5075 BRAVO, H. F. *Las erogaciones en educación; un análisis del caso argentino, fundado en el presupuesto nacional* (Resource allocations in education; an analysis of the Argentine case based on the national budget). Buenos Aires, Centro de Investigaciones en Ciencias de la Educación, 72, 107 p.

5162    STOLZ, P. "Wirtschaftspolitik im Lichte ökonomischer Modelle der Demokratie"
        (Economic policies in the light of economic models of democracy), *Schweizer. Z.
        Volkswirtsch. Statist.* 108(1), mar 72 : 47-58.
5163    TINBERGEN, J. *Politique économique et optimum social.* Paris, Economica, 72, xiii-272 p.


## N.02     THEORY OF ECONOMIC ORGANIZATION
##          THÉORIE DE L'ORGANISATION ÉCONOMIQUE

5164    BARRERA, C.; PISTONESI, H. "Hacia una teoría de la reconversión económica" (Towards
        a theory of economic reconversion), *Economica (La Plata)* 18(1), jul-apr 72 : 3-22.
5165    FISZEL, H. *Teoria gospodarowania* (Theory of economic management). Warszawa,
        Państwowe Wydawnictwo Naukowe, 73, 387 p.
5166    HENSEL, K. P. *Grundformen der wirtschaftsordnung: Marktwirtschaft, Zentralverwaltungs-
        wirtschaft* (Fundamental forms of economic organization; market economy, centrally
        administered economy). München, Beck, 72, 190 p.
5167    LOMBARDINI, S. "Finalità sociali e sistema economico" (Social finalities and economic
        system), *Riv. int. Sci. soc.* 80(5-6), sep-dec 72 : 562-577.
5168    McARTHUR, A. G.; LOVERIDGE, J. W. *Economic theory and organisation.* London, Collins,
        72, 399 p.
5169    SOLO, R. A. "Organizational structure, technological advance, and the new tasks of
        government", *J. econ. Issues* 6(4), dec 72 : 149-170.
5170    VOGT, W. G.; MICKLE, M. H. (eds.). *Socio-economic systems and principles.* Pittsburgh,
        School of Engineering, University of Pittsburgh, 73, xx-349 p.


## N.03     GENERAL THEORY OF PLANNING
##          THÉORIE GÉNÉRALE DE LA PLANIFICATION

        [See also / Voir aussi: 4731, 4990, 5245, 5473]

5171    ANTAL, Z.; KORODI, J. "New methods of national economic planning and regional
        development planning", *A. Univ. Sci. budapest. Sect. geogr.* (7), 1971 : 179-182.
5172    BELKIN, V. D. *Ėkonomičeskie izmerenija i planirovanie* (Economic measurements and
        planning). Moskva, Mysl', 72, 303 p.
5173    BREEV, M. V. *Ėkonomičeskie i metodologičeskie osnovy planirovanija* (Economic and
        methodological planning bases). Moskva, Ėkonomika, 73, 150 p.
5174    BUNGE, M. "The role of forecast in planning", *Theory and Decision* 3(3), mar 73 : 207-
        221.
5175    BURGO Y MARCHAN, A. M. DEL, "Dimensión temporal de la planificación" (Temporal
        dimension of planning), *R. Adm. publ. (Madrid)* 69, sep-dec 72 : 59-107.
5176    CAIRE, G. *La planification; techniques et problèmes.* 2e éd. rev. augm. Paris, Cujas, 72,
        623 p.
5177    CAIRNCROSS, A. "La economia dirigida" (The guided economy), *De Economia* 25(123),
        oct-dec 72 : 605-625.
5178    CARTWRIGHT, T. "Problems, solutions and strategies: a contribution to the theory and
        practice of planning", *J. Amer. Inst. Planners* 39(3), mai 73 : 179-187.
5179    DIMITRIOU, B. "The interpretation of politics and planning", *Socio-econ. plan. Sci.* (1),
        feb 73 : 55-65.
5180    DUDKIN, L. M. *Sistema rasčetov optimal'nogo narodnohozjajstvennogo plana* (System of
        an optimal national economy plan estimation). Moskva, Ėkonomika, 72, 383 p.
5181    FALUDI, A. (ed.). *A reader in planning theory.* Oxford-New York, Pergamon Press, 73,
        xii-399 p.
5182    FALUDI, A. "The 'systems view' and planning theory", *Socio-econ. plan. Sci.* 7(1), feb
        73 : 67-77.
5183    FOXLEY, A. "Objectivos sociales y variables demográficas en la planificación económica"
        (Social objectives and demographic variables in economic planning), *Demogr. y Econ.*
        6(2), 1972 : 221-247.
5184    HARSÁNY, P. *Economic planning or revolution.* Montral, Academic Publishing Co., 72,
        114 p.

5185 HENRY, D. "Differential equations with continuous right-hand side for planning procedures", *J. econ. Theory* 4(3), jun 72 : 545-551.

5186 HOFFMANN, C.; BLAZEJ, K. *Globální metody plánování* (Global methods of planning). Praha, Svoboda; Brno, Rudé právo, 72, 147-11 p.

5187 KEREN, M. "On the tautness of plans", *R. econ. Stud.* 39(4), oct 72 : 469-486.

5188 LEMESEV, M. Ja.; PANČENKO, A. I. *Kompleksnye programmy v planirovanii narodnogo hozjajstva* (Complex programs in national economy planning). Moskva, Èkonomika 73, 167 p.

5189 MADAN, G. R. *Welfare state and problems of democratic planning*. Bombay, Allied Publishers, 72, xii-152 p.

5190 MEHTA, G. L. *Dilemmas in planning*. Bombay, Vora, 72, vi-138 p.

5191 MIRRLEES, J. A.; STERN, N. H. "Fairly good plans", *J. econ. Theory* 4(2), apr 72 : 268-288.

5192 NORDBERG, L. "Beslutsteori och planeringsprocesser" (Decision theory and planning processes), *Ekon. Samfund. Ts.* 25(4), 1972 : 254-260.

5193 OZBEKHAN, H. "Spre o teorie generală a planificării" (Toward a general theory of planning), *R. Filoz. (Bucuresti)* 19(8), 1972 : 1017-1020.

5194 PACKARD, P. C.; WIT, D. "Government and the implementation of economic plans in new and emerging states: an addendum", *Develop. and Change* 4(3), 1972-1973 : 1-11.

5195 RITTEL, H. W. J.; WEBBER, M. M. "Dilemmas in a general theory of planning", *Pol. Sci.* 4(2), jun 73 : 155-169.

5196 ROBINSON, J. N. *Planning and forecasting techniques; an introduction to macroeconomic applications*. London, Weidenfeld and Nicolson, 72, viii-166 p.

5197 SCHUMACHER, A. *Development plans and planning; bibliographic and computer aid to research*. London-New York, Seminar Press, 73, viii-195 p.

5198 SILVESTER, M. S. "The contribution of the systems approach to planning", *Socio-econ. plan. Sci.* 7(1), feb 73 : 91-103.

5199 ŠORIN, V. G. *Èkonomiko-matematičeskie metody i modeli planirovanija i upravlenija* (Economic and mathematical method and planning and management models). Moskva, Znanie, 73, 239 p.

5200 SULMICKI, P. *Planowanie i zarzadzanie gospodarcze* (Economic planning and management). 2nd ed. compl. Warszawa, Państwowe Wydawnictwo Ekonomiczne, 73, 420 p.

5201 TARHANOV, A. V. "O sociologiceskom soderžanii planirovanija narodnogo hozjajstva", on the sociological content of national economy planning), *Plan. Povys. effekt. obšč. Prozivodstva* (1), 1973 : 3-15.

5202 VOLKONSKIJ, V. A. *Principy optimal'nogo planirovanija* (Principles of optimal planning). Moskva, Èkonomika, 73, 239 p.

5203 WATERSTON, A. "Resolving the three-horned planning dilemma", *Finance and Develop.* 9(2), jun 72 : 36-41.

5204 WEBER, W. "Problems of planning in the economics of countries in East and West", *Acta oecon.* 9(2), 1972 : 127-135.

5205 YOUNES, Y. "Indices prospectifs quantitatifs et procédures décentralisées d'élaboration des plans", *Econometrica* 40(1), jan 72 : 137-146.

## N.1 ECONOMIC SYSTEMS AND POLICIES
## SYSTÈMES ET POLITIQUES ÉCONOMIQUES

### N.10 General and comparative studies
### Études générales et comparatives

[See also / Voir aussi: 4585]

5206 ARTIOLI, R. "Dall'economia di mercato all'economia concertata" (From market economy to planned economy), *Impresa* 14(3), mai-jun 72 : 189-195.

5207 BREDOW, W. VON. *Vom Antagonismus zur Konvergenz? Studien zum Ost-West-Problem* (Passage from antagonism to convergence? Studies on the East-West problem). Frankfurt-am-Main, A. Metzner, 72, 218 p.

5208 BUCHHOLZ, A. "Wissenschaftlich-technische Revolution (WTR) und Wettbewerb der Systeme" (Scientific and technical revolution (STR) and systems competition), *Osteuropa* 22(5), mai 72 : 329-390.

5209   Bibl. XXI-5342. ECKSTEIN, A. (ed.). *Comparison of economic systems. Theoretical and methodological approaches.* CR: E. NEUBERGER, *J. econ. Liter.* 11(3), sep 73 : 909-912.

5210   ELLIOTT, J. E.; CAMPBELL, R. W. *Comparative economic systems.* Englewood Cliffs, N. J., Prentice-Hall, 73, xv-540 p.

5211   KLEIN, P. A. *The management of market-oriented economies: a comparative perspective.* Belmont, Calif., Wadsworth Publishing Co., 73, 238 p.

5212   KLINSKIJ, A. I. *Razvitie vnešnih ekonomičeskih svjazej. Ėkonomičeskoe sorevnovanie dvuh mirovyh sistem* (The development of foreign economic relations. Economic competition between the two systems). Moskva, 72, 47 p.

5213   MEISNER, J. *Kapitalizm a socjalizm: wspólzawodniczace systemy ekonomiczne* (Capitalism and socialism: competing economic systems). Warszawa, Państwowe Wydawnictwo Ekonomiczne, 73, 166 p.

5214   PETERS, R. "Hauptsächliche Determinanten von Wirtschaftsordnungen" (The major determining factors of economic systems), *Z. Wirtsch.-u. soz.-Wiss.* 93(4), 1973 : 385-410.

5215   Bibl. XXI-5356. SHERMAN. H. *Radical political economy: capitalism and socialism from a Marxist-humanist perspective.* CR: A. LINDBECK, *J. econ. Liter.* 10(4), dec 72 : 1219-1221.

5216   TEILHAC, E. *Systèmes et structures économiques; les deux moitiés économiques du XXe siècle.* Paris, Aubier Montaigne, 72, 253 p.


**N.11      Present capitalist systems**
           **Systèmes capitalistes actuels**

**N.110     *General studies***
           ***Études générales***

[See also / Voir aussi: **E.42; 2208, 4586**]

5217   ALIA, J. C. *Las leyes del capitalismo actual; segun la teoría de Sweezy y Baran* (Laws of present day capitalism; according to the theory of Sweezy and Baran). Bilbao, Zero; Madrid, ZYX, 73, 142 p.

5218   AMIN, S. *Le développement inégal; essai sur les formations sociales du capitalisme périphérique.* Paris, Éditions de minuit, 73, 365 p.

5219   BALLIVIÁN CALDERÓN, R. *El capitalismo en las ideologías económicas contemporáneas* (Capitalism in contemporary economic ideologies). Buenos Aires, Editorial Paidós, 72, 222 p.

5220   BARTOSIK, J. (ed.). *Procesy integracyjne w wspólczesnego kapitalizmu* (Integration processes in the system of contemporary capitalism). Poznań, Instytut Zachodni, 73, 438 p.

5221   BOKKARA, P. "O krizise gosudarstvenno-monopolističeskogo kapitalizma" (The crisis of state monopolistic capitalism), *Probl. Mira Social.* 14(11), nov 72 : 81-86.

5222   BOSQUET, M. *Critique du capitalisme quotidien.* Paris, Galilée, 73, 341 p.

5223   BRANSTEN, J. H. "Le capitalisme périphérique", *Homme et Soc.* 28, apr-jun 73 : 179-182.

5224   "Capitalisme périphérique (Le)", *Tiers-Monde* 13(52), oct-dec 72 : 689-789.

5225   CAVALLI, A. (ed.). *Le origini del capitalismo* (The origins of capitalism). Torino, Loescher, 73, 258 p.

5226   ČULÍK, J. *Kritika burzuazních teorií o "transformaci" kapitalismu* (Criticism of the bourgeois theory of the "transformation" of capitalism). Praha, SPN, 73, 133-1 p.

5227   FORMAN, J. D. *Capitalism: economic individualism to today's welfare state.* New York, F. Watts, 72, viii-134 p.

5228   GLYN, A.; SUTCLIFFE, B. *Capitalism in crisis.* New York, Pantheon Books; London, Penguin, 72, xxxix-286 p.

5229   GRANOU, A. *Capitalisme et mode de vie.* Paris, Éditions du Cerf, 72, 94 p.

5230   KORČEK, L. *O teóriách "tranformácie" kapitalizmu* (The theory of the 'transformation' of capitalism). Bratislava, Pravda; Žilina, Pravda, 72, 183-3 p.

5231   LEFEBVRE, H. *La survie du capitalisme; la re-production des rapports de production.* Paris, Éditions Anthropos, 73, 273 p.

5232   LEMMNITZ, A. *Politische Ökonomie des Kapitalismus* (Political economy of capitalism). Frankfurt-am-Main, Verlag, Marxistische Blätter, 72, 273 p.

5233    MALININ, S. N.; GRISANOVIČ, P. U. (eds.). *Kurs lekcij po politekonomii kapitalizma* (Conferences on the capitalist political economy). Minsk, Izdatel'stvo BGU, 72, 357 p.

5234    MANDEL, E. *Der Spätkapitalismus; Versuch einer marxistischen Erklärung* (Advanced capitalism: a tentative Marxist exploration). Frankfurt-am-Main, Suhrkamp, 72, 541-1 p.

5235    MAURISCHAT, G. "Der ökonomische Regulierungsmechanismus des staatsmonopolistischen Kapitalismus" (The economic mechanism of regulation of State monopoly capitalism), *Wirtsch.-Wiss.* 21(3), mar 73 : 398-407.

5236    NOWAK, Z. *Procesy dezintegracji i integracji ekonomicznej we wspólczesnym kapitalizmie* (Process of economic disintegration and integration in contemporary capitalism). Poznań, Instytut Zachodni, 72, 229 p.

5237    RUMJANCEV, A. M. (ed.). *Političeskaja ekonomija. Kapitalističeskij sposob proizvodstva* (Political economy. The capitalist way of production). Moskva, Politizdat, 73, 623 p.

5238    SCHLEIFSTEIN, J. "Zur Theorie des staatsmonopolistischen Kapitalismus" (About the theory of State monopoly capitalism), *Blätt. dtsche. u. int. Polit.* 18(4), 1973 : 378-394.

5239    SOKOLOV, P. V. *Političeskaja ekonomija. Kapitalističeskij sposob proizvodstva* (Political economy. Capitalist way of production). Moskva, Voenizdat, 72, 527 p.

5240    TANESKI, V. "Opstestvenoto bitie na sovremeniot kapitalizam" (Social character of contemporary capitalism), *Godis. ekon. Fak. (Skopje)* 15, 1971 : 131-155.

5241    TJUL'PANOV, S. I.; ŠEJNIS, V. L. *Aktual'nye problemy političeskoj ekonomii sovremennogo kapitalizma* (Current problems of the political economy of contemporary capitalism). Leningrad, Leningradskij gosudarstvennyj Universitet, 73, 282 p.

5242    VIÑAS, I. *Capitalismo, monopolios y dependencia* (Capitalism, monopolies and dependence). Buenos Aires, Centro Editor de América Latina, 72, 135 p.

5243    ZIESCHANG, K. "Ursachen und Wesen des staatsmonopolistischen Kapitalismus" (Origins and nature of State monopolistic capitalism), *Wirtsch.-Wiss.* 21(2), feb 73 : 235-244.

### N.111    *Economic management and administrative organs*
### *Gestion économique et organes administratifs*

[See also / Voir aussi: **N.203;** 5301, 5324]

5244    BRIÈRE, R. *Intiation aux institutions et aux mécanismes économiques.* Montréal Lidec, 72, 499 p. [Canada.]

5245    CHILLÓN-MEDINA, J. M. "Formas, técnicas y estructuras administrativas ante la planificación económica" (Administrative forms, techniques and structures facing economic planning), *R. Adm. publ. (Madrid)* 64, jan-apr 71 : 107-178.

5246    JOBERT, B. "Le Ministère de l'industrie et la cohérence de la politique industrielle", *R. franç. Sci. polit.* 23(2), apr 73 : 321-329. [France.]

5247    LA VALLINA VELARDE, J. L. DE; MORELL OCAÑA, L. "Entes territoriales y procedimientos de programación" (Territorial bodies and planning procedures), *Riv. trim. Dir. pubbl.* 23(1), jan-mar 73 : 219-282. [Spain.]

5248    MINOT, J. "La dernière réorganisation du Ministère de l'éducation nationale", *R. adm.* 26(154), jul-aug 73 : 418-420. [France.]

5249    MITCHELL, J. *The National Board for Prices and Incomes.* London, Secker and Warburg, 72, xii-294 p. [UK.]

5250    OGEE, R. A. "Institutional factors to encourage interagency cooperation in the management of natural resources", *Publ. Adm. R.* 32(1), jan-feb 72 : 17-23.

5251    RASMUSSEN, W. D.; BAKER, G. L. *The Department of Agriculture.* New York, Praeger, 72, xii-258 p. [USA.]

5252    WILSON, J. Q. "The dead hand of regulation", *Publ. Interest* 25, 1971 : 39-58. [US governmental regulatory commissions.]

**N.112** *Economic policies*
*Politiques économiques*

**N.1121** *Descriptive studies*
*Études déscriptives*

[See also / Voir aussi: **F.3113**; **J.51**; **M.3**; 1892, 4420, 5319, 5493, 5782]

5253 BALLONI, V. (ed.). *Lezioni sulla politica economica in Italia* (Lessons on the Italian economic policy). Milano, Edizioni di Comunità, 72, viii-413 p.

5254 BHULESHKAR, A. V. (ed.). *Towards socialist transformation of Indian economy.* Bombay, Popular Prakashan, 72, xxvii-422 p.

5255 BRITTAN, S. *Is there an economic consensus ? An attitude survey.* London, Macmillan, 73, 118 p. [UK.]

5256 BUREL, P. *Le déséquilibre de notre système économique.* Caudry, 73, 229 p. [France.]

5257 CAGAN, P. *et al. Economic policy and inflation in the sixties.* Washington, D. C., American Enterprise Institute for Public Policy Research, 72, iv-267 p. [USA.]

5258 CARSON, R. B.; INGLES, J.; McLAUD, D. (eds.). *Government in the American economy; conventional and radical studies on the growth of state economic power.* Lexington, Mass., Heath, 73, xiv-506 p.

5259 CASTELLINO, O. (ed.). *La politica economica italiana dal 1946 al 1970* (The Italian economic policy from 1946 to 1970). Torino, G. Giappichelli, 72, 487 p.

5260 DALIN, S. A. *SŠA: poslevoennyj gosudarstvenno-monopolističeskij kapitalizm* (USA: postwar state monopoly capitalism). Moskva, Nauka, 72, 507 p.

5261 "Development policies in Ceylan: 1966-1971", *Econ. B. Asia Far East* 23(1), jun 72 : 19-36.

5262 ELLINGWORTH, R. *Japanese economic policies and security.* London, International Institute for Strategic Studies, 72, 36 p.

5263 FRANCE. Ministère de l'économie et des finances. Services de l'information. *Le point de la politique économique et financière 1969-1972.* Paris, 73, 63 p.

5264 FUCITO, G. *Aspetti della politica economica della CEE* (Aspects of the economic policy of the EEC). Milano, A. Giuffrè, 73, 114 p.

5265 GALBRAITH, J. K. *Economics and the public purpose.* Boston, Houghton Mifflin, 73, xvi-334 p. [USA.]

5266 GHAI, D. P. "Concepts and strategies of economic independence", *J. mod. Afr. Stud.* 11(1), mar 73 : 21-42. [Africa.]

5267 GLYN, A.; SUTCLIFFE, B. *British capitalism, workers and the profits squeeze.* Harmondsworth, Penguin, 72, 286 p.

5268 GURLEY, J. G. "The future of American capitalism", *Quart. R. Econ. Busin.* 12(3), 1972 : 7-17.

5269 HARRIS, F. R. *The new populism.* New York, Saturday Review Press, 73, viii-209 p. [USA.]

5270 HAVEMAN, R. H.; HAMRIN, R. D. (eds.). *The political economy of Federal policy.* New York, Harper and Row, 73, x-302 p. [USA.]

5271 HENDERSON, R. F. "Australian economic policy", *Austral. econ. R.* 18(2), 1972 : 6-8.

5272 HERZOG, P. *L'union populaire et la maîtrise de l'économie.* Paris, Éditions sociales, 72, 223 p. [France.]

5273 HIROFUMI, U. "Nixon's new economic policy: the Japanese options", *Japan Interpreter* 7(3-4), 1972 : 233-244.

5274 HUSU, E. "The economic stabilization programmes and their political consequences in Finland, 1967-1970", *Scand. polit. Stud.* (7), 1972 : 259-265.

5275 LECHLEITNER, H. *Die Rolle des Staates in der wirtschaftlichen und sozialen Entwicklung Libanons* (The role of the State in the economic and social development of Lebanon). Wien, F. Hirt, 72, 171 p.

5276 LECHT, L. A. *Changes in national priorities during the 1960s: their implications for 1980.* Washington, National Planning Association, 72, ix-53 p.

5277 MARTIN, A. *The politics of economic policy in the United States: a tentative view from a comparative perspective.* Beverly Hills, Sage Publications, 73, 62 p.

5278 MAURO MARINI, R. "La economía del capitalismo brasileño" (The economy of Brazilian capitalism), *Econ. y Adm.* 8-9(19-20), sep-dec 71-jan-apr 72 : 49-55.

5279    NOBLE, C. E.; NOTTLE, R. W. *Case studies in Australian economic policy*. Melbourne, Cheshire, 72, 131-231 p.

5280    PARKER, R. S. "Economics before politics-a colonial phantasy", *Austral. J. Polit. Hist.* 17(2), aug 71 : 202-214. [Australia.]

5281    PERKINS, J. O. N. *et al. Macro-economic policy: a comparative study: Australia, Canada, New Zealand, South Africa*. London, Allen and Unwin, 72, 3-211 p.

5282    PHILIPEAUX, J. "L'évolution de la politique économique en Tunisie", *Études (Paris)* oct 73 : 353-370.

5283    PLAYFORD, J.; KIRSNER, D. (eds.). *Australian capitalism: towards a socialist critique*. Ringwood, Vic., Penguin Books, 72, 380 p.

5284    REYNOLDS, L. G.; GREEN, G. D.; LEWIS, D. R. (eds.). *Current issues of economic policy*. Homewood, Ill., R. D. Irwin, 73, ix-543 p. [USA.]

5285    SCHÖNINGER, K.-E. *Konjunkturstabilisierung als Koordinationsproblem zwischen den Trägern der Wirtschaftspolitik* (Economic stabilization as a coordination problem between the supports of economic policy). Meisenheim-am-Glan, A. Hain, 72, 254 p. [Germany, FR.]

5286    SICAT, G. P. *Economic policy and Philippine development*. Quezon City, University of the Philippines Press, 72, xviii-461 p.

5287    SICAT, G. P.; MAKASIAR, G. S. "Economic policies in Singapore and its growth in the last decade, 1960-1970", *Philippine Econ. B.* 9(1-3), jan-sep 72 : 1-29.

5288    SOLíS M., L. *Controversias sobre el crecimiento y la distribución; las opiniones de economistas mexicanos acerca de la política económica* (Controversies over growth and distribution; opinions of Mexican economists on economic policy). México, Fondo de Cultura Económica, 72, 230 p.

5289    STEINHAUSER, K. *Wohin steuert Österreich? Wirtschaftsfreiheit oder Genossenkapitalismus* (Wither Austria? Economic liberalism or co-operative capitalism). Wien, Institut für Politische Konzepte, 72, 34 p.

5290    TEEPLE, G. (ed.). *Capitalism and the national question in Canada*. Toronto-Buffalo, University of Toronto Press, 72, xv-256 p.

5291    TIXIER, G. "Étude comparée des politiques économiques du Cameroun et de la Côte d'Ivoire", *R. jur. polit.* 27(1), jan-mar 73 : 91-178.

5292    WADHVA, C. D. (ed.). *Some problems of India's economic policy; selected readings on planning, agriculture, and foreign trade*. Bombay, Tata McGraw-Hill Publishing Co., 73, xiv-496 p.

**N.1122**    *Planning under capitalist systems*
           *Les plans en régimes capitalistes*

[See also / Voir aussi: 1927, 5247, 5483]

5293    "Administration et société à la lumière des pratiques planificatrices", *R. franç. Sci. polit.* 23(2), apr 73 : 199-329.

5294    BARBOUR, K. M. (ed.). *Planning for Nigeria; a geographical approach*. Ibadan, Ibadan University Press, 72, vii-228 p.

5295    BARUCCI, P. "The idea of planning in Italian economic thought", *Hist. polit. Econ.* 4(1), 1972 : 232-251.

5296    BEENHAKKER, A. *A kaleidoscopic circumspection of development planning. With contextual reference to Nepal*. Rotterdam, Rotterdam University Press, 73, xiii-170 p.

5297    BHATIA, R. J.; ENGSTROM, P. "Nigeria's second national development plan: a financial analysis", *IMF Staff Pap.* 19(1), mar 72 : 145-173.

5298    BHATTACHARYA, D. "A critical survey of Indian planning and its achievements", *J. contemp. Asia* 3(2), 1973 : 165-180.

5299    CARRANZA, R. G. "Planificación y decisión económica en Argentina" (Planning and economic decision in Argentina), *Criterio* 45(1657-1658), dec 72 : 696-700.

5300    CATANESE, A. J. "Planning in a State of seige; the Colombia experience", *Land Econ.* 49(1), feb 73 : 35-43.

5301    CHARELLI, R. *Gli organi della pianificazione economica* (The organs of economic planning). Milano, A. Giuffré, 73, 272 p. [Italy.]

5302    COURBIS, R. "Les méthods de planification française: évolution et perspectives", *Schweizer. Z. Volkswirtsch. Statist.* 109(3), sep 73 : 317-340.

5303   CRIVELLINI, M.; VACIAGO, G. "Obiettivi e strumenti della programmazione a breve in Italia" (Aims and instruments of short-term planning in Italy), *Moneta e Cred.* 26 (101-102), mar-jun 73 : 76-100.

5304   DAS, N. *The Indian economy under planning.* Calcutta, World Press, 72, vii-140 p.

5305   "Decade of planned development in Egypt (A)", *Econ. B. (Cairo)* 25(3), 1972 : 154-175.

5306   DELEAU, M. *et al.* "Planification, incertitude et politique économique: l'opération optimix", *R. écon. (Paris)* 24(5), sep 73 : 801-836. [France.]

5307   "Deuxième Plan de développement de la Zambie, 1972-1976 (Le)", *Industr. Trav. O.-Mer* 21(236), jul 73 : 583-590.

5308   DUMONTIER, J. "Le système d'indicateurs du VIe Plan", *Consommation* 18(3), jul-sep 72 : 3-30. [France.]

5309   FRIEDMANN, J. *Retracking America; a theory of transactive planning.* Garden City, N. Y., Anchor Press, 73, xx-289 p.

5310   GADGIL, D. R. *Planning and economic policy in India.* Enl. and rev. ed. Poona, Gokhale Institute of Politics and Economics; Bombay, Longman, 72, xx-405 p.

5311   GESSA, C. "Il sistema della programmazione economica nell'ordinamento costituzionale italiano" (The economic planning system in the Italian constitutional structure), *R. Inst. Cienc. soc.* 18, 1971 : 249-258.

5312   GHOSH, R. "Achievements of five-year plans in India", *Econ. Aff.* 17(1-2), jan-feb 72 : 9-24.

5313   GOREUX, L. M.; MANNE, A. S. (eds.). *Multi-level planning: case studies in Mexico.* Amsterdam, North-Holland Publishing Co; New York, American Elsevier Publishing Co., 73, viii-556 p.

5314   Bibl. XXI-5450. GUPTA, S. P. *Planning models in India: with projections to 1975.* CR: P. G. PERIASAMY, *J. econ. Liter.* 11(1), mar 73 : 93-95.

5315   JENSCH, W. *Die afghanischen Entwicklungspläne vom ersten bis zum dritten Plan* (Afghan development in the First to Third Plan). Meisenheim-am-Glan, A. Hain, 73, 377 p.

5316   KOSHAL, M.; KOSHAL, R. K. "Gandhi's influence on Indian economic planning: a critical analysis", *Amer. J. Econ. Sociol.* 32(3), jul 73 : 311-330.

5317   LA ROCCA, S. "Pianificazione urbanistica e pianificazione economica nell'esperienza italiana della programmazione" (Urban planning and economic planning in Italian planning experience), *Civitas (Roma)* 24(6), jun 73 : 23-50.

5318   LEDERER, A. *La plan quinquennal de développement industriel de la République d'Indonésie.* Bruxelles, Académie royale des sciences d'outre-mer, 72, 43-4 p.

5319   LERUEZ, J. *Planification et politique en Grande-Bretagne, 1945-1971.* Paris, A. Colin, 72, xiii-314-3 p.

5320   MAYNARD, G.; Van RIJKEGHEM, W. "Argentina 1967-1970: a stabilization attempt that failed", *Banca naz. Lav. quart. B.* 103, dec 72 : 396-412. [Also published in Italian in *Moneta e Cred.* 25(100), 4 trim 72 : 418-433.]

5321   MOLLER, B. *Employment approaches to economic planning in developing countries. With special reference to the development planning of Ceylon (Sri Lanka).* Lund, Studentlitteratur, 72, 305 p.

5322   NALINI, K. S. "The private sector in Indian planning", *Econ. Aff.* 17(11), nov 72: 493-512.

5323   NAYAR, B. R. *The modernizarion imperative and Indian planning.* Delhi, Vikas, 72, xii-246 p. CR: P. STREETEN, *Amer. polit. Sci. R.* 67(4), dec 73 : 1410-1411.

5324   NIZARD, L. "Le Plan: révélateur d'une définitive impuissance parlementaire ?", *Anal. et Prévis.* 14(6), dec 72 : 1489-1504. [France.]

5325   "Nouveau plan quinquennal irakien 1970-1974", *Syrie Monde arabe* 20(228), jan 73 : 18-40.

5326   "Objectifs et moyens du IVeme plan quadriennal de développement du Sénégal, 1973-1977 (Les)", *Industr. Trav. O.-Mer* 21(235), jun 73 : 507-512.

5327   *Plans de développement des pays d'Afrique noire (Les): Mauritanie, Mali, Niger, Togo, Sénégal, Cote d'Ivoire, Cameroun, Gabon.* Paris, Édiafric-Service, 72, 325 p. [Nº spécial du *Bulletin de l'Afrique noire.*]

5328   "Plan de développement quinquennal, 1971-1975 de la République centrafricaine (Le)", *Industr. Ttav. O.-Mer* 21(238), sep 73 : 761-771.

5329   RULL SABATER, A. *La planificación económica y social en Centroamérica* (Economic and social planning in Central America). Madrid, Confederación Española de Cajas de Ahorros, 71, 342 p.

5330 SANDFORD, C. T. *National economic planning*. London, Heinemann Educational, 72, 8-88 p. [UK.]

5331 SAUL, J. S. "Planning for socialism in Tanzania: the socio-political context", *Develop. and Change* 3(3), 1971-1972 : 3-25.

5332 SAWIRIS, S. B. *Planning economic development in underdeveloped countries with special reference to Egypt*. Cairo-Bruxelles, Université libre de Bruxelles, Faculté des sciences sociales, politiques et économiques, 72, xxxll-453 l.

5333 SINGH, B. "The strategy and pattern of development planning in South Asia. A diagnosis", *South Asian Stud.* 6(1), jan 71 : 1-22.

5334 SURREY, M. J. C. "The national plan in retrospect", *B. Oxford Univ. Inst. Econ. Statist.* 34(3), aug 72 : 249-268. [UK.]

5335 TAAKE, H.-H. "Der dritte Fünfjahrplan, 1972-1976 Koreas (Süd)" (The South Korean third five-year plan, 1972-1976), *Konjunkt.-Polit.* 18(5), 1972 : 295-311.

### N.1123    Armament and defence
         *Armement et défense*

5336 ALBRECHT, U. "Die Struktur von Rüstungsausgaben" (Structure of armament expenditures), *Leviathan* 1(1), 1973 : 43-68.

5337 ALDRICH, M. "The impact of the war in Southeast Asia upon state economies, 1964-1969", *West. econ. J.* 10(4), dec 72 : 449-459.

5338 BIERI, R. "Landesverteidigung und Bundeshaushalt" (National defense and federal budget), *Wirtsch. u. Recht* 24(4), 1972 : 287-301. [Switzerland.]

5339 BRITO, D. L. "A dynamic model of an armaments race", *Int. econ. R.* 13(2), jun 72 : 359-375.

5340 BRUBAKER, E. R. "Economic models of arms races: some reformulations and extensions", *J. Conflict Resol.* 17(2), jun 73 : 187-205.

5341 "Defense spending", *For. Pol.* (6), 1972 : 69-114. [Abstracts 23-269, 23-322, 23-347.]

5342 KALDOR, M. *European defense industries: national and international implications*. Brighton, Institute for the Study of International Organization, 72, 3-79 p.

5343 PURSELL, C. W. Jr. (ed.). *The military-industrial complex*. New York, Harper and Row, 72, x-342 p.

5344 SCHULTZE, C. L. "The economic content of national security policy", *For. Aff.* 51(3), apr. 73 : 522-540.

5345 SUBRAHMANYAM, K. "Indian defence expenditure in global perspective", *Econ. polit. Wkly* 8(26), jun 73 : 1155-1158.

5346 SZYMANSKI, A. "Military spending and economic stagnation", *Amer. J. Social.* 79(1), jul 73 : 1-14.

5347 UDIS, B. "The end of overrun: prospects for the high technology defense industry and related issues", *A. Amer. Acd. polit. soc. Sci.* 406, mar 73 : 59-72.

### N.113    **The co-operative sector**
         *Le secteur coopératif*

5348 FRITSCHE, M. *Planung und Organisation der Beschaffung von langfristigem Kapital im Genossenschaftsverbund* (Planning and organization of long-term capital in co-operative associations). Hamburg, Buske, 72, vi-226 p.

5349 GAIMUSHO (ed.). *Ajia no chiiki kyoryoku kikoo* (Local cooperative organizations in Asia). Tokyo, Nihon Kokusai Mondai Kenkyu-jo, 71, 124 p.

5350 KOWALAK, T. "Spółdzielczość w rozwoju krajów Trzeciego Świata. Możliwości i rzeczywistość" (Co-operatives in the development of the Third World. Their possibilities and reality), *Spóld. Kwartal. Nauk.* (4), 1973 : 47-68.

5351 KRISHNARAO, B. "Cooperation in Thailand", *Ind. coop. R.* 10(1), oct 72 : 119-124.

5352 LOUIS, R. "Co-operative development centres", *Int. Lab. R.* 107(6), jun 73 : 539-551.

5353 LOUIS, R. "Coordination des recherches sur les coopératives des pays en voie de développement", *R. Ét. coop.* 51(169), 3 trim 72 : 294-310.

5354 MAMEDOVA, N. M. *Kooperacija v Irane* (Cooperation in Iran). Moskva, Nauka, 73, 144 p.

5355    "Mouvement coopératif dans les pays du Marché commun (Le)", *R. Coop. int.* 65(6), 1972 : 215-255.

5356    PARMAR, P. S. "Cooperative movement in the Republic of South Korea", *Ind. coop. R.* 10(1), oct 72 : 125-131.

5357    PULINCKX, J.-C. "Analyse des facteurs défavorables à l'implantation de l'institution coopérative en Afrique centrale", *A. Écon. coll.* 61(2), apr-jun 73 : 245-251.

5358    WIDSTRAND, C. G. (ed.). *African co-operatives and efficiency.* Uppsala, Scandinavian Institute of African Studies, 72, 239 p.


**N.12     Collectivist planned systems**
**Systèmes collectivistes planifiés**

**N.120     *General studies***
***Études générales***


[See also / Voir aussi : **I.2124; 6446**]


5359    BATYMURZAEV, (ed.). *Leninskoe učenie o vozmožnosti perehoda otstalyh narodov k socializmu i ego osuščestvlenie* (The Leninist teaching on the possibilities of underdeveloped countries, passage to socialism and its realization). Mahackala Dagknigoizdat, 72, 163 p.

5360    BELYH, A. K. (ed.). *Kommunizm i upravlenie obščestvennymi processami. I. Osnovnye principy socialističeskogo upravlenija. Osobennosti upravlenija ekonomičeskimi i socialističeskogo processami pri socializme* (Communism and social process management. I. Essential principles of socialist management. Characteristics of economic and social processes management under socialism). Leningrad, 72, 272 p.

5361    BORIVIK, F. V. *et al. Leninskie principy socialistčeskogo hozjajstvovanija* (Leninist principles of the socialist economic management). Minsk, Belarus', 72, 200 p.

5362    BRESS, L. *et al.* (eds.). *Wirtschaftssysteme des Sozialismus im Experiment. Plan oder Markt ?* (Socialist economic systems in the experimental stage, planned economy or market economy ?). Frankfurt am-Main, Athenäum-Fischer-Taschenbuch-Verlag, 72, 394 p.

5363    ČIPEK, K. *Teorie a praxe rízení socialistickyh ekonomik* (Theory and practice of socialist economic management). Praha, Svoboda, 72, 353-1 p.

5364    KŁAPKOWSKI, B.; CIĘCINA, Z. *Trójczynnikowy model gospodarki socjalistycznej* (A three-factor model of socialist economy). Warszawa, Państwowe Wydawnictwo Naukowe, 73, 317 p.

5365    KOZLOV, G. A. "Nekotorye čerty razvitogo socializma" (Some characteristics of developed socialism), in: *Ekonomičeskie i social'no-političeskie problemy kommunističeskogo stroitel'stva v SSSR.* Moskva, 72 : 25-47.

5367    LEONT'EV, L. A. *Ekonomičeskie problemy razvitogo socializma* (Economic problems of developed socialism). Moskva, Nauka, 72, 207 p.

5368    LEWANDOWSKI, J. (ed.). *System funkcjonowania gospodarki socjalistycznej* (Functioning system of socialist economy). Warszawa, Państwowe Wydawnictwo Ekonomiczne 73, 378 p.

5369    LOGVINOV, L. D. *O harakteristike ekonomičeskih zakonov socializma* (On the characteristics of socialist economic laws). Moskva, Znanie, 72, 47 p.

5370    LUR'E, A. L.; NIT, I. V. *Ekonomiko-matematičeskoe modelirovanie socialističeskogo hozjajstva* (Elaboration of economic and mathematical models of the socialist economy). Moskva, Izdatel'stvo Moskovskogo Universiteta, 73, 284 p.

5371    MESA-LAGO, C. "A continuum model to compare socialist systems globally", *Econ. Develop. cult. Change* 21(4), *Part I* jul 73 : 473-590.

5372    NOVOZILOV, V. V. *Voprosy razvitija socialističeskoj ekonomiki* (Questions on socialist economic development). Moskva, Nauka, 73, 327 p.

5373    OL'SEVIČ, Ju. Ja. *Effektivnost' ekonomiki socializma. Kritika buržuaznyh i revizionistskih koncepcij* (Efficiency of the socialist economy. Critics of bourgeois and revisionist theories). Moskva, Msyl', 72, 288 p.

5374    OMAROV, A. M. *Naučnye osnovy upravlenija socialističeskoj ekonomikoj* (Scientific bases of the socialist economic management). Moskva, Mysl', 73, 270 p.

5375 OŽEREL'EV, O. I. *Osnovnoj èkonomičeskij zakon socializma i ego ispol'zovanie v upravlenii narodnym hozjajstvom* (The essential economic law of socialism and its utilization in national economic management). Leningrad, Izdatel'stvo leningradskogo Universiteta, 73, 136 p.

5376 POPOV, N. H. "Metodologičeskie problemy teorii upravlenija socialističeskim obščestvennym proizvodstvom" (Methodological problems of socialist social production management theory), in: *Organicija upravlenija.* II. Moskva, 1972 : 5-71.

5377 PORWIT, K. *Methods and techniques of central planning.* Warsaw, Central School of Planning and Statistics in Warsaw, 73, 87 p.

5378 SEVOMSKI, K. "Les prémisses sociales de la politique économique socialiste", *Res. publ.* 15(1), 1973 : 27-45.

5379 SPULBER, N. "On some issues in the theory of the 'socialist economy'", *Kyklos* 25 (4), 1972 : 715-735.

5380 ŠVEC, Ja. G. *Socialističeskoe sovrenovanie na sovremennom etape razvitija* (Socialist competition at the contemporary stage of development). Moskva, Mysl', 73, 124 p.

5381 "Taches d'avenir de l'économie collective (Les)", *A. Écon. coll.* 60(3-4), jul-dec 72 : 327-696.

5382 TIMOFEEV, Ju. N. "K voprosu o suščnosti demokratičeskogo centralizma kak principa upravlenija pri socializme" (On the nature of democratic centralism as a management principle under socialism), in: *Aktual'nye problemy upravlenija social'nymi processami pri socializme.* Moskva, 1972 : 35-49.

### N.121 Soviet regime
### Régime soviétique

### N.1211 Economic policy
### Politique économique

### N.12110 General studies
### Études générales

5383 ABOLIN, E. "Ėkonomičeskaja reforma: nekotorye itogi, problemy i perspektivy" (The economic reform: some balances, problems and prospects), *Kommunist Sov. Latvii.* 28(5), mai 73 : 10-16.

5384 ABOUCHAR, A. "Inefficiency and reform in the Soviet economy", *Sov. Stud.* 25(1), jul 73 : 66-87.

5385 BARYŠNIKOV, N. N.; MARTYNOV, B. M. *Osnovnye napravlenija ekonomičeskoj politiki* (Essential trends of party economic policy). Moskva, Mysl', 72, 126 p.

5386 DELLIN, L.; GROSS, H. *Reforms in the Soviet and East European economies.* Lexington, Mass., D. C. Heath Lexington Books, 72, viii-175 p.

5387 FEIWEL, G. R. "The dynamics of perpetuation: some observations on the efficacity of Soviet economic reforms", *Econ. int. (Genova)* 26(2), mai 73 : 233-260.

5388 GOLDMAN, M. I. "Externalities and the race for economic growth in the USSR : will the environment ever win ?", *J. polit. Econ.* 80(2), mar-apr 72 : 314-327.

5389 GULJAMOV, S. G. *Ekonomičeskaja rol'sovetskogo gosudarstva v sozdanii predposylok socialzma v sel'skom hozjajstve Uzbekistana* (Economic role of the Soviet State in the creation of socialist conditions in Uzbekistan agriculture). Taskent, Fan, 72, 207 p.

5390 HOHMANN, H. H. *Ergebnisse und Probleme der sowjetischen Wirtschaftspolitik; eine Bilanz am Beginn der siebziger Jahre* (Results and problems of Soviet economic policy: a balance-sheet for the beginning of the 1970's). 2 vols. Köln, Bundesinstitut für Ostwissenschaftliche und Internationale Studien, 72.

5391 KATZ, A. *The politics of economic reform in the Soviet Union.* New York, Praeger, 72, viii-230 p.

5392 NEKRASSOV, N. "La politique économique et la répartition des forces productives en U. R. S. S.", *Sci. soc. (Moscou)* (3), 1972 : 40-53.

5393 VISKIJ, E. A.; FEDJUK, V. I. *Voprosy i otvety po ekonomičeskoj reforme* (Questions and answers on the economic reform). Minsk, Belorus', 72, 128 p.

5394    WILCZYNSKI, J. *The economics of socialism; principles governing the operation of the central-ly planned economies in the USSR and Eastern Europe under the new system.* Rev. ed. London, Allen and Unwin, 72, 3-233 p.

N.12111    Economic management and administrative organs
           Gestion économique et organes administratifs

5395    ALBU, V. F.; KISELEV, V. I.; KOŽUHAR', P. V. *Problemy optimizacii razvitija ekonomičes-kogo kompleksa* (Problems of optimization of complex economic development). Kišinev, Štiinca, 72, 163 p.

5396    BENJAMIN, M.; LUNGWITZ, W.; PENIG, L. "Vervollkommung der Wirtschaftsleitung in der UdSSR" (The perfecting of economic management in the USSR), *Staat und Recht* 22(8), aug 73 : 1256-1271.

5397    KAMANKIN, W. P. "Wirtschafts-reform und Planung in der UdSSR" (Economic reform and planning in the USSR), *Wirtsch.-Wiss.* 21(8), aug 73 : 1200-1216.

5398    KAN, A. D. "O metodah upravlenija narodnym hozjajstvom SSSR" (Management methods of the USSR's national economy), *Pravovedenie* 15(5), sep-oct 72 : 21-30.

5399    KRUK, D. M. *Upravlenie obščestvennym proizvodstvom pri socializme* (Social production management under socialism). Moskva, Ekonomika, 72, 233 p.

5400    MULLER, E. *et al. Volkswirtschaftlicher Reproduktionsprozess und dynamische Modelle* (The process of national economic reproduction and dynamic models). Berlin, Verlag die Wirtschaft, 73, 491 p.

5401    SZTARODUBROVSZKIJ, V. "A gazdasági mechanizmus fejlesztésének eredményei és pro-blémai a Szovjetunóban" (Results and problems of the development of economic mechanism in the USSR), *Kozgazd. Szle* 20(3), mar 73 : 271-284.

5402    TAPIOLA, I. *Neuvoltolitton talousuudistus vuosina 1965-1972* (The economic reform in the Soviet Union in 1965-1972). Helsinki, Ulkopoliittinen instituutti, 73, 42 p.

N.12112    Economic plans: aims and realizations
           Plans économiques : objectifs et réalisations

        [See also / Voir aussi: 3199, 3249, 4942, 4965]

5403    BAIBAKOV, N. "La planification sociale et le développement de l'économie en U. R. S. S." *Sci. soc. (Moscou)* (1), 1972 : 18-35.

5404    BARDIN, D. M.; ORLOV, A. V. *Planomernoe razvitija socialističeskoj ekonomiki. Ekonomi-českaja rol'socialističeskogo gosudarstva* (The socialist economy's planned development. Economic role of the State). Moskva, Vyssaja skola, 72, 72, 64 p.

5405    CAPKIN, N. V. *Planirovanie narodnogo hozjajstva v SSSR* (National economic planning in the USSR). Moskva, Mysl', 72, 479 p.

5406    CROSNIER, M. A. "L'analyse séquentielle dans la planification et la gestion en U. R. S. S." *Écon. et Soc.* 7(2-3), feb-mar 73 : 367-389.

5407    EFIMO, A.; SHVYRKOV, Y. *Soviet planning: principles and techniques.* Moscow, Progress Publishers, 72, 193 p.

5408    ELLMAN, M. *Planning problems in the USSR: the contribution of mathematical economics to their solution 1960-1971.* Cambridge, Eng., University Press, 73, xx-222 p.

5409    FEDORENKO, N. P. "O nekotoryh voprosah soveršenstvovanija planirovanija i upravlenija narodnym hozjajstvom" (Some question on improvement of national economy planning and management), in: *Ekonomičeskie i social'no-političeskie problemy kom-munističeskogo stroitel'stva v SSSR.* Moskva, 1972 : 79-99.

5410    GURIN, L. E. *Plan po rudu i zarabotnoj plate* (Plan according to labour and wages). Moskva, Ekonomika, 72, 46 p.

5411    KOVAL', N. S.; MIROSHNICHENKO, B. *Fundamentals of national economic planning in the USSR.* Moscow, Novowti Press Agency, 72, 343 p.

5412    PEDAK, L. "Plany social'nogo razvitija i planirovanie narodnogo hozjajstva" (Social development plans and the planning of the national economy), *Kommunist Est* 29(2), feb 73 : 49-56.

5413    SPINA, E. "La pianificazione economica nell'URSS" (Economic planning in the USSR) *Est-Ouest* 3(3), 1972 : 7-40; 4(1), 1973 : 7-44. [For first part, see Bibl. XXI-5558.]

5414 ŠPINER, R. I. *Svodnoe planirovanie narodnogo hozjajstva oblasti i rajona* (Global planning of the national economy, sector and region). Moskva, Ekonomika, 72, 191 p.

5415 STEPANOV, A. P. *Ekonomičeskie problemy planirovanija narodnogo hozjajstva SSSR* (Economic problems of the USSR national economy planning). Kiev, Isdatel'stvo Kievskogo Universiteta, 73, 221 p.

5416 ZIJADULLAEV, S. K. *Planirovanie i razviti ekonomiki Uzbekskoj SSR* (Planning and development of the Uzbek economy). Taškent, Uzbekistan, 72, 229 p.

### N.12113 The co-operative sector
### Le secteur coopératif

5417 ABÛ AL-ḤAYR, K. Ḥ. *al-Taṭawwur al-ta'âwunî al-ishtirâkî fî Tshikûslûfâkiyâ wa-Miṣr* (The development of socialist co-operatives in Czechoslovakia and Egypt) al-Qâhiraṭ, Maktabaṭ 'Ayn Shams, 73, 494 p.

5418 FOLDES, I. "Genossenschaften und Genossenschaftsverbände in Ungarn" (Cooperatives and cooperative societies in Hungry), *Donauraum* 17(3), 1972 : 143-151.

5419 HOPE, K. R. "Aspects du socialisme coopératif en Guinée", *A. Écon. coll.* 61(3), jul-sep 73 : 347-356.

5420 JAŃCZYK, T. "Spółdzielczośc polska w międzynarodowym ruchu spółdzielczym" (Polish co-operatives in the international co-operative movement), *Spóld. Kwartal. Nauk.* (4), 1973 : 3-21.

### N.122 *People's democracies and other socialist countries*
### *Démocraties populaires et autres pays socialistes*

[See also / Voir aussi: 5386, 5394, 5492, 5498, 5978]

5421 AROJO, Ž. Ž. *Aktualni problemi na ikonomičeskaja politika na BKP* (Topical problems of Bulgarian economic policy). Sofija, Partizdat, 73, 132 p.

5422 AXILROD, E. *The political economy of the Chinese revolution.* Hong Kong, Union Research Institute, 72, ix-541 p. CR: C. HOFFMANN, *J. econ. Liter.* 11(3), sep 73 : 915-916.

5423 BACSURIN, A. V. "Az állami tervezés mint társadalmi termelés hatékonyabbà tételének legfontosabb eszköze" (National planning, main instrument of a better efficiency of social production), *Kozgazd. Szle* 19(11), nov 72 : 1261-1268. [Hungary.]

5424 BAKOS, G. "Az NDK gazdaságirányitasi rendszerének néhány jellemzöje" (Some characteristics of the economic orientation system of the German Democratic Republic), *Kozgazd. Szle* 20(9), sep 73 : 1087-1095.

5425 BARTUŇKOVÁ, M.; ČERVENKOVÁ, A. "Současné petiletky zemi RVPH" (Present five year plans of the CAEM countries), *Plan. Hospod.* 25(4), 1973 : 73-83.

5426 BERNARD, A. et al. "Organisation et méthodes de la planification hongroise", *Écon. et Soc.* 7(2-3), feb-mar 73 : 297-341.

5427 BETZ, H. "The pattern of economic reform in East Germany: return to increased centralization ?", *Econ. int. (Genova)* 26(2), mai 73 : 318-328.

5428 BOLLAND, S. "Freedom of decision within the framework of the Central Plan", *East. Europ. Econ.* 11(1), 1972 : 3-17.

5429 BRETSCHNEIDER, H. "Langfristige Plannung bis 1990" (Long term planning up to 1990) *Einheit* 28(4), 1973 : 448-454. [Germany, DR.]

5430 BREUER, W. M. *Sozialismus in Kuba: zur polit Ökonomie* (Cuban socialism, on political economy). Köln, Pahl-Rugenstein, 73, 293 p.

5431 CEAUSESCU, N. *Report on Romania's short-term and long-term economic and social development, on the improvement of the planned management of society and the development of socialist democracy, the growth of the leading role of the Party in building socialism and communism, on the international activity of the Party and State.* Bucharest, Meridiane, 72, 167 p.

5432 DRECIN, J. "Gazdaságpolitikánk és az 1973, évi terv fö vonásai" (Our economic policy and the main characteristics of our 1973 Plan), *Kozgazd. Szle* 20(2), feb 73 : 129-137. [Hungary.].

5433 FEVERLE, P. "State arbitration in communist countries: the differentiation of functions", *Stud. comp. Communism* 4(3-4), jul-oct 71 : 25-41.

5434 "Enseignements et problèmes de la réforme économique hongroise", *Assoc. Cadres dir. Industr. B.* 278, oct 72 : 499-515.

5435 FEIWEL, G. R. "Aspects of economic policy in postwar Poland", II. *Osteuropa Wirtsch.* 18(3), sep 72 : 145-166. [See part one, Bibl. xxi-5581.]

5436 FLAKIERSKI, H. "The Polish economic reform of 1970", *Canad. J. Econ.* 6(1), feb 73 : 1-15.

5437 GADO, O. "The development of planning and management methods in Hungary", *Acta oecon.* 9(3-4), 1972 : 259-286.

5438 GRANICK, D. "A management model of East European centrally-planned economies", *Europ. econ. R.* 4(2), jun 73 : 135-161.

5439 GRANICK, D. "Hungarian economic reform", *Wld Polit.* 25(3), apr 73 : 414-429.

5440 HOHMANN, H. H. *Die Wirtschaftsordungen Osteuropas im Wandel: Ergebnisse der Wirtschaftsreformen* (Economic organization of Eastern Europe in change; results of economic reforms). Freiburg im Breisgau, Rombach, 72, 2 vols.

5441 HYDEN, G. *Socialism och samhällsutveckling i Tanzania. En studie i teori och praktik* (Socialism and social development in Tanzania. A study in theory and practice). Staffanstorp, Cavefors, 72, 214 p.

5442 JAMPEL, W. "Les grandes organisations économiques (W. O. G.) Contribution à l'étude de la réforme économique actuelle en Polgne", *R. Est* 4(3), jul 73 : 85-99.

5443 KARPINSKI, A. "Problemy organizacji i metodologii prac nad planem prespektywioznym" (Organization and work methodology concerning long term planning), *Gosp. planowa* 27(6), jun 72 : 333-337. [Poland.]

5444 KEREN, M. "The new economic system in the GDR, an obituary", *Sov. Stud.* 24(4), apr 73 : 554-587.

5445 KIERCZYNSKI, T.; RYDYGIER, W.; WOJCIECHOWSKA, U. "Kierunki przebudowy systemu ekonomiczno-finansowego" (Directions of remodelling the economic and finaicial system), *Stud. finans.* 13, 1972 : 5-36. [Poland.]

5446 KLEER, J. "Reformy gospodarcze w krajach socjalistycznych w latach sześćdzuesiątych" (Economic reforms in the socialist countries in the 1960's), *Ekonomista*(1), 1973 : 69-91.

5447 LEVKOVSKIJ, A. I. *Ekonomičeskaja politika i gosudarstvennyj kapitalizm v stranah Vostoka* (Economic policy and state capitalism in Eastern countries). Moskva, Nauka, 72, 403 p.

5448 LIEBER, P.; FEIER, U. *Politische Ökonomie des Sozialismus in der DDR* (Political economy of socialism in the DDR). Frankfurt-am-Main, Makol, 72, 278-1 p.

5449 LUR'E, A. L. *Ekonomičeskij analiz modelej planirovanija socialističeskogo hozjajstva* (Economic analysis of the planning models of the socialist economy). Moskva, Nauka, 73, 435 p.

5450 MANESCU, M. "Institucionalizarea activitatii de planificare în Romania (1948-1973)" (The institutionalization of planning in Rumania 1948 to 1973), *Probleme econ. (Bucuresti)* 26(7), jul 73 : 21-27.

5451 MORAVICK, I. "East European economic reforms: retrospect and prospect", *Ét. slav. est-europ.* 16, 1971 : 14-27.

5452 NICOLAE, N. "Wirtschaftspläne und Aussenhandel Rumäniens" (Economic planning and foreign trade in Roumania), *Aussenpolitik* 24(1), jan 73 : 108-112.

5453 PACIORKOWSKI, K. "Handel w 1973 roku w projekcie Narodowego Planu Gospodarczego" (The basic problems of the project of the National Economic Plan for 1973), *Tryb. Spól.* (2), 1973 : 25-28. [Poland.]

5454 PARASCHIV, G. "Controlul economico-social, parte integrantă a activităii de conducere planificată a vieii economica şi sociale" (Economic and social control, part and parcel of planned direction of social and economic life), *Finanţe şi Cred.* 19(4), apr 73 : 3-10. [Rumania.]

5455 POKORNY, Z. "Développement de l'économie tchécoslovaque et réalisisation du plan en 1972", *Demosta* 6(1), 1973 : 3-10.

5456 PRAVDA, A. "Some aspects of the Czechoslovak economic reform and the working class in 1968", *Sov. Stud.* 25(1), jul 73 : 102-124.

5457 ROBINSON, W. F. *The pattern of reform in Hungary; a political, economic and cultural analysis.* New York, Praeger, 73, xix-467 p.

5458 SCARAMOZZINO(ed.). *L'introduzione delle riforme economiche nei paesi dell'Est europeo* (The introduction of economic reforms in Eastern European countries). Pavia, Istituto di scienze politiche dell'Università, Milano, A. Giuffrè, 72, 294 p.

5459 SCHARNBACHER, K. "Cerflechtungsbilanzierung und Optimierungsrechnung in der zentrallen staatlichen Planung der DDR" (Estimation of the consolidated balance-sheet and optimal calculation in the centralized planning system of Germany DR), *Dtsche Stud.* 11(41), mar 73 : 53-58.

5460 SOBCZAK, K. "Aktuelle Probleme der Wirtschaftsverwaltung in Polen" (Present problems in the administration of the economy in Poland), *Verwaltung* 5(3), 1972 : 336-349.

5461 "Sozialistische Planung" (Socialist planning), *Einheit* 28(3), 1973 : 273-307. [Germany DR.]

5462 TEREKHOV, V. F.; YEVSTIGNEYEV, R. N. "Economic reforms in socialist countries", *Econ. B. Asia Far East* 21(3), dec 70 : 31-40.

5463 TRZECIAKOWSKI, W. *Systems of indirect management in a planned economy. Effectiveness models and their applications in Poland.* Łódz, Państwowe Wydawnictwo Naukowe, 73, 173 p.

5464 WHEELER, G. S. *The human face of socialism: the political economy of change in Czechoslovakia.* New York, L. Hill, 73, xiv-174 p.

### N.123    *Yugoslavia*
*Yougoslavie*

[See also / Voir aussi: 1982]

5465 BIČANIC, R. *Economic policy in socialist Yugoslavia.* Cambridge, Eng., University Press, 73, viii-254 p.

5466 ČERNE, F. "Jugoslovanski samoupravni ekonomski sistem ter njegova učinkovitost" (The self-management economic system in Yugoslavia and its efficiency), *Ekon. R. (Ljubljana)* 22(4), dec 71 : 380-404.

5467 FEUERLE, P. "Yugoslavia's economic courts: between central planning and enterprise autonomy", *Columbia J. transnat. Law* 12(2), 1973 : 274-288.

5468 KORIŠIC, M. "Osnovni kriteriji uspijcha funkcioniranja jugoslavenskog ekonomskog sistema" (The fundamental criterias of success of the functioning of the Yugoslav economic system), *Ekonomist (Zagreb)* 25(3-4), 1972 : 463-479.

5469 PERIC, Z. "Pouke postreformskih privednih kretanja za kreiranje ekonomske politike za 1972 / 1973 godinu" (The lessons of the economic movements following the reform for the elaboration of economic policy in 1972-73), *Ekonomist (Zagreb)* 25(3-4), 1972 : 563-580.

5470 SINGLETON, F. "Yugoslavia: democratic centralism and market socialism", *Wld today* 29(4), apr 73 : 160-168.

5471 TJAGUENENKO, L. "Novye izmenenija v hozjajstvennoj sisteme Jugoslavii" (New changes in the economic system of Yugoslavia), *Ekon. Nauki* 16(8), aug 73 : 71-80.

5472 VOJNIC, D. "Three aspects of development policy in the social plan for 1971-1975", *East. Europ. econ.* 10(4), 1972 : 417-444. [Yugoslavia.]

### N.2    PUBLIC FINANCE
FINANCES PUBLIQUES

### N.20    Generalities
Généralités

### N.200    *General studies*
*Études générales*

[See also / Voir aussi: 3988, 4323]

5473 DAVID, W. L. (ed.). *Public finance, planning, and economic development.* London, Macmillan; New York, St. Martin's Press, 73, 349 p.

5474 DUE, J. F. "Four contributions to public finance-Thurow, Oates, Tait, and Rectenwald: a review article", *Quart. R. Econ. Busin.* 12(4), 1972 : 79-90.

5475 FROMM, G.; TAUBMAN, P. *Public economic theory and policy.* New York, Macmillan, 73, 361 p.

5476     GREFFE, X. *L'approche contemporaine de la valeur en finances publiques.* Paris, Economics, 72, 260 p.

5477     HYMAN, D. N. *The economics of governmental activity.* New York, Holt, Rinehart and Winston, 73, 333 p.

5478     MUSGRAVE, R. A.; MUSGRAVE, P. B. *Public finance in theory and practice.* New York, McGraw-Hill, 73, 762 p.

5479     SHAW, E. S. *Financial deepening in economic development.* New York, Oxford University Press, 73, 260 p.

5480     WAGNER, R. E. *The public economy.* Chicago, Markham Publishing, 73, 240 p.

### N.201     Public finance situation
###            Situation des finances publiques

[See also / Voir aussi: 4112]

5481     ANDERSON, W. H. *Financing modern government; the political economy of the public sector.* Boston, Houghton Mifflin, 73, 354 p. [USA.]

5482     FISHER, G. R.; SHEPPARD, D. K. "The financial sector and the pace of economic activity", *Bankers Mag.* 216(1555), oct 73 : 141-147. [USA.]

5483     FRY, M. J. *Finance and development planning in Turkey.* Leiden, Brill, 72, 231 p.

5484     GOKIELI, A. P.; KIPIANI, N. N. "Voprosy planovogo svodnogo finansovogo balansa sojuznoj respubliki" (Questions of the planned global financial balance of a Soviet republic), *Probl. Ekon. Gruzii* 5(2), 1972 : 135-271.

5485     GRANT, A. T. K. *The strategy of financial pressure.* London, Macmillan, 72, 149 p.

5486     HESS, V. *Finanza pubblica e moneta in URSS.* (Public finance and money in the USSR.) Bari, Laterza, 72, 311 p.

5487     KULIKOV, V. S. *Rol'finansov v povysenii blagosostojanija sovetskogo naroda* (Role of finance in the Soviet people's welfare elevation). Moskva, Finansy, 72, 167 p. [USSR.]

5488     MATHEWS, R. L. "The future of government finance (with special reference to inter-governmental financial relations)", *Publ. Adm. (Sydney)* 32(2) jun 73 : 155-174. [Australia.]

5489     PREST, A. R. "Public finance: backward area or new frontier ?", *Economica (London)* 40(158), mai 73 : 121-135. [UK.]

5490     RENVERSEZ, F. "La situation des finances publiques en 1971", *R. Écon. polit. (Paris)* 82(5), sep-oct 72 : 854-879. [France.]

5491     REVELL, J. *Financial structure and government regulation in the United Kingdom,* 1952-1980. London, Inter-Bank Research Organisation, 72, 65 p.

5492     ROHLIČEK, R. "Le rôle des finances dans la gestion planifiée du développement de l'économie tchécoslovaque", *Aperçus Écon. tchécosl.* (6), sep 73 : 3-61.

5493     SCHNITZER, M.; CHEN, Y.-P. *Public finance and public policy issues.* Scranton, Intext Educational Publishers, 72, 445 p. [USA.]

5494     TAVARES, M. da C. "Naturaleza y contradicciones de la evolucion financiera reciente del Brasil" (Nature and contradictions of the recent financial evolution of Brazil), *R. latinoamer. Cienc. soc.* (4), dec 72 : 55-95.

### N.2011     Treasury and treasury situation
###             Le Trésor et la situation de la trésorerie

5495     HICKS, M. "The Treasury Board of Canada and its clients: five years of change and administrative reform 1966-71", *Cand. publ. Adm.* 16(2), summer 73 : 182-205.

### N.202     Financial policy
###          Politique financière

### N.2020     General studies
###             Études générales

[See also / Voir aussi: J.24; J.5; N.23210]

5496     SCHOPF, A. *Einführung in die Finanzpolitik* (Introduction to financial policy). Berlin, Duncker und Humblot, 72, 212 p.

5497   TKAČUK, M. I. *Problemy finansovogo planirovanija* (Problems of financial planning). Minsk, Nauka i Tehnika, 72, 207 p.

**N.2021**   *Local studies*
              *Études localisées*

[See also / Voir aussi: **N.23211**]

5498   KROPÁČ, L. "K rozvoji finančniho plánováni" (About development of financial planning) *Plan. Hospod.* 25(1), jan 73 : 7-14. [Czechoslovakia.]

5499   LETSCH, H. *Öffentliche Finanzen und Finanzpolitiz in der Schweiz* (Public finance and financial policy in Switzerland). Bern-Stuttgart, P. Haupt, 72, 160 p.

5500   PLOTNIKOV, K. N.; VINOKUR. R. D. "Gosudarstvennye finansy v sisteme funkcioniro-vanija narodnogo hozjajstva" (National finances in the functioning system of the economy), *Vest. Akad. Nauk SSSR* 43(4), apr 73 : 46-54. [USSR.]

5501   SCHMIDT, V. "Finanz- und Aufgabenplanung als Instrumente der Regierungsplanung" (Financial planning and tastes, as an instrument of governmental planning), *Verwaltung* 6(1), 73 : 1-23. [Germany, F. R.]

5502   SITARJAN, S. A. *Finansovye problemy v svete resenij dvatcat' četvertogo s"ezda KPSS* (Financial problems in the light of the decisions of the XXIVth CPSU Congress). Moskva, Finansy, 72, 319 p. [USSR.]

5503   VUČIĆ, N. "Problems der jugoslawischen Finanzpolitik" (Problems of Yugoslavian financial policy), *Osteuropa Wirtsch.* 18(3), sep 72 : 167-182.

**N.203**   *Organization of financial administration*
             *Organisation de l'administration financière*

**N.2030**   *General studies*
              *Études générales*

5504   KUROWSKI, L.; SOCHACKA-KRYSIAK, H. *Podstawy kontroli finansowej* (Basis of financial control). Warszawa, Panstwowe Wydawnictwo Ekonomiczne, 73, 233 p.

**N.2031**   *Local studies*
              *Études localisées*

5505   ALLEGRETTI, U. *Il governo della finanza pubblica* (The governing of public finance). Padova, Cedam, 71, 309 p. [Italy.]

5506   LEVY, V. M. *Public financial administration; a study of the financial and accounting practices of public authorities.* Sydney, Law Book Co., 72, 153 p.

5507   Bibl. XXI-5654. NEUFELD, E. P. *The financial system of Canada: its growth and development.* CR: R. C. McIvor, *J. econ. Liter.* 11(3), sep 73 : 936-938.

5508   PALACIOS MEJIA, H. "La hacienda pública en el derecho constitucional colombiano" (Public finance in Colombian constitutional law), *Universitas (Bogota)* 43, nov 72 : 71-93.

5509   WERALSKI, M. *Socjalistyczne instytucje finansowe* (Socialist financial institutions). Warszawa, Państwowe Wydawnictwo Ekonomiczne, 73, 447 p.

**N.204**   *Public accounting*
             *Comptabilité publique*

[See also / Voir aussi: 5574]

5510   TROTABAS, L.; COTTERET, J. -M. *Droit budgétaire et comptabilité publique.* Paris, Dalloz, 72, 509 p. [France]

**N.21      State budget**
**Le budget de l'État**

**N.211      *Budget economics***
***Économie budgétaire***

**N.2110      *General studies***
*Études générales*

5511   AMSELEK, P. "Note sur la RCB", *R. adm.* 148, jul-aug 72 : 425-438 et 149, sep-oct 72 : 529-535.

5512   BEZDEK, R. H. "The employment effects of counter-budget", *J. econ. Issues* 6(4), dec 72 : 171-186.

5513   SOUMAGNE, J. P. "Les nouveaux budgétaires intégrés", *A. Econ. coll.* 61(3), jul-sep 73 : 357-366.

5514   TRAMONTANA, A. "Política di bilancio, formazione del capitale e sviluppo equilibrato" (Budget policy, capital formation and balanced development), *Riv. Dir. finanz.* 31(4), dec 72 : 622-639.

5515   WERALSKI, M. "Czy zmierzch budżetu państwowego ?" (Is there a decline of the State budget ?), *Finanse* (6), 1973 : 40-47.

5516   WERCHOWSKI, M. "Niektóre problemy norm budzetowych" (Selected problems of budgetary norms), *Finanse* (9), 1973 : 37-48.

**N.2111      *Local studies***
*Études localisées*

[See also / Voir aussi: 4109, 5635]

5517   BIRMAN, A. "Gosudarstvennyj bjudzet SSSR v perspektive ekonomičeskogo razvitija" (State budget of the USSR in the perspective of economic development), *Vopr. Ekon.* 25(9), sep 73 : 14-21.

5518   BLACK, G. "Externalities and structure in PPB", *Publ. Adm. R.* 31(6), nov-dec 71 : 637-643.

5519   BRAVO, J. "L'expérience française des budgets de programme", *R. écon. (Paris)* 24(1), jan 73 : 1-63.

5520   CUTT, J. *Program budgeting for welfare; a case study of Canada.* New York, Praeger, 73, 304 p.

5521   Bibl. XXI-5710. DOH, J. C. *The planning-programming-budgeting system in three Federal agencies.* CR: H. A. HOVEY, *J. econ. Liter.* 11(1), mar 72 : 118-119.

5522   FERNANDEZ, F. D. "Budget process and economic development; the Philippine experience", *Philippine J. Publ. Adm.* 16(1), jan 72 : 58-72.

5523   FEUCHTE, P. "Der Nothaushalt - ein Instrument der Politik ?" (The emergency budget: a policy instrument ?), *Archiv. off. Rechts.* 97(4), dec 72 : 538-567. [Germany. FR.]

5524   GROENEWEGEN, P. D. "The Australian budget process", *Publ. Adm. (Sydney)* 32(3), sep 73 : 251-267.

5525   GURUPRASAD, C. "Planning for tax administration in Canada: the P.P.B. system in national revenue taxation", *Canad. publ. Adm.* 16(3), aut 73 : 399-421.

5526   HIRSCH, W. Z. "Program budgeting in the United Kingdom", *Publ. Adm. R.* 33(2), mar-apr 73 : 120-128.

5527   HOWARD, S. K. *Changing State budgeting.* Lexington, Ky. Council of State Governments, 73, 372 p. [USA.]

5528   JOLLY, R.; WILLIAMS, M. "Macro-budget policy in an open export economy: lessons from Zambian experience", *East. Afr. econ. R.* 4(2), dec 72 : 1-27.

5529   LEE, R. D. Jr.; JOHNSON, R. W. *Public budgeting systems.* Baltimore, University Park Press, 73, 356 p. [USA.]

5530   LORD, G. *The French budgetary process.* Berkeley, University of California Press, 73, 217 p.

5531   NISKANEN, W. A. *Structural reform of the Federal budget process.* Washington, American Enterprise Institute for Public Policy Research, 73, 60 p.

5532   NOVICK, D. (ed.). *Current practice in program budgeting (PPBS); analysis and case studies covering government and business.* New York, Crane, Russak, 73, 242 p.

5533    PACKER, A. H. "A budget structured to reflect economic objectives", *J. Finance* 28(2), mai 73 : 467-480. [USA.]

5534    PICOS, G. "Bugetul de stat al Republicii Socialiste România" (The State budget of the Socialist Republic of Rumania), *Finante și Cred.* 18(9), sep 72 : 35-50.

5535    PIROŻYŃSKI, Z. "Kierunki doskonalenia systemu budżetowego" (Lines of improvement of the budgetary system), *Stud. finans.* (14), 1973 : 5-61. [Poland.]

5536    "Présentation du projet de budget de l'Etat pour 1973 (La)", *B. Docum. (Luxembourg)* 28(6), jun 72 : 1-13. [Luxembourg.]

5537    RAHMANN, B. *Grundlagen konjunkturbeeinflussender Haushalspolitik; ein Beitrag zu einer Theorie der Budgetwirkungen* (The bases of a budgeting policy influencing conjoncture; a contribution to theory of effects on the budget). Berlin, Duncker und Humblot, 72, 148 p. [Germany, FR.]

5538    SCOTTO DI CARLO, G. "La politica di bilancio in Italia, strumento di programmazione europea ?" (Is the Italian budgetary policy an instrument of European planning ?), *Stato soc.* 17(6), jun 73 : 427-445.

5539    SCOTTO DI CARLO, G. "Le politische di bilancio nei paesi della CEE" (Budgetary policies in the EEC countries), *Stato soc.* 16(11), nov 72 : 945-972.

5540    SILVA, J. A. DA. *Orçamento-programa no Brasil* (Program budgeting in Brazil). Sao Paulo, Empresa Gráfica da Revista dos Tribunais, 72, 388 p.

5541    SNYDER, W.; TANAKA, T. "Budget policy and economic stability in postwar Japan", *Int. econ. R.* 13(1), feb 72 : 85-110

5542    SULLIVAN, G. E. "Incremental budget-making in the American states: a test of the Anton model", *J. Polit.* 34(2), mai 72 : 639-647.

5543    THAVARAJ, M. J. K.; IYER, K. B. (eds.). *Readings on performance budgeting.* Delhi, Research Publications in Social Sciences, 72, 154 p. [India.]

5544    VAN LENNER, E. "Politique budgétaire et inflation", *Soc. roy. Écon. polit. Belgique* 369, apr 73 : 25 p. [Belgique.]

5545    WAGNER, A. "Die Auswirkung der öffentlichen Haushalte auf den Konjunkturverlauf in der Schweiz 1955-1970" (The influence of public budgets on the conjunctural situation of Switzerland from 1955 to 1970), *Schweiz Z. Volkswirtsch. Statist.* 109 (1), mar 73 : 17-55.

5546    WEIDENBAUM, M. L.; LARKINS, D.; MARCUS, P. N. *Matching needs and resources; reforming the Federal Budget.* Washington, American Enterprise Institute for Public Policy Research, 73, 114 p. [USA.]

5547    ZLOBIN, I. D.; RODIONOVA, V. M. "Bjudžet Sovestskogo Sojura" (The USSR's budget), *Finansy SSSR* 46(12), dec 72 : 1018.

## N.212    Budget law, budget control
### Droit et contrôle budgétaires

[See also / Voir aussi: 5520]

5548    BOLDT, H. "Haushaltsverfassung im Wandel" (Evolution of budget-making), *Soz.-wiss. Jb. Polit.* (3), 1972 : 281-337. [Germany, FR.]

5549    BOLLAND, S. "Reforma budżetu, czy rekonstrukcja systemu planowania finansowego ?" (Budgetary reform, is there a reconstruction of the financial planning system ?), *Finanse* (3), 1973 : 1-16.

## N.213    Budget situation, by countries
### Situation budgétaire, études localisées

[See also / Voir aussi: 5648]

5550    "Budget de l'Irak pour l'année financière 1972 (Le)", *Syrie Monde arabe* 19(224), sep 72 : 21-32.

5551    "Finances of the government of India: 1973-74", *Reserve Bank India B.* 27(471), apr 73 : 569-610.

5552   ENNERY, S.; ARCHALL, J. L. "Le budget 1973; inflationniste et antisocial", *Écon. et Polit.* 220, nov 72 : 29-50.

5553   FRANCE. Projet de loi de finances pour le budget 1973. *Présentation fonctionnelle du budget de l'État.* Paris, Imprimerie nationale, 72, 67 p.

5554   ITALIA. Ministero del tesoro. Ragioneria generale delle Stato. *Comparazione dei bilanci statali nei sei paesi della CEE* (State budget comparison in the six EEC countries). Roma, MT, 72, 341 p.

5555   JEDRYCHOWSKI, S. "Budzet państwa na 1973 rok" (State budget for 1973), *Finanse* (1), 1973 : 1-9. [Poland.]

5556   LACHMANN, L. M. et al. "The 1973 budget", *South Afr. J. Econ.* 41(2), jun 73 : 146-160. [South Africa.]

5557   LENZ, D. "Haushaltsanalyse 1973" (Budget analysis for 1973), *Städtedag* 26(1), jan 73 : 3-11. [Germany, FR.]

5558   "Loi de finances pour 1973 (La)", *Statist. Ét. financ.* Sér. rouge 25 (295-296), jul-aug 73 : 71-149.

5559   MAHROUG, S. "La loi de finances pour 1972", *R. financ.* (1), mar 72 : 7-41. [Algérie.]

5560   "Presupuesto federal, 1973" (Federal budget, 1973), *Exam. Sit. econ. Mexico* 49(567), feb 73 : 77-86. [Mexico.]

5561   "Projet de loi de finances pour 1973", *Statist. Ét financ. Sér. rouge* 24(286), oct 72 : 1-124. [France.]

5562   "Recettes budgétaires par département au cours de l'année 1972" *Statist. Ét. financ. Sér. rouge* 25(295-296), jul-aug 73 : 151-160. [France.]

5563   "Revised National Budget 1973", *Swedish Econ.* 1973 : 270 p. [Sweden.]

5564   SCHULTZE, C. L. et al. *Setting national priorities; the 1973 budget.* Washington, D. C., Brookings Institution, 72, xx-468 p. CR: H. I. LIEBLING, *J. econ. Liter.* 11(1), mar 73 : 105-107.

5565   SNYDER, W. W. "Are the budgets of state and local governments destabilizing? A six country comparison", *Europ. econ. R.* 4(2), jun 73 : 197-213.

5566   WEIDENBAUM, M. L.; LARKINS, D. *The Federal budget for 1973; a review and analysis.* Washington, American Enterprise Institute for Public Policy Research, 72, 86 p. [USA.]

## N.22   Public expenditures
Dépenses publiques

[See also / Voir aussi: 4017]

5567   ANDRÉ, C.; DELORME, R.; TERNY, G. "Les dépenses publiques françaises depuis un siècle", *Écon. et Statist.* 43, mar 73 : 3-14.

5568   BAYÓN MARINÉ, I. *Aprobación y control de los gastos públicos. Relaciones entre los órganos del Estado en materia presupuestaria* (Approval and control for public spending. Relations between State organs in the budget field). Madrid Ministerio de Hacienda, Instituto de Estudios Fiscales, 72, 434 p.

5569   BUZELAY, A. *Modulation de la dépense publique par les marchés de l'État et de ses satellites.* Nancy, Faculté de droit et des sciences économiques, 72, 11-59 ff.

5570   CASSESE, S. "Controllo della spesa pubblica e direzione dell' amministrazione" (The control of public expenditures and the management of administration), *Polit. Dir.* 4(1), feb 73 : 39-80. [Italy.]

5571   COHN, E. *Public expenditure analysis, with special reference to human resources.* Lexington, Mass., Lexington Books, 72, 157 p.

5572   GORONOWSKI, W. *Klasyfikacja wydatków w budżecie socjalistycznym* (Classification of public expenditures in the socialist budget). Warszawa, Państwowe Wydawn, ctwo Naukowe, 72, 213 p.

5573   GORONOWSKI, W. "O funkcjonalnaj klasyfikacji wydatkow budżetowych" (Functional classification of budgetary expenditure), *Finanse*(5), 73 : 59-64.

5574   ITALIA. Camera dei deputati. V Commissione (Bilancio) - *Problemi della spesa e della contabilità publica* (Problems of public expenditures and public accounting). Roma, Servicio commissioni parlamentari, 72, 780 p.

5575   ORGANIZATION FOR ECONOMIC COOPERATION AND DEVELOPMENT. *Expenditure trends in OECD countries, 1960-1970.* Paris, OECD, 72, 131 p.

5576 ORLANDO, G. "Razionalizzazione della spesa pubblica e programmazione" (Rationalization of public expenditures and programming), *Riv. Econ. agr.* 28(2), mar-apr 73 : mar-apr 73 : 3-27. [USA.]

5577 *Public expenditures and taxation.* New York, Columbia University Press, 72, xx-24 p.

5578 SANFORD, C. T. *Public expenditure and fiscal policy.* Harlow, Longman, 71, 32 p. [UK.]

5579 SEDERBERG, P. C. "National expenditure as an indicator of political change in Ghana", *J. develop. Areas* 7(1), oct 72 : 37-56.

5580 TEIXEIRA MACHADO, J. Jr. "Estimativa da despesa pública" (Estimation of public expenditure), *R. Adm. municip. (Rio de Janeiro)* 19(115), nov-dec 72 : 43-53. [Brazil.]

5581 VIRÉN, M. "Osttaisoptimointi valtion menotaloudessa" (Partial optimization in State expenditure), *Kansantal. Aikakausk.* 68(2), 1972 : 152-162.

5582 ZACCARIA, F. *La spesa pubblica nella teoria giuridica ed economica* (Public expenditures in legal and economic theory), Roma. Stamperia nazionale, 72, 563 p.

### N.23 Fiscal receipts
### Recettes fiscales

### N.231 *Financial economics*
### *Économie financière*

### N.2310 *General studies*
### *Études générales*

[See also / Voir aussi: 2244, 4789]

5583 AHLUWALIA, M. S. "Taxes, subsidies, and employment", *Quart. J. Econ.* 87(3), aug 73 : 393-409.

5584 HAUSSER, K.; PAHLKE, J.; PEFFEKOVEN, R. *Besteuerung und Zahlungsbilanz* (Taxation and balance of payments). Berlin, Duncker und Humblot, 72, 84 p.

5585 THOMAZEAY, Y. *Fiscalité et banque.* Paris, Sirey, 72, 183 p.

### N.2311 *Impact of taxation on economic activity (tax burden)*
### *Action de la fiscalité sur l'économie (pression fiscale)*

### N.23110 *General studies*
### *Études générales*

5586 ATALIBA, G. "Hipótese de incidência tributária (fato gerador)" (Hypothesis of tax burden (generative fact), *R. Serv. pub.* 107 (1), jan-apr 72 : 135-160.

5587 BERGSTROM, T. "A note on efficient taxation", *J. polit. Econ.* 81(1), jan-feb 73 : 187-191.

5588 BROWN, G. A. "Tax incentives for export by developing countries", *B. int. fisc. Docum.* 26(11), nov 72 : 404-412.

5589 DICK, W. "Fighting poverty with simplified tax structure", *R. soc. Econ.* 30(3), sep 72 : 385-393.

5590 HOFFMAN, R. F. "Disaggregation and calculations of the welfare cost of a tax", J. polit. Econ. 80(2), mar-apr 72 : 409-417.

5591 KRAUSS, M. "Differential tax incidence: large versus small tax changes", *J. polit. Econ.* 80(1), jan-feb 72 : 193-197.

5592 KRAUSS, M. B.; JOHNSON, H. G. "The theory of tax incidence: a diagrammatic analysis", *Economica (London)* 39(156), nov 72 : 357-382.

5593 LEVHARI, D.; SHESHINSKI, E. "Lifetime excess burden of a tax", *J. polit. Econ.* 80(1), jan-feb 72 : 137-147.

5594 MANN, F. K. "Der interpersonale und der strukturelle Ausgleich der Steuerlast" (The interpersonal and the structural adjustment of tax burden), *Z. Wirtsch. - u. soz. -Wiss.* 92(4), 1972 : 393-403.

5595 MANNING, R. "Optimal taxation when borrowing alters the foreign supply curve for capital", *Econ. Record* 48(123), sep 72 : 400-410.

5596 SZAKOLCZAI, Gy. "Optimális nyereségszint és termelési adózás" (Optimal profit level and production tax system), *Kozgazd. Szle* 20(7-8), jul-aug 73 : 842-862.

5597 VANDENDORPE, A. L. "Optimal tax structures in a model with traded and non-trade goods", *J. int. Econ.* 2(3), aug 72 : 235-256.

**N.23111**   Local studies
                    Études localisées

5598    DALIP SINGH. *Tax incentives for Indian industry and foreign investment*. Delhi, Atma Ram,
                72, 151 p.
5599    DIXON, D. A. "Techniques of fiscal analysis in the Netherlands", *Staff Pap.* 19(3), nov
                72 : 615-646.
5600    JAO, Y. C. "Tax structure and tax burden in Taiwan", *B. int. fisc. Docum.* 27(3), mar 73 :
                104-114.
5601    JASINOWSKI, J. J. "Great fiscal unknown-subsidies", *Amer. J. Econ. Sociol.* 32(1), jan
                73 : 1-16. [USA.]
5602    KATZ, B. S. "Mexican fiscal and subsidy incentives for industrial development", *Amer.
                J. Econ. Sociol.* 31(4), oct 72 : 353-359.
5603    KRZYZANIAK, M.; ÖZMUCUR, S. "The distribution of income and the shortrun burden
                of taxes in Turkey, 1968", *Finanzarchiv* 32(1), 1973 : 69-97.
5604    POPP, D. O.; SEBOLD, F. D. "Rudistribution of tax liabilities under site-value taxation:
                a survey of San Diego county", *Amer. J. Econ. Sociol.* 31(4), oct 72 : 413-426.
5605    TYLER, W. G. "Incentivos fiscais para a promoção de exportações manufatureiras: o caso
                brasileiro" (Tax incentives for the promotion of export of manufactured products:
                the Brazilian case), *R. Adm. publ. (Rio de Janeiro)* 7(3), jul-sep 73 : 33-54.


**N.232**     *Tax systems and fiscal legislation*
                  *Droit fiscal et législation*

**N.2321**    *Tax systems and policies*
                  *Systèmes fiscaux, politiques fiscales*

**N.23210**   General studies
                  Études générales

      [See also / Voir aussi: **N.23110**; 4318, 4321, 4334, 5577, 6191, 6199, 6206]

5606    BAHL, R. W. "A representative tax system approach to measuring tax effort in developing
                countries", *IMF Staff Pap.* 19(1), mar 72 : 87-124.
5607    BENISHAY, H. "A framework for the evaluation of short-term fiscal and monetary policy",
                *J. Money Cred. Bank.* 4(4), nov 72 : 779-810.
5608    BURCHARDT, M. "Die Koordination von Geldt- und Fiskalpolitik bei festen Wechsel-
                kursen" (Co-ordination of fiscal and monetary policies in fixed exchange rate),
                *Z. Wirtsch.- u. soz.-Wiss.* 93(4), 1973 : 423-444.
5609    CABRAL NOGUEIRA, R. "Alguns aspectos da política fiscal para o desenvolvimento"
                (Some aspects of fiscal policy for development), *R. Fac. Dir. (São Paulo)* 66, 1971 :
                273-294.
5610    DUSANSKY, R.; KALMAN, P. J. "Externalities, welfare, and the feasibility of corrective
                taxes", *J. polit. Econ.* 80(5), sep-oct 72 : 1045-1051.
5611    GEORGAKOPOULOS, T. "Tax harmonisation and international income distribution",
                *Nat. Tax J.* 25(4), dec 72 : 541-555.
5612    HANSEN, B. "On the effects of fiscal and monetary policy: a taxonomic discussion",
                *Amer. econ. R.* 63(4), sep 73 : 546-571.
5613    Bibl. XXI-5806. OATES, W. E. *Fiscal federalism*. CR: G. F. BREAK, *J. econ. Liter.* 11(2),
                jun 73 : 571-573.
5614    RURUP, B. "Handlungsverzögerungen diskretionärer Fiskalpolitik: Konstruktionsfehler
                oder Element rationaler Politik?" (Postponements of discretionary fiscal policy:
                error or element of rational policy?), *Z. Wirtsch.- u. soz.-Wiss.* 93(1), 1973 : 35-49.
5615    SANDLER, T. M.; SHELTON, R. B. "Fiscal federalism, spillovers and the export of taxes",
                *Kyklos* 25(4), 1972 : 736-753.
5616    SHAW, G. K. *Fiscal policy*. London, Macmillan, 72, 76 p.
5617    "Stabilization policy", *Swedish J. Econ.* 75(1), mar 73 : 3-99.

**N.23211**   Local studies
Études localisées

[See also / Voir aussi: **N.23111**; 4123, 4351, 5578, 5752]

5618   AARON, H. J.; RUSSEK, F. S. Jr.; SINGER, N. M. *Tax policy and returns to alternative investments and tax changes and the composition of fixed investment: an aggregative simulation.* Washington, Fund for Public Policy Research, 72, 52 p. [USA.]

5619   AMATO, A. *Il nostra sistema tributario dopo la riforma* (Our tax system after the reform). Padova, CEDAM, 73, 277 p. (Italy.]

5620   ARCHAIL, J. L. "La politique fiscale, aspects recents", *Écon. et Polit.* 222-223, jan-feb 73 : 207-220.

5621   BHARGAVA, P. K. "A critique of the Indian fiscal system", *B. int. fisc. Docum.* 26(9), sep 72 : 327-337.

5622   BLAGOJEVIĆ, S. V. "Poreski sistem kao instrument socijalne politike" (Tax system as an instrument for social policy), *Opstina* 25(6), 1972 : 34-48. [Yugoslavia.]

5623   BRIE, C. de.; CHARPENTIER, P. *L'inégalité par l'impôt.* Paris, Editions du Seuil, 73, 190 p. [France.]

5624   CARBALLO COTANDA, A. *Canarias, region polémica; análisis crítico del regimen económico-fiscal del Archipélago.* (The Canary Islands; a polemic region; a critical analysis of the economico-fiscal regime of the Archipelago). Madrid, Cuadernos para el Diálogo, 72, 335 p. [Spain.]

5625   COLUMBERG, D. *Das Problem des Verteilungsschlüssels im schweizerischen bundesstaatlichen Finanzausgleich* (The problem of distribution codes in Swiss fiscal standardization). Bern - Stuttgart, Paul Haupt, 72, 193 p. [Switzerland.]

5626   COTTON, G. "L'harmonisation de la fiscalité agricole dans le Marché Commun: une tache énorme", *Paysans* 16(97), dec 72-jan 73 : 3343.

5627   DOSSER, D. "Tax harmonisation in the European community", *Three Banks R.* 98, jun 73 : 49-64.

5628   ELVANDER, N. "The politics of taxation in Sweden 1945-1970: a study of the functions of parties and organizations", *Scand. polit. Stud.* (7), 1972 : 63-82.

5629   "Federal fiscal policy, 1965-72", *Fed. Reserve B.* 59(6), jun 73 : 383-402. [USA.]

5630   "Federal revenue system (The)", *J. Finance* 28(2), mai 73 : 467-506. [USA.]

5631   FLEISCHMANN, H. G. *Körperschaftsteuerrechtliche Anrechnungsverfahren* (Fiscal legislation concerning the tax on firms). Bonn-am-Rhein, W. Stollfuss, 72, 117 p. [France and Germany FR.]

5632   GANGADIN, V. J. "Taxation in Guyana", *B. int. fisc. Docum.* 24(11), nov 72 : 416-421.

5633   GIBSON, W. E. "Fiscal and monetary policy: opportunities and problems", *Fed. Reserve Bank St-Louis* 55(1), jan 73 : 14-18. [USA.]

5634   GUPTA, J. R. "Shifting structural emphasis on taxation in India, 1951-1970", *Econ. Aff.* 17(6), jun 72 : 273-280.

5635   HAMDANI, D. H. "Fiscal measures against inflation and unemployment in Canada: 1973 budget and other developments", *B. int. fisc. Docum.* 27(6), jun 73 : 223-240.

5636   HARRISS, C. L. *Innovations in tax policy and other essays.* Hartford, John C. Lincoln Institute, 72, 324 p. [USA.]

5637   HWANKWO, V. O. "Taxation, inflation and company finance", *Banker's Mag.* 214 (1544), nov 72 : 194-198. [UK.]

5638   IWASAKI, H. "Revision of the recent Japanse taxation system and major questions under discussion", *B. int. fisc. Docum.* 26(9), sep 72 : 315-317.

5639   MANSFIELD, C. Y. "Elasticity and buoyancy of a tax system: a method applied to Paraguay", *IMF Staff Pap.* 19(2), jul 72 : 425-446.

5640   MASLOVE, A. M. *The pattern of taxation in Canada.* Ottawa, Information Canada, 73, 189 p.

5641   MATHEWS, R. L.; JAY, W. R. C. *Federal finance; intergovernmental financial relations in Australia since federation.* Melbourne, Nelson, 72, 369 p.

5642   Bibl. XXI-5819. MAY, R. J. *Financing the small states in Australian federalism.* CR: E. A. BOEHM, *J. econ. Liter.* 10(4), dec 72 : 1239-1241.

5643   MEERMAM, J. *Fiscal incidence in empirical studies of income distribution in poor countries.* Washington, 72, 45 p.

5644    NUNEZ MINANA, H. "Federalismo fiscal y política regional: un modelo analítico" (Tax
        federalism and regional policy: an analytical model), *Económica (La Plata)* 18(3),
        sep-dec 72 : 323-351. [Argentina.]

5645    PAKISTAN. MINISTRY OF FINANCE. *Fiscal policy in Pakistan; a historical perspective.*
        2 vols., Islamabad, 72, 791 p.

5646    PETRUCCI, F. "La fiscalità nel sesto piano francese" (Taxation in the Franch Sixth Plan),
        *Riv. Dir. finanz.* 32(1), mar 73 : 85-99.

5647    QUEIROZ RIBEIRO, L. C. de. "Um modelo para a estimativa da receita pública" (A model
        for the estimation of public receipts), *R. Adm. municip. (Rio de Janeiro)* 20(116),
        jan-feb 73 : 28-43. Brazil.

5648    RISTIC, Z. "Aktivna fiskalna i budzetska politika" (An active fiscal and budget policy),
        *Gledista* 14(2), feb 73 : 187-201. [Yugoslavia.]

5649    SCHNEIDER, K. *Entwicklung und gegenwärtiger Stand der Steuerharmonisierung in der EWG*
        (Development and present state of fiscal harmonization in the EEC). Wien, Institut
        für Fiananzwissenschaft und Steuerrecht, 72, 16 p.

5650    STEINAECKER, M. von. *Domestic taxation and foreign trade; the United States-European
        border tax dispute.* New York, Praeger Publishers, 73, 169 p.

5651    STUDER, F. *Wirtschaftsstabilisierende Faktoren im schweizerischen Steuersystem* (Economic
        stabilization factors in the Swiss tax system). Bern, H. Lang; Frankfurt-am-Main, P.
        Lang, 72, 198 p.

5652    "Taxation policy and tax administration in India", *Ind. J. publ. Adm.* 18(3), jul-sep 72 :
        341-480.

5654    WAITE, C. A.; WAKEFIELD, J. C. "Federal fiscal programs", *Survey curr. Bustin.* 53(2),
        feb 73 : 18-28. [USA.]

5655    WILKENFELD, H. C. *Taxes and people in Israel.* Cambridge, Mass., Harvard University
        Press, 73, 307 p.

**N.2322**    *Tax reform*
              *Réforme fiscale*

[See also / Voir aussi: 5678, 5697, 5728]

5656    AMATI, N. D. *Novità e continuità della riforma tributaria* (Innovation and continuity
        of the tax reform). Bari, F. Cacucci, 72, 192 p. [Italy.]

5657    BUCHWALD, H. *Small business incentive and Canadian tax reform.* Don Mills, Ont.,
        CCH Canadian, 72, 72 p.

5658    CEA DOMINGUEZ, L. "Evolución de la fiscalidad en España (Incidencia de la reforma
        tributaria de 1964)" (Tax evolution in Spain; impact of the 1964 tax reform), *Eco-
        nomía* 25(121), apr-jun 72 : 199-297.

5659    COPE, J. M. "Tax reform and the interpretation of financial information", *J. Busin.
        Finance* 4(4), winter 72 : 74-81. [UK.]

5660    GOZZI, L. "Appunti sulla riforma tributaria" (Notes on the tax reform), *Amm. ital.*
        28(1), jan 73 : 20-27. [Italy.]

5661    HALLER, H. "Ideale und weniger ideale Bedingungen für eine Steuerreform" (The
        ideal and less ideal conditions for a tax reform), *Finanzarchiv* 32(1), 1973 : 21-34.
        [Germany, FR.]

5662    HAUSER, W. "Die britische Steuerreform" (The British tax reform), *Intertax* (1-2),
        1973 : 27-37.

5663    "Reforma fiscal, 1973" (Tax reform, 1973), *Examen. Sit. econ. Mexico* 49(567), feb 73 :
        68-77. [Mexico.]

5664    "Réforme fiscale britannique (La)", *R. Dir. gén. Impôts* 28, mar 73 : 47-52.

5665    WALLACE, W. L. C. *Accounting implications of Federal tax reform.* Toronto, Canadian
        Institute of Chartered Accountants, 72, 106 p.

**N.2323**    *Tax collection and evasion*
              *Procédure de recouvrement et fraude*

5666    BROWNLEE, O. "The optimal amount of resources to devote to tax collection", *J. Econ.
        Busin.* 25(1), 1972 : 14-17.

5667 CECCACCI, G. *Forme di evasione e frode fiscale in regime IVA* (Tax evasion and fiscal fraud in the value-added tax system). s.l., A cura della CEMIGO, 72, 204 p. [Italy.]

5668 FRANK, M. "Résorption de la fraude et modernisation du système fiscal belge", *Soc. roy. polit. Belgique* 362, jun 72 : 3-39.

5669 HOLMES, G. W.; COX, J. L. (eds.). *Tax fraud*. Ann Arbor, Mich., Institute of Continuing Legal Education, 73, 260 p. [USA.]

5670 SPRY, I. C. F. *Arrangements for the avoidance of taxation*. Sydney, Law Book Co., 72, 141 p.

**N.233    *Categories of taxes***
        *Différents impôts*

**N.2331    *Income tax***
        *Impôt sur le revenu*

[See also / Voir aussi: 4107]

5671 BILLINGS, R. B. "Income tax credits to reduce the regressivity of state-local tax systems", *Amer. J. Econ. Sociol.* 31(4), oct 72 : 397-411. [USA.]

5672 BROWNING, E. K. "Alternative programs for income redistribution: the NIT and the NWT", *Amer. econ. R.* 63(1), mar 73 : 38-49. [Negative income tax; negative wage tax.]

5673 BUCKLEY, J. W. *Income tax allocation: an inquiry into problems of methodology and estimation*. New York, Financial Executives Research Foundation, 72, 211 p.

5674 CHISHOLM, A. H. "A negative income tax and low income farm families", *Austral. J. agric. Econ.* 16(2), aug 72 : 102-114.

5675 COURCHENE, T. J. "The poverty reports, negative income taxation, and the Constitution: an analysis and a compromise proposal", *Canad. publ. Adm.* 16(3), aut 73 : 348-369.

5676 DUSANSKY, R. "The short-run shifting of the corporation income-tax in the United States", *Oxford econ. Pap.* 24(3), nov 72 : 357-371.

5677 KELLEY, P. L.; OLDMAN, O. (eds.). *Readings on income tax administration; a comprehensive selection of materials on income tax administration drawn from around the world, supplemented by text, questions, and problems of the editors*. Mineola, N. Y., Foundation Press, 73, 675 p.

5678 LEHNER, G. "Zur Reform der Einkommensteuer" (The reform of income tax), *Österr. Inst. Wirtsch. -Forsch. Mber* 46(2), feb 73 : 49-58. [Austria.]

5679 LIDMAN, R. "Cost and distributional implications of a credit income tax plan", *Publ. Pol.* 20(2), spring 72 : 311-334. [USA.]

5680 MARCIREAU, S. M. "L'unicité de l'impôt sur le revenu", *R. Sci. financ.* 65(1), jan-mar 73 : 101-122. [France.]

5681 MARKLE, R. W. *Einkommensteuererklarung* (The income tax declaration). Stuttgart, R. Boorberg, 72, 94 p. [Germany, FR.]

5682 MOLITOR, B. "Negative Einkommensteuer als sozialpolitischer Instrument" (Negative income tax as a social policy instrument), *J. soz. Wiss.* 24(1), 1973 : 38-54.

5683 REIN, M. "Recent British experience with negative income tax", *J. hum. Resources* (8), *Suppl.* 73 : 69-89.

5684 SCHWARTZ, E.; ARONSON, J. R. "How to integrate corporate and personal income taxation", *J. Finance* 27(5), dec 72 : 1073-1080. [USA.]

5685 SMITH, R. S. *Local income taxes: economic effects and equity*. Berkeley, Institute of Governmental Studies, University of California, 72, 220 p. [USA.]

5686 SPIRO, E. "The 1972 and 1973 income tax changes in South Africa", *B. int. fisc. Docum.* 26(9), sep 72 : 318-326; 27(9), sep 73 : 372-378.

5687 TEODORO, B. D.; LEON, H. S. DE. *The law on income taxation*. Manila, Rex Book Store, 72, 332 p.

**N.2332    *Tax on wages and salaries***
        *Impôt sur les traitements et salaires*

5688 FORGARTY, M. P. "Fiscal measures and wage settlements", *Brit. J. industr. Relat.* 11(1), mar 73 : 29-65.

5689 PHELPS, E. S. "Taxation of wage income for economic justice", _Quart. J. Econ._ 87(3), aug 73 : 331-354.

5690 SLEEPER, R. D. "Set and the shake-out: a note on the productivity effects of the selective employment tax", _Oxford econ. Pap._ 24(2), jul 72 : 197-211. [UK.]

**N.2333** _Profit and corporate tax_
_Impôt sur les profits et les sociétés_

[See also / Voir aussi: **2251**]

5691 BUISSON, J. "L'imposition directe des entreprises en France, Grande-Bretagne et Allemagne", _Fiscalité europ._ (1), 1973 : 21-27.

5692 CHAMBAULT, A.; DALIMIER, G. "L'imposition des profits des groupes multinationaux", _intertax_ (1-2), 1973 : 38-45.

5693 COPE, J. M. _Business taxation._ London, Nelson, 72, 328 p.

5694 NAOURI, J. C. "Fiscalité et tarification optimales. Cas de l'impôt sur les bénéfices et de l'IRPP", _R. Econ. polit._ 83(2), mar-apr 73 : 299-326.

5695 TUFQ, A. _Fiscalité de l'entreprise._ Paris, Sirey, 72, 28 p.

5696 WÖHE, G. _Die Steuern des Unternehmens_ (The corporation tax). München, Vahlen, 72, 237 p.

5697 WÖHE, G. "Zur Reform der Körperschaftssteuer" (The reform of the corporation tax) _Wirtsch.-Dienst_ 52(8), aug 72 : 409-415. [Germany, FR.]

**N.2334** _Consumption and sales tax_
_Impôt sur les transactions et la consommation_

[See also / Voir aussi: **5667**]

5698 ALLEN, R. I. G. "The economic effects of the British value—added tax", _Busin. Economist_ 5(1), spr 73 : 24-40.

5699 ANGELI, D. (ed.). _L'I. V. A. e i suoi problemi_ (The problems of the value-added tax). Milano, Consulente delle aziende, 72, 381 p.

5700 BEGIN, C.; DELPECH, J. "La TVA dans la consommation des ménages", _Statist. Et. financ. Sér. orange_ 3(12), 4 trim 73 : 13-23. [France.]

5701 CASILLAS, L. R. "Empleo, inversión y equilibrio externo: un analisis sobre el impuesto al valor agregado" (Employment, investment and external equilibrium: an analysis of the value-added tax), _Trim. econ._ 40(158), apr-jun 73 : 325-369.

5702 DEADMAN, W. B.; STEWART, D. P. _Value added tax._ London, Farringdon Publishing, 72, 31 p.

5703 DOWLING, B. R. "A note on the effect of income growth and changes in the tax rate on consumption and saving ratios", _Econ. soc. R._ 4(1), oct 72 : 1-4.

5704 FERRARI, F. "Il gravame di un'imposta generale sugli scambi a cascata ad aliquota uniforme" (The burden of a general uniform rate turnover tax), _Industria_ (1-2), jan-mar 72 : 82-100.

5705 FREDLAND, J. E. "An estimate of the horizontal burden of a retail sales tax", _Quart. R. Econ. Busin._ 12(4), sum 72 : 39-44.

5706 GOMES DE SOUZA, R. "Os impostos sobre o valor acrescido no sistema tributário" (Value-added taxes in the fiscal system), _R. Dir. adm._ 110, oct-dec 72 : 17-26. [Brazil.]

5707 GUERARD, M. "The Brazilian state value-added tax", _Staff Pap._ 20(1), mar 73 : 118-169.

5708 HIXSON, J. S.; RAMSEY, J. B. "Effects of excise taxes", _Quart. J. Econ._ 86(4), nov 72 : 684-686.

5709 JOSEPH, C. _Value added tax—the British system explained._ Woking, Financial Techniques Ltd., 72, 161 p.

5710 LEHNER, G. "Die Harmonisierung der Mehrwertsteuern in Europa" (The harmonization of value added taxes in Europe), _Cred-Anstalt Bankver. Wirtsch.-Ber._ 8 (2), apr 73 : 8-13.

5711 LENT, G. E. _et al._ "The value-added tax in developing countries", _Staff Pap._ 20(2), jul 73 : 318-378.

5712    MACAULAY, A. J. (ed.). *The Common Market, VAT: second select list, periodicals and books*. Edinburg, Edinburg College of Commerce Library, 73, 1-26.

5713    MCLURE, C. E. Jr.; TURE, N. B. *Value added tax: two views*. Washington, American Enterprise Institute for Public Policy Research, 72, 97 p.

5714    MUSGRAVE, R. A. "Problems of the value-added tax", *Nat. Tax J.* 25(3), sep 72 : 425-430.

5715    SCHOGL, W. *Die Mehrwertsteuer mit praktischen Beispielen* (The value-added tax with practical examples). Wien, E. Weiss-Verlag, 72, 122 p.

5716    SORIENTE, L. "L'IVA, l'inflazione e le responsabilità del governo" (The value-added tax, l'inflation and government responsability), *Polit. Econ.* 4(1-2), jan-apr 73 : 39-46.

### N.2335    Tax on capital and capital income
*Impôt sur le capital et sur ses revenus*

[See also / Voir aussi: 4609]

5717    AGAPOS, A. M.; DUNLAP, P. R. "Elimination of urban blight through inverse proportionnal ad valorem property taxation", *Amer. J. Econ. Sociol.* 32(2), apr 73 : 143-152.

5718    BAILS, D. "An alternative: the land value tax. The argument for continued use of part of the general property tax", *Amer. J. Econ. Sociol.* 32(3), jul 73 : 283-294.

5719    CORD, S. "How land value taxation would affect home-owners", *Amer. J. Econ. Sociol.* 32(2), apr 73 : 153-154.

5720    HIGGINS, J. W. *The tax consequences of the sale of land*. Storrs, Center for Real Estate and Urban Economic Studies, University of Connecticut, 73, 38 p.

5721    JANCSEK, J. P. *Property tax assessment applications of multiple regression analysis*. Berkeley, Center for Real Estate and Urban Economics, University of California, 72, 95 p.

5722    LEWIS, H. W. *The property tax; an introduction*. Chapel Hill, Institute of Government, University of North Carolina, 72, 88 p.

5723    MELLOWS, A. R. *Taxation of land transactions*. London, Butterworths, 73, 269 p.

5724    MITCHELL, W. E. "Equity effects of property tax relief for the aged: circuit-breaker legislation", *Amer. J. Econ. Sociol.* 32(4), oct 73 : 367-378.

5725    PAGLIN, M.; FOGARTY, M. "Equity and the property tax: a new conceptual focus", *Nat. Tax J.* 25(4), dec 72 : 557-565.

5726    PEPPER, H. W. "Taxation of land and real property in developing countries. Some points of practice and policy", *B. int fisc. Docum.* 26(10), oct 72 : 355-373.

5727    PYE, G. "Preferential tax treatment of capital gains, optimal dividend policy, and capital budgeting", *Quart. J. Econ.* 86(2), mai 72 : 226-242.

5728    SAZAMA, G. W.; DAVIS, H. "Land taxation and land reform", *Econ. Develop. cult. Change* 21(4), part I, jul 73 : 642-654.

5729    STATHAM, R. R.; LEHMANN, C. P. *A review of the property tax and its impact on business*, Washington, Chamber of Commerce of the United States, 73, 163 p.

### N.235    Public loan, debt and credit
*Emprunt, dette publique, crédit public*

### N.2350    General studies
*Études générales*

[See also / Voir aussi: 3981]

5730    DAFFLON, B. R. *L'analyse macro-économique de la dette publique*. Fribourg, Editions universitaires, 73, 223 p.

### N.2351    Public debt policy
*Politique de la dette publique*

5731    PAL, D. N. "India's public debt and economic development", *Econ. Aff.* 17(7), jul 72 : 347-356.

**N.24     Local finance**
**Finances locales**

**N.240     *General studies***
***Études générales***

[See also / Voir aussi: 5671]

5732   BOSKIN, M. J. "Local government tax and product competition and the optimal vision of public goods", *J. polit. Econ.* 81(1), jan-feb 73 : 203-210.

5733   KESKUMÄKI, O. "Kaupunkikuntien talous muuttuvassa yhteiskunnassa" (Finances of urban communities in a changing sociéty), *Kansantal. Aikakausk.* 68(2), 1972 : 163-173.

5734   PICA, F. "Problemi di equità e di benessere nella finanza locale" (Problems of equity and welfare in local finance), *Rass. econ. (Napoli)* 36(5), sep-oct 72 : 1315-1335.

5735   STEPANOV, Ja. N.; ČERNYŠEVA É. A.; VIŠNJAKOV, S. A. *Sostavlenie i ispolnenie bjedžeta rajone* (The regional budget elaboration and its execution). Moskva, Financy, 72, 176 p.

5736   VERPRAET, J.; LEFEBVRE, A. *L'action culturelle et le budget municipal.* Paris, Éditions ouvrières, 72, 207 p.

5737   WEICHER, J. C. "The effect of urban renewal on municipal service expenditures", *J. polit. Econ.* 80(1), jan-feb 72 : 86-101.

**N.241     *Particular studies***
***Études particulières***

5738   ADEDEJI, A.; ROWLAND, L. (eds.). *Local government finance in Nigeria: problems and prospects.* Ile-Ife, University of Ife Press, 72, 341 p.

5739   BENAISSA, S. "À propos de l'exécution des budgets communaux en 1969 et 1970", *R. financ.* (2), jun 73 : 3-71.

5740   BROZEK, J.; SADOWY, E.; ZAWADZKI, A. W. "Problemy ustalania obiektywnych norm oglónych dotyczacych finansowania usług niematerialnych z budzetów terenowych" (Problems involved in setting objective general norms in financing non-material services from local budgets), *Stud. finans.* (13), 1972 : 73-117. [Poland.]

5741   CHABERT, L. "Géographie fiscale des Grandes Alpes de Savoie. Essai méthodologique", *R. Géogr. alpine* 61(3), 1973 : 335-370.

5742   FISCHER, G. W. "Problems of financing local government in the United States of America", *Loc. Finance* 2(5), sep 73 : 8-22.

5743   GARNETT, R. W. *Equalization of local govrnment revenues in Alaska.* Fairbanks, Institute, of Social, Economic and Government Research, University of Alaska, 73, 56 p.

5744   GRAMLICH, E. M.; GALPER, H. "State and local fiscal behavior and federal grant policy", *Brookings Pap. econ. Activity* (1), 1973 : 15-65. [USA.]

5745   HASKELL, M. A. "Local government finance in Uganda: taxes, expenditures and grants-in-aid", *East. Afr. econ. R.* 4(1), jun 72 : 75-83.

5746   HOLM, P.; HARSMAN, B. "Long-term planning of municipal finance in a metropolitan region', *Region. Sci. Assoc. Pap. and Proc.* 26, 1971 : 101-128. [Sweden.]

5747   KOBIELSKI, J. "L'influence de la structure administrative des agglomérations et de la couleur politique des municipalités sur les dépenses de fonctionnement des services publics urbains", *R. Sci. financ.* 65(1), jan-mar 73 : 70-99. [France.]

5748   KOMAR, A. "Finanse gmin" (Finances of comunes), *Ruch prawn. ekon. socjol.* (4), 1973 : 187-197. [Poland.]

5749   MALOY, N. G. *Local government accounting in New South Wales.* Sydney, Law Book Co., 73, 232 p.

5750   MAYNARD, A. K.; KING, D. N. *Rates or prices ? A study of the economics of local government and its replacement by the market.* London, Institute Economic Affairs, 72, 66 p. [UK.]

5751   MILLER, S. M.; TABB, W. K. "A new look at a pure theory of local expenditures", *Nat. Tax J.* 26(2), jun 73 : 161-176. [USA.]

5752   MUTHAYYA, B. C. *Panchayat taxes: factors influencing their mobilisation; a study in three panchayats in East Godavari, Andhra Pradesh.* Hyderabad, National Institute of Community Development, 72, 146 p. [India.]

5753 OBERMAN, J.; BINGHAM, R. *Planning and managing the economy of the city; policy guidelines for the metropolitan mayor.* New York, Praeger Publishers, 72, 361 p.

5754 REICHERT, H. *Schuldeinnahmen als Bestreitungsmittel gemeindlicher Ausgaben; Möglichkeiten und Grenzen ihres Einsatzes* (Endebtment, a controvertial form of communal expenses; possibilities and limits of its utilization). Göppingen, A. Kümmerle, 71, 305 p. [Germany, FR.]

5755 RIELLO, G.; SPARANO, E. "Regioni e finanziarie regionali" (Regions and local finance), *Nord e Sud* 20(159), mar 73 : 54-75. [Italy.]

5756 ROHDE, E.; SIEBENHAAR, H. *Haushalts- und Finanzwirtschaft der Städte und Gemeinden* (The budgetary and financial economy of cities and towns). Berlin, Staatsverlag der Deutschen Demokratischen Republik, 72, 201 p. [Germany, DR.]

5757 ROTHBALLER, M. J. "Die Haushalte der kommunalen Gebietskörperschaften im Rechnungsjahr 1970" (The local communal governments budgets during the fiscal year of 1970), *Bayern in Zahlen* 26(12), dec 72 : 445-452. [Germany, FR.]

5758 SARTORATI, G. *La finanza degli enti locali* (Local finance). Udine, Del Bianco, 72, 95 p. [Italy.]

5759 SCOTT, C. D. *Forecasting local government spending.* Washington, Urban Institute, 72, 142 p. [USA.]

5760 SUZUKI, T. *Chiho gyozaisei seido to seisaku* (Local administrative and fiscal systems and policy). Tokyo, Kyoiku Shuppan, 71, 517 p. [Japan.]

5761 WEICHER, J. C. "Aid, expenditures, and local government structure", *Nat. Tax J.* 25(4), dec 72 : 573-583. [USA.]

5762 WIERZBICKI, J. "Budżety terenowe w sytemie wieloletniego planowania budżetowego" (Local budgets in the system of long-term budgetary planning), *Finanse* (7), 1973 : 13-24; (8), 1973 : 1-16. [Poland.]

5763 WIEWIORA, K. "Umocnienie podstaw finansowych gmin" (The consolidation of the financial base of comunes), *Finanse* (3), 1973 : 17-27. [Poland.]

5764 ZANDANO, G. *et al. La finanza pubblica di une grande città* (Public finance of a big city). Torino, Cassa di Risparmio, 72, 365 p. [Italy.]

## N.3 PUBLIC ENTERPRISES, PUBLIC UTILITIES
## ENTREPRISES PUBLIQUES, SERVICES D'UTILITÉ PUBLIQUE

### N.31 Public sector and nationalization policies
### Secteur public et politique de nationalisation

#### N.310 *General studies*
#### *Études générales*

5765 ALBINANA GARCIA-QUINTANA, C. "La empresa pública y la socializacion económica" (The public enterprise and the economic socialization), *De Economia* 25(123), oct-dec 72 : 587-604.

5766 PESTON, M. H. *Public goods and the public sector.* London, Macmillan, 72, 63 p.

5767 Bibl. XXI-5986. PRYKE, R. *Public enterprise in practice.* CR: W. G. SHEPHERD, *J. econ. Liter.* 11(1), mar 72 : 125-127.

5768 REES, M. *The public sector in the mixed economy.* London, Batsford, 73, 240 p.

#### N.311 *Local studies*
#### *Études localisées*

5769 ANDIC, F. M.; ANDIC, S. "Role of the public sector in the economic development of the greater Caribbean; a survey and commentary", *Latin Amer. Res. R.* 8(1), 1973 : 97-134.

5770 BHAMBHRI, C. P. "Public corporations in India: autonomy versus control", *Polit. Sci. R.* 10(1-2), jan-jun 71 : 99-109.

5771 BURRAGE, M. "Nationalization and the professional ideal", *Sociology* 7(2), mai 73 : 253-272. [UK.]

5772 GUPTA, S. "The role of the public sector in reducing regional income disparity in Indian plans", *J. Develop. Stud.* 9(2), jan 73 : 243-260.

5773   PETRAS, J. F. "Chile: nacionalización, transformaciones socioeconómicas y participación popular" (Chile: nationalization, socio-economic transformations and popular participation), *Cuad. Real. nac.* (11), jan 72 : 3-24.

5774   SINHA, J. B. P. *Some problems of public sector organizations.* Delhi, National Publishing House; London, Books from India, 73, 171 p. [India.]

5775   TIVEY, L. J. *Nationalization in British industry.* Rev. ed. London, Cape, 73, 255 p.

5776   TJUL'PANOV, S. I.; VEJC, G. M. "Zur Tätigkeit der staatlichen Unternehmen Indiens" (Public enterprises activity in India), *Jb. Wirtsch. Gesch.* (2), 1973 : 19-36.


## N.32   Public enterprise, nationalized enterprise
Entreprise publique, entreprise nationalisée

### N.320   *General studies*
*Études générales*

5777   DAVANZO, N.; DOBRAN, A. *L'organizzazione amministrativa degli enti pubblici; nuovo metodo* (Administrative organization of public enterprises; a new method). Milano, L. di G. Pirola, 72, 338 p.

5778   FOSTER, C. D. *Public enterprise.* London, Fabian Society, 72, 33 p.

5779   GLENTWORTH, G. "Public enterprises in developing countries", *J. Adm. Overseas* 12(3) jul 73 : 190-205.

5780   STEFANI, G. "La productivité des entreprises publiques", *A. Écon. coll.* 61(1), jan-mar 73 : 15-70.


### N.321   *Local studies*
*Études localisées*

[See also / Voir aussi: **H.1122; 3958**]

5781   CARVALHO, G. "A empresa pública: uma análise administrativa" (Public enterprise: an administrative analysis), *R. adm. municip. (Rio de Janeiro)* 20(116), jan-feb 73 : 5-27.

5782   DAROS, E. J. "A política econômico-financeira e as decisões do setor público" (Economico-financial policy and decisions in the public sector), *Dados* (9), 1972 : 84-91. [Brazil.]

5783   DRESANG, D. L.; SHARKANSKY, I. "Public corporations in single country and regional settings: Kenya and the East African Community", *Int. Org.* 27(3). summer 73 : 303-328.

5784   ÉGOROV, I. I. *Ěkonomičeskaja ěffektivnost' gosudarstvennogo sektora Indii* (Economic efficiency of the Indian state sector). Moskva, Nauka, 72, 251 p.

5785   FRANÇOIS-MARSAL, F. *Le dépérissement des entreprises publiques.* Paris, Calmann-Lévy, 73, 367 p. [France.]

5786   HURET, E. *et al. Les entreprises publiques de 1959 à 1969.* Paris, Institut national de la statistique et des études économiques, 72, 135 p. [France.]

5787   IRIE, K. "Suezu unga gaisha kokuyuka tsuron" (The nationalization of the Suez Canal), *Waseda Hogaku* 47(1), jul 71 : 1-70.

5788   MEDEL CAMARA, B. "La empresa pública no financiera en la economía española" (The non financial public enterprise in the Spanish economy), *A. Econ. (Madrid)* 8(15), jul-sep 72 : 151-177.

5789   MOLINIER, J. "Les expériences britannique et française de contrôle parlementaire des entreprises publiques", *R. int. Dr. comp.* 24(4), oct-dec 72 : 773-790.

5790   NARAIN, L. *Efficiency audit of public enterprises in India.* New Delhi, Orient Longman, 72, 304 p.

5791   NARAIN, L. *Managerial compensation and motivation in public enterprises.* New Delhi, Oxford and IBH Publishing Co., 73, 157 p. [India.]

5792   SELLERI, L. "L'efficienza delle imprese pubbliche: l'esperienza dell' Electricité de France nel suo primo venticinquennio di attività" (The efficiency of public enterprises: the experience of Electricité de France in the first twenty five years of activity), *Econ. int. Fonti Energia* 16(5), sep-oct 72 : 331-352.

5793 ŠIROKOV, G. K.; ÊGOROV, I. I. *Gosudarstvennyj sektor v Indii. (Problemy êffektivnosti)* (State sector in India. Problems of efficiency). Moskva, Nauka, 73, 174 p.

5794 TIVEY, L. J. (ed.). *The nationalized industries since 1960: a book of readings.* London, Allen and Unwin, 73, 329 p.

5795 WAGENER, H. O. *Neue staatswirtschaftliche Funktionen bundeseigener Industriebeteiligungen* (New economic functions of the State: participation of the Federal State in industry). Meisenheim-am-Glan, A. Hain, 72, 245 p.

5796 WERALSKI, M. "Kontrola nad lagalnoscia dzialałnosci przedsiębiorstw panstwowych w Polsce" (State enterprises activity in Poland and the legislation), *Kult. i Społecz.* 16(3), jul-sep 72 : 37-50.

### N.33 Public utilities
### Services d'utilité publique

[See also / Voir aussi: Industrial production, Transports, etc. / Production industrielle, Transports, etc.: 3595]

5797 "Behavior and entry under public utility regulation", *Amer. econ. R.* 63(2), mai 73 *Pap. and Proc.*: 90-105. With contributions by: L. L. JOHNSON and W. G. SHEPHERD.

5798 ELLICKSON, B. "A generalization of the pure theory of public goods", *Amer. econ. R.* 63(3), jun 73 : 417-432.

5799 LOPEZ PELLICER, J. A. "Servicio público municipal y actividades particulares de interés público" (Municipal public service and private activities of public interest), *R. Estud. Vida Loc.* 32(178), apr-jun 73 : 259-306.

5800 MOLITOR, B. "Öffentliche Leistungen in verteilungspolitischer Sicht" (Public services from a viewpoint of income distribution), *Z. Wirsch.-u. soz.-wiss.* 93(2), 1973 : 147-158.

5801 SUELFLOW, J. E. *Public utility accounting: theory and application.* East Lansing, Institute of Public Utilities, Michigan State University, 73, 325 p.

# O INTERNATIONAL ECONOMICS
# ÉCONOMIE INTERNATIONALE

O.1 INTERNATIONAL ECONOMIC RELATIONS
RELATIONS ÉCONOMIQUES INTERNATIONALES

O.12 International economy
Économie internationale

O.120 *General studies*
*Études générales*

[See also / Voir aussi: 2565, 5220, 6180]

5802 ADAMS, J. *International economics: a self-teaching introduction to the basic concepts.* London, Longman, 72, x-a69 p.

5803 AGUILAR NAVARRO, M. *Ensayo de delimitación del Derecho internacional económico* (A tentative delimitation of international economic law). Madrid, Universidad de Madrid, Facultad de Derecho, Sección de Publicaciones, Departamento de Derecho de Trabajo, 72, 71 p.

5804 BIRNBERG, T.; RESNICK, S. "A model of the trade and government sectors in colonial economies", *Amer. econ. R.* 63(4), sep 73 : 572-587.

5805 BONILLA, F.; GIRLING, R. (eds.). *Structures of dependency.* Nairobi, Nairobi Bookstore, 73, 262 p.

5806 CALDERWOOD, J. D. *The world economy.* Bedford Hills, N Y, Teaching Resources Films, 72, ii-79 p

5807 "Capitalism and world economic integration: perspectives on modern imperialism", *R. radic. polit. Econ.* 5(1), 1973 : 1-96.

5808 CHAKRABURTY, B.; SAHA, S. "World income and its distribution, 1957 and 1969", *Econ. Aff.* 17(8), aug 72 : 365-372.

5809 CIAFARDINI, H. "Concepciones 'tercermundistas' en la teoría de las relaciones económicas internacionales" (Third worldist conceptions in the theory of international economic relations), *Econ. y Adm.* 8-9(19-20), sep-dec 71-jan-apr 72 : 77-104.

5810 DEISS, J. *La théorie pure des termes de l'échange international.* Fribourg, Éditions universitaires, 72, 346 p.

5811 DOBOSIEWICZ, Z. *Ekonomiczne aspekty neokolonializmu w Afryce* (Economic aspects of neo-colonialism in Africa). Warszawa, Państwowe Wydawnictwo Naukowe, 73, 200 p.

5812 JANKOWIAK, K. "Zagadnienia umiędzynarodowienia gospodarki światowej" (Problems of the internationalization of the world economy), *Handel zagran.* (7), 1973 : 223-226.

5813 KLEER, J. "Subsystemy w gospodarce światowej i kryteria ich wyodrębnienia" (Subsystems in the world economy and criteria of their distinction), *Ekonomista* (3), 1973 : 661-659.

5814 KLOZA, M. *Aspekty prognostyczne procesu integracji gospodarczej* (Forecasting aspects of the process of economic integration). Wrocław, Politechnika Wrocławska, 73, 65 p.

5815 KNORR, K. E. *Power and wealth; the political economy of international power.* New York, Basic Books, 73, x-210 p.

5816 KRAUSS, M. (ed.). *The economics of integration: a book of readings.* London, Allen and Unwin, 73, 3-300 p.

5817 MARCO, L. E. DI. *International economics and development.* New York, Academic Press, 72, xix-515 p.

5818 McFADZEAN, F. *Towards an open world economy.* London, Macmillan, 72, xvi-181 p.

5819 MEERHAEGHE, M. A. G. VAN. *International economics.* London, Longman; New York, Crane, Russak, 72, xi-259 p.

5820  MEIER, G. M. (ed.). *International economic reform. Collected papers of Emile Despres.* New York-London-Toronto, Oxford University Press, 73, xviii-293 p. CR: N. C. MILLER, J. *econ. Liter.* 11(3), sep 73 : 940-941.

5821  MENNES, L. B. M. *Planning economic integration among developing countries.* Rotterdam, Universitaire Pers Rotterdam, 72, viii-155 p.

5822  MONTI, M. "Riflessi dell'integrazione economica internazionale sulla politica monetaria" (Impact of international economic integration on monetary policy), *Industria* (1-2), jan-mar 72 : 60-75.

5823  NIESS, F. "Imperialismustheorie und politische Ökonomie der armen Welt" (The theory of imperialism and the political economy of the world of the poor), *Polit. Vjschr.* 14(3), nov 73 : 379-383.

5824  PANOV, V. *Ėkonomičeskie metody neokolonializma* (Economic methods of neocolonialism). Moskva, Izdatel'stvo APN, 72, 123 p.

5825  PANOV, V. P. *The economic weapons of neo-colonialism.* Moscow, Novosti Press Agency 72, 106 p.

5826  ROBERTS, P. C.; RABUSHKA, A. "A diagrammatic exposition of an economic theory of imperialism", *Publ. Choice* 14, 1973 : 101-107.

5827  ROBSON, P. (ed.). *International economic integration: selected readings.* Harmondsworth, Penguin, 72, 458 p.

5828  SCHWARZENBERGER, G. "Equality and discrimination in international economic law", *Yb. Wld Aff.* 25, 1971 1 163-181.

5829  ŠIŠKOV, Ju. "Ob'ektivnye predposylki ekonomičeskoj integracii" (The objective conditions of economic integration), *Ėkon. Nauki* 16(3), mar 73 : 41-51.

## O.121  Government organizations
### Organisations gouvernementales

### O.1210  General studies
### Études générales

5830  NÊME, J.; NÊME, C. *Organisations économiques internationales.* Paris, Presses universitaires de France, 72, 482 p.

5831  VIRALLY, M. *L'organisation mondiale.* Paris, A. Colin, 72, 589 p.

### O.1211  World organizations
### Organisations mondiales

[See also / Voir aussi: **O.131; O.1341; O.241;** 6618]

5832  BIJLI, S. M. *Developing nations and the UNCTAD.* Aligarh, International Book Traders, 73, vii-71 p.

5833  DIMITRIJEVIĆ, P. *L'Organisation Internationale du Travail. Histoire de la représentation patronale.* Genève, Georg, 72, x-513 p.

5834  "Future of UNCTAD (The)", *Inst. Develop. Stud. B.* 5(1), jan 73 : 2-53.

5835  KAY, D. A.; SKOLNIKOFF, E. B. (eds.). *World eco-crisis. International organizations in response.* Madison, Wis., University of Wisconsin Press, 72, viii-324 p.

5836  PEŠIĆ, R. *Uticaj radničkih organizacija na stvaranje i aktivnost Medunarodne organizacije rada* (The influence of labour organizations on the creation and activity of the International Labour Organization). Beograd, Knjizevne novine, Redakcija Stručnih izdanja, 71, 227 p.

5837  PROHOROVA, G. N. *Prodovol'stvennaja e sel'skohozjajstvennaja organizacija OON* (Food and Agricultural Organization of the United Nations). Moskva, Nauka, 72, 159 p.

5838  ROWE, E. T. "Financial support for the United Nations: the evolution of member contributions, 1946-1969", *Int. Org.* 26(4), 1972 : 619-657.

5839  RYAN, S. "La crisis financiera de las Naciones Unidas" (United Nations financial crisis), *Foro int.* 13(3), jan-mar 73 : 380-391.

5840  SCHLUTER, B. "Die Kompetenz der UNCTAD, Analyse einer Entwicklung" (The competence of the UNCTAD, analysis of an evolution), *Z. ausländ. öff. Völkerrecht* 32(2-4), dec 72 : 297-338.

5841  ZEMANEK, K. "Die Finanzkrise der Vereinten Nationen" (The financial crisis of the United Nations), *Europa-Archiv* 28(16), aug 25, 73 : 555-562.

5842  WALKER-LEIGH, V. "Was UNCTAD III a failure ?", *Wld today* 28(9), sep 72 : 411-420.


O.1212    *Regional organizations*
          *Organisations régionales*

[See also / Voir aussi: **O.124; O.1342**]

5842a  AKIWUMI, A. H. "The Economic Commission for Africa", *J. Afr. Law* 16(3), 1972 : 254-261.

5843  CARRINGTON, E.; OMAWALE, S. "La solución de problemas económicos por medio de agrupaciones regionales" (The solution of economic problems by means of regional associations), *R. Integr.* 14, sep 73 : 51-77.

5844  DIMITRIJEVIĆ, V. "Postojanje regiona i međunarodne organizacije" (The existence of regions and international organizations), *Medun. Probl.* 24(2), apr-jun 72 : 67-74.

5845  KAMANDA, J. G. "L'Organisation de l'Unité Africaine et le développement économique de l'Afrique", *J. Afr. Law* 16(3), 1972 : 279-294.

5846  PONCE, M.; BREWSTER, H. *Current problems of economic integration; agricultural and industrial co-operation among developing countries.* New York, United Nations, 72, viii-126 p.

5847  ROBANA, A. *The prospects for an economic community in North Africa: managing economic integration in the Maghreb states.* New York, Praeger, 73, xv-206 p.

5848  TAMBOURA, A. "La communauté économique de l'Afrique de l'Ouest", *J. Afr. Law* 16(3), 1972 : 310-338.

5849  VIGAND, V. K. *et al. Dejtael'nost' meždunarodnyh ėkonomičeskih organizacij v Afrike* (The activity of international economic organizations in Africa). Moskva, Nauka, 73, 232 p.


O.122    **Private international organizations (cartels, agreements)**
         **Organisations internationales privées (cartels, ententes)**

[See also / Voir aussi: 3010, 3113, 4077, 6159]

5850  ALEXANDRIDES, C. G. (ed.). *International business systems perspectives.* Atlanta, School of Business Administration, Georgia State University, 73, xiv-293 p.

5851  ARPAN, J. S. *International intracorporate pricing; non-American systems and views* New York, Praeger Publishers, 71, x-126 p.

5852  BEGLOV, S. I. *Monopolii slova* (The world monopolies). Moskva, Mysl', 72, 454 p.

5853  BÉGUIN, J. P. *Les entreprises conjointes internationales dans les pays en voie de développement. Le régime des participations.* Genève, Droz, 72, xxiv-272 p.

5854  BELOUS, T. Ja. *Meždunarodnye promyšlennye monopolii* (International industrial monopolies). Moskva, Mysl', 72, 279 p.

5855  BENOIT, E. "Attack on the multinationals", *Columbia J. Wld Busin.* 7(6), nov-dec 72 : 15-22.

5856  BERTIN, G. Y. *et al. L'expansion internationale des grandes entreprises.* Paris, Documentation française, 72, 123 p.

5857  BLAKE, D. H. (ed.). *The multinational corporation.* Philadelphia, American Academy of Political and Social Science, 72, x-247 p. [The *Annals of the American Academy of political and social Science*, no 403.]

5858  BROOKE, M. Z.; REMMERS, H. L. (eds.). *The multinational company in Europe: some key problems.* London, Longman, 72, xv-194 p.

5859  BRUNDENIUS, C. "De multinationella gruvbolagen i Peru" (The multinational mining corporation in Peru), *Int. Polit. (Bergen)* (4), oct-dec 72 : 681-699.

5860  BRUYN, S. T. "The multinational corporation and social research: the case of the United Fruit Company", *Soc. Theory Practice* 1(4), 1971 : 53-70.

5861  CAMBRE MARIÑO, J. *Nuevo poder del capitalismo; congomerados y empresas multinacionales* (New power of capitalism; conglomerados and multinational firms). Algorta, Zero; Madrid, ZYX, 72, 144 p.

5862    CAMBRE MARIÑO, X. "Las sociedades multinacionales: el capital extranjero en España" (Multinational societies: the foreign capital in Spain), *Cuad. Diálogo* 112, jan 73 : 39-45.

5863    CARTER, W. G. "National support of multinational ventures", *Columbia J. Wld Busin.* 7(5), sep-oct 72 : 6-12.

5864    COPPÉ, A. *De multinationale onderneming* (The multinational enterprise). Antwerpen, Standaard Wetenschappelijke Uitgeverij, 72, 179 p.

5865    COPPEN, M. L. "Avantages et désavantages de l'entreprise multinationale", *R. Soc. Ét. Expans.* 72(255), mai-jun 73 : 223-229.

5866    Bibl. XXI-6090. DUNNING, J. H. (ed.). *The multinational enterprise.* CR: H. G. GRUBEL, *J. econ. Liter.* 11(3), sep 73 : 949-950.

5867    DUNNING, J. H. "Multinational enterprises and domestic capital formation", *Manchester Sch. econ. soc. Stud.* 41(3), sep 73 : 283-310.

5868    DUQUESNE DE LA VINELLE, L. "Le développement des sociétés multinationales", *France-Forum* 122-123, jan-feb 73 : 13-22.

5869    EELLS, R. S. F. *Global corporations; the emerging system of world economic power.* New York, Interbook, 72, 242 p.

5870    EITEMAN, D. K.; STONEHILL, A. I. *Multinational business finance.* Reading, Mass., Addison-Wesley Publishing Co., 73, xv-399 p.

5871    "Entreprise multinationale (L')", *R. écon. soc.* 31(1), mar 73 : 7-141.

5872    EVSER, B. G. "Ontwikkeling van multinationale ondernemingen, ongrijpbaar en onbegrensd ?" (Is the development of multinational enterprises elusive and unlimited), *Econ. soc. Tijds.* 26(5), oct 72 : 355-374.

5873    "Expansion internationale des grandes entreprises (L')", *Trav. et Rech.* 25, 1972 : 3-123.

5874    FRANCE. Délégation à l'aménagement du territoire et action régionale. *Les firmes multinationales.* Paris, La Documentation française, 73, 164 p.

5875    GENNARD, J. *Multinational corporations and British labour: a review of attitudes and responses.* London, British-North American Committee, 72, xv-53 p.

5876    GROCHULSKI, A. *Korporacje miedzynarodowe* (International corporations). Warszawa, Państwowe Wydawnictwo Naukowe, 73, 254 p.

5877    HAHLO, H. R.; SMITH, J. G.; WRIGHT, R. W. (eds.). *Nationalism and the multinational enterprise; legal, economic and managerial aspects.* Leiden, A. W. Sijthoff; Dobbs Ferry, N. Y., Oceana Publications, 73, x-373 p.

5878    HANER, F. T. *Multinational management.* Columbus, Ohio, C. E. Merrill Publishing Co., 73, xii-302 p.

5879    HEISS, P. A. "Multinational corporation and industrial relations; the American approach compared with the European", *Relat. industr.* 28(1), 1973 : 34-55.

5880    HELFGOTT, R. B. "Multinational corporations and manpower utilization in developing nations", *J. develop. Areas* 7(2), jan 73 : 235-246.

5881    HELLEINER, G. K. "Manufactured exports from less-developed countries and multinational firms", *Econ. J.* 83(329), mar 73 : 21-47.

5882    HOGAN, W. P. "Multinational firms, labour utilisation and trade flows", *J. industr. Relat.* 14(3), sep 72 : 225-237.

5883    JANKOWIAK, L. *Przedsiebiorstwa wielonarodowe i ich wpływ na gospodarke swiatowa* (Multinational enterprises and their influence on world economy). Warszawa, Państwowe Wydawnictwo Ekonomiczne, 73, 167 p.

5884    KNICKERBOCKER, F. T. *Oligopolistic reaction and multinational enterprise.* Boston, Division of Research, Graduate School of Business Administration, Harvard University, 73, xiii-236 p.

5885    KRAUSE, L. B. "The international economic system and the multinational corporation", *A. Amer. Acad. polit. soc. Sci.* 403, sep 72 : 93-103.

5886    KUJAWA, D. (ed.). *American labor and the multinational corporation.* New York, Praeger, 73, xxvii-285 p.

5887    LIONS, E. P. *The anational corporation.* Lausanne, Imprimeries réunies, 72, 219 p.

5888    MANSER, W. A. P. *The financial role of multinational enterprises.* New York, J. Wiley, 73, 176 p.

5889    MELLORS, J. "Multinational corporations and capital market integration", *Bankers' Mag.* 215(1551), jun 73 : 255-260.

5890    MICALLEF, A. "Stratégie des firmes multinationales et espace économique", *R. Écon. Gestion* 1(1), jun 72 : 25-51.

5891    MICHALET, C. A. "La politique de financement de l'entreprise multinationale", *Écon. et Soc.* 6(6-7), jun-jul 72 : 1241-1272.

5892    PIATIER, A. "Les sociétés multinationales dans l'économie méditerranéenne", *Mondes en Dévelop.* (2), 1973 : 83-126.

5893    ROBBINS, S. M.; STOBAUGH, R. B.; SCHYDLOWSKY, D. M. *Money in the multinational enterprise; a study of financial policy.* New York, Basic Books, 73, xix-231 p.

5894    ROBINSON, R. D. *International business management; a guide to decision making.* New York, Holt, Rinehart and Winston, 73, xvi-686 p.

5895    ROBOCK, S. H.; SIMONDS, K. *International business and multinational enterprises.* Homewood, Ill., R. D. Irwin, 73, xiii-652 p.

5896    SCHWENDIMAN, J. S. *Strategic and long-range planning for the multinational corporation.* New York, Praeger, 73, xii-150 p.

5897    STEPHENSON, H. *The coming clash: the impact of the international corporation on the nation state.* London, Weidenfeld and Nicolson; New York, Saturday Review Press, 72, 5-189 p.

5898    TSURUMI, Y. "Japanese multinational firms", *J. Wld Trade Law* 7(1), jan-feb 73 : 74-90.

5899    UNITED STATES. Congress. Senate. Committee on Finance. Subcommittee on International Trade. *Multinational corporations.* Washington, United States Government Printing Office, 73, v-968 p.

5900    VAN GINDERACHTER, J. "Les entreprises multinationales et la politique régionale communautaire", *R. Sci. écon.* 48(174), jun 73 : 59-78.

5901    VIITA, P. "Kansainvälisten yritysten etuja ja haittoja" (The pros and cons of multinational corporations), *Kansantal. Aikakausk.* (3), 1973 : 190-203.

5902    VOJNOVIC, M. "Multinacionalue kompanije i promene u svetsioj privredi" (Multinational corporations and world economy changes), *Medun. Probl.* 25(4), oct-dec 72 : 9-141.

5903    ZINK, D. W. *The political risks for multinational enterprise in developing countries, with a case study of Peru.* New York, Praeger, 73, xiv-185 p.


**O.123    *Market conditions***
**         *Conditions du marché***

**O.1232    Specific international markets**
**           Marchés internationaux particuliers**

[See also / Voir aussi: **O.132; 6031**]

5904    CAZZANIGA, V. "Prospettive del mercato petrolifero internazionale" (Prospects of the international oil market), *Futuribili* 6(51), oct 72 : 24-35.

5905    COUTEAUX, D. "Le marché mondial du café", *Reflets Perspect. Vie écon.* 12(3), 1973 : 225-233.

5906    FRIDÉN, L. *Fluctuations in the international steel market 1953-1968; a study of import and export functions.* Stockholm, University of Stockholm, Institute for International Economic Studies, 72, various pagings.

5907    KLAWE, A. J. *Światowy handel surowcami i żywnością* (World trade in raw materials and food). Warszawa, Państwowe Wydawnictwo Naukowe, 73, 312 p.

5908    MAILLARD, J. C. "Les transformations récentes du marché mondial de la banane, 1950-1970", *B. Assoc. Géogr. franç.* 50(406-407), mar-apr 73 : 451-459.

5909    "Marché mondial du café depuis 1968 (Le)", *B. franç. ital. Amér. Sud* (3), mai-jun 73 : 5-48.

5910    MASSERON, J. "Les nouveaux accords sur le prix du pétrole et leurs conséquences", *R. Écon. polit. (Paris)* 82(5), sep-oct 72 : 796-817.

5911    PROBST, F. W. "Entwicklungstendenzen im internationalen Wollmarkt" (Evolution of the international wool market), *Agrarwirtschaft* 22(10), oct 73 : 343-351.

5912    RIDLER, D.; YANDLE, C. A. "Changes in patterns and policies in the international trade in rice", *IMF Staff Pap.* 19(1), mar 73 : 46-86.

5913    SARKAR, G. K. *The world tea economy.* Delhi, Oxford University Press, 72, xviii-237 p.

5914    TEWES, T. "Sugar: a short-term forecasting model for the world-market, with a forecast of the world market price for sugar in 1972-1973", *Busin. Economist* 4(2), 1972 : 89-97.

5915    WIELAND, D. *Organisation des Rauchwarenmarkts* (The organization of the tobacco market). Berlin-Frankfurt-am-Main, CB-Verlag Boldt. 72, xlii-418 p.

5916    WILLIS, J. W. *Review of world rice markets and major suppliers*. Washington, United States Foreign agricultural Service, 72, ii-58 p.

**O.124**    *Economic blocs (descriptive studies)*
         *Blocs économiques (études descriptives)*

**O.1241**    *Western Bloc, Eastern Bloc*
         *Bloc occidental, bloc oriental*

[See also / Voir aussi: 3156]

5917    ILIĆ, B. B. "Intenziviranje kontakata i ekonomska saradnja EEZ-SEV" (The intensification of contacts and the economic cooperation between the EEC and the CMEA), *Ekonomist (Zagreb)* 26(1), 1973 : 91-107.

5918    MALMGREN, H. B. "Europa, die Vereinigten Staaten und die Weltwirtschaft" (Europe, the US and the world economy), *Europa-Archiv* 27(4), feb 25, 72 : 117-128.

5919    PETROVIĆ, N. "Ekonomski razvojzapadne Êvrope i evropska saraduja" (The economic development of Western Europe and cooperation in Europe), *Međun. Probl.* 25(1), jan-mar 73 : 125-131.

5820    VASJANIN, J.-L. "Die Entwicklung der ökonomischen Zusammenarbeit zwischen der DDR und der UdSSR" (The development of economic cooperation between Germany DR and the USSR), *Dtsche Aussenpolit.* 18(5), sep-oct 73 : 1073-1088.

**O.1244**    *Latin America*
         *Amérique latine*

[See also / Voir aussi: 3157, 5843, 6126, 6230, 6415]

5921    AGOR, W. H. "Latin American inter-State politics: patterns of cooperation and conflict", *Inter-Amer. econ. Aff.* 26(2), 1972 : 19-33.

5922    "Asociación de libre comercio del Caribe (CARIFTA) (La)" (The Caribbean Free Trade Association), *R. Banco centr. Venezuela* 32(323-325), jan-mar 72 : 11-40.

5923    AVERY, W. P. "Subregional integration in Latin America: the Andean Common Market", *J. Common Market Stud.* 11(2), dec 72 : 85-102.

5924    AVERY, W. P.; COCHRANE, J. D. "Innovation in Latin American regionalism: the Andean Common Market", *Int. Org.* 27(2), 1973 : 181-223.

5925    BARBANTE, A. "Estructura institucional del Mercado común centroamericano" (Institutional structure of the Central American Common Market), *Lecciones y Ensayos* 42, 1970 : 133-170.

5926    BARBOSA MUTIS, D. "El futuro del grupo andino" (The future of the Andean group), *Universitas (Bogotà)* 43, nov 72 : 177-185.

5927    "Carribbean regional integration", *Guyana J.* 1(5), dec 71 : 5-28.

5928    ČUMAKOVA, M. L. *Integracionnye processy v stranah Central'noj Ameriki* (Integrational processes in Central America countries). Moskva, Nauka, 72, 171 p.

5929    COMMONWEALTH CARIBBEAN REGIONAL SECRETARIAT. *From CARIFTA to Caribbean community*. Georgetown, CCRS, 72, 180 p.

5930    Bibl. XXI-6174. GRUNWALD, J.; WIONCZEK, M. S.; CARNOY, M. *Latin American economic integration and US policy*. CR: R. D. HANSEN, *Amer. polit. Sci. R.* 67(3), sep 73 : 1111-1113; S. DELL, *J. econ. Liter.* 11(1), mar 73 : 122-124.

5931    IRALA BURGOS, J. "La supranacionalidad en el acuerdo de integración subregional andina" (Supranationality according to the Andean subregional agreement), *R. Fac. Der. (Caracas)* 47, dec 70 : 49-64.

5932    KEARNS, K. C. "The Andean Common Market: a new thrust at economic integration in Latin America", *J. inter-Amer. Stud.* 14(2), mai 72 : 225-250.

5933    KNOWLES, Y. K. *Beyond the Caribbean states: a history of regional cooperation in the Commonwealth Caribbean*. San German, Caribbean Institute and Study Center for Latin America, 72, viii-275 p.

5934    LEACH, R. H. "The changing Caribbean Commonwealth", *Wld today* 29(5), mai 73 : 216-226.

5935    MILENKY, E. S. "Developmental nationalism in practice: the problems, and progress of the Andean group", *Inter-Amer. econ. Aff.* 26(4), 1973 : 49-68.

5936    MILENKY, E. S. *The politics of regional organization in Latin America; the Latin American Free Trade Association.* New York, Praeger, 73, xvii-289 p.

5937    "Mouvement d'intégration en Amérique latine (Le)", *Soc. Banque suisse B.* (5), 1972 : 117-130.

5938    NIETO NAVIA, R. "La Organización de Estados Americanos" (The Organization of American States), *R. javer.* 79(395), jun 73 : 434-436.

5939    PAOLILLO, F.; ONS-INDART, C. "Estudio de los procedimientos de hecho utilizados para la solución de conflictos en la ALALC" (Study of de facto procedures used for the solution of conflicts in LAFTA), *Der. Integr.* 4(9), oct 71 : 19-73.

5940    ROSENBAUM, J. J. "El interés norteamericano en la integración económica centroamericana" (North American interest in the Central American economic integration), *Foro int.* 13(1), jul-sep 72 : 27-44.

5941    SELIGSON, M. A. "Transactions and community formation: fifteen years of growth and stagnation in Central America", *J. Common Market Stud.* 11(3), mar 73 : 173-190.

5942    SUNKEL, O. "Capitalismo transnacional y desintegración nacional en América Latina" (Transnational capitalism and national disintegration in Latin America), *Estud. int.* 4(16), jan-mar 71 : 3-61.

5943    SWITZER, K. A. "The Andean group: a reappraisal", *Inter-Amer. econ. Aff.* 26(4), 1973 : 69-81.

5944    WIONCZEK, M. S. "El Grupo andino y la inversión extranjera privada" (The Andean group and foreign private investment), *R. Econ. Estadíst.* 14(1-4), 1970 : 219-248.

**O.1245**    *European Economic Union*
           *Union économique européenne*

**O.12450**   General studies
           Études générales

[See also / Voir aussi: **O.1241**; 6128, 6542]

5945    BERG, H. *Zur Funktionsfähigkeit der Europäischen Wirtschaftsgemeinschaft* (The functionality of the European Economic Community). Göttingen, Vandenhoeck und Ruprecht, 72, x-150 p.

5946    DIERICKX, L. *Het Europese besluitvormingsproces en het Europese integratieproces* (The European decision-making process and the European integration process). Bruxelles, Éditions de l'Université de Bruxelles, 72, 328 p.

5947    NORMAN D'AUDENHOVE, P. DE. *Intégration économique et monétaire européenne.* Bruxelles, Bruylant; Louvain, Vander, 72, 48 p.

**O.12452**   European Economic Community (Common Market, Free Trade Area problems)
           Communauté économique européenne (Marché commun, problèmes de la zone de libre échange)

[See also / Voir aussi: **O.12454**; 2114, 217, 3971, 5062, 5264, 6100, 6631]

5948    BRAUN, G. *Die Rolle der Wirtschaftsverbände im agrarpolitischen Entscheidungsprozess der Europäischen Wirtschaftsgemeinschaft* (The role of economic associations in the decision process in European Economic Community agricultural policy). Berlin, Duncker und Hubmot, 72, 408 p.

5949    EHLERMANN, C. D. "Problèmes institutionnels actuels de la Communauté", *C. Dr. europ.* 8(3), 1972 : 255-271.

5950    "Expansion of the Common Market", *Law contemp. Probl.* 37(2), 1972 : 221-391.

5951    FELD, W. J. "The enlargement of the European Community and Atlantic relations. Economic and monetary implications", *Atlantic Community Quart.* 10(2), 1972 : 215-225.

5952    GÁMIR, L. *Las preferencias efectivas del Mercado Común a España. España, el Mercado Común y el ingreso de Inglaterra* (Effective preferences from the Common Market to Spain, Spain to the Common Market and income of England). Madrid, Editorial Moneda y Crédito, 72, 222 p.

5953    HASENPFLUG, H.; KRÄGENAU, H. "Ökonomische Konsequenzen des EWG-Beitritts für Grossbritannien" (Economic consequences of Great Britain's adhesion to the EEC), *Hamburg. Jb. Wirtsch. u. Ges.-Polit.* 17, 1972 : 31335.

5954    LOPES, J.; PHILLIPS, D. M. Jr. *The European Free Trade Association without the United Kingdom, Denmark, and Norway: implications for agricultural exports of the remaining EFTA countries and the United States.* Washington, Economic Research Service, United States Department of Agriculture, 72, iv-36 p.

5955    MAAS, H. H. "The powers of the European Community and the achievement of the Economic and Monetary Union", *Common Market Law R.* 9(1), feb 72 : 2-12.

5956    SATTLER, A. *Die Europäischen Gemeinschaften an der Schwelle zur Wirtschafts- und Währungsunion* (European countries on the threshhold of economic and monetary union). Tübingen, Mohr, 72, xii-168 p. [Originally published under title: "Die Entwicklung der Europäischen Gemeinschaften von ihrer Gründung bis zum Ende der EWG-Überganszeit", in: *Jb. öff. Rechts Gegenwart* 19, 1970.]

5957    SCHMIDT, S. C. "United Kingdom entry into the European Economic Community: issues and implications", *Ill. agric. Econ.* 12(2), jul 72 : 1-11.

5958    SCHMITT, H. O. "Britain joins the EEC", *Finance and Develop.* 9(4), dec 72 : 24-29.

5959    SEMENOV, É. "Obščij rynok: regulirovanie cen na sel'skohozjajstvennye tovary" (The Common Market and the regulation of agricultural products prices), *Mir. Ėkon. meždun. Otnoš.* 16(10), oct 73 : 132-138.

5960    STOCK, W. *Die europäische Wirtschafts- und Währungsunion: eine integrationspolitische Perspektive?* (European economic and monetary union; a prospect for political integration?). Berlin, Duncker und Hubmot, 72, 183 p.

5961    VITTAS, H. "Effects of changes in EEC currency exchange rates on prices, production, and trade of agricultural commodities in the community", *IMF Staff Pap.* 19(2), jul 72 : 447-467.


**O.12454**   Problems of Eurafrica
         Problèmes de l'Eurafrique

5962    COSGROVE, C. A. "The EEC and its Yaounde associates; a model for development", *Int. Relat. (London)* 4(2), nov 72 : 142-155.

5963    MUTHARIKA, B. W. T. "The enlargement of the European Economic Community and its implications on African trade development", *Afr. Spectrum* 8(2), 1973 : 125-139.

5964    OUATTARA, A. D. "Trade effects of the Association of African Countries with the European Economic Community", *Staff Pap.* 20(2), jul 73 : 499-543.

5965    ROSENTHAL, G. "The EEC and the Maghreb", *Columbia Essays int. Aff.* (6), 1970 : 116-133.

5966    ZAMPAGLIONE, G. "L'associazione tra Mercato comune et SAMA" (The associations between the Common Market and the African Malagasy states) *Aff. est.* 14, apr 72 : 101-112.


**O.12455**   Comecon

[See also / Voir aussi: **O.1241; 1401, 6479**]

5967    AL'TŠULER, A. B. *Sotrudničestvo socialističeskih gosudarstv. Rasčety, kredity, pravo* (Cooperation between the socialist states: calculations, credits, law). Moskva, Mezdunarodnye Otnošenija, 73, 175 p.

5968    AUSCH, S. *Theory and practice of CMEA cooperation.* Budapest, Akadémiai Kiadó, 72, 279 p.

5969    BAJBAKOV, A. A. *Ėkonomičeskoe prognozirovanie v stranah členah SĖV* (Economic forecasts in the Comecon countries). Moskva, Izdatel'stvo moskovskogo Universiteta, 73, 84 p.

5970 BECHER, K.; SEIFFERT, W. "Zur materiellen Verantwortlichkeit der RGW-Staaten als Instrument der sozialistischen ökonomischen Integration" (The material responsabilities of the Comecon member-states, instrument of socialist economic integration), *Dtsche Aussenpolit.* 18(4), jul-aug 73 : 851-864.

5971 BELJAEV, Ju. N.; SEMENOVA, L. S. *Socialističeskaja integracija i mirovoe hozjajstvo* (Socialist integration and the world economy). Moskva, Meždunarodnye Otnošenija, 72, 255 p.

5972 BOGOMOLOV, O. T.; BARKOVSKY, A. N. "Economic co-operation among the Council for Mutual Economic Assistance countries", *Econ. B. Asia Far East* 21(3), dec 70 : 11-29.

5973 BONDARENKO, Ė. L. *Vyravnivanie ėkonomičeskih urovnej stran-členov SĖV* (The equalization of the Comecon countries economic levels). Moskva, Izdatel'stvo Moskovskogo Universiteta, 73, 800 p.

5974 BOŻYK, P. *RWPG. Ekonomiczny mechanizm współpracy* (CMEA. Economic mechanism of co-operation). 2nd ed. compl. Warszawa, Książka i Wiedza, 73, 172 p.

5975 DOBRESCU, E. "Principal bases of collaboration and socialist economic integration of COMECON countries", *Sov. East. Europ. for. Trade* 8(3-4), 1972-1973 : 325-334.

5976 FIUMEL, H. DE. "Les problèmes de la responsabilité matérielle de l'État dans la coopération économique entre les pays membres du CAEM", *C. Dr. europ.* 8(6), 1972 : 623-636.

5977 GALICKOV, A. "Klasni i nacionalni interes u procesu ekonomske integracija socjalističkih zemalja" (Class interest and national interest in the process of economic integration of socialist countries), *Socijalizam* 16(5), apr 73 : 487-512.

5978 INOZEMCEV, N. "Glavye zadači koordinacii narodno-hozjajstvennyh planov stran SĖV" (The important task of coordinating economic plans of the CAEM countries), *Plan. Hoz.* 50(4), apr 73 : 6-14.

5979 IONESCU, I. "Modalities of perfecting collaboration and cooperation among COMECON countries", *Sov. East. Europ. for. Trade* 8(3-4), 1972-1973 : 335-348.

5980 JAKUBOWSKI, J. "Le développement du droit économique communautaire des pays du CAEM et les problèmes posés par son application", *J. Dr. int.* 100(3), jul-sep 73 : 676-699.

5981 KAMECKI, Z. "La coopération économique au sein du Conseil d'Assistance Économique Mutuelle (CAEM) et entre ses membres", *C. écon. Bruxelles* 56, 4 trim 72 : 455-498.

5982 KISS, T. "Progressi e limiti dell'integrazione nel Comecon" (Progress and limits of integration in Comecon), *Polit. Econ.* 4(1-2), jan-apr 73 : 90-100.

5983 KORMNOV, Ju. F. *Specializacija i kooperacija proizvodstva stran SĖV v uslovijah socialističeskoj ėkonomičeskoj integracii* (Comecon countries' production specialization and cooperation under socialist economic integration conditions). Moskva, Ėkonomika 72, 335 p.

5984 KORMOV, Ju. "Mezdunarodnye ekonomičeskie organizacii i ih rol' v sotrudničestve stran SĖV" (International economic organizations and their role in the cooperation between CAEM countries), *Plan. Hoz.* 50(4), apr 73 : 54-63.

5985 KRAKOWSKI, J. "Integracja krajów socjalistycznych i jej mechanizm" (The integration of socialist countries and its mechanism), *Zesz. nauk. wyższ. Szkoły ekon. Katowic.* (44), 1972 : 101-109.

5986 KUBICZEK, F.; SKIBIŃSKI, L. *RWPG. Program socjalistycznej integracji gospodarczej* (CMEA. Program of socialist economic integration). Warszawa, Książka i Wiedza 73, 132 p.

5987 LARIONOV, K. A. "Problemy ėkonomičeskoj integracii socialističeskih stran" (Problems of the socialist countries economic integration), in: *Ėkonomičeskie i social'no-političeskie problemy kommunističeskogo stroitel'stva v SSSR*. Moskva, 1972 : 174-192.

5989 NIKL, M. "International aspects of a new stage in the development of the Council of Mutual Economic Assistance", *Int. Relat. (Prague)* 1972 : 22-29.

5990 OLEJNIK, I.P.; ŠEVJAKOVA, F. N. *Ėkonomičeskoe sotrudničestvo, socialističeskaja integracija i ėffektivnost' proizvodstva* (Economic cooperation, socialist integration and production efficiency). Moskva, Mysl', 72, 327 p.

5991 ŠALAMANOV, S. *SĖV—dostiženija i perspektivi* (Comecon—results and forecasts). Varna, Darzavno izdatel'stvo, 73, 160 p.

5992 SCEGOLEV, V. "Nekotorye aspekty ekonomičeskoj integracii stran SĚV v oblasti valjutno-finansovy otnošenij" (Some aspects of the economic integration of Comecon member countries in the field of monetary and financial relations), *Nauč. Dokl. vysš. Školy ěkon. Nauki* 16(1), jan 73 : 67-73.

5993 ŠIRJAEV, Ju. S.; IOVČUK, S. M. *Proizvodstvennaja integracija stran SĚV* (The production integration between the Comecon countries). Moskva, Nauka, 72, 211 p.

5994 SOLOV'EVA, K. F. "Problemy uglublenija ekonomičeskoj integracii socialističeskih stran" (Problems of the economic integration of the socialist countries), *Trudy Kaf. politěkon. Moskov. ěkon. statist. Inst.* (2), 1972 : 3-44.

5995 ŠTĚPANEK, J. "Further development of cooperation in the Council of Mutual Economic Assistance", *Int. Relat. (Prague)* 1972 : 30-40.

5996 VAN BRABANT, J. M. "The program for socialist economic integration", *Osteuropa Wirtsch.* 17(6), dec 72 : 272-290.

5997 WASOWSKI, S. "Economic integration in the Comecon", *Orbis* 16(3), 1972 : 760-779.

5998 ZOLOTAREV, V. I. *Programma ěkonomičeskogo sotrudničestva socialističeskih stran* (The program of the socialist countries economic cooperation). Moskva, Mezdunarodnye otnošenija, 73, 111 p.

### O.125 *International rivers and waterways*
### *Fleuves et canaux internationaux*

5999 MENON, P. K. "Institutional mechanism for the development of international water resources", *R. belge Dr. int.* 8(1), 1972 : 80-100.

### O.126 *Population movements*
### *Mouvements de population*

[See also / Voir aussi: 1901]

6000 BAUČIĆ, I. "Neka suvremena obilježja i problemi vanskih migracija jugoslovenskih radnika" (Some contemporary characteristics and problems of the emigration of Yugoslav workers), *Sociologija* 15(2), 1973 : 183-216.

6001 BEIJER, G. *Brain drain / Auszug des Geistes / Exode des cerveaux. A selected bibliography on temporary and permanent migration of skilled workers and high-level manpower, 1967-1972.* The Hague, Nijhoff, 72, 84 p.

6002 BERGUES, H. "L'immigration de travailleurs africains noirs en France et particulièrement dans la région parisienne", *Population* 28(1), jan-feb 73 : 59-79.

6003 BÖHNING, W. R.; STEPHEN, D. *The EEC and the migration of workers: the EEC's system of free movement of labour and the implications of United Kingdom entry.* London, Runnymede Trust, 71, 43 p.

6004 CANDEL, F. *Immigrantes y trabajadores* (Immigrants and workers). Barcelona, Planeta, 27, 237 p.

6005 CINANNI, P. "Consequenze economico-sociali dell'emigrazione" (Economic and social consequences of emigration), *Crit. marx.* 11(2), mar-apr 73 : 61-72. [Italy.]

6006 DORAI, G. C. "Study abroad and migration of human capital; an empirical analysis", *Manpower J.* 8(2), jul-sep 72 : 15-52.

6007 FLORES COLOMBINO, A. *La fuga de intelectuales; emigración paraguaya* (The flight of intellectuals: Paraguayan emigration). Montevideo, Tall. Gráf. de la Comunidad del Sur, 72, 255 p.

6008 GEAHCHAN, M. L. "Émigration des cerveaux et le système éducatif au Liban", *Proche-Orient Ét. écon.* 73, mai-aug 72 : 241-258.

6009 GOKALP, C. "L'émigration turque en Europe et particulièrement en France", *Population* 28(2), mar-apr 73 : 335-360.

6010 GONZALEZ PAZ, J. "El futuro de la emigración española" (The future of Spanish emigration), *R. Econ. polít.* 63, jan-apr 73 : 103-122.

6011 HEKMATI, M.; GLASER, W. A. "The brain drain and UNITAR's multinational research project on the subject", *Soc. Sci. Inform. / Inform. Sci. soc.* 12(2), apr 73 : 123-138.

6012    KAO, C. H. C.; LEE, J. W. "An empirical analysis of China's brain drain into the United States", *Econ. Develop. cult. Change* 21(3), apr 73 : 500-513.

6013    KEELY, C. B. "Philippine migration: international movements and emigration to the United States", *Int. Migr. R.* 7(2), 1973 : 177-187.

6014    KUSHNER, G. *Immigrants from India in Israel. Planned change in an administered community.* Tucson, Ariz., University of Arizona Press, 73, xviii-151 p.

6015    OTEIZA, E. "L'exode des cerveaux vers les États-Unis: un cas latino-américain", *Tiers-Monde* 14(55), jul-sep 73 : 515-540.

6016    PFAFF, I. "Die tschechoslovakische Kulturemigration nach 1968" (Emigration of Czechoslovak intellectuals after 1968), *Schweiz. Mh.* 52(11), feb 73 : 806-816.

6017    PLENDER, R. *International migration law.* Leiden, A. W. Sijthoff, 72, xxiv-339 p.

6018    SAVONA, P. "Una analisi logica delle migrazioni di scienziati e di tecnici" (A logical analysis of the migrations of scientists and technicians), *G. Economisti* 31(9-10), sep-oct 72 : 700-704.

6019    SERAYDARIAN, L. "Exode des compétences des pays arabes", *Proche-Orient Ét. écon.* 73, mai-aug 72 : 225-239.

6020    TANIĆ, Ž. "Ekonomska emigracija: klasno odredenje i svest" (Economic emigration: definition of class and consciousness), *Sociologija* 14(3), 1972 : 441-460.

6021    VANDENKAMP, J. "Return migration: its significance and behavior", *West. econ. J.* 10(4), dec 72 : 460-465.

6022    VAN NIEUWENHUIZE, C. A. O. (ed.). *Emigration and agriculture in the Mediterranean Basin.* The Hague, Mouton, 72, 188 p.


## O.13    International economic policy
## Politique économique internationale

### O.130    *General studies*
### *Études générales*

6023    BOCCARA, P. "La crise des relations économiques internationales et les moyens d'en sortir", *C. Communisme* 49(10), oct 73 : 14-26.

6024    TODOROV, T. "Međunarodnite ekonomski odnosi i sovremeni tendencii vo svetskata ekonomija" (Economic international relations and present world economic tendencies), *Godiš. ekon. Fak. (Skopje)* 15, 1971 : 367-392.


### O.132    *International agreements (and agreement schemes)*
### *Accords internationaux (et projet d'accord)*

6025    BARDAN, B. "The Cotton Textile Agreement, 1692-1972", *J. Wld Trade Law* 7(1), jan-feb 73 : 8-35.

6026    BLANC, A. P. "L'accord international sur le cacao", *Ét. Statist. Cameroun Afr. équat. Banque centr.* 181, feb 73 : 76-93.

6027    GALLOWAY, L. T. "The International Coffee Agreement", *J. Wld Trade Law* 7(3), mai-jun 73 : 354-374.

6028    GRENON, J.-Y. "Les traités de commerce, cadre de la libéralisation des échanges", *Canad. Yb. int. Law* (10), 1972 : 65-101.

6029    GWYER, G. D. "Three international commodity agreements: the experience of East Africa", *Econ. Develop. cult. Change* 21(3), apr 73 : 465-476.

6030    KOFI, T. A. "International commodity agreements and export earnings: simulation of the 1968 'Draft International Cocoa Agreement' ", *Food Res. Inst. Stud.* 11(2), 1972 : 177-201.

6031    LAFER, C. "El Convenio Internacional del Café" (The International Coffee Agreement), *Der. Integr.* 6(12), mar 73 : 111-135.

6032    ROY, H. "Some observations on a new international tea agreement", *Econ. Aff.* 17(8), aug 72 : 386-394.

**O.134**  *International co-operation programmes*
           *Programmes de coopération internationale*

**O.1340**  *General studies*
            *Études générales*

[See also / Voir aussi: 6414]

6033  ABBOTT, G. C. "The contradictions and misconceptions of foreign aid", *Co-existence*
      10(1), mar 73 : 64-75.

6034  BONNAMOUR, L. *La capacité d'absorption de l'aide étrangère dans les pays en voie de*
      *développement*. Paris, 73, 377 ff. multigr.

6035  BUTTNER, F. (ed.). *Sozialer Fortschritt durch Entwicklungshilfe ? Kritische Beiträge zur*
      *Praxis westlicher Entwicklungspolitik* (Does aid to developing countries permit social
      progress ?). München, Claudius Verlag, 72, 194 p.

6036  BYRES, T. J. (ed.). *Foreign resources and economic development: a symposium on the report*
      *of the Pearson Commission*. London, Cass., 72, xi-199 p.

6037  FALLAND, J. *Utviklingshjelp og fredspolitikk: utviklingsokonomikk og konfliktforskning*
      (Development aid and peace policy: development economics and conflict research).
      Bergen, Chr. Michelsens institut for videnskap og andsfrihet, 72, 16 p.

6038  FRANK, C. R. Jr. *et al. Assisting developing countries; problems of debts, burden-sharing,*
      *jobs, and trade*. New York, Praeger Publishers, 72, xx-482 p.

6039  GERGEN, K. J.; GERGEN, M. "International assistance in psychological perspective",
      *Yb. Wld Aff.* 25, 1971 : 87-103.

6040  HALBACH, A. J. *Theorie und Praxis der Evaluierung von Projekten in Entwicklungsländern;*
      *eine Bestandsaufnahme* (Theory and practice of project analysis in the developing
      countries; an inventory). München, Weltforum-Verlag, 72, 178 p.

6041  HART, J. *Aid and liberation: a socialist study of aid policies*. London, Gollancz, 73, 287 p.

6042  HOFMANN, O.; SCHARSCHMIDT, G. *Wissenschaftlich-technische Beziehungen mit Entwick-*
      *lungsländern* (Scientific and technological relations with developing countries). Berlin,
      Verlag Die Wirtschaft, 72, 148 p.

6043  IRVINE, R. J. "New approach to foreign aid", *Columbia J. Wld Busin.* 7(5), sep-oct 72 :
      23-30.

6044  MONTRIE, C. "The organization and functions of foreign aid", *Econ. Develop. cult.*
      *Change* 21(4), jul 73 Part I: 697-713.

6045  SEITZ, K. "Die destabilisierende Hilfe—Gedanken über eine neue Entwicklungshilfe-
      politik" (The destabilizing aid—reflections on a new policy for development assis-
      tance), *Europa-Archiv* 26(23), dec 10, 71 : 805-814,

6046  WALL, D. *The charity of nations; the political economy of foreign aid*. New York, Basic
      Books, 73, vii-181 p.

6047  WITTKOPF E. R. *Western bilateral aid allocations; a comparative study of recipient state*
      *attributes and aid received*. Beverly Hills, Sage Publications, 72, 62 p.

**O.1341**  *Technical and financial assistance*
            *Assistance technique et financière*

[See also / Voir aussi: **O.1343; O.2223; O.241**]

6048  AGRAWAL, S. "Objectives and orientations of India's aid diplomacy", *Polit. Sci. R.*
      11(2-3), apr-sep 72 : 232-242.

6049  BALASUBRAMANYAM, V. N. *International transfer of technology to India*. New York,
      Praeger, 73, xiv-143 p.

6050  CHANDAVARKAR, A. G. "Technical cooperation within the Third World", *Finance and*
      *Develop.* 9(4), dec 72 : 17-22.

6051  HENRY, P.-M. "Une expérience de coopération inter-africaine: la CCTA (Commission
      de coopération technique en Afrique du Sud du Sahara)", *CR trim. Acad. Sci. O.-Mer*
      32(3-4), 1973 : 517-526.

6052  KIM, S. "Foreign assistance and Korea's economic growth", *Austral. econ. Pap.* 11(18),
      jun 72 : 89-102.

6053  MORGAN, R. P. "Transfer of technology", *Proc. Acad. polit. Sci.* 30(4), aug 72 : 141-152.

6054  PATEL, S. J. "La transferencia de tecnología a los países en desarrollo" (The transfer of technology towards developing countries), *Foro int.* 13(1), jul-sep 72 : 11-26.

6055  PATEL, S. J. "Transfer of technology and third UNCTAD", *J. Wld Trade Law* 7(2), mar-apr 73 : 226-239.

6056  Bibl. XXI-6308. ROETT, R. *The politics of foreign aid in the Brazilian Northeast.* CR: K. D. FREDERICK, *Amer. polit. Sci. R.* 67(3), sep 73 : 1121-1122.

6057  Bibl. XXI-6309. STREETEN, P. *Aid to Africa. A policy outline for the 1970's.* CR: P. ROBSON, *J. econ. Liter.* 10(4), dec 72 : 1245-1247.

6058  WOLFSON, M. *Aid management in developing countries; a case study: the implementation of three aid projects in Tunisia.* Paris, Development Centre of the Organisation for Economic Co-operation and Development, 72, 49 p.


O.1343   *National plans*
         *Plans nationaux*

O.13432   Foreign aid of the USA
          Aide apportée par les É.-U.A. aux pays étrangers

6059  COOPER, R. V. L. *The additionality factor in tied US development assistance.* Santa Monica, Calif., Rand, 72, xiii-69 p.

6060  DINWIDDY, B. (ed.). *Aid performance and development policies of western countries; studies in US, UK, EEC, and Dutch Programs.* New York, Praeger, 73, vii-139 p.

6061  FRANK, C. R. Jr. *Adjustment assistance: American jobs and trade with the developing countries.* Washington, Overseas Development Council, 73, 49 p.

6062  FULBRIGHT, J. W. (ed.). *Views on foreign assistance policy; comments by individuals and organizations concerning United States foreign assistance policy.* Washington, United States Government Printing Office, 73, vi-345 p.

6063  HINKEL, G. *Die Auslandshilfe der USA; ihre politischen und ökonomischen Aspekte, insbesondere während der Kennedy- und Johnson-Administration* (US foreign aid; political and economic aspects in particular during the Kennedy and the Johnson administration). Berlin, Deutscher Verlag der Wissenschaften, 72, 238 p.

6064  LOOMBA, J. F. "US aid to India, 1951-1967. A study in decision-making", *India Quart.* 28(4), oct-dec 72 : 304-331.

6065  POATS, R. M. *Technology for developing nations; new directions for US technical assistance.* Washington, Brookings Institution, 72, ix-255 p.

6066  STANLEY, R. G. *Food for peace: hope and reality of US food aid.* New York, Gordon and Breach, 73, xiii-355 p.

6067  UNITED STATES. General Accounting Office. *United States interests and activities in Nepal: Department of State, Agency for International Development, Peace Corps, United States Information Agency.* Washington, GAO, 73, 78 p.


O.13433   Foreign aid of the USSR
          Aide apportée par l'URSS aux pays étrangers

[See also / Voir aussi: 3289]

6068  CHERTKOV, D. G. *The Soviet Union and developing countries; (experience and prospects of economic cooperation).* Moscow, Novosti Press Agency Publishing House, 72, 119 p.

6069  OFER, G. "The economic burden of Soviet involvement in the Middle East", *Sov. Stud.* 24(3), jan 73 : 329-347.

6070  TIWARI, J. G. *Basic principle of Soviet economic aid to India; an exposition to Russian theory of non-capitalist development path.* Aligarh, 72, 51 p.

6071  VALKENIER, E.-K. "Die Sowjetunion und die Dritte Welt" (The USSR and the Third World), *Europa-Archiv* 28(5), mar 10, 73 : 162-172.

**O.13434** Foreign aid of other countries
Aide extérieure fournie par d'autres pays

[See also / Voir aussi: 6060]

6072 AGARWAL, J. P. *Direktinvestitionen in Entwicklungsländern und die deutsche Förderungspolitik* (Direct investments in developing lands and the German stimulation policy). Kiel, Institut für Weltwirtschaft, 72, 13 p.

6073 AGLIERI RINELLA, M. "La cooperazione cinese con i paesi in via di sviluppo" (Chinese co-operation with developing countries), *Terzo Mondo* 6(19-20), mai-jun 73 : 28-37.

6074 ALIBONI, R. "Italian aid policy in the 60's", *Spettatore int.* 7(2), apr-jun 72 : 49-68.

6075 AUBENAS, T. "Aide de la Grande-Bretagne au tiers-monde", *Projet* 76, jun 73 : 717-726.

6076 BARTKE, W. *Die Wirtschaftshile der Volksrepublik China* (Economic aid of the Republic of China). Hamburg, Institut für Asienkunde, 72, 251 p.

6077 BODEMER, K. "Entwicklungshilfe und Deutschlandpolitik" (Development aid and German policy), *Vierteljahresberichte* 50, dec 72 : 399-420.

6078 BONDT, J. DE. "Canada's aid to developing countries", *Canad. geogr. J.* 85(5), nov 72 : 165-171.

6079 HØIVIK, T.; REINTON, P. O. "Norge og u-hjelpen. En vurdering og et alternativ" (Norwegian aid to developing countries: an evaluation and an alternative), *Int. Polit. (Bergen)* (1), jan-mar 72 : 31-54.

6080 IQBAL, M. H. "Pakistan—foreign aid and foreign policy", *Pakistan Horizon* 25(4), 1972 : 54-71.

6081 KATINCHAROV, I. S. "Coopération économique de la République populaire de Bulgarie avec les pays en voie de développement", *R. Pays Est* 13(1), 1972 : 99-126.

6082 KIRCHHOF, K.; POPP, U. *Der administrative Aufwand der Entwicklungshilfe* (Administrative expenses for overseas development aid). Berlin, Duncker und Humblot, 73, 198 p. [Germany, FR.]

6083 KOKULINSKY, D.; PARK, S. J. "Die Entwicklungshilfe als ein aussenpolitisches Intrument der Volksrepublik China" (Aid to development as an instrument of foreign policy for the People's Republic of China), *Z. ges. Staatswiss.* 129(3), aug 73 : 559-572.

6084 KUPPE, J. "DDR und Entwicklungsländer" (Germany DR and the developing countries), *Deutschland Archiv* 6(6), jun 73 : 622-633.

6085 LEVIN, N. "Israel and the developing world: new concepts in technical assistance", *Sci. publ. Aff.* 28(9), nov 72 : 37-43.

6086 MARIJSSE, S.; ROOSENS, P. "Kost van de Belgische ontwikkelingsbijdrage tussen 1961 en 1970" (Cost of Belgium's development aid between 1961 and 1970), *Econ. soc. Tijds.* 26(5), oct 72 : 451-492.

6087 MARKIEWICZ, W. *Niektóre problemy współpracy gospodarczej Polski z krajami Trzeciego Świata* (Some problems of Poland's economic co-operation with Third World countries). Warszawa, Polski Instytut Spraw Międzynarodowych, 72, 99 p.

6088 PIKE, C. E. *Japanese overseas aid and investments—their potential effects on world and US farm exports*. Washington, United States Department of Agriculture, Economic Research Service, 72, iv-57 p.

6089 SALVI, F. "Il contributo italiano al progresso del terzo mondo" (The Italian contribution to the progress of the Third World), *Vita e Pensiero* 55(4), jul-aug 72 : 29-37.

6090 SOHN, K.-H. *Entwicklungspolitik—Theorie und Praxis der deutschen Entwicklungshilfe* (Development policy. Theory and practice of German development aid). München, R. Piper and Co., 72, 286 p. CR: U. SIMSON, *Kölner Z. Soziol. u. soz.-Psychol.* 25(1), mar 73 : 194-196.

6091 STANESCU, C. "La Roumanie socialiste et les pays du continent africain", *R. roum. Ét. int.* 6(2-3), 1972 : 189-206.

**O.135** *International relations of specific areas and countries*
*Relations internationales de régions et pays particuliers*

[See also / Voir aussi: O.1241; O.12450; 5930, 6150, 6632]

6092 ALALUUSUA, J. "TTT-yhteistyö Euroopassa. Idän ja lännen välisen taloudellisen yhteistyön keyitys syyt ja muodot" (Development in Europe. Causes and forms of economic co-operation between East and West), *Ulkopolitiikka* 2(4), 1973 : 4-12.

6093 ANCZEWSKI, I. *Ewolucja stosunków gospodarczych Francji z europejskiemi panstwam, socjaliztycznymi po II wojnie swiatowej* (Evolution of the economic relations of France with the European socialist countries after World War II). Warszawa, Polski Instytut Spraw Międzynarodowych, 72, 120 p.

6094 BIEDA, K. *Australia-New Zealand economic relations.* Melbourne, Committee for Economic Development of Australia, 72, i-33 l.

6095 BIRO, G. "Les relations économiques internationales de la Hongrie", *Est-Ouest* 3(3), 1972 : 85-98.

6096 BOCCARA, P. "La crise des relations économiques capitalistes sur le plan international", *Écon. et Polit.* 231, oct 73 : 49-75.

6097 BOLZ, K.; KUNZE, B. (eds.). *Wirtschaftsbeziehungen zwischen Ost und West: Handel und Kooperation* (East-West economic relations: trade and cooperation). Hamburg, HWWA-Institut für Wirtschaftsforschung und Wirtschaftssysteme; Bonn, Europa-union-Verlag, 73, 136-xxxiii p.

6098 BORDAZ, R. "La signification des relations économiques Est-Ouest", *Nouv. R. deux Mondes* (10), oct 73 : 112-117.

6099 BROWN, A. A.; MARER, P. "New options for the United States in East-West trade", *Stud. comp. Communism* 4(2), apr 71 : 119-145.

6000 BRUGMANS, H. *et al. La politique économique extérieure de la Communauté européenne élargie / The external economic policy of the enlarged Community.* Bruges, De Tempel, 73, 249 p.

6001 CALLEO, D. P.; ROWLAND, B. M. *America and the world political economy; Atlantic dreams and national realities.* Bloomington, Indiana University Press, 73, xii-371 p.

6102 "Canadian-United States economic relations", *J. contemp. Busin.* 1(4), 1972 : 1-89.

6103 CHANDRASEKHARA Rao, R. V. R. "Indo-Soviet economic relations", *Asian Surv.* 12(8), aug 73 : 793-801.

6104 COHEN, J. B. (ed.). *Pacific partnership: United States-Japan trade; prospects and recommendations for the seventies.* Lexington, Mass., Lexington Books, 72, xiv-270 p.

6105 DATAR, A. L. *India's economic relations with the USSR and Eastern Europe, 1953 to 1969.* Cambridge, Cambridge University Press, 72, xiv-278 p.

6106 DOBOSIEWICZ, Z. *Ekonomiczne aspekty neokolonializmu w Afryce* (Economic aspects of neocolonialism in Africa). Warszawa, Państwowe Wydawnictwo Naukowe, 73, 200-3 p.

6107 ENGLISH, H. E.; WILKINSON, B. W.; EASTMAN, H. C. *Canada in a wider economic community.* Toronto, University of Toronto Press, 72, viii-151 p.

6108 ENGMAN, H. *Sverige og Europa* (Sweden and Europe). Stockholm, Prisma, 73, 124 p. [European Economic Community and Sweden.]

6109 FÄBL, M. "Die österreichisch-sowjetischen Wirtschaftsbeziehungen" (Soviet-Austiran economic relations), *Österr. Osth.* 15(1), feb 73 : 12-19.

6110 HASAN, M. *India's trade relations with rupee payments countries.* Aligarh, International Book Traders, 72, vi-154 p.

6111 HIERONYMI, O. *Economic discrimination against the United States in Western Europe, 1945-1958. Dollar shortage and the rise of regionalism.* Genève-Paris, Droz, 73, xviii-233 p.

6112 HO, S. P. S.; HUENEMANN, R. W. *Canada's trade with China; patterns and prospects.* Quebec, Private Planning Association of Canada, 72, ix-54 p.

6113 HUDSON, M. *Super imperialism. The economic strategy of American empire.* New York, Holt, Rinehart and Winston, 72, xxxii-304 p.

6114 IIDA, S. *Nichibei keizai kosho* (Economic negociation between Japan and the USA). Tokyo, Sanichi Shobo, 71, 186 p.

6115 "International economic issues and Pakistan", *Pakistan Horizon* 25(4), 1972 : 3-71.

6116 KAJI, M. "Japan-US economics relations", *Japan Quart.* 20(30), jul-sep 73 : 268-274.

6117 KAMECKI, Z. "Possibilities of increasing East-West trade and industrial cooperation", *Sov. East. Europ. for. Trade* 9(1), 1973 : 77-93.

6118 KAMECKI, Z. *Some problems of economic co-operation between Eastern and Western Europe.* Helsinki, Ulkopoliittinen Instituutti monistesarja 37, 73, 12 p. Mimeo.

6119 KISELEVA, V. I. *Afrika: integracija i problemy vnešneěkonomičeskih otnošenij* (Africa: integration and problems of foreign economic relations). Moskva, Nauka, 72, 152 p.

6120 KITAMURA, H. "Japan's economic policy towards Southeast Asia", *Asian Aff.* 59(1), feb 72 : 47-57.

6121    MARER, P.; EUBANKS, G. J. *Soviet and East European foreign trade*, 1946-1969; *statistical compendium and guide*. Bloomington, Indiana University Press, 73, xviii-408 p.

6122    MASNATA, A. *Le destin des échanges Ouest-Est. Problèmes et solutions.* Neuchatel, Éditions de la Baconnière, 72, 175 p.

6123    MOJSIEWICZ, C. (ed.). *Stosunki Polski z innymi panstwami socjalistycznymi* (Relations of Poland with other socialist countries). Warszawa, Państwowe Wydawnictwo Naukowe, 73, 306 p.

6124    MOZEJKO, E. *Włochy a integracja zachodnioeuropejska* (Italy and West European integration). Warszawa, Polski Instytut Spraw Międzynarodowych, 72, 174 p.

6125    MUŃKO, A. *Protekcjonizm w stosunkach gospodarczych między Japonią a Stanami Zjadnoczonymi* (Protectionism in economic relations between Japan and the USA). Warszawa, Polski Instytut Spraw Międzynarodowych, 72, 157 p.

6126    OGELSBY, J. C. M. "Relaciones Canadiense-Latinoamericanas pasadas, presentes y futuras" (Past, present and future Canadian-Latin American relations), *Estud. int.* 5(18), apr-jun 72 : 68-87.

6127    ORŁOWSKA, M. *Szwecja a Europejska Wspólnota Gospodarcza* (Sweden and the European Economic Community). Warszawa, Polski Instytut Spraw Międzynarodowych, 72, 121 p.

6128    PEDERSEN, J. *Danmark og EF. Kommentar og perspektiv* (Denmark and the EEC. Commentary and prospects). København, Aktuelle Bøger, DBK, 72, 176 p.

6129    PERCZYŃSKI, M. (ed.). *Ewolucja stosunków gospodarczych Stanów Zjednoczonych z Europą Zachodnią po II wojnie światowej* (Evolution of the economic relations between the United States and Western Europe after World War II). Warszawa, Polski Instytut Spraw Międzynarodowych, 72, 354 p.

6130    PTASZEK, J. *Polska—ZSRR. Gospodarka, współpraca* (Poland—USSR. Economy, co-operation). Warszawa, Państwowe Wydawnictwo Ekonomiczne, 72, 307 p.

6131    RANA, P. "India and Nepal: the political economy of a relationship", *Asian Surv.* 11(7), jul 71 : 645-660.

6132    SEGERS, J. "Production nationale et relations économiques extérieures du Zaïre", *Zaïre-Afr.* 13(72), feb 73 : 69-79.

6133    SZCZYPIORSKI, S. *Polska-Szwajcaria. Gospodarka, stosunki ekonomiczne* (Poland-Switzerland. Economy, economic relations). Warszawa, Państwowe Wydawnictwo Ekonomiczne, 73, 115 p.

6134    TETTAMANTI, L. H. "Les relations économiques entre l'Amérique latine et la Communauté économique européenne", *Panorama démocr.-chr.* 6(2), apr-jun 73 : 109-122.

6135    TOMALA, M. *Polska-NRF. Gospodarka, stosunki ekonomiczne* (Poland-GFR. Economy, economic relations). Warszawa, Państwowe Wydawnictwo Ekonomiczne, 73, 155 p.

6136    VÁLYI, P. "Hungarian-American economic relations", *New Hungar. Quart.* 14(61), 1973 : 13-20.

6137    WIECZORKIEWICZ, A. *Polska-Jugosławia. Gospodarka, współpraca* (Poland-Yugoslavia. Economy, co-operation). Warszawa, Państwowe Wydawnictwo Ekonomiczne, 72, 132 p.

6138    WINTERBERGER, G. "EWG-Freihandelsabkommen der Schweiz—Bestandaufnahme und Würdigung" (The free trade agreement between Switzerland and the EEC—an examination and an evaluation), *Schweiz. Mh.* 52(6), sep 72 : 403-411.

## O.2    MONETARY ASPECTS
ASPECTS MONÉTAIRES

### O.21    International monetary operations
Opérations monétaires internationales

#### O.210    *General studies*
*Études générales*

[See also / Voir aussi: 6369, 6390, 6440]

6139    ALIBER, R. Z. *The international money game.* New York, Basic Books, 73, viii-236 p.
6140    ASCHINGER, F. E. *Das Währungssystem in der Metamorphose* (The monetary system in metamorphosis). Frankfurt-am-Main, F. Knapp, 72, 79 p.

6141    BARATTIERI, V. "La riforma del sistema monetario internazionale" (The reform of the international monetary system), *Bancaria* 29(5), mai 73 : 568-578.

6142    BEHRMAN, J. N. "The futility of international monetary reform", *Challenge* 16(3), jul-aug 73 : 23-31.

6143    BEYFUSS, J. *Perspektiven der internationalen Währungspolitik* (Perspectives for international monetary policy). Köln, Deutsche Industrieverlags-GmbH, 72, 36 p.

6144    BHAGWATI, J. N. "The international monetary system: issues in the symposium", *J. int. Econ.* 2(4), sep 72 : 315-323.

6145    CATALANO, F. *La crisi del sistema monetario internazionale* (The crisis of the international monetary system). Milano, ETAS KOMPASS, 73, 350 p.

6146    CARREAU, D. *Le systeme monétaire international: aspects juridiques.* Paris, A. Colin, 72, 397 p.

6147    CLEVELAND, H. VAN B. "Reflections on international monetary order", *Columbia J. transnat. Law* 11(3), 1972 : 403-419.

6148    DOMDEY, K. H.; KUHNE, H. D. *Die chronische Krise des kapitalistischen Währungssystems* (The chronic crisis of the capitalist monetary system). Frankfurt-am-Main, Verlag Marxistische Blätter, 72, 238 p.

6149    DROZDOV, V. A. *Kritika buržuaznyh teorij regulirovanija denežnoj sistemy kapitalizma* (Critic of bourgeois theories on the capitalist monetary system's regulation theories). Moskva, Finansy, 72, 104 p.

6150    FEKETE, J. "Some connections between the international monetary system and East-West economic relations", *Acta oecon.* 9(2), 1972 : 153-165.

6151    FIGUEROA, E. DE. "Análisis de la crisis monetaria internacional" (Analysis of the international monetary crisis), *Arbor* 85(330), jun 73 : 185-209.

6152    FLEMING, J. M. "Towards a new regime for international payments", *J. int. Econ.* 2(4), sep 72 : 345-374.

6153    FOCSEANU, L. "Le droit international monétaire à la recherche d'un 'système' ", *J. Dr. int.* 100(3), jul-sep 73 : 644-675.

6154    GARAVELLO, O. "Aspetti distributivi della riforma del sistema monetario internazionali" (Distributive aspects of the reform of the international monetary system), *Riv. int. Sci. soc.* 80(5-6), sep-dec 72 : 535-561.

6155    GARINO, F. "Squilibri, espedienti ed iniziative nel sistema monetario internazionale" (Imbalances, expedients and initiatives in the international monetary system), *Annu. Polit. int.* 24, 1967-1971 : 348-386.

6156    GERACI, F. "La riforma del sistema monetario e i pagamenti internazionali" (The reform of the monetary system and international payments), *Stato soc.* 16(9), sep 72 : 715-734.

6157    GYOMAI, Gy. "Ujabb fejlemények a nemzetközi tőkés monetáris rendszer reformjának előkészítésében" (New development in the preparation of the reform of the international capitalist monetary system), *Közgazd. Szle* 19(12), dec 72 : 1478-1484.

6158    HEIN, J. *Business looks at the international monetary system; recent experience and proposals for reform.* New York, Conference Board, 73, 22 p.

6159    HELLMANN, R. "Reform des internationalen Währungssystems und multinationale Unternehmen. Die Risiken spekulativer Einwirkungen auf das Währungsgefüge" (The reform of the international monetary system and the multinational enterprises. The risks of repercussions of speculations on monetary structures), *Europa-Archiv* 28(3), feb 10, 73 : 85-94.

6160    HERZOG, P. "La réforme du système monétaire international", *Écon. et Polit.* 231, oct 73 : 76-86.

6161    HIRSCH, F. "The development and functioning of the postwar international monetary system", *Finance and Develop.* 9(2), jun 72 : 48-52.

6162    JOHNSON, H. G. "Political economy aspects of international monetary reform", *J. int. Econ.* 2(4), sep 72 : 401-424.

6153    JOHNSON, H. G. "The international monetary crisis of 1971", *J. Busin.* 46(1), jan 73 : 11-23.

6164    JOHNSON, H. G. "The international monetary system and the rule of law", *J. Law Econ.* 15(2), oct 72 : 277-292.

6165    KAHN, R. "The international monetary system", *Amer. econ. R.* 63(2), mai 73 *Pap. and Proc.:* 181-188.

6166 KINDLEBERGER, O. P. "The benefits of international money", *J. int. Econ.* 2(4), sep 72 : 425-442.

6167 KULCZYCKI, M. "Kryzys międzynarodowego systemy walutowego" (International monetary crisis), *Zesz. nauk. Szkoły główn. Plan. Statyst.* 91, 1973 : 71-90.

6168 LUTZ, F. A. *Das Problem der internationalen Währungsordnung* (The problem of international monetary order). Erlenbach-Zürich-Stuttgart, Eugen Rentsch 72, 29 p.

6169 LUTZ, F. A. *et al. Internationales Währungssystem und Inflation* (International monetary system and inflation). Zürich, Schulthess Polygraphischer Verlag, 73, 207 p.

6170 MITZAKIS, M. "Principales causes de la crise prolongée du régime monétaire international depuis 1960", *J. Soc. Statist. Paris* 113(3), jul-sep 72 : 183-197.

6171 MÖLLER, H. *Das Ende einer Weltwährungsordnung ?* (The end of world monetary order ?). München, R. Piper, 72, 158 p.

6172 NARPATI, B. "The international monetary system", *Contemp. R.* 223(1291), aug 73 : 88-95.

6173 NEURISSE, A. *Les règlements internationaux.* Paris, Presses universitaires de France, 72, 128 p.

6174 OSSOL, R. "I problemi monetari internazionali in una prospettiva comunitaria" (International monetary problems in a Community perspective), *Politico* 37(3), sep 72 : 445-453.

6175 POSNER, M. *The world monetary system: a minimal reform program.* Princeton, N. J., International Finance Section, Princeton University, 72, 46 p.

6176 REYNOLDS, G. "Reform of the international monetary system", *Centr. Bank Ireland quart. B.* (3), 1972 : 91-115.

6177 RUEFF, J.; CARLI, G. "Dibattito sulla riforma del sistema monetario internazionale" (Debate on the reform of the international monetary system), *Bancaria* 29(8), aug 73 : 935-946.

6178 SAMUELSON, A. *Économie monétaire internationale.* Paris, Dalloz, 73, 182 p.

6179 SAMUELSON, P. A. "Heretical doubts about the international mechanisms", *J. int. Econ.* 2(4), sep 72 : 443-453.

6180 SCHÖLLHORN, J. *Probleme der internationalen Wirtschafts- und Währungspolitik* (Problems of international economic and monetary policy). Tübingen, Mohr, 72, 29 p.

6181 STAMMATI, G. *Il sistema monetario internazionale* (The international monetary system). Torino, Boringhieri, 73, 304 p.

6182 STAMP, M. "The reform of the international monetary system", *Moorgate and Wall Street* (3), 1972 : 4-21.

6183 THOMAS, L. B. Jr. "Some evidence on international currency experience, 1919-1925", *Nebraska J. Econ. Busin.* 11(4), 1972 : 145-155.

6184 TRIFFIN, R. "International monetary collapse and reconstruction in April 1972", *J. int. Econ.* 2(4), sep 72 : 375-400.

6185 UTKIN, È. A.; PONOMAREV, V. A. *Meždunarodnye valjutno-kreditnye otnošenija razvivajuščihsja stran* (International monetary and credit relations of the developing countries). Moskva, 73, 151 p.

6186 VRIES, T. DE. *An agenda for monetary reform.* Princeton, N. J., International Finance Section, Princeton University, 72, 25 p.

## O.211 *Foreign exchange*
### *Change*

## O.2111 *Theory*
### *Théorie*

[See also / Voir aussi: **O.2320**; 5608]

6187 ALIBER, R. Z. "National interest rates, the forward exchange rate, and international capital flows", *Rech. econ. Louvain* 36(2), jul 72 : 149-155.

6188 ALIBER, R. Z. "Uncertainty, currency areas and the exchange rate system", *Economica (London)* 39(156), nov 72 : 432-441.

6189 BLACK, S. W. *International money markets and flexible exchange rates.* Princeton, N. J., International Finance Section, Princeton University; Washington, Board of Governors of the Federal Reserve System, 73, 67 p.

6190    BOSELLO, F. "Sul potere 'isolante' di un sistema di tassi di cambio flessibili" (On the "isolating" power of a system of flexible exchange rates), *Riv. Polit. econ.* 63(7), jul 73 : 787-808.

6191    BURCHARDT, M. "Die geldfiskalpolitische Kombination und der Zielkonflikt zwischen interner und externer Stabilität im System fester Wechselkurse" (The combination of tax and monetary policies and the dilemma between external and internal stability in a system of fixed exchange rates), *Konjunkt.-Polit.* 19(5), 1973 : 257-276.

6192    CHEN, C. Diversified currency holdings and flexible exchanges", *Quart. J. Econ.* 87(1), feb 73 : 96-111.

6193    CLARK, P. B.; GRUBEL, H. B. *National monetary sovereignty under different exchange rate regimes.* New York, New York University, Institute of Finance, 72, 49 p.

6194    CLESS, K. F."Über rechtliche Probleme bei Wechselkursänderungen" (The legal problems of the modifications of exchange rates), *Verwaltung* 6(3), 1973 : 363-374.

6195    DRABOWSKI, E. *Kursy walutowe w ekonomice wspólczesnego kapitalizmu* (Exchange rates in contemporary capitalist economics). Warszawa, Państwowe Wydawnictwo Naukowe, 72, 261 p.

6196    DUNN, R. M. Jr. *Exchange-rate rigidity, investment distortions, and the failure of Bretton Woods.* Princeton, N. J., International Finance Section, Princeton University, 73, 23 p.

6197    EASTMANN, H. C. "Impersonality in the foreign exchange market", *Canad. J. Econ.* 5(4), nov 72 : 471-485.

6198    FRIED, J. "Inflation—unemployment trade-offs under fixed and floating exchange rates", *Canad. J. Econ.* 6(1), feb 73 : 43-52.

6199    HOLMES, J. M. "Monetary and fiscal policies in a general equilibrium underemployment trade model under fixed exchange rates", *Int. econ. R.* 13(2), jun 72 : 386-398.

6200    LODDO, S. *Struttura dei cambi esteri e condotta del sistema bancario* (Structure of foreign exchange and the conduct of the banking system). Padova, CEDAM, 72, ix-198 p.

6201    MARTIRENA-MANTEL, A. M. "Política de intervención oficial en el mercado de cambio futuro: análisis de su estabilidad" (Policy of official intervention in the future exchange market: analysis of its stability), *Económica (La Plata)* 18(2), mai-aug 72 : 215-235.

6202    OBRADOVIC, S. D. "The problem of exchange rate flexibility", *Int. Probl. (Belgrade)* 1972 : 39-53.

6203    ROOS, F. DE. "Floating exchanges rates", *South Afr. J. Econ.* 41(2), jun 73 : 111-133.

6204    SACCHETTI, U. "Strumenti meccanico-discrezionali per variazioni di partità monetarie" (Mechanico-discretionary tools for variations in monetary parity), *Moneta e Cred.* 25(100), 4 trim 72 : 385-417. [Also published in English in: *Banca naz. Lav. quart. R.* 103, dec 72 : 364-395.]

6205    SHWAYDER, K. R. "Accounting for exchange rate fluctuations", *Accting R.* 47(4), oct 72 : 747-760.

6206    TOWER, E. "The short-run effects of monetary and fiscal policy under fixed and flexible exchange rates", *Econ. Record* 48(123), sep 72 : 411-423.

6207    WEISWEILLER, R. *Foreign exchange.* London, Allen and Unwin, 72, 3-132 p.

6208    WILLIAMS, H. R. "Exchange rate systems, the marginal efficiency of investment, and foreign direct capital investment", *Kyklos* 26(1), 1973 : 58-74.

6209    WILLIAMS, H. R. "Foreign exchange monetary effects of alternative exchange rate systems", *Econ. int. (Genova)* 25(3), aug 72 : 486-493.


O.2112    *International standards: gold problems*
          *Standards internationaux: problèmes de l'or*

6210    CARREAU, D. "L'or", *J. Dr. int.* 99(4), oct-dec 72 : 797-811.

6211    CHEN, C. "Bimetallism: theory and controversy in perspective", *Hist. polit. Econ.* 4(1), 1972 : 89-112.

6212    NIARCHOS, N. A.; GRANGER, C. W. "The gold sovereign market in Greece—an unusual speculative market", *J. Finance* 27(5), dec 72 : 1127-1135.

6213    "Oro y su futuro (El)" (Gold and its future), *R. Inform. econ. mund.* 249, apr-jun 73 :29-39.

6214    STUDENTOWICZ, K. *Perspektywy monetarne złota* (Monetary prospects of gold). Warszawa, Instytut Finansów, 73, 133 p.

6215    TITTA, A. "L'oro ed i problemi monetari internazionali" (Gold and international monetary problems), *Stato soc.* 17(6), jun 73 : 456-469.

6216    WILSON, E. M. "The gold standard and monetary reform", *South Afr. J. Econ.* 41(1), mar 73 : 17-26.

6217    ZOLOTAS, X. "L'or à la croisée des chemins des évènements monétaires internationaux", *R. Sci. écon.* 47(172), dec 72 : 185-193.

### O.2113   *Exchange markets, situation and rates*
           *Marchés des changes, situation et taux*

[See also / Voir aussi: 4171, 4332, 4334, 6255, 6605]

6218    ARGY, V.; HODJERA, Z. "Financial integration and interest rate linkages in industrial countries, 1958-1971", *Staff Pap.* 20(1), mar 73 : 1-77.

6219    ARGY, V.; PORTER, M. G. "The forward exchange market and the effects of domestic and external disturbances under alternative exchange rate systems", *Staff Pap.* 19(3), nov 72 : 503-532.

6220    ARNOULT, É.; LEMAIRE, J.-P. *Euro-émissions; nouvelles perspectives bancaires internationales.* Paris, Mame, 72, 299 p.

6221    BECSKY, Gy. "Az eurodeviza-piac" (The Euro-currency market), *Közgazd. Szle* 19(11), nov 72 : 1340-1357.

6222    COOPER, R. N. "Eurodollars, reserve dollars, and asymmetries in the international monetary system", *J. int. Econ.* 2(4), sep 72 : 326-344.

6223    CUTILLI, B. "Cambi oscillanti, sistema dell'euro-dollaro e politica monetaria" (Floating exchange rates, Euro-dollar systems and monetary policy), *Rass. econ. (Napoli)* 37(1), jan-feb 73 : 7-39.

6224    EDWARDS, S. "Soviet exchange rates: a study in disequilibrium", *Amer. Economist* 16(2), 1972 : 129-132.

6225    FORMUZIS, P. "The demand for Euro-dollars and the optimum stock of bank liabilities", *J. Money Cred. Bank.* 5(3), aug 73 : 806-818.

6226    GEHRMANN, D. "Vom Euro-Dollar-Markt zum EWG-Geldmarkt" (From Euro-dollar market to EEC money market), *Wirtsch.-Dienst* 51(5), mai 71 : 258-262.

6227    GIBSON, W. E. "The Eurodollar market and the foreign demand for liquid dollar assets: a comment", *J. Money Cred. Bank.* 4(3), aug 73 : 684-687.

6228    GISBERT, A.; SARTORIUS, J. *Eurodólares y eurobonos* (Euro-dollars and Eurobonds). Salamanca, Anaya, 72, 302 p.

6229    GRUBEL, H. G.; MORGAN, T. (eds.). *Exchange rate policy in Southeast Asia; papers.* Lexington, Mass., Lexington Books, 73, xxi-109 p.

6230    GRUNWALD, J.; SALAZAR-CARRILLO, J. *Economic integration, rates of exchange, and value comparisons in Latin America.* Washington, Brookings Institution, 72, 228-286 p.

6231    HIRSCH, F. "The exchange rate regime: an analysis and a possible scheme", *IMF Staff Pap.* 19(2), jul 72 : 259-295.

6232    HUDDLE, D. L. "O sistema brasileiro de taxas cambiais flutuantes. Sua eqüidade distributiva, suas relações com a inflação e sua eficiência" (The Brazilian system of floating exchange rates. Its distributive equity, its relations with inflation and its efficiency), *R. brasil. Econ.* 26(4), oct-dec 72 : 149-168.

6233    KEINATH, K. *Geldschöpfung auf dem Euro-Dollarmarkt* (Creation of money on the Euro-dollar market). Tübingen, Mohr, 73, 129 p.

6234    KOZIERKIEWICZ, R. "Rynek eurodolarowy" (The Euro-dollar market), *Finanse* (11), 1973 : 16-28.

6235    KRUBER, K. P. "Wechselkursfixierung—ein geeigneter Weg zur Europäischen Wirtschafts- und Währungsunion?" (Is fixing exchange rates a good solution for an economic and monetary union), *Z. Wirtsch.-u. soz.-Wiss.* 92(5), 1972 : 545-669.

6236    LEFF, N. H. "Modificaciones de los tipos reales de cambio como instrumento de política en la posguerra" (Modifications of the real types of exchange rates as a policy instrument in the postwar period), *Trim. econ.* 40(158), apr-jun 73 : 495-508.

6237    MAKIN, J. H. "Demand and supply functions for stocks and euro-dollar deposits: an empirical study", *R. Econ. Statist.* 54(4), nov 72 : 381-391.

6238   McClam, W. D. "Credit substitution and the Euro-currency market", *Banca naz. Lav. Quart. R.* 103, dec 72 : 323-363.

6239   Mc Clam, W. D. "Il mercato delle eurovalute come 'sostituto' di altre fonti di credito" (The Euro-currency market as a substitute for other credit sources), *Moneta e Cred.* 25(99), 3 trim 72 : 247-290.

6240   Mikesell, R. F. "The Eurodollar market and the foreign demand for liquid dollar assets", *J. Money Cred. Bank.* 4(3), aug 72 : 643-683.

6241   Mourgues, M. De. "Euro-dollar, inflation et système monétaire international", *Écon. et Soc.* 6(6-7), jun-jul 72 : 1273-1294.

6242   *Problemy finansowo-walutowe krajów RWPG* (Financial and currency problems of CMEA countries). Warszawa, Instytut Finansów, 73, 115 p.

6243   Readman, P.; Hoare, M.; Poole, D. *The European money puzzle*. London, Joseph, 73, 165 p.

6244   Rich, G. "A theoretical and empirical analysis of the Eurodollar market", *J. Money Cred. Bank.* 4(3), aug 72 : 616-635.

6245   Schön, S. *Les euro-obligations convertibles ou avec droit de souscription*. Genève, Éditions Médecine et hygiène, 72, vi-186-xv p.

6246   Torrel, R. "Le marché des eurodevises", *R. Écon. Gestion* 1(1), jun 72 : 77-113.

6247   Vinney, L. "Credit creation in the Eurodollar market", *Riv. int. Sci. econ. com.* 20(1), jan 73 : 33-47.

6248   Zabielski, K. "Kurs walutowy a system cen wewnętrznych w gospodarce socjalistycznej" (Exchanges rate and the system of internal prices in the socialist economy), *Finanse* (7), 1973 : 36-48.


O.213    *Methods of financing foreign trade*
         *Méthodes de financement du commerce international*

6249   Haschek, H. H. *Exportkreditgrantien und Exportfinanzierung in Österreich* (Export credit guarantees and export financing in Austria). Wien, Österreichische Kontrollbank, 72, various pagings.

6250   Lavigne, M. "Formes et modalités des subventions directes et indirectes à l'exportation dans les pays socialistes (le cas de la Pologne)", *C. écon. Bruxelles* 58, 2 trim 73 : 161-188.

6251   McKitterick, N. M.; Middletoh, B. J. *The bankers of the rich and the bankers of the poor: the role of export credit in development finance*. Washington, Overseas Development Council, 72, 58 p.

6253   Schnitzel, P. *The role of Euro-dollars in financing United States exports*. Emporia, Kansas State Teachers College, 72, 32 p.

6254   Swedenberg, H. "Exportens finansierung" (Export financing), *Ekon. R. (Stockholm)* 29(7), sep 72 : 306-313. [Sweden.]


O.22     **Balance of payments, balance of accounts**
         **Balance des paiements, balance des comptes**

O.221    *Balances of payments*
         *Balances des paiements*

O.2211   *Theory*
         *Théorie*

[See also / Voir aussi: 5584, 6352, 6437]

6255   Aghevli, B. B.; Borts, G. H. "The stability and equilibrium of the balance of payments under a fixed exchange rate", *J. int. Econ.* 3(1), feb 73 : 1-20.

6256   Berglas, E.; Razin, A. "A note on 'the balance of payments and the terms of trade in relation to financial controls' ", *R. econ. Stud.* 39(4), oct 72 : 511-513.

6257   Bochud, F. "Zur Problematik des Zahlungsbilanzgleichgewichtes" (Towards the problematic of the balance of payments equilibrium), *WIST* 2(1), jan 73 : 1-7.

6258 DASGUPTA, M. "Historical evolution of the concepts of surplus and deficit in the balance-of-payments", *Econ. Aff.* 17(3), mar 72 : 113-127.

6259 JOHNSON, H. G. "The monetary approach to balance-of-payments theory", *Intermountain econ. R.* 3(2), 1972 : 1-13.

6260 PURVIS, D. D. "More on growth and the balance-of-payments: the adjustment process", *Canad. J. Econ.* 5(4), nov 72 : 531-540.

6261 SELLEKAERTS, W.; SELLEKAERTS, B. "Balance-of-payments deficits, the adjustment cost and the optimum level of international reserves", *Weltwirtsch. Archiv* 109(1), 1973 : 1-17.

6262 STERN, R. M. *The balance-of-payments; theory and economic policy.* Chicago, Aldine, 73, xv-436 p.

### O.2212 Descriptive studies
### Études déscriptives

[See also / Voir aussi: 6323, 6514]

6263 BACH, C. L. "Foreign exchange and US balance-of-payments developments in 1972 and early 1973", *Fed. Reserve Bank St Louis* 55(4), apr 73 : 14-20.

6264 BACH, C. L. "US balance-of-payments problems and policies in 1971", *Fed. Reserve Bank St Louis* 54(4), apr 72 : 8-15.

6265 "Balance des paiements de la Côte d'Ivoire, année 1971", *Notes Inform. Statist. Banque centr. Afr. Ouest* 209, aug-sep 73 : 8 p.

6266 "Balance des paiements de la France en 1972 (La)", *Banque* 48(318), mai 73 : 439-442.

6267 "Balance des paiements entre la France et l'extérieur en 1971", *Statist. Ét. financ. Sér. bleue* 288, dec 72 : 210 p.

6268 "Balance des paiements entre la France et l''extérieur en 1972", *Statist. Ét. financ. Sér. rouge* 24(287), nov 72 : 2-17; 25(290), feb 73 : 1-16.

6269 "Balance des paiements extérieurs de la Haute-Volta. Années 1968 à 1971", *Notes Inform. Statist. Banque centr. Afr. Ouest* 208, jul 73 : 8 p.

6270 BARTOLOMEI, J. A. *Balance des paiements et politique monétaire. L'expérience allemande entre 1958 et 1968.* Louvain-Bruxelles, Vander, 72, x-107 p.

6271 "Developments in the US balance-of-payments", *Fed. Reserve B.* 59(4), apr 73 : 243-256.

6272 FRIED, E. R. "The military and the balance-of-payments", *A. Amer. Acad. polit. soc. Sci.* 406, mar 73 : 80-85. [USA.]

6273 LAL, D. "A suggested balance-of-payments policy for less developed countries, with particular reference to India", *Econ. int. (Genova)* 25(3), aug 72 : 459-477.

6274 MAKEEVA, N. P. *Platežnye balansy razvivajuščihsja stran Azii* (Balances-of-payments of the Asian developing countries). Moskva, Nauka, 73, 192 p.

6275 MILLER, E.; SMITH, G. P. "International travel, passenger fares and other transportation in the US balance-of-payments: 1972", *Survey curr. Busin.* 53(6), jun 73 : 12-16.

6276 NOWOTNY, E. "Die kurzfristige Effizienz des aussenwirtschaftlichen Instrumentariums im Bezug auf die amerikanische Zahlungsbilanz—eine priestheoretische Analyse" (The short term efficiency of foreign trade on the American balance-of-payment—an analysis according to price theory), *Aussenwirtschaft (St Gallen)* 27(4), dec 72 : 403-433.

6277 O'HAGAN, J.; NEARY, H. "EEC entry and Ireland's balance-of-payments", *Centr. Bank Ireland quart. B.* (3), 1972 : 116-123.

6278 PARRISH, E. M. "US balance of payments developments: fourth quarter and year 1972", *Survey curr. Busin.* 53(3), mar 73 : 22-44.

6279 PRAET, P. "L'équilibre de la balance des paiements: objectifs-réalisations", *C. écon. Bruxelles* 56, 4 trim 72 : 567-597. [Dans 6 pays de la CEE, le Royaume-Uni et les États-Unis.]

6280 ROBICHEK, E. W.; SANSÓN, C. E. "The balance-of-payments performance of Latin America and the Caribbean, 1966-1970", *IMF Staff Pap.* 19(2), jul 72 : 286-343.

6281 SCHUMANN, C. G. W. "Notes on the balance-of-payments of South Africa", *South Afr. int. Quart.* 3(3), jan 73 : 136-146.

6282 SHENOY, B. R. "Errors and omissions in India's balance-of-payments", *Politico* 37(4), dec 72 : 759-777.

6283    SLIGHTON, R. L.; CHU, D. S. C.; COOPER, R. V. L. *The effect of untied development loans on the US balance-of-payments.* Santa Monica, Calif., Rand, 72, xi-92 p.

6284    TAYLOR, L. "Money, the balance-of-payments and income determination in Jamaica, 1950-1970", *Soc. econ. Stud.* 21(2), jun 72 : 171-183.

6285    "Zahlungsbilanz der Bundesrepublik im Jahre 1972 (Die)" (Germany FR's balance-of-payments in 1972), *Monatsber. dtschen Bundesbank* 25(7), jul 73 : 22-33.


O.2213    *Monetary reserves: dollar gap*
          *Réserves monétaires: pénurie de dollar*

[See also / Voir aussi: 6261]

6286    FRATIANNI, M. *La liquidità internazionale* (International liquidity). Bologna, Il Mulino, 72, 185 p.

6287    GRUBEL, H. G. "The demand for international reserves: a critical review of the literature", *J. econ. Liter.* 9(4), dec 71 : 1148-1166.

6288    GUPTA, R. D. *International liquidity; problems, appraisals, and perspectives.* New Delhi S. Chand, 72, xvi-385 p.

6289    KOZIERKIEWICZ, R. "Niektóre problemy ustalania optymalnych rezerw dewizowych" (Some problems of establishing optimum foreign exchange reserves), *Stud. finans.* 14, 1973 : 161-249.

6290    WILLIAMSON, J. "Surveys in applied economics: international liquidity", *Econ. J.* 83(331), sep 73 : 685-746.


O.222    **Balance of accounts and international capital movements**
         **Balance des comptes et mouvements internationaux de capital**

O.2221    *Theory*
          *Théorie*

[See also / Voir aussi: 6187]

6291    ANTIER, D. "Recherche d'une schématisation des mouvements internationaux de capitaux à court terme", *Statist. Ét. financ. Sér. orange* 3(12), 4 trim 73 : 25-55.

6292    BECHLER, E. *Zur güterwirtschaftlichen Theorie der internationalen Kapitalbewegungen* (A contribution to the economic theory of international capital movements). Bern, Herbert Lang; Frankfurt-am-Main, Peter Land, 72, x-264 p.

6293    "Capitaux internationaux, intégration et croissance", *Écon. et Soc.* 6(6-7), jun-jul 72 : 1205-1460.

6294    CZERWIENIEC, E. "O niektórych czynnikach wpływajacych na międzynarodowe przepływy kapitałów" (On some factors influencing international flows of capital), *Zesz. nauk. wyższ. Szkoły ekon. Poznan.* 44, 1972 : 55-74.

6295    MACHLUP, F.; SALANT, W. S.; TARSHIS, L. (eds.). *International mobility and movement of capital.* New York, Columbia University Press, 72, xii-708 p.

6296    "Mouvements internationaux de capitaux privés à long terme (Les)", *R. écon. Banque nat. Paris* 25, jan 73 : 13-22.

6297    ROGGERO FOSSATI, G. *I movimenti internazionali di capitale* (International capital movements). Milano, A. Giuffrè, 72, 152 p.

6298    RUTKOWSKI, J. *Eksport kapitala* (Capital export). Warszawa, Państwowe Wydawnictwo Naukowe, 72, 324 p.

6299    SHEARER, R. A. "A critical note on two sectors of the financial flow accounts", *Canad. J. Econ.* 5(4), nov 72 : 541-553.


O.2222    *Descriptive studies*
          *Études déscriptives*

[See also / Voir aussi: 6248]

6300    ARCHALL, J. L.; ENNERY, S. "Programme commun et anarchie des mouvements de capitaux", *Écon. et Polit.* 222-223, jan-feb 73 : 61-80. [France.]

6301   DOLGORUKOV, P. D. "Novye tendencii v eksporte kapitala iz Japonii" (New tendencies in the capital exports from Japan), *B. Inostr. kommerč. Inform. Prilož.* (5), 1972 : 3-33.

6302   PRIESTER, H. *Kurzfristige zwischenstaatliche Kapitalbewegungen in der Bundesrepublik Deutschland 1969-1970; eine theoretische und empirische Analyse* (Short-term capital movements between states in the German Federal Republic, 1969-1970; a theoretical and empirical analysis). Berlin, Duncker und Humblot, 72, 216 p.

6303   "Restriktionen im internationalen Zahlungsverkehr wichtiger Industriestaaten (Die)" (Restrictive measures taken by the main industrialized countries with regard to international capital movements), *Aussenwirtschaft (St Gallen)* 28(1-2), mar-jun 73 : 5-130.

6304   SPOONER, F. C. *The international economy and monetary movements in France, 1493-1725.* 2nd rev. ed. Cambridge, Mass., Harvard University Press; London, Oxford University Press, 72, vii-354 p. CR: M. WILFE, *J. econ. Liter.* 11(2), jun 73 : 546-548.

## O.2223   *International investments*
*Investissements internationaux*

[See also / Voir aussi: 5598, 5944, 6088, 6629]

6305   AUSTRALIA. Department of the Treasury. *Overseas investment in Australia: May, 1972.* Canberra, Australian Government Publishing Service, 72, 149 p.

6306   BALLON, R. J.; LEE, E. H. (eds.). *Foreign investment and Japan.* Palo Alto, Calif.-Tokyo, Sophia University, 72, xviii-340 p.

6307   BANDERA, V. N.; CASEY, W. L. "Perspectives on US investments in Europe", *Marquette Busin. R.* 16(1), 1972 : 35-43.

6308   BEJARANO, J. A. *El capital monopolista y las inversiones privadas norteamericanas en Colombia* (Monopoly capital and private North American investments in Colombia). Bogotá, La Oveja Negra, 72, 116 p.

6309   BERGO, J. "Direkte investeringer fra utlandet" (Direct investment from abroad), *Int. Polit. (Bergen)* (2), apr-jun 72 : 236-250. [Norway.]

6310   BERTERO, C. O. "Principais tendências do investimento direto norte-americano na América latina" (Main tendencies of direct North American investments in Latin America), *R. Adm. Emprêsas* 12(4), dec 72 : 6-23.

6311   BODDEWYN, J. J.; GROSSER, D. D. "American direct investment in Italy. Distribution, profitability and contributions", *R. econ. Condit. Italy* 26(5), sep 72 : 362-378.

6312   BRUNS, G. "Restricting foreign investment in Australia", *Round Table* 251, jul 73 : 391-401.

6313   CAMACHO GUIZADO, A. *Capital extranjero: subdesarrollo colombiano* (Foreign capital: Colombian underdevelopment). Bogotá, Punta de Lanza, 72, 143 p.

6314   DOIMI DI DELUPIS, I. *Finance and protection of investments in developing countries.* Epping, Gower Press, 73, x-183 p.

6315   DRYSDALE, P. (ed.). *Direct foreign investment in Asia and the Pacific.* Canberra, Australian National University Press, 72, xiii-360 p.

6316   EKBLOM, H. E. "European direct investments in the United States", *Harvard Busin. R.* 51(4), jul-aug 73 : 16-26.

6317   FIDEL, J. "Antecedentes y perspectivas de la inversión extranjera y la comercialización de la tecnología. El caso argentino" (Antecedents and perspectives of foreign investment and the commercialization of technology; the Argentine case), *Desarr. econ.* 13(50), jul-sep 73 : 285-314.

6318   FIRST, R.; STEELE, J.; GURNEY, C. *The South African connection: Western investment in apartheid.* London, Maurice Temple Smith Ltd, 72, 352 p.

6319   GARNIER, G. "Les investissements directs du Canada à l'étranger", *Actual. écon.* 49(2), apr-jun 73 : 211-235.

6320   GRAY, H. P. *The economics of business investment abroad.* London, Macmillan; New York, Russak, 72, xii-249 p.

6321   GRAY, H. P. *Foreign direct investment in Canada.* Ottawa, Information Canada, 72, xi-523 p. CR: V. N. BANDERA, *J. econ. Liter.* 11(3), sep 73 : 946-947.

6322   GREEN, R. T. *Political instability as a determinant of US foreign investment.* Austin, Bureau of Business Research, University of Texas at Austin, 72, xv-122 p.

6323 HAUBOLD, D. *Direktinvestitionen und Zahlungsbilanzen; Wirkungen der US-Investitionen in Europa auf die amerikanische Zahlungsbilanz* (Direct investments and balance of payments: effects of US investments in Europe on the American balance of payments). Hamburg, Verlag Weltarchiv, 72, 326 p.

6324 HELLMANN, R. "Investimenti diretti internazionali e accordi monetari di Washington" (International direct investments and the Washington monetary agreements), *Moneta e Cred.* 25(99), 3 trim 72 : 341-348.

6325 HEMMER, H.-R. "Die Bedeutung ausländischer Direktinvestitionen für die wirtschaftliche Entwicklung der Dritten Welt" (The importance of foreign investment for the economic development of the Third World), *Z. Wirtsch.-u. soz.-Wiss.* 92(2), 1972 : 155-167.

6326 HERRING, R.; WILLETT, T. "The relationship between US direct investment at home and abroad", *Riv. int. Sci. econ. com.* 20(1), jan 73 : 72-82.

6327 HUMPHREY, D. H. "Private foreign investment in Malawi: a study of the sugar corporation of Malawi", *Afr. R.* 2(3), jan 72 : 283-298.

6328 *Investissement privé, étranger et national, en République du Zaïre (L').* Bruxelles, Centre de recherche et d'information socio-politiques, 72, 63 l.

6329 KAPOOR, A.; COTTEN, J. E. *Foreign investments in Asia; a survey of problems and prospects in the 1970s.* Princeton, N. J., Darwin Press, 72, xvii-198 l.

6330 KILLICK, T. "The benefits of foreign direct investment and its alternatives: an empirical exploration", *J. Develop. Stud.* 9(2), jan 73 : 301-316.

6331 KOLESOV, V. P. "Inostrannyj kapital i bor'ba razvivajuščihsja stran za ekonomičeskuju nezavisimosti" (Foreign capital and the struggle of developing countries for their economic independence), *Vestn. Moskov. Univ. Ser. Ėkon.* 28(3), mai-jun 73 : 13-23.

6332 KRÄGENAU, H. "Direktinvestitionen in der Dritten Welt" (Direct investments in the Third World), *Wirtsch.-Dienst* 52(9), sep 72 : 471-474.

6333 KRETSCHMAR, R. S. Jr.; FOOR, R. *The potential for joint ventures in Eastern Europe.* New York, Praeger, 72, xxvi-153 p.

6334 KWACK, S. Y. "A model of US direct investment abroad: a neoclassical approach", *West. econ. J.* 10(4), dec 72 : 376-383.

6335 LADENSON, M. L. "A dynamic balance-sheet approach to American direct foreign investment", *Int. econ. R.* 13(3), oct 72 : 531-543.

6336 LAU, S. F. *The Chilean response to foreign investment.* New York, Praeger, 72, xx-118 p.

6337 LEFTWICH, R. B. "Foreign direct investments in the United States, 1962-1971", *Surv. curr. Busin.* 53(2), feb 73 : 29-40.

6338 LEVIN, M. *et al. Foreign ownership.* Don Mills, Ontario, PaperJacks, A division of General Publishing Co., 72, 109 p. [US investments in Canada.]

6339 LITVAK, I. A.; MAULE, C. J. "Japan's overseas investments", *Pacific Aff.* 46(2), 1973 : 254-268.

6340 MACKLER, I. *Pattern for profit in southern Africa.* Lexington, Mass., Lexington Books, 72, xv-100 p.

6341 MARAIS, J. S. "Les investissements en Afrique du Sud", *Monde mod.* (2), 1972 : 129-138.

6342 MIHAJLOVA, Z. M. *Inostrannyj kapital v sovremennoj Indonezii, 1966-1971* (Foreign capital in contemporary Indonesia, 1966-1971). Moskva, Nauka, 73, 159 p.

6343 MORAN, T. H. "Foreign expansion as an 'institutional necessity' for US corporate capitalism: the search for a radical model", *Wld Polit.* 25(3), apr 73 : 369-386.

6344 NGANGO, G. *Les investissements d'origine extérieure en Afrique noire francophone: statut et incidence sur le développement.* Paris, Présence africaine, 73, 451 p.

6345 ORGANIZATION FOR ECONOMIC COOPERATION AND DEVELOPMENT. *Investing in developing countries; facilities for the promotion of foreign private invesment in developing countries.* Paris, OECD, 72, 110 p.

6346 PAPANEK, G. F. "Aid, foreign private investment, savings and growth in less developed countries", *J. polit. Econ.* 81(1), jan-feb 73 : 120-130.

6347 RAGAZZI, G. "Theories of the determinants of direct foreign investment", *Staff Pap.* 20(2), jul 73 : 471-498.

6348 RASADI, A. A. *Inostrannij kapital v Irane posle vtoroj mirovoj vojny 1945-1967 gg.* (Foreign capital in Iran after the Second World War, 1945-1967). Moskva, Nauka, 73, 119 p.

6349 ROTSTEIN, A.; LAX, G. (eds.). *Independence: the Canadian challenge.* Toronto, Committee for an Independent Canada, 72, xii-279 p.

6350 SAFARIAN, A. E. "Perspectives on foreign direct investment from the viewpoint of a capital receiving country", *J. Finance* 28(2), mai 73 : 419-438.

6351 SCHARRER, H. E. (ed.). *Förderung privater Direktinvestitionen; eine Untersuchung der Massnahmen bedeutender Industrieländer* (Stimulation of direct private investments; a study of private measures by major industrial countries). Hamburg, Verlag Welt-archiv, 72, xxi-633 p.

6352 SCHUSTER, H. "Direktinvestitionen und Zahlungsbilanz in Entwicklungsländern" (Direct investments and balance of payments in developing countries), *Z. Wirtsch.-u. soz.-Wiss.* 93(2), 1973 : 191-196.

6353 SECCHI, C. "Considerazioni critiche sull'analisi degli effetti degli investimenti esteri diretti nei paesi sottosviluppati" (Critical considerations on the analysis of the effects of foreign investments in underdeveloped countries), *Riv. int. Sci. econ. com.* 19(10), oct 72 : 971-980.

6354 SMETS, P. "La pratique belge en matière de protection bilatérale des investissements privés étrangers", *R. belge Dr. int.* 9(1), 1973 : 28-50.

6355 SOLAUN, M.; CEPEDA, F. "Political and legal challenges to foreign direct investment in Colombia", *J. inter-Amer. Stud.* 15(1), feb 73 : 77-101.

6356 STANLEY, M. I.; STANLEY, J. D. "The impact of US regulation of foreign investment", *Calif. Manag. R.* 15(2), 1972 : 56-64.

6357 SUBRAHMANIAN, K. K. *Import of capital and technology; a study of foreign collaborations in Indian industry.* New Delhi, People's Publishing House, 72, vii-248 p.

6358 SUNKEL, O. *Capitalismo transnacional y desintegración nacional en América Latina* (Transnational capitalism and national disintegration in Latin America). Buenos Aires, Ediciones Nueva Visión, 72, 85 p.

6359 THOMAN, G. R. *Foreign investment and regional development; the theory and practice of investment incentives, with a case study of Belgium.* New York, Praeger, 73, xiii-148 p.

6360 VERNON, R. "US direct investment in Canada: consequences for the US economy", *J. Finance* 28(2), mai 73 : 407-417.

**O.2224** *Foreign debt and credit*
*Dette et crédit extérieurs*

6361 BADE, R. "Optimal growth and foreign borrowing with restricted mobility of foreign capital", *Int. econ. R.* 13(3), oct 72 : 544-552.

6362 DONNELLY, J. T. "External financing and short-term consequences of external debt servicing for Brazilian economic development, 1947-1968", *J. Develop. Areas* 7(3), apr 73 : 411-430.

6363 HORN, N. *Das Recht der internationalen Anleihen* (Lesiglation on international loans). Frankfurt-am-Main, Athenäum, 72, xxvi-572 p.

6364 LIPIŃSKA, A. "Ekonomiczne znaczenie kosztów kredytów srednio i długoterminowych" (The economic importance of the cost of foreign long and medium term credits), *Handel zagran.* (8), 1973 : 259-264.

6365 RHEE, H. Y. "Optimal foreign debt for a developing country", *Amer. Economist* 16(2), 1972 : 94-100.

**O.23** **Monetary policies, monetary areas**
**Politiques et zones monétaires**

**O.231** *Convertibility and multilateralism*
*Convertibilité et multi-latéralisme*

[See also / Voir aussi: 6235]

6366 DEHEM, R. "Le mirage monétaire européen, son coût et ses aléas", *Rech. écon. Louvain* 37(3), sep 72 : 257-266.

6367 FERNANDEZ DE CASTRO, J. "Sobre la teoría de las áreas monetarias óptimas" (On the theory of optimal monetary areas), *Cuad. Econ. (Barcelona)* 1(1), jan-jun 73 : 27-45.

6368 GEHRMAN, D.; HARMSEN, S. (eds.). *Monetäre Integration in der EWG: Dokumente und Bibliographie* (Monetary integration in the EEC: documents and bibliography). Hamburg, Verlag Weltarchiv, 72, 290 p.

291

6369   HANKEL, W. "Europäische Währungsintegration und Reform des internationalen Währungssystems" (European monetary integration and the reform of the international monetary system), *Europa-Archiv* 27(2), jan 10, 72 : 37-43.

6370   HELLMANN, R. (ed.). *Europäische Wirtschafts- und Währungsunion; eine Dokumentation* (European economic and monetary union: a document). Baden-Baden, Nomos Verlagsgesellschaft, 72, 358 p.

6371   INGRAM, J. C. *The case for European monetary integration.* Princeton, N. J., International Finance Section, Princeton University, 73, 33 p.

6372   MAGNIFICO, G. *European monetary unification.* London, Macmillan; New York, Wiley, 73, xvii-227 p.

6373   MARKOWSKI, S. "Money in international communist economics", *Yb. Wld Aff.* 27, 1973 : 257-276.

6374   MCKINNON, R. I. "On securing a common monetary policy in Europe", *Banca naz. Lav. Quart. R.* 104, mar 73 : 3-20.

6375   REITSMA, A. J. "De monetaire crisis, het vraagstuk van het optimale valuta-areaal en de Europese monetaire unie" (The monetary crisis, the problem of optimal currency areas and European monetary union), *Economist (Haarlem)* 120(2), mar-apr 72 : 153-174.

6376   VLERICK, A. "Die europäische Währungsunion" (The European monetary union), 27(22), nov 25, 72 : 757-766.

6377   WYSOCKI, J. 'Währungsunion und Integrationsdynamik" (Monetary union and the dynamics of integration), *Aussenpolitik* 23(12), dec 72 : 718-725.


O.232    *Monetary policies: devaluation, exchange control, specific measures*
         *Politiques monétaires: dévaluation, contrôle des changes, mesures particulières*

O.2320   *General studies*
         *Études générales*

[See also / Voir aussi: 6375]

6378   BENDER, D. *Abwertung und gesamtwirtschaftliches Gleichgewicht* (The devaluation and overall economic equilibrium). Berlin, Duncker und Humblot, 72, 198 p.

6379   BOTHA, D. J. "Some thoughts on devaluation", *South Afr. J. Econ.* 40(3), sep 72 : 197-208.

6380   DORNBUSCH, R. "Devaluation, money, and nontraded goods", *Amer. econ. R.* 63(5), dec 73 : 871-880.

6381   HOWLE, E. S. "On revaluations versus devaluations", *Amer. econ. R.* 63(5), dec 73 : 918-928.


O.2321   *Monetary areas*
         *Zones monétaires*

O.23211  Sterling

6382   COHEN, B. J. "The future role of sterling", *Nat. Westminster Bank quart. R.* mai 73 : 6-19.

6383   COOPER, R. N. *Sterling, European monetary unification, and the international monetary system.* Washington, D.C., National Planning Association, 72, x-34 p.


O.23212  Dollar

6384   ASCHINGER, F. "Die Zukunft des Dollars und der EWG-Währungen" (The future of the dollar and of the EEC monies), *Aussenwirtschaft (St Gallen)* 27(4), dec 72 : 376-391.

6385   "Costs and benefits of the dollar as a reserve currency (The)", *Amer. econ. R.* 63(2), mai 73 *Pap. and Proc.*: 189-214. With contributions by: P. B. KENEN, P. W. MC-CRACKEN, J. HELLIWELL, and H. R. HELLER.

6386   EINZIG, P. *The destiny of the dollar.* London, Macmillan; New York, St Martin's Press, 72, viii-196 p.

6387    FINK, W. H. "Dollar surplus and devaluation", *Riv. int. Sci. econ. com.* 20(7), jul 73 : 625-639.

6388    GHOSH, U. N. "The dollar politics", *Econ. Aff.* 17(1-2), jan-feb 72 : 92-100.

6389    GÖNCÖL, Gy. "A pénz az imperializmusban (a dollár-válság jelentösége)" (Money in imperialism; the meaning of the dollar crisis), *Közgazd. Szle* 20(7-8), jul-aug 73 : 761-784.

6390    JALAKAS, R. *Dollarns kris och världens betalnings-system* (Dollars crisis and the international monetary system). Stockholm, Utrikespolitiska instutet, 72, 32 p.

6391    MANDEL, E. *Decline of the dollar; a Marxist view of the monetary crisis.* New York, Monad Press and Pathfinder Press, 72, 128 p.

6392    MELTZER, A. H. "The dollar as an international money", *Banca naz. Lav. Quart. R.* 104, mar 73 : 21-28. [Also published in Italian in: *Moneta e Cred.* 26(101-102), mar-jun 73 : 22-29.]

6393    STRANGE, S. "The dollar crisis 1971", *Int. Aff. (London)* 48(2), apr 72 : 191-216.

6394    ZANNI, A. "La misurazione delle riserve internazionali e l'alternative tra la svalutazione del dollaro e la rivalutazione del dollaro e la rivalutazione delle altre monete" (The measurement of international reserves and the alternative between dollar devaluation and the reevaluation of other moneys), *Riv. Polit. econ.* 63(1), jan 73 : 3-43.

### O.23213    French franc
Franc

6395    "Zone franc en 1971 (La)", *Statist. Ét. financ. Sér. bleue* 25(293), mai 73 : 295 p.

### O.23215    Ruble
Rouble

6396    REESE, K. "The Soviet Ruble and Comecon countries", *South Afr. J. Econ.* 41(2), jun 73 : 134-145.

### O.2322    *Specific countries*
*Pays particuliers*

[See also / Voir aussi: 6394, 6587]

6397    BHAGWATI, J. *et al.* "Political response to the 1966 devaluation. II. Politicians and parties. III. The press, business groups and economists", *Econ. polit. Wkly* 7(36), sep 72 : 1835-1836; 7(37), sep 72 : 1883-1892; 7(38), sep 72 : 1933. [India.]

6398    BLADES, D. W. "Devaluation and the direction of Malawi's import trade", *East. Afr. econ. R.* 4(1), jun 72 : 63-70.

6399    FRY, M. J.; ILKIN, S. "Devaluation of the Turkish lira", *Turk. Yb. int. Relat.* (9), 1968 : 82-95.

6400    JOVANOVSKI, T. "Kon stabilen i konvertibilen dinar" (Towards stability and convertibility of the dinar), *Godiš. ekon. Fak. (Skopje)* 15, 1971 : 203-229. [Yugoslavia.]

6401    MONROE, W. F. "Management of the yen: the 1971 currency crisis", *J. Wld Trade Law* 6(6), nov-dec 72 : 693-702.

6402    VAN DEN ADEL, M. *Geldentwertung und monetäre Stabilisirungspolitik: eine ökonometrische Studie für die BRD* (Devaluation and monetary stabilization policy; an econometric study for the German Federal Republic). Berlin, Duncker und Humblot, 73, 187 p.

6403    WONNACOTT, G. P. *The floating Canadian dollar. Exchange flexibility and monetary independence.* Washington, D.C., American Enterprise Institute for Public Policy Research, 72, 95 p.

6404    YASER, B. S. *Economic aspects of the devaluation of the Turkish lira of August 10, 1970.* Ankara, Economic Analysis Staff, Agency for International Development, 72, vi-76 l.

### O.24   International monetary relations
### Relations monétaires internationales

#### O.241   *Institutions (IMF, IBRD, EPU, etc.)*
#### *Institutions (FMI, BIRD, UEP, etc.)*

[See also / Voir aussi: 6226, 6620]

6405   CABRERA, H. H. "El Banco centroamericano de integración económica" (The Central American Bank for Economic Integration), *Foro int.* 13(4), apr-jun 73 : 469-489.

6406   CHADENET, B.; KING, J. A. "What is 'a World Bank project'?", *Finance and Develop.* 9(3), sep 72 : 2-12.

6407   DELL, S. S. *The Inter-American Development Bank. A study in development financing.* New York, F. A. Praeger, 72, xvi-255 p. CR: J. E. ZINSER, *J. econ. Liter.* 11(3), sep 73 : 947-948.

6408   GRUBEL, H. G. "Basic methods for distributing Special Drawing Rights and the problem of international aid", *J. Finance* 27(5), dec 72 : 1009-1022.

6409   HIRSCH, F. *An SDR standard: impetus, elements, and impediments.* Princeton, N. J., International Finance Section, Princeton University, 73, 29 p.

6410   HOWE, J. W.; JOHNSON, H. G.; WEXLER, I. "SDR's £ development: $ 10 billion for whom?", *For. Pol.* (8), 1972 : 102-128.

6411   INTERNATIONAL BANK FOR RECONSTRUCTION AND DEVELOPMENT. *World Bank operations; sectoral programs and policies.* Washington, IBRD, 72, xiii-513 p.

6412   ISSING, O. "Sonderziehungsrechte als Instrument der Entwicklungshilfe?" (Are the Special Drawing Rights tools of aid to development?), *Wirtsch.-Dienst* 51(5), mai 71 : 253-257.

6413   JONES, E. "The Fund and the GATT", *Finance and Develop.* 9(3), sep 72 : 30-33.

6414   KAMARCK, A. M. "The allocation of aid by the World Bank group", *Finance and Develop.* 9(3), sep 72 : 22-24.

6415   LAVUT, A. A. "Mezamerinskij bank razvitija" (Inter-American Development Bank), *Latin.-Amer.* (3), mai-jun 73 : 109-121.

6416   LINNAINMAA, H. T. *Sev-maiden pankit MBES ja MIB* (MBES and MIB, the banks of CMEA countries). Helsinki, Ulkopoliittinen instituutti, 73, 35 p.

6417   LOFTUS, M. F. "The International Monetary Fund, 1968-1971: a selected bibliography", *IMF Staff Pap.* 19(1), mar 72 : 174-258.

6418   MASON, E. S.; ASHER, R. E. *The World Bank since Bretton Woods; the origins, policies, operations, and impact of the International Bank for Reconstruction and Development and the other members of the World Bank group.* Washington, Brookings Institution, 73, xxiii-915 p.

6419   MAYNARD, G. *Special drawing rights and development aid.* Washington, Overseas Development Council, 72, 45 p.

6420   MORAWITZ, R. "Der Europäische Fonds für währungspolitische Zusammenarbeit" (The European Monetary Cooperation Fund), *Europa-Archiv* 27(19), oct 10, 72 : 663-673.

6421   PICHLER-STAINERN, H. "Über die Struktur und Funktion der Asian Development Bank" (The structures and the functions of the Asian Development Bank), *Int. Asien Forum* 3(4), oct 72 : 598-603.

6422   SELIHOV, È. I. *Meždunarodnye banki i bankovskie gruppirovki* (International banks and banking groups). Moskva, Mysl', 73, 286 p.

6423   STRATMANN, G. *Der Internationale Währungsfonds; seine Aufsichts- und Lenkungsbefugnisse* (The International Monetary Fund; its competence in the area of control and orientation). Göttingen, Institut für Völkerrecht der Universität Göttingen, 72, 1-328 p.

6424   UCHEGBU, P. E. A. "The Caribbean Development Bank: implications for integration", *J. Wld Trade Law* 7(5), sep-oct 73 : 568-586.

6425   VAHRUŠEV, V. V. "Mezdunarodnyj valjutnyj fond i razirvajuščiesja strany" (The International Monetary Fund and the developing countries), *Latin. Amer.* (5), sep-oct 73 : 46-60.

6426   WHITE, J. *Regional development banks. The Asian, African and Inter-American Development banks.* New York-London, Praeger, 72, vii-204 p.

**O.243** *Agreements*
*Accords*

6427 Ross, L. W. "The Washington monetary agreement", *Yb. Wld Aff.* 26, 1972 : 203-217.


**O.3** **FOREIGN TRADE**
**COMMERCE EXTÉRIEUR**

**O.31** **Theory**
**Théorie**

**O.310** *General studies*
*Études générales*

6428 BALCEROWICZ, L. "Aktywne oddziaływanie handly zagranicznego na gospodarkę narodową" (Active impact of foreign trade on the national economy), *Zesz. nauk. Szkoły główn. Plan. Statyst.* 91, 1973 : 33-52.

6429 BASILE, A. *Commerce extérieur et développement de la petite nation. Essai sur les contraintes de l'exiguité économique.* Beyrouth, Université libanaise; Genève, Droz, 72, xxii-397 p.

6430 BATRA, R. N. *Studies in the pure theory of international trade.* London, Macmillan, 73, xiii-355 p.

6431 BATRA, R. N.; CASAS, F. R. "Intermediate products and the pure theory of international trade: a neo-Heckscher-Ohlin framework", *Amer. econ. R.* 63(3), jun 73 : 297-311.

6432 BHAGWATI, J. (ed.). *International trade.* Harmondsworth, Penguin Books, 72, 414 p.

6433 BHAGWATI, J. N. "The Heckscher-Ohlin theorem in the multi-commodity case", *J. polit. Econ.* 80(5), sep-oct 72 : 1052-1055.

6434 BOŻYK, P. (ed.). *Handel międzynarodowy* (International trade). Warszawa, Szkoła Główna Planowania i Statystyki, 73, 336 p.

6435 BOŻYK, P.; MACIEJEWSKI, W.; PIASZCZYŃSKI, W. *Modele prognoz handlu międzynarodowego* (Forecasting of international trade). Warszawa, Państwowe Wydawnictwo Naukowe, 73, 209-2 p.

6436 CASAS, G. "International trade and economic growth in the presence of factor market distortions", *Amer. Economist* 16(1), 1972 : 112-119.

6437 CAVES, R. E.; JONES, R. W. *World trade and payments; an introduction.* Boston, Little, Brown, 73, xv-574 p.

6438 CHACHOLIADES, M. *The pure theory of international trade.* Chicago, Aldine, 73, xvii-451 p.

6439 CHINOWSKI, K.; SZEWORSKI, A. "Handel zagraniczny jako element nowej strategii rozwoju" (Foreign trade as a factor of new development strategy), *Handel zagran.* (5-6), 1973 : 161-165.

6440 CONNOLLY, M. B.; SWOBODA, A. K. (eds.). *International trade and money.* Toronto-Buffalo, University of Toronto Press; London, Allen and Unwin, 73, 3-264 p.

6441 CRETU, L. *Modalitati de determinare a rentabilitatii comertului exterior* (Modalities for determining foreign trade profitability). Bucuresti, Editura politica, 72, 252 p.

6442 DEGREVE, D. "De la correspondance d'une théorie à l'interprétation des données: la théorie pure du commerce international et les statistiques belges du commerce extérieur", *R. Inst. Sociol.* 45(2), 1972 : 259-303.

6443 ETHIER, W. "Nontraded goods and the Heckscher-Ohlin model", *Int. econ. R.* 13(1), feb 72 : 132-147.

6444 FLØYSTAD, G. "Real wages, factor prices and gain from international trade", *Int. econ. R.* 13(1), feb 72 : 65-84.

6445 HELLEINER, G. K. *International trade and economic development.* Harmondsworth, Penguin, 72, 164 p.

6446 HOLZMAN, F. D. "La théorie du commerce extérieur des économies centralement planifiées", *R. Est* 3(3), jul 72 : 5-36.

6447 HUETH, D.; SCHMITZ, A. "Trade in intermediate and final goods", *Quart. J. Econ.* 83(3), aug 72 : 351-365.

6448 "International trade", *Amer. econ. R.* 63(2), mai 73 *Pap. and Proc.*: 412-427. With contributions by H. B. JUNZ, R. R. RHOMBER, J. N. BHAGWATI and A. O. KRUEGER.

6449 KEMP, M. C.; WAN, H. Y. "The gains from free trade", *Int. econ. R.* 13(3), oct 72 : 509-522.

6450 KOVAČEVIĆ, M. "Teorija spoljne trgovine vis-à-vis empirijskih istrazivanja" (Theory of foreign trade facing empirical research), *Medun. Probl.* 24(2), apr-jun 72 : 37-51.

6451 ŁADYKA, S.; ŁODYKOWSKI, T. *Handel miedzynarodowy i zegluga morksa w gospodarce swiatowej* (International trade and maritime shipping in world economy). Warszawa, Państwowe Wydawnictwo Ekonomiczne, 73, 496 p.

6452 LUCAS, R. E. Jr. "Some international evidence on output-inflation tradeoffs", *Amer. econ. R.* 63(3), jun 73 : 326-334.

6453 MAYOBRE, J. A. "Comercio internacional y desarrollo económico" (International trade and economic development), *R. Econ. latinoamer.* 9(33), 1972 : 53-62.

6454 PABLO, J. C. DE. "El comercio de bienes intermedios en la teoria pura del comercio internacional" (The trade of intermediate goods in the pure theory of international trade), *Trim. econ.* 39(156), oct-dec 72 : 717-725.

6455 PABLO, J. C. DE. "¿Quién se beneficia con el comercio internacional ?" (Who benefits of international trade ?), *R. Integr.* (12), jan 73 : 37-53.

6456 PARRINELLO, S. "Distribuzione, sviluppo e commercio internazionale" (Distribution, development and international trade), *Econ. int. (Genova)* 26(2), mai 73 : 197-228.

6457 PETITH, H. "Vintage capital, joint production and the theory of international trade", *Int. econ. R.* 13(1), feb 72 : 148-159.

6458 ROUMÉLIOTIS, P. *Conjoncture et commerce international.* Paris, Gauthier-Villars, 72, xi-199 p.

6459 RYDYGIER, W. *Handel zagraniczny jako czynnik rozwoju gospodarczego* (Foreign trade as a factor of economic development). Warszawa, Państwowe Wydawnictwo Ekonomiczne, 73, 346 p.

6460 SHONE, R. M. *The pure theory of international trade.* London, Macmillan, 72, 95 p.

6461 SIEBERT, H. *Aussenhandelstheorie* (Foreign trade theory). Stuttgart, G. Fischer, 73, x-99 p.

6462 VELLAS, P. "Problèmes récents du commerce international", *A. Univ. Sci. soc. Toulouse* 20(1-2), 1972 : 8-73.

6463 VICARELLI, F. "Verso un' integrazione tra teoria pura e teoria monetaria del commercio internazionale" (Towards an integration between pure theory and monetary theory of international trade), *Econ. int. (Genova)* 25(3), aug 72 : 431-449; 25(4), nov 72 : 623-649.

6464 WOJCIECHOWSKI, B. "Efektywność handlu zagranicznego a wzrost dochodu narodowego" (Foreign trade efficiency and national income growth), *Handel zagran.* (12), 1973 : 411-415.

6465 ŽIBERNA, M. "Ekspanzija medunarodne trgovine i zemlje u razvoju" (The expansion of international trade and the developing countries), *Medun. Probl.* 24(3), jul-sep 72 : 89-95.

**O.311** *International division of labour, comparative costs, terms of trade Division internationale du travail, coûts comparés, termes de l'échange*

[See also / Voir aussi: 4092, 5810, 6256]

6466 BJERKE, K. "Some reflections on the intersectoral terms of trade of Denmark in the period 1949 to 1965", *R. Income Wealth* 18(4), dec 72 : 341-354.

6467 BRENNINKMEYER, V. C. R. "Internationale arbeidsverdeling en mogelijke gevolgen van herstructurering" (Division of labor in the international field and possible consequences of a restructuration), *Int. Spectator* 27(15), sep 73 : 528-535.

6468 HERMAN, B. "Optimale internationale arbeidsverdeling — schets van het probleem" (Optimal division of labor in the international field—outline of the problem), *Int. Spectator* 27(15), sep 73 : 516-521.

6469 KLAASEN, T. A. "Regional comparative advantage in the United States", *J. region. Sci.* 13(1), apr 73 : 97-105.

6470 KLEIN, R. W. "A dynamic theory of comparative advantage", *Amer. econ. R.* 63(1), mar 73 : 173-184.

6471 KOHT NORBYE, O. D. "Welk soort internationale arbeidsverdeling ?" (What sort of international division of labour ?), *Int. Spectator* 27(15), sep 73 : 507-515.

6472   KOZMA, F. "The effects of the international division of labour on national economies", *Acta oecon.* 9(3-4), 1972 : 343-357.

6473   KROSKE, H. "Afroasiatische und lateinamerikanische Länder in der internationalen Arbeitsteilung" (Afro-Asiatic and Latin American countries facing the international division of labour), *Dtsche Aussenpolit.* 18(4), jul-aug 73 : 950-957.

6474   KRUPER, M. *Wachstum und Terms of Trade* (Growth and terms of trade). Berlin, Duncker und Hubmot, 73, 136 p.

6475   MIMIAM, I. "Sobre la teoría del intercambio desigual" (About the theory of unequal exchange), *Econ. y Adm.* 21(2), mai-aug 72 : 120-137.

6476   PASCALY, F.-J. *Internationale Arbeitsteilung in EWG und COMECON* (International division of labor in the EEC and Comecon). München, Goldmann, 73, 161 p.

6477   PATNAIK, P. "External markets and capitalist development", *Econ. J.* 82(328), dec 72 : 1316-1323.

6478   VAN DRIEL, P.; SALVERDA, W. "International arbeidsverdeling en kapitalisme — een kritiek op de theorie van de optimale internationale arbeidsverdeling" (International division of labor and capitalism—a critic of the theory of optimal division of labor in the international field), *Int. Spectator* 27(15), sep 73 : 522-527.

6479   ŻEBROK, J. "Kompleksowy rozwój gospodarczy a międzynarodowa socjalizacja produkcji państw socjalistycznych" (Integrated economic development and international production specialization of socialist countries), *Zesz. nauk. wyższ. Szkoły ekon. Krakow.* 58, 1973 : 45-67.

O.312   *Import and export trends, foreign trade multiplier*
        *Propensions à importer et à exporter, multiplicateur du commerce extérieur*

[See also / Voir aussi: 3821]

6480   ARAUJO, O. "La política de sustitución de importaciones en Venezuela" (Import substitution policy in Venezuela), *R. Econ. latinoamer.* 9(35), 1973 : 57-84.

6481   ARTUS, J. R. "The short-run effects of domestic demand pressure on export delivery delays for machinery", *J. int. Econ.* 3(1), feb 73 : 21-36. [USA, UK, Germany FR.]

6482   ERNST, D. "Wirtschaftliche Entwicklung durch Importsubstituierende Industrialisierung ?" (Economic development by means of industrialisation through import substitution), *Argument* 15(4-6), jul 73 : 332-403.

6483   ETHIER, W. "Import substitution and the concept of effective rate of protection", *J. polit. Econ.* 80(1), jan-feb 72 : 37-47.

6484   FANE, G. "Consistent measures of import substitution", *Oxford econ. Pap.* 25(2), jul 73 : 251-261.

6485   HSU, R. C. "Changing domestic demand and ability to export", *J. polit. Econ.* 80(1), jan-feb 72 : 198-202.

6486   "Importsubstitution und Exportdiversifierung in ausgewählten Entwicklungsländern—Erfahrungen, Probleme, Aussichten" (Import substitution and export diversification in some developing countries—experiments, problems, prospects), *Weltwirtschaft* (1), 1973 : 26-197. [Mexico, Egypt, Brazil, India, Taiwan, Singapore.]

6487   KAKWANI, N. C. "On the bias in estimates of import demand parameters", *Int. econ. R.* 13(2), jun 72 : 239-244.

6488   KENEN, P. B.; VOIVODAS, C. S. "Export instability and economic growth", *Kyklos* 25(4), 1972 : 791-804.

6489   OJALA, E. M. "Impact of the new production possibilities on the structure of international trade in agricultural products", *Food Res. Inst. Stud.* 11(2), 1972 : 111-128.

6490   PURSELL, G.; SNAPE, R. P. "Economics of scale, price discrimination and exporting", *J. int. Econ.* 3(1), fev 73 : 85-91.

6491   RIEDEL, J. "Importsubstitution, Exportförderung und wirtschaftliche Effizienz in der verarbeitenden Industrie Taiwans" (Import substitution, export promotion and economic efficiency of manufacturing industry in Taiwan), *Weltwirtschaft* (1), 1973 : 141-161.

6492   SAWYER, J. A. "Import forecasts for input-output models", *R. Income Wealth* 18(3), sep 72 : 303-311.

6493    SIEBRAND, J. C. "Potential demand and external trade", *Economist (Haarlem)* 120(3), mai-jun 72 : 260-295.
6494    SULMICKI, J. "Wpływ długookresowych czynników wewnętrznych na rozmiary wymiany zagranicznej" (The effect of long-term domestic factors on the volume of foreign trade), *Zesz. nauk. Szkoły główn. Plan. Statyst.* 91, 73 : 11-32.
6495    TAVARES, M. DA C. *Da substituição de importações ao capitalismo financeiro; ensaios sobre economia brasileira* (Import substitution or financial capitalism; essays on the Brazilian economy). Rio de Janeiro, Zahar Editores, 72, 263 p.
6496    TYLER, W. G. "Importsubstitution, Exportdiversifierung und strukturelle Verflechtungen in der brasilianischen Industrie" (Import substitution, export diversification and structural ramifications in Brazilian industry), *Weltwirtschaft* (1), 1973 : 61-87.


### O.32    Foreign trade relations
###          Relations commerciales internationales

#### O.321    *Balance of trade*
####           *Balance du commerce*

6497    REKOWSKI, M. "Modelowe zmiany eksportu, importu i bilansu handlowego w cyklicznym rozwoju gospodarki kapitalistycznej" (Model changes in import, export and balance of trade during cyclical development), *Zesz. nauk. wyższ. Szkoły ekon. Poznan.* 44, 1972 : 37-54.


#### O.322    *Import-export: descriptive studies, by areas*
####           *Importations-exportations: études déscriptives, par régions*

6498    BHAGWATI, J.; WIBULSWASI, C. "A statistical analysis of shifts in the import structure in LDC's", *B. Oxford Univ. Inst. Econ. Statist.* 34(2), mai 72 : 229-239.
6499    Bibl. XXI-6755. CODONI, R. *et al. World trade flows. Integrational structure and conditional forecasts*. CR: E. THORBECKE, *J. econ. Liter.* 11(3), sep 73 : 941-943.
6500    "East-West trade", *Law contemp. Probl.* 37(3), 1972 : 139 p.
6501    HENKNER, K. "Industrial exports 1954-1967: competitive and structural effects", *Busin. Economist* 4(3), 1972 : 141-150. [USA, Germany FR, Japan, France, Italy, Netherlands.]
6502    HENKNER, K. *Quantifizierung von Wettbewerbs- und Struktureffekten in der Exportentwicklung ausgewählter Industrienationen 1954 bis 1967* (Quantification of competition and structure effects on export development of certain industrial countries between 1954 and 1967). Berlin, Duncker und Humblot, 71, 108 p.
6503    HEROUVILLE, H. D'. "Nouveaux aspects du commerce mondial des demi-produits et des produits fabriqués en 1971 et 1972", *Écon. et Statist.* 49, oct 73 : 21-41.
6504    KUROWSKI, L.; POWAŁKA, A. "Optymalizacja i organizacja importu artykułów konsumpcyjnych" (Optimization and organization of consumer goods exports), *Handel zagran.* (12), 1973 : 415-419.
6505    LUBITZ, R. "Export-led growth in industrial economies", *Kyklos* 26(2), 1973 : 307-321.
6506    O'BRIEN, P. "On commodity concentration of exports in developing countries", *Econ. int. (Genova)* 25(4), nov 72 : 697-717.
6507    "Tendances du commerce international en 1971 et 1972 (1er semestre) (Les)", *Options méditerr.* 6(15), oct 72 : 31-34.


#### O.322(1)    *Africa*
####              *Afrique*

[See also / Voir aussi: 6398, 6529]

6508    "Commerce extérieur du Sénégal en 1971 (Le)", *Notes Inform. Statist. Banque centr. Afr. Ouest* 202, jan 73 : 28 p.
6509    DOBROCZYŃSKI, M. *Afryka a handel międzynarodowy* (Africa and international trade). Warszawa, Książka i Wiedza, 72, 372 p.

6510   GRIESAU, H.-D. "Die Aussichten für desn Agrarhandel Afrikas" (Trade prospects for African agricultural products), *Aussenpolitik* 24(1), jan 73 : 70-84.

6511   NEAL, D. F. "Liberia's foreign trade pattern, 1940-1968", *Liber. Stud. J.* 4(1), 1971-1972 : 1-20.

## O.322(2) *America*
*Amérique*

[See also / Voir aussi: 6523]

6512   BUXBAUM, D. C. "American trade with the People's Republic of China: some preliminary perspectives", *Columbia J. transnat. Law* 12(1), 1973 : 39-55.

6513   "Comércio exterior" (Foreign trade), *Conjunt. econ.* 27(4), apr 73 : 55-128; 27(5), mai 73 : 48-119.

6514   FRANK, H. J.; WELL, D. A. "United States oil imports: implications for the balance of payments", *Natur. Resources J.* 13(3), jul 73 : 431-447.

6515   KAWATA, F. "Patterns of export trade of Argentina and Brazil: a comparative study", *Kobe econ. Busin. R.* 19, 1972 : 1-17.

6516   KINGSTON, J. L. "Export instability in Latin America: the postwar statistical record", *J. Develop. Areas* 7(3), apr 73 : 381-396.

6517   MELGAR, A.; PEGUERO, E.; LAVAGNINO, C. *El comercio exportador del Uruguay, período 1962-1968* (Export trade of Uruguay, 1962-1968). Montevideo, Universidad de la República, Departamento de Publicaciones, 72, 2 vols.

6518   TEIGEIRO, J. D.; ELSON, R. A. "The export promotion system and the growth of minor exports in Colombia", *Staff Pap.* 20(2), jul 73 : 419-470.

6519   UNITED STATES. Tariff Commission. *Comparison of ratios of imports to apparent consumption, 1968-1972.* Washington, United States Government Printing Office, 73, vii-359 p.

6520   WINPENNY, J. T. *Brazil—manufactured exports and government policy: Brazil's experience since 1939.* London, Grant and Culter, 72, viii-136 p.

6521   WOLF, T. A. "A note on the restrictive effect of unilateral United States export controls", *J. polit. Econ.* 81(1), jan-feb 73 : 219-222.

## O.322(3) *Asia*
*Asie*

[See also / Voir aussi: 6512]

6522   BLUMENTAHL, T. "Exports and economic growth: the case of postwar Japan", *Quart. J. Econ.* 86(4), nov 72 : 617-631.

6523   CAHILL, H. A. *The China trade and US tariffs.* New York, Praeger, 73, vi-161 p.

6524   "Commerce extérieur japonais (Le)", *Japon Écon.* 57, jul 73 : 3-46.

6525   KLATT, W. "China's domestic economy and foreign trade", *China Rep.* 9(3), mai-jun 73 : 30-40.

6526   LIM, Y. "ECAFE's trade expansion proposal for Asia: an appraisal", *J. Common Market Stud.* 11(2), dec 72 : 103-119.

6527   Bibl. XXI-6797. MAH, F. *The foreign trade of Mainland China.* CR: Y.-L. WU, *J. econ. Liter.* 11(3), sep 73 : 943-944.

6528   ROBERTS, I. M.; MERINGTON, P. "Growth in the Japanese import demand for rural products", *Quart. R. agric. Econ.* 25(3), jul 72 : 206-222.

6529   SCHRÖTTER, D. VON. "Der Afrikahandel der VR China, 1959-1968" (Trade between China's People Republic and Africa), *Int. Afr. Forum* 8(11-12), nov-dec 72 : 642-651.

6530   STAHNKE, A. A. (ed.). *China's trade with the West; a political and economic analysis* New York, Praeger, 72, xii-234 p.

6531   THOBURN, J. T. "Exports and economic growth in West Malaysia", *Oxford econ. Pap.* 25(1), mar 73 : 88-111.

6532   TULLOCH, P. *The seven outside: Commonwealth Asia's trade with the enlarged EEC* London, Overseas Development Institute, 73, 2-vi-67 p.

6533   YOUNG, A. K. "Japan's trade with China: impact of the Nixon visit", *Wld today* 28(8), aug 72 : 342-350.

**O.322(4)** *Europe*

[See also / Voir aussi: 3323, 3473, 5452, 6442, 6532, 6562, 6586, 6638]

6534   AITKEN, N. D. "The effect of the EEC and EFTA on European trade: a temporal
       cross-section analysis", *Amer. econ. R.* 63(5), dec 73 : 881-892.

6535   BIRÓ, J. "A külkereskedelem árúszerkezetének föbb kérdései" (The main problems of
       the structure of foreign trade), *Közgazd. Szle* 20(3), mar 73 : 253-270. [Hungary.]

6536   BIRÓ, G. "Die Aussenwirtschaft Ungarns. Strukturpolitische Aspekte im Aussen-
       handel" (Hungarian foreign trade. A structural political survey), *Österr. Osth.* 14(4),
       oct 72 : 357-368.

6537   BOGACKA, M.; CIENIUCH, I.; LESZEK, T. "Rozwój handlu wzajemnego w ramach
       RWPG" (Development of trade relations within the CMEA), *Handel zagran.* (11),
       1973 : 374-377.

6538   BOGACKA, M.; LESZEK, T. "Handel Polski z krajami RWPG w latach 1961-1980"
       (Polish trade with the CMEA countries in the period 1961-1980), *Handel zagran.* (10),
       1973 : 335-340.

6539   BRONICKI, A.; GUZ, J. "Prognoza handlu krajów RWPG do 1975 r." (Trade perspectives
       of the CMEA countries till 1975), *Zesz. nauk. Szkoły Plan. Statyst.* 88, 1972 : 167-187.

6540   BURTICĂ, C. "Structural adaptations of Romanian exports to foreign market demand",
       *Sov. East. Europ. for. Trade* 8(3-4), 1972-1973 : 225-237.

6541   CHOCIEJ, S. "Polski eksport do krajów Wspólnego Rynku a mechanizm funkcjonowania
       polityki gospodarczej EWG" (Polish exports to the Common Market countries and the
       functioning of the mechanisms of the European Common Market economic policy).
       *Fol. oecon. cracov.* 14, 1973 : 79-95.

6542   CLARK, C.; WELCH, S. "Western European trade as a measure of integration: untangling
       the interpretations", *J. Conflict Resol.* 16(3), sep 72 : 363-382.

6543   "Commerce en France de 1969 à 1971 (Le)", *Coll. INSÉÉ Sér. C* 21, mai 73 : 144 p.

6544   DOLINŠEK, A.; VERBIČ, B. "Vpliv trgovinske politike EGS na jugoslavenski izvoz"
       (The influence of EEC trade policy on Yugoslav exports), *Teorija in Praksa* 10(7-8),
       jul-aug 73 : 638-654.

6545   FJODOROW, W. "Die Rolle der Aussenwirtschaft für die BRD" (The role of foreign
       trade in the GFR's economy), *IPW Ber.* 2(8), aug 73 : 19-25.

6546   GRABSKI, K. *Handel zagraniczny Polski* (Foreign trade of Poland). Warszawa, Państwowe
       Wydawnictwo Ekonomiczne, 72, 109 p.

6547   GRAZIOSI, D. "Italian foreign trade final results for 1972 and short term prospects",
       *R. econ. Condit. Italy* 27(1-2), jan-mar 73 : 29-42.

6548   JØRGENSEN, B. *Perspektiver for Danmarks undenrigshandel* (Perspectives for Denmark's
       foreign trade). København, Instituttet for Fremtidforskning/Børsen, 72, 185 p.

6549   KOVAČEVIĆ, M. "Neke karakteristike spoljnotrgovinske razmane Jugoslavija u poslerat-
       nom periodu" (Some characteristics of Yugoslavia's foreign trade since the war).
       *Medun. Probl.* 25(4), oct-dec 72 : 43-57.

6550   LUBEN, D. "Aussenhandelsprobleme Jugoslawiens" (Foreign trade problems of Yugo-
       slavia), *Osteuropa* 23(7), jul 73 : 498-510.

6551   POURNAKARIS, E. "New directions for world trade and developing economies: the case of
       the Balkans", *Balkan Stud.* 13(1), 1972 : 31-40. [Rumania, Bulgaria, Greece, Yugoslavia.]

6552   RASNOV, Ju. M. *FRG na mirovyh rynkah* (The GFR in world markets). Moskva,
       Mezdunarodnye Otnošenija, 73, 232 p. [Germany, FR.]

6553   SARNECKI, Z. "Handel zagraniczny Polski w 1972 r." (Polish foreign trade in 1972),
       *Finanse* (6), 1973 : 66-74.

6554   STANKOVSKY, J. "Österreichs Osthandel 1971-1972—Probleme und Entwicklung"
       (Problems and evolution of Austrian foreign trade with Eastern countries), *Cred.
       Anstalt Bankver. Wien Wirtsch.-Ber.* 7(4), aug 72 : 16-25.

6555   SULIMIERSKI, B. "Rozwój handlu zagranicznego Polski na tle handlu swiatowego"
       (Development of the Polish foreign trade and trade in the world), *Handel zagran* 12,
       1973 : 420-424.

6556   TOMZA, R. "Problemy polskiego eksportu płodów rolnych" (Problems of Polish exports
       of agricultural products), *Zesz. nauk. wyższ. Szkoły ekon. Krakow.* 58, 1973 : 5-31.

6557   TRUMAN, E. M. "The production and trade of manufactured products in the EEC and
       EFTA: a comparison", *Europ. econ. R.* 3(3), nov 72 : 271-290.

6558 VAN BARBANT, J. M. "Some observations on recent changes in Poland's foreign trade", *Docum. Europe centr.* 11(2), mar-apr 73 : 99-121.

6559 WIECZOREK, J. "Rola handlu zagranicznego w rozwoju społeczno-gospodarczym Polski Ludowej" (Foreign trade and socio-economic development of People's Poland): *Zesz. nauk. Szkoły główn. Plan. Statyst.* 88, 1972 : 11-26.

6560 WOJCIECHOWSKI, B. "Handel zagraniczny a dochód narodowy Posli" (Foreign trade and the national income of Poland), *Handel zagran.* 11, 1973 : 363-367.


**O.322(5)** *Middle East*
*Moyen-Orient*

6561 GIRGIS, M. "Developpement and trade patterns in the Arab world", *Weltwirtsch. Archiv* 109(1), 1973 : 121-160.


**O.322(6)** *Pacific*
*Pacifique*

6562 HONAN, N. D. "Impact on Australia's agricultural trade of the United Kingdom's accession to an enlarged European Economic Community", *Quart. R. agric. Econ.* 25(3), jul 72 : 191-205.


**O.322(7)** *USSR*
*URSS*

6563 ROSEFIELDE, S. *Soviet international trade in Heckscher-Ohlin perspective: an input-output study.* Lexington, Mass., Lexington Books, 73, xxv-173 p.

6564 SMITH, G. A. *Soviet foreign trade: organization, operations, and policy, 1918-1971.* New York, Praeger, 73, xviii-370 p.


**O.323** *Tourist trade, exchange of services*
*Tourisme international, échanges de services*

6565 ADAMS, J. "Why the Amerijan tourist abroad is cheated: a price-theoretical analysis", *J. polit. Econ.* 80(1), jan-feb 72 : 203-207.

6566 BLAKE, G.; LAWLESS, R. "Tourisme international au Sahara algérien", *Méditerranée* 13(3-4), 1972 : 171-176.

6567 HARROP, J. "The economics of the tourist boom", *J. Wld Trade Law* 7(2), mar-apr 73 : 208-225.

6568 KWACK, S. Y. "Effects of income and prices on travel spending abroad, 1960 III-1967 IV", *Int. econ. R.* 13(2), jun 72 : 245-256. [USA.]

6569 ROGOWIEC, M.; SZUMOWSKI, T. "Wpływ ruchu turystycznego między Niemiecką Republiką Demokratyczną a Poslką na sytuację rynkową a wybranych rejonach naszego kraju" (Impact of tourist traffic between the German Democratic Republic and Poland on the market in selected regions of our country), *Roczn. Inst. Handlu wewn.* (4), 1973 : 97-107.

6570 ZAČINJAEV, P. N.; FAL'KOVIČ, N. S. *Geografija meždunarodnogo turizma* (Geography of international tourism). Moskva, Mysl', 72, 263 p.


**O.33** **Foreign trade policies**
**Politiques du commerce extérieur**

**O.330** *General studies*
*Études générales*

6571 FREYBERG, P.; KUROWSKI, L. *Foreign trade in the theory and practice of economic plan construction.* Warsaw, Central School of Planning and Statistics in Warsaw, Research Institute for Developing Countries, 73, 31 p.

6572 KRUEGER, A. O. "Evaluating restrictionist trade regimes: theory and measurement", *J. polit. Econ.* 80(1), jan-feb 72 : 48-62.

6573    LACHARRIERE, G. L. DE. *La stratégie commerciale du développement*. Paris, Presses universitaires de France, 73, 238 p.

6574    MEIER, G. M. *Problems of trade policy*. New York, Oxford University Press, 73, xv-288 p.

6575    ORGANIZATION FOR ECONOMIC COOPERATION AND DEVELOPMENT. High level Group on Trade and Related Problems. *Policy perspectives for international trade and economic relations*. Paris, OECD, 72, 168 p.

6576    PESTIEAU, C.; HENRY, J. *Non-tariff trade barriers as a problem in international development; a study in two parts*. Montreal, Private Planning Association of Canada, 72, xx-219 p.

6577    ROBERTSON, D. *International trade policy*. London, Macmillan, 72, 79 p.

6578    RYDYGIER, W. "Cele i zadania systemu ekonomiczno-finansowego a problemy handlu zagranicznego" (Objectives and tasks of an economico-financial system and development problems of foreign trade), *Stud. finans.* 13, 1972 : 37-72.

6579    TOKARSKA, B. *Badanie rynków eksportowych* (Export market research). Warszawa, Państwowe Wydawnictwo Ekonomiczne, 73, 292 p.

### O.331    Import-export policies
### Politiques d'importation-exportation

6580    ARAI, M. "La politique économique extérieure du Japon", *Éch. int. Dévelop.* 19, oct 73 : 21-32.

6581    ARIFF, K. A. M. *Export trade and the West Malaysian economy—an enquiry into the economic implications of export instability*. Kuala Lumpur, University of Malaya Co-operative Bookshop, 72, xii-246 p.

6582    BRADGANU, S. "Aspects juridiques de la règlementation du commerce extérieur dans la République socialiste de Roumanie", *R. Pays Est* 13(2), 1972 : 97-119.

6583    COMMITTEE FOR ECONOMIC DEVELOPMENT. *A new trade policy toward Communist countries; a statement on national policy*. New York, CED, 72, 68 p. [USA.]

6584    CORBET, H. "Australian commercial diplomacy in a new era of negotiation", *Austral. Outlook* 26(1), apr 72 : 3-17.

6585    ENGLISH, H. E. (ed.). *Regional and adjustment aspects of trade liberalization* 2 vols. Toronto-Buffalo, University of Toronto Press, 73, vi-203-vi-144 p.

6586    FRANCE. Commissariat général du plan. Comité des échanges extérieurs. *Échanges extérieurs; rapport du Comité*. Paris, Documentation française, 72, 231 p.

6587    HAITANI, K. "Japan's trade problem and the yen", *Asian Surv.* 12(8), aug 73 : 723-739.

6588    HANDKE, W. "Die neue Aussenwirtschaftspolitik der USA" (The new foreign economic policy of the United States), *Z. ges. Staatswiss.* 129(2), mai 73 : 312-332.

6589    HAWKINS, R. G.; WALTER, I. (eds.). *The United States and international markets; commercial policy options in an age of controls*. Lexington, Mass., Lexington Books, 72, xviii-417 p.

6590    HOYA, T. W. "The changing US regulation of East-West trade", *Columbia J. transnat. Law* 12(1), 1973 : 1-38.

6591    IOWA STATE UNIVERSITY CENTER FOR AGRICULTURAL AND RURAL DEVELOPMENT. *US trade policy and agricultural exports*. Ames, Iowa State University Press, 73, viii-228 p.

6592    JONISH, J. E. "Recent development in US anti-dumping policy", *J. Wld Trade Law* 7(3), mai-jun 73 : 316-327.

6593    KOJIMA, K. "Reorganisation of North-South trade: Japan's foreign economic policy for the 1970s", *Hitotsubashi J. Econ.* 13(2), feb 73 : 1-28.

6594    LOUGHEED, A. L. "Australia's policy towards the growth of agricultural protectionism in world trade", *Econ. Anal. Pol.* 3(1), mar 72 : 1-10.

6595    MIKLASZEWSKI, S. "Periodyzacja polskiej polityki importowej w dwudziestoleciu 1950-1970" (Periodization of Polish import policy in the twenty years 1950-1970), *Zesz. nauk. wyższ. Szkoly ekon. Krakow.* 58, 1973 : 33-44.

6596    MILES, C. "US trade policy in the 1970s: the Report of the Williams Commission", *Wld today* 28(3), mar 72 : 102-108.

6597    MOLAVI, M. A. "La nouvelle politique commerciale de l'Iran", *R. Soc. Ét. Expans.* 71(252), sep-oct 72 : 620-638.

6598    NAJLEPSZY, E. *Handel zagraniczny w systemie planowania i zarządzania w Polsce* (Foreign trade in the planning and management system in Poland). Warszawa, Państwowe Wydawnictwo Naukowe, 73, 135 p.

6599    Bibl. xxi-6910. NATIONAL PLANNING ASSOCIATION. *US foreign economic policy for the 1970s: a new approach to new realities.* CR: R. E. ASHER, *Amer. polit. Sci. R.* 67(2). jun 73 : 725-726.

6600    OSIATYŃSKI, L. *Ryzyko w transakcjach handlu zagranicznego* (Risk in foreign trade transactions). Warszawa, Państwowe Wydawnictwo Ekonomiczne, 73, 146 p.

6601    REPETTO, R. "Optimal export taxes in the short and long run, and an application to Pakistan's jute export policy", *Quart. J. Econ.* 86(3), aug 72 : 396-406.

6602    SCHYDLOWSKY, D. "Latin American trade policies in the 1970's: a prospective appraisal", *Quart. J. Econ.* 86(2), mai 72 : 263-289.

6603    SCHYDLOWSKY, D. "Le politiche commerciali dell' America Latina negli anni 70" (The commercial policies of Latin America in the seventies), *Realtà econ.* 5(3-4), mar-apr 73 : 5-27.

6604    STEGEMANN, K.; PESTIEAU, C. *Canadian on-tariff barriers to trade.* Montreal, Private Planning Association of Canada, 73, xi-162 p.

6605    TOWER, E. "Commercial policy under fixed and flexible exchange rates", *Quart. J. Econ.* 87(3), aug 73 : 436-454.

6606    TREJO REYES, S. "Promoción de exportaciones y crecimiento óptimo de la economía. Nuevos resultados" (Export promotion and optimal growth of the economy. New results), *Demogr. y Econ.* 6(2), 1972 : 206-220. [Mexico.]

6607    TRZECIAKOWSI, W. *Foreign trade planning and management in Poland.* Warszawa, Central School of Planning and Statistics in Warsaw, Research Institute for Development Countries, 73, 85 p.

6608    VAN VEEN, P. "Ontwikkelingen in de theorie van de handelspolitiek in Oost en West" (Development in the theory of trade policy in the East and the West), *Economie (Tilburg)* 36(12), sep 72 : 565-583.

6609    VELLAS, P. "La nouvelle politique commerciale japonaise", *Éch. int. Dévelop.* 19, oct 73 : 1-20.

6610    WALTER, I. *US trade policy in a changing world economy.* Tübingen, Mohr, 73, 14 p.

6611    WOLF, T. A. *US East-West trade policy: economic warfare versus economic welfare.* Lexington, Mass., Lexington Books, 73, xx-209 p.

6612    YAKER, L. "La politique commerciale et la règlementation du commerce extérieur", *R. financ.* (3), sep 72 : 17-29. [Algérie.]

## O.332    *Custom tariffs and policies*
### *Tarifs douaniers et politique douanière*

[See also / Voir aussi: 6483]

6613    AHMAD, J. "Trade liberalization and structural changes in Latin America", *J. Common Market Stud.* 11(1), sep 72 : 1-17.

6614    BLACKHURST, R. "Estimating the impact of tariff manipulation: the excess demand and supply approach", *Oxford econ. Pap.* 25(1), mar 73 : 80-87.

6615    BRUNO, M. "Domestic resource costs and effective protection: clarification and synthesis", *J. polit. Econ.* 80(1), jan-feb 72 : 16-33.

6616    CZEPURKO, A. *Cłu w handlu międzynarodowym* (Tariffs in international trade). Warszawa, Państwowe Wydawnictwo Ekonomiczne, 72, 232 p.

6617    FLYSTAD, G. "The impact on allocation and return to labor and capital of a reduction of customs duties in the developed countries in their trade with less developed countries", *Weltwirtsch. Archiv* 109(1), 1973 : 59-68.

6618    HEIDUK, G. *Die weltwirtschaftlichen Ordnungsprinzipien von GATT und UNCTAD* (The principles of world economic organization of GATT and UNCTAD). Baden-Baden, Nomos Verlagsgesellschaft, 73, 314 p.

6619    HENNER, H. F.; LAFAY, G.; LASSUDRIE-DUCHÊNE, B. *La protection effective dans les pays industrialisés; une comparaison internationale.* Paris, Economica, 72, 56-3 p.

6620    KAPLAN, G. G. "Equality and discrimination in international economic law : the UNCTAD scheme for generalised preferences", *Yb. Wld Aff.* 26, 1972 : 267-285.

6621    KELLENSTEIN, E. P. "The free trade agreements between the enlarged European communities and the EFTA countries", *Common Market Law R.* 10(2), mai 73 : 137-149.

6622    ŁAWNICZAK, R. "Strefa wolnego handlu w teorii międzynarodowej integracji gospodarczej" (Free trade area in the theory of international integration), *Zesz. nauk. wyższ. Szkoły ekon. Poznan.* 44, 1972 : 95-109.

6623   LLOSAS, H. P. "Los efectos direccionales de la protección aduanera en la Argentina" (The directional effects of customs protection in Argentina), *Económica (La Plata)* 17(3), sep-dec 71 : 287-298.

6624   MATTSSON, A. *Dumping och antidumpingatgärder* (Dumping and antidumping gate keepers). Stockholm, Almqvist coh Wiksell, 72, iv-82 p.

6625   MURRAY, I. "How helpful is the Generalised System of Preferences to developing countries ?", *Econ. J.* 83(330), jun 73 : 449-455.

6626   RATOWSKA, T. "Problem protekcjonizmu w aspekcie aktualnej sytuacji gospodarczej swiata kapitalistycznego" (Protectionism in the contemporary economic situation of the capitalist world), *Handel zagran.* (9), 1973 : 286-290.

6627   SAUVIGNON, E. *La clause de la nation la plus favorisée.* Grenoble, Presses universitaires de Grenoble, 72, iv-374 p.

6628   SCHMITZ, A. "Tariffs and declining-cost industries", *Economica (London)* 39(156), nov 72 : 419-426.

6629   SCHMITZ, A.; BIERI, J. "EEC tariffs and US direct investment", *Europ. econ. R.* 3(3), nov 72 : 259-270.

6630   SCHUFFT, R.; REID, J. E. "Diagrammatic interpretation of the concept of effective protection", *Econ. Record* 48(123), sep 72 : 433-436.

6631   TAMAMES GÓMEZ, R. *Acuerdo preferencial CEE/España y preferencias generalizadas; un ensayo cuantitativo sobre las relaciones económicas internacionales de España* (The preferential agreement between the EEC and Spain and generalized preferences; a quantitative essay on Spain's international economic relations). Barcelona, DOPESA, 72, 185 p.

6632   WALLICH, H. C. "L'accordo commerciale tra Stati Uniti e Unione Sovietica" (The Soviet-American trade agreement), *Aff. est.* 16, oct 72 : 90-98.


O.333    *Tariff and tax agreements (double taxation)*
         *Accords douaniers et fiscaux (double imposition)*

6633   "Freihandelsabkommen Schweiz-EWG (Das)" (The free trade agreement between Switzerland and the EEC), *Aussenwirtschaft (St Gallen)* 27(3), 1972 : 114 p.

6634   HUDEC, R. E. "GATT or GABB ? The future design of the General Agreement on Tariffs and Trade", *Yale Law J.* 80(7), jun 71 : 1299-1386.

6635   JOHANSSON, B. O. "Den nya GATT-rundan—en lösning av de handelspolitiska problemen" (The new GATT negotiations—a solution to the commercial policy problem ?), *Ekon. Samfund. Ts.* 26(3), 1973 : 167-176.

6636   LUCAS, R. "Das neue deutsch-sowjetische Handelsabkommen" (The new German-Soviet trade agreement), *Osteuropa Recht* 18(4), dec 72 : 255-262.

6637   REUVERS, M. R. *Internationale dubbele belasting* (International double taxation). Deventer, FED, 73, xii-154 p.

6638   SIEBER, H. "Die wirtschaftliche Konsequenzen des Freihandelsabkommens Schweiz-EWG" (The economic consequences of the free trade agreement between Switzerland and the EEC), *Aussenwirtschaft (St Gallen)* 27(3), 1972 : 67-86.

6639   STERN, R. M. "Tariffs and other measures of trade control; a survey of recent developments", *J. econ. Liter.* 11(3), sep 73 : 857-888.


O.334    *Customs unions*
         *Unions douanières*

6640   CORDEN, W. M. "Economies of scale and customs union theory", *J. polit. Econ.* 80(3), mai-jun 72 : 465-475.

6641   HAZLEWOOD, A. "State trading and the East African customs union", *Oxford B. Econ. Statist.* 35(2), mai 73 : 75-89.

6642   NOWAK, Z. "Unia celna jako narzędzie polityki mocarstwowej EWG" (The custom union as a tool of the Common Market's power politics), *Przegl. zachod.* (2), 1973 : 341-350.

6643   WILLIAMS, J. R. "Customs unions: a criterion for welfare gains in the general case", *Manchester Sch. Econ. soc. Stud.* 40(4), dec 72 : 385-396.

Inflation-deflation [*contd.*]
  descriptive studies, 1908, 3911, 3927, 4095-
    4123, 4286, 4429, 4443, 4502, 4577, 5257,
    5544, 5635, 5637
Inland navigation, 3417, 3494-3497
Innis, H. A., 3784
Innovation, *see* Technology
Input-output analysis, *see* Models, economic
Instalment credit, *see* Credit, consumer
Insurance, 4135, 4236-4245
  accident, *see* Work safety
  health, *see* Health insurance
  old age, *see* Old age, insurance
  public, *see* Social security
  unemployment, *see* Unemployment insur-
    ance
Interest rate, 4066, 4074, 4080, 4115, 4262-
    4264, 4266-4271, 4274-4276, 4281, 4283,
    4288, 4300, 4304, 4308; *see also* Discount
    rate
Interindustry relations, *see* Models, economic
International balance of payments, 5584, 6255-
    6285, 6323, 6352, 6437, 6514
International balance of trade, 6497
International Bank for Reconstruction and
    Development, 6411
International capital movements, 6187, 6248,
    6291-6304; *see also* International invest-
    ments
International convertibility of currencies,
    6235, 6366-6377
International division of labour, 6467, 6468,
    6471-6473, 6476, 6478
International economic agreements; 6025-6032
International economic blocs, 5917-5998
International economic co-operation, 6033-
    6091, 6414
International economic integration, 5807,
    5814, 5816, 5821, 5822, 5827, 5829, 5847,
    5889, 6230, 6405; *see also* under Africa,
    Europe, Latin America, etc.
International economic organizations
  governmental, 5830-5842, 6618; *see also*
    European institutions; International mo-
    netary institutions
  private, 3010, 3113, 4077, 5850-5903, 6159
International economic policy, 6023-6138
International economic relations, descriptive
    studies, 5930, 6092-6138, 6150, 6632;
    *see also* International technical assistance
International economics, 2565, 5220, 5802-
    6643
International investment, 5598, 5944, 6088,
    6305-6360, 6629
International Labour Organization, 5833, 5836
International market conditions, 5904-5916,
    6031
International monetary agreements, 6427
International monetary areas, 6382-6404, 6587

International monetary economics, 6139-6427
International Monetary Fund, 6413, 6417,
    6423, 6425
International monetary institutions, 6226,
    6405-6426, 6620
International monetary policy, 6366-6381
International monetary relations, 6405-6427
International monetary reserves, 6261, 6286-
    6290
International monetary standards, 6210-6217
International monetary system, 6139-6186,
    6369, 6390, 6440
International population movements, 1901,
    6000-6022
International rivers and waterways, 5999
International technical assistance, 6048-6058
International tourism, *see* Tourism, inter-
    national
International trade, *see* Foreign trade
Inventions, *see* Technology
Investment
  aggregate amount and policy, 2239, 2240,
    4829-4959, 5891
  and savings, *see* Savings and investment
  by sector, 2624, 2818, 2823, 3155, 3347,
    3453, 3960, 4338, 4860-4876, 5048
  demand, 2227, 2244, 4255, 4789-4828; *see
    also* Capital market
  depreciation and amortization, *see* Capital
    depreciation and amortization
  international, *see* International investment
  multiplier, 4642, 4643
  of the firm, 2218, 2219, 2227, 2228, 2231,
    2234, 2239, 2240, 2243
  trusts, 4246-4250
Iran
  agriculture: co-operatives, 2720, 2727; re-
    form, 2720, 2776
  co-operative sector, 5354
  economic history, 494
  employment, policy, 1654
  foreign trade, policy, 6597
  international investments, 6348
  money, policy, 4351
  oil, 3272
  taxes, system and policy, 4351
  wages, policy, 1654
Iraq
  agriculture, 2589
  economic geography, 775
  economic planning, 5325
  labour, mobility, 1622
  State budget, 5550
Ireland
  balance of payments, 6277
  economic growth, 1213
  foreign investments, 793
  industry: location, 793; policy, 3162; pro-
    duction, 3217

387

*Printed in Belgium.*